The A-Z of
FIRST AID
and
FAMILY HEALTH

The A-Z of
FIRST AID
—— and ——
FAMILY HEALTH

Blitz Editions

Published by Blitz Editions
an imprint of Bookmart Ltd
Registered Number 2372865
Trading as Bookmart Ltd
Desford Road
Enderby
Leicester LE9 5AD

ISBN: 1 85605 226 5

NOTE TO READERS
This book is a work of reference only and should not be regarded
as a source of individual treatments. Readers should consult
qualified doctors for treating specific complaints.

Material previously published in 1992 as part of the encyclopedia set *Know Yourself*
(Fabbri Publishing Ltd).

Editorial and design: Brown Packaging Ltd,
255-257 Liverpool Road, London N1 1LX

Printed in Slovakia
51741

ABDOMINAL PAIN

Abdominal pain is common, usually trivial, but occasionally due to a serious underlying problem.

The abdominal cavity lies between the diaphragm (a dome of muscle attached to the breastbone, ribs and spine) and the pelvis. Within it lie the gut (stomach, small intestine and large intestine), together with its appendages (liver, gall bladder and pancreas) and the genito-urinary systems (uterus, tubes, ovaries and bladder).

Roughly speaking, pain in the upper third of the abdomen is due to problems in the stomach, liver or gall-bladder. Pain in the centre third is due to disease of the small intestine, appendix or kidneys. Pain in the lower third of the abdomen is due to problems in the lower half of the large bowel or rectum. Gynaecological or bladder pain also affect the lower third of the abdomen.

Making a diagnosis

When a doctor is trying to differentiate the causes of pain, he relies on three approaches. First, he asks the patient about any symptoms — nausea, loss of appetite, constipation and so on. The second stage is to look for signs, which are found on examination. A doctor can easily identify a tender liver or swollen bladder, for example. To complete the diagnosis, it may be necessary to make investigations, such as X-rays, blood tests, testing of faeces, or even a laparotomy (an exploratory operation).

As with any pain in the body, you should consult your doctor if the symptoms persist for a number of days. Serious ailments are always best dealt with sooner rather than later.

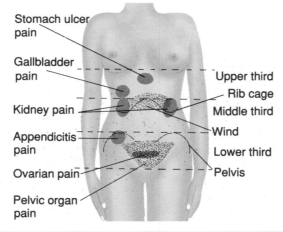

Stomach ulcer pain
Gallbladder pain
Kidney pain
Appendicitis pain
Ovarian pain
Pelvic organ pain

Upper third
Rib cage
Middle third
Wind
Lower third
Pelvis

NOTE

The chart (below) will aid the self-diagnosis of relatively common forms of abdominal pain. If pain does not respond to simple treatment, or persists for more than a couple of days, consult your doctor. Areas where more serious pain occurs are indicated on the diagram (left). If you have severe pain, or if the pain is associated with unexpected loss of weight, see your doctor immediately.

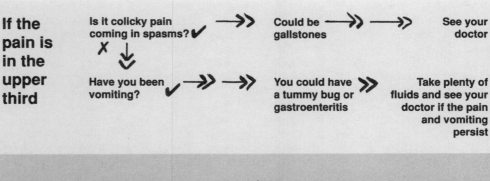

If the pain is in the upper third

Is it colicky pain coming in spasms? ✔ ➤➤ → Could be gallstones ➤➤ → → See your doctor

Have you been vomiting? ✔ ➤➤ → You could have a tummy bug or gastroenteritis ➤➤ Take plenty of fluids and see your doctor if the pain and vomiting persist

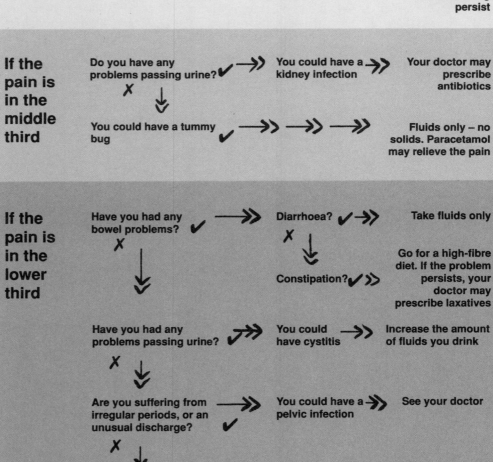

If the pain is in the middle third

Do you have any problems passing urine? ✔ ➤➤ You could have a kidney infection ➤➤ Your doctor may prescribe antibiotics

You could have a tummy bug ✔ ➤➤ ➤➤ → Fluids only – no solids. Paracetamol may relieve the pain

If the pain is in the lower third

Have you had any bowel problems? ✔ ➤➤ Diarrhoea? ✔ ➤ Take fluids only

Constipation? ✔ ➤➤ Go for a high-fibre diet. If the problem persists, your doctor may prescribe laxatives

Have you had any problems passing urine? ➤➤ You could have cystitis → Increase the amount of fluids you drink

Are you suffering from irregular periods, or an unusual discharge? ✔ ➤➤ You could have a pelvic infection ➤➤ See your doctor

Is it a cramping pain on either side of your abdomen around the time of your period? ✔ ➤➤ This is likely to be menstrual pain → Take paracetamol but consult your doctor if the pain is a problem

➤➤ SEE ALSO — Appendicitis, Chest pain, Hernias, Liver, Menstruation, Stomach ulcer, Wind

MEDICAL FACT FILE

ABORTION

An abortion is the premature termination of pregnancy either by spontaneous means (commonly known as miscarriage) or by a medically induced expulsion.

Medically induced abortion is available legally in the United Kingdom up to 24 weeks, but the vast majority of terminations are carried out in the first 12 weeks of pregnancy. The further the pregnancy has progressed, the more risky the procedure and the more difficult it is to obtain .

Under the 1967 Abortion Act you need two doctors to certify that a termination is necessary for medical or psychological reasons. The operation will be carried out at a National Health Service hospital, at a clinic run by a charitable organisation like the British Pregnancy Advisory Service or privately.

The decision to have an abortion is always a difficult one. Women need abortions for a number of reasons — financial or personal, or because the foetus is abnormal. Amniocentesis, the most commonly used test for foetal abnormality, cannot be done until at least 14 weeks after the first day of your last menstrual period. The results take 2–5 weeks to come through, forcing parents to take the agonising choice of having a baby born with an abnormality or going through with a late abortion. Chorionic Villus Sampling is a possible alternative to amniocentesis in some cases. It can be performed as early as eight weeks into the pregnancy and can give results in 5–12 days. It does have some risks, but it gives the woman the choice of an abortion in the first three months.

How to get an abortion

If you think you may be pregnant and you're unsure whether you want to have the baby, it's important to have a pregnancy test as soon as possible. The new do-it-yourself tests are very reliable and some can actually be used as early as the day you missed your period. If you are pregnant, the first step is to visit your GP. She will confirm your pregnancy and discuss your options with you. If you decide on an abortion, she will arrange for you to see another doctor to certify that the termination is necessary. If you'd rather not visit your family doctor, you can go to your local Family Planning Clinic or to one of the specialist organisations listed on the right.

After an abortion

You will probably feel very relieved after the abortion and be glad it's all over. You will be told at the clinic or hospital not to have intercourse for at least three weeks after the abortion and you shouldn't use tampons for about a month. You may experience some light bleeding but it's important that you see your doctor immediately if bleeding is heavy or you experience abdominal pain, vomiting or discharge. Physically, you should be over an early abortion after about a week. For a later termination, physical recovery will take about two to three weeks. You will be asked to return for a check-up after six weeks. Emotional recovery will take longer. You may feel depressed and weepy for weeks or months. If you find it hard to cope, contact the clinic or hospital. They will be able to help by putting you in touch with organisations that specialise in counselling.

Counselling

If carried out by a gynaecologist in a clinic or hospital, complications with an abortion are rare. Infection or severe bleeding occurs in less than 1% of cases.

There is no evidence to suggest that a single abortion will have an effect upon future fertility, however repeated abortions may increase the risk of miscarriage in subsequent pregnancies.

Guilt and grief

The decision whether or not to have an abortion is an emotionally complex one that mustn't be rushed - and yet the time factor is crucial because an abortion should be carried out as early as possible: before 12 weeks, the technique is quick, simple and safe, and emotional and physical recovery tends to be quick. Many women seek counselling to help them make this difficult decision.

Some women need counselling after an abortion. They may experience strong feelings of guilt and in some cases, grief. A few women experience an intense period of mourning after an abortion, and the grief may re-surface regularly at the time of menstruation. Other women may even feel guilty about their feelings of ambivalence towards the abortion.

Types of Abortion

The type of abortion given depends on how far your pregnancy has progressed. The further advanced your pregnancy is, the more difficult and dangerous the procedure. When counting the weeks, start from the first day of your period.

UP TO 12 WEEKS a Vacuum Aspiration can be performed. It's the simplest and safest form of abortion and can be carried out in a clinic or out-patients' department with a local or general anaesthetic. A flexible tube is inserted into the uterus through the cervix and the uterine lining is sucked out. This takes about five minutes.

AT 12-16 WEEKS a Dilation and Evacuation (D&E) can be performed. It can be done under local or general anaesthetic depending on the duration of the pregnancy and can be done on an out-patient basis, although it may mean staying overnight. The operation takes about 30 minutes. The cervix is dilated and a vacuum tube is inserted into the uterus. The tube is connected to a pump which sucks out the womb lining and the foetal material. You may be given drugs to help the uterus contract, and may experience stomach cramps afterwards.

AFTER 16 WEEKS an abortion involves an induced labour which is painful physically and emotionally. A saline solution or the hormone prostaglandin is injected into the amniotic sac through your tummy. You then have to wait for labour to begin, which can take anything up to 24 hours. You will experience painful contractions as if you were in a normal labour and oxytocin may be given or cervical rods used to speed up labour. A Dilation and Curettage (D&C) may then be given to make sure there's nothing left in the uterus and you will probably have to stay in hospital for about three days.

≫ SEE ALSO — Amniocentesis, Contraception, Miscarriage

ABSCESS

An abscess is a collection of pus in tissue or organs caused by a bacterial infection.

The pus is infectious so care needs to be taken to prevent the infection from spreading. Common sites of abscesses include the breast, the armpit, the groin, and the tissue around the root of a tooth that has been damaged, but they may develop in any organ or beneath the skin.

Symptoms

Symptoms include swelling, redness, a fever and pain. The pain is due to the build-up of pus which causes a great deal of pressure as it tries to burst out.

An abscess should be seen by a doctor; usually it will be treated with antibiotics, but if it's very painful the doctor may drain it for you and then take a swab to see what caused it.

A tooth abscess should be treated by a dentist. If the infection has not spread too far, he will be able to drain the pus away without having to remove the tooth.

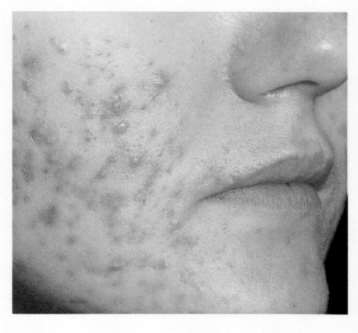

ACNE

Acne is a common complaint, particularly amongst teenagers. It can bring terrible distress at a time when self-confidence needs all the help it can get.

The sebaceous glands, which lie under the skin, continually produce an oily substance called sebum. During adolescence the levels of sex hormones in the blood rise, causing the sebaceous glands to secrete more sebum. Spots form when the

Above: A complexion where pregnancy has made acne worse by increasing the sebum produced by the skin.

ducts, which take the oil out onto the surface of the skin, become blocked with dead skin cells and oil. Blackheads form when the sebum and dead cells oxidise and if they become infected the typical red and swollen spot appears. The spots are usually concentrated on the face, neck, back and shoulders.

There is no simple solution to acne. It's impossible to stop sebum being produced and the more you try to wipe the oil away, the more the sebaceous glands will produce. You can, though, ensure the pores do not become blocked by cleaning frequently with an anti-bacterial cleanser, using a rough flannel or special cleansing sponge like Buf-puf. If this is ineffective you may have to try a special product which will unblock pores.

Products that work

The ingredients to look out for are resorcinol (in Clearasil Cream Medication, DDD Lotion, Acnil and others), salicyclic acid (used in Dermaclear, Clearasil Cleansing Lotion and DDD Lotion) or benzoyl peroxide. Some treatments, however, actually make the problem worse. If you over-use cleansers for oily skin or use alcohol-based astringents, the sebaceous glands will simply pump out more oil.

If the spots become badly infected and unsightly it's worth going to the doctor who may prescribe a short course of antibiotics, ultra-violet therapy or even steroid injections directly into the spots in severe cases.

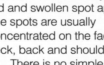

✔ DO

✔ Wash your face regularly. This will help to prevent any acne spreading.

✔ Discuss the problem with your doctor, especially if you have noticed spots have got worse since going on the Pill.

✔ Drink plenty of water.

✔ Eat a healthy, balanced diet, with plenty of fresh fruit and vegetables.

✗ DON'T

✗ Wear too much pore-clogging make-up. Avoid cosmetics that are oil-based.

✗ Pick spots – they may become infected and leave scars on your face.

✗ Allow long hair to become greasy and fall over your face.

✗ Over-stimulate skin with strong products for greasy complexions, as the sebaceous glands will just work harder and produce more oil.

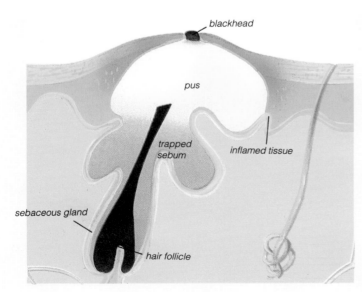

blackhead
pus
trapped sebum
inflamed tissue
sebaceous gland
hair follicle

Left: Spots form when the duct around the hair follicle becomes blocked.

ACTIVE BIRTH

Active birth is the term used to describe childbirth when the mother-to-be is active throughout her labour rather than static and lying in bed.

Over the past few years, more and more women have been adopting this method of childbirth because they claim it's more natural and comfortable than the practices which are widely used in hospitals today. Indeed, the conventional image of a woman confined to bed and lying on her back is something that only came into fashion at the beginning of this century.

Many women also claim that active birth has the added advantage of helping to eliminate pain, and this reduces the use of

Right: In active birth, the mother tries to stay upright.

painkillers which could be potentially harmful to the unborn child. The key to active birth though, is to be relaxed and to understand your body so that you can give birth naturally.

Active childbirth can easily be practised at National Health Service hospitals, as well as private clinics. You should make arrangements early in your pregnancy, and start attending classes weekly. By

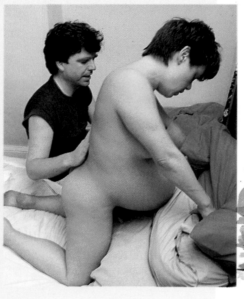

Some exercises for active birth

Above: An exercise for stretching the calf muscles, to help with squatting. Lean against a wall with the upper body relaxed, and push the heel of your back leg against the floor as you breathe out.

Above: If you find it difficult to squat comfortably, practise this supported squat, keeping your heels down and your elbows straight.

Above: Stretch and tone your inner thigh muscles by sitting on the floor with your legs as wide apart as possible. Relax your thighs and push your heels away from you.

embarking upon a specially designed exercise programme during your pregnancy, you can prepare yourself for the event and ensure that everyone involved is aware that you want to follow this method.

Water Birth

The process of birth is a traumatic event for the baby - during birth he is squeezed by muscular contractions and once he is born, he suddenly has to contend with gravity, breathing air, bright light and noise.

Many parents feel that birth into water makes the birth experience as easy as possible as the baby is delivered into a familiar medium where the temperature is similar and early sensations of touch, noise and light are muted.

Many hospitals now offer birthing pools where the mother can relax and give birth naturally and in her own time, but with the security of medical expertise being available if required.

Why Is It So Popular?

A spokesman for the National Childbirth Trust, which has nearly 50,000 members, explains why active birth is so popular:

"Childbirth is something that has become very stereotyped. Turn on any television show or read a book in which a woman is giving birth and the picture portrayed is always of a woman lying in bed, invariably crying with pain as she goes through the final stages of labour. But this is not how it should be, and active childbirth is all about the ideal way to have babies. Women can give birth when they are active. They don't have to lie in bed. When their waters break and their labour starts they can move around, take a bath, keep active and they will find that their labour can be pain-free and the birth easy. It makes sense, you are adopting a natural approach for a natural action.

"You use gravity to draw the baby out naturally. The movement your body makes is up, forward and down as the uterus is contracting. If you're lying down on a bed, you haven't got the pull of natural gravity to draw the baby out. So you're not helping yourself. Many women cry out for painkillers at this point and the problem is not the birth, it is the pressure of the weight on the back."

ADDISON'S DISEASE

Addison's disease is a rare disorder caused by a deficiency of the corticosteroid hormones.

These hormones are produced by the outer part of the adrenal glands and affect the body's use of nutrients. Symptoms develop gradually over months or years and include tiredness, weakness and weight loss. There is no cure, but the deficient hormones can be replaced by regularly taking corticosteroid drugs.

≫ SEE ALSO — Epidural, Labour

ADENOIDS

The adenoids are simply another set of tonsils. They are situated further back and higher up than your normal tonsils at the back of the nasal cavity, rather than in the throat.

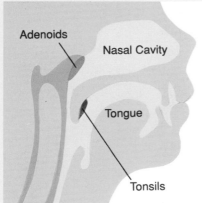

The position of the adenoids.

The adenoids are made up of lymphoid tissue, which is a gland that helps to fight infection. The tissue forms a ring around the throat and gullet and is an important first line of defence against bacteria and viruses.

During the first five years of your life, the adenoids will be very prominent but they will have almost completely disappeared by the time you reach puberty.

Symptoms

The adenoids may become enlarged as a result of repeated infections. Overgrown adenoids obstruct the nasal passage and will force the sufferer to breathe through her mouth. This leads to a vicious circle of repeated infections which in turn increase the size of the adenoids. If the obstruction reaches the drainage tube from the ear, then ear infections occur which may cause deafness. Other symptoms include difficulty in swallowing meat and firm food, and muffled and indistinct speech.

In some cases, enlarged tonsils and adenoids can prevent children from sleeping properly. They will snore and may actually stop breathing for 10 seconds or more at least 30 times a night. In extreme cases, this can lead to heart damage and is an obvious reason for removing the adenoids (an operation known as an adenoidectomy). Another side effect of enlarged adenoids is that children do not fall into a deep sleep, and this chronic infection means that their growth may be restricted. This lack of sleep also makes children prone to temper tantrums.

Some specialists would not advocate removal of adenoids until at least seven, whereas others are prepared to operate on children as young as three, where sleep, hearing and speech are all being interfered with.

ADIPOSE TISSUE

Adipose tissue (subcutaneous fat) is the layer of fat which lies just beneath the skin and around various organs. Adipose tissue is made up of fat which

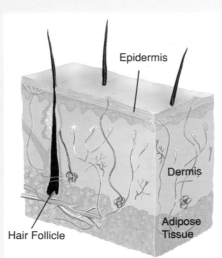

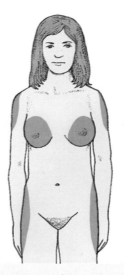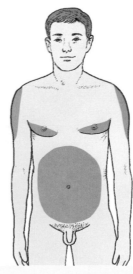

Typical fat distribution in men and women.

stores energy and is deposited in certain areas of the body.

We all have adipose tissue, but the amounts vary according to how much we eat. The layer of tissue helps to insulate the body and keep it warm. It also acts as a cushion in certain areas of the body, such as the feet and bottom, and helps to protect them from sudden pressure.

Where is it found?

The distribution of adipose tissue is different in adult men and women. Women have a larger proportion (18-24%) of adipose tissue in their total body weight than men (who have 12-18%).

It surrounds and cushions various organs such as the heart and kidneys. And in women it also accumulates around the thighs, hips and breasts, while in men it's found on the shoulders, stomach and waist.

ADOLESCENCE

Adolescence is defined medically as the period of physical and emotional development between the onset of puberty and the cessation of bodily growth.

In Western societies, puberty generally starts between the age of eight and 13 in girls, and nine and 14 in boys. Adolescents don't usually stop developing until they're in their late teens or even their early twenties.

Symptoms

Adolescence is not just a period of physical change; it is also a period of psychological and social adjustment that can be painful.

The adolescent will enter this crucial period in her life as a child and emerge from it as an adult who is capable of living independently, and having full sexual and emotional relationships. This period is usually very stressful as the adolescent examines her previous values and ideals and may reject them.

For a number of adolescents, the stresses are so great that they feel the only way to resolve the situation is to run away. The

» SEE ALSO — Tonsils

MEDICAL FACT FILE (vertical, right margin)

MEDICAL FACT FILE

The transition from child to adult can be very stressful for adolescents.

tragedy is that many of today's runaways could be helped if only they were allowed to recognise their own feelings and wishes. With the help of a therapist, they could come to terms with their desires and feelings of deprivation, and lead a happy and fulfilled life.

Adolescents may suffer from the 'Identity Disorder', and become distressed over the uncertainty of various

Internal and External Stress

The stress of adolescence can be divided into two groups: internal and external.

Internal stress tends to centre on concern about physical appearance, and the early/late development of sexual characteristics.

External stresses are usually suffered at school or at home. Adolescents like to think of themselves as being grown-up and independent, while they're still emotionally and financially dependent on their families. This can naturally cause many arguments as the child demands 'more freedom' (late nights, more pocket money) before their parents think they're ready for it.

Physical Changes

The changes that occur in adolescence are due to adult sex hormones which begin to be manufactured by the body at the onset of puberty. In girls, these hormones are responsible for the development of breasts, the growth of pubic and under-arm hair, and the onset of ovulation and periods.

For boys, the physical changes include the growth of facial, body and pubic hair, the enlargement of the penis and scrotum, and the lowering or 'breaking' of the voice.

While these physical changes can be confusing in themselves, the adult sex hormones can also cause emotional upheaval as sexual feelings are awakened.

issues, such as 'what they're going to do with the rest of their lives', their friendships, loyalties and values. They will probably feel very lonely and isolated, and be unable to make decisions. This often leads to them rebelling and choosing a lifestyle that is totally at odds with their families. Luckily, identity crises are short-lived but some may require psychotherapy treatment.

The stresses of adolescence can also lead to 'adult' psychiatric problems such as anorexia nervosa,

schizophrenia and depression, as well as unhappiness and rebelliousness.

ADRENAL GLANDS

The adrenal glands are a pair of small, flattish, triangles of yellow gristle located just above the kidneys.

They consist of two distinct types of tissue which perform completely different tasks.

The medulla
The inner tissue of the adrenal gland is called the 'medulla' and is part of the sympathetic nervous system (a system which controls involuntary activities of the glands, organs and other parts of the body).

During times of stress, the sympathetic nerves are stimulated and the hormone adrenaline is secreted.

The heart rate and blood pressure rise, the body temperature increases and stores of fat or glucose are made ready for rapid use.

This reaction will help you prepare yourself for a fight, for example with a

sabre-toothed tiger, or to run away. If you don't have adrenaline, you won't react to a panic situation.

However, adrenaline also has its disadvantages. All of us have had 'butterflies in the stomach' or have suffered from a 'bowels turning to water' type of fear when sweaty palms and even incontinence can make life a misery. These effects are due to the activities of the sympathetic nervous system

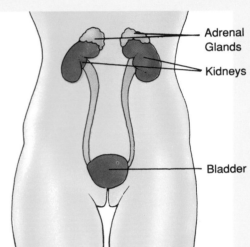

Adrenal Glands

Kidneys

Bladder

The position of the adrenal glands.

and to the effects of adrenaline.

A chronic overproduction of adrenaline can cause panic attacks or generalised anxiety, and this can cause a vicious circle that is difficult to break.

If you suffer in this way, you should see your GP. He may refer you to a specialist who will teach you ways to

Beta - Blockers

● Block the effect of adrenaline and anxiety.
● May be useful before examinations, concerts etc but may cause poor performance due to lack of drive. They are banned from most sports because they may give competitors an unfair advantage.
● Do not cause physical dependency, but should be tailed off slowly because of effects on the heart.
● Must never be taken by asthmatics or anyone with a tendency to wheeze because they can cause fatal asthmatic attacks.
● Are only available on prescription.

≫ SEE ALSO — Addison's Disease

control these panic attacks and thus reduce the production of adrenaline.

In the short term, a drug known as a beta-blocker may be helpful (see box).

The cortex

The outer tissue of the adrenal glands, the 'cortex', is controlled by the pituitary gland and produces two types of hormones: androgens and corticosteroids.

Androgens promote growth, but in excess can cause various problems. In an adult male, they accentuate the development of sexual characteristics, such as the growth of facial and pubic hair, deepening of the voice and enlargement of the genitals. In a boy they can cause early puberty, and in a woman can cause enlargement of the clitoris, shrinking of the breasts and a male pattern of hair distribution. Fortunately these symptoms are extremely rare.

Slightly more common, but still rare, are problems associated with an excess or lack of corticosteroids.

Corticosteroids act on all parts of the body, regulating carbohydrate, fat and protein metabolism, and maintaining the correct balance of fluids and salts. An excess of corticosteroids, known as Cushing's syndrome, causes a long list of problems including obesity, amenorrhoea, high blood pressure and diabetes.

This excess can be due to overactivity of the adrenal glands or to an excess of corticosteroid drugs used for another condition, such as rheumatoid arthritis or asthma. Less commonly, it may be caused by an adrenal tumour secreting excessive corticosteroids.

Long term deficiency of corticosteroid hormones causes Addison's Disease.

AGORAPHOBIA

Agoraphobia is an uncontrollable fear of being in a large open space.

This may lead to panic attacks and sufferers may eventually become housebound.

Treatment includes psychiatric help, such as behaviour therapy, and antidepressant drugs may be prescribed.

AIDS

AIDS (Acquired Immune Deficiency Syndrome) is a complex disease caused by infection with HIV, the Human Immunodeficiency Virus.

The virus, which is spread by the mixing of blood and body fluids, causes the immune system to break down leaving the sufferer open to a variety of infections and diseases. The AIDS patient usually dies of an unusual form of pneumonia or from cancer.

AIDS was first officially recognised in America in 1981, although recent evidence suggests it has been around, unrecognised,

The orange and pink particles are the HIV virus budding in an infected lymphoid cell.

for much longer. In developed countries AIDS is most common amongst gay men, haemophiliacs and those who inject drugs.

The disease now occurs all over the world and in 1989 the World Health Organisation received reports of 203,599 people with AIDS in 177 different countries. They estimate though, that the true figure is likely to be more than 600,000 people with AIDS and between six to eight million people infected by HIV.

The transmission of HIV

It takes time for the virus to develop into full-blown AIDS and some people who were infected more than eight years ago are still healthy. So far researchers have found no way of predicting when the disease will develop although it is unusual for an adult infected with HIV to become ill within three years of infection.

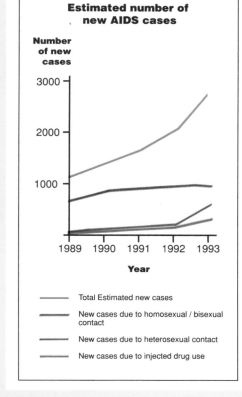

Estimated number of new AIDS cases

Number of new cases

- Total Estimated new cases
- New cases due to homosexual / bisexual contact
- New cases due to heterosexual contact
- New cases due to injected drug use

HIV, unlike other viruses, cannot be 'caught' through casual social contact, coughs and sneezes. It is passed on through sexual contact, shared use of needles and syringes, infected blood transfusions and from mother to child before birth.

In the UK 81 per cent of those with AIDS are gay men

AIDS Symptoms

It takes about three months - and sometimes a year - for a blood test to become positive after infection with the HIV virus. Symptoms at this stage are flu-like, or non-existent.

Symptoms of the next stage, called AIDS-related complex, include fevers, weight loss, diarrhoea, persistent tiredness, and swollen lymph glands. These may appear after a year, or not for many years.

Finally, full-blown AIDS develops when the damaged immune system can no longer fight infection.

» SEE ALSO — Phobias

MEDICAL FACT FILE

but there is also an increasing, though still small, risk for heterosexuals. They are particularly at risk if the man is bisexual, either partner uses intravenous drugs or has had 'high risk' sex in an area of the world where the virus is particularly prevalent such as central Africa or the large cities of America.

The future

There is no cure for AIDS yet, although several drugs are being used to treat HIV infection and the illnesses which it allows to flourish.

Zidovudine, which is marketed as 'AZT' or 'Retrovir', is the best known and is used to try and delay the onset of full-blown AIDS in those who are HIV positive. It does though, have serious side effects and is less effective the longer a person has been infected with the virus. Other drugs are currently being evaluated in the hope of finding one which is cheaper, less toxic and easy to take.

A vaccine against AIDS offers more hope, but so far attempts to find one have proved unsuccessful as the virus has a very complex life cycle and acts on the body's immune system.

But in the fight against AIDS our best hope is in educating people to change their behaviour. HIV is a preventable infection and its spread can be slowed if everyone is properly educated to the risks and behaves responsibly.

ALBINISM

Albinism is a rare hereditary condition, caused by a lack of the pigment melanin in the skin, hair and eyes.

In cases of total albinism, the skin is pale

Top: White rabbits are common albinos of the animal kingdom. Above: Rock star Edgar Winter and brother Johnny used their albinism as part of their distinctive stage presence.

pink, the hair is white and the iris is colourless. The eyes therefore look pink because the blood in the vessels at the back of the eyes shows through the transparent retina and iris.

The skin ages quickly, cannot tan and has a tendency to develop cancer when exposed to the sun. Many albinos suffer with visual problems which should be treated at an early age.

Albinism also occurs in animals. The familiar white rabbits with pink eyes is probably the best known example of albinism.

ALCOHOLISM

When we drink alcohol, it is absorbed into the bloodstream through the lining of the stomach and intestine. Most of it is processed by the liver and the rest is got rid of in sweat and urine.

If you're smaller than average or if you're menstruating, alcohol will affect you more easily. But if you are on the Pill, alcohol is absorbed more slowly and stays in the body longer, so you could find yourself drinking more as the effects aren't felt so soon.

Alcohol dulls your brain functions, affecting your judgment and self-control. You may take risks like driving when you've had a drink too many or you may get into an argument with someone at work or at home. Many family rows are caused by too much alcohol and nearly half of violent crimes are committed by people who have been drinking.

Long term heavy drinking can cause serious diseases such as cirrhosis of the liver, it can affect the nervous system, cause stomach disorders, high blood pressure, breast cancer and brain damage. Too much alcohol can make it difficult to get pregnant and

it can also affect the foetus if you are already expecting.

If you think you are drinking too much, try to break out of your routine. If you usually go to the pub in your lunch hour or after work, arrange to do something different. Go swimming, for example, or join an exercise class. If you have to drink socially, choose low alcohol or alcohol-free drinks. If your problem is more serious and you are finding it impossible to give up alcohol, then see your doctor as soon as possible. There are organisations such as Alcoholics Anonymous who help anyone who wants to give up drinking. Their members have been alcoholics which means they understand your problem.

Alcohol Content

Alcoholic drinks vary greatly in their strength. Beers, lagers and ciders generally contain between 4 and 9% alcohol by volume; wines tend to contain between 9 and 20%; spirits such as gin, vodka, whisky and brandy can contain up to 40%, and liquers up to 60%.

These figures can be confusing, however, in that beer and lager tends to be consumed in large quantities when compared to, say whisky - and so a pint of a strong beer will contain more alcohol than a double whisky.

The unit of alcohol is a good standard measure that enables the alcohol content of different alcoholic drinks to be compared. In this system:

1 unit = ½ pint (284ml) of beer
= a single measure (24ml) of spirits
= a glass (125ml) of wine

Remember that some beers, ciders and lagers may be up to three times stronger than ordinary beers.

ALLERGY

Allergies occur when the immune system produces antibodies and sensitised white blood cells when exposed to substances that are normally harmless.

When the immune system encounters the substances for the second time, it releases histamine and various other chemicals. These chemicals are responsible for the symptoms of allergy, such as sneezing, nasal congestion, itchy swelling, inflammation of the eyes, vomiting or narrowing of the airways in asthma.

Treatment

The best treatment is to avoid the allergen. If this is not possible, a course of antihistamine tablets may be prescribed which may help to relieve the symptoms. They have no effect on asthma or food allergy, however.

On the other hand, sufferers who are allergic to insect venom or some pollens may be desensitised. Desensitisation is the process of administering increasing doses of the allergen in order to trick the immune system into producing antibodies that will

Below: A micro photograph of an allergen. The dark stains are granules that are released in response to an allergy, and contain, amongst other substances, histamine.

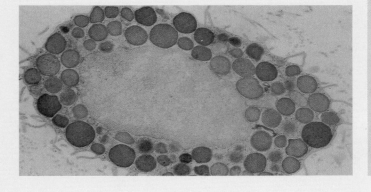

block the allergic reactions. This treatment is successful for two out of three sufferers but may have some side effects, such as itching or swelling.

Types of allergy

Common allergies such as asthma, eczema or hayfever are caused by reactions to substances, such as pollen, particles of animal hair or house dust.

Many people also suffer from skin allergies to substances such as rubber or cosmetic products.

Food allergies are also fairly common and can be very severe. For example, some sufferers develop fatal reactions to nuts and shellfish.

ALOPECIA

Complete loss of body hair, *alopecia totalis,* is rare but most women will suffer from some degree of alopecia, or excessive hair loss, in their lives.

Hair grows in cycles but the length of the cycle depends on the region of the body. For example, scalp hair grows faster and longer than pubic hair.

During pregnancy, scalp hair will grow thicker than normal. But after you have had the baby, your level of hormones will decrease and you may notice a sudden increase in hair loss. Fortunately, by the time the loss is noticeable new hairs

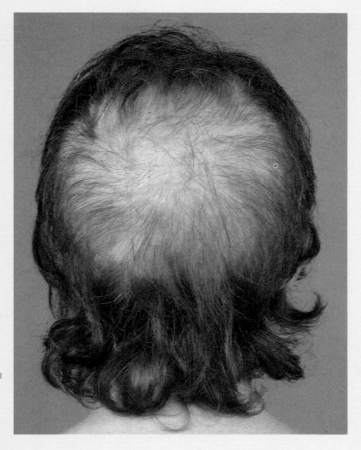

are already appearing to fill the gaps.

Alopecia areata is a distressing condition when hair falls out in distinct round clumps, usually the size of a 10 pence piece. The condition usually cures itself after about six months, but occasionally your doctor may prescribe local injections to speed things up. If you think you are losing too much hair,

Above: Alopecia can be a painfully embarrassing condition, and many women suffer from it.

count the number of hairs on your brush and down the plug hole. If you are losing more than a 100 a day for a week or more, you should see your doctor.

The reasons for hair loss

● The most common form of alopecia is hereditary and usually affects men.
● The precise cause of *alopecia areata* is not known, but it sometimes follows an emotional upset.
● Occasionally, alopecia may follow a severe illness, emotional trauma or an operation. Again this cures itself within two or three months and does not need treatment.
● The hairs themselves may be damaged by bleaches, perms or hair dryers. This damage can cause a dramatic hair loss as all the hair snaps off. Fortunately the roots are unaffected and the hair soon regrows.
● As women get older, especially after the menopause, they tend to lose hair. If this occurs at an early age, it should be investigated but only very rarely is a cause actually found.

➤➤ SEE ALSO — Antihistamine drugs, Asthma

ALZHEIMER'S DISEASE

Alzheimer's disease is one of a group of conditions that cause dementia.

It can occur at any age, but, despite many theories, there has as yet been no convincing explanation as to why it occurs.

The first sign of Alzheimer's disease is a loss of short term memory, but it is something more serious than just the absent-mindedness that we all get from time to time.

For example, the sufferer may be able to remember who came to her fifth birthday party, but will have forgotten what she did this morning.

Gradually, the sufferer will become unable to cope with the problems of daily living. For example, she may become disorientated and lose her way in familiar surroundings. Or she may lose her ability to concentrate and be unable to recognise friends or relatives. Eventually, she will be unable to control her emotions and her speech may make little sense.

Caring for the sufferer

Looking after the elderly who are mentally ill is a stressful and time-consuming task. It usually puts the whole family under a tremendous amount of strain.

This problem has now been recognised though, and help is available in the form of 'meals on wheels', home help, day care and a clean linen service. Social services should be able to organise this.

Voluntary sector organisations such as Age Concern may offer 'granny sitting services' or help with lifts etc. Most geriatric hospitals have one or two beds set aside for respite care which enables the carers to have a short break.

Aluminium Alert

Although not yet proven, it does appear that there is some connection between the amount of aluminium we take into our bodies and the development of dementia.

AMENORRHOEA

Amenorrhoea is a lack of periods. In most cases there is no cause for alarm; just be patient and your periods will start up naturally.

Although a lack of menstrual periods is not dangerous to your health, it usually means that you're not producing eggs and so cannot get pregnant. Don't stop using contraceptives though, just in case!

The 'normal' menstrual cycle of 28 days is relatively uncommon. Anything from 23 to 60 days or more can be considered normal, as long as your periods are regular.

The number of days missed before 'being late' can be labelled as amenorrhoea depends on the previous few cycles. If you have been as regular as clockwork for the past few months, being even a week late should be looked upon as abnormal.

Types of amenorrhoea

Doctors distinguish between two types of amenorrhoea: 'primary' and 'secondary'.

If a woman has never had a period, then she has primary amenorrhoea. But if her periods have been normal and then stop, it is secondary.

If you suffer from amenorrhoea, the first step is to visit your GP. She will ask you when your last period was and, if you've never had a period, will enquire about the periods of your mother and sisters. Women start having periods at different ages, so if your mother and sisters were late starters, your doctor is less likely to worry if you're 15, 16 or 17 years old before your period starts.

Your doctor may examine you for signs of sexual development. She may also measure your height to exclude rare genetic disorders and take a blood sample. It is very rare for these tests to show any abnormality and if they are clear, your doctor will probably reassure you and ask to see you again in six months' time.

However, it is important that you return sooner if you develop severe lower abdominal pain.

Occasionally, the hymen, the

What causes amenorrhoea?

Aside from the menopause, there are a number of reasons you may not have periods.

● Secondary amenorrhoea is surprisingly common – it usually means you're pregnant, unless proven otherwise. Your GP will therefore want to know whether you use contraception, or have noticed breast tingling, nausea and an increased desire to pass water.
● She will also ask if you have noticed any discharge from the nipples. This is fairly common in early pregnancy but may be associated with an excess of a hormone called prolactin. This hormone acts on the breasts to produce milk and on the ovaries to cause amenorrhoea.
● Many women suffer late periods because they are stressed or worrying about something. It is common for women who are worried about pregnancy to experience late periods. This can be especially distressing if you are desperate to have children.
● Weight loss, usually from excessive dieting, will be fairly obvious to your doctor. By the time the periods stop, anorexia nervosa is well advanced and you must

seek expert help. Your own doctor will be sympathetic but if she is not, you could change your GP. New regulations mean that you do not need your old doctor's consent.
● Over-enthusiastic exercise can also delay, or even stop, periods. If you're certain that you're not pregnant, all you need to do is cut back on training.
● Early menopause is rare without either a family history or gynaecological surgery. It is fairly easy to diagnose but your doctor may want to do a blood test to make sure. If you have suffered an early menopause you would almost always be better off on hormone replacement therapy. Ask your doctor or family planning clinic.
● The 'mini-pill' or contraceptive injections often cause menstrual irregularities and it can be difficult to distinguish this amenorrhoea from pregnancy. If you are concerned, you should consult your doctor; a negative pregnancy test will reassure you.
● Occasionally the 'combined pill' can cause amenorrhoea. The Pill, if taken properly, is a very reliable method of contraception but two consecutive missed periods must be investigated. The solution is often just to switch brands.

» SEE ALSO — Dementia, Pregnancy

sheet of tissue at the entrance to the vagina, can stop the menstrual flow, and cause a lot of pain.

Amenorrhoea is rarely serious but it can be very worrying. If you're concerned about your general health or if you think that you might be pregnant you should always consult your doctor.

It's difficult to know when to seek advice; you don't want to leave things too late, but on the other hand women are often frightened of being labelled as 'neurotic'.

Your doctor will be pleased to discuss things and will probably be able to reassure you without too much difficulty. Take along an early morning specimen of urine, even if you don't think you're pregnant. It will save you both a lot of time.

AMNESIA

Amnesia is a loss of memory or an inability to memorise information. It is caused by disease of or damage to the area of the brain concerned with memory functions.

Damage may be inflicted by head injuries, Alzheimer's disease, infections, strokes or brain tumours. A number of people who suffer from amnesia have a big gap in their memories which may go back many years. But, in the majority of cases, amnesiacs manage to get back some of their memory loss.

On the other hand, some amnesiacs cannot remember things that have happened since their illness. This memory gap extends from the time of their illness onwards, to the time when (and if) they get their memory back. This is known as anterograde amnesia and is usually permanent.

AMNIOCENTESIS

Amniocentesis is a procedure used to withdraw a small amount of amniotic fluid from the sac surrounding the foetus.

It was originally used to help with X-ray diagnosis or to induce abortion. Its main role nowadays, though, is to examine for foetal abnormality.

What happens?

Sixteen weeks into pregnancy, the foetus is surrounded by about 130ml of amniotic fluid. The fluid is constantly being swallowed and excreted by the foetus. The aim of amniocentesis is to remove a little of this fluid and either to examine it or the cells in it.

Amniocentesis can be used to obtain information about the baby, including its sex, and to detect some physical abnormalities such as spina bifida or Down's syndrome. Amniocentesis is not without its dangers, however. Even in experienced hands there seems to be a risk of about 0.5-1 per cent of having a miscarriage afterwards, so amniocentesis is reserved for those women whose chance of having an abnormal child is greater than the chance of miscarrying as a result of the test (see box).

Before having the test, you and your partner should have been counselled on the procedure and its risks. You should be aware of the possibility of error and should have given some thought to what to do if the news is bad — whether you would have an abortion (if it is legal in your country).

The test is usually performed at 16 weeks, when there should be enough fluid to spare a little for analysis. The woman lies down and the position of the baby and the placenta is determined by an ultrasound scan. When the gynaecologist is sure that he's found a safe spot, he will inject a little local

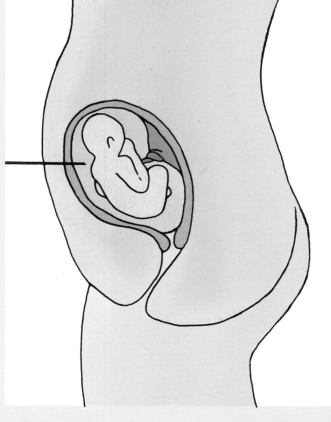

Above: Amniocentesis involves drawing off a small amount of the amniotic fluid that surrounds the foetus.

anaesthetic. Using a long, thin needle he will then draw off about 20ml of fluid.

Most people, though not all, find the whole procedure completely painless. You will be asked to rest for an hour or so and then allowed home, but you will be advised to take things easy for a day or two. Results may take up to three weeks depending on the abnormality being looked for.

Over the past decade, there has been an increase in alternatives to amniocentesis. These techniques are either safer or are performed at an earlier stage in pregnancy.

Chorionic villus sampling, for example, will allow affected foetuses to be aborted (if it is legal) at 10-12 weeks, which is a much safer than the 18-20 week abortion that may follow amniocentesis.

Who should be offered amniocentesis?

● Women over the age of 40. The risk of having a Down's syndrome child is about one in 2000 at age 20 and one in 100 at age 40. All women of 40 would be offered the test but the lower cut off point, 35, 36 or 37 depends on the Health Authority.

● Women with a family history of chromosome abnormalities such as Down's syndrome or who have had such a child.
● Women whose scans or blood tests suggest an abnormality.
● Women known to be carriers of genetic disease.

» SEE ALSO — Down's syndrome, Spina bifida, Ultrasound scan

MEDICAL FACT FILE

AMPHETAMINES

Amphetamines are a group of powerful stimulants that have been used to suppress the appetite.

Unfortunately, they also have some nasty side effects, which include restlessness, anxiety, vomiting, a racing pulse and sweating. In high doses they can cause convulsions and even death.

Uses

Amphetamines were originally used to combat fatigue. They were successful in keeping the subject awake, but the user often found it difficult to concentrate and her work tended to suffer as a result.

A more recent use has been in the treatment of obesity. Amphetamines have the dual role of increasing the rate fat is burnt up and decreasing the appetite. Unfortunately any weight loss is short lived — even if the drug is taken continuously, it soon loses its dieting effect. Worse than this, however, is its powerful addictive effect which will result in the addict suffering all the side effects, but none of the benefits.

Nowadays, amphetamines are almost never prescribed for this purpose except by private slimming clinics whose motives may not always be above reproach.

Who takes them?

Their medical use nowadays is confined to two small groups: patients with 'narcolepsy' who would otherwise sleep all day, and hyperactive children where they exert a calming influence.

Unfortunately their simple chemical structure makes them easy drugs to produce and amphetamines have become one of the most abused drugs because of the temporary 'high' they produce.

Amphetamine Abuse

Amphetamines are often taken by drug abusers for the short period of extreme excitement, cheerfulness and confidence that they produce. This 'high' is followed by temporary feelings of fatigue, depression and irritability.

Acting in a similar way to the body's natural adrenalin, amphetamines speed up the heart and breathing rate and the appetite decreases. A noticeable symptom is that the pupils become dilated.

High doses of amphetamines over a short period of time can produce delirium, hallucinations, fear and panic. Heavy use can cause damage to the blood vessels and heart failure.

ANAEMIA

Anaemia is caused by a lack of the protein haemoglobin, which carries oxygen around the body and is found in red blood cells.

Anaemia is a common problem and most women will suffer from it at one time or another, often without realising it. The symptoms of anaemia depend on the cause as well as the severity of the problem. Anaemic people may suffer from tiredness, shortness of breath, menstrual irregularities and dizziness.

What causes it?

Causes of anaemia have been split into two main groups: either the body does not make enough haemoglobin, or what is made is broken down too quickly.

Iron deficiency is a common cause of anaemia. Before the body can produce haemoglobin it needs adequate supplies of building materials, such as vitamins, iron and protein. If any of these nutrients is missing from your diet, anaemia may result.

Protein is found in most dairy products, beans and pulses; iron is found in red meat, cereals and green vegetables; and the important vitamins required are found in most foodstuffs.

Anaemia may also be the result of excessive bleeding, for example heavy periods. Fortunately these cases are rare but if your periods are heavy, it may be worth having a blood test every year or so.

People at risk

People most at risk are children, pregnant women and the elderly. Premature babies are routinely given iron supplements, as are pregnant women who have been diagnosed as anaemic.

The elderly often skimp on meals, especially if they're only cooking for one, and are probably the group most at risk of anaemia. They should be encouraged to eat a healthy and balanced diet, but failing this may need a mixed iron and vitamin supplement.

Unless you are anaemic though, it is advisable not to take iron supplements as they can have side effects, such as nausea and constipation, and may just mask the problem.

Anaemia is not a disease, only a sign of an underlying problem. If you think you're anaemic, you should consult your doctor before starting any treatment.

Your doctor will ask you a few questions about your lifestyle, diet and periods, and may well then take a blood test.

Below: Anaemia may leave sufferers feeling listless and lacking energy.

MEDICAL FACT FILE

ANAESTHESIA

Anaesthesia literally means 'without feeling' and anaesthetics are divided into two groups: the general anaesthetic and the local anaesthetic.

If you had an operation 150 years ago you would have had every reason to be frightened. The only anaesthetics available were opium, cannabis and alcohol — and the effects were very short-lived! Fortunately

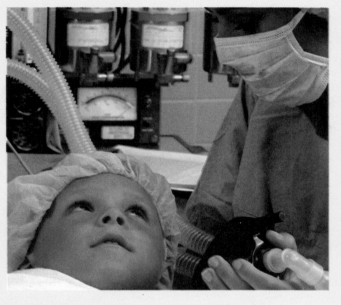

anaesthesia is now much more advanced.

General anaesthetics
A general anaesthetic is administered in the operating theatre, just before surgery, to make you lose consciousness and stop you from suffering any pain.

Once you are asleep the anaesthetist will probably give you further injections of painkillers, paralysing agents

and anaesthetic gases. The painkillers stop your body's unconscious response to pain, such as increasing the pulse and the blood pressure. Paralysing agents allow the surgeons to operate on you without being hampered by your muscle spasms.

Throughout the operation, right up until you are fully awake, the anaesthetist will be there to monitor your condition and treat any unforeseen complication.

Local anaesthetics
A patient given a local anaesthetic remains conscious. These drugs are used to block nerve impulses and thus deaden pain. For example, a common local anaesthetic may be administered by your dentist to numb your gums and prevent discomfort during dental treatment.

Local anaesthesia can be a simple matter of

injecting into a cut before stitching or it may involve 'regional block'.

The idea behind regional block is that nerves are rather like the branches of a tree, with the finest twigs being the nerve endings nearest the skin and the trunk being the spinal cord. For example, injections around the nerve in the jaw will freeze all the teeth supplied by that branch.

ANALGESICS

Analgesics are drugs that relieve pain. They differ in strength and in the way they work, and are divided into two groups: opiates and anti-inflammatories.

For day-to-day pain relief, paracetamol is safe, cheap and effective. It causes fewer tummy upsets than aspirin and should be tried before the more expensive combination analgesics.

Anti-inflammatory drugs
Anti-inflammatories are based on the structure of aspirin, which is a painkiller that has been used for over 80 years.

They are used to treat moderate pain such as headaches, toothache or period pains, and chronic conditions such as arthritis and rheumatism. Anti-inflammatories should only be used for 48 hours, though. If the pain persists, gets worse or is a different kind of pain to the one previously experienced, you should see your GP.

Anti-inflammatory drugs may cause some side effects though, such as abdominal pain, nausea, vomiting, breathing difficulties or even ulcers. You can minimise the risk of side effects by taking the anti-inflammatory drug with food or a glass of milk.

Opiates
Opiates range in strength from codeine to morphine and heroin, and are only available on prescription. Morphine and heroin are extremely powerful painkilelrs. This and their mood-lifting properties make them invaluable in treating cancer and heart attacks.

ANGINA

Angina is a pain in the chest that is due to the heart muscle not receiving enough oxygen in the blood.

The heart is a muscle that needs a regular supply of oxygen to function efficiently. Angina occurs when the coronary arteries, which carry oxygen round the heart, become clogged up by fat deposits. After a critical point, the arteries can no longer supply the heart with enough oxygen, especially if it is forced to work hard. The lack of oxygen causes the build-up of waste products and this causes pain.

Symptoms
Sufferers describe a 'tight' or 'vice-like' pain in the centre of the chest, which often spreads into the left arm or

Pre - Meds
● Are given one to two hours before the operation.
● May be tablet or injection or both.
● Make the patient drowsy and reduce anxiety.
● Dry up secretion; makes the operation easier but will also cause a dry mouth and throat.

Ways to avoid Angina
● Don't smoke – smoking not only encourages the formation of blockages but it also decreases the amount of oxygen in the blood.
● Keep an eye on your weight – obesity puts an additional strain on the heart.
● Take regular exercise.
● Drink alcohol in moderation.
● Stick to a low-cholesterol diet.

➤➤ SEE ALSO — Aspirin, Paracetamol

MEDICAL FACT FILE

MEDICAL FACT FILE

up into the jaw. Symptoms include nausea, sweating and breathing difficulties. Angina is brought on by exercise, emotion or a heavy meal and is eased by rest.

If you're suffering from chest pain, see your GP. She

pain, the next step is either a beta-blocker or a drug called Nifedipine. Both drugs act on the heart itself and on the circulation.

If all these steps prove ineffectual, then the coronary arteries can either be

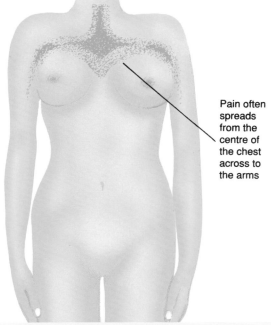

Pain often spreads from the centre of the chest across to the arms

Angina is a 'vice-like' pain felt in the centre of the chest.

will ask you to describe the pain, and will ask whether you smoke, have high blood pressure or whether any members of your family have heart trouble.

Treatment
In most cases of suspected angina, the doctor will perform an ECG or heart trace which records the electrical activity of the heart.

In severe angina it is becoming popular to x-ray the coronary arteries. A dye is fed into the arteries via a small tube inserted into an arm vein. The dye passes through the coronary vessels and shows them up on an x-ray screen. The extent of the blockage and its likely results can be seen at once.

GTN tablets are the mainstay of angina treatment. They cause blood to collect in the legs and this takes the strain off the heart. If these measures do not control the

replaced using veins from the leg or cleaned using a balloon on the end of a tube. Future developments such as tiny lasers are likely to make surgery less common.

ANOREXIA NERVOSA

Anorexia nervosa, the slimmer's disease, is a psychological disturbance which is characterised by the sufferer refusing to eat eat and being terrified of putting on weight.

Anorexia affects one in 100 young women. The group most at risk are 12-30 year–olds, especially those from higher socio-economic classes. No-one knows for sure what causes anorexia, but some doctors argue that anorectics see dieting as a

way to control their lives, while others claim that anorectics have a real phobia about putting on weight (see Anorexia Nervosa Understanding Yourself).

Symptoms
The illness usually starts with normal dieting, but an anorectic eats less and less each day until she loses about one third of her body weight but still thinks she's plump.

When the disease is fairly advanced, the anorectic may stop having periods. She may be tired and pale, and may find she starts to grow downy hair on her body. She may also try to keep her weight down by taking excessive amounts of laxatives and diuretics.

Treatment
The aim of all treatment is to restore the anorectic's body weight to normal and correct the problem that caused the disease in the first place.

If the disease is severe and the anorectic continues to refuse to eat, she may have to go into hospital so her weight can be closely monitored. Sufferers may also need the help of psychotherapy treatment for months or even years after they've achieved a normal body weight.

ANTENATAL CARE

The aim of antenatal care is to produce a beautiful baby and a healthy mother. This is done by monitoring the pregnancy and treating problems as they arise.

The antenatal care you receive may seem tedious, but it's aimed at picking up problems at an early stage and you should make sure you attend your

appointments. Regular check-ups will improve your, and the baby's, chance of a happy delivery.

The first step
If your pregnancy test is positive, your GP will want to examine and advise you on diet, alcohol and smoking.

She will check your urine and blood pressure, and will listen to your heart and lungs. She will also ask you to fill in some forms that will ensure you receive free medical and dental care. Your GP will want to see you every four weeks until 28 weeks, then every two weeks until 36 weeks, and then weekly.

Subsequent steps
Once you've seen your doctor, you may then meet the midwife who's attached to the practice. A midwife is a nurse who has undertaken further training in the care of pregnant women. She is well qualified to see you right

Ultrasound scan

At an early stage in your pregnancy, usually between 14 and 16 weeks, you will have an ultrasound scan.

The scan uses sound waves to build a picture of the baby. For many women it is the first time they really believe they are pregnant. The scan helps to fix the expected date of delivery and will also pick up some abnormalities such as spina bifida, although other conditions such as Down's syndrome cannot be detected. The position of the placenta can be important, especially if it covers the neck of the womb. In about one in 80 pregnancies the scan shows twins!

⟫ SEE ALSO — Amenorrhoea, Diuretic drugs

At antenatal classes you will learn how to relax.

DO

✔ Check that you are immune to German measles (rubella) before getting pregnant - it's a viral infection that may handicap your unborn child

✔ See your doctor once you know you're pregnant

✔ Attend antenatal clinics

✔ Eat a healthy diet

✔ See a dentist - it's free during pregnancy and for one year after

✔ Keep a diary of your periods to help you pinpoint the date the baby is due

DON'T

✗ Smoke – it can stunt your baby's growth

✗ Take any medication without your doctor's or midwife's advice

✗ Drink more than one to two glasses of wine a week

✗ Eat soft cheeses, cooked-chilled food or liver

✗ Run the risk of exposure to x-rays or chemicals

✗ Empty the cat litter without putting a pair of gloves on - a virus found in cat faeces can cause abnormalities

through your pregnancy and will only need a doctor's advice if she thinks there may be a problem.

The midwife will ask you a number of questions about your past medical history. She will also enquire into your social circumstances and can steer you in the direction of housing and other help.

After this initial interview, you will probably be referred to the local hospital consultant. He or she will share your antenatal care until you go into labour.

You, and your partner, will be invited to attend antenatal classes which will help you to understand your labour and the various painkillers available. At most classes you will be encouraged to practise a number of breathing exercises and relaxation techniques. At some stage, usually near the end of the course, you may be invited to look around the labour ward and speak to the staff.

If you have not gone into labour by around week 42, your consultant may suggest you come into the hospital for an induction of labour.

ANTIBIOTICS

Antibiotics are a group of drugs that kill bacteria and fight infection. They were originally obtained from fungus and mould but they are now produced synthetically.

There are many different types of antibiotic drugs, but penicillin is the most well-known. Penicillin has actually been around for 60 years so few people can actually remember the 'bad old days' when you could die from a chest infection.

Antibiotics are not always effective though. Some bacteria may actually develop resistance to the drugs, which is usually a result of a repeated course of antibiotics. They also have no effect on viruses such as AIDS, 'flu or colds.

Side effects
The commonest side effect of antibiotics is diarrhoea. This is usually due to the disturbance of the normal, friendly germ that lives in the bowel. This diarrhoea can cause problems for you if you're on the Pill — use

Why do they do that?

At the antenatal clinic your doctor or midwife will examine you for a number of things.

● Check blood pressure - raised blood pressure can be one of the signs of toxaemia - a serious problem.
● Test urine samples for protein (a sign of toxaemia) and sugar. Diabetes is more common in pregnancy, sugar in the urine is the first sign.
● Weight - excessive weight gain may be due to fat or fluid retention. Poor weight gain may be a sign that the baby is not getting enough nourishment.
● Feeling the abdomen - checking for the position of the baby; is it normal or a breech? Checking the position of the head; is it still free or is it engaged? Checking the size of the womb corresponds with the dates.
● Blood tests - these may be for anaemia or to make sure that the placenta is functioning properly. The alpha-fetoprotein test is usually offered to test for spina bifida.

The fungus Penicillium notatum is a species that was used as an early source of the common antibiotic penicillin.

another contraceptive, as well as the Pill, while you're on antibiotics and for a further 14 days once you've finished the course.

Antibiotic drugs may also make you feel nauseous, cause an itchy rash, or even encourage the growth of oral, intestinal or vaginal fungi. For example, thrush is a frequent side effect of antibiotic therapy. Severe reactions may lead to difficulties in breathing, facial swelling or itching.

Ten per cent of the population think they're allergic to penicillin, but this allergy is actually quite rare. The rash they have is probably a sign of the original illness and not a side effect of the antibiotics.

ANTIDEPRESSANT DRUGS

Antidepressant drugs are frequently prescribed by doctors or psychiatrists for people who are suffering from depression.

Antidepressant drugs come in tablet or capsule form, and need to be taken for at least two or three weeks to have any effect. To be fully effective, they should be taken for eight weeks. They usually work by triggering the release of certain chemicals in the brain which may help to stabilise the depressive's moods.

As with most drugs, antidepressants can cause side effects, such as dizziness, blurred vision, difficulty in passing urine, drowsiness, constipation or a dry mouth. They should not be taken with alcohol and you should try to avoid driving as your reactions may not be as fast as usual.

ANTIHISTAMINE DRUGS

Antihistamine drugs block the effects of histamine, a chemical released during an allergic reaction.

They are used to treat people suffering from symptoms of an allergic reaction, such as sneezing, itchy rashes, redness and swelling. They are also used in some cold and cough medications as they help to relieve discomfort caused by congestion and a runny nose. They have no effect on asthma or food allergy, though.

Some antihistamine drugs (with the exception of the newer ones, such as triludan) can cause drowsiness and impair coordination, so don't drive or operate any potentially dangerous machinery if you are taking them.

ANTIPYRETIC DRUGS

Antipyretic drugs, such as aspirin and paracetamol, help to lower your temperature and are useful for a cold or 'flu.

Take two tablets every four hours, but don't exceed 12 in any 24 hours.

ANTISEPTICS

Antiseptics are chemicals that destroy bacteria.

Antiseptics are commonly used to sterilise equipment which will help to prevent infection.

Antiseptic mouthwashes will also help to relieve discomfort caused by mouth ulcers. They will also ease the symptoms of

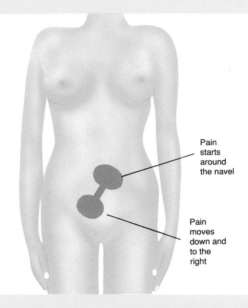

Location of the pain caused by appendicitis.

inflammation. Commonly used antiseptics include iodine, hydrogen peroxide and hibitane.

APPENDICITIS

Appendicitis is acute inflammation of the appendix.

The appendix is a small, worm-like structure leading off the large intestine which has no known function. The cause of appendicitis is usually not known, but it's sometimes the result of a small, hard pellet of faeces blocking the drainage tube.

With luck, the inflammation will settle but if not the infection can spread. If the appendix bursts it causes peritonitis, which is a potentially fatal infection of the abdomen. Peritonitis is very painful and the sufferer will obviously be very ill.

Treatment
Treatment of appendicitis is straightforward and relatively simple. An incision is made in the abdominal wall, the appendix is located and snipped off. The wound is then closed and the patient is usually well enough to go home in three or four days.

Some surgeons have even started removing the appendix using a laparoscope. It is inserted through a small incision in the navel so you'll only get a tiny scar.

Diagnosis
The average GP will see several hundred cases of abdominal pain each year, but only four of these will be due to acute appendicitis.

Appendicitis is difficult to diagnose and dangerous if the GP misses it. If you've been suffering with abdominal pain for an hour or two and are concerned about it, see your GP.

Symptoms

● Pain - starts in the middle, shifts to the right after a few hours. Made worse by pressure.
● Fever - low grade temperature, rarely above 38 degrees centigrade unless peritonitis.
● Loss of appetite
● Vomiting
● The patient often has a coated tongue and bad breath.

≫ SEE ALSO — Analgesics, Aspirin, Paracetamol

Labels on image: Pain starts around the navel / Pain moves down and to the right

ARTHRITIS

Arthritis is an inflammatory disease of the joints that causes stiffness and swelling. It is a common cause of pain and disability.

Forty per cent of people over the age of 65 suffer from it in one form or another. And 45 million working days are lost each year because of it. Unfortunately, there is nothing you can do to stop arthritis, but there are a number of treatments available that will help to ease the pain and slow down the progress of the disease.

Treatment

Pain can be relieved by using treatments such as hot wax, ultrasound and drugs. The drugs prescribed will be either standard painkillers such as paracetamol or anti-inflammatories such as

Arthritis affects the joints, particularly in the hands, resulting in painful swelling and deformity.

aspirin (see analgesics). Anti-inflammatory drugs are more effective but have greater side effects, such as nausea and abdominal pain.

An alternative treatment is an injection of a local anaesthetic and a steroid directly into the joint. This

can be very effective but does need to be repeated every few weeks.

Surgery is becoming an increasingly popular form of treatment. Orthopaedic surgeons can now replace hips, knees, shoulders, elbows and even finger joints.

aim of making the woman pregnant.

Occasionally sperm may be injected through the cervix into the womb itself. The technique can be further refined by concentrating the sperm to artificially raise a low sperm count.

Types of sperm

The sperm can be from the husband (AIH), or an unknown donor (AID).

AIH is useful if the husband's sperm count is low, if penetration is impossible (paraplegics, for example) or if the cervical mucus is 'hostile'. Hostile mucus is when the plug at the neck of the womb is abnormally thick or contains antibodies that kill sperm.

AID is usually reserved for couples with a low sperm count or for those at risk of genetic disorders, such as cystic fibrosis. The obvious advantage of donor sperm is that it's known to be mobile and is hopefully free of genetic disorders, although this cannot be guaranteed.

The risks

The obvious risk involved in artificial insemination is infection from viruses, such as AIDS and hepatitis B. Semen donors must be healthy, and are usually

Forms of Arthritis

Osteoarthritis

Osteoarthritis is the most common form of arthritis and one person in 10 will suffer from it. Sufferers will often be people who have been used to vigorous exercise and who have, quite literally, worn the lining of their joints away.

The knees, hips and spine are usually the first areas of the body to be affected. Pain starts off as an ache that comes and goes. As the disease gets worse, it will become more and more difficult to move these joints – initially due to pain, but later due to deformity. The worn out surfaces, especially of the knee, can be felt grating over each other.

Rheumatoid arthritis

This is the most severe form of arthritis and will affect one person in 100. It occurs when the membrane which lines the joint becomes thick and swollen. Unlike osteoarthritis, this affects the fingers and toes first. The onset is often slow and many joints, particularly the arms, feet, wrists and hands, will become stiff, painful and deformed, inhibiting movement.

Juvenile chronic arthritis

About 1000 children under the age of 16 are affected by juvenile chronic arthritis. It often starts with a severe 'flu-like illness that leaves the joints swollen, painful and stiff. Fortunately, 75 per cent of the sufferers will recover on their own.

ARTIFICIAL INSEMINATION

Artificial insemination is the placing of semen in, or around, the neck of the womb with the

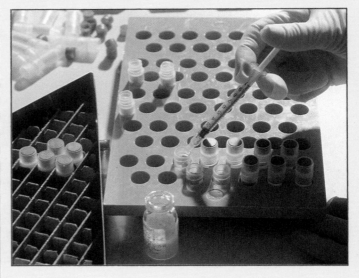

Artificial Insemination centres are specially equipped to store the semen and carry out the insemination.

screened for a number of medical disorders. By law, all donor sperm must be frozen whilst a small sample is analysed to ensure that the donor is clear of infection.

Treatment

The technique of artificial insemination is very straightforward and is no more unpleasant, if it's done sympathetically, than having a smear.

The woman lies on a couch whilst the doctor places the sperm in the neck of the womb using a syringe with a long tube. After lying down for a few minutes, to give the sperm a chance to enter the womb, the woman is then allowed home but advised to take things easy for a day or two.

Artificial insemination is usually repeated three or four times over a period of two to four days. It is essential that it takes place at the right point in the menstrual cycle. The doctor in charge will require an accurate temperature chart or urine tests to determine the time of ovulation.

When fresh semen is used, the chances that the woman will become pregnant over a period of about six months is approximately 60–70 per cent. If semen is used that has been frozen, the success rate is not quite as high — about 35 per cent.

If you think that you may benefit from artificial insemination, then speak to your doctor about referral to a National Health Service infertility clinic or a private clinic such as the British Pregnancy Advisory Service.

ARTIFICIAL RESPIRATION

Artificial respiration is a way of forcing air into the lungs until skilled help can be summoned to start the person breathing again.

Artificial respiration may be given by using mouth-to-mouth resuscitation (see box), mouth-to-nose or by using ventilating equipment.

Respiration can stop for a number of reasons. The commonest causes are heart attacks, electric shocks and drowning. Without oxygen, the adult brain will survive for three minutes. Then it will deteriorate rapidly.

It is usually obvious that breathing has stopped. The patient is blue and lifeless. Act as quickly as possible, following the steps shown on the left.

The likelihood of catching AIDS through mouth-to-mouth resuscitation is remote, but special mouthpieces are available.

Mouth-to-Mouth Resuscitation

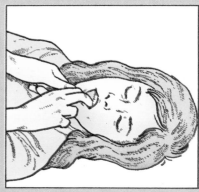

1 Don't waste time feeling for a pulse. Turn the patient on her back, open her mouth, clear out any vomit, remove false teeth.

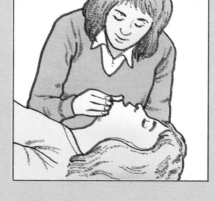

2 Tilt the head back slightly and pull the jaw forward to stop the patient's tongue flopping back.

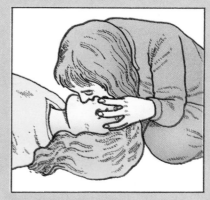

3 Pinch the patient's nostrils with your thumb and forefinger. Seal your mouth around the patient's mouth (mouth and nose if it is a child) and breathe out firmly.

4 Keep an eye on the patient's chest: it should rise and fall with your exhalations. Aim for a rate of about 10 times a minute and keep it up until help arrives or the patient starts breathing.

 DO

✔ Start giving artificial respiration if the victim has stopped breathing
✔ Resuscitate a baby or young child by sealing your mouth over the victim's mouth and nose
✔ Blow gentle breaths of air into the victim's lungs

 DON'T

✗ Tip a child's neck back very far – children's necks and airways are more fragile than adults'
✗ Bother to loosen clothing unless there's a risk of strangulation
✗ Forget to send for medical help as soon as possible

ASPIRIN

Aspirin is a commonly used painkiller that will bring down a high temperature and reduce inflammation

Aspirin is an analgesic that has been used to treat common complaints, such as period pains and headaches for just under one hundred years. Many cold and 'flu remedies contain aspirin as the active ingredient. The benefits of the other ingredients though, are negligible and it would certainly be cheaper to take aspirin on its own. Because of its effects in the stomach though, aspirin should not be used to treat hangovers.

The most common drugs containing aspirin are Anadin, Solprin and Disprin.

Side effects

Aspirin is a remarkably safe medication and is commonly used. But if you have a sensitive stomach, it may give you indigestion or even ulcers. Soluble aspirin is said to cause less upsets than insoluble aspirin but, if taken with plenty of water, the cheaper version is as safe.

Aspirin is no longer recommended for children because of the possible link with Reye's Syndrome, which is a rare, acute disorder of the brain and liver that is usually confined to children under the age of 15. It may be fatal or cause permanent damage. Paracetamol is a safe alternative.

It has been known for many years that aspirin can cause bleeding but in the last decade this fault has been put to good use. Aspirin, even in doses as low as one a day, will decrease the incidence of death from heart disease and may relieve the pain of angina. In a recent study the benefits of treatment were shown to outweigh any side effects.

ASTHMA

Asthma is difficulty in breathing due to narrowing of the small airways in the lungs called the bronchioles.

In older children and adults this narrowing causes a musical wheeze. In younger children the only symptom may be a cough that is usually worse at night.

Most doctors would agree that asthma is on the increase, probably due to rising levels of pollution. Some estimates put the number of sufferers in the UK as high as five million though most of these cases will be mild.

What causes it?

Bronchioles have muscles in their walls. Under normal conditions these muscles are relaxed, allowing air to pass freely. If the airways are irritated, for example by cold air or smoke, the muscle contracts and the tube narrows. The muscle in the airways of asthmatics is abnormally sensitive and will contract at the least provocation.

Apart from straight forward irritation, the three main provocations are infection, allergy and emotion. All will have some effect but the proportion caused by, say, allergy will vary from person to person.It is obviously a good idea to look at the causes before treating the symptoms.

The typical asthmatic will come from a family where hayfever and eczema are common. She will have been 'chesty' as a child and as she grows up she has a tendency to wheeze and she finds that she gets short of breath easily.

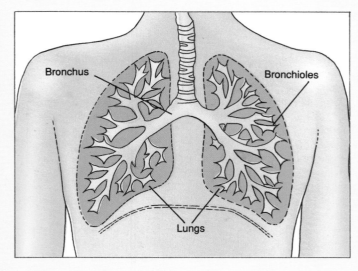

The bronchioles are small, branching airways in the lungs.

Treatment

Modern treatment usually involves two types of drugs The first, a bronchodilator, acts within seconds and causes the airway to relax. The commonest bronchodilator is Ventolin which may be given in tablet or spray form. The aerosol sprays are a bit tricky to master but deliver the drug to the exact spot. They are specially designed with a mouthpiece, and are operated by squeezing so that the spray goes down the air passages as you inhale.

Cardiac Asthma

Cardiac asthma is caused by fluid accumulating in the lungs, making it difficult to breathe.

This usually happens when the pumping action of the left side of the heart is reduced, resulting in congestion and increased pressure in the blood circulation through the lungs. It is usually a result of old age and can be caused by taking beta-blockers.

The sufferer may be treated for heart failure or with bronchodilator drugs.

Inhalers containing bronchodilator drugs are commonly used to treat asthma attacks.

>> SEE ALSO — Analgesics, Antipyretics, Reye's Syndrome

MEDICAL FACT FILE

This means that much smaller doses can be used.

The second group of drugs are the anti-inflammatories such as Becotide or Intal. These block the effects of irritants but take several days to build up in the system. They cannot be used for instant relief but will protect against next week's attack. In severe asthma, steroids can be life-saving, but most doctors would be reluctant to use them every day because of side effects.

Allergic reactions

There is some evidence to suggest that asthmatics are sensitive to particular foods. Sometimes an elimination diet, where specific foods are removed from the diet under medical supervision, may reveal that eggs, wheat, gluten or dairy products exacerbate the problem.

For example, many asthmatics find that goat's milk or soya-based dairy products suit them better than cow's milk, and adapt their diet accordingly.

House-dust Mite

Many asthma sufferers are allergic to the house-dust mite - or, more precisely, their faeces. These miniscule insects feed off household dust so to keep them at bay, keep your house as dust-free as possible.

ASTIGMATISM

Astigmatism is a condition affecting eyesight where the cornea, the tough outer shell of the eyeball, does not bend correctly.

Astigmatism occurs in perfectly healthy eyes and the defect prevents the affected person from focusing on both vertical and horizontal objects at the same time, causing a blurring of lines.

Correcting the problem

To counter the distressing effects of astigmatism, a special spectacle lens is required — one which affects the light rays on either the vertical or horizontal plane.

Sometimes, as an alternative, a hard contact lens is used, which allows the layer of fluid between the lens and the eye to compensate for the cornea. Ordinary soft lenses are unsuitable because they tend to mould to the astigmatic curve.

ATHLETE'S FOOT

Athlete's foot is a common skin disorder. It's caused by a fungal infection that occurs between the toes and on the sole of the foot.

The skin becomes itchy and cracked, with flaking pieces of dead white skin. In severe cases, blisters develop and the toe-nails become thickened and discoloured.

It is highly contagious and is spread either by direct contact or via infected material. Take particular care to use your own towel and not share bathmats.

Easing the symptoms

Athlete's foot is relatively easy to treat. First, you should gently rub away the dead skin. Then apply an anti-fungal treatment — these are available from chemists in spray, ointment or powder form — to the affected area.

You should also keep your feet dry, clean and cool (some doctors believe that wearing open sandals helps), and wear socks made of cotton and shoes with porous uppers. If these measures fail to clear the disorder up within about a week, visit your doctor, who may prescribe a more vigorous type of anti-fungal medicine.

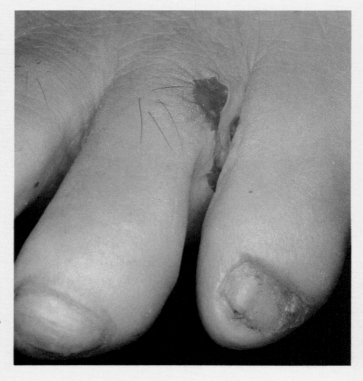

Athlete's foot is an uncomfortable condition, characterised by itchiness, flaking skin and, in severe cases, blisters.

AUTISM

Autism is a condition in which a sufferer is abnormally self-absorbed and unable to relate to people or deal with everyday situations.

Sufferers show an obsessive resistance to any change. Autism is rare though, and only affects about three children in every 10,000, and is more common in boys and in the higher social groups.

What is it?

The exact causes of autism are not known, but it's generally thought to be the result of a subtle form of brain damage, which manifests itself in children when they are about three years old.

The affected child starts to grow aloof from his parents and friends, screams when he's picked up and tries to avoid any contact. The child's behaviour becomes increasingly pathological, displaying a hatred and fear of any change. Delay in speaking is common as is an obsessive devotion to unusual objects.

The child also behaves strangely and finds it hard to learn any manual tasks, although autism does not affect appearance or muscular co-ordination. There is no known effective treatment for autism and only about one in six sufferers is able to lead any kind of independent life. Most autistic children need special and constant care.

Symptoms
• Profound detachment from others.
• Peculiar speech patterns.
• Strong resistance to change.

BACK PAIN

Back ache and back pain are extremely common complaints. Four out of five adults suffer at some time, and about 40 million working days are lost in the UK every year.

There are many more causes of back ache in women than in men but men consult their doctor about it more often.

Causes

Most back pain is due to injury to the ligaments or muscles of the spine. People with heavy manual jobs are particularly at risk. Pain may also come from the joint between the spinal bones or from the joint between the spine and the pelvis. Any of these causes can also produce 'sciatica' — a pain down the leg as a result of pressure on the nerve as it leaves the spine.

A 'slipped disc' is a common diagnosis, but it may be less frequent than first thought. The 'disc' refers to the cushion of cartilage which lies between the spinal bones. It does not actually slip out, but bursts so that the central core presses on nerves and causes pain. The condition usually occurs in fit young adults, often after they have lifted a heavy object.

Acute pain is felt in the lower back and the patient is unable to straighten. The pain is often felt in the legs and buttocks as well. This makes it difficult for the patient to sit in one position for very long.

Disease and back pain

Sometimes, the disc presses on the nerves supplying the bladder, causing difficulty in passing water. This is an emergency and a doctor should be called at once.

Bone disease is a rare cause of back pain, especially in young people. Older women (particularly those in their 70s and above) may suffer from crumbling bones. If this affects the spine the pain is sudden and severe. These days, however, hormone replacement therapy may stop this from troubling today's younger generation.

Treatment

In general, when treating back pain the patient should rest, although there are cases where gentle exercise can help. Sitting should be avoided. When lying down, the patient will be more comfortable in a firm bed with a pillow beneath the knees. Gentle heat from a hot water bottle in the small of the back may also help.

Analgesics will also help to relieve the pain. If the patient is resting, paracetamol may be enough. Occasionally codeine or an anti-inflammatory drug is required.

Osteopathy and chiropractic have been frowned on in the past by conventional medicine, but recent studies show that they may help. It would be reasonable to try them but repeated visits, unless the benefits are clear, are probably a waste of time and money.

Physiotherapy is playing an increasing role in back ache. Not only can physiotherapists relieve the acute pain but, by teaching correct lifting techniques and back strengthening exercises, they may actually prevent further attacks.

If all these treatments fail, a hospital specialist may inject the spine or put the patient on traction.

Surgery is very much a last resort and would only be considered if, for example, a slipped disc was causing nerve damage.

Back pain in women

A common cause of back pain in women is kidney infection. This usually starts with a bout of cystitis but the pain settles in the back just below the ribs. The patient often feels ill, has a temperature and may pass blood in her urine. This condition requires antibiotic treatment but may be relieved by drinking large amounts of water and taking analgesics. Back pain can also be caused by a

The practice of osteopathy was developed by Dr Andrew Still (1828–1917). It is a popular therapy that uses massage and manipulation to ease back problems.

The name 'osteopathy' comes from two Greek words – osteo (bone) and pathos (disease). It is similar to chiropractic, but puts more emphasis on blood circulation than on the nervous system.

Dr Still was a firm believer in man's capacity for self-healing and he argued that in order to be well, our bone structure, particularly the spine, should be in good working order. He claimed that many illnesses, such as headaches and skin complaints, were often the result of the misalignment of spinal vetebrae, and that manipulating the spine would correct the problem.

An osteopath will either use massage to stimulate the supply of blood to the body tissue or manipulation, such as a simple twist, to correct misalignments. Many back conditions can be treated by osteopathy.

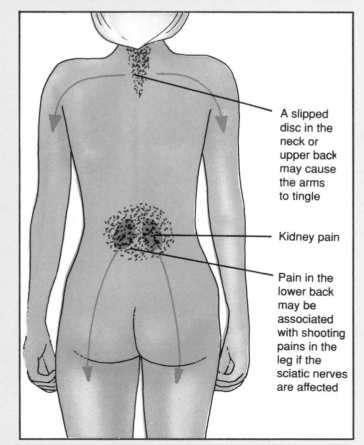

A slipped disc in the neck or upper back may cause the arms to tingle

Kidney pain

Pain in the lower back may be associated with shooting pains in the leg if the sciatic nerves are affected

Exercises to do in the Gym or at Home

Lifting Heavy Objects

When lifting always remember to bend your knees – never bend from the waist as this can damage the spine and the surrounding muscles.

Exercise 1

1 Lie flat on your back on the floor. Stretch your arms out with the palms of your hands on the floor and bring your knees up to your chest.
2 Keeping your knees together and your shoulders on the floor, turn your head one way and your legs the other until they touch the floor. Repeat the other way. Start by doing this six times on each side and build up to 24 times.

Exercise 2

1 Stand with your feet shoulder-width apart and your hands on your hips. Breathe in and as you breathe out, bend as far as you can to one side. Keep your back straight and don't twist your pelvis.
2 Return to the upright position and repeat on the other side. Do this 10 times on each side, remembering to breathe in before bending and out as you bend.

Exercises to do at Work or at Home

Exercise 3

1 Find a surface that is hip height (a filing cabinet or chair back would do). Lean forward with your knees bent until you can rest your folded arms on the chair. Rest your head on your arms and walk backwards until your back is straight and parallel with the floor.
2 Slowly straighten your knees, keeping your back straight. Repeat this bending and straightening six times and gradually build up to 24 times.

Exercise 4

1 Position yourself as for step **2** in Exercise 3 and tilt your pelvis up towards your ribs and back again. Breathe out on the tilt.
2 Breathe in and on the out breath, tilt your pelvis again, this time contracting your tummy muscles and rounding your back. Repeat six times. Do the pelvic tilt and muscle contractions three or four times.

lop-sided pelvis. This can happen to a girl at puberty when her pelvis starts to grow and one side fuses before the other.

Pain from the uterus, the cervix or the Fallopian tubes may be felt in the lower back. These conditions are usually accompanied by other symptoms such as discharge or bleeding and it is uncommon for confusion to occur.

Almost all pregnant women will get back ache at one time or another. This is due to the abnormal load placed on the spine by the weight of the womb, afterbirth and baby. In addition, a hormone is produced during pregnancy which causes the ligaments to relax, putting a further strain on the spine. Rest, simple analgesics and correct posture will all help, but if the condition persists a doctor should be consulted. She should be able to exclude a hidden infection and may suggest referral to a physiotherapist.

Back Care

- Choose a firm, good-quality mattress for your bed.
- Exercise regularly to keep the back muscles toned.
- When standing, keep your weight evenly distributed over both legs.
- Don't allow yourself to become overweight.
- Don't let yourself stoop.

BACTERIA

Under the right conditions a single bacterium can multiply itself a million fold in four hours and a billion fold in six hours.

These microscopic organisms reproduce by splitting in half. Fortunately,

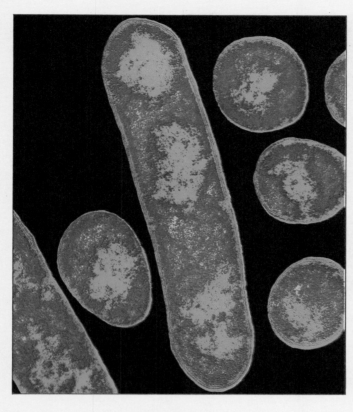

Botulinum grows in badly preserved canned foods, notably meat and fish, and can cause botulism poisoning.

far from being dangerous, the majority of bacteria are our allies. They break down dead plant and animal material into forms which can be used for new growth. A world without bacteria would overflow with the dead bodies of past generations.

There is no environment on earth too hostile for bacteria. Primitive forms have been found in boiling springs and in the depths of the Antarctic wastes.

Bodies teeming with bacteria

Every inch of skin contains millions of bacteria. Some are beneficial, most are harmless but a few are pathological — a word doctors use to describe an organism that can cause disease.

The beneficial bacteria help in at least two ways. For example, *lactobaccilli* live in the vagina and break down glycogen, a natural chemical, to produce acid. This acid, which is nearly as strong as vinegar, prevents pathological organisms such

as thrush getting a hold. Other helpful bacteria live in the gut. They help by breaking down food and producing vitamins the body cannot manufacture for itself.

The vast majority of bacteria in and on the human body are completely harmless and simply see the human body as somewhere

safe and warm to live. Occasionally, however, if the conditions are right (after a serious illness, for example), they may multiply rapidly and cause problems.

Impetigo is a bacterial infection caused by the *staphylococcus* that normally lives on the skin. If the skin is damaged or excessively dry these germs can 'set up shop' in the outermost layers causing the characteristic 'cornflake-like' rash. Impetigo is easily treated by oral or local antibiotics.

Biological poisons

Relatively few bacteria are harmful, and those that are cause problems in two ways: they may produce toxins — biological poisons — or simply cause damage by the sheer weight of their numbers. The latter group destroy cells and tissues in an effort to provide themselves with nutrition.

Bacterial toxins are among the most poisonous substances on earth. *Botulinum*, for example, the toxin produced by botulism, is so toxic that an amount the size of a full stop could kill an adult. Every few years an outbreak of botulism occurs, usually as a result of the incorrect sterilisation of cooked meat, but

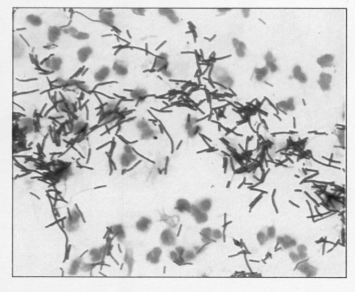

The bacteria Lactobacillus acidophilus lives in the vagina.

The remains of a bacterium destroyed by an antibiotic (above left); and an undamaged bacterium that is in the process of dividing (above right).

occasionally as a result of the home bottling of vegetables.

Fried rice horror

Tetanus and rabies both kill by the production of minute amounts of toxin. Closer to home and much more common is a condition called 'the fried rice syndrome'.

A bacterium called *bacillus cereus* grows in cooked rice and produces a toxin that causes vomiting for up to 24 hours. If the rice is not heated to at least 95 degrees, the toxin will be left intact. Unlike most forms of food-poisoning the onset of symptoms is very rapid, some people have been known to start vomiting before they have finished their meal.

Pneumonia is an example of a disease that is caused by the toxic effects of the growth of bacteria. The lung is overgrown by germs that multiply so rapidly that they destroy the lung structure and block the airways with pus.

Beating bad bacteria

The conquest of pathological bacteria is one of the success stories of 20th-century science, although most doctors would ascribe the benefits to the engineers who built the sewers rather than to great strides in medicine. Taken together, this and the development of antibiotics and mass immunisation programmes mean that bacteria, which once killed millions, are now little more than an irritation.

BALANITIS

Balanitis occurs when the head of the penis becomes inflamed. The area is red and moist and the main symptom is an itchy, sore penis.

Inflammation of the head of the penis can be due to dermatitis (even bubble bath can inflame and irritate sensitive skin) or to infection.

The commonest infection is thrush which is a fungal infection that produces a red glazed appearance especially under the foreskin. Thrush is quickly treated but can be easily passed between sexual partners so both should be treated at the same time.

Herpes, scabies and even syphilis can cause balanitis and it can also be caused by phimosis (tight foreskin). You should wash the penis, especially under the foreskin, and apply a soothing cream, but any inflammation that does not settle within 2-3 days should be seen by a doctor or the local genito-urinary clinic.

BARBITURATES

Barbiturates are sedative drugs that work by slowing down activity within the brain. Although they were once relatively easy to obtain, their use today is strictly controlled.

Barbiturates were originally used as sleeping tablets, but have largely been replaced by the much safer benzodiazepines such as Valium or Mogadon. The main reason why barbiturates fell from favour was that there was a very small difference between a safe dose and a potentially lethal overdose.

Barbiturates go underground

Unfortunately, while the legitimate use of barbiturates has fallen, there has been an increase in their illegal use. Barbiturates have an intoxicating effect, especially if taken with alcohol. Both act by inhibiting the conscious and unconscious parts of the brain and the combination is very dangerous indeed.

Barbiturate and alcohol excess is still a common cause of drug related death. Barbiturate addiction is common and sufferers require increasing doses to avoid the effects of withdrawal. In an effort to receive the same 'high' at less expense some addicts have taken to injecting crushed up tablets directly into a vein. This is particularly dangerous because the drug is highly corrosive and will cause severe tissue damage.

Friends on the take?

If you are concerned that a friend may be abusing barbiturates, then look out for drowsiness, altered sleep patterns, intoxication without the smell of alcohol or general apathy. Barbiturate users are often taking other drugs to try to combat the sleepiness caused. Look out for signs of intravenous injection or the other paraphenalia of drug abuse.

Barbiturate abuse, like all addictions, is expensive and victims may well break the law to satisfy their needs.

Despite the problems of addiction and overdose, barbiturates are still used in two areas of medicine. Long acting forms such as Phenobarbitone are useful in the treatment of epilepsy. They reduce the number of fits, but some people find that they become too drowsy to use them. Most doctors perform regular blood tests to ensure that the right dose is being used.

Short acting barbiturates are used in anaesthesia. Injected into a vein, they reach the brain in seconds and cause sleep equally rapidly. Having induced sleep the anaesthetist may use other drugs to prolong it.

Barbiturates are now classed as controlled drugs, which means that they are subject to the same strict rules as heroin and cocaine.

Dangerous Effects

If you are taking barbiturates, be prepared for the sudden mood changes and loss of behavioural control they can cause. The drugs also depress mental activity so do not drive while under their influence.

BETA-BLOCKERS

Beta-blockers are a group of drugs that are prescribed to block the effects of adrenaline and anxiety. Their main use is in the treatment of heart disorders.

BILE

The human liver produces about one pint of thick, yellow bile per day. Bile breaks down fatty foods and helps with the absorption of the fat-soluble vitamins.

Each cell in the liver produces a minute amount of bile which is collected in the hepatic ducts. These ducts join together and drain into the gallbladder where some of the water is removed and the liquid is stored. When a meal, especially a fatty one, is eaten, the gallbladder contracts and bile is squirted down the common bile duct and into the small intestine. When the meal has been digested, the bile is reabsorbed from the gut and is passed back to the liver. The five per cent that is not reabsorbed is broken down by bacteria to give faeces the characteristic brown colour.

BIOPSY

A biopsy is the removal of tissue or cells from a patient for examination. The tissue can be removed from any organ but probably the commonest areas are the skin, the breast and the cervix.

Most doctors appreciate that the ordeal of having a biopsy is frightening and will take pains to explain what will happen and why. The examination may be uncomfortable but it certainly shouldn't be painful.

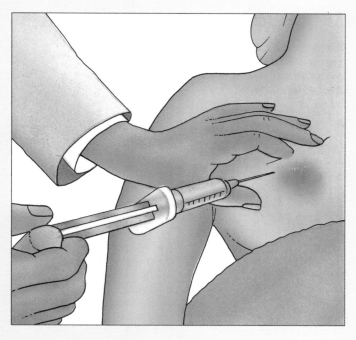

A needle biopsy: cells are sucked into a syringe for examination.

Cervix

A biopsy of the cervix will be performed if the patient's cervical smear is positive. The gynaecologist will examine the anaesthetised cervix and remove two or three small pieces of tissue, about the size of a match-head. These will be sent to a laboratory where a histologist, a doctor specialising in the study of diseased tissues, will examine it. The trained eye can detect the difference between normal and abnormal cells. If the biopsy shows cancers she will be able to tell if it has spread.

Breast

A woman with a breast lump will almost certainly have it biopsied by her surgeon. This may be done in the out-patient clinic or under anaesthetic in the theatre. A few years ago it was common for women to be taken to the operating room and put to sleep not knowing if their breast would be removed or not. The surgeon would locate the lump and remove it. A porter would rush the biopsy to the lab where it would be examined.

If it was malignant the breast would be removed; if not it would be saved.

Fortunately, doctors now appreciate how psychologically damaging this can be. These days a minute sample is removed the first time the patient sees her doctor. This is relatively pain-free and can even be done without a local anaesthetic. The result of the biopsy allows the woman and her surgeon to discuss the various treatments available and arrive at the best course of treatment.

Skin

Biopsies are frequently performed to help skin specialists reach a diagnosis. Perhaps the commonest is the punch biopsy. The area to be biopsied is cleaned and anaesthetised. Using a circular punch, a core of tissue about 5mm wide and 3-4mm deep is removed, usually from the edges of the lesion. The result of the biopsy is vital in determining the severity of the disease and how it can be treated.

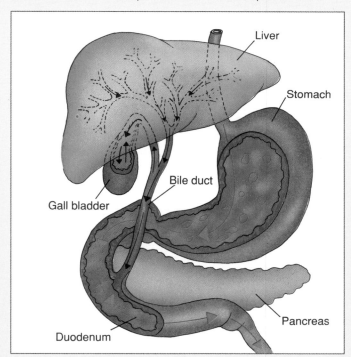

The biliary system: the black arrows show the route of bile from the liver through the hepatic ducts and into the gallbladder where it's stored. When the gallbladder contracts, the bile is squirted into the small intestine. The red arrows show the route of food from the stomach into the duodenum.

Labels: Liver, Stomach, Bile duct, Gall bladder, Pancreas, Duodenum

» SEE ALSO — Adrenaline

BIRTH DEFECTS

Birth defects are abnormalities that become apparent in the first few years of our lives.

The commonest reaction of parents faced with a severe abnormality is similar to those who have been bereaved. The initial response is denial and then anger, either at the spouse or at the medical staff. Sadly, birth defects affect between one in 30 and one in 50 deliveries and only very rarely is anyone to blame.

Types

Birth defects are generally divided into two groups: children damaged at the time of birth and congenital abnormalities. Children damaged at the time of birth are by far the smaller group. Many of these injuries occur if the baby is premature or if there are complications with the delivery, but fortunately these injuries are rare.

The largest group of birth defects are the congenital abnormalities. These occur at the time of conception or at some stage during development in the womb; they may be obvious at birth or may not be noticed until early infancy.

Causes

Of the congenital abnormalities some, such as cystic fibrosis, are simple gene defects. Although they may skip a generation, they can often be traced back through their families. Under these circumstances, the affected couple can be advised on the risk to future pregnancies.

More common are the so-called 'multifactorial abnormalities', such as neural tube defects (spina bifida). Several factors such as genetics and age all combine to cause the defect. Generally speaking, these problems are less likely to affect later pregnancies than the single defects.

Down's syndrome is an example of a chromosome abnormality. In this case, the 21st chromosome has three 'arms' rather than the normal two. The incidence of Down's syndrome increases with the mother's age. At the age of 40, the chance is about one per cent, at 45 it is about four per cent.

Some babies that start life in the womb perfectly healthy may be affected by poisons from the mother's blood stream. Rubella or German measles may cause deafness, brain damage and many other problems, depending on the age of the foetus when its mother catches the disease. By 14 weeks, the foetus is less likely to be affected but can still be damaged by drugs.

One of the commonest drugs to affect the foetus is nicotine. Children of smokers are likely to be smaller and are up to four times as likely to be admitted to hospital in the first year of life compared with the children of non-smokers. Excess alcohol can also cause severe problems and most doctors would not recommend more than one or two units per week. Great care should be taken with drugs in early pregnancy. As a rule nothing other than paracetamol or simple antacids should be regarded as safe unless sanctioned by your doctor.

Just as people live through and accept bereavement, the great majority will accept and love their handicapped child.

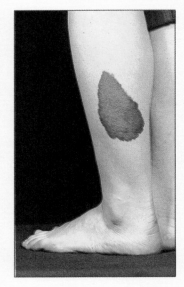

This brown birthmark is the result of a malformation of pigment cells.

skin and are caused by malformed, enlarged blood vessels. Surgery isn't usually recommended because of the dangers of scarring. Some marks can be treated by laser surgery, and there are special cosmetics to conceal these marks.

Strawberry marks are raised, bright red, spongy areas of skin that contain enlarged blood vessels. They are usually small and most vanish after about three years without any treatment.

Vitiligo is a common condition where patches of skin have no colour. It is often due to fungal infection, and occurs on the face, hands, groin and armpits. It can be masked by make-up, but there is no effective cure.

BIRTHMARKS

Birthmarks are various forms of skin blemishes that appear at or soon after birth. They are caused by the malformation of pigment or blood cells.

Moles and freckles are the more common types of birthmarks and become evident in childhood. However, the more serious and easily recognisable types of birthmarks are port wine stains, strawberry marks and vitiligo.

Different types

Port wine stains are dark, purple-red stains that are permanent and appear on the face and neck at birth. They occur over flat areas of

Signs of Malignancy

If you have a mole or a large freckle which begins to grow in size, change colour, bleed or become very itchy or painful, you should see a doctor. These may be signs of a malignant melanoma, or skin tumour, which needs treatment as soon as possible.

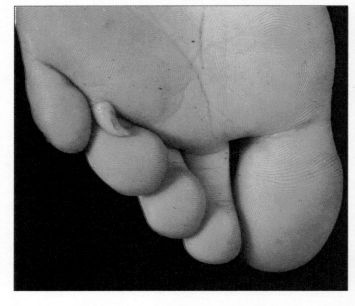

Polydactylism (having a sixth toe) is a relatively common congenital disorder.

» SEE ALSO — Down's Syndrome, Labour, Pregnancy

BITES

Animal bites kill a few hundred people a year, and snake bites kill a few thousand, but insect bites are responsible for at least two million deaths every year worldwide.

With the exception of spiders, the damage caused by insect or mite bites is actually unintended as they are only trying to get some food — in their case human blood. In the UK, serious problems resulting from insect bites are almost unheard of. Bites generally cause disease as a result of an infection or allergy. Insects, for example, are not fussy about what they eat — a horse-fly may leave its meal of horse dung to bite a human. It is hardly surprising that the bite often becomes infected and the whole arm hot, red and painful.

Mosquito bites

Mosquito bites are more troublesome than other insect bites. In order to stop the blood clotting, a mosquito will inject saliva into you as it bites. Unfortunately, certain tropical species may also inject a little blood from their previous victims. This simple fact means that millions of people will die each year from malaria and other related diseases.

The familiar itchy bump caused by mosquito bites is due to an allergic reaction to the anticlotting substance that is injected. It is often intensely itchy, but almost never causes problems unless a bacteria colonises the scratched bump.

Prevention, in the form of mosquito nets, 'cover all' clothing, insect repellents and sleeping with the windows shut is the best form of defence. Failing this, antihistamine tablets and hydrocortisone cream will give some relief. Calamine

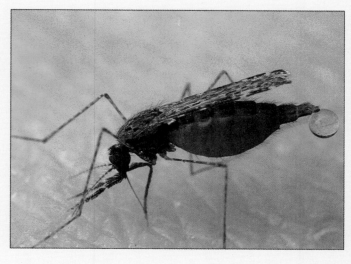

A female, malaria-carrying mosquito feeding on human blood.

lotion or ice will also relieve the intense itching.

Animal bites

Compared with insect bites, animal bites are rare but may cause severe problems. The damage done by tiger or shark bites is obvious but more deaths are caused by infections, such as rabies or tetanus. Dog bites, cat bites and especially human bites are contaminated by millions of bacteria. Unless special precautions are taken, infection is the rule rather than the exception.

All bites should be washed thoroughly with an antiseptic, and anything other than the most trivial bite should be seen by a doctor. She will want to clean it thoroughly, removing any dead tissue, and may well prescribe a course of antibiotics. In addition, a tetanus booster is often needed.

Snake bites

Of the 3500 species of snakes, only about 10 per cent are poisonous but these account for 30,000 to 40,000 deaths per year. The only venomous snake found naturally in the UK is the adder. Fortunately, the adder rarely bites unless it's disturbed. The bite is unpleasant but rarely fatal.

Less than half the victims of adder bites actually receive any venom at all. Treatment consists of keeping the patient at rest, sending for help and applying a tourniquet above the wound, which should be tight enough to stop blood flow along the veins, but not the arteries. Gently wipe or wash the wound to remove any traces of venom. Cutting a cross or sucking out the poison will do more harm than good.

BLADDER

The urinary bladder is located at the front of the pelvis. It is a muscular bag that stores urine until a convenient place is found to empty it.

The bladder receives a constant inflow from the two ureters that come directly from the kidneys. The lower ends of the ureters contain valves to stop back pressure damaging the kidneys. The bladder empties, through a valve, into the urethra.

In small children and some adults with damaged spinal cords, the bladder empties automatically when it reaches a certain volume. With toilet training though, humans and many other animals can learn to control the valve that empties the bladder. The commonest causes of bladder problems are infection (see Cystitis), stones and tumours.

Symptoms of a bladder problem include passing water frequently, pain on passing water and the urgent need to pass water. If you pass blood in your urine, you may have a bladder problem or a kidney problem

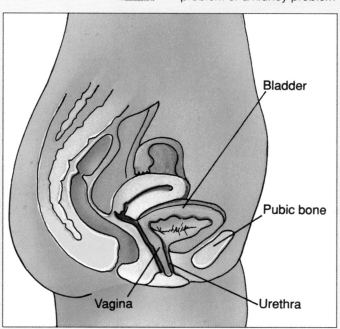

The location of the bladder in the female body.

Labels: Bladder, Pubic bone, Urethra, Vagina

» SEE ALSO — Rabies

and should consult your doctor.

Bladder stones

Bladder stones are commonly caused by an excess of calcium in the urine. Operations to remove bladder stones, usually through the perineum, have been performed for thousands of years.

With the arrival of anaesthetics it became possible to introduce instruments into the bladder, via the urethra. These instruments allowed the surgeon to see, crush and remove stones. Nowadays, increasing numbers of patients are being treated with shock waves to pulverise the stone so that it can be passed in the urine.

Bladder tumours

Bladder tumours are common in the elderly but they are fairly easy to treat. The most common treatment involves viewing the tumour through a telescope and removing it from the wall of the bladder. More advanced tumours may require radio- or chemotherapy. In some cases, the bladder will be removed and the surgeon will fashion a new bladder out of a segment of small bowel. The patient will have to wear an appliance to collect the urine.

BLINDNESS

The World Health Organisation estimates that by the turn of the century at least 80 million people will be blind, mostly in the Third World.

For the eye to see an object, a number of processes have to take place. Firstly, the light from the object must enter the eye. Secondly, the light must react with the retina which is the coating of the back of the eye. Thirdly, the nerve impulses of the retina must reach the brain and, lastly, the brain must be able to interpret the signals. An interruption to any one of these processes can cause blindness.

Causes

Although it's actually very rare in the UK, the commonest form of blindness is infection with trachoma — a disease of the cornea. The cornea is the membrane that forms the front of the eye and it must be transparent so light can pass through it. Blindness may also occur if the cornea is scarred as a result of infection. Ophthalmic surgeons are now able to graft donor corneas onto affected eyes, thereby restoring sight.

Moving further into the eye, a common cause of loss of vision is cataract, or clouding of the lens. This is usually a disease of old age but may affect children who have a rare genetic disorder. Again surgery is usually highly successful.

The portion of the eye that detects light is called the retina and it can be damaged in several ways. For example, a blow from a punch can detach it. Laser beam surgery can now be used to stick the retina back in place.

Thrombosis of the blood vessels that supply the retina is a condition that is untreatable. It may be associated with high blood pressure or smoking but it very rarely affects the younger age group.

Something that does affect young diabetics is the 'diabetic retinopathy' which is when the blood vessels that supply the retina become damaged. Again laser therapy can correct and reverse the process.

Glaucoma, a common cause of blindness, is due to a build-up of fluid inside the eye. This causes a rise in pressure. The high pressure damages the optic nerve as it leaves the retina.

Treatment is simple but

Vitamin Blindness

Lack of Vitamin A can lead to blindness in the form of xerophthalmia, a disease associated with malnutrition.

symptoms are often missed until almost all the sight is destroyed.

Smoking, alcohol or lead poisoning have all been shown to damage the optic nerve. This damage interrupts the signals from the retina to the brain and whilst the eye is perfectly normal the patient is unable to see.

BLISTERS

A blister is a sac of fluid that has collected beneath the outer layer of skin and formed a raised, hardened area, which is usually either circular or oval in shape.

Blisters are comprised of fluid, or serum, which has seeped through from the blood vessels in the underlying skin layers, as a result of minor damage.

Causes

Blisters can be caused by burns, sunburn and friction, for example when we wear new, ill-fitting shoes.

Many skin diseases, such as eczema, impetigo, pemphigus and dermatitis herpetiformis, can also cause blisters. If you have a viral infection, such as chicken pox or shingles, you may also suffer from small blisters — don't scratch them as they contain infectious particles that will quickly spread.

Treatment

If you have a blister, you should let it heal naturally. The fluid is often sterile and the blister serves as a shell to protect the damaged tissue. If you burst it, the damaged tissue beneath the blister may become infected. If you have a large or persistent blister, you should consult your GP.

Guide dogs are a great help to blind people.

MEDICAL FACT FILE

BLOOD

Blood and its circulation is the transport system of the body. It carries food from the gut and oxygen from the lungs to every living cell, and in return takes waste products back to the lungs and the kidneys where they are disposed of.

The blood that circulates in the human body performs many very important functions. One of the most important of these is to help distribute heat from the core of the body to its surface. From there it is eventually lost to the environment.

Blood is pumped around a closed system of blood vessels by the heart and also carries hormones from the glands where they are produced to the organs where they act. In men, blood acts as a rigid skeleton in the erect penis.

In humans, the heart, which sends the blood round the body, is really two separate pumps, working side by side. The left side of the heart pumps blood through the arteries to the branching arterioles and on to the capillaries where it exchanges chemicals with the cells. The capillaries drain into veins and back to the right side of the heart. From the right side of the heart, blood is pumped through the lungs and back to the left. In the lungs, blood gives up carbon dioxide and takes in oxygen.

Red and white cells

Blood is composed of red cells, white cells and platelets, which are suspended in a fluid called plasma. The average 70kg person has about 5.5 litres of blood of which 55 per cent is plasma and 45 per cent is cells. In the adult, the red cells, white cells and platelets are produced in the

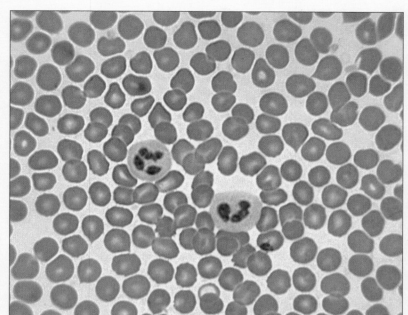

Left: A sample smear of human blood consisting of red blood cells and with two white blood cells situated in the centre. The function of the red cells is distribution and transportation of oxygen and carbon dioxide to and from the cells of the body. The white blood cells perform the important function of protecting your body from infection and disease.

Blood Groups

The science of blood grouping is now so complicated that it has given birth to a new branch of medicine and technology which is known as serology.

The coat of the red blood cell contains the proteins that determine blood groups. If a blood transfusion is required, a serologist will mix a sample of the patient's blood with a sample of the donor's blood and study it for reactions. Only when he is certain that it is safe will he give the go-ahead with the transfusion.

The most important and best known blood groups are A, B, AB and O.
GROUPS A AND B If blood from a group A donor is transfused into a group B patient, antibodies in the blood will rapidly destroy the transfused cells. This reaction may well be fatal.
GROUP AB People with type AB blood can be given any other blood and are therefore called universal recipients.
GROUP O Type O blood is known as the 'universal donor' blood and can be given to anybody without producing an incompatible reaction.

The rhesus group

A group that often causes difficulties is the rhesus group. The rhesus (Rh) factor is an antigen that is commonly found in blood. If your blood contains the Rh factor, you will be Rh positive; if it doesn't contain it you will be Rh negative. Eighty-five per cent of the population are Rh positive, while 15 per cent are Rh negative.

The rhesus factor mainly affects pregnant women who are rhesus negative and are carrying a rhesus positive baby. If an Rh negative woman is exposed to the antigen D that is carried in Rh positive blood, she may produce antibodies that will harm future Rh positive babies. Fortunately, this is now very rare as a simple injection at the time of delivery will stop the mother producing antibodies and will therefore protect future babies.

Transfusion Chart

		BLOOD DONOR			
		A	B	AB	O
PATIENT	A	✓	✗	✗	✓
	B	✗	✓	✗	✓
	AB	✓	✓	✓	✓
	O	✗	✗	✗	✓

Key   **Compatible**   **Incompatible**

The above chart shows compatibility between donor and receiver blood groups.

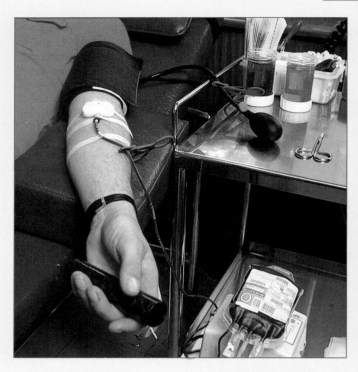

Above: A donor in the process of giving blood. As much as a tenth of the blood in a person's circulation may be donated but most donors do not feel any after effects.

bone marrow which is one of the biggest and most active organs in the body. Each litre of blood contains between 4000 and 11,000 million white cells which mainly protect the body against infection.

The red blood cells carry oxygen around the body. A litre of blood contains about 5000 billion red cells, slightly more in men. Each red cell lives for about three to four months and in this time circulates through the heart about 20,000 times.

Plasma

Plasma is the fluid portion of the blood that contains an immense number of chemicals, proteins, fats and carbohydrates. The largest group is the plasma proteins. These proteins all have a specific function — some help with blood clots, some carry hormones and others fight infection.

Blood disorders

Study of blood and its disorders now forms a branch of medicine which is called haematology. Haematologists are doctors who split their time between the laboratory and the patient. Blood disorders are divided into those affecting the plasma and those affecting the red and white blood cells.

Plasma disorders

Myeloma is a rare disease that usually affects the elderly. It is a malignant condition of the bone marrow that produces an excess of antibodies. This overproduction means that the plasma is exceptionally thick and may sludge up the arteries. It also means that the bone marrow devotes so much of its efforts to producing antibodies that it does not produce red and white cells. The sufferer becomes anaemic and is unable to fight infections. Treatment is usually successful and involves both chemo- and radiotherapy.

Red cell disorders

Red blood cells can be diseased in one of three ways. They may be deficient (see anaemia), abnormal or present in excess.

An excess of red cells occurs in a condition called polycythaemia. This is usually due to over-indulgence in cigarettes and alcohol and commonly affects middle aged men. The sufferer is often short of breath and has a very ruddy complexion. The red cells may become so numerous that they block the capillaries and small arterioles. This can lead to strokes and heart attacks. Haematologists generally treat these patients with regular blood letting or with chemotherapy.

White cell disorders

There may also be an excess or a deficiency of white blood cells. Like the red cells they may be abnormal in shape, although this is usually due to infection, such as glandular fever.

The most serious disease of the white blood cells is leukaemia which occurs when the bone marrow and/or lymphatic cells lose their normal control mechanisms. This means that they work flat out to produce more and more of one particular type of white blood cell. This type of overproduction means that the manufacture of other cells such as red cells or platelets is halted. The victim rapidly becomes anaemic and because of the lack of platelets bruises easily.

BLOOD CLOTTING

Blood clotting occurs at cuts and scrapes both inside and outside the body. It creates a barrier to infection and stems bleeding.

When a blood vessel is severed it bleeds for a minute or two and then stops. The initial bleeding serves to flush dirt and germs from the wound and is an essential part of the process of keeping the area germ-free. The blood then begins to clot. The first stage in the formation of a clot is the contraction of muscles in the wall of the blood vessels. This contraction causes the vessel to narrow and will decrease blood loss. Even arteries as large as the radial, the artery that can be felt at the wrist, may contract so tightly that they do not bleed at all.

Treating a Cut

Occasionally, people bleed to death from small cuts in an artery, but this is usually because first aid is unavailable or the patient has been too scared to help herself.

The first aid treatment for any wound that is bleeding, regardless of the size or cause, is firstly to remove any obvious debris and then to press the edges of the wound together firmly with the fingers or, better still, a clean handkerchief or cloth. The damaged part, if possible, should be raised above the level of the heart and the pressure should be applied for at least 10 minutes.

The use of tourniquets on bleeding wounds is controversial. Most doctors would agree, however, that the average tourniquet is too loose. This will make the bleeding worse rather than better. It is far better to concentrate on pressure than to waste time applying a possibly ineffective tourniquet.

» SEE ALSO — Anaemia, Glandular fever, Leukaemia

Migrating platelets

The damage done to the wall of the blood vessel makes it highly attractive to platelets. Platelets are tiny cell fragments which under normal circumstances circulate in the bloodstream. When they are exposed to the chemicals which are released from a cut blood vessel they become very sticky and migrate to the scene where they begin their indispensable work of healing the wound. Once the platelets reach the damaged blood vessel, they will then become transformed from their usual disc-like shape and will become wholly spherical, a shape that makes them highly effective when blocking a wound. They stick to the damaged walls and to each other, creating a temporary plug. This plug is strengthened by a protein called fibrin that binds the platelets firmly together.

Formation of fibrin is under the control of various enzymes and hormones. Lack of any of these enzymes means that it cannot be produced and damaged vessels will continue to bleed. This lack of fibrin production may occur naturally in haemophilia but may be caused artificially by drugs such as Warfarin. Warfarin was developed as a rat poison but in low doses slow down clotting just enough to stop the formation of unwanted thromboses and is useful in the treatment of deep vein thromboses.

Protective scabs

The clot that has been formed by the platelets and fibrin dries out over the course of two to three days, forming a protective scab over the wound. This scab prevents further damage or infection, while your body is beginning to repair the damage through the formation of new tissue.

» SEE ALSO — Leukaemia

BLOOD POISONING

Blood poisoning, or septicaemia, is a serious condition that occurs when bacteria live and multiply in the blood.

The body's defences would normally destroy bacterial invaders but they can be overwhelmed in two sets of circumstances. Firstly, the number of bacteria can be so great that the defences are simply outnumbered. This can happen, for example, if an infected hand or foot is left untreated.

Secondly, the body's defences can be weakened so much that they are unable to mount an attack on the invaders. AIDS victims often die of septicaemia simply because they lack the antibodies and white cells to stop infection spreading. Leukaemia patients, or those on chemotherapy for other cancers, are also liable to infections and blood poisoning unless great care is taken.

Treatment

Blood poisoning is a serious condition that requires hospital treatment. Signs of blood poisoning are a high fever, 'flu-like symptoms, drowsiness or even a coma. In hospital, you will usually be given a blood test to identify the poisoning germ. Treatment will consist of antibiotics that are designed to kill most of the bacteria responsible for blood poisoning. Before the patient has received her first dose of antibiotics the doctor will try to find the cause of the infection which will mean that further treatment can be carried out.

BLOOD PRESSURE

Blood pressure measures the force with which the heart pumps blood around the body. It has two figures, the higher of which represents the maximum pressure the heart can produce and the lower the minimum.

To carry out the blood pressure test the doctor inflates a cuff which is wrapped round the patient's arm. She then puts a stethoscope over an artery before listening for the first rush of blood past the cuff. The pressure measured on the cuff at this point is the same as the pressure in the artery.

High blood pressure

Most doctors agree that a very high level of blood pressure can cause heart attacks and strokes but few agree on what a high level actually is. Anything below 140/80 or even 160/100 would be looked upon as normal for a middle-aged woman.

Blood pressure gradually changes with age, however, and these figures would be high for a girl and low for an old lady.

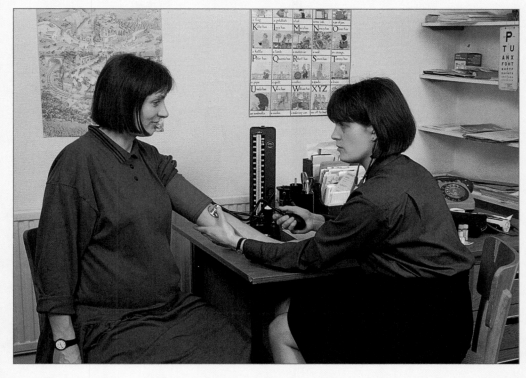

Above: A doctor measuring the blood pressure of one of her patients. Blood pressure is carefully monitored during pregnancy, and in women taking the pill. It is usually lower when the patient is lying down.

Women's blood pressure

Blood pressure in women is, to a certain extent, under hormonal control. It may rise, though very rarely, to dangerous levels because of the Pill. It may also rise during pregnancy, either as a result of hormonal changes or of the disease toxaemia. The measurement of blood pressure at ante-natal clinics guards against this potentially fatal condition.

Treatment

High blood pressure can be treated with drugs but these can cause side effects. It is better to reduce salt and alcohol intake, take regular exercise, lose weight and learn to relax. If all these fail and the blood pressure remains high for several months, then drug treatment may be started. Medicines have been shown to lessen the risk of strokes but so far nobody has proved that they lessen the risk of heart disease. This may be due to the fact that the older remedies were liable to raise the cholesterol and could even cause sugar diabetes, both of which cause heart problems. Modern drugs, however, seem to be safer.

BLOOD TESTS

Blood tests are analyses that are performed on blood samples in order to find out whether the blood is infected or abnormal in any way.

The average hospital blood testing laboratory will receive a thousand blood samples and perform as many as 10,000 tests per day, whereas thirty years ago it would have been unusual for daily tests to reach double figures. This vast increase means that a large part of a hospital's budget now has to be spent on blood tests.

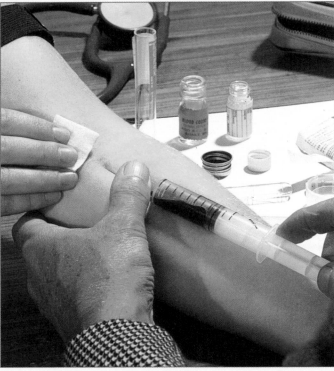

Above: A close-up view of a routine blood sample being taken from a patient. Samples are checked for any blood cells which are irregularly shaped.

Reasons for testing

Tests can be performed for any number of reasons but basically they are done to detect disease and/or monitor its treatment.

Blood tests are commonly performed to measure the amount of sugar in the blood. If a patient has untreated diabetes, for example, the concentration of sugar in the blood will be very high. As a result of a blood test this can be measured, the diagnosis made and treatment given. It is vital to ensure that the right amount of insulin treatment is given — too much is as dangerous as too little. The blood sugar is initially measured regularly and frequently. When the correct dose has been determined, blood tests can be less frequent unless the patient becomes ill.

Other blood tests detect damage to vital organs such as the heart or liver. If an organ is injured, after a heart attack for example, the cells will become leaky and will allow some of their contents to seep out. Blood tests enable the doctor to gauge the extent of the damage to the particular organ.

Training

Although your doctor may suspect you are anaemic or are suffering from leukaemia or any of a hundred other conditions, it is only possible for her to prove it conclusively through giving you a blood test. The people who perform these tests are medical laboratory scientists who have to undergo an intensive period of training which lasts for at least four years. As well as providing them with a thorough knowledge of blood testing, the training stresses the importance of a high degree of accuracy and attention to detail in their work.

Above: Screening blood for sickle cell disease and thalassaemia. The hospital scientist is staining electrophoresis plates in preparation for the screening tests for these inherited blood disorders.

BODY ODOUR

Body odour is the unpleasant smell created when bacteria feed on patches of stale sweat that have been left to fester on the body's surface.

It is a common misconception that the sweat produced by our bodies is responsible for the bitter, pungent smell which we have difficulty noticing but which often results in our friends finding urgent excuses to leave. But in fact, sweat is actually odourless. It is when it has been left to dry on the skin for several hours that it attracts bacterial organisms which create a smell as they go about their essential work of breaking down the chemicals which make up your sweat.

Bacteria are particularly attracted to sweat on the genital areas and the armpits as these parts of the body contain the apocrine glands. These glands secrete the types of fatty substances and proteins that create the favourable conditions under which bacteria thrive.

Treatment

An all-over shower every day should be enough to keep body odour at bay. As extra insurance against BO, an antiperspirant deodorant (See Looking Good, Antiperspirants) should be applied after you have dried yourself to ensure sweat does not get the chance to reach the body surface.

BOILS

Boils are swollen lumps on the surface of the skin and are often the result of a hair follicle having been infected by the bacterium *Staphylococcus Aureus*.

Usually situated on the neck, or on moist areas of the body, such as the armpits or genital areas, a boil begins as a small red lump then grows gradually as it becomes filled with pus. Once a boil has swollen to its full size it usually has a yellow point.

Although boils can be extremely painful it is not advisable to burst them. This may have the immediate effect of relieving the pain, but when the pus from the broken boil flows out and onto the surrounding skin the chances of further infection are greatly increased.

Treatment

A good way to relieve the pain of a boil gradually is to apply a hot hand towel to it every couple of hours.

If the boil becomes too large and painful to bear, consult your doctor who may be able to put you on a course of antibiotics which will kill the bacteria. Alternatively, your doctor may decide to use a sterile needle to burst the boil before draining the pus. The wound must be kept sterile.

BONE

Despite its solid, rock-like appearance, bone is a living tissue with the capability of repairing itself.

Bone consists of two elements: the organic (or living) gristle fibres that form a network and the minerals that lie between them. These are mainly calcium phosphate and calcium carbonate, similar to blackboard chalk. The combination of the elastic gristle and the stony hardness of the chalk makes bone extremely strong.

Functions

Bones serve three main functions. Firstly, they act as a rigid skeleton that supports the body. Muscles act on the bone to produce movement — without them we would be unable to support ourselves, unless we're submerged in water. Secondly, bones provide protection for delicate organs such as the eye or brain and for vital organs such as the heart. Thirdly, they contain bone marrow which is an organ in its own right. Bone marrow produces red blood cells, white blood cells and platelets (see blood).

Structure

The structure of bone is closely related to its needs. It is strongest in areas where the greatest stress is applied. There are three main types of bone: flat, like the bones that make up the skull; cube-shaped like the vertebrae; and long like the femur — the thigh bone.

The joints between bones are either fixed or mobile. Rigid joints occur in the skull and at the front of the pelvis, though even this joint may open by as much as 2cm during childbirth.

The surface of the bone in movable joints is covered with cartilage which acts as a pad and prevents jarring of the bones. Cartilage can be worn away by exercise resulting in painful, creaky joints (see arthritis).

Breaks

When a bone is broken it bleeds and forms a clot around the jagged edge. This clot hardens to form a solid

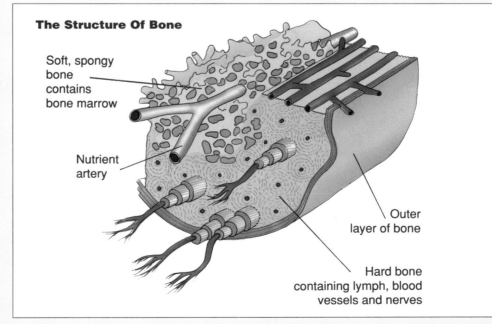

The Structure Of Bone

Soft, spongy bone contains bone marrow

Nutrient artery

Outer layer of bone

Hard bone containing lymph, blood vessels and nerves

The central part of the bone is spongy, with nutrient arteries and the fatty bone marrow. Fine blood vessels and nerves run in canals through the outer part of the bone – which is the bulkiest part of the structure. The casing is a thin layer of hard bone.

» SEE ALSO — Arthritis, Bacteria, Blood, Cartilage

wall around the fracture which holds the ends of the bone together until new bone can bridge the gap. Bones such as the ribs or collar bone, can be left to heal themselves but bones under strain, such as the forearm or thigh, need to be held rigid to allow healing. They can be held in place by a plaster cast or by fixing a plate across the break.

Fractures of the hip used to heal very slowly but surgeons can now replace them with artificial joints.

Elderly women commonly suffer from broken bones as the lack of hormones in their system means that the bone becomes brittle. This condition, known as osteoporosis, can be avoided by hormone replacement therapy after the menopause.

A diet high in calcium is important in repairing and strengthening bones.

BOTULISM

Botulism is a potentially fatal form of poisoning, contracted from food that has not been properly stored.

Fortunately, it is very unusual for food which is contaminated with botulism to be found in the UK as it is extremely difficult to exterminate the bacteria that cause this form of poisoning. They are often strong enough to survive boiling and the other usual methods of fighting bacteria.

They spread most quickly in a sealed, airtight environment, such as the type of tin can that holds many modern food products.

Even a tiny amount of the poisonous substance produced by the botulism bacteria can have serious effects. Within a few hours of eating, the victim may be vomiting and suffering

debilitating physical problems, such as loss of speech or an inability to swallow. Double vision may even occur.

Treatment

The above effects of botulism usually appear within one day of the infected food having been consumed. It is essential for the sufferer to seek medical help immediately as the quick administration of an antitoxin can greatly reduce the possibility of death.

BOWEL

The bowel's purpose is to process food and liquid either into waste matter or into the bloodstream to provide the essential life-force which keeps the body functioning efficiently.

The bowel, or intestine, is composed of two long, snake-like coils that are tightly packed into the bodily cavity immediately beneath the liver and the stomach. The smaller of the two parts of the intestine is surrounded by the outer and wider intestine, which is known as the colon.

The small intestine, which is usually around 6.5 metres in length and 3.5 centimetres wide, is connected to the stomach and completes the initial work of breaking down and digesting food. Blood vessels then move the nutritious parts of the food on to the liver.

Those parts of the food which are not passed to the liver are passed from the small intestine to the large intestine, which is about 1.5 metres long, as fibre and liquids. Useful minerals and vitamins are extracted at this point and waste matter is pushed down into the rectum. It is when your rectum is swollen with waste that you feel the need for

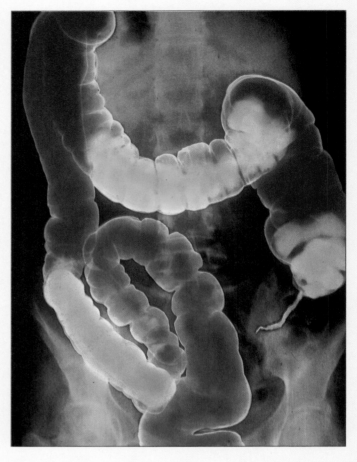

The different sections of the colon fit into the lower part of the rib cage and within the pelvis.

your bowel to open for the purpose of getting rid of the waste matter.

In order for the bowel to function properly, it is essential to follow a well-balanced diet, with plenty of liquid and fibre.

BOWLEGS

Bowlegs are legs which bend outwards away from the hip, then in to the knee and then bend away from the knee and inward to the ankle.

During the early part of the century, bowlegs were very common in the United Kingdom. A child who did not receive enough vitamin D would be very likely to develop rickets and would then grow up with legs which bowed outwards.

Some children still have bowlegs until the age of five or six. If, however, one leg is more bent than the other or if the legs remain bowed after the age of six, a doctor should be consulted.

THE BRAIN

The brain is situated in the skull, and stores and processes all of an individual human's thoughts and emotions as well as controlling the body's physical movements.

There is a great similarity between the brain found in a human and the type found in animals and even fish. All brains, in both humans and animals, have a connected spinal cord and are divided into three parts: the brainstem, the

➤➤ SEE ALSO — Bacteria, Brittle bones

cerebellum and the cerebrum. The brainstem and cerebellum are similar in humans and animals, and these parts of the brain are used in relation to physical functions such as movement and feeling pain or heat.

It is the cerebrum, the egg-shaped part of the forebrain, which greatly distinguishes humans from animals. In the human this part of the brain, which is used for thinking, has been greatly developed, producing the enormous gap in intellectual development between humans and the members of the animal kingdom.

Using your grey matter

The brain is composed of grey and white matter. The grey, surrounding the white, is made up of millions of specialised cells. These cells produce electrical activity which is carried by the nerves of the white matter. The impulses may travel down the spinal cord to the body or around the brain to other cells.

Most of the nerve fibres cross over from one side to the other so the left side of the brain controls the right side of the body and vice versa. In right-handed individuals the left side of the brain controls speech and in left-handers either the left or the right side may be in control.

Strokes

The body has evolved a rigid skull to protect the brain but despite this the brain is commonly the site of serious problems. A third of all deaths are directly related to it. Rupture or blockage of a blood vessel will give rise to a stroke. In the United Kingdom about 200 people in every 100,000 fall victim to a stroke each year. About three quarters of these are over 75.

Symptoms

Most people are familiar with the classic picture of a stroke victim — an elderly man or woman with half the body paralysed. The severity and type of symptoms may vary dramatically from person to person. If you think someone has suffered a stroke you should look closely at the corner of their mouth to see whether it is drooping in any way. More alarmingly, the victim may be unable to speak or even move. In the most severe cases the victim will die instantly.

Treatment

Fortunately most stroke victims tend to make a partial recovery and improve as neighbouring brain cells take over the tasks of the damaged area. This process may take many months but can be helped along by skilled medical care, especially physiotherapy and speech therapy. Most stroke victims are admitted to hospital. This is to aid their recovery and to ensure that the one in 20 strokes which are treatable come to the attention of medical staff.

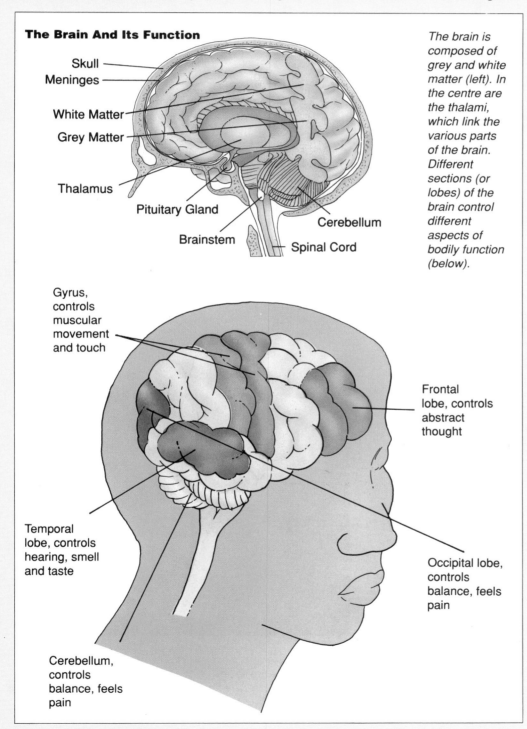

The Brain And Its Function

- Skull
- Meninges
- White Matter
- Grey Matter
- Thalamus
- Pituitary Gland
- Brainstem
- Cerebellum
- Spinal Cord

The brain is composed of grey and white matter (left). In the centre are the thalami, which link the various parts of the brain. Different sections (or lobes) of the brain control different aspects of bodily function (below).

- Gyrus, controls muscular movement and touch
- Frontal lobe, controls abstract thought
- Temporal lobe, controls hearing, smell and taste
- Occipital lobe, controls balance, feels pain
- Cerebellum, controls balance, feels pain

BRAIN ABSCESS

A brain abscess is a localised infection unlike encephalitis, which is an inflammation of the brain and which is a generalised infection.

An abscess may be a complication of a head injury or it may have spread to the brain from other organs. It may spread locally from the middle ear or sinuses although this is very rare. It may also have spread, by the blood, from infections in other parts of the body such as the heart. Symptoms are usually similar to those of tumours. The abscess is often so well walled off that fever and general upset are rare. Treatment is with high doses of intravenous antibiotics but surgery is often needed as well.

BRAIN DAMAGE

Head injuries are usually obvious although occasionally the skull may appear undamaged.

This is especially true if the damage was caused by a forceful blow from a cushioned object such as a gloved fist. The classic knock-out punch causes the skull to fly backwards until stopped by the neck. The brain continues backwards until it bounces off the back of the skull. This movement can tear blood vessels and, if repeated often enough, can lead to the shambling punch-drunk appearance of the ex-fairground boxer.

A severe blow to the head may cause the blood vessels on the brain surface to tear. A bruise may take several days to develop but will eventually cause pressure and ultimately death. If recognised, the clot can be removed by a relatively simple operation.

The danger signs to look out for when a person receives a moderate to severe head injury are when he seems to recover and then loses consciousness again. This is an acute emergency and if you notice someone in such a condition you should lose no time in taking them to a fully equipped accident department.

BRAIN TUMOURS

A brain tumour is a growth that develops either in or on the brain. Like all other tumours, brain tumours may be malignant or benign, and are either primary or secondary growths.

There are many different symptoms of brain tumours, which depend on its site and the speed of its growth but in general headaches are not usually an indicator. Common symptoms include visual disorders, speech difficulties, loss of muscular control and epileptic fits.

A tumour is looked upon as malignant if it has the ability to spread to other parts of the body, although this is uncommon in brain tumours. Unfortunately, even benign brain tumours may cause problems because the rigid skull restricts their growth and causes pressure damage to the delicate grey matter (see diagram on previous page).

Treatment may be by surgery or radiotherapy but with the exception of a few special cases drugs are not really useful.

BRAIN SCANS

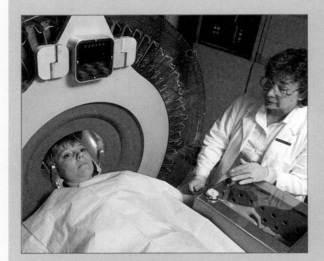

Brain scans are performed for a number of reasons: to detect the extent of brain injury, tumours and to diagnose the cause of other unexplained symptoms, such as fits.

X-rays have long been used to look at head damage, but they are really only useful in diagnosing fractured skulls and damage to the skull due to tumours, aneurysms or abscesses. Other ways of looking at the brain include CT scanning, which gives images of the fluid-filled cavities in the brain to help differentiate abnormal brain tissue; MRI scanning, which does a similar job to CT scanning, without using radiation; ultrasound scanning is used on very young babies, who do not have such hard skulls as older children and adults; and PET scanning which gives more information about the activity of the brain.

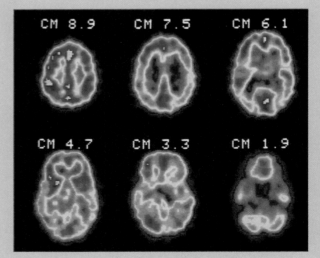

Above left: The circular detector is used to scan the brain using Positron Emission Tomography (PET). The results appear as slices across the brain – those above are the results of a PET scan on a normal brain.

BREASTS

The breasts are milk secreting glands which are dormant until pregnancy.

Before pregnancy most of the breast consists of fat and connective tissue. In between these tissues lie the mammary glands.

The size and shape of the breast varies from woman to woman and from age to age. Size has nothing to do with the ability to produce milk. Big breasts have more fat, nothing else.

Structure

On the surface of the breast, about the middle, is the nipple. The skin around the nipple is pigmented and is called the areola. The areola of women who have had children is brown rather than pink. The areola skin contains a number of small glands which produce an oily secretion that keeps the nipple supple during breast feeding. The nipple contains muscle fibres which, when contracted, cause it to stand out. The nipple may also stand out as a result of suckling or sexual arousal.

The tubes from the mammary glands, about 15 per breast, empty onto the surface of the nipple. The mammary glands themselves resemble bunches of grapes, all coming together to a single stalk or duct. The glands are arranged around the nipple like the segments of an orange. Each segment is surrounded by a thick fibrous band.

Puberty

The secretion of the female sex hormones oestrogen and progesterone, which starts at puberty, begins to prepare the breast for milk production. The breasts enlarge and the mammary glands begin to develop. This development is slight compared with the changes of pregnancy. After puberty

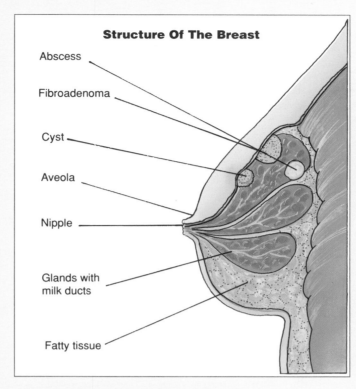

Structure Of The Breast

Abscess
Fibroadenoma
Cyst
Aveola
Nipple
Glands with milk ducts
Fatty tissue

Breast lumps may be benign or malignant.

you should check your breasts regularly for unusual lumps or unexpected changes in colour or texture.

Non-cancerous lumps

Most breast lumps are not due to cancer. Hormonal imbalance is thought to be the cause of lumpy, painful and tender breasts — a condition known as fibroadenosis (also known as chronic mastitis or fibrocystic disease). The condition is usually noticed in the week or so before a period. Hormones may ease the pain, and diuretics are also prescribed in some cases.

Fibroadenoma is a benign growth, which is round, painless, and can be moved around beneath the skin. This may grow very large, and is usually removed surgically.

Lumps may also be fluid filled cysts which develop when breast ducts get blocked. Treatment normally involves draining the cyst, and sending a sample of fluid for analysis to check there are no cancerous cells.

Another cause of lumps (which occurs during breast feeding) is a breast abcess. This is a collection of pus which may develop in the

breast if mastitis is not treated (see overleaf).

BREAST CANCER

Breast cancer is a tumour which is found most often in the upper and outer part of the breast. It is normally first noticed as a painless lump.

Breast cancer is one of a group of tumours that metastasize, or spread, to other parts of the body. The speed of spread varies from person to person and with the age of the patient. Tumours spread faster, and are therefore potentially more harmful in young women. Early diagnosis is essential; therefore you should examine your breasts regularly for lumps (see Your Health, Cancer).

Malignant tumours

Cancerous lumps may be accompanied by a puckering of the skin and a

Mammograms are a way of examining the breast for cancerous tumours, using an ordinary, low-dose x-ray.

➤➤ SEE ALSO — Abscess

MEDICAL FACT FILE

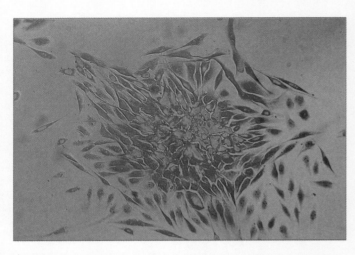

Human breast cancer cells grown in the laboratory, showing how the outer cells spread (or metastasize).

dark discharge from the nipple. In most cases, only one breast is affected.

Ten years ago the death rate from breast cancer had not changed in 50 years. The discovery of Tamoxifen has changed that. Tamoxifen is a drug that stops oestrogens acting in the breast tissue. This blocking effect means that tumours grow much more slowly than they otherwise would.

Statistics and Breast Cancer

No-one knows exactly what causes breast cancer but one or two statistics have emerged from recent studies.

● One in 14 women will develop breast cancer at some stage in their lives.
● Breast cancer is commonest in older women.
● Breast cancer tends to run in families.
● Breast cancer is least common in women who have had children and breast fed them.
● Taking the contraceptive pill does not increase the risk of breast cancer.

Treatment

Most cancer specialists would now suggest a combination of surgery and Tamoxifen in most cases of cancer of the breast.

The choice of what type of surgery is not clear. Mastectomy (removal of the breast) or lumpectomy (removal of the lump) seem to have similar cure rates, especially if radiotherapy is used at the same time to control any further spread. Surprisingly, women who have had the whole breast removed seem to suffer less psychological harm after surgery. The reason for this is unclear but it may be due to the fact that after mastectomy there is less fear of recurrence.

BREAST FEEDING

Breast feeding is the most natural way to feed a baby, and it is generally agreed that it is best for the baby. Breast milk contains all the nutrients a new baby needs, and also helps to build up a baby's antibodies to fight infection.

In the first half of pregnancy the breasts enlarge and in the second half the glandular tissues

increase. The production of milk is switched on by a hormone, prolactin, produced by a gland in the mother's brain. During pregnancy the effects of prolactin are swamped by the vast amounts of oestrogen and progesterone produced by the placenta.

When the baby, and afterbirth, are delivered the amounts of oestrogen and progesterone fall dramatically. Prolactin acts unopposed and milk begins to fill the glands and ducts.

Before milk can be released from the breast another hormone, oxytocin, must play its role. When a baby first sucks on the nipple it releases no milk for half a minute or so. Milk then appears from both nipples. The act of suckling, or even the sound of a crying baby, cause the pituitary gland to produce oxytocin which causes muscles in the duct to contract.

Establishing breast feeding

This production cycle is easily disrupted, by worry for example. Perhaps even fear of being unable to breast feed will stop the production

of oxytocin. If the breasts are not emptied regularly the production of prolactin and therefore of milk will stop within two or three days.

It is often said that breast feeding is natural; unfortunately it may not come naturally and may need working at. It is worth some effort to try and establish a pattern you and your baby are happy with.

Most mothers get conflicting advice about what to do. Choose one person you feel at ease with and who has time to help you. This could be a midwife, a National Childbirth Trust counsellor or a friend or neighbour. Listen to her advice and no-one else's.

If you can, put the baby to the breast straight after birth. The baby sucking produces a powerful bond, and as an added bonus, produces a hormone that helps expel the afterbirth.

For the first two days the baby will receive colostrum rather than milk. This thick, yellowish fluid is full of antibodies that will protect the child for the first few weeks of life.

Demand feeding,

Breast feeding helps to build up antibodies. It is also a time when babies become bonded to their mothers.

allowing the baby to decide when it should feed, is the easiest way to establish successful feeding. If the breast is not producing enough milk, the baby will suckle more frequently and for longer. This produces the best possible stimulus to increase the flow of milk.

Engorgement

In the early stages of feeding, before a rhythm is established, the breasts may become overfull. The nipple no longer stands out from the breast, and the baby cannot 'latch on'. By expressing a little milk at the start of each feed, you will ease the tightness and make it easier for the baby to feed.

Sore nipples

While you are establishing feeding, you may find that your nipples become sore or cracked. It is important to wash and dry your nipples before and after feeding, and you may find it helpful to hold the baby at a different angle (lying under your arm, with her head towards the centre of your body, for example). If the problem becomes very bad, you may have to rest the affected nipple for a few days, and express milk to prevent further problems. Breast shields, to wear inside your bra, and special creams may help to alleviate the problem.

Mastitis

Mastitis is an infection in the breast, almost always as a result of a blocked milk duct. The duct may be blocked by a plug of solid milk, often the result of some external pressure such as clothing that's too tight.

The affected area will become hard and tender and may become red. At the first sign of trouble, feed your baby from that side, even if it is a little painful, and if possible from that segment. This may be achieved by positioning and gentle

massage. If the problem persists, or gets worse, consult your midwife or doctor. An abscess may develop in the blocked duct. Antibiotics may be needed but you can still breast feed (double check that your GP knows that you are breast feeding) provided milk from the affected side is discarded for a day or two.

Boosting the milk supply

The stimulation of sucking will encourage and increase the supply of milk. But it is essential to drink a lot to keep the supply going.

An old-fashioned remedy, but one that works, for boosting the milk supply is Guinness. Successful as this may be, limit yourself to two bottles per day. They can be taken at any time but before a feed may be best, to help you relax.

Excess milk production can be a problem, especially at weaning. Try to cut down on breast feeding gradually, running down the supply naturally. Firm pressure from a tight bra and simple pain killers are usually enough to stop overproduction with a minimum of discomfort. If this fails try sage tea. Your doctor may prescribe hormone tablets if there is a real overproduction problem.

Feeding Tips

- Make sure you are comfortable and your back is well-supported.
- Support the baby's head with your hand or in the crook of your arm.
- Always raise the baby up to your breast rather than bending over the baby.
- Ensure that the entire areola is taken into the baby's mouth.
- Offer alternative breasts first at each feed.
- Ask for help and advice.

BREATHING

Three things are essential for life, oxygen, water and food. We can survive for many days without food, many hours without water but only a few minutes without oxygen.

Eating and drinking are under conscious control: we choose when and where we do these. Breathing is too important to leave to chance and happens automatically, under subconscious control.

The purpose of breathing is to exchange oxygen from the air for carbon dioxide from the blood. The actual exchange occurs in minute, sac-like structures called alveoli, in the lungs. These alveoli give the lung its characteristic honeycomb appearance and vastly increase the surface area available for the exchange of gases.

In order for efficient breathing to occur, three things must happen. Firstly, the air must contain oxygen. Secondly, the air must reach the alveoli and thirdly, blood must be pumped to the alveoli and back to the heart.

The mechanics

The body has two mechanisms for moving the air in and out of the lungs. The ribs and diaphragm are efficient enough to allow a normal life on their own. The diaphragm is a muscular sheet between the abdomen and the chest. Because of its dome-like shape, contraction causes it to flatten and pull the lungs down. This sucks air down the windpipe and into the alveoli. Tightening the muscles between the ribs causes the rib cage to lift and the ribs are pivoted on the spine, a bit like a bucket handle. As the handle is raised the volume is increased and again air enters the lungs. To breathe out the procedure is

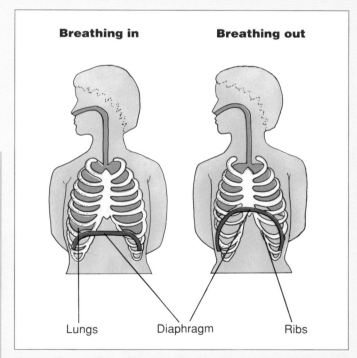

Breathing in **Breathing out**

Lungs   Diaphragm   Ribs

The mechanism of breathing: as the diaphragm tightens it flattens (above left), enlarging the cavity so the lungs are pulled down. At the same time the muscles between the ribs tighten, again increasing the volume of the rib cage so that air is drawn into the lungs. As the muscles relax air is expelled from the lungs (above right).

Causes of Breathlessness

Breathlessness has several different causes, many of which are serious problems.

● Lack of oxygen due to high altitude: the air becomes thinner the further we climb up mountains. In practice this is not a problem for the average adult but may cause difficulties in those with breathing disorders.

● Obstruction of the windpipe, by a peanut for example, will cause acute breathlessness. Try three sharp blows between the shoulder blades or the Hemlich manoeuvre if this fails. Stand behind the victim and grip your left hand in your right hand, around their midriff. Jerk your hands up towards their diaphragm.

● Pneumonia will cause breathlessness. The pus-filled alveoli do not work properly and more breaths are needed to exchange the normal amount of gases. Pneumonia can be treated with antibiotics but in severe cases oxygen is needed. Pure oxygen, from a mask, allows the exchange of gases to occur more efficiently.

● Heart failure may cause breathlessness, though this is rare in the young. If the heart is not working properly blood will dam up behind it. Fluid from the blood leaks into the lungs and they slowly fill up. Diuretic, or water tablets will help clear the lungs.

● Severe anaemia will cause breathlessness. Air enters the lungs normally but the blood is so thin it is unable to carry enough oxygen for the body's needs.

reversed. The normal rate of respiration varies according to age, sex and illness. Children breathe faster than adults and women breathe faster than men.

Problems with breathing

Illness affects breathing in two ways. Any infection that raises the body temperature, like 'flu for example, means we need more oxygen and must breathe faster. This is particularly noticeable in small children.

Breathlessness is a feeling of needing to fight to draw breath and an awareness of the process of breathing. According to their state of fitness most people will become breathless with exercise. Young adults should be able to climb two flights of stairs at a brisk pace and still be able to hold a normal conversation at the top. The box (left) explains causes of breathlessness.

BREECH BIRTH

Breech delivery is when a baby is born with the lower half of its body emerging from the womb first.

Although most babies are delivered with the head emerging first, breech delivery happens in about three per cent of pregnancies. In such cases the delivery is trickier; in a normal (or cephalic) presentation, the head moulds to the mother's pelvis, and once the head has emerged, the rest of the baby's body is easily delivered. In a breech presentation, the danger is that once the body has been delivered, the head will get stuck in the pelvis. Often, therefore, obstetricians will attempt to switch the baby's position in the womb, usually about a fortnight before the anticipated birth.

Caesarean section

If attempts to change the baby's position have been unsuccessful, and it appears that complications are likely to arise at birth (due to a large head, or the mother having a narrow pelvis), the baby will often be delivered by Caesarean section.

Vaginal delivery

If the obstetrician feels that it is safe to go ahead with a normal vaginal delivery, extra care will be taken. The

midwife's assistant may use physical pressure to push the baby's head from inside the womb to compensate for the difficulty of the feet or bottom emerging from the womb first. An epidural (an anaesthetic injected into the lower back which acts on the lower part of the body) is often advised, and an episiotomy (a cut in the opening of the vagina to ease delivery) may be necessary.

BRITTLE BONES

Brittle bones are those which break easily.

In the years following her menopause, a woman may find her bones become more fragile and breakable. This is likely to be as a result of osteoporosis, where the bones have a tendency to become reduced in thickness. Brittle bones may also develop because of hormonal problems or may even be inherited.

Old people should take particular care, as an ordinary fall may cause broken bones.

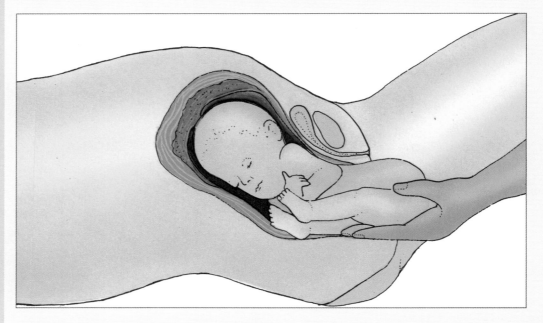

In a breech birth, the baby's feet or bottom are delivered first.

➤➤ SEE ALSO — Childbirth, Osteoporosis

BRONCHITIS

Bronchitis is a sudden or continuous infection which blocks the airways of the lungs.

Bronchitis is a good example of an illness that means different things to different people. To the writer of a medical dictionary it is sufficient to describe it as an 'inflammation of the

Elements in your surrounding environment, such as cold weather, pollutants in the atmosphere or smoke, can often cause or prolong coughs and cigarette smoking is probably the most common cause of bronchitis in the adult population. In some cases an allergy may cause bronchitis, although this is usually called asthma.

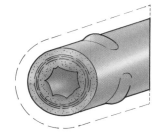

Cross Section Of Bronchioles

A normal bronchiole (left) and a bronchiole after drug treatment to relax the muscles and open the airway (right).

bronchus'. In plain language this means irritation of the larger air passages. To a doctor it is an acute or chronic infection in the lungs. To the patient, bronchitis can often simply mean an irritating cough.

Causes of bronchitis

Bronchitis may be due to an infection. In the great majority of cases the illness is brought on by a virus and only lasts for about two or three days. It is one of the most annoying of short-term illnesses, however, as it is characterised by a cough or wheeze which is usually most severe at night, interrupting the precious sleep of the recuperating patient. Some viruses do, however, increase the risk of a bacterial infection. If you have a bronchial cough and it becomes 'productive', that is when coloured phlegm is brought up by the coughing action, then you should make sure that you consult your doctor.

The 'smoker's' cough is one form of bronchitis that is all too familiar to doctors. The patient is usually in her thirties and complains of shortness of breath. This and the production of phlegm has gone on for so long that the patient has accepted it as normal. Unless smoking is stopped at once the condition inevitably deteriorates into chronic bronchitis or severe breathlessness.

Treatment

Most cases of bronchitis can be treated at home. A regular intake of fluids including honey, lemon or even a little alcohol at night will provide some soothing relief. Also recommended is a sharp intake of some moisture in the form of steam just before you go to bed. Once you are actually in bed, try sleeping with an extra pillow. If the cough persists or if breathing becomes difficult, your doctor may prescribe a

course of antibiotics or a drug that will relax the muscles and open up the airways and make breathing easier (see diagram).

BRUISING

A bruise is a discoloration of the skin where blood has leaked out of damaged capillaries.

Bruises usually appear bluish-black to start with, turning red and yellow as the haemoglobin in the blood breaks down. This may also be accompanied by swelling, and a dull ache or throbbing.

Treatment

A cold compress (a cloth soaked in ice-cold water, or a bag of ice wrapped in a cloth) will help to ease the pain associated with bruising. The discoloration will disappear with time.

Related problems

A disorder of the blood platelets, thrombocytopenia, may cause spontaneous bruising, as the blood leaks from the capillaries without any injury. The disorder may be caused by diseases such as leukaemia or cancer, or as a side effect of particular drugs, such as certain antibiotics or anti-inflammatory drugs.

Common purpura, also known as senile purpura, is also similar to bruising, and mainly affects middle-aged and elderly women. Large discoloured areas appear, particularly on the thighs

Black Eyes

Bruising is particularly noticeable around the eye, where the skin is thin and loose, giving rise to spectacular black eyes.

Treat black eyes in the same way as other bruises, by applying a cold compress to ease the pain. The only danger is that there may have been some damage to the brain so if your vision has become impaired or you are a little confused, you should seek medical help.

» SEE ALSO — Asthma, Breathing, Coughs

MEDICAL FACT FILE

and on the forearms. They are caused by rupturing of the blood vessels that are located beneath the skin, which is due to a thinning of the surrounding tissue with age. The condition may be helped by hormone replacement therapy.

BSE

Bovine spongyform encephalopathy (BSE) is a disease that affects cattle. It is not yet known whether human beings can get the disease.

Affected animals become unsteady on their feet, don't feed properly and quickly die. When viewed under a microscope the affected cow's brain is seen to be riddled with holes like a Swiss cheese. Scientific experiments on cows have proved little about the dangers of BSE to human beings despite the public scare over the disease in the summer of 1990.

There is no evidence of any transmission of the disease from cows to human beings, although it will be at least 20 years before anyone can be completely sure about the extent of any connection between BSE and human beings. Meanwhile, the good news is that the risk appears to be so remote that it seems reasonable for you to continue to enjoy eating beef so long as you avoid the brains and the spinal cord.

Roots of the disease
It was not until the late 1980s that scientists actually began to make some inroads into full recognition of this disease. It is therefore possible that BSE has always been around but that no-one has ever recognised the disease before. However, a similar condition has actually been recorded

in sheep for many years so this seems unlikely.

The most likely, and the most generally accepted, explanation is that modern animal feeding techniques have caused the problem. Until fairly recently, cows were fed on protein feeds which were made from processed cow offal. It is this form of feeding cattle which appears to have been a major factor in the development and spread of BSE, as some agent seems to have been passed from the foodstuffs to the cattle. In experiments to try to establish the cause of the disease, scientists have killed infected cows and injected their ground-up brain matter into animals that are unaffected. These experiments have produced identical symptoms in the living animals.

BULIMIA NERVOSA

Bulimia nervosa is a condition that usually affects young women. The sufferer binges and then makes herself sick after she has eaten in an attempt to lose weight.

In common with anorectics, the victims of bulimia nervosa often have a distorted image of themselves as being excessively fat (See Anorexia Nervosa, Understanding Yourself). There is, however, one major difference between the two conditions. While anorectics actually lose weight and become painfully thin, bulimics often find that their eating habits result in little or no overall loss in weight.

Bulimic behaviour
Often, a bulimic will overindulge in food or drink before deliberately making

herself sick and bringing it all back up again. Such behaviour will have a serious effect on the sufferer's health and not only because her body is not receiving essential vitamins and proteins. The repeated action of bingeing and vomiting can seriously damage the oesophagus, the teeth and even the gums.

Ulcers are likely to develop in the oesophagus, which is the muscular channel that carries food from the mouth to the stomach. The damage is caused when the stomach acid used to break down food is unnaturally brought back up to the mouth to be vomited out with the food that was originally consumed. This stomach acid can also wear away the bulimic's teeth and gums. In the most serious cases the stomach acid eventually creates holes in the oesophagus.

Treatment
Recommended treatment for bulimia nervosa is similar to that recommended for

anorexia. Once the bulimic has been convinced of the need to visit a doctor she will undergo close scrutiny to ensure that she is eating regularly and is not regurgitating her food.

As this is a psychological disorder, psychotherapy may also be recommended to treat the compulsion itself as well as any resulting side effects, such as depression. Anti-depressant drugs may also be prescribed.

BUNION

A bunion is a swollen pad of flesh at the base of the big toe which is frequently caused by the sufferer wearing shoes that do not fit her well.

Ill-fitting shoes may be fashionable and stylish in appearance but they do not have enough room for your toes to fit comfortably without being pinched and squeezed. Consequently,

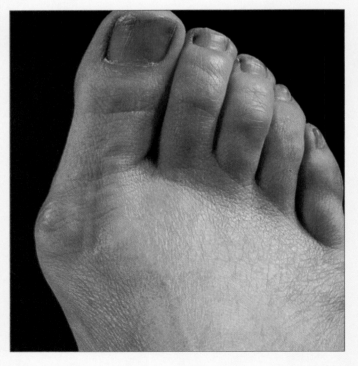

A bunion is a swelling of the joint between the big toe and the first metatarsal bone of the foot. It is often caused by ill-fitting shoes and may require surgical treatment.

➤➤ SEE ALSO — Anorexia nervosa, Callus

the big toe is crammed up against the other, smaller toes and this causes friction and, eventually, bunions. Sometimes, however, bunions cannot be avoided. A weak big toe joint may simply be hereditary in some people and the big toe will consequently flop towards the other toes.

Treatment

Normally, the best long-term solution for the discomfort that is caused by bunions is for the sufferer to choose a new and more comfortable pair of shoes. In the meantime, and while the bunion is still inflicting great discomfort and pain, special pads can be fitted at the base of the big toe to help to alleviate the pain.

Should the pain suffered from bunions become so bad that the sufferer can no longer move about freely, an operation may be recommended to straighten the toe. However, recovery from this operation can take some considerable time so it is only undertaken in the most serious cases.

BURNS

A burn is an area of the skin that has been damaged by heat, radiation or by corrosive chemicals.

Burns are divided into three groups according to their severity. The main problem with this system of classification, though, is that most burns will have a mixture of first, second and third degree damage and this can cause difficulty for your doctor as she attempts to prescribe some treatment and predict the outcome of your injuries.

A first degree burn produces an extremely painful redness of the skin. Second degree burns show severe blistering to the skin surface whilst third degree damage extends through the full thickness of the skin.

If you have received a third degree or 'full thickness burn' you may find that the affected area of skin is so numb you can't even feel the prick of a pin as the nerves have all been totally destroyed. This destruction may involve the loss of cells that would normally produce

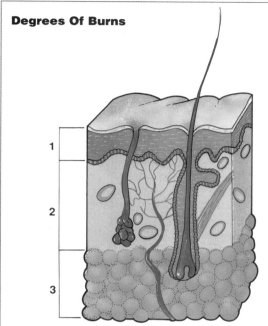

Degrees Of Burns

Burns are classified according to how far they burn into our skin: 1) first-degree burns affect only the top layer of skin (epidermis); 2) second-degree burns go down to the second layer of skin (dermis) and 3) third-degree burns destroy all of the skin and require hospital treatment.

the new skin. If this occurs, healing is a long and complicated process. Your doctor may advise that for your full recovery to be speeded up significantly, the application of skin grafts may be necessary.

Treatment

First Aid treatment for all types of burns is similar. The burn must be drenched in large amounts of cold running water. This has the immediate effect of cooling the affected area while stopping any further damage. It will therefore restrict the spread of the burn. Superficial scalds and burns can be treated with a 0.5 per cent hydrocortisone cream, which should be obtainable, without prescription, from your local chemist. Blisters should not be burst and should be covered with a clean, dry dressing.

More severe burns, especially those on the face or on the palms of the hands, should be treated straight away by a doctor. She may leave the burn exposed to the air in the expectation it will heal from the bottom upwards. Or she may refer you to a hospital Burns Unit for skin grafts. If you are administering First Aid to a burns victim don't use butter,

First Aid for Burns

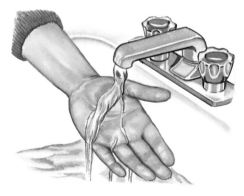

1 *The first step to take in the treatment of any burn is to pour cold water over it. This should prevent the burn from spreading and affecting the surrounding areas and will also ease the pain.*

2 *Cover the burn with a clean bandage. Make sure that the dressing you use on the burn is smooth and is not fluffy like cotton wool as this will cause friction and fluff will stick to the damaged skin.*

» SEE ALSO — Blisters

MEDICAL FACT FILE

bicarbonate of soda or anything other than clean water to ease the pain. Water is the only element guaranteed not to stick to a burn make it worse!

CAESAREAN SECTION

Caesarean section is the delivery of a baby through an incision in its mother's abdomen when vaginal birth would be difficult or dangerous.

Caesarean sections are usually performed for two main reasons: either because problems are expected with the mother if she were to give birth naturally or problems with the baby are anticipated. The mother's pelvis may be too small for her to give birth comfortably or she may have become too ill during her pregnancy to stand the enormous physical strain of the effort involved in a delivery. Pre-natal tests may have shown that the baby is likely to be too weak to stand a normal delivery or there may be a reason, such as severe haemorrhaging on the part of the mother, why an emergency operation should be carried out to enable the baby to be delivered at once.

The actual operation to perform a Caesarean section is fairly simple. A cut is made through the mother's lower abdomen. This cut is then continued through the wall of the uterus and into the amniotic sac. The baby is delivered through the gap created by the incision and the umbilical cord is cut. The surgeon then peels the afterbirth off the inside of the womb. The uterus is stitched up and the abdomen is closed. The whole operation should take about 40 minutes and can safely be

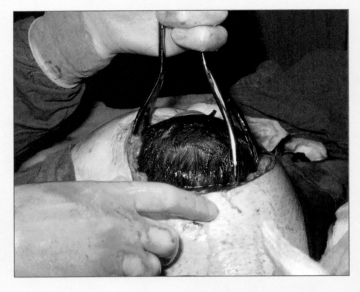

Above: Caesarean sections are performed when vaginal birth would be difficult or dangerous.

done under either a local or a general anaesthetic. If an epidural (local) anaesthetic is used, the recovery may be quicker.

Background

This method of delivering babies is so called because it was widely believed that the Roman emperor Julius Caesar was brought into the world in such a fashion. The main reason for this belief, however, was because the name Caesar is similar to the Latin verb 'to cut'. It was not until the 1500s that the first well-documented case of delivery of a live baby by Caesarean section occurred. A Swiss farmer called Jacob Nufer operated on his wife when the doctor could do no more! Mrs Nufer survived this traumatic ordeal and became pregnant several more times.

Caesarean section was a last resort until the 1940s. By then antiseptics, antibiotics, anaesthetists and blood transfusions had made all types of surgery safer. In the 1990s 10 per cent of babies are delivered by this route, but many midwives feel that some Caesareans are unnecessary.

CALLUS

A callus is an area of the surface of the skin which has become thickened and hardened through frequent use.

Although calluses may look unattractive they are generally harmless unless the particular area of skin in question is subjected to extreme overuse. Then the callus may begin to cause discomfort. Calluses are most commonly found on the hands and feet as those are the parts of the body which most frequently tend to come into physical contact with external surfaces.

Treatment

If you find that the callus has become unbearably painful you should visit a chiropodist. She will be able to scrape away the painful skin and will advise on such matters as whether you are wearing incorrect footwear. It may even be possible with calluses that are less severe for you to keep them at bay yourself. Rub the affected area with a pumice stone while in the bath to smoothe out the skin.

CANCER

A cancer is a group of cells which have continued to grow despite the body's efforts to stop them.

This growth may cause problems according to the cancer's site or size. Cancers may be malignant or benign, although most doctors would avoid using the word 'cancer' for benign conditions. Malignant tumours spread around the body by growing into and around neighbouring structures, (it is said that cancer 'the crab' refers to the 'pincer-like' growth of the tumour) or by metastasising. Metastases or secondaries are tumours that are identical to the first tumour but are in different parts of the body. Secondaries are usually carried by the blood. Nobody knows why one person rather than another develops cancer. There seems to be a genetic link but this is not the whole story. Environmental factors, such as radiation, chemicals or infections act on susceptible individuals to cause cancer.

Treatment

With one or two notable exceptions, the increasing cure rate for most cancers has been caused by better use of existing treatments. The three mainstays of modern treatment are surgery, radiotherapy and chemotherapy. The surgeon aims to remove as much of the tumour as possible. Specialists then use drugs and radiation to kill the remaining cells. Cancer, because it grows so fast, is more sensitive than normal tissue to poisons. With luck, and skill, the cancer cells will be destroyed and the normal cells spared. A fourth, equally important tool, is psychological support.

» SEE ALSO — Chemotherapy, Epidural

CAPILLARIES

Capillaries are tiny vessels that transport the blood between the arteries and the veins. Life-giving substances such as blood and oxygen flow through them around the bloodstream.

One of the most important roles played by capillaries is in the control of the flow of blood around your body. When you are taking part in strenuous exercise, such as aerobics, your capillaries will open to ease the flow of blood to your muscles. Once you have stopped exercising, and your muscles no longer require a constant supply of blood, the capillaries will slow down the blood supply.

Capillaries also serve the function of controlling the temperature on the skin's surface, helping to keep you warm when the weather is cold and cooling your body when it becomes hot.

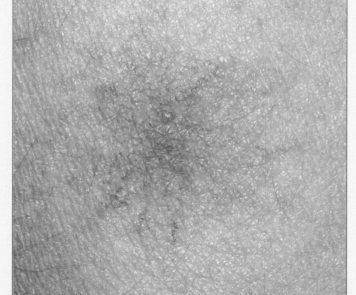

Above: Some birthmarks are produced by a group of capillaries on the skin's surface becoming dilated.

CARBON MONOXIDE

Carbon monoxide poisoning occurs when a reaction takes place between carbon monoxide fumes you have inhaled and haemoglobin in the bloodstream. Such a reaction stops oxygen circulating efficiently around the body.

The most common source of carbon monoxide is actually car exhaust fumes, but fumes may also come from some home heaters such as those that are fuelled by supplies of bottled gas. However, most people can tolerate small doses of carbon monoxide such as the emissions from car exhausts which most city dwellers have to put up with every day.

It is only when we are exposed to concentrated doses of carbon monoxide over a sustained length of time that it can cause serious side effects. Symptoms of carbon monoxide poisoning are headaches, light-headedness and a general feeling of sickness. The sufferer may pass out if she is exposed to the fumes over a considerable length of time. Unless it is treated swiftly, inhalation of carbon monoxide may be fatal.

Treatment

The best immediate treatment for someone who has inhaled carbon monoxide fumes is to get them out into the open air. But even if they appear to have made a complete recovery you should make sure they visit a doctor.

CARDIAC ARREST

Cardiac arrest is the technical term for the heart ceasing to beat.

When someone's heart stops it is just one event in a whole series that can eventually end in brain death. Sometimes the heart can be restarted but this depends on why it stopped in the first place.

Normally your heartbeat is regular and rhythmic but in cardiac arrests one of two things can happen: either the heart starts to beat irregularly with one small area contracting whilst another relaxes, or else the heart stops altogether. In either case the body is soon starved of oxygen. Oxygen starvation usually occurs if a heart attack affects the pacemaker part that regulates the pulse. It is probably one of the most common causes of death in the first few hours after having occurred.

Treatment

Cardiac arrest can be treated as long as the body has not been starved of oxygen. From a First Aid point of view it is vital to carry out artificial respiration and heart massage until skilled help arrives. Such on-the-spot assistance should be carried out because if the patient's brain is deprived of oxygen for longer than three or four minutes it will then become irreparably damaged.

Once the patient comes under medical supervision an electric current is passed through the heart. The sudden shock jolts the heart into beating rhythmically again. All hospitals, some ambulances and a few GPs now have the equipment to deliver such a shock.

It is much harder for doctors to treat a patient who has suffered a cardiac arrest where the heart has stopped beating completely. This may happen after the irregular contractions of a heart attack or it may be the end result of a fatal illness. Treatment involves injecting drugs, often into the heart itself, to establish some form of contraction. The contractions are then converted into a regular rhythm by the use of a series of electric shocks.

In towns and cities throughout the country, where a suitably trained general public is backed up by a skilled ambulance service, and where instant shock treatment has become available, more and more people are surviving cardiac arrests.

Symptoms of Cardiac Arrest

- Searing pain in the centre of the chest.
- Sweating
- Pallor
- Feelings of nausea.
- Breathing difficulties and wheezing.
- Intense fear or shock.
- Collapse

MEDICAL FACT FILE

▶▶ SEE ALSO — Blood, Oxygen, Veins

Treating Cardiac Arrest

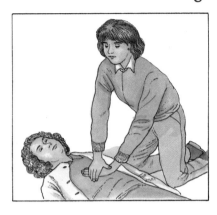

If attempts at mouth-to-mouth resuscitation fail, press rhythmically and firmly on the breastbone with both hands to restart breathing.

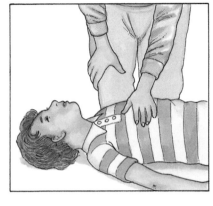

With a child, it is important that only one hand should be used, to avoid the risk of causing damage to either the ribcage or the breastbone.

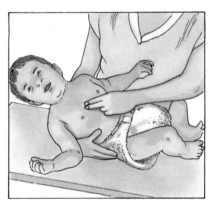

When dealing with cardiac arrest in a baby you should be even more careful than usual. Only two fingers should be used when applying pressure to the breastbone.

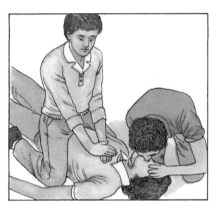

If there are two of you, one should supply oxygen through mouth-to-mouth resuscitation, and the other should then expel it by exerting pressure on the breastbone.

CARIES

Caries is tooth decay which is caused when plaque has eroded the enamel which protects the teeth.

Dental caries is a disease which is typically characteristic of the heavily industrialised societies in the developed world where people follow diets which contain many highly refined carbohydrates such as sugar. However, sugar is not the only cause of caries. To cause decay the sugar must first react with plaque.

Plaque is a hard substance which gathers over a period of time on the surface of the teeth, usually collecting in spots which are difficult to clean. Plaque is a combination of food and debris from the organic substances in the mouth.

The process of decay

Plaque contains bacteria which react with sugars in the diet to form acids which have the effect of dissolving the enamel on the teeth. Once the enamel is destroyed, the substance of the tooth is attacked, giving rise to a painful cavity. Fortunately, dental caries is

How Tooth Decay Starts

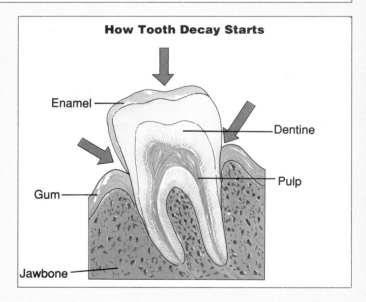

Enamel

Dentine

Gum

Pulp

Jawbone

Preventing Caries

We all hate going to the dentist, particularly if we need to have a filling. Here are some tips on how to look after your teeth and prevent decay.

● Use a toothpaste that contains fluoride. Some dentists advocate using fluoride drops but check that your water supply doesn't already contain it. Too much fluoride can produce fluorosis, where the teeth become stained with ugly, brown spots.
● Brush your teeth thoroughly and regularly – at least twice a day.
● Buy some plaque disclosers from your local chemist. They are tablets that dissolve in your mouth and lightly stain the areas of plaque you missed with your toothbrush. The stain and plaque can be removed with a little more brushing.
● Eat sweets at meal times but never just before you go to bed.
● Don't give children sweets – encourage them to eat plenty of fresh fruit.

≫ SEE ALSO — Plaque, Teeth

not as common as it once was. This may be due to many factors but fluoride has played an active part. Fluoride in the water supply or in toothpaste protects the enamel and fights decay.

CARTILAGE

Cartilage is a pliable substance which provides padding between the bones of the body and eases movement of the joints.

There are three types of cartilage: fibrocartilage, hyaline and elastic. Women who play sport are most likely to have problems with their hyaline cartilage as it allows joints such as knees to move freely and without restriction. Sports such as squash place heavy demands on the joints, and can lead to cartilage damage.

Fibrocartilage is tougher than hyaline and reinforces the joints under pressure. Elastic cartilage is situated in the arteries. It gives them elasticity and enables them to expand or contract when the heart beats.

Cartilage problems

The most common cartilage problems are a result of overuse or strain of the hyaline cartilage, general wear and tear of which may cause osteoarthritis. It is difficult, though, to gauge the damage you're doing to your cartilage as it tends to be done over a long period.

Torn cartilages may be operated on but remember the surgeon will often not know the exact location of the problem until your knee is opened up. It is important to realise that once your knee has been operated on it will never be the same again.

But with a modern arthroscopy a small incision is made in the knee and a pencil-thin telescope is inserted. Damage is then assessed and cartilage removed. The patient can be up and walking around later on the same day.

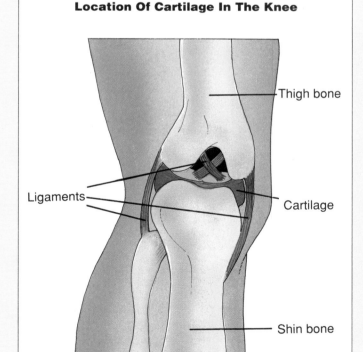

Location Of Cartilage In The Knee

Thigh bone

Ligaments

Cartilage

Shin bone

CASTRATION

Castration is a surgical operation to remove either one or both of a woman's ovaries or, in men, either one or both of the testes.

Although the word castration has long struck fear into the hearts of men, modern reality dictates that castration is simply a necessary step in reducing the risk of certain cancers. It is also, despite popular belief, an operation that can be carried out on women as well as on men.

Should a woman be in danger of breast cancer the removal of one or both ovaries restricts the production of the hormone oestrogen which spreads the cancer. In men, one or both testes may be removed to prevent the spread of prostate cancer. Castration may also be carried out if the ovaries or testes have become so badly infected that they are beyond repair.

Sex after castration

It is commonly assumed that castration means the end of a person's sex life. However, surgical castration does not involve the entire removal of the genitals, and an individual's sex drive is unlikely to be affected.

Once a woman has been castrated, there should be no loss of sexual drive. In fact, many women enjoy an increase in sexual desire as, if both ovaries have been removed, the fear of pregnancy is no longer present. The psychological effect is similar to that of the menopause, and some women may experience hot flushes. There may also be dryness of the vagina, but this can be easily treated by your doctor. Men who undergo castration, however, do lose their libido in almost every case.

CATARACT

Cataracts occur when the lens of the eye loses its transparency. This impairs the sufferer's vision.

Surprisingly, the lens of the eye is made up of the same fibres as gristle. Unlike gristle, however, the fibres are laid down side by side and this allows light to pass through. Any loss of transparency, whatever the cause, is known as cataract. World-wide, cataract is the most common cause of blindness but, thankfully, it is also the type of eye condition that is most frequently treated with a degree of success.

Cataract classification

Cataracts can occur at any age. They may be present at birth: viral infections such as German measles can affect the baby while it is in the mother's womb. If the damage occurs when the baby's lens is being formed, between three and 12 weeks after conception, a cataract will form. Babies may also inherit other cataracts that are rarer, but these may not develop until a few weeks or months after the birth.

Traumatic cataracts are caused by parasitic infections or through a direct injury to the eye and can develop at any age. Diabetes may also cause cataracts. Thankfully, however, modern diabetic management has assured that this is becoming less and less of a problem.

By far the most common cause of cataract in the UK is old age. Elderly people often find that their blood circulation tends to slow down. A poor blood supply to the eye means that the lens is starved of oxygen, causing what medical people call a senile cataract. As the lens' fibres die they will change from being clear to opaque.

» SEE ALSO — Eyes, Ovaries

MEDICAL FACT FILE

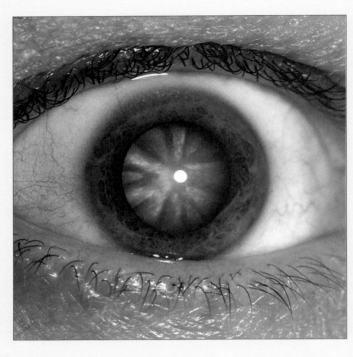

Above: A close-up of an eye, showing a cataract – a clouding of the lens that results in blurred vision.

Treatment

The surgical treatment of cataracts was initially attempted over 2000 years ago during Babylonian times. A sharp knife would be used to cut around the lens and the lens would then be pushed into the eye. A modern surgeon will carefully remove the lens completely and may then insert a plastic lens into the patient's eye.

CEREBRAL PALSY

The cerebral palsies are a group of disorders of movement and posture that are caused by damage to the immature brain.

The cause of the damage may also affect the eyes or ears as well as leading to fits or mental retardation. Many children with cerebral palsy have a normal or even a high IQ. Christy Brown, the Dublin novelist gives a striking description of his own cerebral palsy in the book 'Down all the Days'.

Cerebral palsy is becoming less common, probably as a result of better care during labour. It has not disappeared entirely, though, and still affects one in 500 births. It is more common in premature babies or those who, despite being on time, are very small. Damage from meningitis or head injury may cause cerebral palsy.

Symptoms

The commonest form of cerebral palsy, which used to be called spasticity, affects the legs more than the arms. The muscles are held tight and so restrict movement. The strong calf muscles mean that the feet point downwards, which makes it difficult to walk.

Cerebral palsy may not be detected at birth. In some cases the child will be slow to develop but in mild cases failure to raise an arm or leg properly may be the only sign. If a doctor or health visitor suspects cerebral palsy she will refer the baby to a specialist unit. The staff of the unit will be able to make the diagnosis and care properly for the child. They will also be able to counsel the child's parents.

Treatment

Treatment using drugs and surgery may be useful to correct a patient's muscular contractions. The mainstay of treatment, however, is physiotherapy, which helps the child to make the best possible use of her limited physical powers and co-ordination. Whether intensive physiotherapy will cause other parts of the brain to take over the function of damaged regions is a matter which has produced a great deal of controversial debate inside medical circles. Conventional wisdom says it is impossible but the results to date are encouraging. Speech therapy to assist with communication and feeding can be a tremendous help, as can an occupational therapist, who will provide their specialist advice on adapting the home.

Avoiding Cataracts

There is medical evidence which suggests that cataracts can be caused by prolonged exposure of unprotected eyes to strong sunlight. Take precautions to shield your eyes, therefore, when you are in bright sunshine.

Wear either a hat with a wide brim which shades the eyes, or sunglasses. Choose a good-quality pair of sunglasses which have lenses that are specially treated to darken and screen out the dangerous rays of the sun.

Above: Cerebral palsy patients using a computer for writing exercises and games.

Causes of Cerebral Palsy

Prematurity - the baby being born before 37 weeks or with a birthweight of less than 5.5lbs (2.5kg) - is the most common single associated factor in cerebral palsy. Other causes include:
• Maternal infections such as toxoplasmosis, rubella or herpes being passed on to the unborn baby.
• Umbilical cord problems.
• Injury to the baby's head during or after birth.
• Severe infection such as meningitis or a brain abscess.
• Carbon monoxide poisoning.

➤➤ SEE ALSO — Brain, Muscles

MEDICAL FACT FILE

CERVICAL CANCER

Cervical cancer grows in the neck of the womb. it is always malignant and will spread to other internal organs unless it is treated medically.

The cancer which grows in the cervix is the second most common form of the disease to affect women. It accounts for about 10 per cent of all female cancers but is completely curable if found at an early stage. There is a period of five to 15 years between the first changes to the affected cells and the development of cancer.

After the initial development of cervical cancer, cells become more and more abnormal but they will eventually return to their normal state with medical treatment. If you suspect that you have cancer, you must always make sure you consult your GP.

Doctors recommend women should have regular smear tests. In Scotland, women are advised to have their first test when they reach the age of 20, while in England the recommended starting age is 25. A general rule is that you should go for your first smear test about two years after you first have sexual intercourse. If you have not had sex, there is no need for you to have a smear test. After the first test you should have one every three to five years before you reach the age of 35 and then every two to three years.

Taking the test

The smear test used to diagnose cervical cancer is often described, although usually by men, as painless although some women do feel some discomfort and a very few suffer real pain. In order to take a smear your doctor will ask you to lie down with your legs bent and your knees flopped apart. An instrument called a speculum, shaped a bit like a duck's beak, will be placed into the vagina and opened to view the cervix. A shaped wooden spatula is used to remove the top layers of cells from the cervix for analysis.

Many women find that insertion of the speculum, especially if it is cold or poorly lubricated, is the most painful part of the test. In fact, some women find it very much easier to insert the speculum themselves.

Up to 20 per cent of women who have a smear

Causes Of Cervical Cancer

Nobody knows what actually causes cervical cancer but there are a number of factors which seem to be connected.

● Genital warts. Of the 40 or so strains of wart virus, four or five seem to have malignant effects on the cells of the cervix. It is vital that any woman who has, or whose partner has, genital warts should have an annual smear.
● Intercourse. Prostitutes, before the present era of safe sex, had a one hundred times greater chance of developing cancer of the cervix than nuns. The damage may be caused by sperm or by infection in semen.
● Early age of first intercourse. The immature cervix seems particularly prone to malignant damage from sperm. Women under the age of 17 must make sure that a condom is used during sex regardless of whether they are using the contraceptive pill or not.
● Giving birth. Childbirth seems to raise the risk about four-fold.

test are recalled. This is usually due to technical difficulties or may indicate an infection. Usually the repeat smear is fine but it may show some early changes. Your GP may then refer you to a gynaecologist for a colposcopy. A colposcope is a microscope for examining the cervix. By using this colposcope a gynaecologist can remove, or destroy through the use of a laser, any abnormal cells.

CHEMOTHERAPY

Strictly speaking, giving drugs of any sort to treat any disease, is chemotherapy. It is accepted, however, that chemotherapy refers to drugs used to treat cancer.

Cancer cells differ from normal cells in that they grow at a much faster rate. Therefore, most of the drugs used to treat cancers are highly toxic to growing cells. Cancerous cells, which grow faster than normal cells, are affected more than the surrounding tissues. Therefore, cancer cells will become poisoned while the normal cells will remain relatively undamaged.

Other chemotherapy drugs

The other group of chemotherapy drugs are those that block the effects of hormones. Certain tumours, those of the prostate or breast for example, depend on sex hormones for their growth. If the effects of the sex hormones can be blocked, by drugs with a similar chemical formula for example, the tumour will grow more slowly. Tamoxifen used in the treatment of breast cancer is the most widely used example. Patients are often more worried by the thought of having chemotherapy than

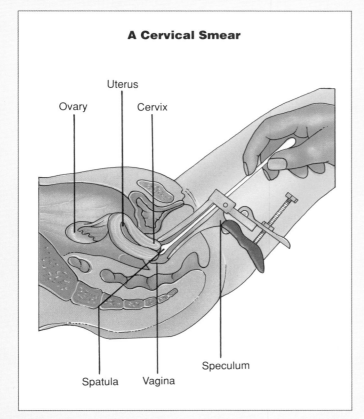

A Cervical Smear

Uterus
Ovary
Cervix
Speculum
Spatula
Vagina

➤➤ SEE ALSO — Cancer

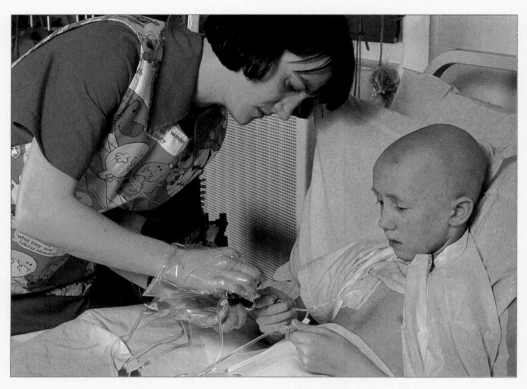

Above: A young patient suffering from hair loss, one of the side effects of chemotherapy. Drugs kill cancer cells but can also destroy healthy body cells.

they are of the cancer itself. Many of the drugs that attack and poison the cells can cause side effects such as nausea or hair loss. Chemotherapists recognise these problems and, by careful calculations of the dose and through the use of other drugs, can minimalise or abolish them. Despite its drawbacks and its bad image, chemotherapy can often be a life saver.

CHEST PAIN

Pain in the chest is a worrying symptom but is rarely due to a serious problem. It is most commonly a result of straining the bones, muscles or the cartilages of the rib cage.

In a recent survey five per cent of the people who took part were found to have suffered from chest pains during a two-week period. Yet proportionately far fewer than this number of people ever attend their own doctor when they suffer chest pains and even fewer will know the exact cause of the pain. Muscle pain is usually described by sufferers as 'knife like', is often in one spot and usually lasts for a few seconds. Pressing firmly in the painful area of the chest should bring the pain back which is a reassuring sign as it means the damage has been done to the muscle, bone or fat just under the body's surface and is unlikely to be heart disease. Chest pain can be treated with analgesics and by avoiding the exercise that caused the problem in the first place.

Indigestion
One of the most common everyday causes of chest pain is indigestion, although it is often confused with heart disease. The pain is usually located behind the breast bone and is brought on by such things as spicy foods, alcohol, smoking, stress and worry. If the pain is rapidly relieved by antacids, even if it comes back after a few minutes, then the problem is likely to be indigestion. Indigestion is caused by an excess of acid or is due to acid burning the lining of the gullet. The treatment is usually fairly simple: all sufferers form indigestion should do is quickly make an appointment to visit their own family doctor.

Serious chest pain
About one fifth of patients who consult their doctor about chest pain will find it has some sort of connection with the way they breathe or with a mild chest infection. Even the most simple coughs and colds are capable of causing quite severe pain if a muscle has been torn or a rib has been cracked. The effort of coughing or sneezing may aggravate the injury. Pleurisy, for example, is an infection of the space in between the chest wall and the lung, and causes a characteristically severe pain that becomes worse when the sufferer is breathing in.

Laryngitis may have the effect of causing a burning sensation with each breath. The pain is felt behind the breast bone and up into the ribs but the cause is usually quite obvious. Occasionally blood clots from the legs can move upwards and settle in

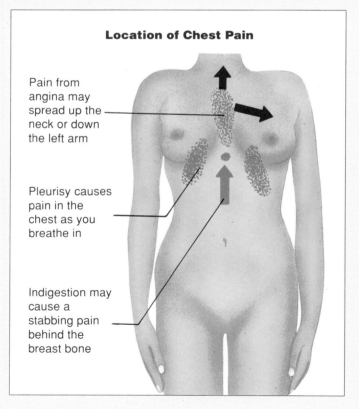

Location of Chest Pain

Pain from angina may spread up the neck or down the left arm

Pleurisy causes pain in the chest as you breathe in

Indigestion may cause a stabbing pain behind the breast bone

>> SEE ALSO — Angina

the lungs and cause severe pain and even death. These clots are more common in women who are on the pill, especially if they smoke.

Real heartache

Heart disease is actually a comparatively rare cause of chest pain. The pain is often described as 'clutching' or 'tight' and may be mild or severe. Angina, for example, is brought on by insufficient oxygen reaching the heart. This pain usually comes on with exercise, especially if it is vigorous or unexpected. Apart from the breast bone, the pain is often felt in the throat and left arm.

Angina can be relieved by plenty of rest but pain from a heart attack, which occurs when a part of the heart muscle dies, may not be. If pain is accompanied by sweating, nausea, shortness of breath or faintness, a doctor should be called urgently. If the patient stops breathing, call an ambulance immediately and start artificial respiration.

CHICKENPOX

Chickenpox is caused by the common varicella zoster virus which usually strikes children under 10 years of age, producing a rash and a fever. Once someone has had chickenpox they are then almost certain to be immune.

For most people, chickenpox is just a fading memory of early childhood. But although this infection is most often associated with the early part of the life cycle, it may remain in a passive form inside the body, eventually re-emerging during old age in the painful form of shingles.

Chickenpox is easily transmitted and, as such, it is almost inevitable that

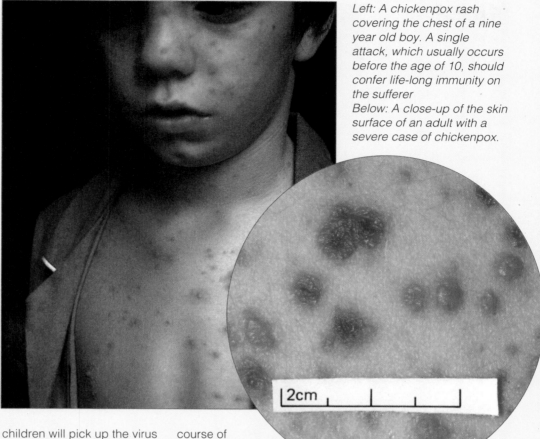

Left: A chickenpox rash covering the chest of a nine year old boy. A single attack, which usually occurs before the age of 10, should confer life-long immunity on the sufferer
Below: A close-up of the skin surface of an adult with a severe case of chickenpox.

2cm

children will pick up the virus from one another at some time. Its spread is also helped by it being very infectious for about five days before it first becomes visible on the sufferer's body in the form of a rash. It can therefore be spread by a carrier even before they begin to suffer its symptoms. In children, chickenpox first appears in the form of irritable red spots on the upper body, arms, legs, face, behind the ears and in the mouth. These spots become blisters and about five days after they first appear they dry and become scabs which, in turn, remain on the body for about another five days. There are unlikely to be any serious aftereffects for the child.

Chickenpox in adults

The best way to avoid catching chickenpox is to avoid those who have the infection. The infection has similar symptoms in adults but complications can occur if you are pregnant, taking a

course of prescribed drugs or are suffering from a blood disorder. If that is the case you should make sure you consult your doctor immediately.

Although you should only suffer chickenpox once, the virus does not actually leave your body completely. Some parts of the virus will remain in your nerve cells and these can, from late middle age onwards, develop into shingles. This is a painful condition which is very similar to chickenpox in that the skin becomes covered in blisters, although these blisters will be concentrated on a small area of the upper body.

Treatment

It is important to prevent the infected child scratching her spots as this can result in ugly marks remaining on the body after the infection has passed. One of the simplest methods of treatment is to cut the child's fingernails. Dabbing calamine lotion on

the spots will also soothe the pain and paracetamol can be used to ease suffering.

One new and very effective treatment for chickenpox is a bath oil called Aveeno. This is a blend of soya oil and oatmeal and is quite beautifully soothing. It moisturises the skin and smoothes out the rough coating on the chickenpox spots. The same advice for attention to chickenpox in children applies to infected adults and they should also ensure they increase their intake of liquids.

At the first sign of shingles make sure you consult your doctor. If this infection is spotted quickly, prescribed drugs can attack it effectively. If not, the sufferer is likely to undergo serious pain for weeks or months afterwards.

CHILBLAINS

Chilblains are small swollen areas of skin that are most often found on fingers or toes. They are caused by the contraction of tiny blood vessels underneath the skin.

As their name might suggest, chilblains most often strike during chilly weather. Women are actually more likely to suffer from chilblains than men but they most often affect either old people or children. Although chilblains cause great irritation, making the sufferer constantly wish to scratch them, they do not normally require any sort of medical attention.

Chilblain relief

A little talcum powder applied to the affected areas will probably go a long way to relieving the irritation caused by chilblains. The simplest way to make sure you do not run the risk of suffering from chilblains is to keep your fingers and toes well protected during the winter months. Try wearing a warm pair of gloves and sturdy footwear.

CHILD ABUSE

in the US, where the reporting of suspected child abuse is legally mandatory, one in 10 children suffers abuse. The exact figures for the UK are not known but at least 100 children die each year through child abuse.

Since 1979 the figures have shown a steady rise but this may well be due to increased public awareness. What is child abuse and what makes adults deliberately harm children? Children may be abused physically, sexually or mentally. Sexual abuse, where an adult indulges in sexual acts with a child which are disapproved of by society, has only become publicised in the last few years, though it is very likely that is has existed for centuries. Mental abuse is caused by the child being deprived of love and care. Some parents, however, may not be aware of the mental abuse they are inflicting because they do not appreciate the child's needs. Striking a child violently is now considered by some people to be abuse, although hitting a child as a means of discipline used to be widely accepted and even approved of by society. Indeed, in some cultures what we would regard as abuse is looked upon as perfectly normal and understandable behaviour.

Broken homes

No two abuses are the same but some features seem common to most of them. In general, abused children are members of families where there is little or no love and care. The parents are often young, isolated and depressed. Broken marriages are common. The NSPCC claim that fewer than half of all physically abused children are still living with both natural parents. Financial problems can often lead to family instability — a state of affairs which may actually result in child abuse. However, children who are in families which are poor but stable, even those which are heavily in debt, are no more likely to suffer abuse than other children.

Who are the abusers?

People from all walks of life may abuse children. Abusers are likely to come from any race, creed, colour or class. It seems likely, therefore, that social factors are less important than behavioural ones.

Parents who abuse may have had impossible expectations of their child. The child's failure to live up to these standards may lead

Above: Child abuse leads to great sadness, not only during childhood but also as abused children grow up.

to a point where even a minor problem can cause the parent to snap. Feeding problems and toilet training accidents may cause outbursts of temper. Parents often say that the child is deliberately provoking them.

If you are worried that you might be about to abuse your own child you must seek help from your GP or a social worker. Admitting you have a problem does not mean your children will be taken away from you, usually the reverse.

CHILDBIRTH

Childbirth is the process through which a baby is ejected from its mother's womb then pushed through the birth canal and out of the vagina to begin the first stage of its life as a separate being.

A full understanding of the process of childbirth is a phenomenon of the 20th century. An interest in reproduction has always been very common but the actual process of childbirth has been shrouded in myth and mystery.

The initial developments of childbirth are triggered by the actions of the foetus rather than by the mother. A hormone called cortisol is produced by the foetus's adrenal glands. The cortisol acts on the placenta to alter the proportion of the other hormones it produces. This hormonal reaction then increases the strength and frequency of the contractions of the womb.

When these contractions become strong enough to dilate the neck of the womb, they will cause quite severe pain to the mother and childbirth has begun.

Labour

Most hospitals advise that the right time to summon medical attention is when the contractions become regular and are occurring at intervals of less than 10 minutes.

Other signs of the beginning of childbirth are fresh bleeding or the 'waters breaking'. This commonly used term refers to a sudden gush, often a pint or two, of amniotic fluids. This happens when the baby's head and the dilated cervix break the bag that surrounds the baby, allowing the fluid contents to flow out.

Labour is established (likely to progress to a delivery) if the contractions are painful and regular. They should also last more than 45 seconds and occur every two to three minutes.

Comfortable position

The most natural method of delivery is for the mother to squat on her haunches. Given the choice, many women instinctively adopt this position. This squatting position allows the mother to push most effectively. It also tilts the pelvic bone forward and makes the passage of the head easier.

In developed countries women have been encouraged to lie flat. This is often more painful for the mother but it does allow the midwife or obstetrician access when they are helping with the delivery.

Natural childbirth

Some women like to feel they can give birth 'naturally', ie using relaxation techniques and a minimum amount of

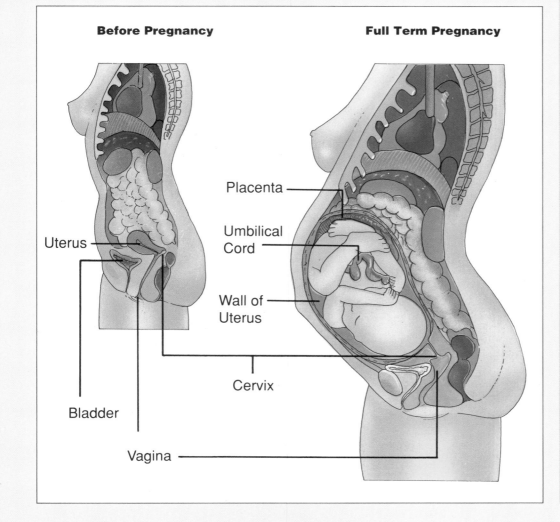

Before Pregnancy

Full Term Pregnancy

Placenta

Umbilical Cord

Wall of Uterus

Cervix

Uterus

Bladder

Vagina

Methods of Pain Relief During Childbirth

Several drugs are effective in soothing childbirth pain.

PETHIDINE Usually given as an injection. The main side effects are nausea and vomiting in the mother and breathing difficulties in the baby. Both these side effects can be treated and this remains a safe and popular method.

ENTONOX Also known as 'Gas and Air', this is a 50:50 mixture of nitrous oxide and oxygen. It is administered through a face mask with a safety valve. This form of pain relief may be very effective in some people but can have almost no effect on others. Its main advantages are that it has no serious lasting effects and is safe to use.

EPIDURAL This is an injection of local anaesthetic into the space around the spinal cord. It deadens the nerves that conduct pain and lasts for several hours. Its main disadvantage is that it must be administered by an experienced anaesthetist and may relax the woman so much that she loses the desire to push. Its major advantage is that it is highly effective in numbing pain, especially in deliveries where forceps are used.

≫ SEE ALSO — Delivery, Epidural, Labour

Emergency Childbirth

Thankfully, totally unexpected deliveries are rare as there is usually enough time to summon help.

If you are assisting with an emergency childbirth you should tell the mother to push if she wants to. The baby's head appears first. After the head emerges there will be a delay, often of a minute or two, before the next set of contractions. When the mother starts pushing again the baby's shoulders will appear. Then, when the shoulders are visible, grasp the head and gently pull it down to release the upper arm. Once the first arm is free it will be easy to deliver the rest of the baby. When it has been delivered, the baby should be placed on the mother's abdomen and wrapped up to keep it warm.

Immediately after birth leave the umbilical cord untouched. After a few moments, tie the cord tightly about 30cm from the baby's tummy with two pieces of string. There is no need to cut it at this stage. Do not pull on the cord because the knack of not snapping it takes practice! Between two minutes and two hours later the afterbirth will be delivered. Essentials for emergency childbirth are:

● Something clean for the baby to be born on. Clean newspapers are ideal.
● Something clean to wrap the baby in – a clean towel is fine.
● Clean ties for the umbilical cord. Household string which has been boiled for a few minutes is perfect for this.

drugs. However, some supporters of natural childbirth have extended their definition so that any form of active treatment, even pain relief, is regarded as 'unnatural'. This is an extreme view, and a disservice to women who want to give birth naturally but who also prefer some form of pain relief during labour.

Pain relief

Childbirth can be extremely painful. Ante-natal classes will help explain what is going to happen and will also go a long way towards dispelling any fears. Women who have attended such classes tend to have easier deliveries and need less pain relief.

Even as recently as the last century clergymen were preaching that the pain endured during childbirth was God's will. Opium and alcohol had been used but it was not until Queen Victoria allowed Doctor Snow to give her chloroform that the concept of pain relief was widely accepted. One complication of the type of pain relief given during modern childbirth, however,

is that the painkilling drugs given to the mother pass rapidly from her bloodstream into the baby's own system.

There are some other, more unusual ways of helping the mother cope with

childbirth pain, including acupuncture, massage and Transcutaneous Nerve Stimulation machines which administer electric currents.

Pack Your Bag

From about the 36th week of pregnancy, there is the chance that you could go into labour at any time. Have a bag packed and ready with:

● An old nightdress, to wear during labour.
● A couple of nightdresses and a couple of daytime outfits which are suitable for breastfeeding (just because you are in hospital there is no need to stay in your nightclothes, but do remember that hospitals can be uncomfortably hot).
● Several pairs of knickers and a couple of front-fastening bras.
● Sanitary towels (not tampons).
● A washbag with your flannel, toothbrush, toothpaste, moisturiser, deodorant, etc.
● Make-up and your usual hair-care equipment.
● Towels for yourself and the baby.
● Plenty of change for the telephone.
● Notepaper, envelopes and stamps – and something for you to write with.
● Three or four outfits for the baby.

The hospital usually provides anything you forget, and most hospitals supply nappies, cream, etc for changing the baby, but you may prefer to take your own.

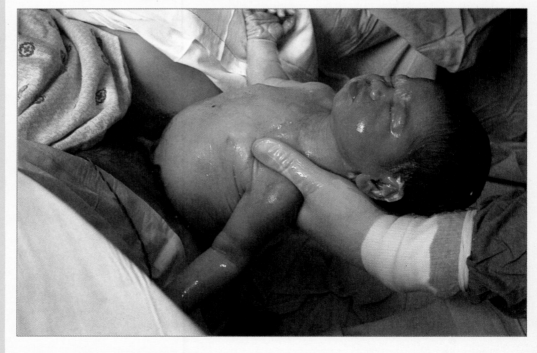

Above: After all the pushing and shoving, the moment that really makes it all worthwhile as a new-born baby emerges kicking and screaming from its mother's womb.

CHIROPODY

Chiropody is the examination and cure of all types of problems and injuries relating to the feet and hands.

Your feet and hands are in constant use and undergo a lot of everyday wear and tear. As a result, they can often become affected by a greater number of niggling infections and impairments than most other parts of the body. If you find you have any sort of foot problem which requires treatment, such as bunions or ingrown toe-nails, it is almost inevitable that you will be referred to a chiropodist by your doctor.

Footsure treatment

Every UK registered chiropodist will have spent a period of three years studying their speciality at one of the exclusive chiropody schools which must be judged satisfactory by the standards of the Society of Chiropodists. Once they have finished this training they are then qualified to deal competently with all manner of problems affecting your feet. Some will have the knowledge and ability to carry out surgery on your feet but most feet problems normally require quite simple treatment. Surgery is not usually necessary in most cases of foot problems.

CHIROPRACTIC

Chiropractic is one of the most popular forms of alternative medicine. A chiropractor manoeuvres the patient's spine to relieve pressure on a specific area through rearrangement of the surrounding nerves.

Although many doctors do not have any faith in chiropractic it has become extremely popular with people who suffer from serious back pain, most particularly in the United States. Unlike conventional treatment for back pain, the chiropractic technique is largely concentrated on manipulating small, specific areas of the spine in order to relieve the pain.

CHLAMYDIAL INFECTIONS

Chlamydial infections are caused by tiny micro-organisms which thrive by taking up residence in the cells of other living beings.

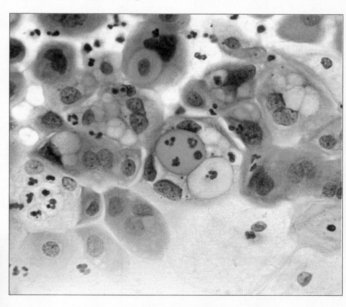

Above: A close-up of a cervical smear with cells infected by Chlamydia Trachomatis in the centre of the picture.

cervix and swelling of the fallopian tubes, known as pelvic inflammatory disease. The sufferer will have a painful lower abdomen.

Eventually, this condition, which is passed on through sexual intercourse, may lead to infertility both in men and women but if caught in time it can usually be treated quite swiftly with some prescribed antibiotics.

Eye disease

If a pregnant woman has suffered a chlamydial infection to her cervix her child may suffer neonatal ophthalmia, an infection which causes pus to be discharged from the baby's eyes at regular intervals. This irritation, which usually starts three weeks after the birth, can be treated by your GP.

In the Third World poor sanitation spreads an eye disease called trachoma, a strain of Chlamydia Trachomatis which can end in blindness.

Chlamydia Psittaci, the other chlamydial infection, is highly unusual and is a form of pneumonia.

The two types of chlamydial infections which affect human beings are Chlamydia Trachomatis and Chlamydia Psittaci. The most common condition caused by Chlamydia Trachomatis is nonspecific urethritis (NSU), which causes pain in the urethra, the tube through which urine flows out from the bladder. This is particularly uncomfortable for men, causing the testes to swell and producing unpleasant discharges from the penis.

In women it may initially cause a mild unnoticeable discharge. If left unattended it can cause irritation of the

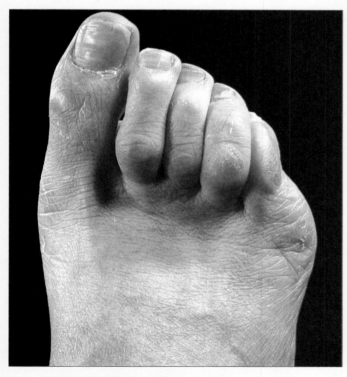

Above: An adult's foot requiring treatment from a chiropodist to remove the hard skin on the tops of the toes.

➤➤ SEE ALSO — Back pain, Bunions

CHOKING

Choking occurs when the windpipe becomes blocked and the sufferer is then unable to breathe.

There is no doubt that the sight of a child, or even an adult, choking is quite terrifying. It may be due to a piece of food, a small toy, or some inhaled vomit, but the result and the treatment required are the same.

Treatment

Firstly, don't waste time trying to pick the object out of the throat as it will probably be too slippery and you might well push it further down. To clear a baby's or a small child's throat, turn them upside down, holding them firmly by the legs, and slap them smartly between the shoulder blades. The object should come shooting out but if it doesn't, try again. If this hasn't worked and the child is quite obviously choking to death then try giving their stomach a short, sharp squeeze.

For any bigger children, or adults, bend them forwards over the arm of a chair and give them two hard thumps between the shoulder blades. Try this four or five times.

The Heimlich Manoeuvre

If thumping the person's upper back fails to remove the cause of the choking, then consider trying the Heimlich Manoeuvre. To carry out this manoeuvre stand directly behind the patient with your hands around their tummy, then bend them forward and join your hands together to make a double fist in the pit of their stomach. Squeeze the stomach by giving it a quick, hard hug first upwards and then backwards.

CHOLERA

Cholera is a disease found mainly in tropical countries. It is a serious infection of the bowel and can be fatal.

Although cholera was widespread in Western Europe during the last century it now tends to spread in those towns and villages in the Third World where there is a general lack of hygiene. The cholera bacteria are usually passed on through water which has been infected by the waste matter of someone who is already suffering from the disease. It is also sometimes contracted through eating similarly infected food although it is less usual for food to become infected in this way. One of the other most common ways of catching this disease is by eating seafood which has been contaminated by the cholera bacteria.

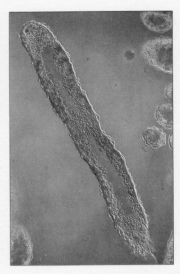

Above: A microscopic slide of one cholera bacterium known as vibrio cholerae.

Symptoms

Once inside the body the cholera bacteria find their way into the small bowel. After a short time, usually only three or four days, the victim will begin suffering constant diarrhoea and vomiting. As much as 500 millilitres of fluid can be lost in this way every hour by an individual who has contracted cholera. This enormous loss of fluid may cause irreparable damage to the body and can result in death if it is not replaced swiftly. It is possible the victim may perish within a day of the diarrhoea and vomiting beginning.

Treatment

It is essential that a cholera victim should have the fluid they have lost replaced quickly. This process, which is called rehydration, can be done by passing drinks through the patient's mouth or by a drip. Liquids given to the patient must include sufficient doses of life-sustaining salts and sugars. Antibiotics may be prescribed to counter the effects of the cholera and should reduce the diarrhoea and vomiting.

Techniques To Relieve Choking

Above: With older and bigger children, it may be necessary to bend them over your knee or the back of a chair before giving them two hefty thumps on the back.

Above: With adults, the Heimlich Manoeuvre can be used. Standing behind the victim, squeeze the bottom part of their stomach upwards and backwards.

≫ SEE ALSO — Bowel, Diarrhoea

CHORIONIC VILLUS SAMPLING

Chorionic villus sampling is removal, for genetic tests, of the tissue known as chorionic villus, which surrounds the foetus, during the first 12 weeks of pregnancy.

The purpose of carrying out chorionic villus sampling is to determine whether the baby inside the womb has any genetic defects. If, for example, your doctor believes there is an increased risk of you giving birth to a handicapped baby, and you are concerned about this, she will probably recommend that you attend hospital for chorionic villus sampling. The sampling is a simple procedure and, although you may be given a sedative, it will probably take less than an hour for the doctor to complete her work.

Sampling
The most simple way for the doctor to take some chorionic tissue from a pregnant woman is for her to insert a needle and syringe through the lower abdomen and into the womb. By using an ultrasound machine the doctor can see inside the womb and can guide the needle towards the chorionic villus. Once in place the needle is used to suck samples of the chorionic tissue into the syringe. Another way for the doctor to remove the chorionic villus is for her to insert the needle through the vagina and into the womb.

Pros and cons
The testing can cause problems. The insertion of the needle into the womb may, in a very small number of cases, cause damage to it, reducing its efficiency in protecting the foetus and causing some complications at birth. In about two per cent of cases chorionic villus sampling may cause nutritional and growth problems at a later stage in the pregnancy. It also increases the chances of miscarriage, but only slightly.

If the tests show the baby will be handicapped or will suffer from some deformity, the parents are given the choice of whether they wish to have an abortion (if abortion is legal in their country of residence). As the chorionic villus sampling is usually performed during the first three months of pregnancy, abortion (if legal) is less traumatic at this stage than later on.

CHROMOSOMES

Chromosomes are tiny bodies found in the nuclei (the central portion) of all plant and animal cells. Each chromosome consists of two separate strands – one from the mother and one from the father

The 23 pairs of chromosomes in the cells of an unborn child will determine whether the child will be born black or white, tall or short and will even determine what diseases it will suffer from in later life. The strands come together at the time of conception and each carries some of the features of each parent.

The characteristics the child will inherit from each parent depend on the particular genes that go together to form the chromosomes. For example, the child will have blue eyes if it inherits that particular gene, and brown if it does not. There are hundreds of thousands of genes in every chromosome and each gene will influence the cell to produce one characteristic. Genes consist of two tightly bound spirals of amino acids, which are the building blocks from which all proteins are made.

Determining the sex
The sex of a baby is determined by the X and Y chromosomes. The child may inherit either an X or a Y chromosome from its father (who must himself be XY) but only an X from its mother (who must be XX). The baby that is XX will be female and XY will be male (See the box shown overleaf).

The sex chromosomes can be identified under a microscope, thus giving doctors and parents the chance of knowing the baby's sex at a very early stage of the pregnancy. This can be important if the couple are at risk of having a child with a condition linked to its sex such as haemophilia or muscular dystrophy. In these particular conditions the genes that carry the faulty information are found on the Y chromosome and will only affect male children. Armed with the vital information of the baby's sex, the parents can decide whether to continue with the pregnancy or have an abortion (if it is legal in their country).

Detecting congenital conditions
A number of other congenital conditions can be detected by examining the baby's chromosomes. Down's syndrome is due to a defect in the 21st set of the chromosomes. Instead of having the normal pair the sufferer has three. This causes a whole host of problems as practically every organ is damaged in some way, but the severity of the damage depends on

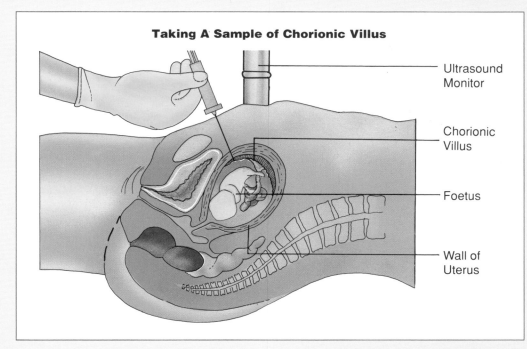

Taking A Sample of Chorionic Villus

- Ultrasound Monitor
- Chorionic Villus
- Foetus
- Wall of Uterus

» SEE ALSO — Genes

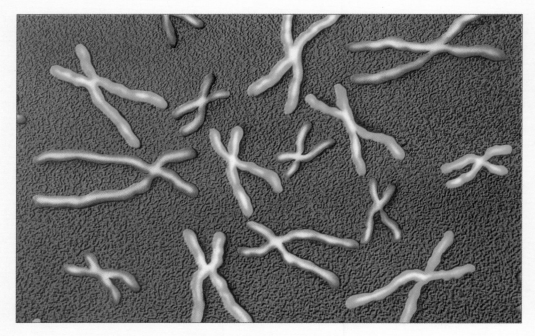

Left: Human chromosomes, are thread-like structures essential in the formation of human characteristics. Each has two strands and is capable of constructing an exact copy of itself. These are from the red blood cell of a healthy female.

If you think you are at risk of bearing a child with a chromosome abnormality, because of a problem with an earlier pregnancy or due to your age, consult your GP before you get pregnant. She should be able to reassure you or refer you to a genetic counsellor who can advise of the risk in your case.

which of the functions were under the control of chromosome 21.

Other chromosomes may be damaged at the time of the formation of an egg or a sperm, which can result in bits of chromosomes being lost or duplicated. This damage may appear to be very extensive but it is likely to have little or no effect on the baby. On the other hand, it may only affect a small part of one chromosome, but if this is in a vital part the effects can be potentially quite disastrous.

Chromosome analysis
Material from a foetus for chromosome analysis can be obtained in one of two ways: amniocentesis or chorionic villus sampling.

Amniocentesis is when a small sample of the fluid surrounding the baby is removed. Floating in this fluid are a few cells from the baby's skin or intestines. These cells can be grown in a laboratory and the chromosomes stained for microscopic analysis. An alternative approach is the passing of a thin needle

through the abdominal wall into the chorionic villus (the tissue which is present in the early stages of pregnancy and which becomes the placenta) of the foetus and the removal of some cells which can be analysed at once. This test can be arranged at a much earlier stage of pregnancy than the one carried out for amniocentesis, which means that decisions about terminations can be made at a time when the less traumatic suction method can be used.

CIRCULATION

The circulation is the continuous movement of blood and oxygen around the body by the heart's pumping action.

People have a tendency to blame circulation problems for any number of the physical difficulties and ailments which afflict them, from cold feet to fainting (See Your Health, Circulation). This frequently expressed concern with the importance of the circulation

How A Baby's Sex Is Determined

FEMALE
- Each cell has 23 pairs of chromosomes, of which one is XX.
- Each egg has 23 single chromosomes, of which one is always an X.
- An egg fertilised by a sperm carrying an X chromosome produces a girl.

46 (XX)

X   X X   =

X

MALE
- Each cell has 23 pairs of chromosomes, of which one is XY.
- Each sperm has 23 single chromosomes, of which one is either X or Y.
- An egg fertilised by a sperm carrying a Y chromosome produces a boy.

46 (XY)

X   X Y   =

Y

» SEE ALSO — Amniocentesis, Chorionic villus sampling, Down's syndrome

MEDICAL FACT FILE

The Circulatory System

Heart

Lungs

Liver

Kidneys

Aorta

is fully justified as it serves a whole number of vital interrelated functions which keep the human body alive and healthy.

The purpose of the smooth passage of blood around the body is quite simple. It allows oxygen from the lungs and processed food from the gut to be distributed efficiently to the organs that need them. In return it takes waste products such as carbon dioxide back to the lungs and spent food to the liver and kidneys.

The aorta

There are several vital processes which ensure that the blood circulates efficiently around the body. Initially, the heart pumps blood into the aorta, the main artery of the body. The aorta serves a dual role, carrying blood to the smaller arteries

but also ironing out the change in pressure which is caused by the heart's stop-go pumping action. As the heart squirts a jet of blood into the aorta its elastic walls will stretch and then, while the heart rests between beats, the aorta squeezes the blood around the body.

The arterioles

From the aorta the blood passes down smaller and smaller vessels until it reaches the smallest arteries of all: the arterioles. The arterioles have muscle fibres in their walls and these can be tightened or relaxed when necessary. Relaxing the muscles increases the blood flow and contracting them decreases it. This system, which is under the control of the autonomic nervous system, ensures that the blood can be directed wherever it is needed in the

body. A man slumbering in an armchair after Sunday lunch, for example, will switch most of the circulation from his muscles to his guts.

Problems can arise if more than one activity is undertaken at once. Swimming after a heavy meal, especially if alcohol has been drunk, is potentially disastrous as the circulation cannot keep up with the demands of the muscles (swimming), the gut (digestion) and the skin (effect of the alcohol).

The capillaries

From the arterioles the blood squeezes through the narrowest vessels of all, the capillaries. The walls of the capillaries allow dissolved gases, such as oxygen, carbon dioxide and molecules such as glucose to pass into the cells. As the blood passes slowly through the capillaries it is busy giving up those substances which the body needs and is equally busy in taking up waste products.

Veins and valves

After that part of the process the blood is low in oxygen and rich in carbon dioxide and other waste products. On reaching the end of the capillaries it flows into the veins. Veins usually run inside muscles and, as these contract, blood is forced back towards the heart. A series of one-way valves keeps the blood moving round in the right direction.

End of the journey

When the blood arrives back at the heart it is not immediately returned to the circulation. Instead, it goes through a second, smaller system before reaching the lungs. The oxygen-rich blood returns to the heart and is then recirculated. The whole journey round the body takes about a minute to complete.

CIRCUMCISION

Circumcision is an operation to remove the labia and clitoris in females and the foreskin in males.

In males, circumcision is carried out for medical reasons such as the condition of phimosis (tight foreskin). It is also frequently administered as part of the Muslim and Jewish religions and in hot countries for reasons of hygiene.

Although there are often medical reasons for male circumcision, there are absolutely none which can be advanced for performing this operation on females. Yet the practice of female circumcision remains astonishingly common in Africa where young girls are circumcised as part of traditional religious custom.

The aftereffects can be quite severe — difficulties will probably arise when the circumcised woman is giving birth and sexual intercourse can lead to damage of the vagina. An inability to pass urine is also possible, leading to potentially serious infections of the woman's bladder or even to damage to the kidneys.

CIRRHOSIS

Cirrhosis is severe liver damage. After sustained punishment the liver stops producing cells and begins producing scar tissue instead.

Most people imagine that cirrhosis of the liver is invariably due to chronic alcohol excess. This is often the case but cirrhosis may also affect children or life-long tee-totallers. Even prolonged bouts of heavy drinking may not produce cirrhosis as the liver has quite remarkable powers of self-regeneration.

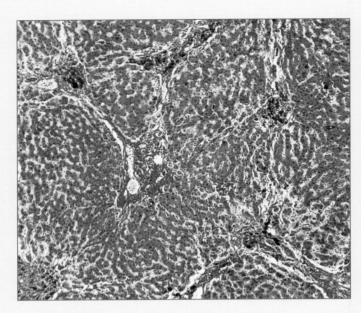

Above: The blue fibrous tissue on the surface of this liver indicates cirrhosis damage to the healthy pink liver cells.

It is even possible to surgically remove half of your liver and it will continue to function efficiently. In fact, the remaining half will grow to fill the newly created space. If it suffers a severe dose of poisoning the undamaged cells will multiply to repair the damage. Eventually, however, even the liver can only take so much punishment and is unable to regenerate.

Results of cirrhosis
The scar tissue which replaces the damaged parts of the liver is unable to fulfil the liver's vital functions of detoxifying poisons and making protein. Once fewer and fewer fully functioning liver cells remain the signs of cirrhosis will become apparent. The victim is then likely to suffer from jaundice and anaemia, they will bruise easily and will generally feel fairly lethargic. Swelling of the legs and abdomen will gradually worsen until the victim will eventually die of liver failure.

The alcohol connection
As far as alcohol is concerned, there is a grey area between the amount that is known to be harmful and the amount that is known to be safe. To be certain, you should make sure you drink no more than 14 units of alcohol per week (See Your Health, Alcohol). One unit of alcohol is the equivalent of a small glass of sherry or half a pint of lager. If you must drink more, try and have at least two 'alcohol free' days per week to give your liver a chance to recover.

Middle-aged women may be affected by a form of the disease known as primary biliary cirrhosis. This is similar to alcoholic cirrhosis but its cause is unknown. Wilson's Disease, a rare inherited disorder causing an excess of copper, may produce cirrhosis in children.

Treatment
Cirrhosis, by its very nature, is difficult to treat. Other than avoiding the cause, treatment is mainly dietary. A dietician will choose a diet that gives the remaining liver cells as little work to do as possible. In the end, unfortunately, a liver transplant may be the only hope of restoring the patient to complete health.

CLEFT PALATE

A cleft palate is a gap along the roof of a new-born baby's mouth.

Approximately one in every 1000 babies is born with either a cleft lip or a cleft palate. A cleft lip is a small indented ridge in the top lip which may cause a speech defect but a cleft palate is easier to deal with, although it requires surgery to correct it. This defect may result in the baby being unable to feed at its mother's breast.

Coping with a cleft palate
However, medical accessories can be fitted to the palate during the first year of the baby's life which will make feeding possible. When the baby is about one year old, however, its mouth will by then be strong enough to undergo the operation required to mend the palate. This operation should remove difficulties which the child may have in eating. A speech defect may remain with the individual although this can be eradicated in later life.

CLUB FOOT

Club feet are a birth defect where one or both of the baby's feet will be set at an abnormal angle to the rest of the body.

The reasons for some babies being born with their feet pushed away at an angle from their ankles are still not fully known. For some time, however, it has been suspected that large babies may not have enough room inside the womb and that their feet are consequently squashed over a considerable period. The result is that by the time they are born their feet are permanently at an unorthodox angle from their ankles and shins. It is a condition which is considerably more common in males than in females.

Treatment
The treatment for club feet should begin as soon as possible after birth and involves massage of the point where the ankle joins with the foot.

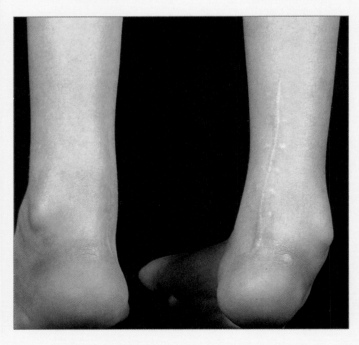

Above - A child with club feet, the congenital deformity in which the victim cannot stand with the feet flat on the ground.

▶▶ SEE ALSO — Birth Defects

COELIAC DISEASE

Coeliac disease is a serious digestive disorder caused by the body being sensitive to gluten — a protein found in cereals. It is most commonly found in young children.

The symptoms of coeliac disease do not occur until cereals containing gluten are introduced to the diet. When someone who is gluten-sensitive begins eating wheat, rye and other cereals their normally highly folded gut lining becomes flat and featureless. As a result, the surface area inside the intestines, which is available for the digestion and absorption of food, is greatly reduced. Undigested food reaching the large bowel will then cause the frothy, greasy diarrhoea which is such a distressing feature of this disease. As well as suffering from the fatty diarrhoea, children with coeliac disease will become thin and miserable and will have a bloated stomach. In contrast with cases of cystic fibrosis, another digestive disorder, children with coeliac disease usually have very poor appetites.

Some experts would suggest that putting babies who are aged less than four months on foods containing gluten increases the risk of them later becoming sensitive to foods which contain gluten.

Dealing with coeliac

If you are looking for an alternative, gluten-free foods are marked on their packets by a symbol of an ear of corn with a line across it. If your doctor suspects your child may have coeliac disease she will refer her for specialist advice. As well as carrying out a full examination the specialist will arrange some simple tests. These tests, which usually involve analysing samples of urine and faeces, may make a successful diagnosis more or less likely but will not be conclusive. To be absolutely sure, a tiny biopsy must be taken from the wall of the bowel. This is done by passing a small capsule into the intestine, opening it in the upper part of the small bowel and taking a sample. The capsule, complete with the biopsy, is then retrieved and analysed.

Treatment

The treatment of coeliac disease is simple, consisting of the exclusion of wheat, rye and possibly some other foods containing glutens. The results are often dramatic with a rapid weight gain and an improvement in the child's temper. The results may take two or three weeks to develop. At first, it may appear that avoiding gluten is a difficult task but fortunately all general hospitals have dieticians who can offer advice on this subject. There is also a wide range of special gluten-free bread, biscuits and cakes which are readily available on the NHS.

Some children's gluten sensitivities can appear to be resolved by the age of two but most doctors would suggest the child is retested at some stage.

Later life developments

Coeliac disease may develop in later life, causing a highly irritating skin condition. The rash associated with adult coeliac disease resembles scabies but fails to respond to the normal medication. As well as a special diet, drug therapy may be needed.

Early Treatment

Early treatment of coeliac disease is vital as it can prevent stunted growth.

COLDS

Colds are common infections which cause mild discomfort to the ears, eyes and nose. They are caused by viral infections of the mucous lining around the throat and in the nasal passages.

Everybody expects to suffer from a cold or two during the chilly winter months and because of the name most people believe that colds are actually brought on by cold, damp weather. This, however, has never been proven. The reason for colds being widespread during the winter is more likely to be due to people being indoors and in close confinement — factors which aid the spread of any infection, especially one which, like the cold, is extremely common.

Symptoms and treatment

The most obvious symptoms of a cold are a running nose, a sore throat and a general feeling of malaise. It is considerate of the sufferer to keep away from other people to prevent spreading their cold but unfortunately there is little a cold sufferer can do to attack their own infection. There are, however, various medicines which can be purchased at your local chemist which will at least go some way towards relieving the symptoms.

COLD SORES

Cold sores are small blisters on the skin's surface which are caused by the Herpes simplex virus.

After you have been infected for the first time by Herpes simplex, which usually appears initially in the form of 'flu, the virus will move into your nerve cells where it will remain inactive for long periods of time. It will then reappear at a later time but usually only once or twice a year and most commonly as a cold sore on the lips of the sufferer.

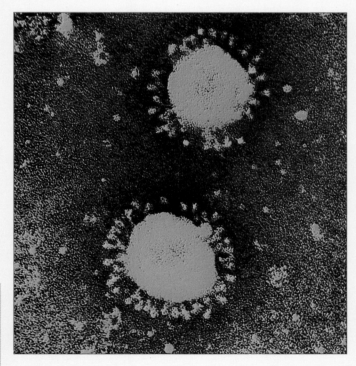

Above: Two human cold viruses greatly magnified. In humans, such cold viruses cause common colds and gastroenteritis. Similar infections occur in animals.

➤➤ SEE ALSO — Bowel, Diarrhoea

MEDICAL FACT FILE

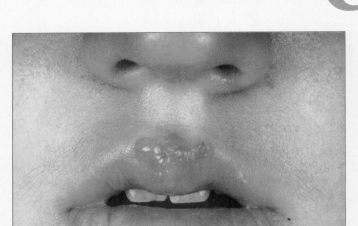

Above: A young girl who has been affected by a particularly ugly cold sore which is located on the edge of her upper lip.

If you suffer from cold sores you will probably find that they afflict you when you are already feeling a bit under the weather. It may be that you are already suffering from a severe cold or you may be finding it difficult to cope with either extremely hot or cold temperatures such as a heat wave or a cold snap. You may be able to relieve some of the pain from a cold sore with an ointment from your chemist.

It is unlikely the sore should bother you for any longer than two weeks and although it will itch and annoy you there should not be any serious or long-lasting side effects. If, however, you find that a cold sore is causing you some serious discomfort you should make a point of consulting your GP as soon as possible.

Dealing With Cold Sores

Although it is almost impossible to avoid getting cold sores, there are several things which you can do in order to ensure you minimise the discomfort.

● Do not touch any part of the cold sore.
● Do not touch your eyes when you have a cold sore infection and take extra care when applying or removing make-up.
● Do not kiss people, especially children, when you have a cold sore.
● Do not have oral sex when either you or your partner are suffering from a cold sore — this may lead to genital herpes.
● Do not break the blister or pick at the scab which

appears on your cold sore. Not only are you likely to infect your fingers with the virus but you may infect the sore with other germs.
● Do not share your eating or drinking utensils, especially with children.
● Do not share towels or face cloths with other people in your household.
● Do wash your hands thoroughly if you accidentally touch a cold sore or when applying any medication you may be using on it.

COLECTOMY

Colectomy is the surgical removal of all or part of the large bowel or colon.

When a total colectomy is performed the rectum is removed and a new opening for waste material must be made in a further operation known as an ileostomy. This is different from a colostomy (see page 64) as a bag is attached to the end of the small bowel rather than the large one. This means that waste material collected in the bag will be much more fluid than with a colostomy. Total colectomies, however, are much less common than partial ones.

Partial colectomies

When performing a partial colectomy the surgeon is likely to have two options, depending on the nature of the disease and the area of the colon removed. The two cut ends of the bowel can be joined together or an artificial opening can be fashioned in the abdomen for a colostomy. Many colectomy patients dread the thought of a colostomy but relatively few will need one and even then many patients are quite surprised at just how easy they are to cope with.

Colectomies may be performed for a variety of reasons. Cancer and gangrene from a twisted bowel are most common in the elderly while people in their twenties and thirties are more likely to be suffering from ulcerative colitis or complications which have resulted from it.

Modern surgery, with its strong emphasis on prevention and its use of flexible telescopes which can visualise the whole of the colon should mean that colectomies will become less common in the future.

COLIC

Colic is a type of spasmodic pain caused by internal muscles fighting to overcome an obstruction.

Colic is not actually a disease in itself. It is, instead, a form of pain which comes and goes, usually building up to a minute or so of real agony and subsiding to a dull ache before building up to another crescendo. The site of the pain as well as the time interval in between each attack can give your doctor some very useful clues as to whether or not you have been struck by colic. Many organs, such as the gut and the ureter (the passage through which urine travels from the kidneys to the bladder) contain the type of smooth muscle which is usually affected by colic.

Classic colic

Pain from the ureter, renal colic, is felt in the back, just below the ribs. The pain is severe and often seems to travel into the groin. Renal colic is due to the presence of a stone in the ureter. Waves of contractions pass down the ureter to try and push the stone along. Often they succeed and the stone passes into the bladder causing immediate relief of the pain. Before Nature does the trick a painkilling injection, such as pethidine, may be needed. Biliary colic is very similar but in this case the stone will be stuck somewhere en route from gall bladder to intestine.

The commonest colic

The commonest type of colic is intestinal in origin. This may be due to constipation or inflammation in the bowel wall. Inflammation and swelling fool the gut into thinking it is full and powerful waves of contraction build up to try and shift the obstruction. Simple

⇒ SEE ALSO — Bowel

painkillers, hot-water bottles and peppermints may help to relieve the discomfort. If not, your doctor may decide to prescribe an anti-spasmodic drug.

Baby colic

Every parent can remember sleepless nights with a screaming baby. This is 'three-month colic', so-called because it should get better at that age. Nobody knows the cause, though it does seem commoner in families which are under stress. It is certainly commoner in the children of smokers. Warm drinking water may help as may 'colic drops', available from your chemist, or gripe water. This condition can be very distressing for mother and baby alike so make sure you seek advice from your GP.

COLITIS

Colitis is a severe inflammation of the colon or large bowel.

The symptoms of colitis are diarrhoea or a pain, which may be severe, below the navel. The diarrhoea may arrive every few minutes or may even consist of loose motions once a day. It may also be possible to identify colitis from inspection of your faeces when you go to the toilet. Everybody passes some mucus with their bowel action but if this is present in large amounts, especially if it is tinged with blood, it may indicate that you are suffering from colitis.

Most diarrhoea attacks are due to some form of irritation of the wall of the large bowel either as the result of an infection or after someone has eaten spicy food. The cause is usually fairly obvious such as a severe attack of gastroenteritis that affects the whole family or even a particularly hot Vindaloo!

The Digestive System

- Oesophagus
- Liver
- Stomach
- Small intestine
- Colon or large intestine
- Rectum

Uncommon colitis

Two rare but important causes of colitis are ulcerative colitis and Crohn's disease. Ulcerative colitis usually produces bloody diarrhoea which is very rich in mucus.

Although doctors describe Crohn's disease as colitis it is not, strictly speaking, a colitis at all as the region of the gut affected is usually the end of the small bowel rather than the colon. The sufferer usually has abdominal pain and diarrhoea which lasts for many months. A diagnosis can be made by passing a flexible telescope into the bowel and inspecting the lining. Treatment for both of these conditions is with medicine but occasionally some surgery will be needed.

COLON, CANCER OF THE

Many growths in the colon are benign, but if they are not removed then there is a possibility of them becoming cancerous at a later stage.

Cancer of the colon is usually a disease of middle or old age but occasionally those aged under 50 can also be affected. Men are more likely to be affected by this cancer than women.

Symptoms of colon cancer depend on the part of the colon affected. Tumours in the rectum often show themselves early by causing constipation or obvious bleeding. Cancer of the first part of the colon may not be discovered until late on; the faeces in this part of the bowel are too soft to be easily obstructed and any blood loss is hidden in the faeces. Abdominal pain is a common symptom of all sorts of bowel cancer as is a change in a person's bowel

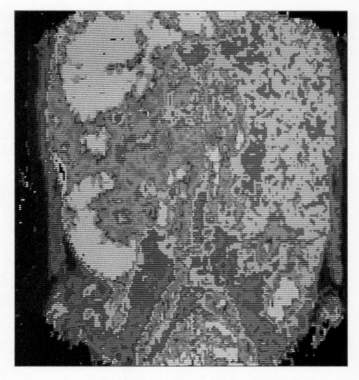

Above: A cancer sufferer's abdomen with the diseased areas, including the colon and liver, highlighted in white.

➤➤ SEE ALSO — Crohn's Disease, Diarrhoea

MEDICAL FACT FILE

habits (usually increasing constipation) or weight loss. Chronic blood loss may cause anaemia.

Although these are all signs of cancer of the colon, they are also features of some commoner and less serious conditions. Do not assume, therefore, that one, two or even all of them mean you have cancer, especially if you are under 40.

Examining the colon

A doctor has several options as to how she goes about investigating a patient whose symptoms might suggest cancer of the colon. The simplest is an examination, with a gloved finger, of the rectum itself. This may reveal a tumour or the presence of blood may suggest a problem further up the bowel. A medical telescope can be used to view the first 15cms and can provide vital clues to the diagnosis. Tumours higher up than this can only be seen using a flexible telescope or x-rays. Another test for cancer is a barium enema where the colon is emptied using powerful laxatives. A dye that will reveal any abnormality is then squirted into the patient's rectum.

Occasionally tumours may be burnt away completely by using an operating telescope but surgery offers the most realistic hope of a cure.

COLOSTOMY

A colostomy is an artificially created hole in the large bowel. Its purpose is to drain solid or semi-solid waste matter when the rectum and anus are unable to cope adequately. The waste is collected in a bag.

A colostomy may be either permanent or reversible. As the name suggests, a reversible colostomy is usually a temporary measure, often to give the bowel something of a rest or to remove an obstruction further down its length. This type of temporary colostomy is made by bringing a loop of the bowel up to the surface of the abdomen, which will then be opened.

It is most often performed to remove the obstruction of either a tumour or an abscess. When the obstruction has been removed the colostomy will then be closed off and the patient will be able to use her bowels as normal.

Permanent colostomies

A permanent colostomy is usually made if cancer has forced the surgeon to remove the rectum. The site at which the colostomy is brought to the surface must be carefully chosen to allow a bag to be attached without interfering with clothing.

Most district hospitals have a special nurse or therapist who can advise on this and all other aspects of colostomy care.

Living with a bag

Many patients dread the thought of 'having a bag' more than they dread the disease that makes it necessary. Surprisingly they and their families often accept it very easily, especially if the surgeon and nurses have explained the situation fully beforehand.

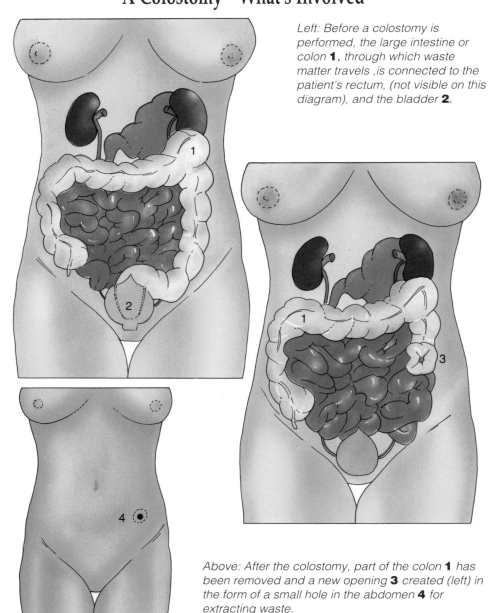

A Colostomy – What's Involved

*Left: Before a colostomy is performed, the large intestine or colon **1**, through which waste matter travels, is connected to the patient's rectum, (not visible on this diagram), and the bladder **2**.*

*Above: After the colostomy, part of the colon **1** has been removed and a new opening **3** created (left) in the form of a small hole in the abdomen **4** for extracting waste.*

➤➤ SEE ALSO — Bowel

COLOUR BLINDNESS

People described as colour blind cannot distinguish as many different colours as most people.

The term 'colour blind', although widely used, is actually misleading. It is commonly used to refer to people who have difficulty in telling the difference between particular colours as well as those who are able only to see their surroundings in black and white. Many so-called 'colour-blind' people are able to distinguish a variety of other colours as easily as people who do not have colour vision problems.

A black and white outlook?

There are several varieties of colour blindness. Some of the colours which people have difficulty trying to distinguish between are: red and orange; green and yellow; and blue and green. Strangely the most frequent confusion is caused by people being unable to tell the difference between purple and grey. It is even quite possible for someone who has great difficulty telling the difference

between green and yellow to have no problem making out the difference between red and orange.

Colour blindness is usually inherited with the male chromosome: eight per cent of men are affected but only 0.4 per cent of women suffer from colour blindness. The condition may also be caused by damage to the back of the eye or its nerves.

Being colour blind can have serious repercussions. For example, colour blind people often confuse red and green and may also have difficulty distinguishing the brightness of certain colours. This could lead to danger when dealing with such things as information

about electrical cables, which is often colour coded. Getting the colours mixed up and interchanging the live wire for the earth wire could be fatal. Even in the natural world there are certain colour codes. Bright colours are often a sign of danger.

Most people with defective colour vision confuse two colours, seeing them as the same. Very rarely, they may even view their surroundings as black and white with no colour.

Methods of testing

There are two main tests for colour blindness and one or other makes up a vital part of the medical examination for new employees in many

Above: A typical exercise in testing for colour blindness. Those with normal vision will see the number 57, those with red-green deficiency will see the number 35.

fields. A colour blind telephone engineer, for example, could cause havoc.

One series of such tests gives the subject the chance to match colour plates of various hues. This is the most accurate method of testing someone's colour vision but it takes too long for it to be adopted for practical use. A more straightforward method, especially for the red-green defect is the use of 'dot

cards'. These are a series of plates filled with coloured dots which form figures that can only be seen if the viewer has normal vision.

COMA

A coma is a sleep which is unnaturally deep, caused by damage to the brain by poisons or by severe physical trauma such as a bang on the head.

The depth of sleep induced by a coma will vary from case to case as will the duration and treatment. The damage, which can be permanent or temporary, may be caused by poisons from outside the body such as alcohol or from inside the body such as the waste products which circulate after kidney failure. Repeated alcohol or drug abuse can result in chemicals overpowering the brain tissues, eventually producing a coma.

In many ways, poison damage is easier to treat than that inflicted by head injuries. Given time, the liver will break the poisons down and the doctor's task is to allow the brain to survive until this has been achieved. This life support for the brain may well involve artificial respiration and some intravenous feeding.

A really deep sleep

The depth of coma after a head injury depends on the degree of brain damage and the length of time since the accident. Doctors use the Glasgow Coma scale to try and quantify the depth of unconsciousness. This may range from the deeply unconscious who can't feel pain to those who can be woken by a familiar voice.

The last sense to leave the unconscious patient, and the first to return, is hearing. Even apparently deeply

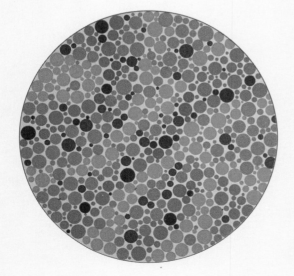

Above: In this test, those with normal vision see a random pattern, while those with red-green deficiency see a number.

➤ SEE ALSO — Bowel

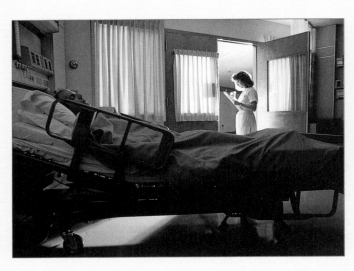

Above: A nurse taking some of the essential readings which are used to carefully monitor the progress of coma patients.

CONCUSSION

Concussion is temporary, minor damage to the brain frequently caused by a knock to the head.

Following a head injury the victim may be dazed or knocked out for a few seconds. For several hours afterwards, however, they may appear completely normal and may carry out complicated tasks perfectly well. Despite this, they will have no later memory of their actions during this time. They will have been acting on 'remote control.' Most people make a complete recovery but occasionally a severe headache may persist for several days after other symptoms of the concussion have vanished.

At one time it was believed that concussion occurred when there was no visible damage to the brain.

unconscious patients may hear and be able to remember later on, the exact words which have been spoken to them. There are also many cases of patients, who have been comatose for many months, being revived by the sound of the voice of a loved one.

However, it is now known that this definition is not an accurate one as any form of disturbance of brain function must be accompanied by some form of damage even if it is only visible under a microscope.

Danger Signs

There are certain signs you should look for which will tell you if a head injury patient is suffering from a more serious condition than concussion.

● Unequal pupils. One pupil will appear either considerably larger or smaller in size than the other one.
● Vomiting. This is common, but if frequent, severe or unaccompanied by nausea, it may be a sign of brain damage.
● Unusual behaviour or excessive drowsiness. If the patient seems to recover well and then gets worse this may indicate a blood clot. They should be taken to the nearest hospital accident. department immediately.

CONJUNCTIVITIS

Conjunctivitis is an irritation of the membrane which covers the inside of the eyelid and the white part of the eye's surface. It produces pain and the release of fluid discharges.

Conjunctivitis is very common in adults and is usually contracted when the eye comes into close contact with a substance it is allergic to — such as pollen or eye make-up. It is easily treated by delicately bathing the eye in a bicarbonate of soda solution (available from most local chemists) or by using eye drops.

In new-born babies, however, it can be somewhat more serious as the type of conjunctivitis of the eye which is known as neonatal ophthalmia can, if it is allowed to infect the main part of the eye, end in blindness. This type of conjunctivitis is passed on to the baby at birth due to infections such as gonorrhoea or genital herpes in the mother's cervix.

CONSTIPATION

Constipation is the term used to describe irregular bowel actions, hard motions or difficulty in passing faeces. It is twice as common in women as it is in men and increases with age.

A recent study revealed that 10 per cent of adults believed they had suffered from constipation during the previous fortnight. Those results may have stemmed from the widespread belief that the bowels should be opened daily and that failure to do so will cause any number of complaints ranging from headaches to depression. In fact, one medical study has shown that the average person may pass faeces as little as twice a week or as often as three times every day.

Constipated children

Children are often taken to a GP by a parent who is worried that their child's bowel frequency is not normal. This is common in parents who use laxatives, probably because their idea of the norm is unrealistic.

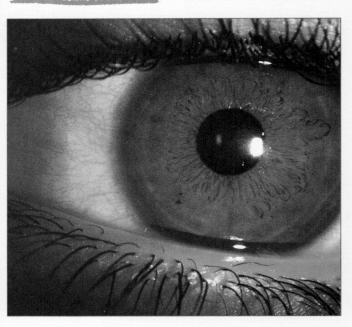

Above: A close-up of an eye's surface showing a severe red inflammation which indicates acute chlamydial conjunctivitis.

Constipation in infancy is usually due to the child not having been given sufficient fluids or having been given cows' milk formula feeds. Very rarely, constipation in early infancy can be due to Hirschsprung's disease. In this case, a segment of the bowel lacks the nerves that provide an individual's bowels with the strength to pass faeces on and out of the body. Occasionally surgery may be the only hope of curing this condition.

If your child is constipated the treatment is usually fairly easy. First, offer them extra fluids, preferably as fruit juice. This is especially important in hot weather. If this fails then extra sugar in one or two of their feeds may do the trick. If your child is still struggling to pass a hard motion you should then consult your GP, who may pass a well vaselined finger into the rectum. This often has spectacular results!

Dietary constipation

The commonest cause of constipation in young adults is dietary, often at times when they are dieting to excess and not receiving enough fibre. Irritable bowel syndrome may cause constipation but this usually alternates with diarrhoea and is accompanied by abdominal bloating and pain. Treatment consists of a high fibre diet and anti-spasmodics such as peppermint oil. Irritable bowel syndrome is much more common in women and seems to be stress related.

If you are elderly and have been constipated for two weeks or more, especially if it is associated with weight loss or bleeding, you should consult a doctor. She may be able to reassure you but may wish to take a few simple tests first. In the elderly, perhaps more than in any other age group, constipation may be due to a

dietary cause. Cooking for one is never very interesting, especially if old age has robbed you of your appetite.

Natural treatment

There is no doubt that as far as treatment is concerned, the natural way is the best by far. The standard western diet consists of far too few foods which provide fibre. An apple a day, an orange or a meal consisting of some lightly cooked vegetables will certainly keep the doctor away. Only rarely will laxatives be required to help ease your bowel movements and in such cases your doctor's advice should be sought immediately.

CONTRACEPTION

Contraception is a general term used to describe the methods that reduce the chance of sexual intercourse resulting in a woman becoming pregnant.

The only way you can be completely sure of avoiding pregnancy is simply to avoid having sexual intercourse. Just as there is no completely foolproof way of planning a pregnancy, there is no perfect method of contraception. Even those methods which are the most successful in preventing unwanted pregnancies have certain disadvantages. However, the most efficient and effective methods of contraception are more than 99 per cent effective.

For example, the most drastic but also the most effective means of contraception, is sterilisation. In the female this entails the fallopian tubes being closed off to prevent the egg travelling down them to connect with sperm. In males, the tubes down which sperm travels from the testes to the penis are cut or blocked. This means that

sperm can no longer enter the semen that is ejaculated when the man climaxes during sexual intercourse. If either partner in a relationship undergoes sterilisation the chances of the woman becoming pregnant are about one in 1000. However, this is almost always a permanent method of contraception and unless the individual concerned is absolutely sure that they do not wish to become a parent in the future, sterilisation should not be undertaken. In certain circumstances, attempts at reversing both male and female sterilisation may be made, but this is inadvisable as it is often complicated, expensive and has a low rate of success.

The human factor

In contrast, *coitus interruptus*, the least complicated method of contraception, and the one which relies entirely on judgement and self-control, is the least successful.

Many men believe that if they withdraw their penis just before they climax when making love they eliminate the possibility of their partner becoming pregnant. However, once the penis is

There is also the chance that one or both of the partners will be unable to exercise the necessary restraint to stop short of a climax once they have become involved in the passionate business of making love!

Another nonscientific method of contraception, which was particularly popular during pre-industrial times, is breast-feeding. The process of infants feeding at the breast during the first three years of life has the effect of altering hormone levels in their mother's body. This can prevent an egg being released from the woman's ovary. This method is no longer widespread as there is no guarantee that breast-feeding will have the desired effect on ovulation.

Pills and thrills

The Contraceptive Pill was introduced in the early 1960s and the freedom it gave women to enjoy sex without worrying about pregnancy was one of the major factors in the sexual revolution of that decade. Twenty years later the Pill began to suffer some bad publicity when some experts suggested that it could be linked to an increased incidence of

The Pill

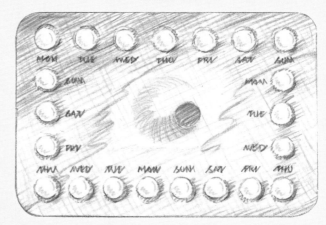

erect there may be sperm in the drops of lubricating fluid at its tip so a climax is not necessary to produce an unwanted pregnancy.

breast and cervical cancer. However, this has not been proven conclusively and the Pill remains the most popular method of birth control. This probably has a great deal to do with the Pill's success rate — fewer than one per cent of women using the Pill will become pregnant.

There are three types of pill in use in the UK: the combined pill, the mini-pill, and the so-called 'morning-after pill'. The combined pill contains two hormones: oestrogen and progestogen. If it is taken regularly it prevents a woman releasing an egg every month. If it is used carefully and consistently it is very effective and fewer than one woman in every 100 per year will become pregnant. It is not suitable for smokers over 35, diabetics, women who have raised blood pressure or women who are from a family which has a history of heart-related trouble.

For women who cannot use the combined pill for health reasons, the mini-pill, which has fewer side-effects, may be the answer. This pill is composed purely of progestogen and taken every day it prevents both sperm and fertilised eggs implanting in the womb.

The last resort

If you have had sex without using birth control and you wish to avoid the risk of pregnancy then you may wish to use the morning-after pill. This name is a bit misleading as this method of preventing pregnancy can be effective if taken within 72 hours of sex. It should also not be strictly described as contraception as the process of fertilisation of the egg may already have begun and the morning-after pill may have the effect of aborting the foetus. This treatment is prescribed by a doctor and two pills must be taken 12 hours apart.

It is usually very effective with a success rate of between 96 and 99 per cent. Your period should turn up at the expected time or even slightly earlier. However, you

Coil

may feel sick because of the treatment and not all women will be suitable as users of this pill.

Putting up barriers

If you feel you cannot trust yourself to remember to take a pill every day or if the Pill is likely to affect your health, you may wish to use a device which can be fitted inside your vagina or womb.

The most effective of these is the intra-uterine device (IUD), also known as the coil, which is a small copper and plastic device which is inserted into the womb by a doctor. It works partly by preventing the egg and sperm meeting, and by preventing an egg settling in the womb. This method is not advisable for a woman who has never been pregnant. Drawbacks include the danger of the coil coming out of place and the increased likelihood of the user suffering from some serious infections of the pelvis.

Between two and five per cent of women who use a coil become pregnant.

Condoms

Apart from sterilisation and the withdrawal method, the only other means by which a man can take responsibility for contraception is by using condoms. These rubber tubes are shaped to fit the man's erect penis and should prevent sperm entering his partner. This is fine in theory but if there is a small hole in the tip of the condom or if it has not been properly fitted over the penis, sperm may escape. Among women who regularly have sex using condoms approximately one in six will become pregnant.

Cap

Spermicide Cream

Caps and sponges

The cap, or diaphragm, is a soft rubber device which is put into the vagina before intercourse. It covers the cervix and forms a barrier which prevents sperm from meeting the egg. A cap must be used with a spermicide

Condom

and left in place for six hours after intercourse. As well as preventing pregnancy in 98 per cent of women using this method, the cap reduces the risk of cancer of the cervix.

A less reliable vaginal method of contraception is the sponge. Tests show that for every 100 women who use the sponge very carefully

Sponge

and consistently, nine will become pregnant every year. With less careful and consistent use, the rate of pregnancy increases to between nine and 25 women in every 100.

The sponge is made of soft foam, contains a spermicide and is circular in shape. It is inserted into the vagina before intercourse to cover the cervix and left in place for six hours after. It is important you do not leave the sponge in your vagina for longer than 30 hours.

One old-fashioned method of contraception was the douche, where cleansing fluid and spermicide would be squirted into the vagina. Doctors recommend this type of contraception is avoided as it leaves the vagina susceptible to bacterial infection.

CORONARY HEART DISEASE

Coronary heart disease is caused by the narrowing or blockage of the arteries that carry blood to the heart muscle.

The heart is a muscle and, to function like any other muscle, requires a regular blood supply to provide it with food and oxygen. The arteries that supply the heart are known as the coronary vessels. In a baby these arteries are smooth and supple, but a lifetime of the wrong foods can leave them looking like the inside of an old kettle.

Heart failure

Coronary artery disease is the narrowing or furring up by cholesterol of the arteries that supply blood to the heart muscle. This furring up gradually slows down the blood flow to the heart, starving the heart of the proper oxygen supply it needs to work normally and causing the cramping chest pain of angina. Coronary artery disease that is severe enough to affect the working of the heart results in coronary heart disease, which may show itself as angina or as an irregular heart beat. Once the heart begins to be starved of oxygen, the electrical mechanism that controls its pumping rate also stops functioning properly.

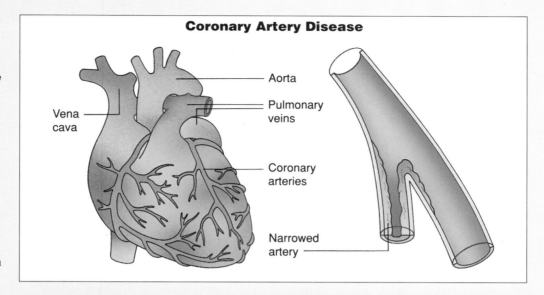

Coronary Artery Disease

Aorta
Pulmonary veins
Vena cava
Coronary arteries
Narrowed artery

Severe coronary heart disease may cause heart failure, a condition in which the heart contracts so inefficiently that it fails altogether to act as a pump. Heart failure results in a state of extreme tiredness, which is accompanied by swelling of various parts of the body, particularly the ankles. This is caused when the blood slows down so much that it begins to collect in the veins, Fluid is forced to seep out into the surrounding tissues, producing the swelling. Heart failure may also cause shortness of breath and chest pain, when excess fluid leaks out on to the lungs.

Treatment

Treatment of coronary artery or heart disease is usually carried out with drugs. This is principally aimed at controlling the symptoms rather than reversing the

Coronary Thrombosis

A coronary thrombosis is a clot in one of the coronary vessels, and is the final stage of coronary heart disease. It is the main cause of a heart attack or 'coronary'.

Blood can find its way around the cholesterol deposits on the narrow, furred-up walls of the arteries, but the uneven flow makes it more likely to clot. When it does so, the oxygen supply to an area of the heart is cut off or so badly reduced that a heart attack occurs. The effect of acute oxygen starvation depends on the area affected. With luck, the area damaged will be replaced by scar tissue without any appreciable loss of efficiency. If a vital area is affected it may prove fatal.

Coronary thrombosis is normally treated with drugs, aimed at dissolving the clot and allowing blood to return to the damaged area. If this is done within the first few hours any acute damage can be reversed. Otherwise bypass surgery may be necessary to help the blood flow around the blocked artery section.

process, so that drugs can improve the blood flow through the arteries in order to relieve angina and even reduce the heart's workload during exercise. If the heart's pumping action is weak, it may also sometimes be improved with drugs. The actual furring up can be tackled in two ways. Firstly, a balloon on the end of a tube can be passed along the artery and inflated to press the cholesterol into the wall and out of harm's way. Not all cases are suitable for this treatment and some sufferers may have surgery

to replace the damaged arteries with normal vessels taken from the leg.

Prevention of Heart Disease

Coronary disease is sometimes hereditary, and therefore rather difficult to guard against, but otherwise can be largely minimised by:

- Taking regular exercise
- Learning how to relax
- Not smoking
- Cutting down on alcohol
- Eating fewer fatty foods
- Keeping your blood pressure under control
- Staying within a few pounds of your ideal weight

Bypass Surgery

Surgery for coronary arteries may consist of a bypass operation where a vein is removed from the body - often the leg - and grafted on to the damaged artery below the narrowing. The other end of the vein is then connected to the aorta.

➤➤ SEE ALSO — Angina

CORTICOSTEROID DRUGS

Corticosteroid drugs are a group of drugs that are used in the treatment of allergies and inflammations.

Corticosteroids, more commonly known as 'steroids', resemble the naturally occurring hormone cortisol, which is produced in the adrenal gland. These steroid drugs are quite different from the infamous anabolic steroid drugs, used by athletes and body builders to improve speed and strength, which mimic the male hormone testosterone.

Cortisol has several effects, and synthetic steroids are designed to emphasise one or more of these properties, usually their anti-inflammatory action. An anti-inflammatory drug is one that acts on the body's immune system to weaken its natural defences. This has obvious disadvantages, but does mean that in certain conditions, such as allergic reactions, the body's over-reaction can be modified. When they were first synthesised in the 1950s the corticosteroid drugs were looked upon as every bit as miraculous as antibiotics had been 10 years before. But side effects have limited their use to several main areas.

Uses

Corticosteroids given in the form of a cream or by inhaler produce very little in the way of adverse effects, since only small amounts are absorbed into the blood.

Creams containing steroids have a very powerful effect on the skin. For example, they can remove the itching and redness of eczema in a day or two. However, apart from the very mild hydrocortisone creams, they can't be bought across the counter. This is because the wrong cream used on the wrong sort of skin can prove disastrous. Ringworm, for example, which looks like eczema, would be made much worse by their use.

Inhalers containing steroids are very effective in controlling asthma. One minute's treatment twice a day can completely abolish the lung inflammation which is often found to be the main asthmatic problem.

Serious side effects such as diabetes, weight gain and brittle bones mean that steroid tablets are only used for serious conditions such as rheumatoid arthritis where the benefits positively outweigh the risks.

Corticosteroid drugs are also prescribed as hormone replacement therapy to patients with an inadequate level of natural corticosteroids as a result, for example, of Addison's disease, or following the surgical removal of the adrenal gland, or after the destruction of the pituitary gland. They are sometimes used in the treatment of intestinal disorders, such as Crohn's disease.

COSMETIC DENTISTRY

Cosmetic dentistry is used to improve the appearance and strength of damaged or badly positioned teeth.

Many children and adults benefit from the techniques of cosmetic dentistry in the form of a brace or bridge, and often through techniques such as crowning or bonding.

Crowning is used to improve the appearance of damaged or discoloured teeth, and can also help guard against further deterioration in decay. A crown is an artificial replacement for the crown of a tooth. Porcelain crowns are normally used on front teeth, due to a colour similarity, whereas metal or gold ones are used at the back where greater strength is needed.

Bridges

A bridge normally consists of one or more false teeth, attached to crowned normal teeth on either side of a gap left by a missing tooth or teeth. A bridge helps the patient bite properly and, often, speak more clearly. It can also stop the problem of teeth shifting or drifting.

Bonding

The recently developed process of bonding is quite similar to crowning, but involves the use of mainly plastic resins and veneers. It is generally used to treat malformed teeth, to close gaps, and to cover up discolourations or stains.

Building A Bridge

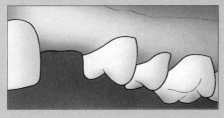

1 To enable better chewing and biting, the gap between two good teeth will be filled by a bridge, consisting of two false teeth and three crowns.

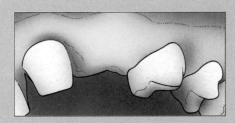

2 The three natural teeth beside the gap, which are still in a healthy condition, are reshaped so that the crowns can be fitted onto them.

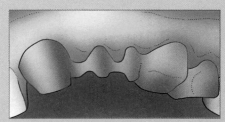

3 A mould is made of the gap and the newly shaped teeth. A metal base for the bridge is then produced from this mould, enabling alterations to be made before the final fitting.

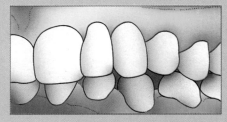

4 The finished version of the bridge is slotted in place. There is no longer a gap, since the two false teeth and porcelain crowns are firmly attached to the metal base.

▶▶ SEE ALSO — Addison's Disease, Asthma

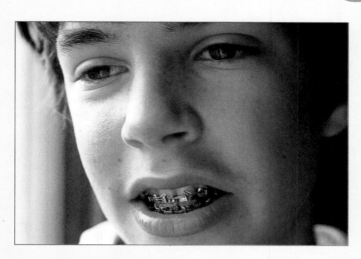

Braces move the teeth very gradually, to position them more correctly. They may need regular readjustment.

Braces

Teeth can be hard to keep clean and develop decay if they are not well aligned and fail to bite together properly. Braces may be fitted in adults, but they are more normally fitted during childhood, while the teeth and jaws are still developing and adapt better to change.

COT DEATH

Cot death is the sudden and unexpected death of an infant, usually when she's asleep in her cot at night.

Cot death, also known as sudden infant death syndrome, normally occurs in apparently healthy babies, who seem perfectly well when they are put to bed, but who are later found dead. In developed countries it is now the most common cause of death between the ages of one month and one year, although the causes are still not properly understood.

Possible causes

It is generally thought that there is no single cause of cot death, but that problems in a baby's breathing or heart rate are the important factors. Blockage of the mouth or nose is always potentially dangerous. But some babies do seem to have throats that close up more easily than others, and something simple like an infection or a cold with a stuffy nose can also cause breathing problems.

Other unproven theories abound for the cause of cot death. These include the possibility that some houses have fungal growths in their furnishings that give off arsenic gases, which could affect sleeping children. And overheating, caused by excessive amounts of bedding or clothing, might also cause problems.

Prevention

• Put your baby to sleep on its back, and never use a pillow.
• Don't overheat the baby's bedroom - an even temperature of 65°F (19°C) is ideal for night and daytime.
• Choose a firm mattress.

COUGHS

A cough is a normal, reflex reaction to irritation and congestion in the throat and lungs.

The purpose of a cough is to move and, if possible, expel the irritant. In babies under six months coughing is an unusual symptom and can be a sign of a serious lung infection, but in older children and adults it is quite normal. According to a recent survey, the average adult has four or five coughs and colds per year, so it is hardly surprising that a cough is one of the most common reasons for visiting the doctor. But most of these visits could be avoided by a better understanding of what makes us cough.

Causes

Most common coughs are due to minor infections of the nose and throat, usually caused by a virus, as in the common cold or influenza. Viruses have the ability to lower our immunity levels, and lowered immunity makes the patient more likely to get bacterial pneumonia.

A viral infection can also cause inflammation of the respiratory tract, which in children might lead to breathing difficulty or croup. Croup is normally characterised by noisy breathing, hoarseness and a barking cough. Whooping cough is now much less common than it used to be, but it may still cause a severe, prolonged cough in the unimmunised child.

Coughs may sometimes be due simply to habit or nervousness, as in the case of the perpetual throat clearer, but are more commonly due to irritation of the airways by dust, smoke or gases. Allergic coughs usually occur at night. As well as asthma, an allergic reaction may cause a runny nose. When a child is asleep the mucus runs down the back of the throat and sets up a cough reflex that often wakes the child and half the family. Coughs are said to be productive when they bring up mucus or sputum (phlegm), and are unproductive or dry when they do not. Any cough that suddenly becomes productive may indicate a worsening of the condition.

Symptoms

A cough that lasts only a short time will not normally be serious at all, but just a feature of an acute infection such as a cold. Many children seem to get cold after cold just after they start school. This is normal and just reflects the fact that they are meeting and coming into contact with many other children. A serious illness, such as heart failure, is often suggested by an abnormally persistent cough, accompanied by chest pain, breathlessness, or a very pale or bluey complexion.

Treatment

Treatment at home will obviously depend on the

Smoker's Cough

Smoking comes second only to viral infections as a regular, common cause for coughing.

The smoker's cough is so common that many sufferers think it is normal to be breathless after climbing two flights of stairs. Smokers may cough up phlegm without recognising this coughing as a sign of a potentially serious condition.

Smoking and lung cancer are often associated, though lung cancer is very rarely the cause of a cough. Weight loss and coughing up blood may be a sign of lung cancer, and a heavy smoker with either of these symptoms needs a chest X-ray to exclude the possibility of disease. To receive proper treatment for lung cancer, an early diagnosis is necessary.

➤➤ SEE ALSO — Cancer, Croup

MEDICAL FACT FILE

cause of the cough, but one or two simple measures may help. Smoking will certainly make things worse. This is especially true of childhood asthma, when even a parent smoking in the same room will worsen a child's wheezing. A moist atmosphere is usually more soothing than a dry one. The easiest way to add moisture to the atmosphere is to put wet towels on the radiator, or to leave a clothesdryer full of wet clothing in the room.

A cough caused by a runny nose, known as 'post-nasal' drip, is treated normally with an anti-inflammatory spray. A dry cough can often be relieved by sucking throat lozenges and warm, soothing drinks like honey and lemon can often be very effective for immediate relief. Cough mixtures such as 'Simple Linctus BPC' will help, and can be especially useful at bedtime to permit sleep. If the cough is part of a 'flu-like illness, aspirin or paracetamol should be given every four hours. Codeine-based pain killers or linctuses may help a dry cough, but there is no real evidence that they work and so are worth avoiding. In choosing any over-the-counter cough remedy it is worth finding out whether it is intended for a dry or a 'productive' cough. The wrong sort of medicine may even delay recovery, or actually interfere with proper diagnosis of a potentially serious disorder.

Consultation

The doctor should be consulted if the patient is obviously unwell, especially if she complains of chest pain or breathing difficulty.

Coughing up phlegm, unless it is blood-stained, is not usually a sign of serious illness. If the patient feels well, then wait and see what happens over the next day or so. A cough that lasts for over a week or is severe probably deserves medical attention. Babies and small children are prone to respiratory infections, but unless the baby seems unwell or is breathing faster than normal it is usually advisable to wait until the morning to see the doctor.

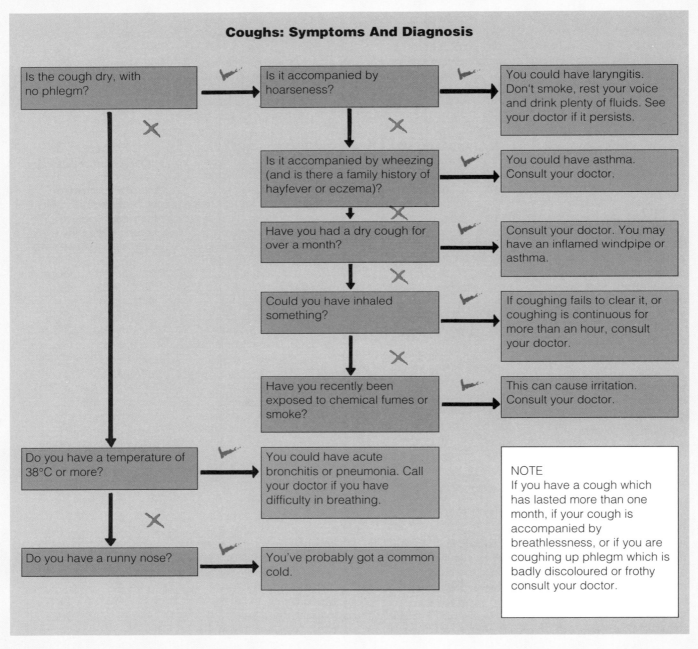

Coughs: Symptoms And Diagnosis

Is the cough dry, with no phlegm? → Is it accompanied by hoarseness? → You could have laryngitis. Don't smoke, rest your voice and drink plenty of fluids. See your doctor if it persists.

Is it accompanied by wheezing (and is there a family history of hayfever or eczema)? → You could have asthma. Consult your doctor.

Have you had a dry cough for over a month? → Consult your doctor. You may have an inflamed windpipe or asthma.

Could you have inhaled something? → If coughing fails to clear it, or coughing is continuous for more than an hour, consult your doctor.

Have you recently been exposed to chemical fumes or smoke? → This can cause irritation. Consult your doctor.

Do you have a temperature of 38°C or more? → You could have acute bronchitis or pneumonia. Call your doctor if you have difficulty in breathing.

Do you have a runny nose? → You've probably got a common cold.

NOTE
If you have a cough which has lasted more than one month, if your cough is accompanied by breathlessness, or if you are coughing up phlegm which is badly discoloured or frothy consult your doctor.

CRAMP

Cramp is a sharp pain felt in a muscle, due to prolonged muscular contraction.

Cramps are generally quite a common occurrence, often as a result of unaccustomed or excessive exercise and usually last only a few moments. Prolonged muscular contraction causes lactic acid and other chemicals to build up in the muscle fibres, producing the characteristic cramping pain.

Repetitive physical movements, such as writing, or remaining in an awkward position for a long period, can also result in cramp. Cramps at night are a common problem, especially for old people. There is no known cause for this, but it often seems to occur in people who have circulation problems in their legs.

Massaging and stretching the cramped muscles can provide relief, but the only known medical treatment comes in the form of calcium or quinine-based drugs. These help the muscle recover from the cramp and can help prevent painful recurrences.

CROHN'S DISEASE

Crohn's disease is an inflammatory disease of the bowel, which can cause pain, fever, diarrhoea, and even loss of weight.

The disease may affect any part of the bowel from the mouth to the anus, but most commonly affects the lower end of the small intestine where it joins the large intestine. The intestinal wall becomes thick and inflamed, producing ulcers and cracks, and may even cause abnormal

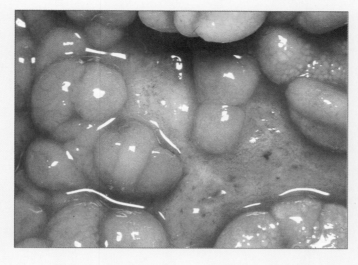

Above: The inflamed wall of the small intestine is often a characteristic symptom of Crohn's disease.

passageways to form between adjacent parts of the intestine. The intestinal space becomes so narrow that the passage of food may become obstructed.

Crohn's disease usually starts in the teens or early twenties. Its cause is still unknown. An abnormal allergic reaction or an exaggerated reaction to an infection like a virus may play a role in the onset of the disease. At one time it was thought that swallowing toothpaste caused the condition, a theory since disproved. When examined under a microscope Crohn's disease resembles an infection, but no actual germ has ever been found.

Symptoms

Crohn's disease can produce symptoms similar to those of appendicitis, but more commonly produces pain in the lower abdomen, accompanied by diarrhoea. In extreme cases the diarrhoea may contain blood and pus. The body's ability to absorb food may also be affected, resulting in a loss of weight and general tiredness.

Diagnosis

Fortunately Crohn's disease is rare, but if a doctor suspects it she can organise one or two simple tests to confirm the condition. A barium meal introduces dye into the intestine, which will help show up ulcers on an x-ray. If this fails a colonoscopy may be necessary. A colonoscope is a long fibre-optic telescope that can be passed the length of the large bowel. Occasionally a patient with Crohn's disease will have to have an exploratory operation to help diagnose the condition.

Treatment

A few cases of Crohn's disease get better spontaneously. The rest need long term treatment with corticosteroid and other anti-inflammatory drugs. A high protein, low roughage diet may be beneficial. Surgery is only required if the disease causes a bowel obstruction.

CROUP

Croup is a barking cough, caused by narrowing and inflammation of the upper airways.

Croup is most common in infants and children up to the age of four. The cough is normally violent and very alarming. It is sometimes accompanied by hoarseness, wheezing and 'stridor', a grunting noise during breathing. The sufferer may even turn blue due to lack of oxygen.

Croup is normally caused by a viral or bacterial infection which affects the voice box or the windpipe. Infectious croup is most likely to occur in winter. Croup may also be caused by an allergy, by a spasm as a result of lack of calcium in the blood, or simply by the inhalation of a 'foreign body' like a peanut.

In older children and adults the airways are wider and stronger, so that inflammation does not have such a strong effect.

Treatment

In most cases croup is mild and passes quickly. The best thing is for the parent to remain calm and comfort the child, who will be able to breathe more easily once the initial shock of the cough has worn off. After that the best treatment is to humidify the air, by putting on the kettle, placing wet towels on radiators, or by taking the child into the bathroom and turning on the taps. If a child is in obvious difficulties with her breathing, or is turning blue, a doctor should be consulted immediately.

CRYOSURGERY

Cryosurgery is a form of surgery which involves temperatures of below freezing, used to destroy tissues with minimal scarring.

Cryosurgery is a relatively new form of surgery, only becoming widely used within the last decade. In certain cases cryosurgery has proved to be more effective than traditional methods. Due to the minimal amount of scarring it produces, cryosurgery has been used extensively in operations on

▶▶ SEE ALSO — Appendicitis, Bowel

MEDICAL FACT FILE

malignant (cancerous) tumours of the cervix, liver and intestines. Heavy scarring in these areas can be dangerous and possibly lead to blockages.

Cryosurgery has also been used to deal with smaller problems like warts, birthmarks and some sorts of skin cancer. And it has even been used to help in the intricate treatment of eye problems like cataracts and detached retinas.

Methods

Cryosurgery is normally carried out at temperatures as low as that of liquid nitrogen (–160°C). A growth can be destroyed quite simply, by applying to it a metal probe called a cryoprobe, cooled to the temperature of liquid nitrogen, or by spraying it with liquid nitrogen.

Exterior body operations, on the skin for example, can be performed quite quickly with cryosurgery and are sometimes even painless, since the low temperatures involved paralyse the nerves in the skin for a short time.

CUSHING'S SYNDROME

Cushing's syndrome is a hormonal disorder which results from an unusually high level of corticosteroid hormones in the blood.

The corticosteroid hormones are produced by the adrenal glands, and Cushing's syndrome can be caused by overactivity of the adrenal glands or the pituitary gland. Prolonged use of corticosteroid drugs can also cause the condition. Cushing's syndrome is most common in people who are middle-aged, but in fact can occur at any age.

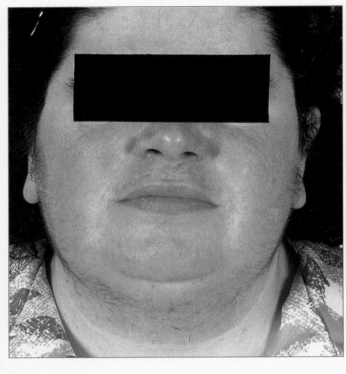

Above: Cushing's syndrome can cause reddening of the face and neck, and the growth of unnatural facial hair.

Physical signs

Cushing's syndrome changes people's physical appearance. The face becomes round and red, the upper body overweight and hump-backed, and the limbs thin and wasted. The condition generally weakens the body, lowering its resistance to infection. The skin becomes thin, bruises easily and develops acne. Purple stretch marks may appear on the breasts, thighs and abdomen. And women may even become more hairy as a result of the syndrome. Problems such as insomnia and high blood pressure often occur, and in children growth can be suppressed.

When Cushing's syndrome results from the use of corticosteroid drugs, the problem can usually be eradicated by a steady reduction in the drug dosage. If it results from a tumour of the adrenal gland or pituitary gland, surgery is necessary to reduce or to even remove the tumour.

CUTS AND GRAZES

Cuts and grazes are a part of everyday life and are normally quite easy to treat.

Cuts are normally inflicted in one of three ways: by incision, stabbing or laceration. An incision is a straight cut, caused when a sharp edge is drawn across the skin. A stabbing injury occurs when a sharp edge punctures the skin in a downwards direction. A laceration is a torn, irregular cut caused by the famous 'blunt object' so beloved by crime writers.

A graze is a number of scratches or superficial cuts, all in the same place and all in the same direction. A graze is caused by contact with a number of sharp points, such as when someone falls over on gravel. The depth of the graze depends on the number and the size of the points.

Tetanus

Tetanus is a serious and sometimes fatal disease of the central nervous system, caused by bacterial infection of a wound.

The most common symptom of tetanus is 'lockjaw', which makes it difficult for the sufferer to open the mouth. Muscle stiffening and spasms can also result from the condition, which can normally be relieved and then reversed by prompt diagnosis and treatment with antitoxin drugs.

Any cut or graze, however small, may cause tetanus. Every year about 10 people die in the UK from the disease, and worldwide about half a million cases of tetanus occur. So, if you have not had a tetanus immunisation in the past 10 years, it is worth seeing your doctor now!

Hospital Treatment

In the case of severe bleeding that refuses to stop, or a wound that is obviously deep, it is likely that hospital treatment will be necessary.

Stitching certainly requires an immediate visit to the accident department. A deep wound caused by something dirty, such as a nail or an animal's tooth, may also require hospital care. Such accidents carry a high possibility of infection, and thus frequently need antibiotics and a tetanus injection to be on the safe side.

➤➤ SEE ALSO — Adrenal Glands, Corticosteroid Drugs

Treatment Of Cuts And Grazes

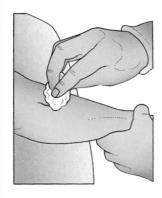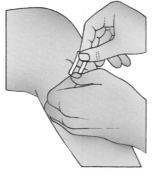

1 Press a clean pad over wound to stop bleeding. Once the bleeding has stopped, apply antiseptic to a cleaning swab (and not directly to the wound) and clean around the cut, wiping from the edges outwards

2 Leave the wound uncovered and open to the air, unless it is dangerously large. Gaping edges of up to 1cm long can be held together with strips of surgical tape, which will help the healing process

Treatment
The treatment of cuts and grazes is essentially the same. Differences in treatment normally depend on the severity of the injury, rather than its cause. In most cases the only treatment needed for slight cuts and grazes is to rinse the wound thoroughly in clean water and then to leave it open to the air. Unless the wound is likely to get dirty and possibly infected there is no real reason or need for it to be covered up.

Grazes
Grazes need to be cleaned with a mild antiseptic solution, and all traces of dirt and grit should be removed. If it is not possible to remove all the dirt, and especially if the wound is to the face, the patient may need to be taken to the hospital for treatment. A local or even a general anaesthetic may be required. Grazes heal quickest if left open to the fresh air, but if a dressing is required a special Vaseline impregnated gauze will help healing and won't be too painful to remove.

Cuts
Deep cuts, especially if arteries are severed, may bleed a great deal and be very alarming, but first aid is simple and effective. First of all, the victim needs to be calmed and reassured, so it's probably best for her to sit or lie down. The wound then needs looking at, and if there are any obvious pieces of glass in it they should be removed, if at all possible. The cut should then be raised above the level of the heart. And using a clean cloth, such as a handkerchief, the edges of the wound should be kept pressed firmly together for at least ten minutes.

If blood seeps through the cloth don't take it off to have a look, but instead put another one on top, and another if necessary. Cuts severe enough to continue bleeding for some time will almost certainly require stitching. And if this is the case the patient should be taken to the hospital after the bleeding has been sufficiently controlled.

CYSTS

A cyst is an abnormal lump or swelling, containing liquid or semi-solid matter.

Cysts are normally harmless, if unsightly, and can be removed by a minor surgical operation. Cysts are formed in various ways, for example when the outlets of fluid-forming glands become blocked. Therefore, a sebaceous cyst may form in

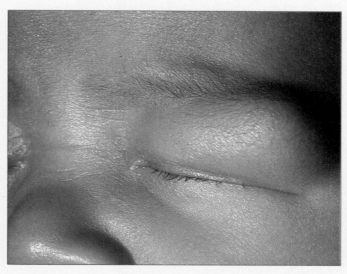

Above: A dermoid cyst on a child's eyelid. Cysts like this are normally harmless, but treatment is still by surgical removal.

a sebaceous gland in the skin. Other cysts may form around parasites in disease.

Ovarian cyst
Ovarian cysts rarely cause any obvious symptoms, and often are only discovered when they become large enough to be detected in a routine vaginal examination. They can, however, sometimes cause abdominal pain, menstrual irregularities and pain during intercourse. Some ovarian cysts are relatively simple and will go away on their own, but other more complicated ones need fully diagnosing and removing by surgery. An undetected cyst may grow so large as to make a woman appear pregnant, and a burst cyst can cause infection and peritonitis.

Dermoid cyst
Dermoid cysts develop in between the layers of tissue in the growing embryo and are therefore usually congenital (present from birth). They have a skin structure similar to that of normal skin, but may sometimes contain a variety of different tissues like hair, sweat glands, nerves and teeth! Dermoid cysts most commmonly occur on the head or neck, and cause a small but painless swelling. Dermoid cysts are generally not malignant (cancerous), but surgical removal is still recommended in most cases to remove the possibility of infection or complications.

CYSTIC FIBROSIS

Cystic fibrosis is a hereditary disease that causes lung infections and problems in the digestive system.

In Britain an average of one baby a day is born with cystic fibrosis, a serious and potentially fatal disorder. Yet until 40 years ago it was not even recognised as a separate condition. It is a 'recessive' genetic condition, which means that

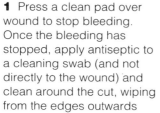 SEE ALSO — Clotting, Ovaries

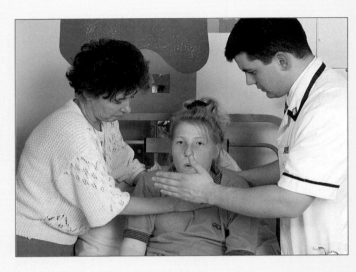

Aove: A physiotherapist teaches essential massage techniques to the mother of a young cystic fibrosis patient.

both parents have to carry the faulty gene for it possibly to be passed on. On average one person in 20 carries the gene, so the chances of any couple both carrying the faulty gene is one in 400. And even if both parents do carry the faulty gene, only one in four children will actually be affected as a result.

Gene Discovery

The discovery, in 1989, of the gene responsible for cystic fibrosis has offered real hope to sufferers and their families.

The faulty gene can now be used to study the disease in the laboratory and should allow the development of an effective drug treatment. It might even become possible to replace the faulty gene, in the living cell, with an artificially produced one.

The introduction of antenatal diagnosis by foetal cell analysis has been the most immediate benefit of this recent gene discovery. Diagnosis like this can be used to determine whether a baby will be born with cystic fibrosis or not, a great help to parents known to be carriers of the recessive gene that causes the debilitating condition.

Causes

The gene defect which is characteristic of cystic fibrosis causes an abnormality in the system that governs how salt and water move in and out of the body's cells. It causes problems with the glands that secrete mucus, sweat and digestive juices.

Mucus is normally produced to act as a lubricant, but in cystic fibrosis the mucus becomes very thick, and is unable to flow freely in the nose, throat, airways and intestines. This results in blockages, with the worst problems occurring in the pancreas and the lungs.

Pancreas

The pancreas normally produces digestive enzymes which are released into the small intestine and break down food. Cystic fibrosis hampers this process, the enzymes remaining in the pancreas, which damages the pancreas itself and hampers digestion. Undigested food then reaches the large bowel, where it is broken down by bacterial action, producing

the diarrhoea that is one of the most common symptoms of cystic fibrosis.

Lungs

The thickening of mucus also results in blockages of the small airways, which can cause bronchitis, repeated bouts of pneumonia, constant coughing and breathlessness. The lungs then become damaged, which can prove to be fatal.

A few years ago anyone who reached the age of 20 with cystic fibrosis was regarded as something of medical marvel. But the average life expectancy nowadays is at least 30, and over two-thirds of cystic fibrosis sufferers now survive to adult life, although few of them are in perfect health.

Treatment

Cystic fibrosis is normally treated with antibiotic drugs and physiotherapy. Lung damage can be minimised if the treatment is put into action as soon as possible after diagnosis. However, it may be necessary for the patient to take as many as 60 tablets a day, including capsules and vitamin supplements designed to replace the lost digestive enzymes and help regain weight. The physiotherapy is used principally to loosen and remove the thick mucus that builds up in the lungs.

Symptoms of Cystic Fibrosis
• Hacking cough, sometimes with vomiting.
• Wheezing and shortness of breath.
• Loss of appetite and consequent weight loss.
• Loose, greasy stools with an unpleasant odour.
• Abdominal pain.
• Rectal prolapse.

CYSTITIS

Cystitis is an inflammation of the bladder, usually due to bacterial infection.

Cystitis is often caused by the incomplete emptying of the bladder when urinating, since urine left stagnating in the bladder or urethra (the tube from the bladder to the outside) easily becomes infected. And anything that obstructs normal urination, such as a stone in the bladder, can also make the condition more likely to occur.

Common condition

Cystitis is very common in women, mainly because their urethra is short and therefore bacteria can more easily reach the bladder. Bacteria can also come from the intestine via the anus, or from the vagina.

In men cystitis is rare, because the urethra is longer, and infection is more likely to be due to an obstruction. In children cystitis is often due to an abnormality in the tubes carrying urine from the kidneys to the bladder.

Symptoms

Cystitis often occurs suddenly and produces an urge to urinate frequently. Urinating is normally accompanied by a sharp, stinging pain. And if it is severe, cystitis may even lead to fever, blood in the urine and back ache.

Treatment

People with cystitis symptoms should drink large quantities of fluid, and the bladder ought to be emptied regularly and completely. If bacteria are confirmed as the source of infection, antibiotic drugs are normally prescribed to destroy them. The drugs will usually settle the infection within 24 hours.

SEE ALSO — Bladder

D AND C

This is a minor operation in which most of the lining of the uterus is scraped away and removed.

D and C is an abbreviation for dilation and curettage, and is commonly used to diagnose problems of the uterus, such as heavy menstrual bleeding,

The patient undergoing D and C will usually remain in hospital overnight, and in some cases she may even be able to leave hospital the same day. The pain resulting from the operation will not normally be too severe and will usually be similar to a mild period pain. D and C causes few side effects. The uterus lining soon grows again during menstruation.

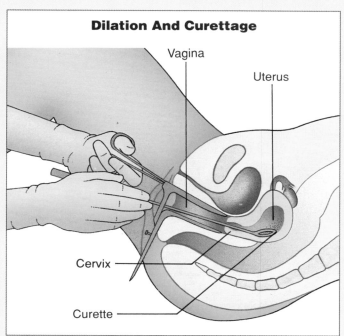

Dilation And Curettage

Vagina

Uterus

Cervix

Curette

bleeding between periods, or bleeding from the vagina after the menopause. D and C is also used for abortion in early pregnancy, in countries where it is legal. After a miscarriage it may be carried out to free the uterus of any remaining fragments of tissue. And a limited D and C can be useful in an investigation of infertility.

Methods

D and C is usually carried out under general anaesthetic and lasts about 30 minutes. The vagina and the cervix are dilated (stretched out) so that a curette (a spoon-shaped instrument) can reach into the uterus to scrape away the necessary tissue. This tissue will then be examined under a microscope.

D and C is sometimes beneficial in itself, such as when heavy periods have been caused by thickening of the uterus lining.

DANDRUFF

Dandruff is a common condition in which small flakes of dead skin are shed from the scalp.

Dandruff is harmless, but irritating, and occurs when the fine cells from the outer layer of the skin are shed at a faster rate than normal. This often produces unsightly white or yellow flakes which stick to the hair whenever it is brushed or combed, and which may also cling rather undecorously to the collar and shoulders of clothes.

The condition is usually caused by a fungal infection or by dermatitis. Dermatitis is also often accompanied by inflammation and itching on the face, chest and back, as well as on the scalp.

Treatment

The hair should be shampooed frequently, at least two or three times a week, with an antidandruff product. This should be a mildly medicated detergent shampoo, and preferably not soap based, as soap seems to exacerbate the condition. Regular treatment will normally cause dandruff to disappear, but only constant control will stop it recurring.

Dandruff caused by dermatitis may require a cream or lotion containing a corticosteroid drug. And severe dandruff may require an antifungal shampoo.

DEAFNESS

Deafness is a partial or complete loss of hearing in the ear.

It is a common condition that affects over one per cent of the population in the UK. Total deafness is rare and usually congenital (present from birth). Partial deafness is normally caused by an ear disease or injury. Deafness can also result from the degeneration of the hearing mechanism with age.

Hearing

In order to understand deafness it is necessary to appreciate how the normal person actually hears sound. First of all, sound waves travel through the air and reach the outer ear. The minute changes in pressure then cause the eardrum to vibrate, and in turn these vibrations are transmitted across the middle ear by three interconnecting bones, the *malleus, incus* and *stapes* (more commonly known in Engish as the hammer, anvil and stirrup). From the middle ear the sound passes to the inner ear, where an arrangement of minute hairs picks it up. Nerve impulses then pass to the brain, where they are interpreted as sound.

Conductive deafness

Deafness which results from the faulty transmission of sound from the outer to the inner ear is called conductive deafness. This is usually caused by an obstruction to the passage of the sound vibrations. In adults, conductive deafness

Above: Sign language and lip-reading can prove to be essential skills for deaf children and adults.

➤➤ SEE ALSO — Uterus, Dermatitis

MEDICAL FACT FILE

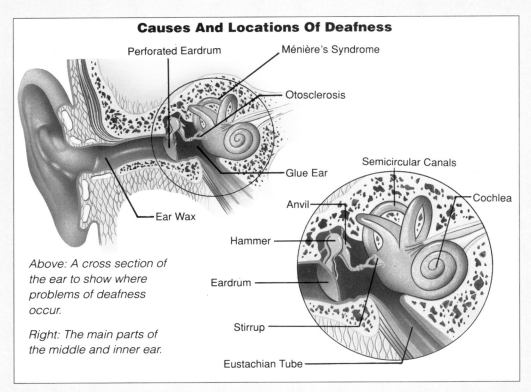

Causes And Locations Of Deafness

Perforated Eardrum

Ménière's Syndrome

Otosclerosis

Glue Ear

Ear Wax

Semicircular Canals

Cochlea

Anvil

Hammer

Eardrum

Stirrup

Eustachian Tube

Above: A cross section of the ear to show where problems of deafness occur.

Right: The main parts of the middle and inner ear.

happens most commonly when ear wax accumulates and blocks the outer ear canal, stopping sound from ever reaching the eardrum. Ear wax is secreted, as a liquid, by the outer ear. In normal circumstances it solidifies on contact with the outside air to form a waterproof layer which protects the eardrum, rather than blocking it.

Conductive deafness is sometimes caused by a lack of mobility in the stirrup bone, which normally vibrates to transfer sound from the eardrum to the inner ear. This problem is called otosclerosis. Temporary deafness may be caused by a change in pressure on either side of the eardrum. This can occur if the eustachian tube, which

leads from the middle ear to the throat, becomes blocked, or even as a result of a sudden change in air pressure, as can happen in aircraft or deep-sea diving. A perforated eardrum, resulting from middle ear infection or injury, can also produce conductive deafness.

Perceptive deafness

Perceptive deafness, also known as sensorineural deafness, is caused by problems in the nervous system, nerve impulses failing to reach the brain from the inner ear. It is often a congenital condition, caused perhaps by injury or damage to the foetus while it is still developing, or due to the mother being infected with German measles (or some other viral disease) during pregnancy. Fortunately, congenital deafness is rare, and only occurs in about one in 1000 babies.

Perceptive deafness can occur in later life, and frequently does so in old people as a result of the natural ageing process. This affects roughly 25 per cent of over-65-year-olds. This form

of deafness can also result from drug overdoses, from damage to the auditory nerve, or from diseases like Meniere's disease.

Exposure to excessive noise levels may also produce perceptive deafness. A UK study in the 1960s showed that more men were deaf than would usually be the case. The conclusion was that the noise of rifles experienced during National Service was largely to blame. Similarly, some people have recently been found to have hearing problems following excessively loud rock concerts or after using personal stereos.

Diagnosis

Babies who are born with perceptive deafness do not react to sounds in the normal way, and usually fail to make the characteristic pre-speech babbling noises, even though they may cry.

Older children and adults who suspect they may have deafness problems will probably have obvious trouble hearing. In this case not only do all noises generally become quieter, but also high-pitched tones and softly pronounced sounds, such as 'f' or 's', become difficult, or even impossible, to hear.

Treatment

Congenital deafness needs special care so that the affected child can learn to cope with everyday life as soon as possible. Sign language and lip-reading can be learnt and can prove very effective in helping deaf people communicate.

Hearing aids are sometimes used to help sufferers of otosclerosis, although this is normally treated by the damaged stirrup being replaced by an artificial substitute. More normally hearing aids are used to treat perceptive deafness, amplifying the

Glue Ear

Middle ear infection and 'glue ear' (the collection of sticky fluid in the middle ear) are the most common cause of conductive deafness in children.

Middle ear infection normally follows a cold and can be very painful. It can also sometimes be caused by water getting into the ear while swimming, or due to something, like a nut or even a cotton bud, being pushed into the external part of the ear.

As the name suggests, 'glue ear' happens when the middle ear gets excessively blocked up, due normally to inflammation and an accumulation of pus. This stops the eardrum and the bones that transfer sound from moving adequately. Unfortunately many young children are quite deaf before anyone actually notices. Slow speech development may provide a clue, but many mothers instinctively know that something is wrong. If you think that your child is affected, it is worth consulting your doctor.

▶▶ SEE ALSO — Ear

sound that reaches the inner ear with an ear-phone. However, an aid can occasionally cause some problems in that it also magnifies background noises, causing distortion. If the patient's deafness is due to damage to the inner ear, the distortion may cause considerable pain. Aids which only amplify certain wavelengths can help alleviate this problem.

Wax blockage can normally be syringed clear, but 'glue ear' usually necessitates a draining operation. Deafness can also cause problems with things like doorbells and 'phones. British Telecom can provide flashing lights and extra-loud bells to try and improve this.

Lipreading

Lipreading, or speechreading as it is increasingly being called, is the reception of spoken messages through the medium of vision. Lipreading involves watching the jaws, tongue, and total facial expression as well as the lips.

Brain Death

Brain death is the term now used to describe a state in which not only the heart and lungs have naturally stopped functioning, but also in which the brain has totally ceased to function.

The development of medical technology in the 1960s led to a reassessment of the way doctors and hospitals approach the concept of death. These technological developments include sophisticated life-support systems. These systems now enable breathing and heartbeat to be maintained artificially in circumstances where before the lungs and heart would have naturally stopped functioning due to structural brain damage.

Brain death is normally evident due to a number of factors: a persistent deep coma, for example, or a total lack of reflex or electric activity in the brain. Ultimately brain death shows itself in a failure to breathe once the life-support system is disconnected. But disconnection only ever takes place after extensive testing, and following consultation with the patient's relatives.

DEATH

Death is the end of life, when the body's organs cease to function.

The classic, traditional symptoms of death are an absence of spontaneous breathing, a loss of heartbeat, and dilated (wide open) pupils which are no longer responsive to light, though only the onset of *rigor mortis* is really a sure sign of death. In normal circumstances a doctor will certify death when the heart and lungs permanently cease to function.

Sudden death

The unexpected death of someone who previously seemed to be in perfectly good health is referred to as sudden death. This category does not include those who are killed in accidents.

A sudden death victim will not normally have complained of illness symptoms. After a postmortem examination many young victims of cardiac arrest are discovered to have had an undiagnosed congenital heart abnormality. In older victims (over 35), the most common causes of death, apart from a heart attack, are an irregular heartbeat or coronary artery disease. By law, sudden death cases must always be reported to the coroner, who will decide if an autopsy is necessary.

DECONGESTANT DRUGS

Decongestants are drugs used to reduce and relieve congestion of the nasal passages.

Irritation or infection of these passages can cause the blood vessels that line the nose to become enlarged. The enlargement of the blood vessels produces swelling and the excess secretion of mucus, all of which causes congestion. Patients who are prone to sinus or middle-ear infection are particularly likely to need decongestant drugs. These are designed to reduce the swelling of the blood vessels, thus reducing the nasal congestion.

Types of drug

Decongestant drugs are contained in various cough and cold remedies, which are generally available over the counter from the chemists. They are often antihistamine preparations and come in tablet or nose-drop form.

Decongestants need to be prescribed and taken with care, since there are various problematic side effects. Prolonged use of decongestants can actually increase the symptoms and even damage the lining of the nose. The drugs should therefore only be taken for as short a time as possible, whatever form they come in.

Taken in tablet form the drugs can produce tremors or palpitations in the patient, and accordingly should not be given to patients who are known to suffer from heart disease. Nasal-drop treatment is usually less of a problem, since the quantities of decongestant absorbed into the blood stream are then much smaller.

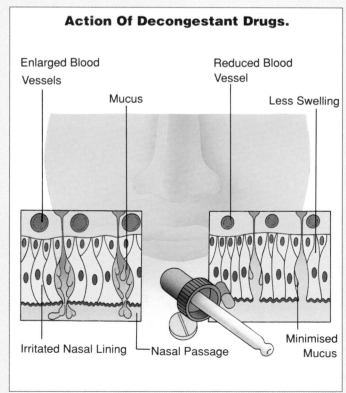

Action Of Decongestant Drugs.

Enlarged Blood Vessels

Reduced Blood Vessel

Mucus

Less Swelling

Irritated Nasal Lining — Nasal Passage

Minimised Mucus

▶▶ SEE ALSO — Brain

DEFORMITY

When a body, or part of a body, is abnormally formed, misshapen or distorted in any way it is said to be deformed.

Sometimes deformities are present from birth (congenital). Most people have heard of the more common congenital deformities, like 'cleft lip and palate' and 'club foot'. 'Club foot' refers to a baby's foot which is twisted out of its natural shape. 'Cleft lip and palate' (a split upper lip and a gap along the roof of the mouth) can occur either together or separately. However, these deformities are generally more rare than those which result from accident, disease or misuse.

Injuries to muscles or bones can frequently result in deformity, as can burns and other accidents. Muscle damage deformity is a quite common problem with people who are bed-ridden or who are forced to spend large amounts of time in a wheelchair, when muscles become stiffened and shortened due to underuse.

Deformity may also be caused by other disorders, like paralysis of the facial nerves, or nutritional deficiency diseases such as rickets, which causes skeletal deformity in children due mainly to a lack of Vitamin D.

Prevention and treatment

Prevention of forms of deformity caused by nutritional deficiencies can be partly countered by eating a well-balanced, vitamin-rich diet. Problems involved with lack of exercise or movement can normally be aided by a programme of regular exercise to keep muscles in a relatively fit condition.

Some deformities may ultimately require (plastic) surgery to try and improve the patient's health, mobility or even appearance. 'Cleft lip and palate', for example, are regularly and succesfully operated on in childhood. On the other hand, surgery on 'club foot' is much more difficult, and therefore needs to be performed before the age of two to stand a good chance of success.

DEGENERATIVE DISORDERS

Degenerative disorders occur when part of the body gradually starts to deteriorate and fails to function properly.

This can be caused by a number of different factors, including infection, disease, inflammation, a defect in circulation, or even problems with the body's natural immune responses. Something as natural as the

loss of memory, confusion, and ultimately an inability to cope with life in general.

Parkinson's disease affects the part of the brain which controls movement and balance, and mainly occurs in the elderly. The disease causes muscles to become weak and stiff, and also produces trembling. Motor neuron diseases affect the part of the central nervous system which controls muscular activity, causing muscle wastage and subsequent weakness.

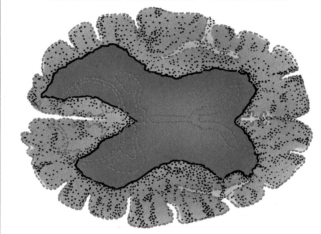

Alzheimer's Disease – Brain Scan

The brain substance (grey area) has shrunk noticeably: the red dotted line shows its normal, healthy position.

wrinkling of skin through age is actually caused by degeneration of tissue; but the changes that occur in degenerative disorders, such as Alzheimer's or Parkinson's disease, normally occur more rapidly

Nervous disorders

Alzheimer's disease and Parkinson's disease, probably the best known of degenerative disorders, are caused by problems in the nervous system.

Alzheimer's disease is the most common cause of dementia, but nobody has up to now provided a full explanation of why it occurs. In Alzheimer's disease the grey matter of the brain gradually shrinks, leading to

Other disorders

Degenerative disorders can affect other parts of the body, apart from the brain. The most familiar disorder is osteoarthritis, which affects the lining of the joints, causing considerable pain and possible deformity. Osteoarthritis particularly occurs in people who are involved in a lot of sport or vigorous exercise that puts strain on the joints.

There are also certain genetic disorders which can cause premature blindness, by causing vital cells to be lost from the retina; and others, called muscular dystrophies, which cause muscular weakness.

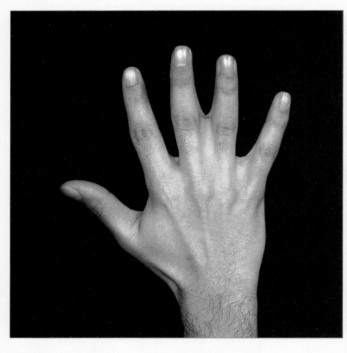

Above: Deformity can affect many parts of the body. Here two fingers are webbed together.

» SEE ALSO — Birth defects, Bowlegs

DEHYDRATION

The body is said to be dehydrated when it becomes dangerously short of water.

The average man is made up of about 60 per cent water, and the average woman about 50 per cent. The figure is even higher in children, but declines in old age. An adequate intake of water is essential for the healthy functioning of the body. There are actually two main causes of dehydration: either the body can take in too little water, or it can lose too much.

Water intake

Normally a poor intake of water is due either to poor water supplies or to difficulties with swallowing. In the UK the commonest difficulty is connected with vomiting. Many people who are being sick think that the best remedy is to drink nothing at all. But in fact it is far better to take regular sips of cold, clear fluids.

Water loss

In a temperate climate, like that of the UK, the adult body normally loses about 1.5 litres of water a day, simply through the natural processes of sweating, breathing and urinating. In a hot climate between two and

Above: Dehydration can be greatly helped and even reversed by special sugar and salt solutions.

five litres of water can be lost daily, which can in fact be doubled if hard physical work is involved.

Diarrhoea is the most common cause of an increased fluid loss from the body, particularly if the diarrhoea is unusually watery, as occurs in cholera. The cholera patient may possibly lose up to 10 or 15

litres of fluid in 12 hours. This sort of fluid loss can prove to be a fatal problem, especially in children. As a result, dehydration persists as one of the main causes of death in the Third World.

Treatment

Dehydration treatment is usually quite simple. The main thing is to try and keep up a regular and adequate fluid intake. Under normal circumstances this should be at least enough to produce urine that is consistently pale. In hotter climates, especially in direct sun, it needs to be very much more, possibly as much as half a litre of water every hour.

Diarrhoea and vomiting should not normally cause dehydration problems in adults. However, if problems do occur, rehydration can be aided and essential minerals replaced by a special sugar and salt solution, like Dioralyte, which can be bought at the chemist's.

Diabetic Dehydration

There are two different forms of diabetes – *diabetes mellitus* and *diabetes insipidus*. Both of these can cause problems with dehydration.

Diabetes mellitus (or sugar diabetes), caused by a lack of the hormone insulin, produces a very high level of sugar in the blood. The body rids itself of the excess sugar by passing it in the urine.

Diabetes insipidus, which is much rarer, is due to a hormone imbalance that stops the kidneys concentrating the urine. Many of the 'morning after' (hangover) feelings are due to dehydration, when alcohol makes the kidneys pass large amounts of dilute urine. A pint of liquid, preferably with a small amount of salt and sugar in it, may relieve the symptoms.

Treatment Of Children

Children have much smaller water reserves than adults and can run into dehydration difficulties if they suffer from diarrhoea and vomiting.

If a baby has diarrhoea and becomes listless, has a shrunken 'soft spot' on the top of its head, or has a dry tongue or sunken eyes, it is advisable for the doctor to be consulted.

Lost fluid can be replaced by using a nasogastric tube or an intravenous drip. The nasogastric tube passes down the throat and into the stomach, and is useful in children who are unable to drink. An intravenous drip gives the doctor the opportunity to completely bypass the gut, so that any lost fluid can be replaced without difficulty.

DELIRIUM

Delirium is a serious state of mental disorder and confusion, normally caused by physical illness.

The brain is a very sensitive organ. Its normal functioning can quite easily be disrupted and thrown into confusion by any rapid transformations in the body's chemistry or metabolism.

Delirium sufferers experience dramatic changes in their perception of everyday reality. Time and place can become confused for them, and loss of memory can result. Delirium can also produce severe mood swings and an unnatural state of agitation and excitement. The sufferer may

MEDICAL FACT FILE

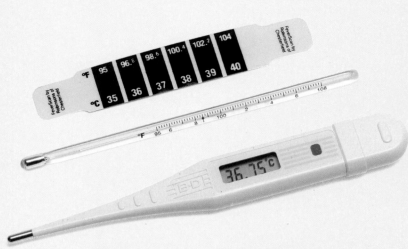

Above: Types of thermometer (heat sensitive strip, mercury and digital) useful for testing the severity of delirium fever.

even hallucinate, and speech and sight are occasionally impaired.

Treatment
Simple procedures, such as close supervision of diet, calm surroundings and attentive nursing, may aid the delirium sufferer. Tranquilliser drugs are often prescribed to reduce the symptoms, but only the removal of the cause will actually stop delirium from recurring.

Delirium Tremens

Delirium tremens is a form of delirium that usually occurs after withdrawal from alcohol or drug addiction.

Delirium tremens is a type of psychosis and produces the confused state that is characteristic of delirium. An attack of delirium tremens, often known as 'the DTs', is normally accompanied by trembling, insomnia and nausea, and sometimes even frightening hallucinations. The classic hallucinations are of vividly coloured insects. Fever and excessive sweating may also result. Treatment for delirium tremens normally consists of plentiful rest, sedative drugs, and rehydration if necessary. Psychiatric help might also be involved to help resolve the psychotic element of delirium tremens.

DELIVERY

Delivery is the ejection of a baby from the uterus during birth.

A baby is normally delivered head first. Uterine contractions first dilate the neck of the womb. These contractions then become more frequent, causing the baby to move down the birth canal to complete delivery. The mother may assist with voluntary pushing.

Operative delivery
A so-called 'operative' delivery may be necessary if certain problems arise. These can include insufficient contractions, or the baby's head being too large for its mother's pelvis, which can result in the necessity of a forceps delivery or vacuum extraction. A vacuum extraction involves the use of a suction cup, which is carefully attached to the baby's head to enable the doctor to guide the baby more easily out of the mother. It is generally safer than using forceps.

The baby lying in an abnormal position in the uterus may require a breech delivery, in which the bottom comes out before the head. And when a vaginal delivery is judged to be of potential danger to either mother or baby, a Caesarean section will be performed. The baby is then delivered through an incision in the abdomen.

DEMENTIA

Dementia is a decline of mental ability, usually irreversible, that results from physical changes in the brain.

Dementia affects about 10 per cent of the UK population over the age of 65, when it is referred to as 'senile' dementia. Middle-age dementia is said to be 'presenile'. Dementia is mainly caused by injury, infection, drug or alcohol addiction, or by brain diseases, like Alzheimer's disease. It can even develop in the late stages of conditions such as syphilis. Dementia has also been found to be a hereditary condition in some cases.

Symptoms
In the early stages, senile dementia sufferers may become restless and begin to lose their short-term memory. Insomnia also results, accompanied by confusion over times, days and dates. Everyday habits and events lose their natural logic in dementia, and unexpected mood changes may well occur. Ultimately the dementia patient may lose any sense of responsibility, both for themselves and others. This normally requires careful, probably full-time, nursing.

DENTAL PROBLEMS

Dental problems are the infection of, and even injury to, teeth and gums.

Such infection and injury will lead to the need for dental examination and treatment, and to decay and the possible loss of individual teeth.

Tooth decay
Tooth decay (also known as dental caries) is today one of mankind's most common diseases, although even the teeth of cavemen were decayed to some extent. In spite of the fact that teeth are the hardest things in the human body, they are also usually the first to begin to wear out.

Tooth decay is caused by a complicated reaction between sugars in the diet and bacteria in plaque. Accordingly, the large amounts of sugar to be found in Western society diets can only make the problem of decay worse. Such decay does seem to run in families, though no one is sure whether this is due to hereditary factors,

Dental Pains

Not all toothache is due to dental disease, though it usually is.

Infections of the sinuses, ears, eyes or throat can all cause pain around the mouth. Sinusitis can cause toothache, but the pain is often more widespread. The pain of sinusitis often gets worse as the day wears on, and it is also made worse by stooping down or by blowing the nose. Treatment is with painkillers, steam inhalations and antibiotics.

▶▶ SEE ALSO — Alzheimer's Disease, Caesarean Section, Childbirth

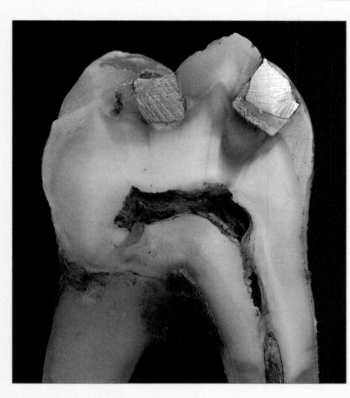

Above: A cross-section of an extracted molar, with two amalgam fillings. The channel that leads up from the root to the centre of the tooth is the pulp.

Common Dental Terms

ABSCESS A collection of matter or pus in a cavity, resulting from infection.

AMALGAM A powdered metal alloy, based on mercury, used for filling cavities. Alternatively, a translucent silicate cement may be used on surfaces other than those required for grinding.

BRIDGE The means by which a missing tooth or teeth are replaced and linked to surviving ones.

CALCULUS This deposit of hard salt on the teeth is also known as tartar.

CARIES Decay of a tooth.

CAVITY A hollow in the tooth, as a result of decay.

GINGIVITIS Inflammation of the gums.

HALITOSIS Bad breath.

IMPACTED TOOTH One so wedged that it cannot emerge through the gum.

MALOCCLUSION An abnormal alignment of the jaws and the teeth.

OCCLUSION The 'bite' or position in which the upper and lower teeth meet.

ORTHODONTICS A branch of dentistry dealing with the prevention and treatment of tooth irregularities.

PALATE The roof of the mouth.

SCALING Removal of deposits from the teeth with the help of dental instruments.

FISSURE SEALANT A watertight varnish for coating crevices of the biting surfaces of back teeth, sealing them against acid attack. A number of dentists carry out this treatment with children.

diet or to the way different families look after their teeth.

Bacterial infection

Plaque is a china-like layer of micro-organisms which develops on the teeth. Plaque contains bacteria which change carbohydrates in the mouth into acids. These are usually strong enough to attack and penetrate the hard, outer layer (enamel). After breaking down the protective enamel the bacteria are then able to enter and invade the living tissue, normally causing inflammation of the tissue and a cavity to form.

Infection of the inside of a tooth causes pain. To start with, this pain comes and goes, often as a result of hot or cold drinks, since the living part of a tooth is very sensitive to changes in temperature. However, after a few days or weeks the infection sets in properly and the pain becomes constant and very painful.

Gum disease

Receding gums and gum disease are the commonest cause of tooth loss in the UK. The condition is caused by the build-up of plaque on the teeth. Bacterial infection from plaque can cause inflammation of the gums (gingivitis), which in turn can cause bleeding and swelling. According to recent surveys nine out of 10 people suffer from gingivitis to some extent.

Gingivitis is a reversible condition, but if it is ignored it can lead to further teeth and gum problems, such as periodontitis and 'trench' mouth. Periodontitis occurs when the swelling of the gums becomes so bad that it allows bacteria to attack and enter the tissue that holds the teeth in position. Once this tissue is attacked the teeth may become loose. 'Trench' mouth occurs when gum infection develops, producing ulcers on the inside of the mouth.

Dental health

A dental problem, such as plaque, can be treated and removed by a dentist, but the best thing is to prevent the problem occurring and building up in the first place.

Mouth washes can help the prevention of dental problems, but the mainstay

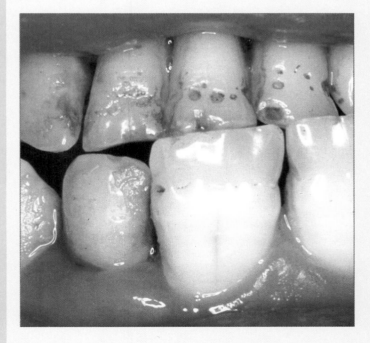

The teeth above are damaged due to insufficient development of the protective enamel layer.

▶▶ SEE ALSO — Caries, Cosmetic Dentistry

Dental Abscess

If the inside of a tooth becomes severely infected, the infection may form an abscess around the roots of the tooth.

This causes a severe toothache that is worsened by pressure on the overlying tooth. The infection may even spread to the surrounding lymph glands, causing swelling of the face and neck. A severe dental abscess can also cause 'flu-like symptoms and a high temperature. Dental abscesses are treated with antibiotic drugs, though the abscess will very often require surgical drainage.

of prevention is twice-daily toothbrushing. A fluoride toothpaste will also help prevent decay, particularly in children's developing teeth, as will the daily use of dental floss help fight plaque.

A well-balanced diet will also help to guard against dental problems. Sweets and sugar-based foods should be limited, and even then only be eaten at meal times. This is because, in between meals, the mouth produces less saliva, which normally acts as a defence against bacteria, and so infection is more likely to set in.

Treatment

If tooth decay is quite severe it may be necessary to fill the empty cavity with a filling, or even to extract the tooth in extreme cases of decay.

Sensitive teeth, whatever their cause, may be helped by a paste containing chemicals that bind to the exposed living tissue of the teeth. A dentist may also prescribe similar sorts of ointments to apply to the painful areas.

Wisdom teeth are a common cause of dental problems, especially in the early 20s. They often erupt and emerge at an abnormal angle, as a result of pressure from the other teeth that surround them. Occasionally they do not emerge at all, but rather grow into the other teeth. In either case, treatment is usually by surgical removal.

One of the major complications of dental treatment can be an infection of the heart valves. This only affects diseased valves, but can be fatal. Dental work causes bacteria from the mouth to be forced into the blood stream. They pass around the body until they reach the damaged valve, where they can settle. Unless treated they can then form a growth causing serious circulation problems.

Tooth Care

- Brush teeth twice a day with a fluoride toothpaste.
- Buy a new toothbrush every two months.
- Use dental floss regularly.
- Gently brush the gums as well as the teeth.
- Visit your dentist every six months.

DEPRESSION

Depression occurs when someone experiences feelings of sadness and hopelessness, and life seems to be worthless.

Everyone feels 'down', or experiences grief or sadness at one time or another, often as a result of bereavement or personal disappointment. This can frequently be just a natural case of unhappiness. Or perhaps it could be minor (neurotic) depression. This kind of depression is quite common and can affect up to 15 per cent of the population at some time. On the other hand, manic or major (psychotic) depression is very much less common.

Women seem to be affected by depression twice as frequently as men, although this high figure may be due in part to the fact that women are more likely to go to their doctor with their depressive symptoms. The worst depressive conditions generally occur after the age of 60, but no age group is totally immune to depression, so that even small children, for example, can become profoundly depressed, a fact that has only recently been appreciated.

Symptoms

The various sorts of depressive illness are quite difficult to differentiate between, but there are certain common symptoms. A general state of anxiety and uncharacteristic mood changes generally occur. And tiredness and a tendency towards hypochondria will often accompany this. It will be normally possible, however, for the minor depressive to be coaxed out of her condition by a positive, change of surroundings and cheerful company.

More serious depression is usually accompanied by physical and more marked behavioural symptoms, and can last for months or even years. Sleeplessness, constipation, loss of appetite and diarrhoea can all occur, sometimes along with phobias and hallucinations. Suicidal thoughts may even result, and movement and speech can be noticeably slowed down. The severely depressed patient may ultimately show no interest in work or in socialising, and may spend the whole time indoors, alone.

Causes

Nobody knows what exactly causes depression. It is thought that some physical problems, like viral infections or hormonal imbalances, can play a part in the onset of a depressive condition.

Physical challenges such as the strain, and possibly the hormonal upset, of childbirth can cause the first attack of depression in a normally well-balanced person. Chronic illness can certainly cause depression, something that is often overlooked by relatives and doctors, thereby causing much unnecessary suffering.

Manic depression is sometimes hereditary, and in many cases is almost certainly caused by a chemical imbalance in the brain. Drugs can also precipitate depression. The oral contraceptive pill for example, especially when it contains a high level of the hormone progesterone, is frequently to blame.

Treatment

Given sufficient time and support many depression sufferers are able to recover on their own. Fortunately this process can be speeded up considerably with medical care and attentive nursing.

Psychotherapy is used to help depression sufferers when their symptoms seem to have been caused by psychological factors. Antidepressant drug therapy is used to deal with more physically-based problems.

Electroconvulsive therapy, in which a small amount of electric current is passed through the brain, is a less popular form of treatment than it once was. But it is still regarded as a very effective form of treatment for post-natal depression. The patient is anaesthetised and given a muscle-relaxing drug before ECT is performed.

▶▶ SEE ALSO — Psychotherapy

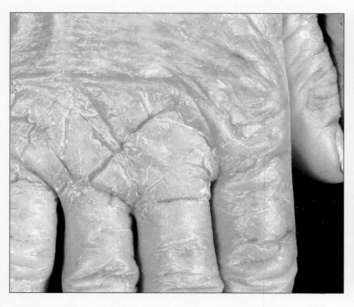

Above: Dermatitis of the hand, in this case caused by the sufferer's allergic reaction to rubber gloves.

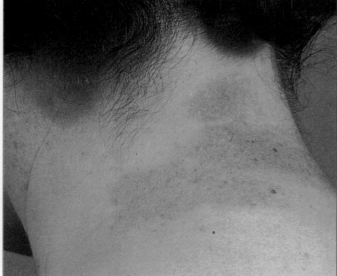

Above: Phytophoto dermatitis, caused by an allergy to certain plant substances, is triggered by sunlight.

DERMATITIS

Dermatitis is an inflammation of the skin, sometimes severe enough to cause the formation of blisters.

When acute, dermatitis causes a red, blistery rash. The rash is often weepy and may be covered by scales and crusts. Chronic dermatitis, on the other hand, is less angry, may be brown in colour and is covered in layers of thick skin. Both these forms, acute and chronic, are itchy and both are most commonly found in the creases of the elbows and knees.

External causes

The most common external causes of dermatitis are irritants, such as detergents. Common symptoms include inflammation, itching and raised spots. Everyday materials, such as wool, nylon, certain metals, and some chemicals found in quite common perfumes or cleaning products, can all produce allergic reactions that lead to dermatitis. The classic example of this 'contact' dermatitis is the irritated patch under a nickel bra hook or watch strap.

Nappy rash, also known as ammoniacal dermatitis, is caused by a chemical reaction to the ammonia in urine. The sun can cause dermatitis in people whose skin is ultrasensitive to light. And dermatitis can also be self-induced, as a result of excessive scratching.

Treatment

Treatment for 'contact' or 'allergic' dermatitis is usually by avoidance of the irritant and by the application of

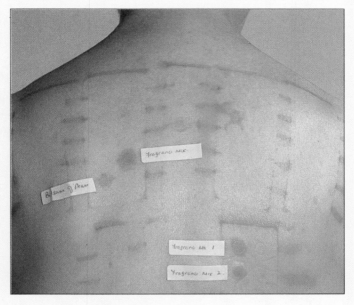

Above: Patch skin testing is used to help discover the exact cause of allergic dermatitis.

corticosteroid creams. If the allergy is unknown, the doctor may wish to perform a skin test to discover the cause. Skin tests are performed by potential irritants being attached to the skin for two days. An attack of dermatitis will normally show itself during that time.

Internal causes

Dermatitis that comes from within used to be called eczema, but this term is being employed less and

less. This form of dermatitis is due to the presence of excessive amounts of an immune protein in the blood. It is often associated with hay fever and asthma, and affects about 15 per cent of the UK population.

Internal dermatitis often starts in infancy, and is usually present as dry skin on the face. The rash may then progress and develop into blisters, but it usually spares the nappy area. As the child becomes older, the dermatitis becomes thick and leathery. The rash is similar in adults, but tends to affect more of the body. The itching involved may be so bad that the patient is unable to get any sleep, and scratching the rash can also cause bacterial infections.

Treatment

Internally caused dermatitis is best treated by avoiding known irritants, such as wool, soap, or biological washing powders. Bath oils can help, as do moisturising lotions. Corticosteroid creams can have very dramatic effects, but the benefits must be carefully weighed against the side effects, such as the thinning of the skin. Antihistamine

▶▶ SEE ALSO — Dandruff, Eczema

tablets may help, if only by improving sleep.

Many doctors feel that the effects of diet are minimal in relation to dermatitis, though it is thought that some babies may stand less chance of developing dermatitis if they are kept off dairy products in the first six months of life.

Seborrhoeic Dermatitis

Seborrhoeic dermatitis is generally thought to be caused, like acne, by a disorder of sebum production.

Seborrhoeic dermatitis produces a red, itchy rash, sometimes with weeping blisters. It occurs mainly on the face, scalp, chest and back, and can sometimes be exacerbated by anxiety or stress. On the scalp it is the most common cause of dandruff. It is usually treated with corticosteroid drugs or a special prescription shampoo.

DESIGNER DRUGS

Designer drugs are a form of drugs that imitate other drugs, such as LSD or amphetamines.

These designer drugs are produced from chemicals and are illegal in the UK. They are cheap to produce and thus are found on the high street as a cheap alternative to already available drugs.

Chemically, they are sometimes made up in a slightly different way from the drugs that they are designed to imitate. This means that in some countries they are not subject to the normal restrictions and laws that control the drug trade.

Effects

By imitating types of drugs like LSD (acid), amphetamines (speed), or even narcotic painkillers, designer drugs can produce dramatic physical and mental changes in the user. They can increase energy levels, giving the user a 'high', a temporary sensation of well-being and happiness.

But designer drugs also provoke depression, cause hallucinations and distort perceptions of reality. In turn this can lead to dangerous behavioural problems, aggression and abnormal mood swings. Frequent use may eventually lead to addiction, drug poisoning, permanent brain damage and even death.

DEVELOPMENT

Development is the process in which mental and physical growth takes place.

The first, and probably most dramatic, stage of development is in the first two months of pregnancy when the fertilised egg is transformed into the embryo and then into the foetus, and takes on recognisable, human characteristics.

Pre-natal development

The fertilised egg develops in the fallopian tube and takes six days to reach the womb. After four weeks the embryo is the size of a grain of rice. It already has a recognisable heart, and the arms and legs are beginning to appear as minute buds. Within another four weeks, the embryo is the size of a jelly baby and has arms, legs and a head, though the eyes and ears are rudimentary. At the end of the 10th week the embryo is termed a foetus,

and at this stage even the nails and teeth are beginning to appear. The last major change occurs in the 14th week with sexual differentiation. Until this stage, male and female development is identical. From now on the emphasis is on the development of the major organs.

Bone develops early in pregnancy, but doesn't start to harden until just before birth. This process continues through childhood and is not complete until the early 20s.

Childhood development

The second significant stage of development is during the child's first five years of life. It is during this time that the child usually learns to walk, speak and control her physical movements. Up to the age of five the brain develops more and the child learns more than at any other stage in her later life.

It is the development of the nervous system that determines how a child develops in general. Genetic factors dictate how fast this development takes place. But this can be changed by environmental factors, even in the womb, so that a premature baby is likely to develop less rapidly than would normally be the case. A baby's first reactions are

reflex, but these soon develop into voluntary and imitative actions, once muscles and coordination begin to develop. Sight and sound abilities progress by concentrating on individual objects and noises, as the child learns to focus and differentiate. Speech advances from a stage where crying is the only sort of language used, to imitation and repetition of the parents' word sounds.

Physical control and coordination start with the head and slowly move down the body. This means that most babies only walk after a series of lying, sitting, crawling and standing movements, followed by a few first hesitant steps being taken. Most babies learn to walk between the ages of nine and 15 months.

Puberty

The third major stage of development is during puberty and adolescence. Puberty refers to physical change, when the sexual organs develop and mature. It usually occurs between the ages of 10 and 15, often slightly earlier in girls than in boys. Changes occur due to hormonal changes in the pituitary gland, causing the secretion of oestrogen in girls and testosterone in

Development delay

Development delay is a source of worry to many parents. If you think your child is 'delayed', consult your doctor.

But as a general guideline it is worth noting the general child development characteristics:

● 6 weeks – responds with a smile, especially to mother; unable to support head
● 7 months – responds to name; may sit unaided for a few moments; makes simple sounds like 'ma', but without any clear meaning
● 15 months – uses a few simple words; points to what she wants; spoons food into mouth; may stack a couple of bricks together
● 30 months – uses three or four word sentences; builds a tower of six to eight bricks; runs, climbs and jumps

▶▶ SEE ALSO — Embryo, Foetus, Puberty

Stages Of Physical Development In Boys And Girls

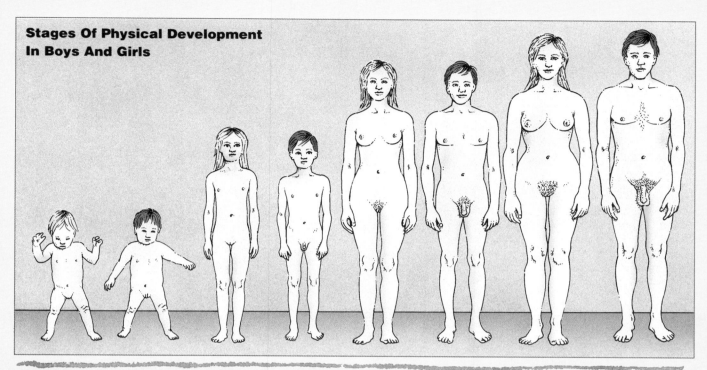

Aged one: *First steps; head disproportionately large.*

Aged eight: *Growth of limbs; girls similar shape to boys.*

Aged 14: *Sexual organs begin to develop.*

Adult: *Development of sexual organs complete.*

boys. In girls the first sign of puberty is 'breast budding', which is followed by the growth of pubic hair. The first menstrual period does not begin until about a year after the first signs of puberty. Girls also then begin to put on weight and fat, and the pelvis widens. In boys the testes and scrotum begin to grow, reaching their full size after about two years. The hormone testosterone also causes the production of reproductive sperm. The shoulders become wider and the voice deepens.

Adolescence

Adolescence normally refers to the teenage years when puberty starts and physical and mental changes take place. In adolescence she must begin to come to terms with these changes, which signal the changeover from childhood to adulthood. She will begin to form a greater sexual awareness and sense of self-identity, and start to assume a position of relative independence.

DIABETES

The most common form of diabetes, *diabetes mellitus,* is due to an excess level of sugar in the blood.

Also known as sugar diabetes, *diabetes mellitus* is very common and tends to run in families. Most estimates suggest that between 500,000 and a million people are affected by it in the UK alone.

Sugar levels

Glucose is the sugar which is present in the body, following the breakdown of carbohydrates, and helps provide the body with vitally required amounts of energy. The level of sugar in the blood is normally controlled by the hormone insulin. But this level can be disrupted if the pancreas produces an insufficient amount of insulin, so that the body is unable to process the glucose. As a result of this the body's blood sugar level rises and the energy-producing sugar fails to be absorbed into the body's tissues.

This high sugar level causes a constant and excessive thirst, resulting in large quantities of urine to be passed. Tiredness and moodiness may well also result, as may blurred vision, hunger and weight loss.

Insulin-dependent diabetes

Diabetes mellitus, which is caused by a lack of insulin, is most common in children and young adults. The onset is usually sudden. If the condition is not treated, the patient can soon lapse into unconsciousness and a coma, and will eventually die.

The exact cause of the onset of *diabetes mellitus* is unknown, though some cases certainly seem to follow infections of the pancreas. And other attacks of this sort seem to be caused by the body's attempt to fight off the onset of viral infections.

Treatment

Insulin-dependent diabetes is treated with injections, normally two or three times a day. Dietary control is also used to keep sugar levels in check. To make sure that they get the right level of insulin, diabetes sufferers have to have regular blood and urine tests.

The results of getting the insulin and blood sugar levels wrongly balanced can provoke short- and long-term problems. In the short term, too much or too little insulin can cause a coma, especially when there is too

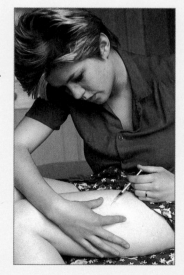

Above: Insulin-dependent diabetes is treated with self-administered injections.

SEE ALSO — Coma

much insulin present; the blood sugar level is forced down to such a low level that the brain stops functioning properly. As a result the sufferer becomes sweaty, confused and may lapse into unconsciousness. Temporary treatment for this problem may be given in the form of sugar lumps that sufferers sometimes carry with them.

The long term results of too high a blood sugar level can also be very serious, in that the high sugar level affects the functioning of the small arteries. This means that blood supply to the eyes, kidneys and legs can be disrupted, possibly leading to blindness, kidney failure and gangrene. However, modern medication and the development of, and emphasis on, home blood tests and regular check-ups by diabetic specialists means that these complications very rarely occur nowadays.

Non-insulin-dependent diabetes

A milder form of *diabetes mellitus* can also be caused in adults, normally over the age of 40. Usually this comes as a result of the pancreas not supplying the body with a sufficient amount of insulin, and even when it does so the action of the insulin seems to be ineffective.

This happens most frequently in overweight people, almost as if there were not enough insulin to go around the body. It is quite often a hereditary problem. The onset of this form of diabetes is not sudden, and symptoms may be delayed for many years after the start of the condition.

Insulin-replacement injections are not usually employed to deal with this sort of diabetes. Treatment with a weight-reducing diet may be enough to bring the blood sugar level back to normal. Failing this, a low sugar diet, accompanied by tablet treatment, will usually avoid the need for injections.

Diabetes Insipidus

***Diabetes insipidus* is a rare metabolic disorder that is characterised by an excessive thirst and large quantities of urine being passed.**

Diabetes insipidus most commonly results from a failure of the pituitary gland to produce ADH (antidiuretic hormone). ADH usually regulates the amount of water that is absorbed by the kidneys.

This form of diabetes is usually caused by damage to the pituitary gland, sometimes as a result of an injury or a tumour, or even following brain surgery or radiotherapy. In very rare cases it is caused by the kidneys failing to react to the effect of ADH.

Initially *diabetes insipidus* must be differentiated from *diabetes mellitus*, with which it shares certain symptoms. It is then possible to treat the condition, which is normally carried out with ADH replacements in the form of nasal sprays.

Symptoms of Diabetes

• Tiredness and weakness.
• Very frequent urination.
• Enormous thirst.
• Itching around the genitals, caused by excess sugar in the urine.
• Blurred vision.

DIALYSIS

Dialysis is a technique that artificially performs the kidneys' natural functions in cases of kidney failure.

The kidneys normally clear waste products from the blood and help to maintain the level of fluids in the body. Twenty per cent of the blood that gets pumped by the heart actually passes through the kidneys. The kidneys act as filters, vital to the maintenance of good health. The kidneys' semi-permeable membrane reabsorbs important products and elements such as water, sodium and calcium, and gets rid of unnecessary waste products, partly in the form of urine. Kidney failure means that these vital filtering processes begin to fail themselves, corrupting the quality of the blood and possibly threatening the sufferer's life.

Techniques

The most common form of dialysis is haemodialysis. which involves the fitting of a needle into an artery in the arm. The blood is redirected through an artificial kidney machine where it is filtered and cleaned, then returned via another vein. This is done two or three times a week, for up to eight hours at a time. Some patients have their own machine at home.

The more convenient method is peritoneal dialysis, during which the patient is able to be mobile. Dialysing fluid is fed into the abdomen via a catheter, with the peritoneum (the membrane that surrounds the intestines) acting as the cleaning filter. After a while the waste fluid is drained off. This technique is repeated about four times a day, and enables the patient to continue a more normal life style than is possible with haemodialysis.

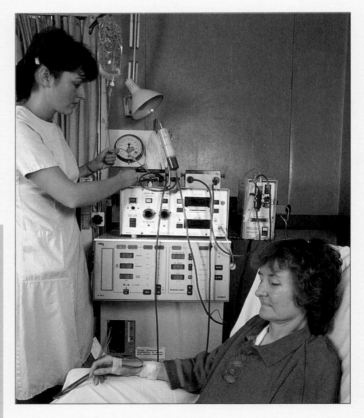

Above: A nurse prepares a patient for the use of a kidney dialysis machine, designed to clean the blood.

DIARRHOEA

Diarrhoea is the passing of frequent, watery stools.

Everyone has a different idea of a 'normal' bowel habit. But a good working definition of diarrhoea is 'a looser, more frequent bowel action than expected from past experience'. In a recent survey, seven per cent of a cross section of the population in the UK said that they had had diarrhoea in the past two weeks.

A short bout of diarrhoea, lasting a few days, is known as acute diarrhoea, but if the condition persists for more than two weeks it is described as chronic. However, diarrhoea is not actually a disorder in itself, but is a symptom of another problem.

Acute diarrhoea

Acute diarrhoea is usually due to infections or dietary upsets, but the cause may also be emotional. Foods which are unusually hot or spicy, or which contain an excess of fibre are common causes of acute diarrhoea.

Bacterial infections — 'food poisoning' — include campylobacter, giardia or salmonella. Campylobacter is characterised by abdominal cramps and 'flu-like symptoms, coupled with foul-smelling, blood-stained diarrhoea. Giardia and salmonella have less distinctive symptoms. The presence of these bacteria can only be diagnosed by testing a sample of the motion. Your doctor may ask you to take a specimen to the local health office, and you may be questioned about what you have eaten, to trace the source and prevent a widespread outbreak.

When you are nervous, because of exams, an interview or a new date, for example, you may also experience a bout of diarrhoea. Antibiotics can cause diarrhoea, because the antibiotics act on the 'good' bacteria in the digestive tract. And diarrhoea is also a symptom of some rare — in the UK — but serious diseases, such as dysentery, typhoid and cholera.

Treatment

Acute diarrhoea can usually be treated with a carefully controlled diet, plenty of water (or a salt and sugar solution like Dioralyte), and rest. The symptoms should go away by following a careful diet of easily digested food, avoiding all fats, acids and dairy products. In more severe cases, stop eating altogether, drinking only clear fluids — an easily prepared mixture is lemonade mixed with an equal quantity of water.

If diarrhoea is due to a bacterial infection, antibiotics may be prescribed, but such treatment should be applied carefully, as there is a danger that the bacteria will become 'super bugs', resistant to the drugs, and patients treated in this way may become chronic carriers of the infection.

Chronic diarrhoea

If diarrhoea is chronic, several investigations may

Diarrhoea And The Pill

Diarrhoea can sometimes disrupt the effectiveness of the oral contraceptive pill.

If stools are very frequent, your digestive tract may not have the chance to absorb the necessary hormones, and the pill may be ineffective. Consult the leaflet supplied with your oral contraceptive.

Diarrhoea In Infants

In babies under six months, diarrhoea may be a reaction to too much sugar in the diet, or a sign that there is a serious problem involved, such as gastroenteritis.

● Young babies are particularly at risk from diarrhoea, because of the danger of their small bodies becoming dehydrated.
● Consult your doctor without delay if the problem persists for more than 24 hours, or if the baby is unwell, in pain or has a temperature.
● Whatever you think the cause may be, the first thing is to cut out all milk apart from breast milk, all solids, and increase the amount of water given to the baby. Avoid all types of fruit juice.
● Your doctor may prescribe drinks of Dioralyte, a sachet containing salt and sugar (available over the counter), which should be added to boiled water.

Gastroenteritis is an inflammation of the intestine that causes vomiting and loose, watery stools, and can affect babies and children. The symptoms vary in severity, and are less common in breast-fed babies, as breast milk contains antibodies which shield the intestine from possible infection.

Treatment involves cutting out solids and bottle feeds. Antidiarrhoeal drugs may be prescribed. If the condition persists, and the baby becomes badly dehydrated, hospital admission may be necessary, so that an intravenous drip can be given. All foods (including baby milk) should be re-introduced slowly, over a couple of days, and stopped again if the diarrhoea recurs.

Diarrhoea in babies may also be a reaction to a change in diet, medicines prescribed for some other problem, and the same 'food poisoning' bacteria which affect adults.

Avoiding Diarrhoea Abroad

Travellers to parts of the world where hygiene levels are not very high should follow these simple rules:

● All water, including that used for ice cubes, must be regarded as infected unless you know that it has been boiled prior to use.
● Food must be piping hot (partially re-heated meat is particularly prone to salmonella).
● Peel fruit and vegetables yourself before eating. Avoid prepared fruit from restaurants or markets, that may have been handled by unwashed hands.
● Do not swim in fresh water – you do not know what is being thrown in upstream.
● If you get a bad upset stomach, stop eating and drink a lot of liquid – preferably containing a little sugar and salt; sachets are available from the chemist's, but remember to add them to freshly boiled water.

» SEE ALSO — Cholera, Dehydration, Dysentery, Typhoid

MEDICAL FACT FILE

be necessary to find the cause. The first step is to check that it is not caused by bacteria, and stools may need to be analysed.

If there is blood in the faeces, and if the diarrhoea alternates with bouts of constipation, the condition may be caused by diverticular disease or bowel cancer. These conditions normally only affect those over the age of 35.

In those under 35, the condition is more likely to be caused by an irritable colon, Crohn's disease or ulcerative colitis, although the latter two are both quite rare. Crohn's disease is an inflammation of the digestive tract, and its cause is unknown.

In women, a commonly overlooked cause of diarrhoea is an overactive thyroid. This speeds up a lot of the body's activities, producing emotional and physical symptoms.

Treatment

Diagnosis of the causes of chronic diarrhoea may take some time, and include hospital tests such as barium enemas, x-rays, and laparoscopy (examination with fibreoptic telescopes). The treatment will depend on the causes, and includes dietary control, corticosteroid drugs to treat inflammation of the digestive tract, pain killers and, if the problem is serious, surgery.

DILATION AND CURETTAGE

Dilation (also known as Dilatation) and Curettage, is normally abbreviated to D and C: a minor operation in which most of the uterine lining is removed for medical examination.

DIPHTHERIA

Diphtheria is a serious, highly infectious bacterial disease that affects the nose and throat areas.

Diphtheria is caused by rod-shaped bacteria that develop in the nose and in the skin. These can produce a dangerous toxin (poison) that is released into the bloodstream. Being highly infectious it can spread very quickly, which normally happens when the infected person sneezes or coughs.

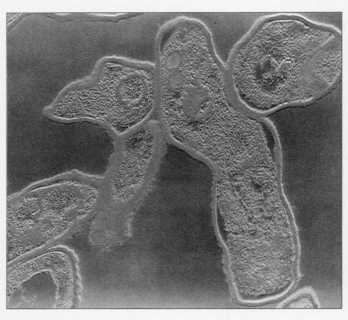

Above: A coloured image of the slightly curved diphtheria bacteria that are sometimes known as 'Chinese characters'.

Endemic problem

Until the Second World War diphtheria was one of the world's most common causes of childhood death. But since then, the development of new drugs and mass immunisation have virtually eradicated the disease from developed countries, as in the UK, where only one child has died from diphtheria in the last 10 years. But it still remains a serious problem in some Third World countries.

Symptoms

Initial symptoms of diphtheria often include an unusually high temperature, an increased pulse rate, slight fever and even swollen glands in the neck. When the throat is affected, a grey membrane may well develop over the tonsils, and can spread to the voice-box and the windpipe. This can result in a sore throat and hoarseness. Life-threatening illness results from toxin infection. Death may follow within a day if this occurs.

Treatment

Immunisation, during the first year of life, with the vaccine DPT (which acts against diphtheria, pertussis or 'whooping cough', and tetanus) usually provides most people with an immunity against the condition. But people are always advised to check up on their immunisation details before travelling to parts of the world known to be affected by diphtheria.

Penicillin will usually kill off diphtheria if it is present as a throat infection. If it has entered the blood as a toxin the only remedy is for an antitoxin to be administered.

DISCHARGE

A discharge is the production and elimination of a substance from a wound or from one of the body's orifices.

Some discharges are normal and harmless. Some are a natural response to the body's healing mechanism; and others indicate that treatment is necessary.

Wounds

Discharges from wounds are usually clear, colourless and odourless. Such 'weeping' is part of the body's mechanism for repairing and cleaning the damaged tissue. If the discharge becomes thick, yellow or smelly it may mean that the wound has become infected.

Some wounds, notably severe burns, produce such large amounts of discharge that the patient is in danger of dehydration. Usually an intravenous drip is used to replace the lost fluid.

The nose

Nose discharges are a common problem: the runny nose seems to be a permanent problem for some infants. Discharges from the nose may be due to an infection or an allergy.

Those due to infection may take a wide range of forms: they may be clear or thick, colourless, yellow or green. The causes include colds, 'flu and sinusitis. Allergies, such as hay fever, cause a profuse, watery discharge that is worse at certain times of the year and in certain conditions.

Vaginal discharge

Normal vaginal discharges, between periods, are clear and almost odourless. The normal discharge is the method by which the vagina and cervix keep themselves clean. The discharge is rich in glucose, and certain bacteria in the vagina turn

▶▶ SEE ALSO — Bacteria, Crohn's Disease, D and C

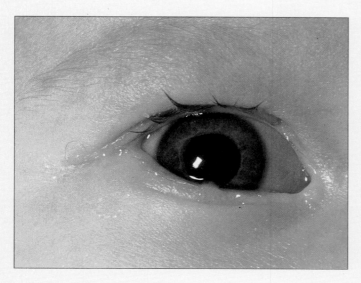

Above: Conjunctivitis often causes a sticky eye discharge that makes the eyelids difficult to separate in the morning.

this glucose to acid, which kills off harmful germs.

The amount may increase when you are sexually excited. You may also notice that the discharge is heavier midway between periods; this is due to ovulation, and is part of the body's effort to aid fertilisation. Discharge will, of course, differ from woman to woman. The coil also increases the amount of discharge; and hormonal changes, due to being on the Pill or pregnancy, also increase the quantity.

Thrush

Thrush (candidiasis), a fungal infection, produces a thick, white and very itchy vaginal discharge. The thrush bacteria are usually killed off by the normal, acid discharge, so the white discharge indicates that the acid-producing bacteria have been killed off.

Thrush may be the result of a course of antibiotics, a change in the normal conditions in the vagina (due to hormonal changes in pregnancy or when on the Pill), or it may result from using douches or vaginal deodorants. Consult your doctor, who will prescribe treatment in the form of tablets or pessaries.

Bacterial infections

Trichomoniasis is a bacterial infection spread by sexual contact. It causes a grey frothy discharge, which smells strongly of fish. A short course of tablets will kill off the infection, but your partner must be treated as well, because it is contagious. Gonorrhoea and chlamydial infection also cause discharges, but these are less noticeable.

An abnormally discoloured (likely to be green or yellow) and offensive smelling discharge, coupled with pain in the abdomen, may be caused by an acute infection of the fallopian tubes or uterus, and you should consult your doctor immediately.

Bloody discharge

A bloody discharge may have several different causes. It may be caused by one of the above infections, or by cervical polyps. These are normally harmless, but you should consult your doctor immediately, since the symptoms are similar to those of cervical cancer. Cervical polyps are easily removed without an anaesthetic, and a D and C may be necessary.

A bloody discharge in post-menopausal women is

usually a result of thinning of the vaginal wall. However, it may be a sign of more serious problems in the uterus, and you should consult your doctor.

Watery discharge

Watery, urine-like discharges during pregnancy may be an indication that the waters have broken. This is normal at the end of pregnancy, and a sign that labour is under way. Earlier in pregnancy, it may lead to premature labour, and a danger that an infection may enter and affect the baby: hospital admission is usually necessary.

Foreign bodies

Foreign bodies left in the vagina by mistake (a tampon, cap or contraceptive sponge, for example) may cause an infection coupled with an extremely offensive discharge. Removal of the forgotten item should clear the problem up.

DISC PROLAPSE

The discs in the spine are thick pieces of cartilage which join the bones, acting as shock absorbers.

The centre of the disc is like a very tough jelly, and it is surrounded by a thick fibrous capsule. In everyday language, the term 'slipped disc' is used to describe a wide range of back aches. But, in actual fact, the discs cannot slip.

Prolapsed disc

The disc is fused with the bones above and below it, and it is impossible for it to just slip out, like a slice of cucumber from a sandwich. Indeed, if a disc could slip out, it could equally be pushed back again.

What actually happens is that the fibrous shell bursts (or ruptures), letting the gelatinous centre seep out (or prolapse). The prolapse and the fibrous debris press on the surrounding nerves,

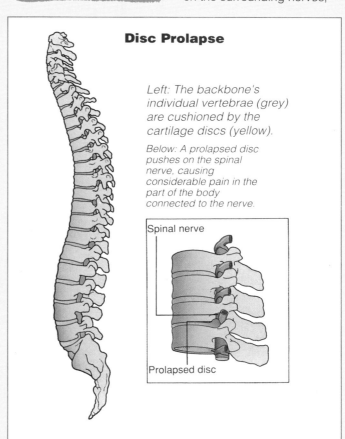

Disc Prolapse

Left: The backbone's individual vertebrae (grey) are cushioned by the cartilage discs (yellow).

Below: A prolapsed disc pushes on the spinal nerve, causing considerable pain in the part of the body connected to the nerve.

Spinal nerve

Prolapsed disc

⟫ SEE ALSO — Childbirth

causing considerable pain. A prolapsed disc can occur in any part of the spine, but it is most common between the bottom two joints, where the spine takes the stresses of tilting forwards. Prolapsed discs can occur at any age, but are most common between the ages of 20 and 50, and are slightly more common in men than women.

Research has shown that in normal spines the bones will crumble before the disc bursts, usually through a natural process of degeneration with age, which results in the discs becoming dehydrated and weakened. A disc may also have been weakened in some other way causing it to prolapse; this can occasionally result from a sudden movement or from strenuous exercise, such as unaccustomed lifting of heavy weights. It is also more likely to occur in people who spend large amounts of time in a sitting position.

Symptoms

Often, there is a day or two of vague aches and pains in the back before a disc prolapses. The actual injury may be slight, but after prolapse the pain becomes so severe that the victim cannot straighten up. After an hour or two the pain may affect the buttocks or legs, as the prolapse presses on more and more nerves. In some rare cases the nerves affecting the bowel or bladder may be damaged, leading to incontinence or difficulty in passing water. Full diagnosis is carried out with medical tests, including x-rays, scans, and electrical activity tests to measure nerve damage.

Treatment

Strict bed rest is the best treatment. Pain killers may be prescribed if needed. The back must be well supported, and a small pillow or hot water bottle in the small of the back may be

helpful. Bending the knees may also ease the pain.

Recovery may take several weeks, depending on whether the disc has actually burst, or is just bulging out. Physiotherapy will help once the initial stage has passed, and careful, gentle exercise is important in helping the back to return to a healthy condition. If you consistently contort or twist your back in an effort to relieve the pain, the disc will not heal properly. On the other hand, manipulation too early may be dangerous.

Surgery to remove the damaged disc is becoming less popular, but your GP may refer you to a specialist if the condition is unimproved after a couple of weeks. In some cases, traction may be applied — the spine is stretched to take pressure off the healing disc.

DISLOCATION

Dislocation occurs when the two bones that make up a joint become detached from their normal position.

Dislocation most frequently occurs as a result of an accident or injury, but may sometimes also occur without any obvious cause. This happens most often when the capsule that surrounds the joint is too loose in the first place; or when there is a congenital problem with the joint structure — most commonly with the hip joint.

When the dislocation results in the bones no longer being in contact at all it is referred to as a luxation. If, however, there is still partial contact between the dislocated bones, it is known as a subluxation.

Symptoms

Dislocation is often accompanied by other injuries. The bones involved

in the dislocation can get fractured if the injury is severe. The attached ligaments can easily be torn, causing a considerable amount of pain; and the capsule that surrounds the joint can also get damaged.

As well as the pain that accompanies the tearing of ligaments, swelling and discolouring occur, and movement of the joint is severely restricted.

Treatment

Most dislocated joints are quite obvious and easy to diagnose, but some may require an x-ray for a satisfactory diagnosis (as is often the case with hip joint dislocations), or to make sure there has been no fracture or any other such complication.

After diagnosis the dislocated bones are eased back into place by the doctor or surgeon, usually under general anaesthetic.

Repositioning ought not to be performed by an untrained person, as this can simply make the injury worse. Accompanying support and immobilisation with bandages, or even a splint or plaster cast, will generally help the joint to heal to its former, healthy condition within a few weeks.

Problems

Serious, long-term damage, inflicted upon the joint or bones, can sometimes occur and hinder the healing process. Problems can also occur if the dislocation affects the back and particularly the spinal vertebrae. If the spinal cord is damaged paralysis may occur below the point where the dislocation takes place. Paralysis can also result from major nerve damage in hip or shoulder dislocation.

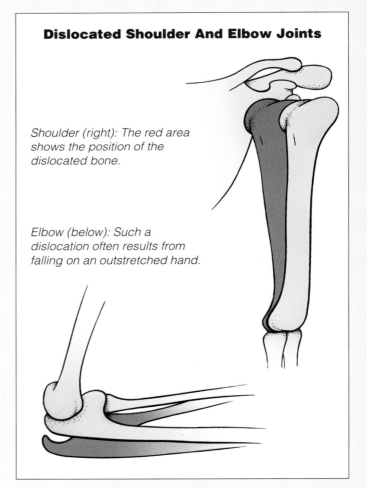

Dislocated Shoulder And Elbow Joints

Shoulder (right): The red area shows the position of the dislocated bone.

Elbow (below): Such a dislocation often results from falling on an outstretched hand.

▶▶ SEE ALSO — Bones

DIURETIC DRUGS

Diuretic drugs help rid the body of excess fluid in the form of urine.

Diuretic drugs work upon the kidneys, which normally act as filters of the salts, water and waste products present in the blood. Under normal circumstances most of the water and salts are returned to the bloodstream by the kidneys, the waste products being discarded. Diuretic drugs alter this filtering process, causing different proportions of water and salts to be saved or lost according to the drugs.

Types

Thiazide, loop and osmotic diuretic drugs all reduce the amounts of salts and water that are reabsorbed into the bloodstream, with the result that the volume of urine is increased, and the problem of oedema (fluid retention in the body) is reduced.

Thiazide drugs cause only a moderate increase in urine production and are therefore able to be administered for prolonged periods of time. Loop drugs, which act on the 'loop' region of the kidneys, are powerful, rapid action drugs. Osmotic drugs are powerful and are commonly used to help maintain the steady production of urine following major surgery or injury. There are also other drugs, like caffeine, that increase the quantity of blood that flows through the kidneys, in turn increasing the amount of water that is passed quite naturally as urine.

Uses

Diuretic drugs are used to help treat heart failure in an emergency, as heart failure can cause the lungs to become saturated with fluid (pulmonary oedema). They are also used to counter the effects of kidney and liver disorders that cause oedema. Oedema normally shows itself as the physical symptoms of swollen ankles and breathlessness. Diuretics can also help to reduce high blood pressure and glaucoma, which occurs when a build-up of fluid on the eyeball causes a problem of abnormal pressure.

Side effects

Diuretics were used in the past as a slimming aid, but this is no longer so, since side-effects — such as dizziness, nausea, rashes, weakness and tingling in the hands and feet — can sometimes result from their use. These effects are caused by chemical imbalances that the diuretic drugs induce in the body. This is frequently due to the reduction in the level of potassium after diuretic treatment. The level of uric acid can be increased, bringing with it the possibility of gout. Sugar levels may be raised, which can lead to *diabetes mellitus* problems.

DIVERTICULAR DISEASE

Diverticular disease involves the presence of small pouches (diverticula) in the wall of the intestines.

The intestine wall consists of several layers. The outer layer is made up of strips of muscle that contract to force the food along. In the sufferer the muscle layer is pierced by the blood vessels that supply the inner wall (the mucosa). Where the blood vessels enter, it is quite possible that an area of weakness will develop.

Diverticula

If the pressure in the intestine is high enough, the mucosa will be forced out through the gaps. This excessive pressure is thought to be caused by the attempt of the body to push the hard stools, that are characteristic of a low-fibre diet, through the intestines. The intestine then comes to resemble a worn bicycle tyre with the inner tube bursting out. These pouches of the mucosa are called diverticula. They can be found in any part of the intestines, but are most common in the lower part of the colon (part of the large intestine) where they cause diverticular disease.

Incidence

Diverticular disease is a disease of middle and old age. It is very rare in Africans and Asians who eat a high fibre diet. In the UK, however, five per cent of 40-year-olds have the disease and the number increases with age. Diverticular disease is most common in people who have overactive gut muscles. This can be caused by stress, constipation or the excessive use of stimulant laxatives.

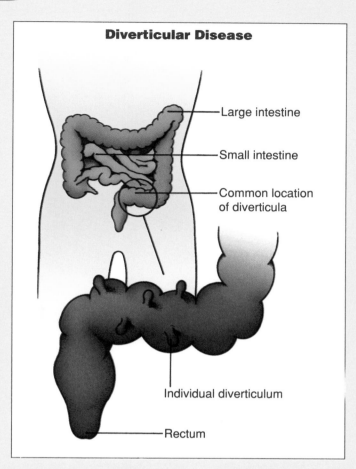

Diverticular Disease

- Large intestine
- Small intestine
- Common location of diverticula
- Individual diverticulum
- Rectum

Diverticulosis

The first stage of diverticular disease is diverticulosis.

In the early stages of diverticulosis the diverticula are relatively small and painless. But the warning signs of raised pressure in the bowel can be detected by the use of a measuring gauge. Many people with diverticulosis have no symptoms, but they may complain of wind and bloating.

On occasions, diverticulosis will result in a severe colicky pain in the lower abdomen. Diverticulosis is usually treated with a high-fibre diet and the avoidance of laxative medication. Unless treated properly it can quite easily progress to diverticulitis.

▶▶ SEE ALSO — Diabetes, Oedema

MEDICAL FACT FILE

DIVERTICULITIS

Diverticulitis is caused by inflammation of the diverticula, and causes severe abdominal pain.

The abdominal pain normally occurs low down on the left hand side of the patient. The patient will usually feel ill, experiencing physical symptoms such as nausea and an abnormally high temperature.

In severe cases the abdominal cavity can become infected, causing peritonitis (inflammation of the lining of the abdomen) or abscess formation. The inflamed diverticula may bleed and this is a common cause of rectal bleeding in the elderly. In about five per cent of cases the diverticula will burst into the surrounding tissues, such as the bladder or the vagina. This can cause a chronic condition where the bowel empties via an unnatural route. Constipation and diarrhoea can also result from diverticulitis.

Diagnosis

Diverticulitis is very common, but most doctors will only diagnose it once they have excluded all the other causes of abdominal symptoms. The best means of diagnosis is with a barium enema, in which dye is fed into the patient's intestines, to help show up the condition on x-ray, as the individual diverticula begin to fill up with the dye.

Treatment

Diverticulitis is treated with bed rest, anticolic drugs and antibiotic drugs. Occasionally surgery may be necessary to treat an abscess, or to remove a particularly badly affected section of bowel. It can generally be avoided in the first place by keeping to a healthy, high-fibre diet.

DIZZINESS

Dizziness is a sensation of light-headedness, faintness and unsteadiness.

Dizziness is a very common condition. In one recent survey six per cent of men and 10 per cent of women claimed to have suffered from it in the previous two weeks.

Like so many common complaints, dizziness means different things to different people. Therefore, doctors try to differentiate between a relatively simple feeling of light-headedness or faintness, and a more dramatic feeling that the room or the patient is spinning round. Doctors normally refer to the latter as vertigo, which is thought to be a more serious condition.

Common problems

Attacks of dizziness are generally quite harmless, normally being caused by a temporary lowering of the blood pressure to the brain. This can occur when you get up too quickly from a sitting or lying position, causing a rush of blood, and is called postural hypotension.

Elderly patients who have developed hardened arteries may well experience light-headedness and postural hypotension. This is especially true if they are taking blood pressure tablets, as this results in blood pooling in the legs and deprivation of oxygen to the brain. A similar condition occurs in early pregnancy, since the blood pressure is naturally lower at this time. And the symptoms are similar if there is a momentary blockage in the arteries that supply the brain.

Diabetics will feel light-headed and sweaty if their blood-sugar level is low. This condition is referred to as hypoglycaemia. This is rapidly relieved by an intake of food or sugary drinks.

Light-headedness or faintness can also both be caused by anxiety.

Viral infections such as 'flu may cause fever and tiredness, which are often accompanied by symptoms of dizziness and light-headedness. Anaemia will also cause it, but only if the blood count is very low. Anaemia occurs when the flow of the blood's oxygen-carrying haemoglobin becomes disrupted, often as a result of iron deficiency in the diet. And a heart block, which happens as a result of an insufficient level of electrical activity in the heart muscle, can equally cause an attack of dizziness.

Vertigo

True vertigo usually involves a problem with the three semi-circular canals of the labyrinth of the inner ear, where the organ of balance is located. Inner ear problems are commonly accompanied by nausea, sweating, vomiting or fainting. Some people can also experience problems with the brain stem, the nerve path that connects the lowest part of the brain to the spinal cord and transfers brain messages to and fro.

Old people who suffer from hardening or narrowing of the arteries that supply blood to the brain stem, may experience the sensations of vertigo when they look up or turn their heads too quickly. This happens because the artery that supplies the back of the brain becomes squashed as it travels up the spine, often as a result of arthritis in the neck area of the spinal cord.

Vertigo can be incapacitating, with the sufferer unable to get out of bed or even lift her head. Alcohol is a common cause of vertigo, as are drugs, such as aspirin, that affect the inner ear. In very rare cases, vertigo in a young person may be a sign of a benign tumour in the inner ear nerve, or of a serious condition like multiple sclerosis.

Vertigo can also sometimes be caused by various psychological

Ear Problems

The inner and middle ears are very sensitive to any sort of change or infection.

The inner and middle ears are separated by a thin membrane. Occasionally bacterial ear infections cross this membrane to cause an acute reaction in the balance organ. Such an infection produces severe symptoms, rather like sea-sickness, sometimes with uncontrollable vomiting every time the head is moved. Similar symptoms can sometimes follow a cold. The acute symptoms usually resolve themselves in a day or two, but they may recur, on moving suddenly, for several weeks afterwards.

Ménière's disease and labyrinthitis are the most common causes of inner ear disorders. Both these can cause vertigo, accompanied by fainting and vomiting. Ménière's disease is a degenerative disease of the inner ear that is frequently linked to deafness, abnormal (whistling) noises in the ears, unsteadiness and jerky eye movements. It's quite possible for months or years to go by between attacks, but some people suffer it continually.

In labyrinthitis the fluid-filled inner canals of the ear, which are vital for balance, become inflamed due to viral infection, affecting the way that the sufferer is able to retain their balance.

➤➤ SEE ALSO — Anaemia, Deafness, Ear disorders

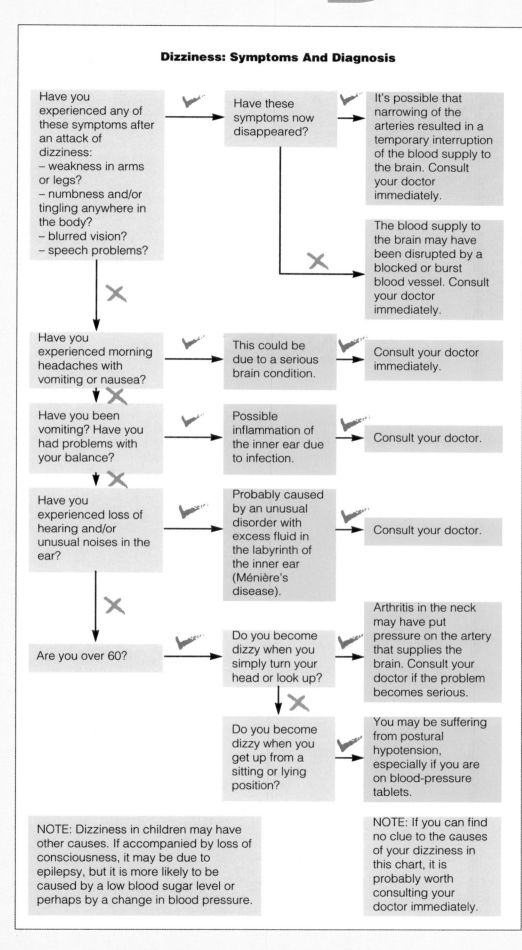

Dizziness: Symptoms And Diagnosis

Have you experienced any of these symptoms after an attack of dizziness:
– weakness in arms or legs?
– numbness and/or tingling anywhere in the body?
– blurred vision?
– speech problems?

Have these symptoms now disappeared?

It's possible that narrowing of the arteries resulted in a temporary interruption of the blood supply to the brain. Consult your doctor immediately.

The blood supply to the brain may have been disrupted by a blocked or burst blood vessel. Consult your doctor immediately.

Have you experienced morning headaches with vomiting or nausea?

This could be due to a serious brain condition.

Consult your doctor immediately.

Have you been vomiting? Have you had problems with your balance?

Possible inflammation of the inner ear due to infection.

Consult your doctor.

Have you experienced loss of hearing and/or unusual noises in the ear?

Probably caused by an unusual disorder with excess fluid in the labyrinth of the inner ear (Ménière's disease).

Consult your doctor.

Are you over 60?

Do you become dizzy when you simply turn your head or look up?

Arthritis in the neck may have put pressure on the artery that supplies the brain. Consult your doctor if the problem becomes serious.

Do you become dizzy when you get up from a sitting or lying position?

You may be suffering from postural hypotension, especially if you are on blood-pressure tablets.

NOTE: Dizziness in children may have other causes. If accompanied by loss of consciousness, it may be due to epilepsy, but it is more likely to be caused by a low blood sugar level or perhaps by a change in blood pressure.

NOTE: If you can find no clue to the causes of your dizziness in this chart, it is probably worth consulting your doctor immediately.

factors, and particularly agoraphobia (the fear of wide-open spaces).

Diagnosis
The doctor's examination of the dizziness sufferer will be intended to distinguish the many trivial causes of dizziness from the few severe ones. She would usually check the temperature, pulse and blood pressure, but the rest of the examination will depend on clues from the patient. A history of diabetes or a late period will prompt the doctor to perform the relevant tests.

True vertigo requires an examination of the ears, the eyes and the nervous system in general. The doctor will look in the ears for signs of infection and may use a tuning fork to distinguish between deafness due to Ménière's disease and due to infection. A brain scan may also be necessary to eliminate the possibility of more serious conditions.

Treatment
Infections will often get better on bed rest, paracetamol and regular fluids, but an obvious ear infection is usually treated with antibiotics. Occasionally, vertigo is severe enough to need treatment in its own right. In these cases the doctor will usually give an injection of a drug called prochloperazine. This can be given in tablet form, when the vertigo is less severe.

Elderly patients with dizzy spells may benefit from a neck support. Ménière's disease is not very easy to treat. Tablets may help the dizziness and masking music may help the whistling, but overall little can actually be done. Occasionally a low salt diet will help. Dizziness due to psychiatric illness may be helped by psychotherapy or antidepressant drugs.

M E D I C A L   F A C T   F I L E

SEE ALSO — Epilepsy, Fainting, Ménière's disease

DOGS AND DISEASES

There are a number of parasitic and infectious diseases that can sometimes be caught from dogs by humans.

Some of these infections and parasites are common to both humans and dogs. But some are more common to dogs and can be transferred to people by the fur being stroked or contaminated faeces being touched. The diseases normally come in the form of living worms, insects and mites, or as viruses, bacteria or fungi. The diseases that can be acquired from dogs are actually quite rare, but can, in some cases, be quite dangerous. Generally, however, the possibility of contracting any dog-related disease must be weighed against the great pleasures and positive benefits that can be gained from owning a fit and healthy dog.

Diseases

The most serious and well-known disease that can be caught from dogs is rabies. Two less well-known diseases are toxocariasis and hydatid disease, which are contracted when worm eggs from dogs are somehow taken into the body. These diseases are both very rare, but can both cause very serious conditions in the sufferer.

Toxocariasis

Toxocariasis is a condition that mainly affects children. The worm that causes it is small and thread-like, and lives in dogs' intestines. Children may become infected with the worm if they come into contact with an infected dog. This infection can occur if they touch the dog's fur, but more usually would result from coming into contact with infected faeces in soil or on the grass

Above: Dogs are sometimes carriers of serious diseases, like toxocariasis, that may be transferred to humans.

in the park. The child has only then to put her hands in her mouth for infection to become a possibility.

Toxocariasis does not usually result in symptoms more serious than pneumonia or seizures. But it can occasionally cause asthma and other allergic reactions to develop, and can even result in loss of vision when the worm larva enters the eye. Dogs should be dewormed regularly, especially if they spend a lot of time around children, and particularly when they and the children are young.

Hydatid disease

Hydatid disease develops from something very similar to the tapeworm larva. It is contracted in the same way as toxocariasis, but is normally only found in places such as New Zealand and Australia where dogs are used to work with sheep. The disease is maintained in a regular cycle of infection between dog and sheep.

Hydatid disease results in the growth of cysts in the liver and lungs, and

generally in the body's muscle fibre. Occasionally a cyst will develop in the brain. The cysts generally develop very slowly and may cause inflammation, lumps and sometimes seizures. In very rare cases a severe allergy

can result from a cyst and may prove to be fatal.

Other problems

Contact with dogs can cause other problems, including hookworms, fleas and allergic reactions. Hookworms, which enter the body as larva, are small blood-sucking worms. They are predominantly a problem in the countries of the developing world, where even just walking around barefoot on dog-faeces-infected ground can result in infection. Hookworm can cause an itchy rash to occur, and can lead to pneumonia and even anaemia through loss of blood.

Mites, ticks and fleas can all be caught from dogs. Fleas can be very annoying, jumping on to humans from dog hair and causing irritating bites. Humans can also develop allergic reactions, like asthma, to the dander (small scales that come from the skin or fur of cats and dogs) that is often found in household dust.

Rabies Infection

Rabies is a viral infection that is usually transferred by an animal bite.

Rabies acts on the central nervous system, causing delirium, throat spasms, paralysis in parts of the body and hydrophobia. Hydrophobia means that the sufferer becomes very thirsty, but is unable to drink due to muscle spasms in the throat. A rabies-infected bite will result in certain death, unless immunisation treatment is given immediately.

Rabies is not a problem in the UK these days, but travellers to the Continent will be familiar with the rabies warning signs that greet them at customs, advising against the illegal importation of animals from across the Channel without quarantine.

Rabies is still a problem in some countries, especially developing countries, and therefore a dog bite sustained whilst abroad should be regarded very seriously, particularly if the dog involved seems to be a stray. Dog bites usually require rapid treatment since, even if rabies is known not to be a possibility, tetanus can always develop. Dog bites can also cause shock and sometimes severe bleeding problems.

>> SEE ALSO — Tetanus

DONOR

A donor is someone who donates their body, or part of it, for the medical benefit of another person.

Donors most commonly give blood for transfusions during operations, or following an accident. Organs such as the kidneys, heart, lungs, liver, pancreas and cornea are also donated for transplantation, to replace organs that have been injured or have stopped working properly. And semen is frequently donated to be stored and potentially used for artificial insemination purposes.

Conditions of donation

Many people now carry donor cards on which is printed the part or parts of their body that they are willing to donate for the treatment of others in the event that they should die unexpectedly. If necessary, permission for donation may also be given by the dead person's next of kin.

In general, donors have to be free of serious infections and viruses, such as HIV, hepatitis or cancer. Organs that are to be used in a donation operation must be in perfect condition. Organs are usually removed for donation within two days of 'brain death' being certified, and frequently much sooner. This is so that the heart has only recently stopped beating or, in cases such as brain death, is still actually beating, meaning that the organ to be donated is still in a very healthy condition. Brain death also often means that the vital organs can be kept 'alive' on special life-support machines.

Suitability

Organs that are to be donated are always tested for their capacity to match the organ that they are replacing. In kidney replacement operations up to 30 per cent of the kidneys donated come from living donors. Often kidneys come from a member of the same family, since they may well possess the same tissue and blood types. (This also occurs in the case of bone marrow transplant). Donating a kidney should not normally have any effect on the donor's life, since the other kidney that is left will grow to compensate for the loss.

DOUBLE VISION

Double vision occurs when a single object is seen not as one single image but as two.

Also known as diplopia, double vision is quite a rare condition. It normally results in the double images seeming to stand side by side, although in vertical diplopia they are aligned on top of one another.

Children

In babies, double vision can occur when the mechanism that governs the eyes' combined alignment has not fully developed. In slightly older children, double vision sometimes occurs if this aligning mechanism breaks down in some way.

And double vision in children can also result from a squint or a 'lazy' eye. In this case these children are not actually seeing double. The apparent double vision is really caused by the brain trying to compensate for the failure of one of the images to fall on the retina properly. It does this by 'turning off' one of the images, causing lack of sharpness of vision. Long-sightedness can also occasionally cause double vision in children: problems in focusing lead to one eye turning inwards (converging). A squint is said to be 'divergent' when one eye turns abnormally outwards.

Adults

In later life, double vision can occur as a result of damage or paralysis to one of the muscles that control the movement of the eye in a particular direction. This sort of double vision can sometimes be helped, if not cured, by tilting or turning the head to one side.

This paralysis and restriction of movement may be caused by a stoke or a tumour that is pressing upon the nerve that controls the eye muscle. A tumour in the

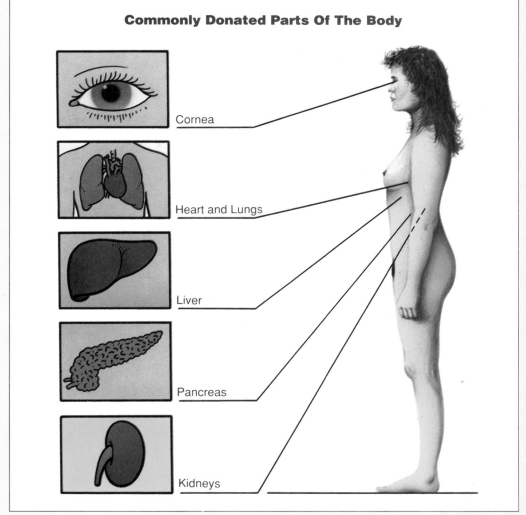

Commonly Donated Parts Of The Body

Cornea

Heart and Lungs

Liver

Pancreas

Kidneys

>> SEE ALSO — Artificial insemination, Blood

eyelid may also cause double vision by pressing on the eyeball and causing the light-rays that enter the eye to be misdirected, in turn distorting the normal alignment of the two received images.

An overactive thyroid can cause double vision. The hormonal imbalance causes a build-up of fat behind the eye and weakness and swelling of the eye muscles, which makes it difficult to move the eyes together and causes abnormal alignment. A similar problem may also occur if there has been damage to the floor of the eye socket, perhaps as a result of a blow to the cheek, where swelling causes one of the eyes to be pushed out of alignment.

In adults, double vision can also occasionally result from psychological problems, and from abnormal quantities of drugs or alcohol. Double vision, even if it is only a momentary problem, can sometimes be a sign of a much more serious condition, such as *diabetes mellitus* or multiple sclerosis. Therefore, it is always worth consulting the doctor if you have a problem with double vision.

DOWN'S SYNDROME

Down's syndrome is a chromosomal abnormality that results in mental and physical handicap.

Down's syndrome is a congenital condition (present at birth), that used to be called Mongolism, because it was thought that the condition produced facial features similar to those of Mongolians. The term Mongolism is no longer used in medicine. Down's syndrome affects about one

in 650 births, but it was not until 1959 that scientists discovered its actual cause.

Down's syndrome is due to a fault in the chromosome content of the body's cells. Normally, every cell in the body contains 46 chromosomes, which carry the body's genetic information. In Down's syndrome the cell content is 47 chromosomes.

In 95 per cent of cases, this abnormality is a new problem that occurs in the formation of an individual sperm or egg, and is therefore very unlikely to affect the same family twice. The chances of having an affected child increase with the mother's, but not the father's, age. The risk at the age of 35 is about one in 150, but potentially as high as one in 40 at the age of 45.

Diagnosis
Down's syndrome is usually diagnosed at birth — the doctor will base the diagnosis on physical characteristics, but may need a chromosome analysis of the baby's blood to be certain. Down's syndrome babies usually have round heads that are flat at the back, with characteristically

slanted eyes that turn upwards at the outer corners.

Often a Down's syndrome child will only have a single crease that crosses the palm, rather than the normal two. In some cases the little finger will be curled abnormally inwards. The most striking feature to the experienced doctor or midwife is that the baby is very floppy and the joints have an exaggerated range of movement.

Characteristics
Children affected with Down's syndrome are mentally retarded, usually in the IQ range of 30-50. Some

Left: Down's syndrome produces small facial features, with eyes that slope upwards at the outer corners.

Below: Down's syndrome sufferers are also characterised by their hands – they have little fingers that curve slightly inwards, and an unusual crease across the top of the palm.

children have IQs of 70 or more, however, and may even hold down jobs in later life. Almost all of those affected are happy, friendly children, and often show an unusual enjoyment of music.

Heart defects are common in Down's syndrome, as are chest and gut problems. This, coupled with the accelerated ageing process that affects them, means that the life expectancy of Down's

Life Improvement

There is no cure for Down's syndrome, but much can be done to help those who are affected with the condition.

All Down's syndrome children can learn certain things, even if they never learn to read or write. And they can be taught how to care for themselves and how to shop. Despite their handicaps, children and adults with Down's syndrome seem to experience far happier, more contented lives than 'normal' adults. Local authorities should be able to equip the home with aids, such as handrails for toilets, that can make daily living easier.

▶▶ SEE ALSO — Chromosomes, Diabetes, Genes, Multiple sclerosis

syndrome babies is reduced, though many do actually live to middle age or even beyond.

Pre-natal care

In most parts of the UK the standard practice is to offer those at high risk of having an affected child the chance of ante-natal screening. This is done by amniocentesis at 16 weeks. Amniocentesis involves the removal of a small amount of fluid from the sac that surrounds the foetus to check for abnormalities in the foetus.

However, the risks of miscarriage and the expense involved means that, as a rule, the test is only offered to women above a certain age (usually 35 – 37), or who have had an affected child in the past.

In an ideal world screening would be cheap and accurate, and backed up by adequate therapy, giving all couples the right to choose whether to continue an affected pregnancy or not. Such a test is not yet available, but a new blood test, the 'triple screen', solves some of the problems. This test measures the three factors in the mother's blood and gives an idea of who may be at risk. They can then be offered the amniocentesis for a firm diagnosis. By the mid-1990s it is hoped that the test will be widespread, but even now it may be worth discussing it properly with your obstetrician.

Development

Down's syndrome children will develop and learn new skills throughout their life, but their development is slower than that of the average child and consequently their behavioural age is younger than their physical age.

DPT VACCINATION

DPT are the initial letters of diphtheria, pertussis (whooping cough) and tetanus.

Babies are protected from these diseases by vaccination. The DPT vaccine (also known as the triple vaccine) results in the body producing antibodies that protect the individual against the infections of diphtheria, whooping cough and tetanus. The vaccine is administered in injection form in early childhood. It is given at about eight weeks of age, with two further doses at monthly intervals. There is no need to give whooping cough boosters, but diphtheria and tetanus are reinforced at age four.

The reinforcement booster given to children normally lasts a very long time. But people who are intending to travel to countries, especially in the Third World, that are known to house the conditions of diphtheria, whooping cough or tetanus, are well advised to check their immunisation position with the doctor before travelling.

Whooping cough

Whooping cough is caused by a form of bacteria that results in a severe cough, spasms and vomiting. In small children it may lead, in rare cases, to their breathing stopping as a result of such a spasm. It can also cause dehydration and general breathing difficulties.

Routine immunisation began in the 1950s, so that the number of cases of whooping cough fell from 150,000 a year to just 2400 in 1973. However, during the mid-1970s and the early 1980s there was a scare over the safety of the vaccine, and more and more cases occurred as fewer and fewer children were

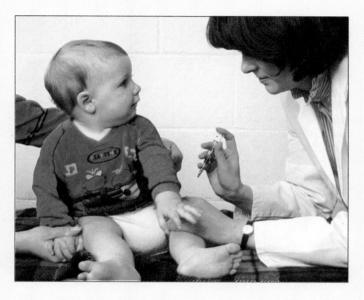

Above: Babies are immunised, when only a few months old, to guard against the danger of DPT infection.

immunised. Several hundred children actually died from the whooping cough epidemic that followed this period of parents refusing to have their children immunised. Thankfully, modern treatment of whooping cough means that few children actually die of the disease, but it is still a source of grave concern.

Diphtheria

Diphtheria is an extremely serious and infectious bacterial infection of the nose and throat areas, that leads to toxin (poison) being released into the blood.

Diphtheria is so highly infectious that it can be transferred quite simply by someone sneezing or coughing. Before the Second World War, it was one of the most common causes of childhood death in the world. In 1940, before immunisation was actually introduced, 46,281 cases were reported in the UK, and 2480 children died. In the last 10 years, only 31 cases have been reported and only one child has died.

Immunisation Worries

Despite the obvious advantages of immunisation many parents still worry about whether they should have their child immunised or not.

Most of the concerns about DPT immunisation are over the whooping cough part of the vaccine. There is no doubt that brain damage has occurred in certain cases after this particular vaccine has been used, but equally it is recognised that brain damage can occur at the same rate in the unvaccinated child. Indeed, brain damage is sometimes a result of whooping cough itself.

Whooping cough vaccine should not be given to a child with a fever, nor should it be given to a child who has had a serious reaction to a previous dose. Many children with epilepsy or brain damage can be immunised, but most doctors would seek specialist advice before proceeding with such treatment. Immunisation often causes a mild fever, but this can be treated with paracetamol.

➤➤ SEE ALSO — Amniocentesis, Diphtheria, Tetanus, Whooping cough

MEDICAL FACT FILE

Tetanus

Tetanus or 'lockjaw' is a bacterial infection that causes muscle spasms and death. The bacteria normally live in the soil but they may grow in dirty wounds. Routine immunisation means that a disease that used to kill thousands of people every year has been virtually eliminated in the countries of the western world.

However, tetanus immunisation does not last forever, so it needs to be boosted with another injection every 10 years, especially in cases where travel is involved to affected countries. Deep or unusually dirty wounds also need a tetanus injection to guard against possible infection. This is especially the case when the wound or cut has been inflicted by an animal.

Types Of Drowning

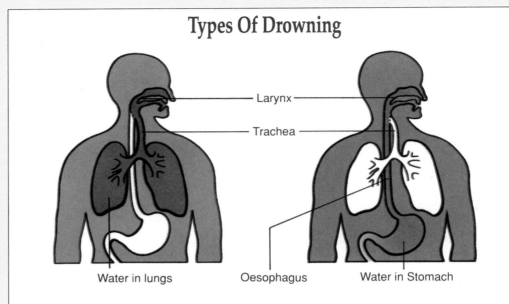

Larynx — Trachea — Oesophagus

Water in lungs — Water in Stomach

Wet drowning: This form of drowning occurs when water enters the lungs. This happens in approximately 80 per cent of all drowning accidents.

Dry drowning: Suffocation occurs in this case when liquid enters the stomach, rather than the lungs. This is less common, but equally dangerous.

DROWNING

Drowning is death caused by lack of oxygen, due to fluid in the lungs or stomach.

Approximately 80 per cent of drowning cases are caused by fluid entering the lungs and are said to be 'wet' drownings. The other 20 per cent are referred to as 'dry' drownings. In these cases water enters the stomach, rather than the lungs. Both types of drowning involve the fluid impairing normal breathing, which in turn leads to suffocation, and to the end of life if the lack of oxygen is great enough.

Causes

Unlikely as it may seem, a large number of drowning victims are actually competent swimmers, who have run into difficulties while swimming, often due to their underestimating the actual swimming conditions. Swimmers can easily get into difficulty in the sea or in rivers as a result of unseen currents, strong waves or tidal movements. Fatigue and panic can follow on from this, leading to an inability to swim properly and safely, resulting in drowning.

Drowning can obviously occur in non-swimmers, but it happens more due to accidents around water, than due to direct swimming problems. Drownings can be caused by floods, ships sinking, and plunging into very cold water (especially after falling through ice). Infants can drown in shallow levels of water, such as when they are having a bath, and therefore they need close supervision when they are around water.

Alcohol is closely linked with many drowning cases. Alcohol can affect physical coordination and interferes with judgment, and if this is combined with swimming it can end in tragic results.

Drowning Mechanism

Once someone in water becomes tired or starts to panic they become incapable of keeping afloat properly and the body will then start to take in water, leading possibly to death.

To begin with, a reflex reaction of the throat muscles causes the water to be redirected into the oesophagus and stomach, rather than the lungs. But this in itself can result in breathing difficulties and subsequent suffocation, in which case it is known as 'dry' drowning.

In most cases water does, in fact, ultimately enter the lungs, which automatically impairs breathing and may cause damage to the lining of the lungs. Water may pass from the lungs into the blood, causing further problems.

Treatment Of Drowning

Someone who is on the point of drowning can be helped, and even saved, if some calm steps are taken.

The person drowning in open water should be thrown something to help them keep afloat, and they should be encouraged to keep as calm as possible. Panic can only make the situation worse and can even lead to the rescuer being drowned.

The victim's head should be kept above the water level and they should be taken to dry land, so that their exact condition can be properly assessed. Artificial respiration may then be necessary to get the victim breathing normally again. Whatever happens, hospital care is always necessary after a near-drowning incident.

➤➤ SEE ALSO — Artificial respiration

DRUG ABUSE

Drug abuse is the use of drugs for reasons other than those for which they were medically created.

Such abuse can be carried out for varying reasons, from the desire to escape everyday reality to the attempt to extend the body's physical capabilities.

It may lead to drug dependence, and even drug poisoning. Abuse-related drugs include amphetamines (speed), LSD (acid), and narcotics such as heroin and cocaine. Recently, anabolic steroids have made big news as top athletes attempt to push themselves to unnatural physical limits.

Above: A man smoking the highly addictive drug 'crack'. This drug is made from cocaine and is taken as a vapour.

Signs of Drug Abuse

- Drastic weight loss or gain.
- Problems with concentration, and reduced attention span.
- Erratic sleeping and eating habits.
- Victim becomes verbally abusive and physically violent.
- Loss of motivation and self-esteem.
- Victim steals, cheats and becomes deceitful.

DRUG DEPENDENCE

Drug dependence is a condition that makes the sufferer want to carry on taking a drug.

This dependent condition may result from someone's desire to continue to experience the effects that a certain drug normally has upon them, or from an inability to cope with life when the drug is removed. Drug dependence can be both physical and psychological.

Psychological drug dependence results in a great craving for the drug concerned, whereas physical dependence produces physical symptoms, which are often part of 'withdrawal syndrome', when the drug is taken away from them.

Drug dependence can result in serious problems and even death. Lung and liver problems, for example, can be a direct result of dependence on tobacco and alcohol. And indirectly, dependence on narcotic drugs like heroin, for example, can sometimes lead to hepatitis or HIV infection — normally through infected needles used in the intravenous administration of these drugs.

Causes

The number of people addicted to, and dependent upon, drugs such as nicotine, alcohol and caffeine is surprisingly high. Dependence on caffeine, especially, goes unnoticed by many, until they are forced to go without it, even for just a short time.

The most serious sort of dependence is caused by drugs which produce significant physical and mental changes in the sufferer. The rapid effect that intravenous drugs — like heroin — have on the taker means that the dependence is simply reinforced, every time the drug is taken.

Symptoms

Mild physical symptoms can include a runny nose, sneezing and sweating. More serious symptoms might reveal themselves as vomiting, diarrhoea, trembling and even coma. Such symptoms are part of withdrawal syndrome. This is caused by the body becoming steadily accustomed to a certain drug, which disrupts the body's chemical balance. For example, nicotine has an effect on the body's natural production of adrenaline. Subsequent withdrawal of that drug will only confuse the body even more. This confusion is revealed in the form of physical symptoms.

DRUG POISONING

Drug poisoning is poisoning that can affect various parts of the body following a drug overdose.

Drug overdoses account for about five per cent of all emergency admissions to hospital. The overdose may be accidental or deliberate.

Occasionally drug poisoning can follow someone's 'idiosyncratic reaction' to a normally harmless drug, which they happen to be allergic to in some way.

Drug overdose

Accidental poisoning as a result of an overdose is most common in children under the age of five, who are attracted to the colours of tablets and pills and swallow them like sweets. Recently, such a problem of overdose has been reduced, as a result of the childproof medical containers that have been widely introduced.

Accidental overdose also occurs in the elderly, or in confused people, who are not sure about the exact quantity of a drug that they are supposed to be taking. Elderly people are often unsure of whether they have taken their last dosage of the day, and end up taking an extra one 'to be on the safe side'. Drug abuse may also result in drug poisoning.

Deliberate self-poisoning is becoming more and more common. Rarely do those involved actually want to die, but rather they want to draw attention to

⮞⮞ SEE ALSO — Adrenaline, Alcoholism, Hepatitis, HIV

MEDICAL FACT FILE

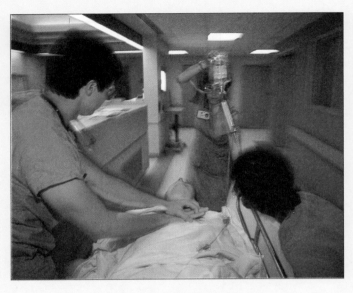

Above: A medical team rush a patient to emergency care on a stretcher. Drug overdoses account for about five per cent of all emergency admissions to hospitals in the UK.

themselves, as if crying for help, or even to punish someone else. Deliberate self-poisoning is rarely successful, although there is a tragically fine line that separates a 'safe' overdose from a fatal one.

Diagnosis
Most patients who take overdoses are still conscious when they see a doctor and can give quite an accurate account of what sort of drug they have taken, which is the vital information needed for the right treatment to be given by the doctor.

If the patient is unconscious the doctor must rely on the accounts from the emergency services to learn what the victim might have taken. On the whole, there is very little effective first-aid for drug overdoses, although it is essential that anyone found unconscious should have their airway cleared and artificial respiration should be given if necessary. Drinking milk may initially help a patient who has become poisoned with a corrosive substance.

Treatment
Hospital treatment normally begins with a stomach washout. In order to remove as many tablets or poisonous elements as possible, a tube is passed down into the stomach and jugs of water poured in, which helps to flush the system clean.

Depending on the drug taken, there may be an antidote that can be used. In general, the aim is to keep the patient alive until the liver and kidneys can remove the poison. This often involves the use of advanced, artificial life support techniques, along with kidney dialysis and artificial ventilators.

Most hospitals have a rule that all overdose patients are seen by a member of the hospital psychiatric team.

DUODENITIS

Duodenitis is an inflammation of the duodenum. Its exact cause remains uncertain, but it is thought to be due to a bacterial infection.

The duodenum is the first part of the small intestine, where digestive enzymes from the liver, pancreas and gallbladder help to break down food.

Duodenitis produces inflammation and sometimes considerable pain, as well as redness and swelling in the lining of the duodenum. Bleeding may also occur. Duodenitis is normally diagnosed by means of a gastroscopy. A gastroscopy involves the use of an endoscope (a flexible viewing instrument), which is inserted in the mouth and passed through the stomach and into the duodenum.

DYSENTERY

Dysentery is a form of severe intestinal infection, usually resulting in abdominal pain and diarrhoea.

Dysentery can be caused either by bacterial or by parasitic infection. It is a common problem in Third World countries, especially in areas where hygiene standards are low, and it causes many deaths amongst children and babies. Cases of dysentery do also crop up in places like the UK — in institutions, such as hospitals and children's homes.

Bacillary dysentery
Also known as shigellosis, bacillary dysentery is caused by infection with the shigella bacteria. This form of dysentery is passed on via human faeces, and therefore is frequently due to dirty hands infecting food.

The effects of bacillary dysentery are sudden, producing watery diarrhoea, vomiting, nausea, abdominal pain and fever. The diarrhoea will become more regular and persistent after a few days, and may contain blood and pus. Bacterial toxins (poisons) may enter the bloodstream, leading to high fever and delirium.

Amoebic dysentery
Amoebic dysentery is caused by an amoebic parasite, which is found in

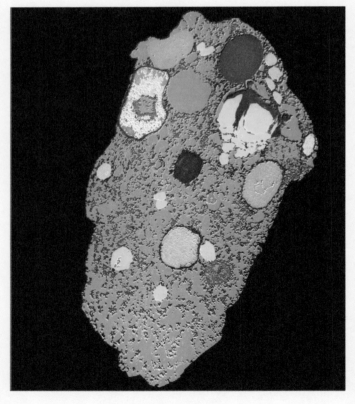

Above: A specially coloured and magnified image of the amoebic parasite that causes amoebic dysentery.

▶▶ SEE ALSO — Dialysis, Diarrhoea, Endoscopy

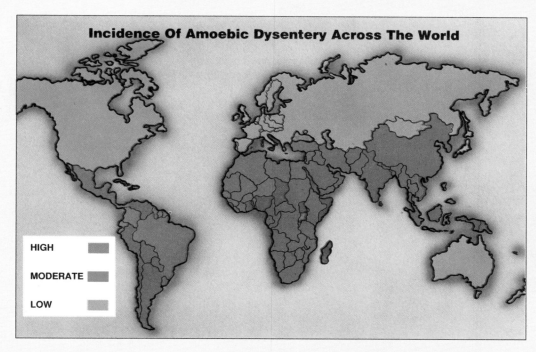

Incidence Of Amoebic Dysentery Across The World

HIGH

MODERATE

LOW

Above: Amoebic dysentery is caused by an amoebic parasite that is found in contaminated water and food, particularly in parts of the world where general food hygiene is not of a very high standard. It can cause problems of severe diarrhoea, dehydration and even high fever.

cyst form in contaminated water and food. The cyst enters the intestines where the amoeba hatches out, passing from person to person via the faeces.

Amoebic dysentery produces more gradual symptoms than the bacillary form, but can often persist for far longer. It may cause only mild symptoms in some people, while in others it produces severe symptoms of high fever and diarrhoea. The diarrhoea can also often contain blood and mucus. In extreme cases, amoebic dysentery may lead to the formation of liver abscesses.

Treatment

Both forms of dysentery result in dehydration, and therefore large quantities of fresh, clean water should be administered to keep up the body's fluid levels. Bacillary dysentery may be treated with antibiotic drugs, whereas the amoebic form is treated with drugs that act upon, and aim to eliminate, the parasite.

DYSLEXIA

Dyslexia is the term used to describe a group of disorders that all cause great difficulty in learning to read and write.

Dyslexia usually becomes apparent at infant school, where the sufferer may occasionally be referred to as backward or lazy. However, IQ tests show that dyslexic children are of normal intelligence. But, such an unfair stigma can cause problems of its own, in that some children and adults can become almost neurotic in their efforts to hide their dyslexic disability.

Cause

The controversy over the cause of dyslexia may soon be over. Painstaking post mortem examinations and brain scans of sufferers show that an abnormality of the brain's structure may be the root cause.

Incidence

Dyslexia has been recognised as a problem for over 100 years. Indeed, a survey conducted as long ago as 1905 declared that one in 2000 London school children were affected with the condition. The true figure these days is probably much higher than this. Dyslexia tends to run in families and often more than one generation are affected. About 90 per cent of dyslexia sufferers are male.

There seem to be two distinct groups of dyslexics. One group is able to make sense of visual, rather than spoken, images. The other group seems unable to break the spoken word into syllables, or the written word into letters and their corresponding sounds. This means that the spoken word is spelt incorrectly and the written word mispronounced.

Treatment

Treatment of dyslexia is based on recognition of the problem. The child affected is taught to associate syllables with specific mouth movements. Phonetic spelling, with the emphasis on the sound of a letter,

rather that its name, is important. The emphasis should always be placed on reading for fun.

Allowances are usually made by education authorities for dyslexia sufferers in exam situations, and many sufferers hold down high-powered jobs.

Famous Dyslexics

- Albert Einstein
- Woodrow Wilson
- Leonardo da Vinci
- Hans Christian Andersen
- Auguste Rodin

DYSMENORRHOEA

Dysmenorrhoea is the medical term for painful menstruation.

Many women suffer from dysmenorrhoea. In five per cent of these cases it is bad enough for them to seek help from their doctor, and in about two per cent of women the pain is bad enough for them to have to take time off work.

Different types

Gynaecologists usually talk about primary and secondary dysmenorrhoea. The primary variety is more common and generally starts soon after puberty. Secondary dysmenorrhoea can occur after years of painless periods.

The discomfort of dysmenorrhoea is usually characterised by pain in the lower abdomen, rather like cramp, which rarely lasts for more than a day. The pain may sometimes also be felt in the back or down the thighs. And in some cases it may even be accompanied by vomiting and fainting.

Causes

There are several theories as to the main causes of dysmenorrhoea, none of

SEE ALSO — Dehydration

which has been completely proved. Hormonal changes which occur during menstruation certainly play a major part in the onset of dysmenorrhoea. It is also thought that dysmenorrhoea is linked to a level of prostaglandins that is abnormally high. These prostaglandins are substances that are similar to hormones and stimulate muscle spasms in the uterus. Psychological factors can also play a part in the condition. A girl who is afraid of her periods is far more likely to suffer pain than her friend who is relaxed and calmly prepared for it.

Treatment

Education and stress placed on the normality of menstruation are the most important primary aids to relieving dysmenorrhoea. Thereafter simple pain killers, such as paracetamol, or anti-inflammatory drugs, may help relieve the discomfort. In more severe cases, ovulation can be suppressed using the contraceptive Pill. Childbirth can also ease the problem. In about a quarter of cases of dysmenorrhoea, a D and C (Dilation and Curettage) operation helps to cure the problem.

DYSPAREUNIA

Dyspareunia is the medical term for painful sexual intercourse.

Dyspareunia is usually considered to be either primary or secondary. Primary dyspareunia is the term used if sexual intercourse has always been a painful experience. If pain develops after years of a painfree sex life, it is said to be secondary dyspareunia.

The two forms of dyspareunia may be due to physical or psychological factors, but most cases of

primary dyspareunia have a psychological basis.

Psychological factors

The couple will often complain of difficulty with penetration, even though both partners are willing. The woman may say something like 'I'm sure I'm too small', or 'his penis is much too big for me'. These psychological fears mean that physical symptoms occur, so that, for example, the woman's pelvic muscles may well go into spasm, often completely blocking the vagina.

Secondary dyspareunia may sometimes be caused by fear of pregnancy or by changing emotions within a couple's relationship.

Physical factors

Primary dyspareunia is occasionally caused by an extra thick remnant of hymen. But more commonly it results from inadequate or unskilled sexual stimulation, which leaves the cervix and the vagina very dry. Such dryness makes for painful intercourse and may even make it impossible. Simple lubricants such as KY jelly will help, but mutual understanding and advice to the partner can often be the most rewarding medication for both partners.

If dyspareunia occurs after previously painfree intercourse it is very likely to have a physical cause, though this may be made worse by psychological factors. Endometriosis can also cause dyspareunia. This involves fragments of the uterine lining becoming lodged elsewhere in the pelvic cavity (such as the vagina, the ovaries or the cervix). The exact cause of endometriosis is unknown.

Superficial pain

Dyspareunia may cause pain at either the opening of the vagina or deeper inside the pelvis. Pain at the opening, 'superficial pain', is more

common. The commonest causes of this sort of pain are pelvic infections or, in older women, thinning of the vaginal walls.

Infections, such as thrush, may not be obvious and can easily be missed if a swab test is not performed to find the source of the infection. And an infection in a Bartholins gland, which usually helps to secrete moisturising fluid in the vagina, can cause an acute abscess or a generalised swelling and soreness. Both these types of infection can cause painful intercourse and both require antibiotics, though the abscess may need surgery as well.

After the menopause the walls of the vagina become thinner and the production of the normal vaginal secretions slows down. This can be eased by lubricants and a greater emphasis on foreplay and sexual stimulation. Hormone replacement therapy, in the form of tablets, patches or local creams, will help remedy the problem of vaginal secretion.

Episiotomy scars may also cause pain, but surgery to help the problem can often be avoided if the lubrication involved is adequate.

Deep pain

Deeper pain may be due to psychological causes, but usually is more likely to be due to infections, damage to an ovary or endometriosis.

Uterine Problems

The uterus normally tips slightly forward. If it does not, pain can result.

Pain is most likely to occur if the uterus tips backwards, especially if it drags the ovaries down with it. This causes pain in sexual intercourse due to compression during thrusting. The pain involved is often described as 'sickening', and usually only occurs in certain sexual positions. Advice about sexual positions can normally solve the problem, though occasionally a gynaecologist will decide to do an operation to put everything back in its correct natural position.

Pelvic inflammatory disease, due to chlamydia or gonorrhoea, will cause a deep ache that may last for several hours after intercourse. The infection irritates the womb, the fallopian tubes and the ovaries. The physical activity of intercourse inflames these organs causing pain. Treatment consists of identifying the cause of the infection and prescribing appropriate antibiotics.

In very severe and persistent cases pelvic clearance, which involves the removal of the uterus, the fallopian tubes and the ovaries, may prove to be a last-resort treatment.

Dyspareunia In Men

Dyspareunia in men is relatively rare.

Impotence or premature ejaculation are the usual signs of psychological problems, whereas pain is usually due to a physical cause. Infections of the foreskin (balanitis), testes urethra, or epididymis may all cause pain. All of these are treated with antibiotic drugs. In rare cases a hernia may cause pain during sexual intercourse.

>> SEE ALSO — Chlamydial infections, D and C, Endometriosis, HRT

DYSTROPHY

Dystrophy refers to a number of disorders, normally inherited, in which wastage of tissues occurs.

This wastage results from a disruption of the normal action and structure of the cells within the tissues involved. Nutritional inadequacies are the usual cause of such abnormalities, frequently as a result of insufficient blood supply to the tissues. But it can also occur as a result of nerve damage, and also sometimes as a result of an insufficiency of certain enzymes in the tissues.

Different dystrophies

The most well-known sort of dystrophy is muscular dystrophy, in which muscle cells fail to develop properly. This results in weakness and paralysis, as the muscle fibres gradually deteriorate and waste away.

In leukodystrophy, the sheath that surrounds the nerves in the brain wastes away, which can result in disturbances of physical movement and coordination, problems with thinking and mental agility, and general sensory problems.

A much rarer, usually inherited, form of dystrophy is corneal dystrophy in which the cells inside the cornea are damaged, causing sight to be impaired. Especially bad damage may even result in blindness.

EAR DISORDERS

There are various disorders that can affect the ear, and can cause pain, loss of balance and can sometimes even lead to deafness.

The most common disorder of the ear is earache, which affects

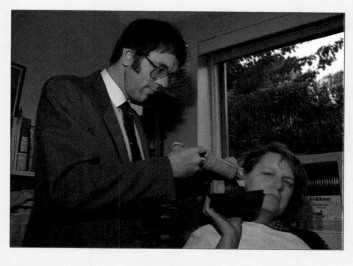

Above: A doctor is syringing a patient's ear to remove wax from the outer ear canal. A build-up of wax can sometimes cause temporary deafness. Pain can also result, especially when the sufferer attempts to remove the wax herself.

children more than adults. The term earache covers a wide range of different problems. The pain from earache can be due to problems in the outer ear, the middle ear or the surrounding tissues, such as the teeth or gums.

Outer ear

The outer ear, the canal between the outside and the eardrum, is a common site of ear infection. The problem is often due to simple boils that thrive in the warm, moist atmosphere of the ear. The boil has no way of expanding and the pressure that results can cause excruciating pain.

Treatment with painkillers will usually help to alleviate this problem, as will a hot water bottle held against the ear. Lancing the boil can be a difficult operation to carry out, but will give immediate relief to the sufferer. Antibiotics are often prescribed, but they are not actually of any great use or relief.

Otitis externa

Another problem of the outer ear is a generalised inflammation known as otitis externa. This is an acute or chronic condition with a

variety of causes. The original problem may be a form of eczema, but the cracked skin rapidly becomes infected with a mixture of bacteria and fungi.

Otitis externa is more common in hot climates and in people who swim a lot. Treatment with drops from the doctor is usually effective, but the sufferer must avoid swimming and should not poke things, such as cotton buds, into the ear.

Wax can cause pain, although the main problem is not usually the wax itself. The main problem is caused by clumsy attempts to remove the wax, often with cotton buds. The safest way to remove troublesome wax is with bicarbonate drops, supplemented, if necessary, by syringing.

Middle ear infection

Middle ear infection is a common cause of earache, especially in children. The main feature of middle ear infection is pain. It usually follows a cold, and the child often seems to be over the worst of it before being noticeably affected. Infection usually works its way up the tube that connects the middle ear to the back of the throat. Overenthusiastic nose blowing may hasten the process — children who are prone to middle ear problems should be encouraged to wipe, rather than blow, their noses.

The doctor is usually able to see the eardrum using a special torch with a built-in viewing lens. The eardrum, which is usually white and shiny, becomes red and dull when infected. If left untreated, the eardrum may burst allowing blood and pus to flow out of the ear. Alarming as this may sound, it rarely causes long-term problems and does actually provide immediate pain relief. Antibiotics and pain killers solve the problem in most cases. And a hot water bottle, wrapped up in a towel and pressed against the ear, can be very soothing and pain-relieving.

A middle ear infection may become a chronic 'glue ear' condition, if it goes untreated. 'Glue ear' causes temporary deafness, but it is not usually too painful. If nose drops fail to clear up the condition, a grommet

Children And Swimming

The question of whether children with ear problems should go swimming or not is nearly always a difficult one for parents.

When swimming, water only very rarely gets into the ear as far as the eardrum. Providing that they do not dive, children with grommets should be able to go swimming as usual. However, a child with an acute infection should stay out of the water, though it is unlikely they will feel much like entering the water in any case.

▶▶ SEE ALSO — Deafness, Muscular dystrophy

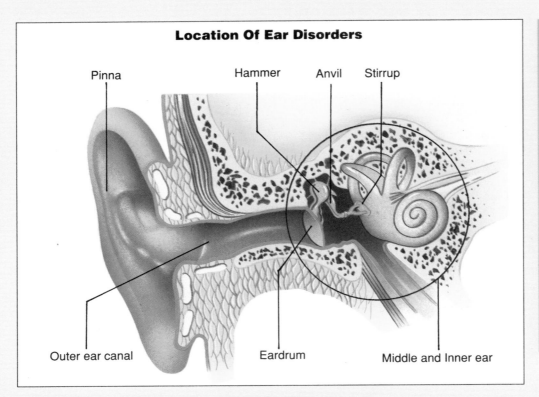

Location Of Ear Disorders

Pinna

Hammer   Anvil   Stirrup

Outer ear canal

Eardrum

Middle and Inner ear

Above: The outer ear canal is a common site for infections. Infections and other problems may also affect the middle and inner ears, sometimes resulting in deafness and loss of balance.

operation may be needed. This involves little plastic tubes called grommets being pushed through the eardrums to allow the fluid to be drained off safely.

Pressure problems

Flying in aeroplanes is quite a common cause of ear problems and of earache in particular. This problem is usually worse on landing. As the aeroplane descends, the air pressure in the cabin rises. Air passes up the tube from the back of the throat to the ear, to keep the pressure on the eardrum maintained at a constant level.

Beyond a certain pressure difference, the tube will not function properly. This, in turn, causes severe pain and temporary deafness, as the eardrum is unable to function in its normal way. A similar problem sometimes arises with swimming or diving to great depths.

Sucking hard on a boiled sweet, chewing gum or blowing the cheeks out hard may well help alleviate this problem, which is often made worse by a cold or hay fever. In such circumstances decongestant nose drops should be used an hour or two before the flight.

Referred pain

Not all earache is caused by direct problems in the ear. Pain can often be caused by problems outside the ear. 'Referred pain', or pain that is felt a long way from the source of the problem, is quite common in the ear. Earache may be due to sinusitis, gingivitis, toothache, infections of the salivary glands, arthritis of the jaw, shingles or even a heart attack.

Fortunately, examining the ear is a relatively simple procedure, so that the doctor should be able to make a relatively fast diagnosis.

Congenital Problems

Babies are occasionally born with problems that affect their ear mechanisms.

Congenital problems often result in the very structures of the ear being malformed or underdeveloped. The external ear canal, for example, may sometimes have failed to widen and grow properly to allow for the hearing mechanisms to function normally.

Similarly, the bones of the middle ear (the hammer, the anvil and the stirrup) that conduct sound waves can also fail to develop sufficiently to function as they ought to do. And in a few rare cases a mother's infection with German measles (Rubella) during the first three months of pregnancy can result in underdevelopment of her growing baby's ear structures.

Ear Tumours

Ear tumours are very rare, but when they do occur they can affect the ear and the hearing mechanism.

Cancerous tumours can sometimes affect the pinna (outer, visible part of the ear), and the ear canal. Only in extremely rare cases do tumours develop in the inner parts of the ear. Tumours can also develop on and around the acoustic nerve, pressing on the inner ear structures. This can result in tinnitus, lack of balance and deafness.

ECG

ECG is an abbreviation for electrocardiogram, a special device that is used to measure and monitor the heart's electrical activity.

The heart muscle's regular contractions are controlled and preceded by electrical impulses that spread through the muscle, and that can be detected by an ECG. The ECG techniques are extremely sophisticated and sensitive, and are normally used to help diagnose heart disorders, such as heart failure, coronary artery disease, coronary thrombosis and inflammation of the heart muscle.

Method

An ECG involves small electrodes being attached to the skin of the patient. This process takes place in two stages. First of all, the electrodes are connected to the wrists and ankles. The conduction is aided at this point by the application of special conductive jelly. These electrodes are

➤➤ SEE ALSO — Gingivitis, Rubella, Sinusitis, Tumours

MEDICAL FACT FILE

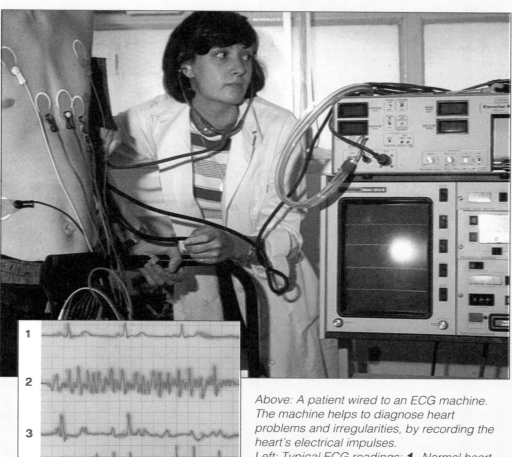

tube may stop the egg from passing into the uterus, as may damage to the tube itself. Infection and surgery are the most common ways in which the fallopian tubes can become damaged. Whatever the cause, ectopic pregnancy can mean that the embryo eventually grows too big for the tube that has been forced to contain it, causing it to burst in some cases. This is often accompanied by profuse blood loss and can be fatal.

Infection
Infections of the fallopian tubes, such as chlamydia or gonorrhoea, may damage the normal, healthy lining of the tubes. This damage may mean that the hair cells that move the egg along the tube do not work properly. As a result the fertilised egg may be big enough to become embedded in the tube before it has a chance to reach the womb.

Contraceptive problems
Similar problems to those associated with fallopian

Above: A patient wired to an ECG machine. The machine helps to diagnose heart problems and irregularities, by recording the heart's electrical impulses.
Left: Typical ECG readings: **1.** *Normal heart-beat;* **2.** *Irregularity in lower chambers of the heart;* **3.** *Complete heart block;* **4.** *Irregularity in upper chambers of the heart.*

removed and electrodes are then connected to the patient's chest. These electrodes detect the heart's electrical impulses, which are amplified and recorded. The impulses are then traced out as electrical patterns on a special printing machine. The procedure can be carried out in hospital or in the home, with lightweight, portable ECG machines.

Heart disorders usually produce electrical deviations that differ from the normal electrical activity of a healthy heart. These deviations are picked up as characteristic patterns on the print-out from the ECG machine. Even a very minor heart attack will show up as a noticeable pattern when tested on an ECG machine.

ECTOPIC PREGNANCY

An ectopic pregnancy is a pregnancy that develops not in the uterus, but elsewhere in the pelvis.

In a normal pregnancy, the fertilisation of the egg takes place in the fallopian tubes, from where it passes into the uterus. In rare cases, an ectopic pregnancy can also occur in the ovary itself, the cervix or the abdominal cavity, as well as in the fallopian tubes.

Causes
There is no single known cause of an ectopic pregnancy, although it has been found to occur in approximately one in 500 pregnancies. A congenital abnormality in the fallopian

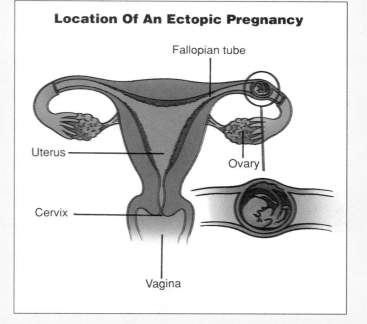

Location Of An Ectopic Pregnancy

Fallopian tube

Uterus

Ovary

Cervix

Vagina

Above: An ectopic pregnancy is a pregnancy that has developed not in the uterus, as it usually does, but elsewhere in the pelvis (for example, in the cervix, the ovary itself, or most commonly in the fallopian tubes). The cause of the condition is not fully known.

➤➤ SEE ALSO — Coronary heart disease, Pregnancy, Sexually transmitted diseases tube infection also sometimes seem to arise from irregularities following the use of certain methods of contraception. Ectopic pregnancy has been connected with the use of an IUD (intra-uterine contraceptive device) and the sort of oral contraceptive Pill that only contains the hormone progesterone.

Symptoms

The symptoms of ectopic pregnancy depend on where the embryo has settled and how much blood has been lost. The first symptom is obviously of pregnancy itself — the patient's period is late and she begins to suffer from morning sickness.

Lower abdominal pain is always present, no matter where the location of the misplaced embryo, and is followed after a few hours by vaginal bleeding. In severe cases, the internal bleeding can be so bad that the abdomen distends quite visibly and the patient may actually faint.

Treatment

Ectopic pregnancy is a gynaecological emergency that requires immediate admission to hospital. Most doctors would not want to perform an examination in the home because of the possibility of further bleeding. In hospital an ultra-sound scan may be helpful to diagnose the exact problem, but in most cases a laparoscope examination (viewing of the abdominal cavity with a special instrument) will be needed. If the fallopian tube is bleeding, the surgeon will normally need to remove all or part of the tube. Fortunately, this has little adverse effect on the possibility of future fertility, as the other fallopian tube compensates and can take over the job of fertilisation.

ECZEMA

Eczema means 'bubbling up' and refers to an inflammation of the skin that is often accompanied by itching and sometimes blisters.

Eczema used to be considered different from dermatitis, but most dermatologists now accept they both mean one and the same thing. Originally, eczema was thought to be due to problems within the body, and dermatitis caused by exterior irritants.

The old view of eczema was that it was due to an excess of allergic protein in the blood. As such, it was closely associated with asthma and hay fever. This is true of certain types of eczema, such as atopic, but not of all the different types.

Symptoms

The fact that eczema means 'bubbling up' is very relevant to the symptoms of the condition. The eczema rash starts as a raised, red patch. This rapidly develops into blisters that weep and crust over. The open sores are very itchy and may well become infected. If left untreated, the skin becomes thicker and may begin to resemble cracked leather.

Types of eczema

Atopic eczema is closely associated with allergic conditions, such as asthma and hay fever. It is especially common in infants between the ages of two to 18 months. It is characterised by extremely itchy rashes, accompanied by small red pimples that usually occur in creases of the joints, such as in the elbow and behind the knee. Weeping sores may sometimes also develop.

Hand eczema normally crops up as a result of an allergy to chemically based products, such as washing-up liquids and detergents. Itchy patches and blisters usually result from this form of eczema, developing on the palms, and becoming very painful when they start to crease and crack.

Nummular eczema is a type of eczema usually restricted to adults. Nobody knows exactly what causes it, but it results in characteristic symptoms of circular itchy patches that are rather similar to those produced in ringworm.

Treatment

If it is chronic, eczema is usually treated with corticosteroid creams and moisturising bath oils. Steroid creams vary in their strength, and the aim is to use the very strong ones for as short a period of time as is possible.

Eczema that is weeping is best treated with liquid applications. A useful, if messy, treatment is potassium permanganate solution, followed by more conventional treatment with a corticosteroid cream.

Bacterial infections can be treated by mixing the corticosteroid-based cream with an antibiotic drug. If itching at night becomes a problem, one of the older, more sedating, anti-histamine medications, such as Piriton, may help.

Caution

Take care not to overuse steroid cream. Regular use can damage the epidermis and the dermis, resulting in thinning of the skin.

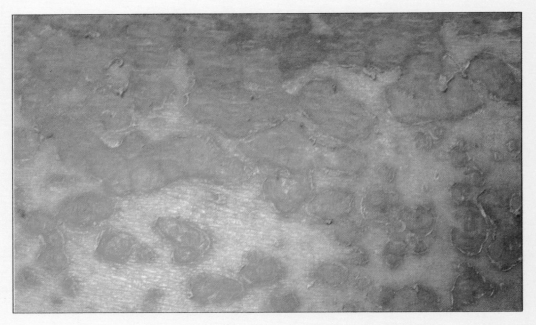

Above: A close-up of an eczema condition, known as herpeticum eczema, which occurs when the eczema sufferer's rash becomes infected with the herpes simplex virus.

⏵⏵ SEE ALSO — Contraception, Dermatitis, Ringworm

MEDICAL FACT FILE (side margin)

EJACULATION

Ejaculation is the process of semen being discharged from the penis at the point of orgasm.

Ejaculation is a reflex reaction to stimulation of the penis, normally during sexual intercourse or during masturbation. This usually involves pressure on the penis that is regular and rhythmic. This pressure triggers off a reaction of the receptive nerves in the spine, which in turn results in the ejaculation reaction.

Process of ejaculation

The semen is produced by the testes, stored in special ducts (the epididymides) and emitted from the penis via the urethra. The stimulation that results in orgasm causes regular contractions in the muscles that surround the urethra, forcing about a teaspoonful of semen to be pumped out of the body through the opening of the urethra. This semen normally contains about 350 million sperm, one of which will play the vital role of fertilising the egg from the woman's ovary.

Ejaculation And Urination

The urethra is the route via which both semen and urine leave the man's body.

However, the two can never actually be emitted at the same time – during ejaculation the opening to the bladder automatically closes, so that no urine can be passed from the bladder. This means that semen cannot enter the bladder, except in the case of retrograde ejaculation, and also that the semen cannot be contaminated.

Premature ejaculation

Premature ejaculation is the most common ejaculation disorder, and the most well-known sexual problem in men, especially in adolescents. The disorder involves ejaculation taking place very quickly, normally just before or after penetration. Premature ejaculation is usually due to psychological causes, especially anxiety over sexual performance. It may also be due to over-stimulation. Premature ejaculation is normally helped by sexual methods and counselling, designed to delay ejaculation and thus alleviate the problem.

Two techniques can be used to help premature ejaculation. The 'squeeze technique' involves the glans (the head of the penis) being pressed between the thumb and two fingers just before ejaculation. The other technique requires the man to stop thrusting just before ejaculation. These techniques aid control over the ejaculation reflex.

Inhibited ejaculation

Inhibited ejaculation is much less common than is premature ejaculation. In this case ejaculation does not take place at all or is delayed for an abnormally long time, even though erection of the penis is perfectly normal, and sometimes even prolonged.

The cause of this disorder can also sometimes be psychological based. But there are cases in which the cause is more physically linked — for example, *diabetes mellitus* and the long-term effects of dependency on alcohol can both lead to problems of inhibited ejaculation.

Retrograde ejaculation

When the opening of the bladder fails to close spontaneously during sexual intercourse, ejaculation may result in the semen emitted being forced back into the bladder. This disorder is known as retrograde ejaculation and is usually caused by complications following surgery on the bladder or on the prostate gland. There is no real treatment for this disorder.

ELBOW DISORDERS

The elbow is the joint between the upper-arm bone and the forearm bone, and is quite susceptible to a number of disorders.

The elbow joint is made up of muscles, tendons, bone and ligaments that stabilise the bone. Damage and injury can quite easily happen to these different parts, and disorders, such as arthritis, dislocations and fractures, can also occur.

Tennis and golfer's elbow

There are two main types of inflammatory problems that affect the elbow. They occur where the tendon of the forearm muscles is attached to the upper-arm bone. Excessive movement and tugging of these muscles causes the tendon to be strained, resulting in the characteristic symptoms of pain and tenderness in the affected area.

Tennis elbow affects the outside of the elbow and often results from playing tennis — and other racket sports like squash — with a faulty grip. More commonly, it results from less obviously strenuous activities like gardening. The lifting of heavy objects makes the condition worse.

Golfer's elbow produces similar symptoms, on the inside of the elbow. It can result from playing golf with a faulty grip or swing, but can also result from the twisting movements involved in something as innocuous as using a screwdriver.

Both tennis and golfer's elbow can be treated with a few months' rest from the activity that originally caused the symptoms to be produced, especially if sport is the cause of the problem. Ice-packs may be applied to the affected area to ease the discomfort involved, and

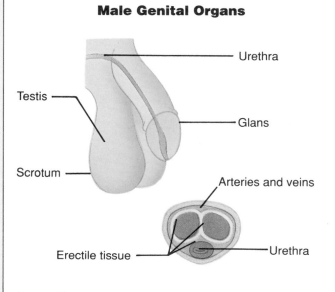

Male Genital Organs

- Urethra
- Testis
- Glans
- Scrotum
- Arteries and veins
- Erectile tissue
- Urethra

Above: The arteries and veins provide the blood that fill up the tissue, as the penis becomes erect.

►► SEE ALSO — Arthritis, Dislocation, Orgasm, Sexual problems

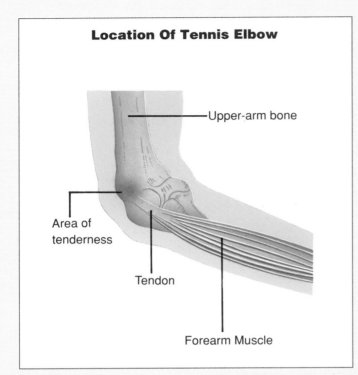

Location Of Tennis Elbow

Upper-arm bone

Area of tenderness

Tendon

Forearm Muscle

analgesic drugs (painkillers) may also be prescribed to help. Surgery may occasionally be required to ease the pain of the tendon.

Other disorders

Olecranon bursitis is an inflammation of the olecranon (the bone at the tip of the elbow). This occurs normally as a result of pressure against the end of the elbow, such as during prolonged periods spent with the elbow leaning on a desk or hard surface. The condition is more commonly known as 'student's elbow'.

Occasionally, it can be caused by damage to the membrane that lines the elbow joint. There is a build-up of fluid that produces swelling and consequent pain. Rest is normally the best treatment.

A very temporary disorder can result from pressure on the tip of the elbow (the 'funny bone'), causing the nerve in the elbow to get trapped and shooting pains to pass down the arm into the hand. 'Pins and needles' may also result.

ELECTRICAL INJURY

The first recorded death by electrocution was in 1879. Electric shocks still kill several hundred people a year, mostly in industrial situations.

The damage caused by electricity depends on the intensity of the electrical current involved, and on the part of the body it passes through — and not on the voltage involved.

Conduction and resistance

The voltage is 'the pressure' and is normally fixed, and the current is the variable amount of power involved. The current decreases as the resistance rises.

The resistance of a certain tissue or organ depends on its water content. Blood and nerves have a relatively low resistance, whereas skin and bone have a relatively high · level of resistance.

The resistance of the body, and therefore the degree of damage caused by an electric shock, also depends on the environment. An electric shock in a damp

bathroom is much more likely to be fatal than one in a dry bathroom. For this reason, it is never advisable for electrical items to be taken into a damp bathroom.

The electric shock will travel to earth along the line of least resistance. Even quite small currents across the chest can upset the heart's own electrical activity, causing a fatal heart attack. A large current across the head can cause the brain to malfunction for several minutes. If this affects the centres of activity that govern the breathing mechanism, death may occur. A high current across a hand or foot will cause a deep electrical burn, identical to one caused by a naked flame.

Treatment

The most important part of first aid treatment, in cases of electrical injury, is for the person who is treating the victim not to get electrocuted themselves. The current must be turned off or, failing this, the victim must be moved away from the electrical source. This should be carried out with something that does not conduct electricity — an insulator — such as a dry broom handle. Treatment of cardiac arrest and burns may also need to be carried out.

EMBOLISM

Embolism is the medical term for the sudden blockage of an artery with a clot of material that is contained in the bloodstream.

The material clot involved, called an embolus, can be made up of a number of things, including air, fat, a foreign body, amniotic fluid, bone marrow, a piece of tissue or tumour, or a clump of bacteria. It circulates in the bloodstream until it

becomes wedged somewhere in a blood vessel and blocks the flow of blood, a condition that is medically known as ischaemia.

Pulmonary embolism

Blood clots are the most common sort of embolus — and the most common form of embolism is pulmonary embolism, which occurs in the pulmonary artery of the lung. Blood clot emboli usually break off from a larger blood clot somewhere else in the body. In pulmonary embolism such a fragment normally breaks off from a thrombosis (a blood clot formed in a deep vein, frequently in the leg). The fragment then travels via the heart to the arteries that supply the lung and may cause a blockage.

Such a blockage can prove to be fatal, often in a sudden and unexpected manner. This is because the flow of oxygen to the blood is restricted. Consequently, the lungs may collapse, blood pressure falls quickly and the rate of the heartbeat speeds up. The functioning of the heart is seriously impaired and death of tissue in the lungs may well occur.

Other clots

Similar sorts of blood clots may result from a heart attack. In this case, fragments of clots that form on the lining of the heart are transferred to the brain itself, where they cause cerebral embolism. This is in turn one of the most significant causes of a stroke.

Air embolism is a very rare condition in which a bubble of air causes a small artery to become blocked. This usually only results from air entering a vein, either following a serious injury, such as a stab wound, or during surgery. In fat embolism an artery may become blocked when fat globules get lodged, sometimes as a result of

» SEE ALSO — Cardiac arrest, Coronary heart disease

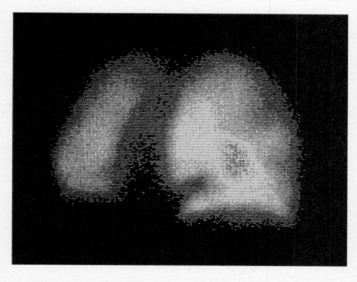

Above: A scan showing restricted blood supply to the lungs (dark blue patches) in a case of pulmonary embolism.

complications following a major fracture of an arm or a leg. Amniotic fluid embolism is an even more rare condition and occurs when some of the amniotic fluid that surrounds the baby in the uterus gets forced into the mother's circulatory system. It is usually the result of a complication at the end of pregnancy.

Clots can be found in other parts of the body. Embolism of the kidney may cause ischaemia, and the kidney may eventually fail to function if the lack of oxygen is serious enough. Gangrene can also develop if there is a lack of oxygen supply to limb extremities, such as toes.

Symptoms

The exact symptoms depend on the form of embolism involved. Pulmonary embolism, the most common form, produces faintness and breathlessness in the sufferer, which is usually accompanied by chest pains. When embolism results in a stroke the symptoms depend on which part of the brain has been affected; speech, movement, sight can all be disturbed, as can consciousness.

In very rare cases, fat embolism may develop into a very serious condition — the sufferer's breathing and heartbeat rates increase and speed up. In this case, confusion, drowsiness and restlessness may also result.

Treatment

Embolism is usually treated with anticoagulant drugs, which work to prevent the formation of blood clots, or with thrombolytic drugs, which dissolve the clot that has caused the problem in the first place. When embolism is very serious and causes the sufferer to lose consciousness, emergency first aid will be necessary.

Surgery is sometimes performed to get rid of severe blood clotting. This operation is called an embolectomy. If the embolism is not too serious, but the embolus involved still needs removing, the operation will be carried out with a balloon catheter.

EMBRYO

The unborn child is termed an embryo during its first eight weeks of growth after conception. Thereafter, it is known as a foetus.

After ejaculation, millions of sperm enter the vagina and swim up through the uterus into the fallopian tube. Fertilisation begins when just one of these sperm penetrates a mature egg that has been released from the ovary. As soon as the sperm enters the egg, it sets off a chemical reaction that stops further sperm entering. This fusion of sperm and egg takes place in the fallopian tube. The four-day journey of the fused egg and sperm along the fallopian tube and into the womb produces a remarkable change in the fertilised egg.

Primitive development

Initially, inside its capsule, the egg is made up of a single cell (or zygote). This then divides and divides again to form a ball of cells. At this stage of development the egg has reached the womb and produces an enzyme that allows it to burrow into the wall of the womb. Within another 10 days, it is completely buried and is termed the embryo.

Early days

At its most primitive, the embryo consists of three layers of cells arranged like a sandwich. The outer layer develops more rapidly than the inner, and the embryo takes on a 'C' shape. About four weeks after fertilisation, tiny limb buds start to appear, growing into flipper-like structures over the next seven days.

At this stage the outer layer of cells has curved in on itself, to form the face and neck. Eyes and nostrils also begin to become apparent at this stage.

Initially, most of the growth takes place at the head end, as the brain and primitive heart develop. During the fifth and sixth weeks the head is as large as the rest of the body put together. The primitive flipper-like limb buds elongate and start to develop their characteristic shape. By the end of the sixth week, fingers and toes can be seen, although the whole embryo is no bigger than a jelly baby.

Human characteristics

By the end of the seventh week, the embryo is undoubtedly human. The

Process Of Embolism

Deep vein   Thrombus

Embolus   Blood flow

SEE ALSO — Development, Gangrene

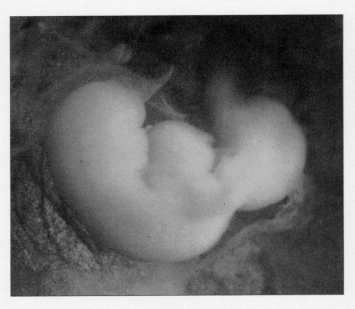

Above: The human embryo after 28 days' growth. The head is on the left – by this stage, most of the primitive organ systems are formed and the heart has begun to beat.

head is round, erect and held on a recognisable neck. The head is still as big as the trunk, but it is now equipped with ears, a nose and even eyelids. The abdomen is formed, but at this stage the intestines are still found in the umbilical cord. From the eighth week onwards, the embryo becomes a foetus and the emphasis is now actually on growth, rather than on development.

EMPHYSEMA

Emphysema is a stage in the progression of bronchitis, a condition in which an acute or chronic infection blocks the airways of the lungs.

Emphysema and bronchitis cause 30,000 deaths a year in the UK. Doctors define bronchitis as 'a daily cough with the production of sputum for at least three months per year, over a period of at least two years'. Emphysema is a part of this process.

Lung deterioration

Emphysema actually occurs when the condition of the lungs deteriorates to such an extent that the lungs' bronchioli (tiny air passages) and alveoli (small air sacks), where gas exchange takes place, break down to form small cavities. Strictly speaking, the condition of emphysema can only be diagnosed at post-mortem, but doctors often use the term to describe the final stages of bronchitis.

Smoker's cough, essentially the first stage of bronchitis, often goes quite unnoticed by the sufferer. However, over the years, the patient becomes shorter of breath and develops a wheeze. At this early stage the lungs start to overexpand to make up for the space that has been lost. This leads finally to the barrel-chested appearance that is characteristic of the patient with advanced emhysema.

Causes

Although lower social class, an industrial environment and even just being British are all recognised risk factors, the most important factor by far in the causes of emphysema is cigarette smoking. The increased risk is the number of cigarettes smoked a day divided by two, so that if 20 cigarettes are smoked, the risk of emphysema is increased 10 times. Only one in 20 cases of emphysema is inherited and is usually attributed to an enzyme deficiency.

Diagnosis

The diagnosis of emphysema is usually fairly easy to make, but if the doctor is unsure, she may order a chest x-ray. Lung function tests are more helpful, but are not available at all hospitals.

Treatment

The most effective treatment for emphysema is to stop smoking — to halt the progression of the disease, and to lose weight — to take the strain off the heart and the lungs. Antibiotics help fight infections, but these infections become more common and harder to treat as the disease progresses. Corticosteroid drugs and anti-asthma inhalers are also sometimes prescribed.

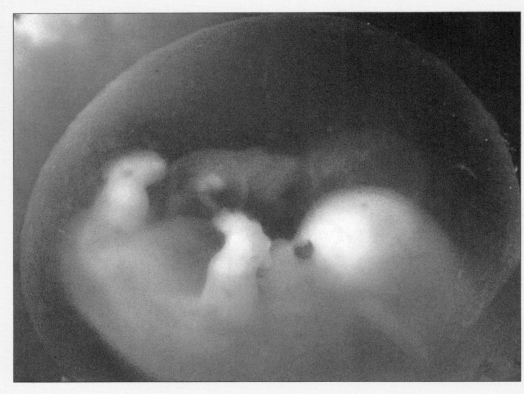

Above: The human embryo at about seven weeks, held in the amniotic sac. External limbs have begun to develop – the arms and legs have budded (even the fingers are visible). The eyes and the nose have also started to develop and can clearly be seen.

▶▶ SEE ALSO — Bronchitis

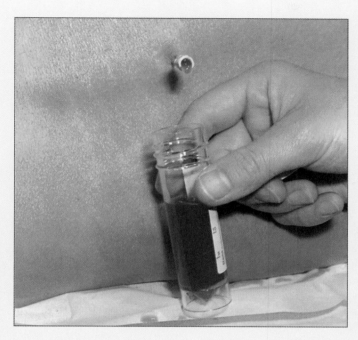

Lumbar puncture may be used to diagnose encephalitis. Cerebrospinal fluid is drawn from the spine for examination.

ENCEPHALITIS

Encephalitis is an infection of the brain which may occur on its own, but is more often seen in association with viral infections.

In many cases, meningitis is also present (the meninges, or membranes that enclose the brain and spinal cord are affected), and if it is, the symptoms will differ.

Viral connections

Many different viruses may lead to encephalitis, (including herpes simplex and HIV), or the condition may occur as a complication of childhood viral diseases, including measles, mumps and chicken pox. Polio and rabies viruses are also causes of encephalitis, targeting the brain directly rather than the whole body.

Bacterial infection

When bacteria are the cause of encephalitis, meningitis is also usually present. Bacterial infections may also cause brain abscesses, leading to inflammation of the brain (for example, when a bacterial infection spreads from the middle ear).

Symptoms

The symptoms vary according to the cause and the severity of the infection. In some cases, encephalitis passes almost unnoticed, but in others — particularly the very old or young, it is a life-threatening disease.

The patient will be confused, speech may be affected and the patient may be drowsy or even comatose. If meningitis is also present, the patient will be complaining of a headache, of a stiff neck and that light hurts the eyes.

Infections of specific parts of the brain will cause specific problems such as loss of balance or paralysis of part of the body.

Diagnosis

If the symptoms are present, diagnosis is usually confirmed by hospital tests, including CT scans, EEGs (electroencephalograms) and lumbar puncture (which involves taking fluid from the spinal canal for testing).

Treatment

The main treatment consists of supportive therapy — caring for the patient until the body's own defences can fight the infection. There has been some progress in developing anti-viral drugs to treat encephalitis (particularly when it is caused by herpes simplex).

Some patients fail to recover, some suffer permanent brain damage, which causes mental disturbance, physical impairment or epilepsy. But 90 per cent of patients make a complete recovery.

Encephalitis lethargica

This form of encephalitis, sometimes known as 'sleepy sickness', occurs without other viral infections being present. The symptoms are as described above, with very noticeable lethargy and drowsiness. There have been no major outbreaks of this form of encephalitis since the 1920s, although it does still occur sporadically.

Many of the people who survived the epidemics of the 1920s developed Parkinson's disease in later life.

ENDOCRINE SYSTEM

The endocrine system produces hormones in various parts of the body which are delivered into the blood stream and control many of the body's mechanisms.

The main endocrine glands are the thyroid, the pancreas, the pituitary and the adrenal glands, together with the testes or ovaries. The main difference between the endocrine and other (exocrine) glands is that their products (hormones) are delivered directly into the blood stream rather than travelling through ducts.

These hormones may act on organs that are distant from the site of the gland where they are produced. Many of the glands work together to keep the body's chemistry on course. For example, the pancreas, the pituitary gland and the adrenal glands produce hormones which work to control the blood sugar levels; the pituitary gland produces hormones which help to regulate the ovaries, and so on.

Disorders

The commonest disorders of the endocrine system are diabetes mellitus and over- or underactivity of the thyroid.

Diabetes mellitus is a result of underproduction of the hormone insulin by the pancreas, resulting in high blood sugar levels.

Thyroid disorders may be due to either an over- or underactive thyroid gland. Too high a level of the thyroid hormone in the blood causes excessive sweating, a dislike of warmth, weight loss and palpitations. If the disorder is unchecked, the patient may develop visual symptoms — an enlarged gland in the neck and bulging eyes. Treatment may be prolonged, to get the balance back to normal, and involves drug treatment, radiotherapy, and even surgery to remove part of the gland to prevent over-production. Overactivity of the thyroid gland can lead to problems with the heart and circulatory system.

Underproduction by the thyroid gland causes the opposite symptoms — lethargy, a tendency to gain weight and a dislike of the cold. Hair loss may also occur. Treatment is simpler — the hormone is replaced with a daily tablet.

Rare disorders

Failure of the pituitary gland produces differing symptoms, depending on

The Endocrine System

The endocrine system is a complicated one. Each of the glands responds to changes in the content of the blood, including the levels of hormones which may have been produced by other glands. This diagram explains some of the functions of the system.

The Pituitary Gland

Position: Attached to the base of the brain, behind the nasal cavity.
Functions: Produces hormones which: control many of the other endocrine glands; stimulate the growth of body cells; maintain the volume of blood in the body; control the uterine muscles during and after childbirth; control the breastfeeding mechanism.

The Adrenal Glands

Position: In the abdomen, one on top of each kidney.
Functions: Produce hormones which: prepare the body for fight or flight in times of stress by increasing the heart rate and the amount of sugar in the blood (as well as dilating the pupils and making hair stand on end); control the volume of blood and fluids in the body by regulating the amount of salt in the blood, in combination with the kidneys; help to reduce inflammation and to reduce allergic reactions. They also produce some sex hormones, but far less than the ovaries or testes.

The Testes

Position: In the scrotal sacs.
Functions: Produce sperm and secrete hormones which control all aspects of sex and reproduction in men.

The Thyroid Gland

Position: In the neck, in front of the windpipe.
Functions: Produces hormones which: affect the metabolic rate of cells – the way they use oxygen, protein and other foodstuffs; control the level of calcium in the blood (which affects nervous response in the body).

The Pancreas

Position: Lies across the body, below the stomach.
Functions: Produces hormones which help to control the level of glucose in the blood (monitoring of blood sugar and production of insulin is carried out by specialist cells in the pancreas, called the islets of Langerhans). The pancreas also secretes enzymes into the digestive tract.

The Ovaries

Position: In the abdomen, on either side of the uterus at the end of the fallopian tubes.
Functions: Produce eggs (ova) and secrete hormones which control all aspects of sex, reproduction and childbirth in women.

---

which hormones are lost. Lack of sexual function, with loss of libido and amenorrhoea may result. In this case, the ovaries are perfectly normal but lack any stimulation and control.

An overactive pituitary gland in childhood will cause overproduction of the growth hormone, resulting in gigantism. These unfortunate people, because of their great height, were often employed as bodyguards in the past. Their overactive glands often gave up at an early age and they would be left physically weak with no aggression or interest in sex. Other disorders of the endocrine system include Cushing's syndrome and Addison's disease.

Special tests

If you suspect a problem with your endocrine system, it is usually fairly easy to diagnose with a blood test, since the hormones produced by the glands go directly into the blood stream — although this may not bring out the actual cause of the disorder. If there is a problem, your GP may refer you to a specialist called an endocrinologist. Disorders of the ovaries or testes are usually dealt with by other specialists.

MEDICAL FACT FILE

Sites Of Endometriosis

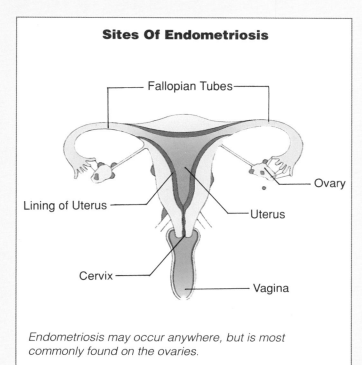

Fallopian Tubes

Ovary

Lining of Uterus

Uterus

Cervix

Vagina

Endometriosis may occur anywhere, but is most commonly found on the ovaries.

ENDOMETRIOSIS

In endometriosis, the endometrium, or lining of the womb, is found in other places, such as the ovaries.

The endometrium is under the hormonal control of the ovaries. Oestrogen and progesterone cause it to grow and fall away in time with the menstrual cycle.

Very rarely, the same type of tissue is found on the outside of the body — on the stomach or the arms and legs. In these cases, the spots will bleed in time with the periods, but other than cosmetic difficulties will cause little problem. However, if parts of the endometrium are inside the body, on sites other than the internal wall of the womb, there may be a number of severe symptoms.

Causes

Endometriosis may occur as the result of an abnormality at the time of the formation of the reproductive organs, or by menstrual blood flowing back up the fallopian tubes. Spots of tissue can be found anywhere, but the ovaries are the commonest site. The womb, fallopian tubes and bowel are frequently affected. In these sites, the monthly bleeding causes intense irritation and the body tries to wall the problem off. This sets up a vicious circle that ends up in the formation of blood-filled cysts that may be two or three inches across.

Symptoms

The most noticeable symptoms of endometriosis are pain, particularly during intercourse, and ovarian problems. These may include short cycles and infertility. There may be tender nodules which the doctor feels when she makes an internal examination, but the diagnosis is difficult to make unless the organs are examined using a medical telescope known as a laparoscope.

Treatment

The two ways of treating the problem are through hormones and surgery. Drugs (in the form of the contraceptive pill, or other hormones) may be given to stop the normal menstrual cycle, thus preventing the abnormal tissue from bleeding. This is highly effective and the benefits often continue for many months after the drugs have been stopped.

Surgery may be necessary to remove large cysts; and if the woman has completed her family and the disease is widespread, she may be offered surgery in the form of a hysterectomy, with removal of the ovaries, to prevent monthly bleeding.

ENDOSCOPY

Endoscopy is a method of examining certain internal parts of the body without the need for major surgery.

The gadget used for endoscopy is an endoscope: a long tube of optical fibres with a lens on the end, which carries light into the area being examined, and back to the viewer. The endoscope may be rigid or flexible. There are several different types of endoscope, with different names, designed to be used to examine different parts of the body. In most cases, special attachments can be used for minor operations.

What is it used for?

Endoscopy was first developed for examining the digestive tract, but is now used for many other parts of the body. A gastroscope is used for the oesophagus, stomach and small intestine; a broncoscope is used for the airways in the lungs; a colonoscope is used for the large intestine; a cytoscope for the bladder; a laparoscope for the female internal organs and an arthroscope for the knee. In some cases the endoscope is inserted through one of the orifices, and in others a small incision is made.

Special attachments

As well as simply examining the area for abnormalities, endoscopes can be used to treat some disorders. For example, special attachments such as scissors and wire loops can

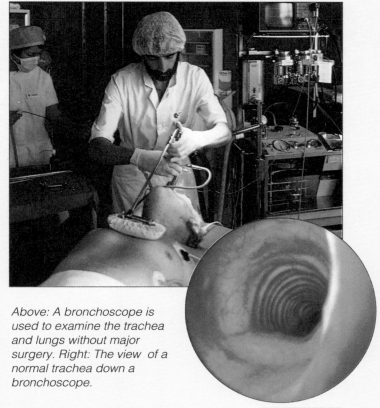

Above: A bronchoscope is used to examine the trachea and lungs without major surgery. Right: The view of a normal trachea down a bronchoscope.

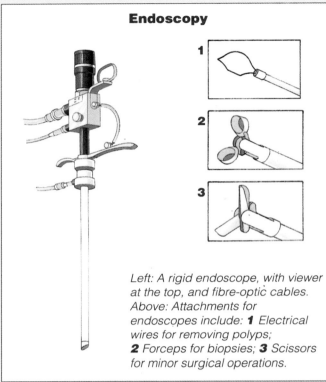

Endoscopy

*Left: A rigid endoscope, with viewer at the top, and fibre-optic cables. Above: Attachments for endoscopes include: **1** Electrical wires for removing polyps; **2** Forceps for biopsies; **3** Scissors for minor surgical operations.*

be used to cut out small growths, polyps or stones in the biliary system; and in some cases an electric current is passed through a wire to treat affected areas; endoscopes can also be used in laser therapy. More commonly, however, the endoscope is fitted with an attachment for removing a sample of tissue or cells from the affected area for further testing (a biopsy).

ENEMA

An enema is a procedure whereby liquids are passed into the rectum through a tube which is inserted in the anus.

The liquids clear the lower part of the intestine of solids. Enemas are carried out both as treatment and as an aid to diagnosis. The patient lies on her side and a lubricated flexible tube is inserted in the anus. Warm liquid is used to prevent sudden contraction of the intestine.

Treatments
Traditionally, soapy water was used to clear the bowel when constipated, but now specially prepared sachets are used. Enemas are only used to clear constipation in cases where diet (plenty of liquids and fibre) cannot cure the problem.

Some drugs and special treatments (for ulceration in the lower digestive tract, for example) are administered as enemas.

Enemas may also be used to treat a rare disorder found in children, known as intussusception. In this condition, part of the intestine telescopes back on itself, causing a blockage. A barium enema may be used for diagnosis, but the enema may actually force the intestine back into its correct position.

Diagnosis
In some cases, enemas are used as an aid to diagnosis: barium enemas are given when diagnosing disorders in the large intestine.

ENTERITIS

Enteritis is the term for inflammation of the small intestine. It is usually associated with diarrhoea.

Enteritis may be caused by food poisoning (due to bacterial infection), viral infections or inflammatory conditions such as Crohn's disease.

Enteritis is also caused by exposure to radiation, through too many x-rays, during radiotherapy for cancer, or following exposure to radioactive substances.

ENURESIS

Enuresis is the medical term for bed-wetting.

By the age of five, about 90 per cent of children remain dry at night. However, some children, particularly boys, continue to wet the bed until they are about 10, when better bladder control enables them to last the night without an 'accident'.

Causes
The main cause of bed-wetting is simply that the bladder control mechanism is not mature enough. Occasionally, psychological stress can cause a child who is normally dry to start wetting the bed again.

In a few cases, there is a a definite physical problem (including a malformation of the urinary system, diabetes mellitus or spina bifida), in which case there will be incontinence or excessive urination during the day as well as at night.

Treatment
Unless there is a physical cause, bladder control is nearly always mastered as the child develops. If you consult your doctor, she will be able to investigate or eliminate any possible physical causes.

There are several simple measures to help prevent the problem: restricting drinks during the evening and waking the child a few hours after it has gone to sleep are helpful in preventing accidents and unnecessary washing of bedlinen.

If the problem persists, it may be worth investing in a special alarm: these consist of a pad which is placed over the mattress but under the sheet. As soon as the child begins to urinate, the alarm sounds, waking her up so that she can control her bladder and go to the bathroom. Like Pavlov's dogs looking for food, eventually the child will wake up before the alarm sounds, as the child recognizes the feeling which indicates she is about to pass urine.

Drug treatment is also possible, but the drugs used generally have side effects and are dangerous if the child takes an overdose.

DO

✔ Make sure the child goes to the toilet last thing at night.

✔ Restrict drinks after five in the evening.

✔ Praise the child every time she has a dry night – or encourage her by putting up a chart with a star for every dry night.

✔ Wake the child and 'pot' her if she urinates at a regular time (about three hours after she has gone to sleep).

DON'T

✘ Punish a child for bed-wetting.

✘ Make the child anxious or worried about the problem.

EPIDURAL

An epidural is a method of anaesthetising the chest and lower part of the body, which may be used during childbirth and some minor operations.

The anaesthetic is injected into the lower part of

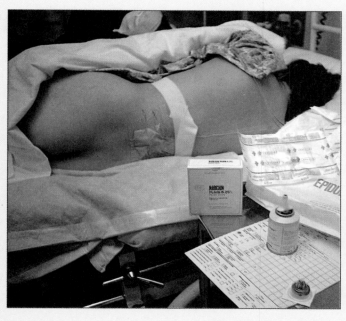

Above: For an epidural, the mother has to lie on her side, and a needle carrying a tube is inserted between the vertebrae into the epidural space at the base of the spinal chord.

the back so that it envelops part of the spinal cord, blocking the messages to the brain about the pain in the chest and lower part of the body.

Advantages
In theory, all the pain of childbirth is relieved, but the mother is still conscious. Relieving pain during childbirth may help the mother to relax. If there are problems during labour, the anaesthetic can be topped up so that an emergency Caesarean section can be performed. The method can also be used for mothers who have Caesarean sections for other reasons.

Disadvantages
The mother has to remain 'attached' to the catheter

which supplies the anaesthetic, and the legs are numb, so the mother has to remain lying down. The anaesthetic may have the effect of slowing down labour. The pain relief can only be administered by an anaesthetist, and has to be done before pain is a problem because it is such a

precise operation. If the mother is too relaxed, labour may be prolonged. In the second stage of labour, when the mother has to push, the loss of sensation may make it difficult for her to push at the right time, so that forceps delivery is more likely.

In some cases the epidural does not work properly, so that pain relief is only partial. There is also the risk that the needle may be inserted in the wrong place, and partial, usually temporary, paralysis may result. Some women complain of headache and extra discomfort on the day after the epidural — just when they should be feeling good and enjoying their new-born child.

EPILEPSY

Epilepsy is a disorder of the brain in which the patient suffers fits, or convulsions. There are several different forms of the disorder.

Epileptic convulsions may be mild or severe, and may be accompanied by loss of consciousness. It is estimated that one in 20 people will have an epileptic fit at some time in their lives, and of these one in eight will suffer repeated convulsions.

Causes
The convulsions are due to a surge of overactivity in the brain's electrical system. Usually there is no obvious cause, and the mechanism is not fully understood. However, in some cases the fits are due to scars on the brain from injury or sugery, or even a tumour. Suddenly withdrawing from an excessive intake of alcohol is likely to cause fits, and most doctors would put patients who were 'drying out' on a short course of anti-epileptic medication. Some sufferers find that certain stimuli, such as flickering fluorescent lights or television screens, spark off a fit.

Grand mal
Half the cases are of the classic grand mal type, where the sufferer has a few seconds warning, loses consciousness and then jerks rhythmically for up to a minute or two. Incontinence is common, as is tongue biting. When the fit is over the patient is usually drowsy for two or three hours.

First aid consists of making sure the patient does not harm herself. Turn her on her side (into what is known as the recovery position) and protect her head with a pillow. Trying to put something between the teeth is completely useless: it does no good and may cause injury to both parties.

Petit mal
The other common form of epilepsy, petit mal, occurs in childhood. The child is perfectly well most of the time but is subject to absence attacks in which she seems to switch off for a few seconds. Petit mal virtually never continues past puberty but it may be replaced by the adult, grand mal, form.

Temporal lobe epilepsy
In temporal lobe epilepsy the electrical overactivity occurs in a part of the brain that governs thought. Hallucinations may occur and the patient is often left in a state of automatism where complex tasks can be performed without any later recollection.

Investigation and treatment
A good eye-witness account of the fit is invaluable in diagnosis. X-rays of the head and a trace of the brain's electrical activity may also provide vital clues as to the cause of the fit. Treatment is with drugs, to keep the sufferer free of fits. In some cases, surgery may be necessary to remove tumours and scar tissue.

EPISIOTOMY

An episiotomy is a cut made in the outer rim of the vagina during labour to create a large enough opening for the baby's head.

There is some debate among obstetricians as to whether or not such a cut is a good idea. Some do it almost routinely, on the basis that a cut heals more easily than a tear — but this means that women who may not have suffered a tear still have to suffer the discomfort of the cut and the stitches. Other obstetricians feel that a small tear heals more easily than a cut, and only

➤➤ SEE ALSO — Caesarean section

MEDICAL FACT FILE

advocate an episiotomy if there is likely to be a large tear, or if the baby is in distress. It is more often necessary in breech or forceps deliveries.

How is it done?

If the obstetrician considers an episiotomy is needed, the patient may be injected with a local anaesthetic, but this is not always done, since speed is essential, and the mother may not be able to keep still for the injection. Scissors are used to make a cut in the vaginal opening towards the anus, cutting into the perineum (between the vagina and the anus). The cut is made at an angle.

After the birth, the cut has to be stitched up — further anaesthetic may be given. The vagina is checked for further tearing or damage and the wound is repaired, with absorbable stitches. Although the mother may get up and walk as soon as she feels able to, she may feel pain or discomfort for some weeks.

EUTHANASIA

Euthanasia is the term given to taking the life of someone who is terminally ill in order to bring pain and suffering to an end.

Euthanasia is illegal in all countries and is a point of great controversy. While no one would condone taking someone else's life in most circumstances, some would argue that for old people who see no reason to live — because of the pain and the burden on those around them — euthanasia is a welcome release. Most doctors, and members of the hospice movement, argue that with proper care and control patients should never feel they are a burden. In the Netherlands, attitudes are more relaxed and some

doctors prescribe medicines so the terminally ill can take their own lives (voluntary euthanasia).

Drawing the line

It is difficult to define exactly what constitutes euthanasia. In many terminal illnesses the doses of pain-relieving drugs are increased steadily, until the lethal dose is reached. Doctors in maternity wards may have to make the decision whether or not to treat horrifically deformed new-born babies for respiratory problems — when they know that most other bodily functions are seriously defective. If a patient is brain dead, however, switching off a life-support system is not considered to be euthanasia.

EYE DISORDERS

The eye is a complex organ, and has a whole branch of medicine devoted to it.

Specialists in eye medicine, or ophthalmology,

spend many years studying the eye and its problems.

How does it work?

Light rays pass through the cornea, the transparent window at the front of the eye, and then pass through the lens and the aqueous humour, the fluid in the eyeball, to be focused on the retina at the back. The retina produces electric impulses that travel along the optic nerve to the visual cortex at the back of the brain.

Each of the different parts of the eye can suffer disease or injury that can interfere with vision. The eye patient may complain of 'something in the eye', decreased or double vision, pain, redness or watering. Some of the most serious eye problems may cause no symptoms at all.

Foreign bodies

It is usually obvious when something has gone into the eye. Occasionally eyelashes lodge under the lid and cause a similar sensation. Contamination with

chemicals should be treated by washing with plenty of water. Hold the eyelids open under a trickling tap for at least five minutes.

Dust and sand may be removed in the same way as chemicals. Even if they are easily visible, it is often best to leave foreign bodies alone: the eye has a very efficient tear system which will wash most things out. If foreign bodies are not washed out naturally, the eyelid can be pulled away from the eye and the object wiped out with a clean handkerchief. It is very important not to touch the pupil or iris, as this can cause pain and scarring.

A problem sometimes arises if the foreign body hits the eye with some force. A piece of metal from a drill, for example, may pass clean through the cornea and rust in the eye itself. If there is any suspicion that this may be the case, or if the object is not easily removed, the patient should go straight to the nearest casualty department. Do not let them

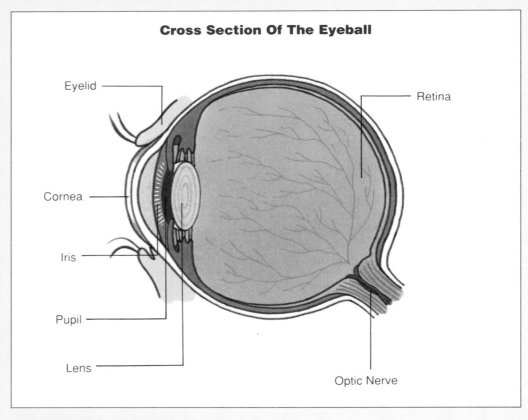

Cross Section Of The Eyeball

Eyelid

Cornea

Iris

Pupil

Lens

Retina

Optic Nerve

SEE ALSO — Breech birth, Forceps delivery

eat or drink as they may need an anaesthetic.

Red eye

A redness of the white of the eye is called conjunctivitis. It is usually due to irritation. Irritation of the cornea is called keratitis. Such irritations may be due to an infection, an allergy or may be a symptom of a serious disease such as acute glaucoma (see below).

Infections may be caused by viruses or bacteria. As a first aid measure, the eye can be bathed in a weak solution of bicarbonate of soda (one level teaspoon in a mug of cooled, boiled water). Antibiotic or antiviral drops may be needed, so see your doctor as soon as possible.

Hay fever or an allergy to animal fur is a common cause of conjunctivitis. In this case, the eye usually feels gritty and the discharge is watery. Antihistamine tablets or drops are often very useful, but sometimes antiallergy drops from the doctor are needed. If a red eye is painful or if it is associated with a loss of vision it may be a sign of raised pressure in the eye. Consult your doctor at once.

Watery eye

This is a common problem, and is either due to an over-production of tears or a problem with their drainage. The commonest cause of overproduction is emotion (crying or even laughing). Other causes include irritation by conjunctivitis, a foreign body, or, in some people, irritation by bright light. Eyes may water as a result of going into a smoky room: this is the natural response to the smoke, which is, in effect, a foreign body in the eye. Failure to drain tears properly is common in babies where the duct is not fully developed, and the problem may occur in adults due to trauma.

First Aid For Eyes

Foreign bodies are best left to be washed out naturally by the tears, but it may be necessary to wash the eye.

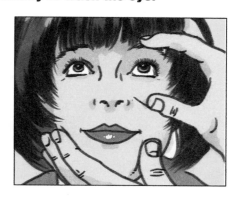

1 To wash out chemicals, lay the patient down, hold the eye open and trickle clean, cold water into the eye for five minutes.

2 If you cannot wash out a foreign body, lift the lids away from the eye and ask the patient to roll the eyes around to shift it.

3 If the foreign body is under the upper lid, pulling the lid down over the lower lid may help to wash it out.

4 If the object still hasn't shifted, turn the lid out and use the corner of a clean cloth to lift it out. Don't touch the cornea.

Pain

Foreign bodies or conjunctivitis are the commonest cause of pain in the eye, but it may be due to many other conditions either inside or outside the eye, including acute glaucoma.

Migraine, neuralgia, sinusitis and eye strain can all cause pain in the eyes. Your doctor should be able to advise you about further treatment. She may send you to have your eyes tested before making a diagnosis.

Loss of vision

Another eye disorder is loss of vision, which may be slow or sudden, and may affect both eyes or only one. If loss of vision is gradual, it may be some time before it is noticed, so regular trips to an optician are essential.

One cause of loss of vision is cataract (clouding of the lens). The only treatment is surgery. In old age, the retina may wear out. Usually the portion that controls fine vision goes first. Little can be done other than help with visual aids.

Loss of vision due to problems with the visual cortex (the part of the brain which interprets the messages from the optic nerve) are rare. However, occasionally the nerves are damaged as they pass over the pituitary gland in the base of the brain. This is usually due to a tumour, but can be helped by surgery.

Sudden loss of vision may be as a result of damage from an accident, but this is surprisingly rare as the eye is well protected by the surrounding bone. Problems with the blood vessels of the eye or with its nerves cause instantaneous loss of vision.

Any sort of visual loss is serious. If it is sudden consult a doctor at once.

Acute glaucoma

One of the most serious eye disorders is acute glaucoma. In this condition, the pressure of the fluid in the

SEE ALSO — Conjunctivitis, Glaucoma, Styes

Self-help For Eyes

Soreness and tired eyes – a grittiness and constant desire to blink – are common among those who read a lot or do detailed work.

The feeling is caused by lack of blinking, due to concentration, tension of the muscles which move the eyeball, and overuse of the muscle which alters the shape of the lens.
● If you are doing close work, raise your eyes and focus on a distant object every five or 10 minutes, to relax the ciliary muscle.
● Every now and then, close your eyes and count up to 60 to relax the eye muscles.
● Blink whenever you remember to.
● Help to relax your eyes by covering your eyelids with slices of cucumber or pads of cotton wool soaked in witchhazel.

cavity of the eyeball rises to the point where it kills the optic nerve, causing severe pain. In acute glaucoma the pupil does not change its size according to the amount of light entering the eye. The eye is often red and feels hard to the touch. Prompt treatment may save the sight of the eye. Take the patient to the nearest casualty department without any delay.

FAINTING

Fainting is a loss of consciousness, usually accompanied by loss of colour in the skin.

Although a faint occurs suddenly, it is often preceded by feelings of lightheadedness and nausea. Fainting is twice as common in women as in men, and peaks in the teens and during pregnancy. Faints in older people may be a sign of serious disease.

Causes

Fainting is the body's response to a reduction in blood, and therefore oxygen, to the brain. The brain uses the faint to bring the head down to the level of the heart to make the best use of the available blood.

The reduction in the flow of blood to the brain may be due to sudden blood loss, either internal or external. The brain responds in exactly the same way if blood pressure drops for a reason other than blood loss.

Many people faint at the sight of blood — in extreme cases even at the sight of other people's. This is because the body's mechanisms see the blood loss and assume that it is going to reduce the amount of oxygen to the brain.

Blood pressure

As well as psychological factors, faints may be due to low blood pressure. This is especially true of the elderly patient on treatment for high blood pressure. Most blood pressure drugs work by slowing the heart and pooling blood in the legs. When the patient rises from bed, not enough blood — and hence not enough oxygen — gets to the brain and a faint follows. Doctors encourage sufferers to get up slowly and to leave at least a minute between sitting up and standing up. Pregnant women faint for the same reason and the same advice applies.

A sudden change in heart rhythm (in the elderly) can also cause fainting. In this case the attack really is 'out of the blue' with no warning. Disturbance of the blood supply inside the brain itself (a stroke) may cause fainting in the elderly. This should be suspected if, on recovering consciousness, the patient has a weakness or difficulty speaking.

Blood sugar

A very low blood sugar level can also cause faintness or even fainting. This is usually as a result of too much insulin or not enough food in a known diabetic. However, even people who are not diabetic may faint if the gap between meals is too long.

Hysteria

Hysterical fainting is commonest in young women with immature personalities. They always occur in company and are used by the victim as a way of drawing attention to herself.

Diagnosis

If there is any doubt as to the cause of fainting there are several things a doctor will want to do. An account of the few minutes before the attack is important: was the patient injured or stressed in any way? Did the sufferer feel (or onlookers see) limbs jerking? The pulse and blood pressure should be measured to check that the heart is working normally and to give clues about blood loss. If diabetes is suspected, blood sugar will be tested to exclude hypoglycaemia. If there is a possibility of epilepsy the brain's electrical activity may be tested.

First Aid For Fainting

There is little that can be done once someone has fainted, except to make them comfortable until they recover.

Left: If you feel a faint coming on, sit down and lower your head between your knees, to allow blood to circulate to the brain.

Below: If someone faints, ensure that she is lying on her side (in the recovery position). Loosen clothing around the neck. If possible, raise the feet slightly.

FALLEN ARCHES

Fallen arches occur as a result of a weakening of the muscles and ligaments in the feet, and lead to flat-feet.

In many cases, the condition is painless, but it may cause the feet to ache, particularly if the patient stands or walks a lot.

Causes

In most people, the arches do not form until they are about six years old. At this age, the muscles and ligaments have gained the strength needed to lift the arches, giving the foot the bounce it needs. Fallen arches in adult life occur due to a sudden increase in weight, or due to a weakening of the muscles and ligaments in the feet as a result of neurological or muscular disorders (including poliomyelitis).

Treatment

Arch supports inside the shoes may help to relieve aches as a result of fallen arches, and physiotherapists may be able to recommend exercises to strengthen the affected areas.

FAMILY PLANNING

Family planning is the use of contraception (or abstension from sexual intercourse) by parents to plan the number of, and age gaps between, children.

In the UK, most GPs will give advice on family planning, but there are also specialist clinics which you can visit — these usually have sympathetic staff and are open at convenient times for working men and women.

The term family planning has essentially come to mean contraception — and

Above: Your family planning clinic will be able to give you advice on all the available contraceptive methods.

family planning clinics are open to fertile women and men of all ages.

FERTILITY

Fertility is the ability of someone to produce children without any undue problem.

Fertilisation occurs the instant a male sperm enters the female egg. The process by which the sperm and egg come together, in the right place and at the right time, is what governs fertility. By the time the female foetus is 20 weeks old, its ovaries already contain 20 million primitive egg cells. This number falls to half a million by puberty, and of these potential eggs only 300 or 400 are used.

Ovulation

Each month, in the adult woman's ovulation cycle, hormones from the pituitary gland stimulate about 20 eggs to start to develop. Each egg produces its own supply of the hormone oestrogen, which then promotes the growth of the individual egg. The egg is the largest cell in the human body and is just about visible

to the eye. Soon one of these primitive eggs is seen to develop at a faster rate than its rivals, which then begin to dwindle away. This strong egg surrounds itself with a layer of cells, and hormones are produced. Within a few days, a swelling about the size of a pea develops on the surface of the ovary. At the time of ovulation this swelling bursts to release the egg into the end of the fallopian tube.

From here, the egg is carried along the dilated part of the fallopian tube towards

the womb. The egg is moved along by a combination of contractions of the tube itself and tiny hairs that engulf the egg and waft it down along the tube. The egg cells that are left behind on the ovary multiply rapidly to become the 'corpus leuteum'. This produces the hormone progesterone, which keeps the lining of the womb in a condition to receive the fertilised egg.

The egg only lives for 24 hours, and its condition actually starts to deteriorate before that day ends. Ideally, for fertilisation to take place, sperm should already be in the fallopian tube awaiting the arrival of the egg.

Development of egg

If the egg is not fertilised, the hormone-producing 'corpeus leuteum' lives for 14 days and then dies. When it dies, the production of progesterone stops. Deprived of progesterone, the lining of the womb falls away and the menstrual flow starts. It is this that allows doctors to calculate the time of ovulation. Regardless of the cycle length, an egg is always released 14 days before the first day of the period. This allows the time of maximum fertility to be

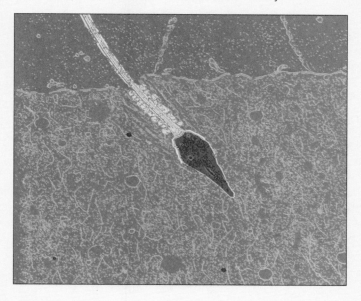

Above: A specially coloured and magnified photograph of a sperm as it penetrates the surface of the egg.

➤➤ SEE ALSO — Contraception, Foetus, Poliomyelitis

MEDICAL FACT FILE

The Male Reproductive System

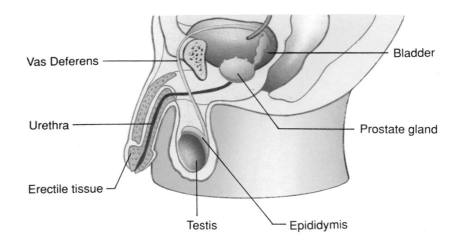

Vas Deferens

Urethra

Erectile tissue

Testis

Bladder

Prostate gland

Epididymis

Journey of The Sperm

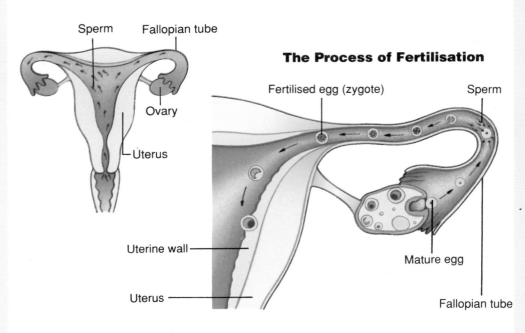

Sperm

Fallopian tube

Ovary

Uterus

Uterine wall

Uterus

The Process of Fertilisation

Fertilised egg (zygote)

Sperm

Mature egg

Fallopian tube

occur during the two weeks or so that it takes the sperm to travel along the epididymis to the outside.

Mature sperm

The mature sperm is often described as being like a tadpole, but in fact it is much longer, thinner and more graceful. The head of the sperm is capped by an area that is rich in digestive enzymes. These enzymes give the sperm its ability to burrow through the wall of the egg. The body of the sperm contains the genetic material that determines the characteristics of the off-spring. The tail lashes to and fro, from side to side and propels the sperm along in a purposeful manner.

During ejaculation, sperm in the 'vas deferens' and the end of the epididymis are forced into the urethra. Here they are mixed with the nutrient-rich secretions of the prostate gland and the Cowpers gland to form semen. The second stage of ejaculation sees rhythmic contractions of the base of the penis. During intercourse the semen is forcibly expelled by the contractions to lie in the vagina next to and around the cervix.

Of the two or three hundred million sperm contained in each ejaculation only tens of thousands make it through the cervix, and only a few thousand actually reach the womb. Only 200 or 300 reach the fallopian tube and the awaiting egg. The journey from the 'vas deferens' to the fallopian tube may take only five minutes.

Sperm count

The most important part of male fertility is the number of sperm per ejaculation (the sperm count), how well the sperm swim and the percentage of mature specimens. A sperm count of greater than 20 million per ml in an ejaculation quantity of

worked out, provided the cycle is adequately regular.

Sperm production

Sperm are produced in the testes, in the seminiferous tubules. The cells that produce sperm develop in early embryological life but remain dormant until puberty, becoming active between the ages of 12 and 15.

Sperm are 2000 times smaller than the size of the (female) egg. The production and maturation of the sperm

are under the control of the hypothalamus, a part of the brain which is vital for the production of sperm that are capable of fertilisation. It takes about three months to actually produce a mature sperm. During this time, the sperm is attached to cells that act almost like parents, supplying all the natural nutrients the sperm needs to grow. During this time of development, the sperm may be damaged if the nutrients they receive are sub-

standard. The commonest cause of such damage is excess alcohol. Men may increase their fertility by cutting back the amount of alcohol they consume. 14 units (seven pints) or less a week is probably an advisable limit.

When sperm are first released from their supporting cells, they are immature and lack both the ability to swim and the capacity for fertilisation. The final stages of maturation

▶▶ SEE ALSO — Ejaculation

at least three ml is looked upon as the minimum requirement for male fertility. Below this level, the man may not actually be sterile, but his fertility is certainly reduced.

Fertilisation

For fertilisation to occur, a number of factors must all work together. For 85 per cent of the population, this very complicated fertilisation process is all too easy.

The woman must produce a normal egg that passes into, and down, the fallopian tube at the right rate. If it is too slow, an ectopic pregnancy may result. If it is too fast, the fertilised egg will not be mature enough to embed itself in the womb. To maintain the pregnancy and adapt the womb for its new role, she must produce the correct hormones, in the correct quantities.

The man must produce sufficient healthy sperm and these must be delivered to the right place at the right time. Delivering to the right place presupposes the ability to maintain an erection long enough to ejaculate inside the vagina. The vulva must be distensible enough to take the erect penis and the womb must be situated so that sperm can enter easily.

Calculation of the right time for intercourse is more difficult. For the best chance of fertilisation, the timing is absolutely vital. The fertile days in the woman are those when the egg is ripening and just as it released by the ovary. Insemination must occur within 12 hours of ovulation if the fertilisation is to succeed. Sperm can survive for up to three days in the fallopian tube, so intercourse just before ovulation may result in pregnancy.

Pin-pointing ovulation may not be easy, as it depends on the next period, rather than the last. This is fine if the periods are as regular as clockwork, but if not, other methods must be used. Traditionally, body temperature has been used, and whilst this is slowly being replaced by blood and urine tests, it is still widely used. The body temperature rises by about 0.2°C at the time of ovulation. Careful and accurate measurement may be enough to reveal the fertile time. In the early stages of the cycle, the mucus at the opening of the vagina is thick, sticky and cloudy. At the time of ovulation, it becomes thin and stringy to allow the sperm easy access to the cervix. If the woman can recognise this stage she will probably be able to predict her fertile periods.

Fertility drugs

These are drugs that improve fertility and increase the chance of pregnancy.

All fertility drugs have potentially serious side effects, so it is recommended that their use is restricted to specialist clinics. If the problem is lack of ovulation, a drug called clomiphene may induce the ovary to produce an egg. This often works in women who are having periods, even if they are very irregular. Other women may need injections to produce a period, but this is very expensive and runs a real risk of multiple births. In 'test tube baby' clinics fertility drugs are used to overstimulate the ovaries, so several eggs can be harvested at one time.

FEVER

Fever, also known as pyrexia, is an abnormally high body temperature.

Humans belong to the group of animals that maintain their body temperature at a constant level, whatever the environmental conditions. This allows the body to perform complex biological reactions that would fail at low temperatures. To maintain a constant temperature, the body produces heat by burning fuels such as fat and sugar. Excess heat is lost through sweat evaporation.

In certain circumstances, usually infections, the body temperature rises above the normal 37°C. This may be perfectly normal — babies, and women in the second half of their menstrual cycle, have a temperature that is up to half a degree above the average. Doctors reserve the term fever, or pyrexia, for a raised temperature that is due to illness.

Fever, therefore, is not a disease in itself, merely a sign that an illness is present.

Causes

The commonest cause of fevers in adults and children are viral infections, such as colds and 'flu. In children, the commonest infections normally start with a fever and this, linked to the length of time before the rash appears, may help the diagnosis. Chickenpox appears on the first day of fever, German measles on the third and measles on the fourth.

Probably the most common bacterial fever is caused by infections of the urinary tract. This is usually fairly obvious, with the sufferer complaining of a frequent desire to pass water and a stinging pain when she does. Children and babies may have urinary infections without these symptoms. A urine examination is a standard part of the investigation of children with an unexplained fever.

There are many other, rarer, causes of fever. Of these, glandular fever, infective hepatitis and chest infections are the most common in young adults. 'Pyrexia of unknown origin', where the cause of the fever is unknown, is a favourite exam question for medical students. Most doctors have a mental check list of 20 or 30 conditions that they can rapidly exclude by physical examination of blood, urine or stool tests.

Fever is not always caused by an infection. Some of the more common, non-infectious causes are malignant disease (such as leukaemia), coronary thrombosis and rheumatoid arthritis, and certain drugs such as barbiturates can cause fever.

Children between the ages of six months and five years are prone to 'febrile convulsions'. These epilepsy-like fits affect up to six per cent of children. They are due to a rapidly rising temperature and whilst they are very frightening, they are completely harmless and are not connected to any disorder such as epilepsy.

Treatment

Fever that is caused by a common cold or 'flu is quite simple — little need be done other than keeping the patient comfortable and waiting for nature to take its course. Paracetamol or aspirin will lower the temperature and make the patient feel better. A child with a temperature should be put in a comfortably warm room, but only wearing a vest and pants. A bed in front of the fire is a comforting thought, but actually makes things worse. If the fever has not subsided after a week in adults, or two days in children, consult the doctor.

▶▶ SEE ALSO — Chickenpox, German measles, Influenza, Measles

MEDICAL FACT FILE

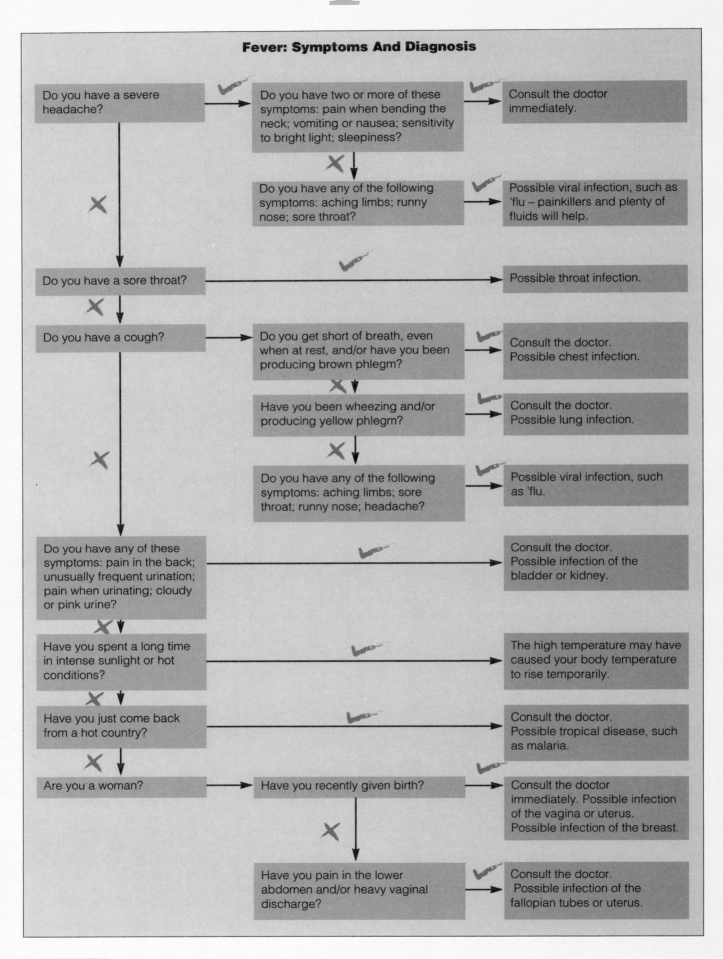

Fever: Symptoms And Diagnosis

Do you have a severe headache? → Do you have two or more of these symptoms: pain when bending the neck; vomiting or nausea; sensitivity to bright light; sleepiness? → Consult the doctor immediately.

Do you have any of the following symptoms: aching limbs; runny nose; sore throat? → Possible viral infection, such as 'flu – painkillers and plenty of fluids will help.

Do you have a sore throat? → Possible throat infection.

Do you have a cough? → Do you get short of breath, even when at rest, and/or have you been producing brown phlegm? → Consult the doctor. Possible chest infection.

Have you been wheezing and/or producing yellow phlegm? → Consult the doctor. Possible lung infection.

Do you have any of the following symptoms: aching limbs; sore throat; runny nose; headache? → Possible viral infection, such as 'flu.

Do you have any of these symptoms: pain in the back; unusually frequent urination; pain when urinating; cloudy or pink urine? → Consult the doctor. Possible infection of the bladder or kidney.

Have you spent a long time in intense sunlight or hot conditions? → The high temperature may have caused your body temperature to rise temporarily.

Have you just come back from a hot country? → Consult the doctor. Possible tropical disease, such as malaria.

Are you a woman? → Have you recently given birth? → Consult the doctor immediately. Possible infection of the vagina or uterus. Possible infection of the breast.

Have you pain in the lower abdomen and/or heavy vaginal discharge? → Consult the doctor. Possible infection of the fallopian tubes or uterus.

SEE ALSO — Malaria, Meningitis

FIBROIDS

Fibroids are benign tumours of the muscular tissue in the uterus. They are mainly made up of muscle and fibrous tissue.

Fibroids either grow into the muscular wall of the uterus or grow outwards into the uterine cavity. Fibroids develop very slowly over a number of years. Eventually, they may grow to be no bigger than a pea, but in some cases their growth is far greater and they may become as large as, if not larger than, a grapefruit.

Problems arise due to the distortion of the wall of the uterus. There are other complications. Occasionally fibroids become cancerous; they may calcify (into what used to be known as womb stones); and they can be a (rare) cause of acute pain during pregnancy.

Causes

The exact cause of fibroids is still not known, although they are amongst the most common sort of tumour. The hormone oestrogen is thought, on occasions, to be responsible. Oral contraceptives that contain oestrogen may cause fibroids to increase in size. This may also occur during pregnancy. After the menopause, the reduced level of oestrogen production may cause the fibroids to reduce in size.

They are reckoned to occur in about five per cent of women overall. In women over the age of 40, this figure rises to about 20 per cent. Before the age of 20, they are quite rare. Statistics show that women who have not had a child or who have had only one are more at risk.

Symptoms

In many cases, especially if the fibroid is small, there may be no noticeable symptoms. Larger fibroids may cause the lining of the uterus to be distorted (and therefore larger) which may lead to prolonged or heavy periods. Severe bleeding may result in iron deficiency and anaemia. There may also be a discharge and dysmenorrhoea.

If the fibroid pushes into the uterine wall, infertility may result, as the distortion makes it difficult to receive and retain the fertilised egg. This variety of fibroid may well also put pressure upon the bladder, provoking pain and discomfort during urination, and it may also cause backache and constipation.

Treatment

The smaller fibroids are normally quite harmless and will require no treatment at all. However, if the fibroids start to grow and cause serious problems or complications, surgery may be necessary. A myomectomy operation will remove the fibroid and save the uterus, but older women, particularly if they already have a family, are likely to be offered a hysterectomy — it is a more satisfactory treatment, with no chance of recurrence, and better recovery times.

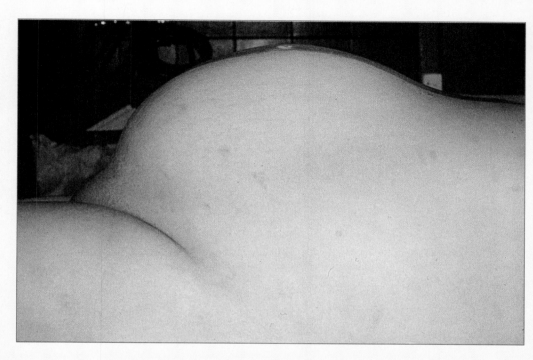

Fibroids can grow very large, distorting not only the uterus, but the whole of the abdomen.

FIBROSIS

Fibrosis is an excessive growth of tissue (either the body's normal connective tissue or scar tissue).

The condition may be part of a disease (such as cystic fibrosis or asbestosis) or it may occur as a response to the body's healing mechanism. It may also occur as a result of a lack of oxygen supply to a tissue, which can sometimes happen as a result of having a heart attack.

What happens?

If there is fibrosis, some of the specialised cells in the body (in the heart muscle or in the kidneys, for example) are replaced by normal fibrous tissue, so the organ does not work so well. Fibrosis may also cause blockages in some parts of the body — if it puts pressure on hollow parts such as the ureters, for example.

Treatment

If fibrosis occurs as part of the healing process, it does not normally need treatment. When it occurs as a result of disease, however, it is very difficult to treat, particularly if it is in the lungs, heart or kidneys. It may be fatal.

FIBROSITIS

Fibrositis is a term used to describe inflammation of the body's muscular connective tissue, causing aching pains.

Fibrositis most commonly affects the back and trunk, particularly in older people. It is not a medical term.

Fibrositis may be a symptom of pressure on the sciatic nerve (sciatica), but more often the inflammation seems to be due to bad posture and tension.

Treatment

The disorder is best treated with hot baths, proprietary rubs and analgesics. You may be able to get a nonsteroid anti-inflammatory cream from your doctor. Keep up regular, gentle exercise, to tone the muscles and to prevent further attacks or worsening inflammation.

 SEE ALSO — Anaemia, Discharge, Dysmenorrhoea, Hysterectomy

MEDICAL FACT FILE

First-Aid Check List

What should you do if you are the first person on the scene of an accident? Here is a quick guide, together with information on where to find out more. Brush up on your first-aid knowledge now.

● The first thing to do is to check whether or not the victim is breathing: give mouth-to-mouth resuscitation (see page 18).
● Next look for severe bleeding. Try to stem the flow by putting pressure on the wound and raising it above the level of the heart (see pages 30 and 75).
● Treat burns (see page 43).
● Lay the victim on their side in the recovery position (see page 120) and summon help if you have not been able to do so already.
● For more information on electrical injury, see page 110.
● For more information on choking, see page 56.
● For more information on cardiac arrest, see page 46.

First-Aid Kits

A first-aid kit is an essential piece of equipment – whether you are at home or out and about. Here's a quick guide to the essentials.

Car/camping kit (right): Antiseptic cream; insect repellent; calamine lotion/cream, paracetamol, antiseptic wipes, triangular bandage (sling), 2-inch-wide crepe bandage, sterile gauze, self-adhesive strip, strip of self-adhesive plaster, Melolin (non-adherent) dressing, padded dressings (for blisters), scissors, tweezers, safety pins.

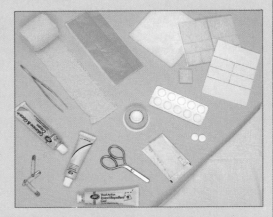

First-aid kit for the home (left): Antiseptic cream, sting relief cream, paracetamol, anti-septic wipes, triangular bandage, selection of gauze and crepe bandages sterile gauze, self-adhesive strip, eye dressing, wide selection of self-adhesive plasters, cotton wool, eye bath, scissors, tweezers, safety pins.

Warning: Keep out of the reach of children.

FIRST AID

There is no substitute for formal first aid training, but if you are first on the scene of an accident of any type, there are certain procedures to follow.

The main problem is assessing the condition of the victim(s) when you have limited medical knowledge. Remember that comfort and reassurance are two of the victim's major needs.

Look out for further dangers (oncoming traffic, corrosive or explosive chemicals, live electrical cables) as you approach. Move the victim to safety if necessary (using something which does not conduct electricity if there has been an electrical accident).

FLAT-FEET

Flat-feet is a condition in which the foot (usually both feet) has no arch, so the whole sole of the foot rests on the ground.

Flat-feet are normal in small children, but most people develop arches as they grow up, giving the feet spring. Occasionally there are hereditary problems, which means that the muscles that form the arch never develop. The condition is normally painless and does not require any attention.

FLATULENCE

Flatulence is the production of excessive wind (flatus) in the digestive tract.

The wind may cause embarrassing rumbling noises, which usually recede once the wind has been expelled — either through the mouth or the anus (often with further embarrassment).

Causes
Flatulence develops as a result of eating high-fibre foods, swallowing air while you are eating or in an attempt to relieve discomfort in the digestive tract, or as a symptom of a more serious complaint, such as a hiatus hernia, an irritable bowel, or an imbalance in the digestive system which upsets the normal process of breaking down food.

Self-help
If flatulence is accompanied by pain in the lower abdomen, if you also pass pale or foul-smelling faeces, or if it persists with no obvious cause, you should

consult your doctor.

However, normally it is a social problem rather than a medical one. There are certain precautions to take to avoid flatulence. Eat slowly, sitting upright, and relax after meals to prevent indigestion. Take care not to swallow air as you eat. Spicy foods will make the smell worse, but do not produce more gas than other foods. Experience will teach you which foods to avoid if you are going out to meet someone special.

FOETUS

During the first eight weeks after conception, the growing baby is known as an embryo. From eight weeks until birth, the growing baby is called a foetus.

During the embryonic period the emphasis is on the development of primitive organs and their transformation into something resembling those in the fully formed baby. The foetal period is a time of growth and maturation.

By the time a baby is born, it is six billion times heavier than the egg it grew from. In contrast, it will only increase its weight twenty fold during the rest of its life. It has been calculated that if a baby grew as fast as the foetus, it would weigh two trillion times as much as the earth by the time it reached its sixteenth birthday.

Changing proportions

At nine weeks the head accounts for almost half the length of the foetus. This disproportion corrects itself over the next four weeks as the body enters a relative growth spurt at the expense of the head. At the same time the neck lengthens and straightens to lift the chin off the chest. The eyelids grow towards each other, meet and fuse. They will not

reopen until the twenty-fifth week of pregnancy.

Although the sex of the baby is determined at the time of conception, the external genitals do not appear until the tenth week. They are fully formed by the twelfth week and can be distinguished by an ultrasound scan. Perhaps the greatest change at this time occurs in the digestive system. Up until the tenth

week the intestines are actually inside the umbilical cord. From then onwards they fill the rapidly expanding abdominal cavity.

Strange looks

At this stage the face looks quite bizarre. The eyes are at the side of the head and the ears are low down on the neck. By 12 weeks they are in their normal position although the eyes are still set far apart.

Rapid growth continues with the foetus doubling in size every three weeks until the twentieth week. By this time the normal relative proportions have been reached and the mother may well have felt the baby move.

From the twenty-first to the twenty-fifth week the eyebrows and eyelids develop. The face now resembles that of a newborn baby. The body has very little

Foetal Monitoring And Foetal Distress

The foetus is monitored in many ways to check its development during pregnancy, and specific types of monitoring are used to check its condition during labour.

Throughout pregnancy, the foetus is monitored by means of observation, scans and blood tests. Doctors and midwives will feel the mother's abdomen for clues about the baby's size and postion, and listen to the baby's heart beat.

During labour, two items are monitored to determine the well-being of the foetus – the heart rate and the acidity of the blood. The foetal heart slows down with every contraction. The speed and the manner in which it picks up afterwards can give vital information about the welfare of the foetus. The rate can be measured with a stethoscope, or using a type of ultrasound,

with the monitors held in place on the abdomen. If the cervix is open an electrode can be put on the scalp of the foetus and an ECG recording made.

Blood samples can be taken from the foetus's scalp for testing. If the acidity, and hence the amount of oxygen in the blood, is low, it is a sign that it is time for the doctor to intervene.

Foetal distress

Delivery is obviously a difficult and dangerous time for the foetus. With each contraction of the uterus the blood supply to the baby is cut off. The normal foetus is equipped to deal with this, but if it is already under stress or if the delivery is unusual or prolonged, the result is known as foetal distress. The monitoring methods indicate that all is not well and that the doctor or midwife may need to intervene.

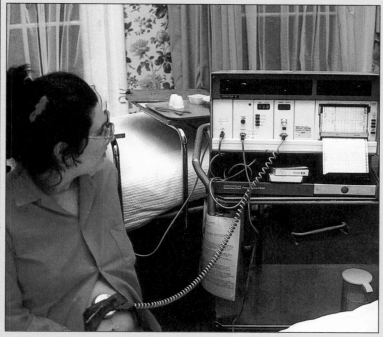

During the later stages of pregnancy, ultrasound is often used to monitor foetal movements and heartbeat. Two discs, which pick up the readings, are held in place on the mother's abdomen with a broad elastic band, and the readings show up on a digital display. The readings are recorded on a continuous roll of graph paper so they can be checked later.

The Growing Foetus

From the eighth week of pregnancy, the growing embryo becomes known as the foetus. The organs form at an early stage, and then the growing baby starts to stretch the mother's abdomen, pushing the mother's organs out of the way. The foetus turns around within the uterus until about 32 weeks, when it normally settles head down.
At nine weeks the foetus weighs less than 30g (1oz); by 20 weeks (half-way through the pregnancy) it normally weighs about 450g (1lb) and at full term the normal foetus can weigh anything from 2300g (5lbs) to 4000g (9lbs).

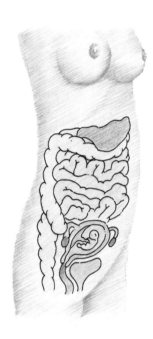

The foetus at nine weeks.

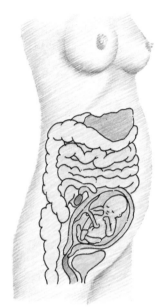

The foetus at 13 weeks.

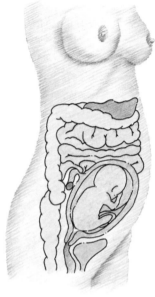

The foetus at 20 weeks.

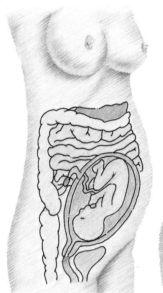

The foetus at 25 weeks.

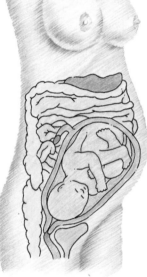

The foetus at 30 weeks.

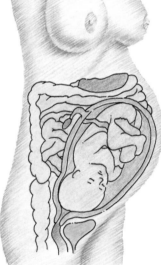

The foetus at 35 weeks.

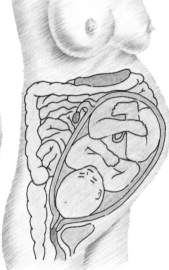

The full-term foetus.

fat and as a result the skin looks wrinkled.

Sustaining life

Twenty four weeks is a landmark in the development of the foetus. If it were born now it could survive, even though it would need sophisticated life support for several weeks. The recent changes in the Abortion Act in the UK recognized this fact and routine abortions after this time are now illegal.

Between 26 and 29 weeks the eyes open and the hair on the scalp begins to grow. As more and more fat is laid down the foetus looks less wrinkled. Around 34 weeks the testes descend (in boy babies). The ovaries (in girls) are still in the abdomen and will not enter the pelvis until after birth.

A foetus of 35 weeks resembles a full-term baby, but even now, premature birth can cause problems — most often with the lungs.

During the last month of pregnancy, the foetus lays down fat stores against the first two or three days of life when its mother's milk is full of protective antibodies, but is not very nutritious.

▶▶ SEE ALSO — Development, Embryo, Pregnancy

FOOD POISONING

Food poisoning is defined technically as 'the contamination of food with toxic chemicals or bacteria'.

It is a term that doctors try to avoid using it. Some infections, such as typhoid, which are undoubtedly carried by food, do not come under the definition. On the other hand, many cases are diagnosed by doctors under the label of 'gastric 'flu'.

Toxic chemicals

Toxic chemicals may be present naturally, in toadstools, for example. They may also be the result of changes in what normally is a perfectly safe food. Potatoes, for example, contain a toxin that is usually present in such small amounts as to be completely harmless. But if the living potato is exposed to sunlight the toxin rises to dangerous levels and the potato turns green.

Accidental contamination with pesticides and other poisons can cause food poisoning on the farm, at the warehouse or even in the shop. Fruit and vegetables should be washed thoroughly before being eaten. Even the kitchen is not safe: boiling apples in a zinc saucepan can cause dangerous levels of the metal to be absorbed. Normally harmless chemicals, such as monosodium glutamate (a flavour enhancer widely used in Chinese cooking) can cause poisoning if taken in excess.

Bacteria

Most cases of food poisoning are due to bacteria. Food is an ideal environment for the growth of bacteria. Any food will eventually go bad if left unprotected — some foods obviously take longer than others. Not all bad food is poisonous and not all fresh food is safe. Bacterial food poisoning can be due to the production of toxins in the food or by the multiplication of harmful germs in the patient's intestines.

Milk and cream products can easily become contaminated with the

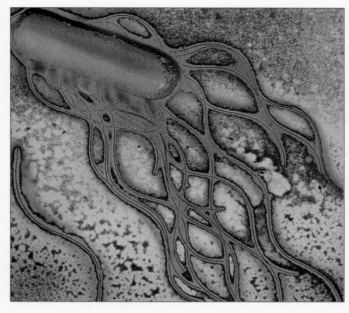

A specially coloured image of a single salmonella bacterium, a form of intestinal parasite. The thin strands are the 'flagellae' that allow the bacterium to move.

staphylococcus germ. This is normally found on the skin and is the cause of boils. If it multiplies in cream it produces a toxin that can cause severe vomiting for several hours. The onset is rapid, usually no more than an hour or two after the meal.

Much more deadly, but less common, is botulism. A germ, *clostridium botulinum*, which normally lives in the soil, may contaminate tinned meat or vegetables. As the germ grows it produces *botulinum* toxin, an extremely dangerous chemical. When eaten, this chemical rapidly attacks the brain and nerves and is usually fatal.

The majority of food poisoning germs cause problems by multiplying once they are located in the body. We all eat one or two food poisoning germs every day. Luckily, our bodies can cope with small doses and we suffer no ill effects. Problems arise if the dose of germs is very high. For this to happen the food must be contaminated, the germs must be given the right conditions for their multiplication, and the food must be eaten without adequate cooking.

Symptoms

The symptoms vary according to the type of food poisoning involved, but they may include vomiting, diarrhoea, sweating and stomach cramps.

Food Poisoning Germs

There are several common food poisoning germs, all of which cause slightly different symptoms.

● Salmonella – There are many sorts of salmonella germs, some more serious than others. They usually live quite happily in the guts of animals. But we run into difficulties if we eat the meat of an animal that has itself been contaminated with the germ. This may occur at the time of slaughtering, or contamination may cross from raw to cooked food if they are stored together. The salmonella germ can also get into eggs laid by infected hens. Salmonella is readily killed by heat. Cooking will make the meat safe, but only if the temperatures are high enough for long enough (over 60°C for more than 10 minutes). Remember if you are re-heating food, that this temperature must be reached at the centre of the dish, not just around the edges. Salmonella poisoning causes vomiting, diarrhoea and a 'flu-like illness.

● Campylobacter – These organisms, usually found in the guts of sheep, cows and chicken, are probably the commonest cause of food poisoning. Infection causes severe cramping and abdominal pain with bloody diarrhoea.

A doctor may prescribe antibiotics, which have been found to work on campylobacter, but only when tests have proved the diagnosis.

● Listeria – This bacteria is found in unpasteurised milk and cream, and in cheese made from unpasteurised milk. It has also been found in pâté. It is relatively harmless in most cases, but puts pregnant women and their unborn child at risk. For this reason it is best to avoid these foods if you are pregnant.

● Cholera – The germ that causes cholera only affects humans. It causes severe diarrhoea and is often fatal. Large epidemics may occur after disasters such as floods, especially if the sewage system has been disrupted.

⟫ SEE ALSO — Bacteria, Cholera, Listeria, Salmonella

Rules For Avoiding Food Poisoning

There are two basic rules to follow to avoid food poisoning:

● Never store raw food with cooked food.
● Cooked food should be kept at a temperature that is either too low or too high for germs to multiply.

If you are eating out, especially in a country with poor hygiene levels, it is impossible to ensure that these rules are followed. Under such circumstances the safest option is to eat food that is fresh and served piping hot.

MEDICAL FACT FILE

Forceps Delivery Technique

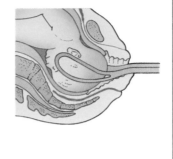

The forceps blades are placed alongside the baby's head. The baby is then eased out.

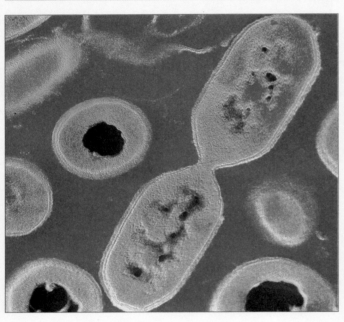

A specially coloured image of listeria bacteria. These bacteria can put pregnant women and their unborn child at risk.

Treatment

In most cases of food poisoning, the best treatment is to stop eating all food until diarrhoea and vomiting have stopped, taking care to drink plenty of water to prevent dehydration. Special rehydration sachets of glucose and salt (available over the counter) may be added to the water, especially if babies or old people are affected. In some extremely serious cases, hospitalisation is necessary.

Antibiotics should, in theory, kill off the bacteria and end the illness, but in practice they often make matters worse, as they kill off the 'helpful' bacteria.

FORCEPS DELIVERY

If the delivery of a baby becomes difficult, forceps may be used to ease the process.

The forceps used in this kind of delivery are made up of two wide, blunt blades that are designed to fit snugly around the baby's head.

Uses

There are various reasons why a forceps delivery is employed. Sometimes the mother herself may have become overtired and is no longer really capable of pushing sufficiently to enable her baby to be born without technical intervention. The

forceps are therefore used to ease the baby's head out.

Usually, however, it is problems with the baby and its position in the womb itself that precipitate the use of forceps. This is especially true in the case of a breech birth, when the baby's bottom, rather than its head, is in position to be delivered first. In either case, if problems become evident before the second stage of labour, the decision may well be taken to perform a Caesarean section instead.

Techniques

Painkillers and an anaesthetic are often given to the mother before the doctor can inspect her to see if a forceps delivery is the best method to employ. For a forceps delivery to be performed, the neck of the uterus must be adequately dilated and the baby must be in a position that means it is near to being born. An episiotomy is also frequently used to make a forceps delivery easier to perform.

Once the doctor has decided that forceps are to be used, they are postioned carefully around the baby's head — the two blades just in front of the ears. Rotation may be necessary to get the baby's head and body in the correct position. The baby is then eased out.

FRACTURE

A fracture is the medical term for a break — almost always for a broken bone.

Fractures are the result of violence, either directly to the site of the break, or indirectly. Twisting the body around a trapped foot, for example, can cause a spiral fracture up and through the great bones of the leg. It is important for the doctor to know how the injury occurred — not only will she be able to make a diagnosis more easily, but she will be able to apply the best treatment.

Types of fracture

The most basic, and from a first aid point of view, the most useful distinction is between simple and compound fractures. Simple fractures occur if the skin is intact, whereas the compound variety are said to occur when the the skin has been broken.

A comminuted fracture occurs if the bone breaks into more than two fragments. A greenstick fracture is a form of fracture particularly common in children, and affects the forearm bone more than any other. In children, these bones are slightly springy and when stress is placed on the bone, one side of it may bend enough to cause the other side to splinter.

▶▶ See also — Dehydration, Delivery, Diarrhoea, Episiotomy

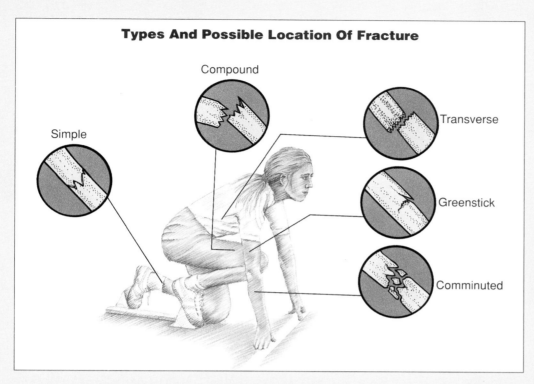

Types And Possible Location Of Fracture

Compound

Simple

Transverse

Greenstick

Comminuted

Stress or 'march' fractures usually occur in long, thin bones that are repeatedly flexed. The most commonly affected bones are in the forefoot, hence the expression a 'march' fracture, meaning that the injury has resulted from a long march.

A pathological fracture, unlike other sorts of fractures, is not associated with excessive force. In this case, the bone is weakened in some way until a point is reached when any slight knock will inevitably break it. The weakness may be the result of the very rare 'brittle bone disease', or it may even be due to deposits of cancer.

Diagnosis

The first sign of a fracture is, of course, pain. If the patient complains of pain in the bone at the site of an injury, a fracture should be suspected. The broken bone is often noticeably different from its normal shape and is tender to the touch.

Some first-aid books suggest that bending the bone and hearing the grating noise made as the two ends rub together is the only sure way of diagnosing a fracture. This is very painful and should be avoided.

The easiest way to diagnose a fracture is to treat all suspected cases as though they were breaks, and so x-ray them at the earliest opportunity.

Treatment

From a first aid point of view, the treatment of all fractures is the same: the affected part of the body should be immobilised, and the patient made as comfortable as possible. She should be given nothing to eat or drink.

If the damage is so great that the limb involved is distorted out of all normal recognition, it may be necessary to straighten it. This may be difficult and will certainly be painful, but it may help to save the limb. Obviously, this should only ever be used as a very last resort and not at all if there is a chance of skilled medical help arriving.

A compound fracture should be covered with a clean, dry dressing. Do not attempt to clean it, as this will have to be done at the hospital in any case.

From a treatment point of view, fractures fall into three groups. The first group encompasses those fractures which need little to be done to them, because the break will heal itself. Broken shoulder blades fall into this category, as even when they go untreated full recovery is almost a certainty. Another group, which is by far the largest, includes the fractures in which the blood supply is good and a cure is expected as long as the bone is held in the right position. A third group are the bones with a poor blood supply where a prolonged period in plaster is needed before any hope can be held out for a cure.

Treatment consists first of 'reduction' in which the bone is restored to as near its normal position as possible. This reduction may be closed, where the bone is manipulated from the outside, or open. Open reductions need surgery to immobilise the fragments and then return them to their rightful, original place.

'Immobilisation' allows the break to heal without it being moved. This can be done by means of a plaster cast or plates and screws around the site of the injury.

The last stage of treatment is rehabilitation. The patient must learn to use her newly healed limb. In the case of a serious break, this may take many months.

FROSTBITE

Frostbite is damage to skin and the tissues beneath, as a result of exposure to temperatures below freezing point.

Frostbite most commonly affects exposed parts of the body, such as the nose, fingers, toes and ears. Frostbite is quite a common problem for mountaineers and explorers who tend to spend long periods of time in sub-zero conditions.

Development

Frostbite first reveals itself as a pins and needles sensation. This then develops into complete numbness in the affected areas, the skin gradually becoming hard and turning white and cold. The area will eventually become red and swollen. If only the skin and the superficial tissues are affected, the damage may not be too great.

The sufferer must be returned to a warm environment as soon as possible, and the affected areas must be immersed in water at 40°C to help them thaw out. Massage of the affected area is not a recommended treatment.

If the damage has worked its way through to the blood vessels, the problem may be more serious and difficult to reverse. Once the tissue has died, it turns black and will blister. If gangrene develops amputation may be the only 'treatment' possible.

▶▶ See also — Gangrene

MEDICAL FACT FILE

FROZEN SHOULDER

Frozen shoulder is a condition that causes pain and stiffness in the shoulder area.

Frozen shoulder arises from problems of inflammation and thickening of the lining of the capsule in which the shoulder joint is held. The exact causes of the condition are difficult to pin down — they are often thought to result from other problems, such as a muscle injury, a stroke, bronchitis, angina or diabetes mellitus.

Treatment

Moderate symptoms are normally relieved by painkillers and an ice-pack. Severe symptoms may call for corticosteroid injections, or shoulder manipulation under anaesthetic.

FUNGAL INFECTIONS

When most people think of germs, they usually think of viruses or bacteria. There is, however, another group that can cause disease and that is fungi.

Fungi are generally larger than bacteria and unlike them are often made up of many cells. Most fungi are either harmless or positively helpful. Of the fungi that cause disease, there are two main groups — the moulds and the yeasts. The moulds grow as very fine, fluffy hairs. Look closely at an old piece of bread and you will probably see some. The yeasts are oval in shape and reproduce very quickly.

Candidal infections

Candidal infections belong to the group of yeasts. They are found in the mouth, lungs and guts as well as on the skin and in the vagina. Normally they do not cause problems but if the individual becomes run-down, a wide range of diseases can result.

Common reasons for candida causing problems are poor nutrition, sugar diabetes and the regular use of antibiotics. As well as killing off harmful bacteria, antibiotics tend to kill the germs that keep the candida infection at bay. Without any competition, the candida yeast may take over.

Thrush

The most common form of candidal infection is thrush. This can affect the mouth and appears as white patches against a red background. It usually affects babies or the old and frail, and can be very painful. It may well be painful enough to stop a child feeding and is one of the the first things a doctor would look for in a fractious baby. It is easily treated with drops. If it recurs, it may be a sign of faulty sterilisation technique.

Thrush may also affect the vulva and the vagina of young women, causing a yeasty smelling, white discharge. Thrush is intensely irritating. It may also cause balanitis in men.

Diagnosis and treatment

All women have candida living in their vagina. It may never cause problems, but it may be the source of constant misery. Regular sufferers should avoid washing in bubble baths, washing the vulva with soap, or using vaginal deodorants. Skirts are better to wear than trousers, and cotton (as opposed to nylon) underwear is a must. Self-treatment with live yoghurt, smeared on the vulva, may help.

Your doctor will probably want to examine your vagina and may take a swab if the diagnosis is in doubt. Treatment consists of either pessaries and cream, or a single tablet. The tablet may keep the sufferer free for up to eight weeks and is theoretically the ideal treatment. The tablet treatment is relatively new, however, and most doctors would try the cream first.

Other candidal infections

Some types of candida cause whitlows — painful, pus-filled swellings around the nail bed. These are commonly found on the fingers of barmaids and others whose hands are constantly in water. The condition is usually cured by a few days of keeping the hands dry.

Athlete's foot

Athlete's foot is another candidal infection, and causes the skin between the toes to soften and split. It is commonest in young people, usually due to wearing shoes that do not allow the feet to breathe sufficiently. Creams and powders will help the sufferer, but the sufferer can help by wearing leather shoes and cotton socks. The feet should be washed and dried twice a day.

Ringworm

Another kind of infection that produces similar symptoms to those of athlete's foot is ringworm. Ringworm fungi are spread in the superficial layers of the skin and nails. Ringworm gets its name from

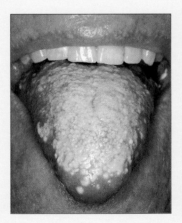

In this severe case of oral thrush, the white spots have merged to cover the tongue.

its appearance. It starts as a small spot that slowly widens to form a near circular lesion with a centre of normal skin. But it is not a worm and cannot be treated with medication for worm infestations. It is infectious and can be passed from person to person or from animals to humans.

Athlete's foot that is caused by the ringworm fungus may be harder to treat than the candidal sort, as it is often infected with a bacteria as well. If it does not clear up with simple treatments your doctor may prescribe a combination antifungal/antibiotic cream. Ringworm itself is usually treated with creams, though in difficult cases or where the nails are involved, tablets may be needed. Whatever treatment is used, it should be continued for some time after an apparent cure so as to make sure that all the spores are destroyed.

It is now thought that many cases of dandruff are due to ringworm-like infections of the scalp. The fungus concerned, *pityriasis ovale*, can be destroyed with coal-tar-based shampoos which can be bought over the counter. If the dandruff does not respond, or is very severe, your doctor may be willing to prescribe an antifungal shampoo.

Serious infections

Occasionally, often in patients whose immunity is lowered for some reason, fungi may be more than skin deep. Aspergilla moulds are found everywhere — in rare cases they may fill the ear canal, in which case treatment is long and difficult. They may also settle in the lungs where they can cause a fungal abscess or start an allergic process that ends in asthma. Treatment may require surgery to remove the affected area.

≫ SEE ALSO — Bronchitis, Diabetes, Heart, Thrush

GALL BLADDER

The gall bladder is a pear-shaped organ about 7 – 10cm long. It concentrates the bile, also acting as a reservoir for it.

Bile is a waste product, which also helps to break down globules of fat into smaller fragments that can be digested more easily. It is produced in the liver as a break-down product of blood, and travels down a duct into the gall bladder. The wall of the bladder is very spongy and absorbs most of the water, leaving the concentrated thick, dark brown bile. When fatty food reaches the intestine, hormones are released which make the gall bladder contract and empty the bile back down the bile duct, into the intestine.

If there are no fats in the gut, and the hormones are not released, the bile is still released, because the gall bladder becomes overfull. Without the fatty globules present, this concentrated bile can cause problems.

There are various

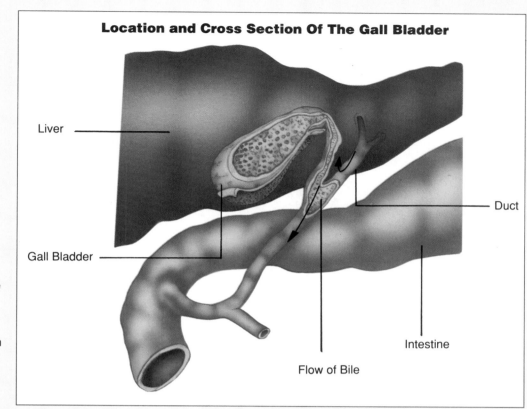

Location and Cross Section Of The Gall Bladder

Liver

Gall Bladder

Duct

Intestine

Flow of Bile

disorders of the gall bladder, of which the best known is probably gall stones.

Gall stones

As the gall bladder removes water from the bile, there is a danger that the concentration of salts in the gall bladder becomes so high that they crystallise out and start the process of stone formation. Gall stones vary in shape and compostion, but are usually composed of pigments from the bile, cholesterol or calcium. The exact trigger mechanism which starts the formation of the stones is not fully understood. They may form in the gall bladder itself, or in the duct.

They are a very common problem: 20 per cent of women of child-bearing age have one or more stones. It used to be said that the classic sufferer was fair, fat, 40 and fertile.

Problems with gall stones

Many people have gall stones without even knowing about them. However, they can cause an excruciating pain, known as gall-stone colic. The pain is felt in the upper abdomen, and sometimes in the back, and can be so severe that the patient rolls around in agony. The pain often comes on at night, and may last several

hours. It is due to small stones accumulating in the narrow neck of the gall bladder. The pain is caused by the muscle fibres in the wall of the bladder contracting in an effort to expel the stone.

Treatment

Most cases of gall-stone colic settle after a few hours. Injections of morphine and a drug to relieve the spasm alleviate the symptoms until the body can move the stone on. When the pain has settled, most doctors would suggest some form of surgery. This may involve the complete removal of the gall bladder, or the opening of the bladder may be enlarged to allow stones to pass through more easily. This is done using an endoscope, passed through the stomach and into the small intestine.

In the elderly or weak, treatment is more often with drugs, to try to dissolve the stones. Unfortunately, the drugs used often cause gastric upsets and they need to be taken for at least two

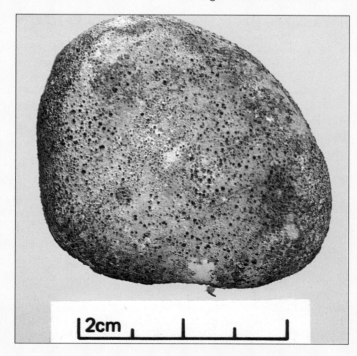

This gall stone, which is 8cm in diameter, was clearly large enough to cause problems and required surgical removal.

This diagram shows how small gall stones can collect in the gall bladder and block the duct.

years — and often for life, as the stones tend to recur if the treatment is stopped.

Infections

About half the gall bladders with stones in them are also the seat of chronic infection. If a gall stone blocks the drainage of an infected duct, an acute infection may result — causing pain which builds up slowly. Fever, nausea and vomiting are common. Treatment consists of rest, antibiotics and pain killers. If the condition settles, the gall bladder can be removed at a later date, but if the patient's condition continues to deteriorate, surgery is necessary at once.

Complications

In some cases the stones in the gall bladder find their way into the duct that drains both the liver and the gall bladder. If this happens, bile builds up in the liver and is eventually released into the blood stream, causing jaundice (a yellow staining of the skin). The urine becomes a very dark brown, like stewed tea. The stools, without their normal pigment, become very light in colour. Surgery may be needed to remove the stone, but this can often be done with endoscopy.

New developments

A new technique using powerful ultrasound waves to pulverise the stones is still being evaluated. This has the advantage of avoiding surgery, but the stones still tend to recur.

More promising is the so-called 'keyhole surgery'. Three small incisions are made in the abdominal wall. The first is used to fill the abdomen with gas to allow the surgeon a clear view. A telescope is inserted in the second opening, and operating instruments in the third. The surgeon removes the gall bladder without leaving a scar and the patient is fit to leave hospital after only a day or two.

Congenital abnormalities

Very rarely, the gall bladder fails to develop at all. This is not a major problem, as the digestion can still function reasonably well. More serious is a condition where the ducts fail to develop. This results in back pressure on the liver, which swells up causing an enlarged abdomen. The bile seeps out of the liver to give the infant a dark yellow colour (jaundice). Surgery offers the only hope of a cure. This surgery may be fairly easy or very difficult, depending on where the blockage is and how much of the duct is affected. In some cases, the liver becomes damaged and a liver transplant is needed.

Cancer

Cancer of the gall bladder accounts for less than one per cent of all cancers. It is very rare under the age of 40, but because it is associated with gall stones it is more common in women than men. The main symptom is painless jaundice, though sometimes it is found after routine gall-bladder surgery. The treatment is to remove the cancerous growth, but in most cases this only relieves the symptoms, and as few as one sufferer in 50 survives more than five years after diagnosis.

GANGRENE

Gangrene is the death of tissue, usually due to the lack of circulation of blood to a particular part of the body. It may affect a small area of skin, toes or fingers, or a whole limb.

There are two forms of gangrene, known as dry or wet gangrene.

Dry gangrene

In dry gangrene the affected area dies because the blood supply is blocked — there is no bacterial infection, and the gangrene does not spread to other areas. The main causes are arterio-sclerosis, diabetes mellitus, frostbite or a thrombosis or embolism. The affected area turns black as the tissue

---

Investigating the Gall Bladder

If a doctor suspects a disorder of the gall bladder there are several tests that can help her to reach a diagnosis.

● **Ultrasound** This is a cheap, easy and painless method of examination. The stones and position of the obstruction show up clearly.
● **Cholangiongram** This is a more complicated investigation, which involves the use of a dye, either in the form of an injection or a drink, to show up the gall bladder in an x-ray.
● **ERCP** This uses a flexible fibre-optic cable to view the inside of the gall bladder. Combined with x-rays and dyes it is very useful for detecting and removing stones and treating blockages.

dies. There is pain as the tissue is dying, but then numbness takes over. The condition takes months to develop, and is more common in older people.

Wet gangrene

This develops when an area of dry gangrene or a wound becomes infected with bacteria. The area swells and oozes pus. This type of gangrene may occur in the digestive tract if the blood supply is cut. (This may happen due to a strangulated hernia or a volvulus — a loop or twist in the bowel.) The area becomes infected because of the bacteria in the digestive tract.

One form of wet gangrene, known as gas gangrene, caused many deaths during the First World War. It is due to infection of wounds by a bacteria of the Clostrida family, which is found in the soil. It produces a foul-smelling gas as the tissue is destroyed.

Treatment

In dry gangrene, the treatment is to improve the circulation before the body tissue dies. Antibiotics may be prescribed if there is any infection, to prevent wet gangrene from taking over.

In wet gangrene, surgery

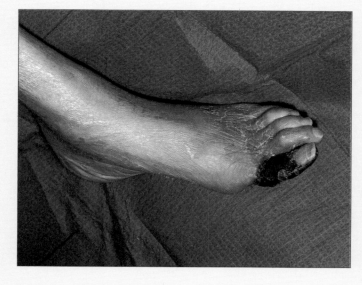

In dry gangrene, a constriction or blockage of the blood supply causes tissue to die and turn black.

is necessary to remove the infected tissue. This may involve removing a limb.

GASTRECTOMY

Removal of the stomach: gastrectomies may be partial or complete.

Gastrectomy may be carried out for several reasons: partial gastrectomy is used to treat peptic ulcers which have not responded to other forms of treatment, ulcers which bleed or perforated ulcers (those which have made a hole in the wall of the stomach). Stomach cancer may also be treated by gastrectomy: in rare cases, total gastrectomy has to be performed.

What's involved?

Gastrectomy is a major operation, carried out under general anaesthetic.

First, the stomach has to be emptied, by passing a tube down the nose into the stomach and pumping out the contents. The part of the stomach which has to be removed is cut away, and the remaining stomach is formed into a smaller bag. An opening is formed to re-connect the duodenum (the

first part of the intestine) to the stomach. If the gastrectomy is total, the oesophagus is joined directly to the duodenum.

The tube remains in the nose and continues to drain the stomach until the system is able to cope again. Gradually, the patient is given small amounts of water to drink, and if these go down without too much discomfort or nausea, then a light diet can be introduced.

Patients who have had a gastrectomy will have to watch their diet carefully in future. Their digestive system will not break down food or absorb certain minerals and vitamins as well as it did before. In particular, vitamin B12 has to be given, by injection, to those who have had a total gastrectomy.

A Partial Gastrectomy

Stomach

Part of stomach removed and re-connected to intestine

Small Intestine

Large Intestine

GASTRITIS

Gastritis is an inflammation of the lining of the stomach.

The condition may be acute, due to food poisoning or a viral infection, a drug (such as alcohol or aspirin), or extreme physical stress, such as a head injury. It may be a sign of a serious disorder, such as liver failure.

Chronic gastritis may come with age, or through prolonged exposure to irritants, including tobacco smoking, alcohol and aspirin.

Symptoms and diagnosis

The symptoms include nausea, vomiting and pain (particularly after eating). Faeces may be dark, due to bleeding in the stomach. The symptoms are similar to a gastric ulcer.

If the condition persists,

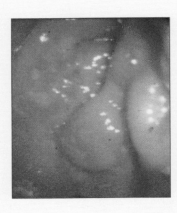

Above: This view through an endoscope shows gastritis – inflammation of the lining of the stomach.

it may be necessary to use a gastroscope (a medical telescope) to examine the stomach, and a sample of tissue (biopsy) may be taken for analysis.

Treatment

As long as the doctors find no serious underlying cause, the treatment for gastritis is through a carefully controlled diet: in particular, sufferers should not drink alcohol or smoke, and use paracetamol rather than aspirin.

GASTROENTERITIS

Gastroenteritis is an inflammation of the stomach (gastritis) and intestine (enteritis). It may cause diarrhoea, vomiting, pain or, more usually, a combination of all three.

Gastroenteritis is very common. In a random survey of adults, up to 5 per cent had suffered some form of gastroenteritis in the previous two weeks. Twice as many children as adults are affected and the worst hit group is the under fives.

Causes

The commonest cause of gastroenteritis is probably an ill-considered diet. This may well follow a holiday abroad and is often labelled as food poisoning. Alcohol, even in quite modest amounts, can cause loose motions. Most people are aware of the emetic effect of too much alcohol but it can also cause gastroenteritis for many days after a binge. Apart from moderating the alcohol intake the risk of developing gastroenteritis can be lessened by avoiding neat spirits and not smoking.

Some forms of gastro-enteritis are caused by bacteria — campylobacter is probably the commonest.

Viruses are another common cause of gastroenteritis. Only a few of these viral infections can be positively identified, but the fact that there are epidemics with consistent features — even when sufferers have not been eating the same food — means that they are almost certainly due to a virus.

In some cases, gastroenteritis is due to drugs prescribed for other conditions. For example, if a doctor prescribes antibiotics (for an ear infection, for instance) they may cause mild nausea and a few loose motions. Very rarely, antibiotic therapy is followed by acute diarrhoea and a generalised illness. This is due to the overgrowth of one particular type of germ. This condition can be fatal and the patient needs immediate hospital treatment. Other drugs, such as aspirin or ibuprofen (Neurofen) may

Warning Signs

Dehydration, as a side effect of gastro-enteritis, is more likely to affect the very young and the very old.

● Dry mouth and tongue.
● Loss of skin tone.
● Less frequent urination.
● In severe cases, confusion and coma.

Gastroenteritis and Bacteriology

Bacteriology (the study of bacteria) has developed rapidly over the last decade.

A few years ago, when stools of sufferers were analysed, it seemed that they were clear of infection. However, it is now known that this was not the case. Hospital laboratories were unable to test for disease-causing germs that died very quickly outside the body. This meant that bacteria like campylobacter were never reported as the cause of gastroenteritis.

Bacteriology is also recognising that some germs which normally live quite harmlessly in our gastrointestinal tract have different strains in different parts of the world. These different strains do no harm to the local population, but cause gastroenteritis in holidaymakers.

As laboratory science progresses, doctors will be given the chance to identify the cause of most cases of gastroenteritis. This will make little difference from a treatment point of view but may mean that public health measures will be easier to apply.

cause a gastric upset in some people.

Many chronic (long term) conditions, such as ulcerative colitis or Crohn's disease, will also cause some degree of gastroenteritis. Unlike the acute, infective diarrhoeas, these conditions do not clear up in a day or two.

Treatment

The treatment of gastroenteritis depends on the severity of the condition. The vast majority of adults do not need to see a doctor unless the problem persists for more than 48 hours. Exceptions from this rule would include anyone who has a serious pre-existing condition such as sugar diabetes or kidney failure; anyone who works in the catering industry, when stool tests and time off work are important public health measures; anyone who seems badly affected or dehydrated (see left).

The main aim in treating gastroenteritis is to avoid dehydration. Keep up an adequate fluid intake: if there is vomiting, regular small sips of water are better than glassfuls. Special sachets of glucose and salt, for mixing with water, are available at chemists or on prescription. They are more important for children than for adults. In mild cases, lemonade mixed 50:50 with water is good for rehydration.

If vomiting is so bad that fluid cannot be kept down, or if diarrhoea is so bad that fluid intake cannot keep pace, intravenous fluid has to be used. When fluids are administered intravenously, salts and glucose can also be given.

Gastroenteritis is made worse by eating — especially dairy products or anything fatty. Avoid all food for at least 24 hours. Then start with something easy to digest, such as dry toast with a smear of jam.

Certain specific conditions may be treated with antibiotics, but in most cases they have no role to play and may only make the problem worse. Anti-diarrhoeals are also likely to prolong the infection, and are best avoided (unless you have a special engagement or are travelling and do not want the inconvenience of diarrhoea).

GASTROENTEROSTOMY

This is the technical term for an artificial opening between the stomach and the duodenum or jejunum.

This operation is sometimes carried out in conjunction with a partial gastrectomy (removal of the lower part of the stomach).

The operation was previously used to treat duodenal ulcers, but this is no longer the case. It is now used to allow food to pass directly from the stomach to the small intestine, when there have been problems with the digestive system. It is also used to bypass a duodenum that may be damaged, scarred or obstructed in some way.

Technique

The patient is put under general anaesthetic. The stomach is then emptied by means of a tube that is passed through the nose and down into the stomach via the oesophagus. The first part of the jejunum is pulled up and stitched to the lower part of the stomach. A new opening is made which allows food to pass through to the small intestine.

The tube that has been used to empty the stomach is left in position for a few days after the operation to allow any digestive secretions to drain off.

GENES

Genes are the basic units of inheritance contained in every chromosome in the human body.

Our genes determine how we develop physically and mentally, and dictate what diseases we may be predisposed to (including cancer and heart disease). Every cell in the body carries 46 chromosomes, each carrying the string of genes which holds the inheritance information. The sperm and eggs normally each carry 23 chromosomes. When the sperm and egg combine the embryo produced receives a normal full adult complement of genes.

Within the genes the information is carried in the DNA (deoxyribonucleic acid) which makes up the genes. DNA consists of a double spiral made up of thousands and thousands of amino acid molecules. These amino acids are the building blocks of protein and they always combine in the same way. The sequence of amino acids in the DNA acts as a code that enables the cell to build proteins and to develop and grow normally.

If the DNA is thought of as a string of beads, then the body will recognise a sequence — red, red, blue, red, for example — as one particular code. Each separate and distinct sequence is called a gene. One gene will determine the colour of the eyes, another the colour of the hair, and so on. Many thousands of genes are held together in a string that is coiled and twisted in on itself. One of these collections is called a chromosome.

Hereditary sequences

If the sequence of amino acids in a gene is altered in any way, the cell will read the code incorrectly. This is the case in many serious and often fatal diseases where the sequence is wrong by only one amino acid.

Many common diseases tend to run in families. Heart disease, for example, is more common in the children of sufferers than in those of non-sufferers. Some diseases follow a regular pattern, because it is carried in a particular gene or group of genes and the chance of the child being affected can actually be calculated beforehand. The science of heredity is called genetics.

Not all congenital problems or diseases are genetic however. This has been proved recently by tests on pregnant mothers, which show that some infections can affect the embryo and result in problems from birth. So damage to unborn children caused by German measles, for example, is not inherited, even though it is present from birth.

Not only do genes determine what diseases we may or may not suffer from, they also determine almost everything else, from our sex to the colour of our eyes. At the moment of conception, genetic material from the mother and father mix to make a unique cocktail so that two individuals with the same parents can look totally different from each other.

Genetic determination

Most characteristics are determined by several genes acting together, but sometimes it is the combination of a single pair of genes that determines the way we look or develop.

Such a pair combination is normally governed by the nature of the individual genes, which may be dominant or recessive. In the case of eyes, for example, brown eyes are dominant and blue eyes are recessive.

The Structure of DNA

Individual amino acids (shown in different colours) link together in a series and specific groups form patterns which are recognised as genes. A long spiral of genes forms each chromosome (represented at the top of the diagram as an X).

DNA (deoxyribonucleic acid) was discovered by two scientists, Watson and Crick, working during the 1940s and early 50s. They produced a three-dimensional model to illustrate its complex structure. Once the structure of DNA had been established, scientists were able to analyse how an irregularity in the sequence of amino acids could cause genetic disorders.

Dominant And Recessive Genes – Eye Colours

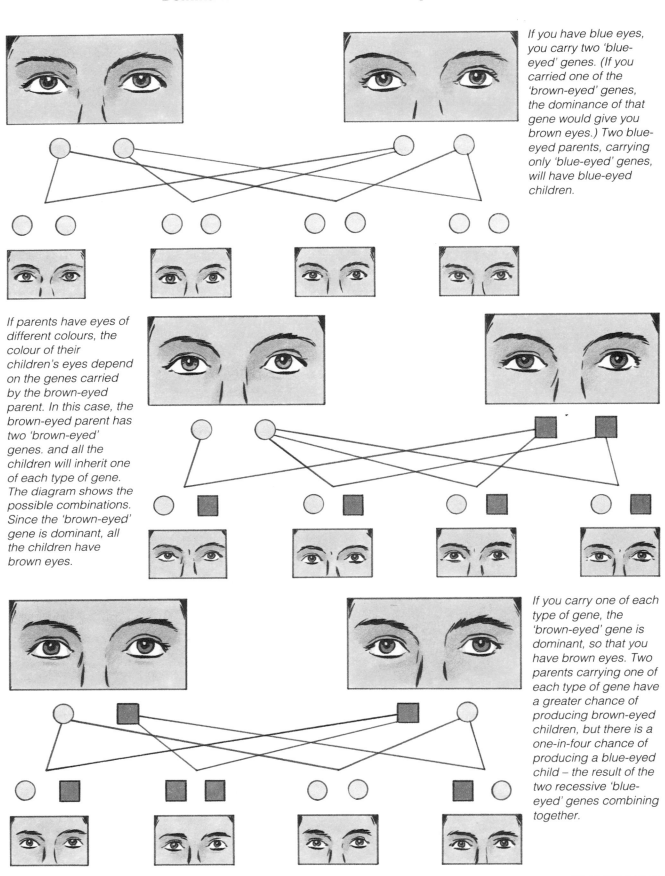

If you have blue eyes, you carry two 'blue-eyed' genes. (If you carried one of the 'brown-eyed' genes, the dominance of that gene would give you brown eyes.) Two blue-eyed parents, carrying only 'blue-eyed' genes, will have blue-eyed children.

If parents have eyes of different colours, the colour of their children's eyes depend on the genes carried by the brown-eyed parent. In this case, the brown-eyed parent has two 'brown-eyed' genes. and all the children will inherit one of each type of gene. The diagram shows the possible combinations. Since the 'brown-eyed' gene is dominant, all the children have brown eyes.

If you carry one of each type of gene, the 'brown-eyed' gene is dominant, so that you have brown eyes. Two parents carrying one of each type of gene have a greater chance of producing brown-eyed children, but there is a one-in-four chance of producing a blue-eyed child – the result of the two recessive 'blue-eyed' genes combining together.

What this actually means, therefore, is that a person with one gene for brown eyes and one gene for blue eyes will have brown eyes, as brown is the dominant force involved. The various combinations are shown in the diagrams on the opposite page. This means that two brown-eyed parents may in fact produce blue-eyed children if they are both carriers of the genes responsible for blue eyes.

Faulty genes

The embryo receives its DNA from both parents. If there is an abnormal dose from one parent it is possible that a normal dose in the other parent will cancel it out. But there are three main ways in which faulty genes can be inherited and cause disease.

Dominant gene disorders

Dominant gene disorders are carried by either the mother or the father and affect both sexes equally. It is only necessary for one of the parents to carry the disease for it to be passed on to a child. If a parent does have the condition, a child who inherits the gene will contract the disease. Huntingdon's chorea, a degenerative disease which does not usually show itself until the sufferer is in his or her late 30s, is a condition caused by a dominant gene.

Recessive gene disorders

Recessive gene disorders will only affect children if both parents are carriers of the condition. Carriers are entirely healthy themselves but have one abnormal gene. This gene, as far as the carrier's health is concerned, is cancelled out by a healthy gene from their other parent. If the mother and father are both carriers, there is the potential for an affected child (1 in 4 chance). If the child inherits one normal and one abnormal gene, she will be a carrier (2 in 4 chance). If the child inherits two normal genes she will be a healthy carrier (1 in 4 chance). Cystic fibrosis and albinism are examples of recessive gene disorders.

Sex linked

Chromosomes are long strands of genetic material. Using a special stain, they can be seen under the microscope. A normal cell contains 46 chromosomes — 22 in pairs and two sex chromosomes, X and Y, which determine the sex. A male has XY and a female XX. A sperm contains 22 single chromosomes and either an X or a Y sex chromosome. An egg will also contain 22 single chromosomes, but only the X chromosome.

An abnormal gene on the X chromosome of a girl (who is XX), will be cancelled out by the normal gene on the other X chromosome, so she will be a carrier. An abnormal gene on the X chromosome of a boy has nothing to balance it and will cause disease. The best known example is haemophilia (see above).

Chromosome Disorders

If there are problems with the combination of the sex chromosomes, several abnormal conditions may arise:

XO Turner's syndrome: This involves the sufferer, always a woman, being short of an X sex chromosome. Affected women are very short with webbed skin on their necks. They do not develop secondary sexual characteristics and do not have periods. Sex hormones will produce breasts, but there is no specific treatment to cure the condition.

YO Foetuses with this condition, in which there is an X sex chromosome missing, are miscarried at an early stage in pregnancy.

XXX An extra X chromosome produces a near normal female who may well be fertile.

XXY Kleinfelter's syndrome: In this case the extra chromosome gives rise to adults who look and act like men, but develop breasts and do not need to shave. They are infertile.

XYY 'Supermen': with a double dose of the male Y chromosome, these men are taller and stronger than normal. It used to be thought that they were more violent as well though this does not seem to be the case.

Haemophilia: Carriers and Sufferers

- **X** Normal X chromosome
- **X** Defective X chromosome
- **Y** Normal Y chromosome
- Female carrier
- Unaffected female
- Affected male
- Unaffected male

Haemophilia is a genetic disorder caused by a defective X chromosome. The condition only affects males, but females carry the disease. If a woman is known to be a carrier of the disorder (if she has a defective X chromosome), she can pass it on to her sons, and her daughters may be carriers. However, she can also produce normal, unaffected children.

▶▶ SEE ALSO — Chromosomes, Down's Syndrome

GENETIC COUNSELLING

Parents who have had an abnormal child, or those whose relatives have an abnormal child, should be offered the chance to see a genetic counsellor (or geneticist).

By definition, congenital abnormalities are present at birth. There is, therefore, a natural tendency on the part of the parents to think that all such conditions are inherited — some are, but most are not. Sorting them out is the job of the genetic counsellor. A genetic counsellor is a specialist in all aspects of congenital disorders. She will usually split her time between patients and the laboratory.

Genetic advice

The genetic counsellor may be able to pin-point abnormalities present at birth to problems during pregnancy, such as rubella, radiation, diet and even problems with certain drugs. In this case, the problem can be avoided in the next pregnancy and the chance of another affected child will be largely minimalised.

In some cases, and these are in fact the majority, no cause can be found. The genetic counsellor can use her experience of similar cases to predict figures for subsequent pregnancies.

In a few cases, and these are becoming more common as the field of genetics expands, the abnormality is due to a single gene defect. The genetic counsellor can arrive at precise odds on subsequent children being affected.

Family tree

The genetic counsellor will construct a family tree to see if any pattern emerges — all the boys dying young, for example. She will examine the parents, any affected children and any non-affected children. She will also want to examine genetic material from all the members of the family. This material can be obtained from the blood or from a few cells found in mouth washouts. Unless a specific disease is suspected, she will only be able to pin-point abnormalities of the chromosomes, but this will give information about many of the commonest disorders. Once the disorder has been recognised, she will be able to give some idea about the effects of the disease, though the treatment will be in the hands of a child specialist.

Constructive advice

The role of the genetic counsellor comes to the fore when the couple are planning another pregnancy. She will be able to advise them of their chances of having a normal baby. If the risk is substantial she may be able to offer an antenatal diagnosis — by chorionic villus sampling or amnio-centesis. The results give the parents the option of an abortion, if they wish, and if it is legal in their country.

Modern advances

Human genetics is developing so fast that by the turn of the decade, we may know about the function and position of every gene in the human cell. Using this knowledge, we may be able to avoid illness. The smoker who knows he has the gene associated with lung cancer will think twice before lighting up. Even today, knowledge is such that genetic scientists are already experimenting with the idea of replacing an abnormal gene with a healthy one. Such technology will herald the end of many diseases, in the same way that the discovery of anti-biotics wiped out TB.

Common Disorders

There are a number of quite common problems that a genetic counsellor can help with:

Spina bifida The cause of this is unknown, though many theories have been put forward, from potato blight to vitamin deficiency in early pregnancy. Recent research suggests that a deficiency in folic acid may be the cause. This is found in liver. It is essential to ensure that folic acid is included in the diet for at least six weeks before trying to start a pregnancy.

The idea that spina bifida is due to a vitamin deficiency is an easily assumed theory, in that babies from lower social classes, where the diet is poorer, are more prone to it than babies from higher social classes where the levels of nutrition and hygiene are better. This cannot, however, explain the whole story, because the condition is more common in English cities than in Indian ones, despite the fact that vitamin deficiency is more common amongst ethnic Indians. The risk of a secondary pregnancy being affected works out at about three per cent. This risk is acceptable to some couples but not to others. The genetic counsellor will help them make a decision and can arrange the tests that can reveal the answer in early pregnancy.

Sugar diabetes Analysis of family trees shows that of the two sorts of diabetes mellitus, the type that comes on with age and can be treated with dietary changes and pills, may be inherited. The counsellor will be able to assess the risk of a healthy individual, with an affected parent, contracting the disease. This may not be very important in the case of diabetes, where effective treatment exists, but may alter the whole life of someone at risk of contracting other conditions, such as Huntingdon's chorea.

Cystic fibrosis This is the commonest single gene defect in the UK. The inheritance is well understood and, using a simple blood test, relatives of affected individuals can be screened to see if they have the abnormal gene. If both they and their intended partner are the carriers, they must think very carefully before embarking on a pregnancy as there is a one-in-four chance of the child being affected.

Cystic fibrosis is a well-known genetic disorder. CF sufferers tend to get chronic lung infections, due to the sticky mucus secreted in the throat and lungs.

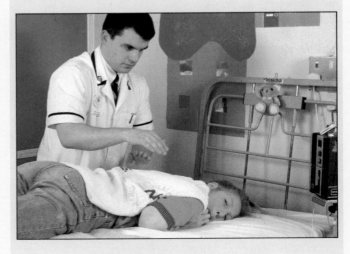

GERMAN MEASLES

German measles, or rubella, is one of a group of illnesses often referred to as childhood diseases.

A mild infection that usually affects older children and adolescents, rather than babies, German measles is due to a virus that is spread by droplets. It is less infectious than measles or chicken pox, which are spread in a similar fashion. One attack usually confers natural, lifelong immunity, though some people do suffer a second time, so do not assume you are immune if you have had the disease.

The course of illness

The incubation period (the time between picking up the virus and developing the disease) is two to three weeks. The first symptoms are usually vague aches and pains and a runny nose. Often these symptoms are so mild that they go unnoticed and the first sign is the appearance of a rash 24 hours later.

The rash consists of tiny pink spots, which may be so close together that they give the appearance of a solid mass of pink. They start behind the ears and spread down over the trunk and on to the limbs. The feature that distinguishes German measles from other causes of a rash is the presence of lymph nodes on the back of the head. These are felt as pea-sized, tender lumps just above the point where the neck meets the skull. There may also be a mild fever — up to 38°C (100°F).

German measles is a mild disease that is over in two or three days, though it should be borne in mind that the sufferer is infectious for a week after the appearance of the spots. No treatment is necessary, other than paracetamol to keep down any fever. You do not need to have the diagnosis confirmed by a doctor, and should certainly not visit the waiting room, where there may well be pregnant women.

Risks

The most serious effect of rubella is on the pregnant woman. If the foetus is affected during the period of organ growth (the first 10 weeks) serious damage may occur. The actual damage caused depends on the exact stage of development at the time of infection, but may include blindness, deafness and brain damage.

GERMS

A germ is a microorganism that causes disease.

The term is not usually used in medical circles, as there is more precise, technical terminology. What we refer to as germs may be viruses or bacteria. (In medical science, the term 'germ cell' is sometimes used to describe simple cells which are capable of growing into complete organisms.)

GESTATION

Gestation is the length of time it takes for a fertilised egg to develop, from conception until birth.

In humans, the gestation period is 40 weeks. During the first few weeks of gestation, the unborn child is known as an embryo, and after the eighth week it becomes known as a foetus.

GINGIVITIS

Gingivitis is the term given to inflammation of the gingiva (or gums). Gingivitis may be chronic or acute.

Chronic gingivitis may be present for many years, and affects almost all adults.

Chronic causes and symptoms

Chronic gingivitis is caused by the germs that live on dental plaque. The bacteria, and there are many different sorts, do not invade the gums, but cause damage by the release of toxins.

If chronic gingivitis is left unchecked, it will cause a breakdown of the structures that hold the teeth in place. After the age of 40, as dental decay becomes less of a problem, the complications of gingivitis are the most common cause of tooth loss.

The symptoms of gingivitis may be so mild as to go unnoticed. It may, however, cause painful teeth and gums, loose teeth and bleeding. These symptoms tend to be more of a problem during eating.

The lack of severe symptoms may mean that the disease progresses to an irreversible condition before help is sought. This is one of the reasons why it is necessary to visit the dentist regularly — at least once every three months for children and once a year for

---

Immunisation and Blood Tests

It is important to ensure you are immune to rubella if you are considering starting a family.

Immunisation against German measles used to be offered to all 13-year-old girls, but this has recently been changed to include all children at 14 months. If you missed your injection it is not too late to ask your doctor for it now. If you are contemplating pregnancy, even if you think you are immune, it is worth checking that you are safe. This can be done by a simple blood test and your doctor or family planning clinic will be pleased to help. If you are already pregnant and think you may have been exposed to risk, ask your midwife about the blood test that can show if you are infected or not.

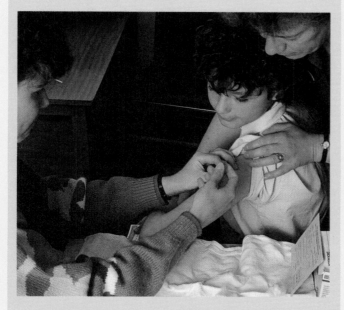

A simple injection will give you protection against rubella if you do not have natural immunity.

➤➤ See also Embryo, Foetus, Pregnancy

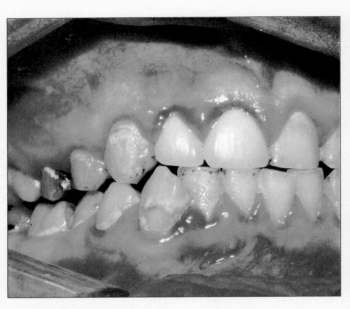

When gingivitis takes hold, the gums become very sensitive, with pus-filled areas and red patches.

adults are the latest recommendations.

Treatment and prevention

The treatment for gingivitis is to remove the plaque which collects around the base of the teeth. By the time it is causing gingivitis, the plaque is so hard that it needs to be scraped off by a dentist or dental hygienist.

Prevention is more effective than cure and consists of regular, careful brushing. Disclosing tablets should be used to reveal any plaque which has not been cleared, to help train you to brush thoroughly.

Acute gingivitis

This condition is much rarer. It is commonest in young adults, especially smokers or those with weakened resistance. The bacteria causing acute gingivitis actually invade the gums, so the damage is much quicker. The disorder occurs as a result of poor dental hygiene, and may be coupled with a throat infection or emotional stress.

The symptoms of acute gingivitis are sudden onset of pain, bleeding gums and foul breath. The temperature may rise as high as 39°C (102°F),

and the patient feels ill. An examination of the mouth reveals indented pus-filled ulcers and sore, red areas on the gums.

Treatment is with penicillin and mouth washes. Although treatment is effective, the condition will almost certainly recur unless there is meticulous attention to oral hygiene.

GLANDS, SWOLLEN

Swollen glands are a common symptom of many disorders.

Although commonly referred to as glands, it is the lymph nodes which become swollen when we talk about swollen glands. Since they do not secrete chemicals (hormones or enzymes), the lymph nodes are not strictly glands. The function of the lymph nodes is to release white blood cells, which are important in fighting infection.

Swollen glands near the surface of the skin (at the top of the neck, in the armpit and in the groin) can usually be felt as tender lumps, but elsewhere in the body you may not be aware of them.

Causes

The lymph nodes may become swollen for a number of reasons. They may be overloaded with white blood cells when fighting infections, particularly in children. If the infection is localised, the swelling may also be localised. For example, a throat infection is likely to cause swollen glands in the neck, and an infection of the breast is likely to cause swollen glands in the armpit. But some types of infection (in the pelvic cavity, for example) cause swollen glands in other parts of the body, away from the site of the infection. Generalised swelling of the lymph nodes may be caused by glandular fever. Some secondary infection following allergies also cause swollen glands.

Rarer causes

Some forms of cancer affect the lymph system, causing the lymph nodes to swell. These include Hodgkin's disease and leukaemia. Cancer may also spread to the lymph system from other parts of the body, particularly the breast.

Diagnosis and treatment

In most cases, it is clear what is causing the glands to swell, and treatment of the infection will relieve the condition. However, if there is

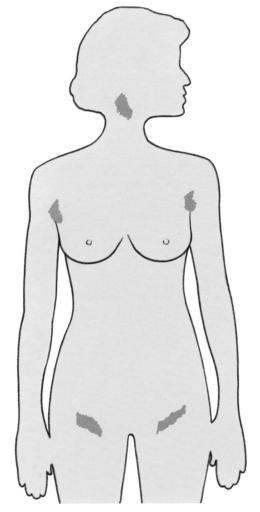

Common Sites for Swollen Glands

Common areas for swollen glands are at the base of the skull, in the armpits and in the groin.

no obvious cause, and the condition persists, blood tests and x-rays may be necessary (or a biopsy).

The treatment will depend on the cause, and may range from rest (for glandular fever) to antibiotics (for infection) or antihistamine (for allergic reactions). If the cause is cancer, the doctor will probably refer you to a specialist for further investigation and treatment, including radiotherapy and chemotherapy.

GLANDULAR FEVER

Glandular fever is a viral infection, most commonly found in adolescents. Its medical name is infectious mononucleosis.

In the USA, glandular fever is known as the kissing disease. It was thought that only teenagers were affected, and that it was spread by the mixing of saliva during kissing. Epidemics may appear after school camps or at colleges,

One virus which may cause glandular fever is the Epstein-Barr virus, shown here as round red and gold particles. This virus is a herpes virus. In central Africa, where malaria is common, the malaria may affect the virus so that a more serious disease develops. In some cases, African children infected with the Epstein-Barr virus develop a type of face cancer known as Burkitt's lymphoma.

but it is now known that younger children are also affected. In younger children the disease may be so mild as to pass unrecognised.

Symptoms

Glandular fever has an incubation period of four to seven weeks. The onset of symptoms is sudden, with sore throat, fever and tiredness. The tonsils are very swollen and may be covered with a thick, foul-smelling layer of pus. All the lymph glands in the body can be affected, though the ones in the neck are usually the most swollen. (These signs may be present with other diseases — tonsillitis for example.) The two features that a doctor would look for to confirm the diagnosis are the presence of spots on the palate and the fact that, despite any treatment, the disease lasts for several weeks.

It is important to call the doctor to have diagnosis confirmed, as the recovery period may be so long that school or college work is affected, or you may need a certificate if you have to take a long period off work. Confirmation is by means of a

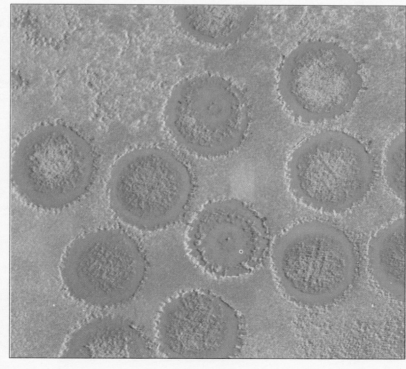

blood test, but it is at least seven days from the onset of symptoms before this becomes positive.

Treatment

Treatment is aimed at relieving the symptoms. Because it is a viral disease, glandular fever is not affected by antibiotics. Indeed, some forms of penicillin react with the disease to cause a very unpleasant, itchy rash. In severe cases, where the patient is unable to swallow, the doctor may prescribe steroids to try to reduce the swelling of the tonsils. Rest is essential — the disease is often more prolonged in those patients who try to resume their normal activities too soon.

Recovery is often slow. Most people take several months to return to normal. Some patients may take two or three years. This prolonged recovery may be due to infection spreading from the tonsils to the liver and heart. Despite all this, glandular fever is a benign disease and complications are almost unheard of.

GLASSES

Glasses or spectacles are frames holding lenses which are needed to correct visual defects.

In normal vision, muscles in the eye adjust the natural lens to ensure rays of light are focused on the retina. The lenses of glasses alter the point at which rays of light are focused as they enter the eye. The lenses may be glass or plastic: glass lenses have the advantage of not scratching easily, while plastic lenses are lighter and virtually unbreakable.

The ophthalmologist

If you think you have anything wrong with your vision it is important to have your eyes properly tested by a qualified ophthalmologist. He will not only be able to prescribe the correct lens for you, but also may be able to advise on suitable frames — and on any 'extras' like tinted glass, bifocals, or contact lenses if you cannot bear the idea of wearing glasses.

Types of lenses

Different types of lenses are prescribed for different defects: longsightedness, for example, requires convex lenses to shorten the focal length, while shortsighted people require concave lenses (see overleaf). In astigmatism, the eye's lens is distorted so that the corrective lens only has to be curved in one plane.

It is also possible to get special types of lenses to help with problems at different focal lengths. For example, if you cannot see things close to, but your distance vision is good, you may only need 'reading' glasses. In such cases, many people find it easier to use bifocals, which have different types of glass in different parts of the lens in order to cater for the needs of the

How Glasses Correct Long- and Shortsightedness

Longsightedness

Convex lens

Retina

Close object

Shortsightedness

Concave lens

Retina

Light from distant object

Defect:
Light from near objects (shown in blue) focuses beyond the retina.
Correction:
A convex lens bends the rays of light from a near object further inwards, so that they focus on the retina (shown in red).

Defect:
Light from distant objects (shown in blue) focuses in the eyeball before it reaches the retina.
Correction:
A concave lens bends the rays outwards, so that the natural lens focuses the light on the retina (shown in red).

viewer. Bifocals like this can be adapted to suit many different needs and visual problems. But they take some time to get used to. Because of the split lens they are not suitable for people in some occupations: if you need to be able to see at a distance while looking downwards, for example, it will not help to have bifocals with a 'close-up' lens in the lower part of the frame.

Tinted lenses
Some glasses have tinted lenses to cut out glare: this is not usually part of the ophthalmist's prescription, except in special conditions. It is, however, a useful option if you wear glasses and also like to wear sunglasses. You can have a tint added to prescription glasses. Photochromatic lenses, which get darker as the light gets brighter, are also a useful alternative. Tinted glasses also help to disguise unsightly conditions, such as cataracts or squints.

GLAUCOMA

Any condition in which the fluid pressure inside the eye rises is called glaucoma.

The fluid itself is produced in the main chamber of the eye and passes through the iris to be absorbed where the iris and cornea meet. The effect of this raised pressure is damage to the blood supply to the optic nerve.

Visual loss
The nerve is pressed out of shape and vision is lost. This visual loss usually occurs at the edges of the field of view. If left unchecked, it will cause tunnel vision and eventually leads to blindness.

The different types of glaucoma are classified in several ways but the most important distinction is between acute (sudden onset) and chronic (slow onset) glaucoma.

Acute glaucoma
Acute glaucoma is a medical emergency which requires

immediate hospital treatment, day or night, if the sight is to be saved. Acute glaucoma is rare and almost never affects people under 60.

The patient complains of severe pain in the eye and head which may be bad enough to cause vomiting or even collapse. The vision is greatly reduced and the victim may even be unable to count fingers. The eye becomes red and swollen; the pupil is fixed and does not change with the light. If the eyelid is closed and the eyeball gently pressed it feels stony hard.

Treatment
Treatment of acute glaucoma is initially with eyedrops and intravenous drugs. When the condition is under control surgery is performed. This involves drilling a tiny hole in the iris to allow the fluid to drain freely. Surgery may be done with a laser.

Chronic glaucoma
Chronic glaucoma is much more common than the acute variety. It affects about two

per cent of those over 40. It usually affects both eyes and tends to run in families, so children of sufferers are particularly at risk.

Most cases are found by routine eye testing. The optician notices the change in the nerve or measures the loss at the edges of the field of vision. A simple pressure test using a puff of air will confirm the condition. For those who are not helped by eye drops, surgery will offer an immediate cure.

Glaucoma may be the result of several diseases of the eye. It can also be caused by trauma, for example a blow to the eye, which damages the normal drainage mechanism.

Preventive action
The best way to guard against glaucoma is to have an eye check every two years. This is free to the immediate family of glaucoma sufferers but not until they have reached their 40th birthday.

▶▶ SEE ALSO — Astigmatism, Hypermetropia, Myopia

GLOSSITIS

Glossitis is an inflammation of the tongue, which may be caused by irritation, or certain deficiencies.

When the tongue swells, it usually becomes smooth and dark red, as well as feeling sore and uncomfortably swollen.

Causes

The condition is most often caused by burning the tongue on hot food. It can be caused by eating spicy food, irritation from dentures, excessive alcohol and tobacco consumption. Pipe smoking causes glossitis, and is associated with increased cancer of the tongue. Oral thrush may also cause a swollen tongue, together with the white spots which are characteristic of thrush. More seriously, glossitis may be a sign of iron deficiency (anaemia), or vitamin B deficiency. In addition, glossitis is occasionally a symptom of infections of the mouth such as herpes simplex.

Treatment

As long as an infection or deficiency is not responsible, then the main treatment is to avoid spicy foods and other irritants until the swelling has gone down. It is important to maintain good oral hygiene, and regular rinsing with a salt solution may help.

GLUE EAR

Glue ear is the common name for a build-up of pus in the middle ear, which leads to deafness.

The condition affects children, particularly between the ages of 18 months and three years. The pus builds up in the middle ear as a result of repeated infections, usually caused by

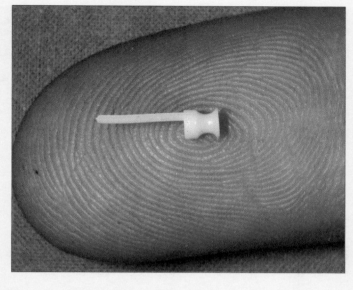

Above: Tiny grommets inserted in the ears of children suffering from glue ear help to clear the condition.

common colds and 'flu. Because the tubes within the ear are not fully developed they do not drain so easily as in later life.

Symptoms

Many children who suffer persistent ear infections during their early childhood show signs of deafness: they are slow to learn to speak, have difficulty differentiating certain vowel sounds, and, unless you shout, may not respond to what you are saying if they are unable to see you. They may also find it difficult to tell where sounds are coming from.

Treatment

It is advisable to get children's ear infections looked at by the doctor as soon as you notice them: this may be difficult, because young children find it hard to identify where the pain is, and it may not be clear that it is their ear which is bothering them. Doctors may prescribe antibiotics to clear the infection if it is severe.

If glue ear does develop, the child will be referred to a specialist. The normal treatment is to make a small incision in the eardrum (under anaesthetic) and drain the fluid. A small valve, known as

a grommet, is then inserted to prevent further build-up of fluid. The operation is small, only requiring a day in hospital. The grommets gradually work their way out of the ear after about six months, and further out-patient checks are necessary. In some cases, the deafness returns after the grommets have come out,

and a repeat operation is performed. In many cases, abnormally large adenoids and tonsils are involved in the pattern of infection, and a tonsillectomy and/or adenoidectomy may be performed at the same time, requiring approximately three days in hospital.

GOITRE

Goitre occurs when the thyroid gland on the neck becomes visibly swollen and manifests itself as a small lump which sometimes presses on the trachea or oesophagus.

There are several factors which can cause an enlargement of the thyroid gland. Natural causes are the onset of puberty or pregnancy although the condition may be induced as a side effect of taking the oral contraceptive pill. However, in many parts of the world, particularly in the Third World, goitre is a result of a

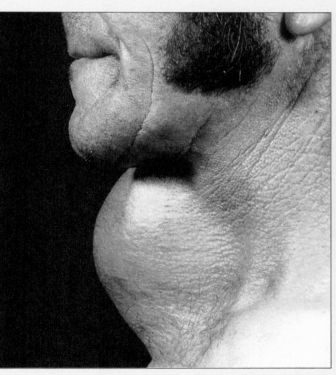

Above: A large goitre on the throat of a man suffering from Graves' disease, a disorder which causes thyrotoxicosis.

diet which is lacking in sufficient iodine. The condition also used to be common in Derbyshire and Switzerland, because they are a long way from the sea (so traditionally there was little fish included in the diet) and the geology is such that there is no iodine in the underlying rock.

The thyroid gland needs iodine to create the hormone thyroxine and without this hormone the thyroid begins to swell.

Thyrotoxicosis

Thyrotoxicosis is an overactive thyroid gland (known as hyperthyroidism). A sufferer from thyrotoxicosis will undergo several uncomfortable symptoms of physical dysfunction. These will include sudden reduction in weight, itchy and dry skin, and a strange combination of twitching muscles which is also accompanied by a lack of muscle strength. In some cases they may develop goitre and bulging eyes.

Treatment

If goitre has been brought on by drugs then it should normally disappear once the sufferer ceases to use the drugs. Thyrotoxicosis requires prolonged treatment to control the production of thyroid hormones. It may be possible to aid recovery with a diet which contains an increased amount of fish and specially iodized salt.

GONORRHOEA

Gonorrhoea is a painful bacterial infection which is transmitted by sexual contact and which can affect any part of the body that is not covered by skin. This includes the urethra, the cervix, the mouth and the anus.

The discovery of penicillin in 1928 led to a

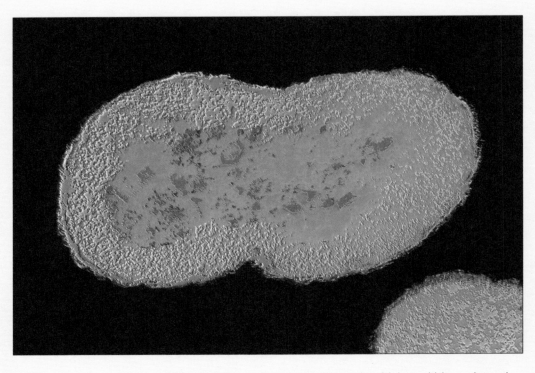

Above: A microscopic view of the Neisseria gonorrhoeae bacteria which are kidney-shaped and often occur in pairs. They cause the sexually-transmitted disease gonorrhoea.

dramatic fall in the number of cases of gonorrhoea. Unfortunately, this trend was reversed over the 25 years after the introduction of the pill in the early 1960s. The resultant increased sexual activity brought about an increase in gonorrhoea. Nowadays, apart from the common cold, it is still the most prevalent infectious disease in the world.

Now, however, the growth of the AIDS epidemic and the practice of 'safe sex' mean that gonorrhoea is once again on the decline. Such is the nature of the disease that more women than men are infected, and in the UK the average age of the women infected is falling. Now, 25 per cent are less than 20 years old.

Transmission and symptoms

In theory, it might be possible to catch gonorrhoea from a toilet seat but in reality this may be a convenient let-out for those who don't want to admit to sexual indiscretions.

The disease may take anything from two days to two months to develop and in

men the symptoms are obvious. These are a discharge from the penis and pain when passing water. There is often a stinging pain when urinating after drinking alcohol. Women may be infected and have no symptoms at all. The usual complaint is of pain on passing water, increased frequency of passing water and a vaginal discharge.

In women with severe infection the whole vulva can be red and painful and the patient will generally feel unwell. If left untreated the condition may be infectious for years. It will cause chronic damage to the urethra, cervix and fallopian tubes. Severe cases may cause pelvic peritonitis. It may spread, causing inflammation of tendons and joints.

Diagnosis and treatment

Diagnosis is suggested by the symptoms and the patient's recent sexual behaviour and is confirmed by recognising the bacteria under a microscope.

Sexually transmitted diseases tend to hunt in

packs. If you think you may be infected you should seek advice to exclude other diseases. This is one of the few occasions when it may be better to by-pass the GP and go direct to the special clinic of the local hospital (the telephone number will be in your local directory).

Not only can all the tests be carried out on the spot but there will be no record in your doctor's notes. This can be important if you apply at a later stage for life insurance policies. Treatment is simple because penicillin is highly effective in most cases.

Preventive measures

If you are diagnosed as having any sexually transmitted disease, all recent partners should be told, so that they can be treated. Many special clinics have counsellors to help trace sexual contacts.

As with most diseases, prevention is better than cure. If you use condoms and avoid casual sex you should not catch 'the clap'.

GOUT

Gout is a malfunction of the metabolism which results in arthritis, initially in only one of the body's main joints.

Gout is caused by uric acid crystallising out of the blood supply, as a result of eating certain foods (containing purines) or as a result of the sufferer getting hot and sweating. The crystals of uric acid form in the parts of the body with the worst blood supply, which includes the joints, causing very painful arthritis.

Although an attack of gout may be extremely painful, it can be easily treated and the sufferer may never experience the symptoms again. The joint which is most often attacked by gout is the one which joins the big toe to the main part of

the foot. Other joints which may be affected are the knee, ankle and the various joints of the hand.

Once gout strikes, the affected joint becomes swollen and painful to the touch. At its peak, this pain makes any contact between the joint and external objects very painful. Happily, the inflammation is only likely to last for between a day and a day and a half. One unfortunate side effect for the sufferer is likely to be a feverish condition.

Repeated attacks

After the first attack of gout, some people are fortunate in never having to undergo another one. For most victims of gout, however, the affliction will repeat itself any time between six months and two years later. With continued attacks, the body's

joints will become progressively weakened and the gout will spread to previously unaffected joints.

Treatment

The effects of gout can be countered by use of a nonsteroidal anti-inflammatory drug. If this doesn't work, a corticosteroid drug can be injected into the offending joint. Sufferers should cut down on foods such as chicken and liver, which contain uric acid — a major contributor to gout. Certain drugs can also reduce the body's production of uric acid.

GRAFTING

Any transplanted tissue or organ is called a graft.

Grafts may come from a different part of the same individual, identical twins, unrelated living or dead donors, from cells grown in the laboratory or even from animals of different species.

Skin grafts have a very long history. In India, during the 13th century, there was an enormous demand for reconstrucive surgery as mutilation was a common punishment. For example, adulterers would have their noses cut off.

Tile makers from the lowly seventh caste developed the necessary skills and passed them on from father to son. From contemporary accounts the techniques sound very similar to those used today.

Skin graft techniques

In 1800 an Italian surgeon found that skin transplanted from one part of a sheep to another part of the same animal survived but that skin transplants between different animals did not. It was not until 150 years later that this rejection was shown to be due to an immunilogical

MEDICAL FACT FILE

Skin Grafts

How do specialists treat bad burns?

Third-degree burns heal inwards from their edges. This time-consuming process can be speeded up by grafting some healthy skin from another part of the body on to the burnt area.

The top 15/1000th of an inch of a patch of healthy skin is shaved off and cut to form a mesh. The mesh covers the damaged area and stops blood clots pushing it off. The graft is stitched or held on with bandages and allowed to 'take'.

In more complicated cases, skin and the underlying muscle are freed on three of their four sides and swung around to cover the missing area.

reaction. The host skin rejects the graft as foreign tissue and then uses all its powers to destroy it.

Organ transplants

In 1955 kidney transplants were attempted between unrelated dead donors and renal patients. Before rejection occurred the new kidneys produced urine. This showed that they functioned and if the problem of rejection could be overcome the technical skills were available to fit a new kidney. In 1958 transplants between identical twins worked successfully. Some of them have been working ever since.

Grafting gets results

Successful grafting followed the discovery of tissue typing, which allowed transplantation to occur between individuals who had a similar genetic make-up. The closer the match, the greater the chance of success. Drugs have since been developed

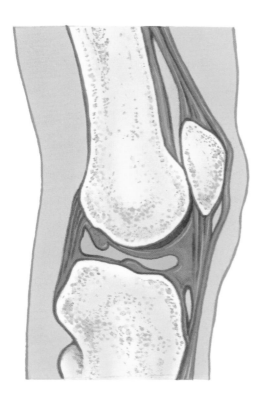

Gout On A Knee Joint

Above: Crystals of uric acid have formed in the centre of the knee joint, causing friction, immobility and pain.

which suppress the body's immune response but these can cause problems by bringing on infections.

There is not an organ in the human body which has not been transplanted. If, at some time in the future, rejection can be overcome, then diabetes could be treated by a pancreas transplant, cirrhosis by liver transplant and even sterility by testis transplant! If this day ever does dawn, the demand for donors will far

GROWTH

Growth is the process by which a body becomes larger, usually following the assimilation of food.

The term growth refers to an increase in the size of the body (or part of the body) while the term development is usually used to describe an increase in complexity. The rate of growth varies throughout childhood. It is at its fastest during the first few weeks after birth and then falls off over the next two years. Up until puberty, growth is slow and steady. The onset of puberty and the adolescent growth spurt cause growth to accelerate before it gradually slows down to zero in adult life. Growth is greater in the spring than in the autumn.

Feeding the growth
The size of a new baby is a very poor predictor of adult height. The major factor determining the size of a baby at birth is its nutrition in the last two months of pregnancy. Problems such as growth hormone deficiency do not become apparent for a year or two. During a period of illness or starvation growth will be reduced, but when the problem is overcome a period of faster than average 'catch-up' growth occurs.

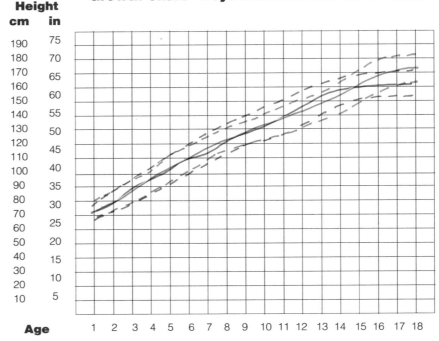

Growth Chart - Boys And Girls One to 18 Years

Above: The solid lines (girls pink, boys blue) show the average height for growing girls and boys. The dotted lines show the usual parameters of height for both tall and short children.

The overall effect of poor nutrition on growth is difficult to determine. It needs to be quite severe before growth is affected and there are usually other factors such as chronic infections present at the same time. Improved social conditions in the UK over the past 50 years have caused a dramatic increase in average height. This increase would now appear to be tailing off, and it seems quite possible that we have reached the limit of our potential growth.

Growth factors
The hormonal control of growth during childhood is under the influence of thyroid hormones and the growth hormone. Thyroxine, a thyroid hormone, seems to control the development of bones and the growth hormone controls height. The growth hormone is produced in the pituitary gland and performs the function of regulating the metabolism of fat, carbohydrate and protein produced in our bodies.

Short stature
Short stature (occasionally referred to as dwarfism) is defined as a height which is exceeded by at least 97 per cent of the population. Often, genetic factors are believed to be the cause of this and a person with short parents is quite likely to be on the short side herself. Various other factors are also likely to play a significant part in inhibited growth: emotional deprivation, poor nutrition, physical illness, and hormonal deficiencies.

Treatment for height deficiency using growth hormone is very expensive and is also usually time consuming. It can really only be justified in cases where there is a proven hormone deficiency, which is very rare. Treatment of the other causes of height deficiency is usually aimed at prevention, by correcting the underlying problem.

Children of mothers who smoke more than 10 cigarettes a day are, on average, half an inch shorter than the children of non-smokers even when all the other contributing factors to height deficiency are taken into account.

Gigantism
The most common cause of excessive height in people, a condition known as gigantism, is caused by the individual having tall parents. This may be a problem for adolescent girls in particular. In such cases, oestrogens can be prescribed for them and these mimic the end of puberty and prevent the bones continuing to grow.

In some very rare cases, a tumour of the pituitary gland will produce an excess of growth hormone and this will cause gigantism. Removal of the tumour stops the excess growth but will not reverse it. Painful surgery can be carried out to remove a few inches from the thigh bone but surgeons will only resort to this in quite exceptional cases.

➤➤ SEE ALSO — Development

HAEMOPHILIA

Haemophilia is a blood clotting defect, which means that when an affected individual bleeds, the bleeding will not stop.

The blood of haemophiliacs is missing one of the 'ingredients', known as factor VIII, which makes blood clot.

There are two forms of haemophilia, A and B (the latter is also known as Christmas disease). The condition is hereditary and is sex-linked recessive. This means that it is carried by women, but affects males: half the male children of female carriers will be affected. The condition is very rare in females.

All blood from donors is thoroughly tested before use. Factor VIII is separated out for use in treating haemophiliacs.

Symptoms

The condition doesn't usually cause problems until the child is active, commonly the second year of life. Minor injuries tend to bleed for a long time and bruises tend to spread. Bleeding into joints is a major problem. Not only is it intensely painful but the presence of so much blood damages the joint causing severe arthritis.

Diagnosis and treatment

Once suspected, the diagnosis is simple. A blood test will reveal the absence of a clotting factor, usually factor VIII. Treatment of bleeding involves the intravenous injection of the missing factor. Unfortunately, these factors are rapidly used up and each haemorrhage needs a fresh injection. This problem has been overcome to a certain extent by training haemophiliacs to administer their own factor VIII at home.

Problems and control

One of the hardest decisions that doctors and parents of haemophiliacs are faced with is how much activity the child should be allowed. The risk of damage needs to be balanced against the dangers of wrapping them in cotton wool. However, it is generally agreed that contact sports, such as rugby and judo, are not a good idea, but exercise in the form of swimming and walking should be encouraged.

Surgery and dental treatment can be performed on haemophiliacs as long as specialists are aware of the problem and factor VIII is administered after the operation or treatment.

As if all this was not enough, the haemophiliac has been dealt another cruel blow of late. Stocks of factor VIII produced in the USA in the early 1980s were contaminated with HIV. As a result, many haemophiliacs, usually in their 20s and 30s and often with young families, face the prospect of developing AIDS.

New manufacturing methods have removed the risk of infection, but this is sadly too late for those who are already infected.

HAEMORRHAGE

Haemorrhage is the term that doctors use for bleeding, which may be internal or external. It is usually reserved for sudden, unexpected blood loss.

Haemorrhage is due to one of four causes: trauma or injury, leaking capillaries, coagulation disorders, or a low platelet count.

Trauma

Trauma may have an obvious cause: it is clear that when a motorcyclist hits a brick wall he will suffer both internal and external haemorrhages. However, there are less obvious causes; 20 per cent of strokes are also due to haemorrhage. In such cases a blood vessel in the brain, which has already been weakened as a result of structural abnormality, bursts because of increased blood pressure. Cerebral haemorrhage (bleeding within the brain) is a very serious condition, and 80 per cent of victims are dead within a month.

One form of cerebral haemorrhage that affects young adults is the sub arachnoid haemorrhage. This results from the bursting of a small swelling on one of the arteries at the base of the skull, usually with no warning. The patient may or may not lose consciousness. If not, they describe a severe headache, 'Like being hit over the back of the head'. If the patient survives the attack, surgery may be needed to stop the bleeding.

Another form of traumatic haemorrhage, which looks very alarming but is in fact completely harmless is the subconjunctival haemorrhage (bleeding in the white part of the eye). One of the very fine vessels across the white of the eye turns bright red. This often occurs after very mild injury — rubbing the eyes

---

How Blood Clots

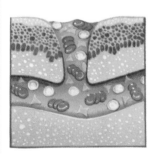

1. When skin and blood vessels are damaged, the blood has a mechanism for stemming bleeding. First, the platelets become sticky and clump together.

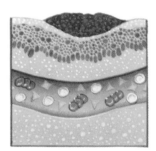

2. Platelets release chemicals which stimulate coagulation, and filaments of fibrin enmesh the blood cells, finally contracting to form a clot.

MEDICAL FACT FILE

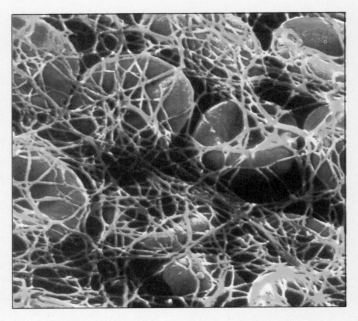

Normally, blood clots when fibrin strands enmesh the cells.

may do it, or sneezing or blowing the nose. This is painless and does not interfere with the vision. There is no treatment, but the blood will take several weeks to disappear.

Leaking capillaries
Capillaries are the very fine blood vessels, and these may sometimes start to leak, causing bleeding. The commonest form of leaking capillaries is called senile purpuras. This affects the elderly, as the name suggests. Senile purpuras appear as purplish blotches on the forearms and they are completely harmless. Similar haemorrhages can occur in patients taking long-term steroid therapy.

A rare condition that only really affects children is Henoch-Schoenlein purpura. This is due to an inflammation of the blood vessels in the skin. Blood leaks out to such an extent that it can be mistaken for a skin condition. As well as the skin problems, patients may have difficulty because of bleeding in the joints and kidneys.

Coagulation disorders
The commonest coagulation (or clotting) disorder occurs

as a result of warfarin medication. Warfarin is a drug that interferes with the enzyme systems that produce a blood clot. In the right dose, it slows down, but does not stop, the formation of a clot. This is very important if the user is prone to thrombosis or has an artificial heart valve, when a blood clot could be fatal. Getting the dose right may take several weeks of regular blood tests. Even when the dose seems to be right the blood must be checked every few weeks.

Haemophilia A and Christmas disease are inherited disorders of clotting. They are treated by infusions of the missing clotting factors. Many of these clotting factors are produced in the liver.

Liver damage (cirrhosis, for example) means that these factors are missing and the patient is liable to bleed more than normal.

Low platelet count
Platelets are minute particles in the blood, much smaller than the red and white cells. They are produced by the bone marrow and broken down by the spleen. If a blood vessel is cut or

damaged the platelets respond to hormones released from the raw edges by becoming sticky. This is the first stage of clotting.

If the production of platelets is decreased, as in leukaemia, for example, the patient will bruise and bleed very easily.

Occasionally, children are affected by a condition known as idiopathic thrombocytopenic purpura, or ITP for short. This commonly follows a viral infection. The spleen breaks down too many platelets and the patient starts bruising or, in severe cases, bleeding into the gut or brain. The chances of full recovery are good, but in severe cases blood and platelet transfusions may be needed.

HAEMORRHOIDS

Haemorrhoids, or piles, are varicose veins in the anal canal.

The cause of haemorrhoids is unknown, but they do tend to run in families. Whether this is due to hereditary or dietary considerations is not clear, but the condition does tend to be associated with a low-fibre diet.

Looking for causes
The veins in the rectum normally become congested with blood as the bowels are opened. Chronic constipation or straining to pass a motion will mean the veins are congested for longer and piles may result.

Piles are often worse in pregnancy due to the extra pressure on the veins caused by the weight and size of the baby. And muscular straining during childbirth may also cause piles.

Any condition, such as a tumour, which causes congestion, may cause piles. This is even true of conditions such as ovarian cysts which,

whilst they are outside the bowel, press on it and cause congestion with blood.

Degrees and symptoms
There are three 'grades' of haemorrhoids: first, second and third degree. First-degree piles stay inside the anal canal. Second-degree piles prolapse (come down the anal canal) when the bowels are being opened, but then return, while third-degree piles prolapse but then stay down. The worry with second- and third-degree piles is that the blood supply may be cut off by the action of the anal sphincter. If this happens, the piles swell, the blood supply is made worse and the piles swell more. This vicious circle, known as strangulation, is only broken when the piles die and fall away or a surgeon operates.

Haemorrhoids tend to come in attacks, every few months, with very little trouble in between. The first sign is usually bleeding when the bowels are opened. There may also be a feeling of minor irritation. If left untreated, these first-degree piles tend to prolapse, causing a fullness in the rectum, a mucous discharge and intense itching. Piles only become painful if they become strangulated.

During an attack of piles there may be very little to see. If the piles prolapse they appear as tense, dark swellings. If they strangulate they become very swollen and painful, making it impossible to sit down. In addition to examining the piles, a doctor will examine the rectum further to ensure there are no other problems.

Treatment
Treatment of first-degree piles is aimed at reducing the chances of their prolapsing. This is done by increasing the amount of fibre in the diet and, if needed, taking the occasional mild laxative.

Ointments or suppositories containing a mild anaesthetic and astringent may help. Patients are encouraged to accept that their bowels may not need to open daily, and they must not strain in order to 'stay regular'.

If bleeding is a problem a surgeon may inject the piles with a chemical that causes them to shrivel up. As the area the piles come from has no nerves this is a painless procedure.

Prolapsing piles tend to recur, even if injected, but rubber bands can be fitted around the base of the piles, causing them to shrivel away. For third-degree piles, haemorrhoidectomy may be performed. The piles are pulled down the anal canal, cut off and the stumps are stitched. An alternative treatment is an anal dilatation. Under a general anaesthetic the surgeon stretches the anus by inserting the fingers of both hands into it. The patient can go home when he recovers from the anaesthetic, and the piles rarely return.

HAIR

There are three types of hair – lanugo, vellus and terminal hair. It is terminal hair (the hair on our heads, under our arms and in the pubic area) which concerns us most.

In the second half of pregnancy, embryos are covered in fine, downy hair called lanugo, which disappears before or soon after birth. Children's bodies are covered in fine, colourless hair, called vellus hair, until puberty.

All hair consists of dead cells and a protein called keratin. It has a central core (or medulla), a cortex and a cuticle around the outside. It grows from a root, buried in a follicle in the skin, and each

How Hair Grows

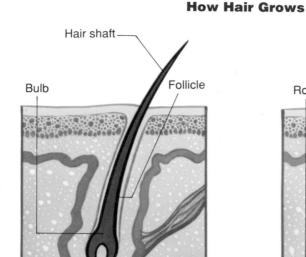

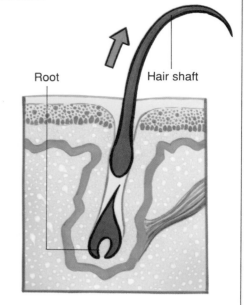

1. Each hair grows from the root at the base of the follicle.

2. After the rest period, the hair comes out and is replaced by a new one.

follicle has a sebaceous gland which secretes a lubricant called sebum. This helps to keep what is actually a dead cell flexible and healthy-looking. There is no way of 'bringing hair back to life', whatever lotions and potions you use on it.

Terminal hair
The terminal hair which grows on our heads, eyebrows and eyelashes is normally pigmented, and may have different textures, depending on the shape of the hair follicle. Curly hair, for example, has an oval follicle. After puberty, terminal hair develops in the pubic and underarm area, and on the face, trunk and limbs of men (and sometimes women).

Growth
On average, hair grows at the rate of about 1cm per month and there are up to 300,000 hairs on every scalp. Most hairs have a growing period of about three years, followed by a rest period of about three months.

During the rest period, the root of the hair becomes detached from the base of

the follicle, and a new hair starts to develop in its place. Most people lose 150 hairs from their scalp per day.

Hair disorders
Hair is no longer necessary to humans (to keep us warm or help with sweating

functions), although the eyelashes and hairs in the nose help to keep out dust and dirt. However, there are some disorders which may become a problem, which is, in most cases, cosmetic.

Excessive hairiness is usually genetic, but may be a

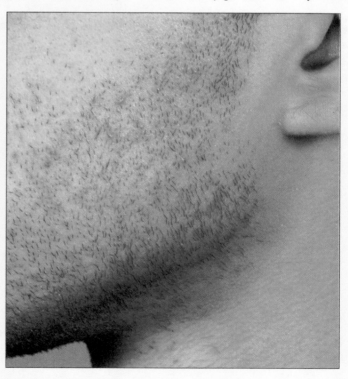

An ingrowing hair causes inflammation and soreness.

symptom of a hormonal disorder. Brittle hair may be a symptom of a vitamin or mineral deficiency, or of an underactive thyroid gland. Dry hair may be caused by dietary deficiency, but is more often the result of using too many chemicals (colorants and perms) and heated appliances (such as rollers and blow-dryers).

Alopecia (baldness) may be a normal part of the ageing process, but also occurs as a result of stress (including surgery, illness or pregnancy) and as a side effect of anticancer drugs. Radiotherapy also causes burns which may stop hair growth. Sometimes alopecia occurs with no clear reason, but the hairs grow back.

Ingrowing hairs occur in people with very curly hair: a hair grows back into the skin close to the point at which it came out, causing inflammation. The problem is treated by moisturising and shaving the hairs.

HAIRINESS

An excess growth of hair can be a cosmetic problem for women. It may be a symptom of a hormonal disorder.

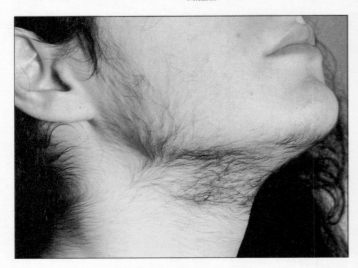

Hairiness, showing on a woman's face, may be a normal condition, particularly in certain racial groups. On the other hand, it may be an indication of a hormonal disorder.

Coarse, dark hair sometimes grows on a woman's face, trunk and arms, like a man. This may be natural and normal growth, particularly when it happens after the menopause, or in Hispanic or Asian women.

However, excessive hairiness (hirsutism) may be a symptom of an underlying disorder, such as polycystic ovary syndrome, or a disorder of the pituitary or adrenal gland. Such disorders upset the balance of hormone production so there is overproduction of the male hormone. Hirsutism sometimes results from taking anabolic steroids.

Treatment

It is fairly easy to investigate hormonal disorders by doing some blood tests, and it may be possible to correct the imbalance.

If the hairiness is natural, cosmetic treatment is necessary. Bleaching will make the hairs less obvious, but the only way to get rid of them altogether is through electrolysis, which can be a very costly process. Shaving is only a short-term solution, which usually makes the hairs feel coarser.

HALITOSIS

Halitosis is the medical term for bad breath.

In most cases, bad breath is the result of poor dietary habits and lack of oral hygiene. Sometimes it is a result of bad tooth decay. It may, occasionally, be a side effect of a disorder of the sinuses or bronchioles which produces thick, smelly phlegm, affecting the breath.

Prevention, not cure

If you know that you have a tendency to get halitosis, you should avoid highly spiced food, or food laced with garlic. Smoking and drinking alcohol may also aggravate the problem.

It is essential to be meticulous about oral hygiene, not only to prevent halitosis but to protect your teeth from decay and your gums from gingivitis. Mouthwashes and breath-freshening sprays may help in the short term, if you had a rich, continental dinner the night before an important office meeting, for example.

Parsley is reputed to counteract the smell of garlic, and strong peppermints can help to mask bad breath.

However, eating a healthy diet which includes plenty of raw vegetables is the best solution. Try to cut down on animal proteins, and avoid foods which give you indigestion, which may contribute to the problem.

HALLUCINATION

Hallucination is the term used to describe the process of seeing (or hearing) something when there is no stimulus (that is, there is nothing there).

Hallucinations are sometimes experienced by patients suffering from fever, and by those suffering delirium as a result of alcohol

withdrawal. They may be a symptom of a mental disorder, such as schizophrenia, and auditory hallucinations are often reported by manic depressives. They may also be an effect of temporal lobe epilepsy. Some drugs cause hallucination, notably the psychedelic drugs which were popular with drug abusers in the 1960s.

HAMMER-TOE

Hammer-toe is a malformation of a toe. It is usually the second toe which is affected.

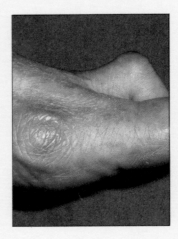

Hammer-toe can lead to calluses and corns.

The middle joint of the affected toe is bent almost at right angles, due to a problem with the ligaments in the toe. The condition may be congenital, or develop with age.

A corn often develops on the top of the affected joint, and the sufferer has considerable difficulty in buying shoes which allow for the misshapen toe. A pressure pad will help to relieve pressure and pain.

The condition may be corrected surgically, but operations involving ligaments are not always successful.

➤➤ SEE ALSO — Polycystic ovary syndrome

HAMSTRINGS

The hamstrings are the muscles which connect the pelvis to the knee.

Located in the rear of the thigh, the hamstring muscles provide the elasticity which enables humans to bend the knee with ease. Connected by tendons to the shin bones and to the pelvis, hamstrings are vital in allowing the free movement of the legs.

Pulled hamstrings

One of the most common injuries to afflict athletes is a pulled hamstring. Often this is caused by the sudden jerking of the thigh which occurs when someone launches into a sprint.

If the muscles are cold and unprepared they can be torn rather easily. Further movement of the leg will then be virtually impossible. The most straightforward way of avoiding this type of injury is to ensure that you go through a thorough warm-up exercise programme before taking part in sports.

HARDENING OF THE ARTERIES

The hardening of the arteries is caused by the accumulation of plaque inside the arteries, which goes in between and on top of healthy muscle fibre.

Hardening of the arteries, or atherosclerosis, is the most common cause of death in the UK, being the main factor in approximately one in every three deaths.

The plaque which builds up inside the arteries consists of such bodily waste matter as decaying muscle cells, fibrous tissue and blood platelets, and it tends to be found most often in people who have a high blood cholesterol content.

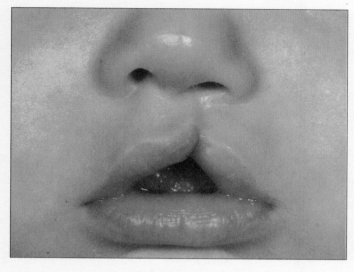

Above: A young child with a cleft, or hare, lip located almost in the centre of her upper lip. This condition is easily treated.

HARE LIP

Hare lip is a condition present in babies at birth where there is a vertical tear in the upper lip.

According to an Old Wives' Tale, if a mother gave birth to a child with a hare lip it meant that she had been scared by a hare during pregnancy. Although a hare lip may look unattractive on a new-born baby, it is not as serious a condition as the closely-related cleft palate. The hare lip may be located anywhere on the upper lip and will differ in size from one baby to another.

In most cases of hare lip, a surgical operation can be carried out under a general anaesthetic within three months of the child's birth which will eliminate the condition successfully.

HAY FEVER

Hay fever is caused by an allergic reaction to the pollen emitted by grass and flowers and is often at its worst during the summer.

When pollen enters the nose of a hay fever sufferer it sets off a reaction with the lining of the nose which causes irritability and inflammation. The symptoms, which tend to be concentrated on the nose, sinuses and eyes, are, mainly, sneezing and a blocked or runny nose and streaming eyes. The symptoms are worse during hot, unsettled weather.

Fighting hay fever

The easiest way for your doctor to establish whether you are suffering from hay fever is for her to take a skin test. Unfortunately, because of the nature of the disease, it is difficult for sufferers to avoid repeated attacks.

Top: Magnified pollen grains of Timothy grass, a major cause of hay fever, which are dispersed by the wind.
Above: A field of flowering rape seed, a valuable crop to farmers, but one of the commonest causes of hay fever.

Your doctor may prescribe decongestant or antihistamine drugs and there are now eye drops and nose sprays available on prescription. These are likely to relieve some of the hay fever symptoms. The new antihistamine drugs on the market these days have the advantage of not causing drowsiness and they need to be taken only once a day.

An alternative to drugs is a course of desensitisation injections which make the sufferer immune to the effects of pollen. Tests are carried out to establish which type of pollen is affecting the individual concerned and small doses of the same pollen are then injected into the sufferer's bloodstream. This should have the effect of preventing further allergic reaction to the pollen.

However, desensitisation is now illegal and since 1987 such tests have been carried out only in hospitals. The injections are usually given once every three months but as there may be side effects from the steroids, they are usually avoided.

HEADACHE

Headache is pain which affects all or part of the head and is produced by tension or tautness in the membranes around the brain, scalp or neck.

Doctors recognise that all illnesses are caused by a combination of physical, psychological and social factors. This is best exemplified by the way headaches affect people. The patient with migraine may find it is brought on by an infection, made worse with worry and used as an excuse to avoid social functions.

Numerous sufferers
It is very difficult to get an accurate picture of how many people suffer from headaches as most sufferers tend to treat themselves. One study suggested that nearly 40 per cent of the population had had a headache in the two weeks prior to the survey. Twenty per cent of the population believe they suffer from migraine but the actual figure is far lower as many people use the term to express the severity of the symptoms rather than as a specific diagnosis.

The causes
There are many causes of headaches. Physical examination is rarely helpful and the doctor has to rely on the patient's story to a large extent. If you have to consult a doctor about a headache, arm yourself with a few basic facts such as when it is at its worst, what brings it on and what makes it better.
By far the most common cause of early morning headaches and nausea are hangovers!

Tension headaches
The most common cause of headaches is tension. The pain is often described as 'band-like' or 'like a pressure inside the head'. The pain is due to cramp of the neck and scalp muscles and may be very severe. Standard painkillers such as aspirin or paracetamol are usually of little help.

The pain often lasts all day but is usually worse in the evenings. The cramp is due to stress. Indeed, many people describe themselves as feeling 'uptight'. In some cases, the pain is made worse by the fear that it is a symptom of high blood pressure or a brain tumour. Reassurance about the benign nature of the complaint may help.

Other remedies that sometimes work are a walk in the fresh air or a gentle neck massage. One curious treatment which sometimes works is to apply gentle pressure with the thumb at the junction of the hard and soft palate in the mouth.

Migraine
Pain that is present every day is not migraine as migraine is a condition which attacks the sufferer only on occasion. The headache is one-sided and throbbing. There may be nausea and vomiting as well as photophobia — light hurting the eye. Occasionally, there is numbness or weakness down one side of the body. An onset of migraine may be associated with periods, the Pill, eating certain foods or emotional upsets. It is often worse at the weekends.

Treatment
Treatment is aimed at removing the cause if possible. Food diaries can be very useful but they must be kept for several months before a pattern begins to emerge. Attacks may be treated with simple analgesics although the associated stomach upsets may mean that the drugs are not absorbed properly. This can be overcome by adding an antiemetic. This combination can be bought over the counter at chemists but it is expensive.

Different drugs
Many different drugs have been used to try to prevent migraine. Beta-blockers may help as may a drug known as Sanomigran. If you suffer frequent attacks of migraine it might be worth discussing these preventive treatments with your doctor.

Sinusitis
An infection of the sinuses may also cause severe, one-sided headaches. The infection usually occurs a day or two after a cold or a bad bout of hay fever. The pain is often described as 'a feeling of pressure' and is made worse by lying or bending down. There is often an accompanying nasal discharge. Antibiotic treatment of the underlying infection is helpful but the pain may be relieved more quickly if the sinuses can be drained. In severe cases, this may be done surgically but inhaling menthol vapours will often be just as efficient. The opening of the sinuses is located at a high point on the nose and they will drain more successfully if the head is tipped forward.

Trigeminal neuralgia
This very painful condition is almost unheard of in people under the age of 50. Pain shoots across the face for only a split second but this may happen many times a day. There is often a 'trigger spot' on the side of the face and even a gentle breeze on this spot can precipitate an attack. As a rule, drug treatment tends to be unsatisfactory and many patients end up having the nerve killed by an injection.

Brain tumour
Some people with headaches are worried that they may have been caused by a tumour or an abscess. Both are actually rare causes of headaches. The pain of a brain tumour is caused by pressure exerted by its growth. The pain is at its worst after the sufferer lies down and only gets better after an hour or two. It is made worse by coughing or sneezing and is usually followed by vomiting.

If the tumour is large enough it may upset the eyesight. Treatment is with surgery, chemotherapy or radiotherapy according to the type of tumour present and its position.

Rare causes
Temporal arteritis is a rare condition which affects the elderly. It is caused by inflammation of the scalp arteries and may be accompanied by

Headaches – Symptoms and Causes

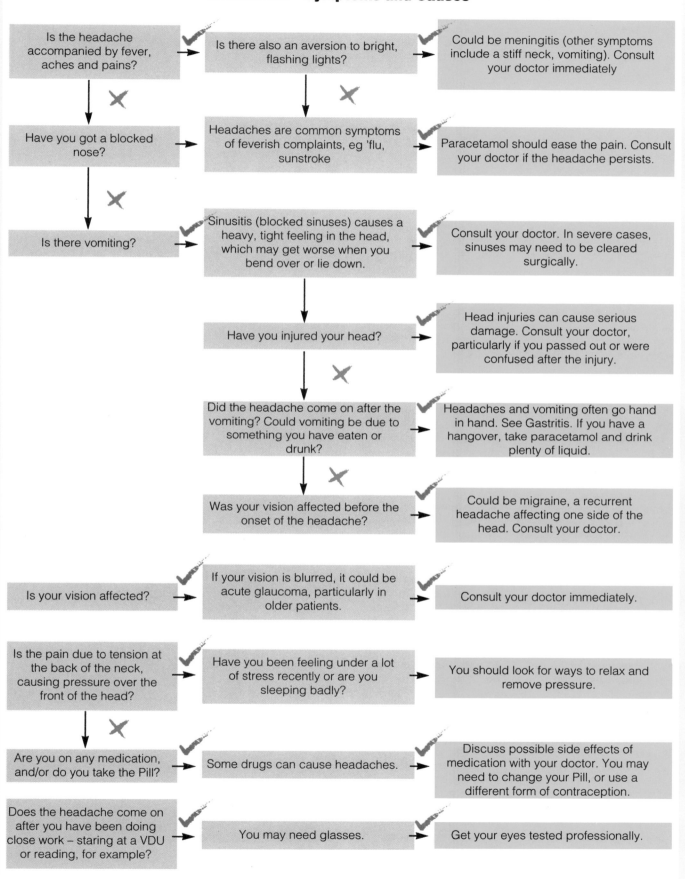

Is the headache accompanied by fever, aches and pains?	Is there also an aversion to bright, flashing lights?	Could be meningitis (other symptoms include a stiff neck, vomiting). Consult your doctor immediately
Have you got a blocked nose?	Headaches are common symptoms of feverish complaints, eg 'flu, sunstroke	Paracetamol should ease the pain. Consult your doctor if the headache persists.
Is there vomiting?	Sinusitis (blocked sinuses) causes a heavy, tight feeling in the head, which may get worse when you bend over or lie down.	Consult your doctor. In severe cases, sinuses may need to be cleared surgically.
	Have you injured your head?	Head injuries can cause serious damage. Consult your doctor, particularly if you passed out or were confused after the injury.
	Did the headache come on after the vomiting? Could vomiting be due to something you have eaten or drunk?	Headaches and vomiting often go hand in hand. See Gastritis. If you have a hangover, take paracetamol and drink plenty of liquid.
	Was your vision affected before the onset of the headache?	Could be migraine, a recurrent headache affecting one side of the head. Consult your doctor.
Is your vision affected?	If your vision is blurred, it could be acute glaucoma, particularly in older patients.	Consult your doctor immediately.
Is the pain due to tension at the back of the neck, causing pressure over the front of the head?	Have you been feeling under a lot of stress recently or are you sleeping badly?	You should look for ways to relax and remove pressure.
Are you on any medication, and/or do you take the Pill?	Some drugs can cause headaches.	Discuss possible side effects of medication with your doctor. You may need to change your Pill, or use a different form of contraception.
Does the headache come on after you have been doing close work – staring at a VDU or reading, for example?	You may need glasses.	Get your eyes tested professionally.

inflammation of the artery which runs to the eye. In this case, blindness may ensue unless treatment with high doses of steroids is started immediately.

Shingles may cause headaches but until the rash appears a day or so later this can be confusing. Meningitis also causes headaches but is accompanied by severe neck stiffness, photophobia and vomiting. The irritation of the covering of the brain throws the neck into spasm, making it impossible for the sufferer to flex their neck. Treatment is a matter of urgency but with intravenous antibiotics most patients make a full recovery.

High blood pressure, eye strain and glaucoma rarely cause headaches.

HEAD INJURY

A head injury is any damage which is done to the scalp, brain or skull.

Serious head injuries are surprisingly common. On average, one person in every thousand will be admitted to hospital every year as the result of head injury. Of these injuries, 75 per cent are due to road accidents.

Assessing head injuries is very difficult. The skull may be fractured and the scalp severely lacerated but the brain may have escaped unscathed. On the other hand, an injury which has left no outward mark on the victim's head may have fatally damaged the brain.

Brain damage
Serious damage to the brain happens when acceleration and deceleration forces act together at the moment of impact. If the skull stops dead, after hitting a road or some hard ground, for example, the brain will continue with its forward momentum for an instant,

tearing the blood vessels that supply it.

The most severe brain damage is caused by the brain bouncing back and causing further damage as it bounces violently off the back of the skull.

The most trivial injuries may cause no signs or symptoms at all. Under these circumstances, it is not necessary to consult a doctor so long as someone responsible can observe the patient over the 24 hours following the injury. Signs that complications may be arising are: vomiting, severe headache, drowsiness, slurred speech, loss of consciousness or unequal pupils. Any of these may indicate a serious problem and a doctor should be consulted at once. As a general rule, any injury severe enough to cause a laceration or loss of consciousness, even if only for a second or two, is serious enough to warrant taking some professional medical advice.

A severe knock
Concussion is a loss of function to the brain without unconsciousness or any apparent damage to the brain itself. The victim will always have a period of amnesia from a few moments before the injury to some time afterwards. The longer the period of amnesia the worse the concussion.

Cerebral cuts and bruises
The damage may range from a minor bruise to extensive lacerations according to the type and force of the injury sustained. As a result of the most severe head injuries, the brain may be badly bruised and cut.

Symptoms vary according to the area of the brain which is damaged. Loss of consciousness is the rule and this may last for weeks or even years. As the patient recovers she often

shows signs of brain damage such as weakness or difficulty with speech, although these will improve, to a certain degree, with time. The main components involved in the expert care of these patients are skilled nursing, physiotherapy, speech therapy and occupational therapy.

Even after a year of normal recovery, many such patients are left with epilepsy and many need to be on anti-epileptic drugs for the rest of their lives.

Haemorrhage
Tearing the arteries and veins between the skull and the brain causes the bleeding and pressure on the brain known as a haemorrhage. If an artery or a major vein is involved, the pressure build-up will be very rapid and the patient will not recover consciousness.

If a minor blood vessel is torn, the patient may appear to be making a recovery but will then lose consciousness again. This indicates a serious rise in pressure inside the skull which can only be relieved by surgery which

releases the blood clot and ties off the bleeding vessel.

This is an acute emergency situation and the patient must be admitted to hospital at once.

Fracture
Skull fractures do not usually require treatment unless the fractured segment is causing bleeding or compression. In this case, surgery must be performed at once.

HEARING

Hearing is the process by which sound waves are picked up by our ears and sent to the brain in the form of nerve impulses.

Sound waves are caught on the outer ear then pass to the middle ear from where a complex system of membranes and bones channels the sound into the inner ear. There, the sound is converted into nerve impulses which are passed to the brain.

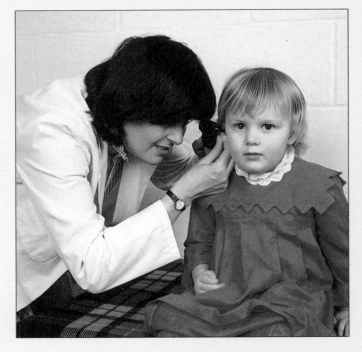

A doctor checking for hearing defects by carrying out a thorough examination of a young girl's ears.

THE HEART

The heart, a powerful muscular sac, beats roughly 70 times per minute when the body is at rest, driving approximately five litres of blood out into the arteries and around the circulatory system.

Structure and circulation

The heart comprises two separate and distinct pumps, right and left, contracting and relaxing simultaneously.

Each pump consists of a thin-walled upper chamber or atrium communicating by means of a one-way valve with a thick, powerful lower chamber or ventricle (see diagram). Oxygen-rich blood from the lungs reaches the left atrium via the pulmonary veins, and passes into the left ventricle.

Each time the heart beats, blood is squeezed out into the body's largest artery, the aorta, which subdivides many times into numerous smaller arteries that carry it to

Blood flow around the heart

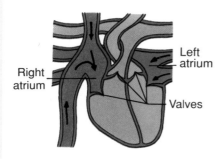

Right atrium — Left atrium — Valves

1 The right atrium fills with (blue) deoxygenated blood, while the left atrium fills with (red) oxygenated blood.

Right ventricle — Left ventricle — Septum

2 Blood flows through the valves from the atria to the ventricles.

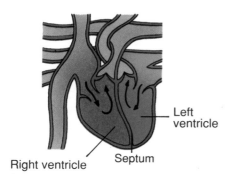

Aorta — Circulation — Lungs — Pulmonary vein

3 Deoxygenated blood flows out of the heart via the pulmonary vein to the lungs. Oxygenated blood flows out of the heart via the aorta to nourish the blood vessels.

Glossary

The following are some of the more common terms used when discussing heart conditions.

● The aorta is the main artery, carrying oxygen-rich blood from the heart, out to the body.
● The atria are the upper chambers in the heart. The wall of each atrium relaxes to draw in blood from the veins, then contracts to pump the blood into each ventricle.
● Coronary arteries carry blood to the cells in the muscular wall of the heart, to provide the energy for contraction.
● The pacemaker is a bundle of specialised cells on the surface of the right atrium which sends out electrical signals to make

the muscular walls of the heart contract and relax.
● The pulmonary artery carries blood with a low oxygen content from the heart to the lungs.
● The pulmonary vein carries oxygen-rich blood from the lungs to the heart.
● The septum is the wall between the two pumping sides of the heart. Normally it is impermeable to blood: it is this wall which is faulty in 'hole in the heart' patients.
● The veins carry blood from the body (including the lungs) to the heart.
● The ventricles are the lower chambers of the heart. The muscular walls relax to draw in blood from the atria, and then contract to pump the blood into the arteries, which carry the blood around the body and to the lungs.

all the tissues and organs of the body.

Here, oxygen — vital for releasing energy from food fuel — is exchanged for carbon dioxide and other waste products of metabolism in vast networks of minute vessels, known as capillaries. The thin-walled veins draining the capillaries return the blood to the right atrium, those in the legs being helped to transport blood upwards against gravity by small valves in their walls, and by the massaging action of surrounding muscles. From the right atrium, the blood passes into the right ventricle and out through the pulmonary artery and its branches back into the lungs, where it gives off carbon dioxide and picks up a fresh supply of oxygen.

Cardiac muscle

Interlinking branches of specialised cardiac muscle fibre enable the heart to

contract and relax rhythmically by conducting the electrical current controlling its action. This current originates in a specialised nodular area in the right atrium, called the pacemaker, and spreads downwards and outwards in waves through the atria and ventricles.

The heart's contraction or pumping phase (systole) is followed by a relaxation phase (diastole), during which its chambers refill with blood. Elastic fibres in the walls of the main arteries allow them to expand during systole, when blood pressure reaches its highest point; while the resistance to blood flow afforded by the smallest arterial branches (arterioles) maintains blood pressure at a minimum level during diastole.

Heart beat

The double thud of the heart — lubb dupp — is due to the closure, first of the valves between the atria and ventricles, and then of the valves in the arteries leaving the heart.

The heart rate is controlled by the nervous system and the body's chemical balance, and increases or decreases according to the body's needs. It reaches its lowest level during sleep, when the body's metabolism slows down and the need for oxygen is minimal.

Exercise, fever and other forms of stress create a demand for extra oxygen, causing the heart to beat more rapidly, and the breathing to deepen and/or quicken.

Examining the heart

Doctors usually examine the heart in one of two ways: the pulse (normally taken at the wrist) reflects the heart beat, and the beats are counted to give the heart rate.

Most people have a heart rate of between 60 and 100 beats per minute when at rest. This may increase to as much as 200 during heavy exercise. The heart rate is a useful guide to general fitness: the fitter your heart, the less your pulse rate will go up when you exert yourself.

The stethoscope is used by doctors to listen to the heart beat and to detect any abnormalities, such as echoes, a variable rate, and extra beats and clicks, which could indicate problems such as damaged heart muscle, faulty valves, holes in the heart, high blood pressure, and so on.

Heart murmurs

Sometimes, a doctor hears a murmur as the blood swirls through the chambers, rather than flowing smoothly. This may be a symptom of many conditions, including congenital heart defects and defective valves.

HEART ATTACK

A heart attack, or myocardial infarction, is damage to the heart due to a blockage in the coronary arteries, which cuts off the supply of blood and oxygen.

Heart attacks are usually accompanied by severe pain in the chest, often radiating into the neck and arms. (See Coronary Heart Disease, Heart Disease.)

HEARTBURN

Heartburn is the common name for dyspepsia — the pain associated with indigestion.

Heartburn is a burning pain behind the breastbone, which is usually caused by gastritis, one of several common causes. It is possible to trace the cause to a particular food you have eaten, or to eating too much. The condition is made worse by smoking.

Repeated attacks

If the pain is more than just an occasional twinge, it may be that gastritis has caused ulcers. Heartburn is also caused by hiatus hernias and gall stones.

HEART DISEASE

The term 'heart disease' covers a wide range of disorders — congenital defects, damaged heart muscle, conditions brought on by a lack of oxygen supply to the heart, faulty heart valves, and problems caused through alcohol abuse and drugs.

Heart disease is very common in the western world — in one form or another, it accounts for 20 per cent of all deaths. Many of these deaths from heart disease are in the younger age groups.

Congenital heart disease

Congenital heart disorders are surprisingly common. One per cent of babies are affected and of those who die in the first month of life, 10 per cent are found to have a congenital heart defect.

Causes of heart defects are not clear, but they may stem from the mother catching German measles during pregnancy, and are often present in chromosome disorders such as Down's syndrome.

'Hole in the heart' is the commonest problem. In this condition the septum has a defect which allows oxygen-rich and oxygen-poor blood to mix, putting a strain on the heart and lungs. Small holes may close without treatment, but severe cases need open-heart or transplant surgery.

Other congenital problems include distorted valves and arteries, and 'wrongly connected' arteries or veins.

Lack of oxygen

Ischaemic heart disease is the result of lack of oxygen to the tissues (ischaemia). Angina (heart pain) and heart attack are its usual complications.

The heart is a muscle and the oxygen it needs is carried in arteries that run across its surface (the coronary arteries). If these arteries get clogged up with atheroma, a fatty deposit high in cholesterol, the flow of blood is reduced and the heart is deprived of oxygen.

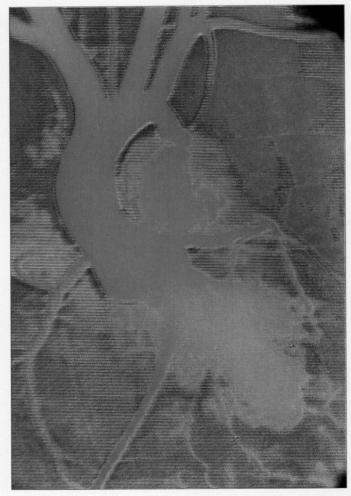

A false-colour image showing a large septal defect, a type of hole-in-the-heart condition, in a seven-month-old child's heart.

➤➤ SEE ALSO — Coronary heart disease

Risk Factors

There are certain factors which could increase the risk of ischaemic heart disease.

1 Sex. More men than women are affected.
2 Heredity. Heart disease runs in families.
3 Diet. A high consumption of cholesterol and saturated fats increases atheroma formation.
4 Emotion. Stress may increase the risk.
5 Smoking. Increases the risk of ischaemia by about 300 per cent.
6 Medical conditions. Recognised risk factors include high blood pressure, sugar diabetes and obesity.
7 Alcohol abuse.

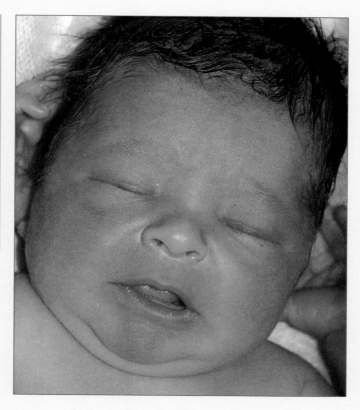

A blue baby suffering from a congenital heart defect resulting in deoxygenated blood not being oxygenated in the lungs.

This causes a tight chest pain (angina) that may also be felt in the arm and neck.

A heart attack is caused by a blood clot (coronary thrombosis) or spasm in the coronary arteries, cutting off the blood supply to an area of heart muscle, with resultant tissue damage. The pain is similar to angina but it lasts longer and is more severe. Thirty per cent of heart-attack victims die within four weeks.

Treatment of angina is aimed at reducing the work of the heart by weight reduction and drugs. Low-fat diets can help to prevent further cholesterol deposits.

Rheumatic heart disease

Some heart disease is the result of rheumatic fever, usually caught in childhood, but not making its effects known until later in life.

Rheumatic fever is due to an acute infection with the streptococcus bacteria and usually follows a severe sore throat. Since the advent of penicillin, it has become very rare, but still affects some children. There are, however, many elderly people who had rheumatic fever as

Diagnosing Heart Disease

If the doctor suspects that a patient's heart is not functioning normally, she may refer the patient to a cardiologist (heart specialist).

Many diagnostic tests may be carried out to establish the cause and extent of the problem.

The doctor's first step in diagnosing heart disease is to listen to the patient's description of the symptoms. For example, a description of the pain of angina is a much better diagnostic aid than the stethoscope or an ECG. The patient's medical and family history will also be taken into consideration.

● ECG (Electrocardiogram) is the commonest investigation. Electrodes are placed on the chest, wrists and ankles and a tracing produced of the heart's electrical activity. It can be interpreted to give a picture of muscle damage, defective electrical conduction – for example abnormal rhythm patterns, and other conditions.

It is particularly useful in detecting rhythm disturbances in which the heart beats in an uncoordinated fashion. Because damaged muscle has a different electrical resistance, it can also be used to detect heart attacks and angina.

The main disadvantage of the ECG is that it is a 'snapshot' that only lasts a few seconds. This problem is overcome by linking the ECG to a mini computer that can be worn like a Walkman. The computer analyses and records the heart tracing and can pick up any rhythm disturbance in a 24-hour period. Many angina sufferers only suffer pain during vigorous exercise. Running a continuous ECG trace whilst the patient runs on a treadmill may show up problems missed by the usual, resting, ECG.

● X-ray examination of the chest is used to detect any increase in the heart size, possibly due to heart failure. It is also possible to see a change in the outline of the heart, suggesting valve problems.

● NMR (nuclear magnetic resonance) also known as MRI (magnetic resonance imaging) gives a picture of the heart in action. The NMR machine uses a magnetic field and radio waves to create an image of a 'slice' through the body (and heart).

Coloured dyes, which are injected into the wall of an artery or the pumping chambers of the heart, are used in conjunction with NMR to detect abnormal function in both sides of the heart.

● CAT (computed axial tomography) scans, also known as CT (computed tomography) scans, combine x-ray techniques and computer technology to create an image of part of the body.

➤➤ SEE ALSO — Angina

children. Sixty per cent of these are left with damaged heart valves. The commonest problem is tightening of the valves so that blood can only be forced through under pressure. This puts a strain on the heart muscle, which can result in an abnormal rhythm, fatigue, shortness of breath and angina. Patients with rheumatic heart disease — or any other sort of valve problem — are especially liable to infections of the valve itself. Under certain circumstances, (when undergoing dental treatment, for example) antibiotic cover is needed to prevent this.

HEART FAILURE

Heart failure can either affect the whole heart or one side. It occurs when the heart muscle becomes incapable of pumping sufficient blood around the body and through the lungs.

The body's attempt to compensate by increasing the volume of blood helps for a while but eventually it aggravates the problem by increasing the heart's workload.

Causes and symptoms
Causes of left ventricular failure include high blood pressure and a diseased aortic valve, both of which make the ventricular muscle pump harder, and coronary arterial disease, which damages the ventricular tissue by reducing its oxygen supply.

The left atrium fails when it is prevented from emptying its blood completely during diastole, either because the intervening (mitral) valve is diseased, or because of increased pressure inside a failing left ventricle.

Symptoms of left-sided heart failure include weakness and lethargy due to a decreased blood supply to the tissues, and breathlessness caused by congestion in the lungs due to back pressure from an overtaxed left atrium.

Right ventricular failure is most often caused by a pressure backlog from left-sided heart failure, but can also be triggered by lung diseases such as emphysema, congenital heart defects, or conditions that interfere with the inflow of blood into the right side of the heart, for example a damaged tricuspid valve. The principal symptoms are enlarged veins — again due to back pressure — leading to oedema (fluid swelling) in the feet and ankles, and an enlarged liver.

The basic treatment for heart failure aims at reducing the heart's workload. Measures include rest and sleep, weight reduction where necessary, and drugs, especially digitalis compounds, which improve the heart muscle's efficiency, reduce the heart rate and act as a diuretic, marshalling excess fluid from waterlogged tissues to be excreted as urine.

Surgery may be required for problems involving heart valves or coronary arterial disease.

HEART MURMUR

A murmur is an additional sound over and above the normal 'lubb dupp', which is heard by means of a stethoscope or indicated on ECG.

A heart murmur is due to a fast and turbulent blood flow in the heart's chambers. Causes of a heart murmur include damaged valves, abnormal communicating channels, and an abnormally swift circulation, for example in pernicious anaemia or overactivity of the thyroid gland.

Treatment
This depends on the cause. Some murmurs are harmless; damaged valves may be treated surgically

HEART SURGERY

Cardio-thoracic (heart and chest) surgery is an expanding field, and surgery is used to treat a wide range of conditions.

Heart surgery is divided into three main types: open heart surgery, closed heart surgery and transplant surgery.

Open heart surgery
Open heart surgery is used to describe operations where the heart is cut open. It is used to deal with faulty or leaky valves (which can be replaced with artifical valves of metal, plastic or specially treated pig tissue), and it

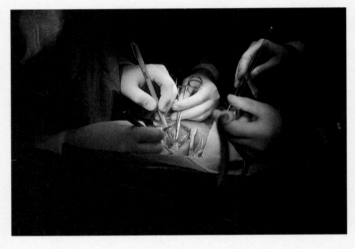

A 48-day-old boy, suffering from a potentially fatal congenital heart defect, undergoing heart transplant surgery.

treats some types of congenital heart disease.

Closed surgery
Closed surgery is used for diseases of the coronary arteries. If a blockage is present, it can be by-passed using a graft taken from the patient's leg vein. This operation is now so common in the USA that more by-passes are performed than appendectomies.

Transplant surgery
Heart transplant, or heart and lung transplant, is used when the heart is badly damaged or defective (including, sometimes, congenital defects in new-born babies). Since the first heart transplant in 1967, the operation has been refined to the point where it has become almost routine.

Life-saving machines
The heart by-pass machine made heart surgery possible. It is a machine that enables the surgeon to operate on a heart that has stopped beating and has been drained of blood.

The heart by-pass machine (or heart-lung machine) is a pump and an oxygenator and enables the surgeon to work on the heart for extended periods. Before surgery can start, the beating of the heart is stopped by applying an ice-cold solution. The low temperature also reduces the heart's need for oxygen, which gives the surgeon a longer period of time to operate. After surgery is complete, the heart is restarted by means of a small electric shock.

≫ SEE ALSO — Cardiac arrest

HEAT CRAMPS

Heat cramps are a form of severe cramp, or muscular spasm, caused by a loss of salt from the body's system.

Closely related to heatstroke, heat cramps are most often caused by excessive vigorous physical activity during very hot weather. Through increased sweating, the body loses the vital salts which are necessary for the efficient working of the muscles.

Treatment

As soon as the condition is diagnosed, the sufferer should attempt to replace the lost salt by taking salt tablets. An alternative way of restoring salt to the muscles is by drinking a mixture of salt and water. Mix a half teaspoon of salt with a litre of water and drink as much as possible. It is important not to exceed the recommended dosage of salt as this is likely to cause an upset stomach.

HEAT EXHAUSTION

Heat exhaustion is caused by the body overheating as a result of exposure to unusually hot conditions.

The symptoms of heat exhaustion include queasiness, tiredness and, sometimes, loss of consciousness.

As with heat cramps, heat exhaustion is most often caused by a person taking part in vigorous activity under unfamiliar conditions of extreme heat.

Treatment

The treatment is similar to that for heat cramps. The sufferer should be removed from exposure to the heat and kept in cool conditions. A salt solution (half a teaspoon of salt mixed in with a litre of water) should be gently administered to them. It is very important, however, to call a doctor immediately to check that the condition has not developed into heatstroke.

HEATSTROKE

Heatstroke is a potentially fatal disruption of the body's normal cooling processes which is caused when the body is unable to function efficiently after being exposed to unusually high levels of heat.

The human body is best able to function at a temperature of 37 degrees centigrade. In extreme heat, the body's temperature can increase to 41 degrees or higher. The skin will dry out and the sufferer may develop heatstroke and become severely ill.

In some cases, for example when the atmospheric humidity is very high, sweating will cease entirely and the body will be unable to cool itself. The sufferer will feel faint, have difficulty in breathing and may lose consciousness. Death may follow.

Dealing with heatstroke

The best way to deal with heatstroke is to take steps to avoid possible exposure to excess heat. If you are travelling in a very hot country, for example, a process of gradual acclimatisation should be followed: stay in the sun for short periods initially then a bit longer each day; wear cool clothes; avoid alcohol and heavy meals; drink plenty of fluids.

If someone is suffering from heatstroke remove their clothes and cover them with a thin cotton or linen blanket which should then be continually soaked in cold water. A doctor should be called and the process of cooling the sufferer's body should continue until the body temperature has been reduced to its normal level.

HEMIANOPIA

Hemianopia is the loss of sight in half of the visual field.

Hemianopia may impair vision in one of two ways. Either the same half of each eye will be affected or the two different halves will blank out the vision.

The condition may be permanent, in which case it is likely to have been caused by a stroke damaging the nerve tracts which run from the eye to the brain. Other brain disorders or internal pressures on the brain may also be responsible.

Alternately, it may be a temporary condition which, especially in young people, is often caused by migraine headaches.

Anyone suffering from impaired vision in this way, whether they suspect it to be hemianopia or not, should make sure they consult a doctor immediately.

HEPATITIS

Hepatitis is inflammation of the liver and is usually caused by chemical poisons or infections.

Unlike cirrhosis, which may follow it, there is no scarring of the liver involved with hepatitis. For those who are infected, therefore, recovery is usually complete.

The most common forms of viral infection of the liver are known as hepatitis A and hepatitis B. The other causes of viral infection to the liver are therefore classified as 'non-A' and 'non-B'.

Hepatitis A

Hepatitis A is caused by a virus that normally lives in the gut. Small epidemics occur and the infection is spread from person to person through contaminated food and drink.

The incubation period is between two and six weeks and the onset is gradual with malaise and 'flu-like symptoms, often followed by loss of appetite, nausea, vomiting and pain in the upper abdomen. Jaundice, when it occurs, develops after an interval of between two days and two weeks, and is accompanied by dark urine and pale stools.

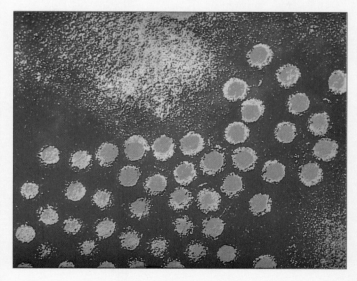

The blue dots highlight the Hepatitis A virus, which is transmitted by flies, food and contaminated drinking water.

As a rule, once the patient develops jaundice they will begin feeling better although itching all over can be a problem for several weeks. The symptoms should disappear after a week or two and a second attack then becomes extremely unlikely.

Treatment and prevention

Treatment is simple. Rest during the jaundiced phase and be sure to avoid alcohol entirely for a year.

As Hepatitis A is rife in many tropical countries you should ask your doctor about a gamma globulin injection if you are travelling anywhere off the beaten track. This will offer some protection against possible sources of infection but it will only last for three or four months.

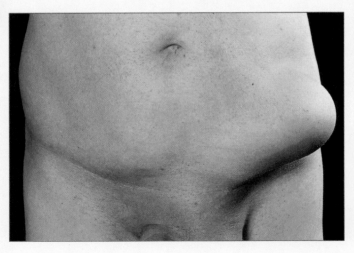

Above: An image of the Hepatitis B virus – one of six different viruses which infect the livers of humans and animals.

Hepatitis B

Hepatitis B is less common but is a much more serious disease. The virus is present in nearly all the body fluids and in the stools. It is usually spread by infected blood and is most frequently caught by intravenous drug users who share contaminated needles. It can also be passed on between sexual partners, and from mothers to newborn babies.

Health workers used to be a high risk group but the introduction of an effective vaccine has reduced the incidence in this group.

The incubation period for Hepatitis B is between four weeks and six months.

The symptoms

The symptoms of Hepatitis B are similar to those of Hepatitis A but can also cause rashes, arthritis and kidney problems and in uncomplicated cases the treatment is the same. Unlike Hepatitis A, however, complications can arise from Hepatitis B. The condition may progress to chronic hepatitis where the inflammation and the jaundice do not improve.

Chronic hepatitis may progress to cirrhosis, a condition in which most of the liver is replaced by scar tissue. In some cases of hepatitis the liver damage is so great that it can no longer function. If a transplant organ is unavailable, death is almost certain.

Immunisation

Hepatitis B is a serious condition which can be avoided by immunisation. At present, the vaccine is reserved for those who are at most risk. High risk groups are health workers such as doctors, dentists, nurses and cleaners, as they are likely to come into contact with contaminated blood. Others at risk of coming into contact with contaminated blood and saliva are staff and inmates of mental institutions and homes for the handicapped; homosexual and bisexual men; intravenous drug users and members of the police and other emergency crews.

Chemical poisons

The most common poison which causes hepatitis is alcohol. Exceed the weekly total of 14 units for women and 21 units for men and you are at risk. The features of alcoholic hepatitis include pain under the right ribs, jaundice, cirrhosis and liver failure. Alternately, there may be no symptoms at all.

Organic solvents such as carbon tetrachloride can also cause hepatitis if inhaled in quantity. The treatment required depends on the stage reached but alcohol is forbidden. If cirrhosis is present, a low protein diet, vitamins and drug treatment may be needed.

Drugs

Drugs are another form of chemical poison which may bring on hepatitis. The most common cause is sensitivity to a drug which is perfectly harmless in other people.

Hepatitis caused by drugs is uncommon but the mortality rate of those affected is very high. Up to 20 per cent of sufferers die from drug-induced hepatitis.

It usually occurs two or three weeks after starting a drug and may be caused by some antidepressants and the antibiotics used for tuberculosis. Halothane, an anaesthetic gas, can cause hepatitis if used repeatedly.

In much the same way as with alcohol, drug-related hepatitis can be caused by direct damage to the liver cells. For example, the drug paracetamol, usually safe in normal use, can cause a fatal hepatitis in overdosage.

Death may take over a week, during which time the patient becomes more and more ill. An antidote can be given but, for this to be effective, it must be administered during the first few hours after the overdose.

HERNIA

Hernia occurs when a part of the body's internal tissues or organs protrudes through the wall of the abdomen.

Above: A man suffering from a hernia – a protrusion of an organ or tissue out through the wall of the body cavity.

»» SEE ALSO — Alcohol, Cirrhosis, Jaundice, Liver

HERPES

Abdominal hernias are caused when the abdominal wall is too weak to take the strain of the internal components of the body pressurising it. A hernia is likely to occur when an individual attempts some form of physical exertion which puts great strain on the abdominal wall. A typical cause of hernia is straining to lift a heavy weight in a way which puts severe pressure on the lower body.

The hernia will bulge through the abdominal wall, protruding visibly and often causing a degree of pain. In some cases, it may be possible for the sufferer to press on the affected area and push the organ or tissue back into place. When the tissue or organ cannot be pressed back into place it may become strangulated, causing the victim to suffer from a reduced blood supply. This brings the danger of gangrene so it is essential that a person who suspects they have suffered a hernia of any sort should consult a doctor immediately.

Treatment

If the hernia can be replaced, and is not particularly painful, a supportive truss may be used to keep the intestine in place until it heals. Otherwise, surgery is likely to be performed.

HERPES

Herpes is a blister-like rash caused by infection with any of a group of viruses responsible for many common illnesses, including chickenpox, shingles and glandular fever.

Herpes simplex is probably the most common viral parasite which lives off man. It exists in two forms, type 1 and type 2. Type 1

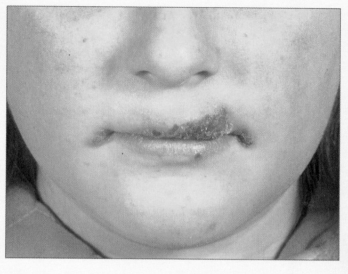

Above: Cold sores around the lips and mouth, caused by an oral infection with the herpes simplex virus.

usually causes cold sores, spots and blisters on the face, lips and eyes but oral sex with a partner who has cold sores could cause genital herpes. Herpes simplex type 2, is transmitted sexually, causing genital herpes in men and women, and can affect non-genital skin areas in the new-born babies of mothers who are carrying the infection.

In the past, the majority of children would have been infected with cold sores at an early age. Increasing hygiene standards have meant that

more and more children are reaching sexual maturity with no antibodies against type 1 herpes. As antibodies to type 1 offer some protection against type 2, this may help to explain the increasing incidence of genital herpes.

Symptoms of genital herpes

The incubation period (the length of time between picking up the infection and developing the disease) is short: only five or six days. The first attack usually consists of blisters on the genitals. Initially the affected

parts of the body start as areas of visible redness and then rapidly change, first of all into blisters, then ulcers and finally scabs. The blisters may also appear on those areas which are near the genitals such as the anus, buttocks or thighs as well as on the fingers.

In women, the cervix is a common site of infection and in homosexual men the anus and the rectum are often affected. If the rectum is affected, herpes can cause

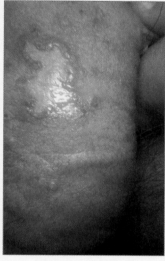

Above: Genital herpes – a cold sore located on a penis and caused by infection by the herpes simplex virus.

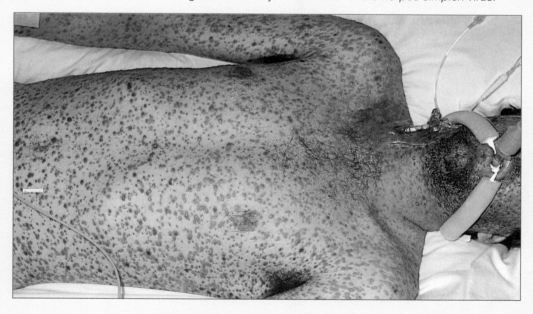

Above: An adult with a severe case of chickenpox, caused by the herpes zoster virus. This is unusual as the disease infects the majority of children and usually confers a life-long immunity.

▶▶ SEE ALSO — Cold sores

severe pain, discharge and constipation.

The degree of pain depends on the number and site of the blisters, although some of the areas likely to be affected will probably be more painful than others. The blisters will usually take about 10 days to heal completely but throughout that time they will be constantly shedding viruses.

A range of symptoms

Approximately half of the people who suffer herpes for the first time actually feel unwell. This can range from a mild feeling of lethargy to the 'flu-like symptoms of fever and headache.

Second and subsequent infections are less severe. They are caused by a recurrence of the original infection rather than a new one. Frequent sufferers can often identify a precipitating factor such as menstruation, sexual intercourse or stress, which they know will almost certainly bring on an attack. Type 2 infections will tend to recur more frequently than type 1 infections.

Genital herpes is an incurable condition with long-term implications for both the sufferer and her partner. For this reason, doctors will always try to confirm the diagnosis before voicing their suspicions. Fluid from a blister can be examined by the doctor to give a definite diagnosis.

Finding a cure

There is no cure for genital herpes although trials are underway. An antiviral agent (a drug that kills viruses rather than bacteria) called Zovirax shortens the course of the disease but does not cure it. Long-term treatment may prevent a second attack. This drug is expensive and is only used in particularly severe cases.

Sheaths offer some protection from genital herpes but the blisters can be so widespread that infection can still occur even if safe sex is strictly observed. Sexual intercourse between attacks is usually safe but there is a small risk that viral particles can still be shed. Under these circumstances, contraceptive sheaths may be needed all the time.

Herpes zoster/varicella

Herpes zoster and varicella are different names for the same virus. It is related to the virus which causes cold sores and genital herpes but, unlike them, it is transmitted by droplets of saliva.

Varicella causes chickenpox, a mild disease that commonly affects children. Zoster causes shingles, a more serious condition that usually affects adults. The main features of shingles are pain followed by a rash of blisters along the course of the nerve in whose root the virus has lain dormant, often for many years, probably since an attack of chickenpox during childhood.

As with genital herpes, the herpes zoster virus seems to flare up after periods of particularly serious physical or emotional stress for the individual infected. There is no specific cure for herpes zoster but Zovirax, painkillers and physiotherapy will all help the condition.

Curative Diet

Although there is no medical proof, many sufferers of herpes believe that outbreaks can be reduced by regulating the intake of two amino acids, lysine and arginine, which occur naturally in foodstuffs. Foods high in lysine are believed to reduce attacks, while those high in arginine, for example nuts and rice, should be avoided.

HIATUS HERNIA

Hiatus hernia is caused when a section of the stomach is forced up through the space in the lower part of the diaphragm which is normally occupied by the oesophagus.

The most likely sufferers of hiatus hernia are women in middle age, particularly if they are overweight or are suffering from increased pressure on the abdomen such as multiple pregnancy or constipation. It can also be found in new-born babies.

Often, an individual who has a hiatus hernia will be unaware of their condition as it sometimes does not produce any pain or visible symptoms. The symptoms include heartburn, upper abdominal pain and regurgitation of partially digested stomach contents, especially on bending forwards or lying down flat.

Diagnosis and treatment

If hiatus hernia is suspected, the patient will be required to attend hospital. They will be given a barium meal, and then asked to put their head between their knees. X-rays taken while they are in this position should enable medical staff to establish whether the oesophagus is functioning efficiently or is hampered by a hiatus hernia.

Hiatus hernia victims can usually treat themselves. A reduced consumption of rich food and a healthy diet help. Smokers should give up and all sufferers should sleep with their head tilted above their body by raising the head of the bed by 2-3ins.

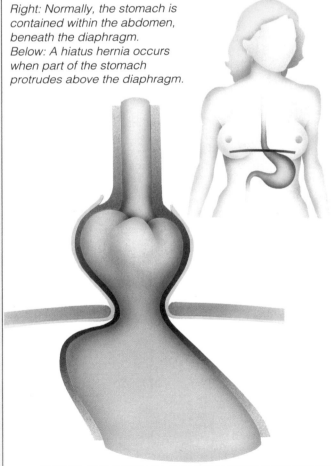

Position of hiatus hernia

Right: Normally, the stomach is contained within the abdomen, beneath the diaphragm.
Below: A hiatus hernia occurs when part of the stomach protrudes above the diaphragm.

HICCUPS

Hiccups are spasmodic, sharp emissions of air through the mouth, caused by minor disruption to the normal working of the diaphragm.

The initial trigger for an attack of hiccups is usually difficult to trace but is unimportant as the condition is usually short-lived and is not serious. The actual hiccups are caused by muscular spasm in the diaphragm. This forces air rapidly through the vocal cords and produces the hiccup sound.

Treatment

There are many folk remedies for a burst of hiccups, such as holding your breath, drinking a glass of water or standing on your head. Some of these work for some people but there is, as yet, no universal cure.

If hiccups continue over a long period, and become a serious problem, drugs can be prescribed and surgery may eventually be carried out. However, these methods of treatment are also often of only limited success. A prolonged attack may be a symptom of kidney failure.

HIP DISORDERS

The hip joint is a ball and socket which connects the top of the thigh bone, the femur, with the pelvis. It is one of the strongest joints in the body, but is prone to a number of diseases.

Although hip problems tend generally to affect middle-aged and older people, one condition, known as congenital dislocation of the hip, usually occurs soon after birth. In this condition the head of the femur slips out of its normal position. It is

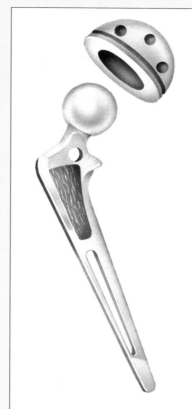

Hip Replacement

Left: A replacement socket and cup are fitted during a hip-replacement. Above: Incisions are made around the site, without damaging muscles.

rarely dislocated at birth but slides out as the baby becomes more active. The cause is not known, but there is a tendency for the condition to run in families. It is also commonly found in breech-birth babies.

Babies with congenital dislocation of the hip are usually treated as soon as the condition is diagnosed. If not, they are likely to experience great difficulty in walking. Treatment, if it is caught early enough, consists of fitting the baby with a harness to hold the hip in position. If this does not work, or if the condition is not detected until later on, an operation may be needed.

Perthe's disease

Perthe's disease occurs in children between the ages of four and 10. Boys are more often affected than girls. The growing end of the bone fails to develop properly, usually because of problems with the blood supply. The child then develops a limp as the hip becomes more and more painful. The condition can be

diagnosed by x-ray. Fortunately, the pain should disappear without treatment although this may take up to three years.

Osteoarthritis

A very common condition of the hip is osteoarthritis, which is due to degeneration of the weight-bearing surfaces. Instead of being smooth and flat, the cartilage between the bones becomes rough and uneven. Osteoarthritis may be due to a pre-existing condition such as a dislocated hip. It is often, however, simply a result of excessive wear and tear.

The main symptoms of osteoarthritis are pain and deformity. The pain is often severe enough to wake the patient at night and as the condition progresses any form of movement is acutely painful. X-rays are of little value in the diagnosis as the most important factor in analysis of the condition is the degree of disability rather than the appearance on an x-ray plate.

Osteoarthritis sufferers can help themselves by losing weight. Medical help consists of physiotherapy, pain killers and sometimes non-steroid anti-inflammatory drugs. This often keeps the condition at bay for several years but some patients will eventually have the entire joint replaced. Current practice is to replace the end of the thigh bone with a metal ball and the socket with a plastic cup. Both parts are cemented in place.

Variations, if this ideal operation is not possible, are to remove the joint completely or to screw the bones together. However, these operations are usually reserved for bedridden patients and the main aim is to relieve pain rather than to restore function.

Fractured neck of femur

Old people, particularly women, tend to have crumbling bones as a result of osteoporosis. In people with this condition, even a light fall can fracture the

>> SEE ALSO — Arthritis, Breech birth

neck of the thigh bone. Surgery to replace the joint or to plate the fracture is usually technically possible but many frail old people cannot survive the post-operative period. The increasing use of HRT should make fractures of the femur less common in the future.

HISTAMINE

Histamine is matter which is stored under the skin and in the mucous membranes and is released to help repair damaged tissue.

Histamine is often associated only with the uncomfortable reaction it causes in hay-fever sufferers. Its importance in mending damaged tissue therefore tends to be overlooked.

When tissue is damaged by, for example, a bee sting, histamine causes blood vessels to widen, allowing more blood to reach the damaged area. However, as part of this process, histamine narrows the bronchi, making breathing more difficult.

Those who suffer from hay fever are often prescribed antihistamine drugs. If taken before an attack, these drugs can lessen the effects.

HIV

The Human Immuno-deficiency Virus attacks the body's immune system and may develop, in some people, into Acquired Immune Deficiency Syndrome (AIDS).

The title Human Immuno-deficiency Virus was created in the 80s to describe a virus which came to the attention of American scientists. Homosexual men and haemophiliacs in the US had

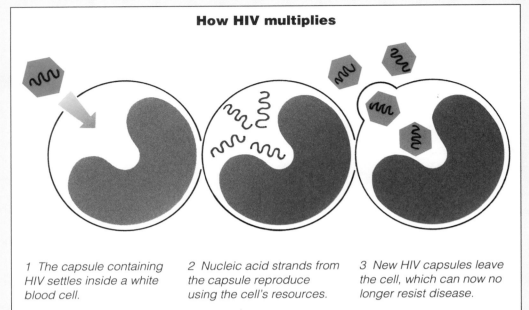

How HIV multiplies

1 The capsule containing HIV settles inside a white blood cell.

2 Nucleic acid strands from the capsule reproduce using the cell's resources.

3 New HIV capsules leave the cell, which can now no longer resist disease.

begun developing an unusual infection of the lung. The same symptoms were found in heterosexuals in Africa, and among drug abusers using needles.

The American scientists who investigated the infection concluded that it was being contracted by these people through blood or homosexual activity.

HIV settles in the T4 white blood cells which play an important role in regulating the body's immune system. The virus may lie dormant for years but once it becomes active it attacks and weakens the T4 cells. It may then lead to AIDS and several other serious diseases including some types of cancer.

Transmission
It has now been established that HIV can be transmitted only in blood, semen and vaginal secretions. It may be found in other substances, such as tears and saliva, but there is no evidence that it can be passed on through them.

The virus can be passed on during sexual contact, and through sharing hypodermic needles. It can even be passed on from a pregnant infected woman,

through the placenta, to her child while it is in the womb.

Identifying the virus
Sudden and unusually great weight loss, persistent diarrhoea or fever may be early signs of HIV. Anyone with such symptoms should consult a doctor immediately and if HIV is suspected, a blood test will be carried out. Alternatively, there may be no symptoms at all.

Prevention
Safe sexual practices (including using condoms) will help to prevent the spread of the virus. And drug abusers should never share needles.

HOARSENESS

Hoarseness is an unnaturally deep and rough sounding voice caused by strain on the vocal cords. Because speech is produced in the larynx, hoarseness is often called laryngitis.

Many people have a voice that sounds hoarse but this should only be regarded as a problem if it differs from their normal one.

How the voice works
Air from the lungs passes upwards through the vocal cords and then soundlessly through the larynx. The vocal cords are pulled towards one another and the air from the lungs causes them to vibrate.

The vibration causes a sound which varies in pitch when the length of the vocal cords is altered. The sounds become speech through the workings of the palate, tongue, teeth and lips. The vocal cords of a baby are 5mm long, those of an adult female 15mm and those of an adult male 20mm. This helps explain the depth of a man's voice.

Anything that interferes with the delicate process of producing vocal sounds can result in hoarseness.

Acute laryngitis
Acute laryngitis is the result of an infection, usually viral. It is often part of an upper respiratory tract infection though it can occasionally be due to lower airway infections such as pneumonia. It is most common in smokers and those who live or work in polluted environments. The most important aspect of treatment is to rest the voice. Whispering is not enough as

SEE ALSO — Aids

Diagnosing Hoarseness

By answering the following questions, you may be able to work out what the most likely cause of your hoarseness is.

● Have you recently developed the hoarseness?
It is likely to be due to a recent cold or using your voice more than usual. In both cases, avoid smoking and alcohol, rest the voice and drink lots of fluids.

● Do you use your voice a lot in your daily work?
Teachers and singers may develop chronic laryngitis. Your voice may need prolonged rest. Consult your doctor.

● Do your drink or smoke a lot?
Both of these tend to contribute to chronic laryngitis, in which case your doctor will recommend that you should give up the habits immediately.

● Have you noticed any other symptoms?
Hoarseness associated with a dryness of skin or hair, an unexplained weight increase, excessive tiredness and feeling the cold more than usual suggests hypothyroidism.

● Has your hoarseness increased gradually?
Hoarseness may simply be a symptom of the normal hormonal changes which come with age. In some rare cases, it may also be an indicator of a growth.

Left: Smoking is a major cause of acute laryngitis and smokers should give up the habit immediately if they are diagnosed as suffering from hoarseness.

it puts even more of a strain on the vocal cords. Use a pencil and paper.

Steam inhalations soothe the vocal cords. The steam can be sweetened by menthol crystals or by Friar's Balsam. Simple analgesics such as aspirin should be adequate to deal with any fever or discomfort.

Croup
Croup can cause hoarseness and a barking cough in children. It is due to a viral infection and affects infants under three years old.

Small epidemics occur most winters and the symptoms are often worse at night. The child may become ill very rapidly, developing a high temperature and a painful cough. Steam inhalations, particularly if carried out in the atmosphere of a steamy bathroom, rapidly relieve the symptoms but may need to be repeated many times in one night.

Allergic laryngitis
Inhalation of an allergen such as pollen may result in allergic laryngitis. It may also be part of a general reaction to a bee or wasp sting. A sting which brings on allergic laryngitis is an acute emergency requiring urgent hospital admission. When produced by pollen inhalation it can be treated with antihistamines such as Piriton, which are available over the counter.

Chronic laryngitis
Some cases of chronic laryngitis may be the result of repeated acute infections, but the majority appear to be without any obvious cause. Again, smokers and those who work in a dusty environment are most likely to be affected but the removal of these particular risk factors is no guarantee that you will not contract chronic laryngitis.

The best treatment is to rest both the voice and body. Failure to rest the voice may cause scarring to the vocal cords. Speech therapists are able to help by teaching voice patterns which do not strain the cords.

Acid laryngitis
Under some circumstances, with a hiatus hernia for example, acid from the stomach can be forced up the oesophagus and into the larynx. This can cause burning in the throat and hoarseness.

Sleeping propped up helps but if this and simple antacids do not remove the condition a doctor should be consulted. She may prescribe a drug to stop the production of stomach acid.

Vocal strain
The optimum pitch for a voice is a third of the way up that person's range. If this pitch is deliberately ignored, by screaming at a pop concert for example, hoarseness will probably be the result. Again, the only treatment is to rest the voice.

Singer's nodules
Singer's nodules are sometimes called screamer's nodules — usually by people who do not like rock music. This provides a clue to the cause of the problem.

If a singer wishes to raise the pitch of her voice she can only do so by tightening the muscles which shorten the vocal cords. If the singer then raises the volume of her voice the result is a greatly increased vibration of the vocal cords. This produces serious swellings on the vocal cords which can eventually only be removed surgically — an operation which can have the effect of ruining a voice.

Rare causes of hoarseness
Cancer of the larynx does exist but it is very rare in young people. The first sign is often persistent hoarseness. Most doctors will seek a specialist's advice if hoarseness lasts more than three weeks. Lung cancer and strokes can both create hoarseness by damaging the nerves which control the vocal cords.

An underactive thyroid may also cause hoarseness and this should be borne in mind if the hoarseness is accompanied by weight gain, hair loss and a general slowing down of activity.

HODGKIN'S DISEASE

Hodgkin's Disease is a cancer of the lymphoid tissue, which is found in the lymph nodes and the spleen.

There is no known cause of Hodgkin's Disease. It is uncommon, and affects more men than women. The age groups most often affected are 20 to 30 and 55 to 70 years.

Symptoms and treatment

Often, the only symptom is visible, rather than painful, lumps under the skin, frequently in the neck or armpits, caused by swollen lymph nodes. The enlargement of the lymph nodes, which are a vital part of the body's system of immunity to disease, may cause other problems: sufferers may feel generally unwell, with night sweats and loss of sleep, appetite and weight; a minor infection, which would be easily fought off by a healthy person, may be fatal in a person with

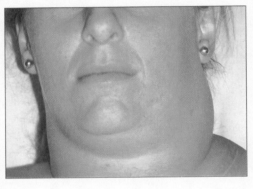

Above: Swollen lymph glands in the neck of a sufferer from Hodgkin's Disease.
Below: The illuminated discs over this patient's chest indicate areas which are to receive radiotherapy for Hodgkin's Disease.

Hodgkin's Disease.

Diagnosis is normally by biopsy. If diagnosed at an early stage, radiotherapy should be effective. If, however, it has spread to other organs around the body, a course of drugs may be prescribed to be followed for a lengthy period. It may be necessary to remove the spleen, if the lymphoid tissue there is affected.

HORMONES

A hormone is a chemical substance produced by a gland and secreted into the bloodstream.

Hormones act on organs distant from the site of their production. The nervous system can be likened to a computer, with a vast network instantly connecting all parts of the body. In this maze, the hormones are the postal system. Some messages take longer to travel than others but the same message can be sent to many different places at once. Hormones affect our digestive system, our reproductive system, our growth — indeed, all the body's processes.

The body produces many hundreds of hormones but medical scientists have only managed to identify a few of them. Of these, they are only sure about the purpose and function of a small number.

Growth hormone

The process by which growth hormone is produced and distributed is a good example of how hormones work.

It is one of the half dozen hormones produced in the anterior lobe of the pituitary gland, which is situated in the brain. Its secretion (the process by which it is produced and released) is controlled by two other hormones produced in the hypothalamus, another gland inside the brain.

The actual amount of growth hormone secreted depends on several factors and it can fluctuate wildly over the course of a day. Secretion is increased by a wide variety of factors including sleep, fear, starvation and exercise.

Stemming growth

Growth hormone is decreased by growth hormone itself. The more growth hormone there is in the blood, the less growth hormone is produced in the pituitary gland. This so-called negative feedback system is very common in hormones and is a useful brake on their overproduction. It is also closely related to some of the hormones found in placenta and it may be that both placental and growth hormones are derived from a common hormone.

On average, the pituitary gland produces about one thousandth of a gram of growth hormone daily. In children, growth hormone causes an increase in bone length. In older children and adults it causes an overgrowth in most organs, leading to deformity.

Growth hormone increases the amount of protein in the body and decreases the amount of fat. It also counters the action of insulin. Insulin decreases the amount of glucose in the blood, growth hormone increases it.

Tumours

Over- or underproduction of growth hormone, in common with many other hormones, is usually due to a tumour. In children, this has the effect of producing giants (if the tumour causes enlargement of the gland) or dwarfs (if the tumour is non-productive and crowds out the hormone-producing cells).

» SEE ALSO — Endocrine system, Growth

HOT FLUSHES

These usually occur during or after the menopause, and they are caused by decreased oestrogen production by the ovaries.

Women experience a reddening of the face, neck and upper trunk, accompanied by a sensation of heat, often followed by sweating. Hot flushes are also aggravated by stress.

If hot flushes are severe, they can usually be alleviated by hormone replacement therapy (see HRT). Women can also experience hot flushes if they have their ovaries removed. Occasionally men suffer from them if they have their testicles removed, as this causes a reduction in testosterone levels.

HRT

HRT (Hormone Replacement Therapy) is used to help alleviate the adverse side effects of changes in the hormone levels at the menopause.

Most women reach the menopause between the age of 46 and 54. For some, the end of the monthly chore of periods and the final elimination of worries over pregnancy mean that this is a positive time in their lives.

On the other hand many women suffer the effects of decreased levels of oestrogen: hot flushes, a dry vagina (which may make intercourse uncomfortable), loss of the typical female fat distribution and, in the long term, crumbling bones.

The therapy
These symptoms can largely be eliminated by replacing the missing hormone, oestrogen. In short-term use — for only a few weeks —

oestrogen is perfectly safe. However, to prevent hip fractures and crumbling spines it must be used for at least five years, and then there is a danger of cancer of the womb.

To overcome this risk doctors will always prescribe a progestogen as well as an oestrogen. This combination may cause period-like bleeding which some women find unacceptable.

Administering hormones
Oestrogens can be taken in several ways. Daily tablets, similar to the Pill, are probably the most popular. These have the added advantage that half the pills can be made up to contain progestogen as well. Patches that allow a minute amount of hormone to cross the skin can be kept on for four days but progesterone pills still have to be taken for half the month. The third alternative is implants that last up to three months. They have similar problems to patches, and are probably best suited to women who have had a hysterectomy and do not need progesterone.

HYDROCEPHALUS

Hydrocephalus or 'water on the brain' as it is commonly known, is an increase in cerebrospinal fluid inside the brain.

About one in 500 babies is born with a degree of hydrocephalus, which is frequently associated with spina bifida. Hydrocephalus can also arise in later childhood as a result of brain damage caused by a tumour or infection.

The skull swells because of a blockage in the normal circulation of spinal fluid which prevents the fluid from draining away into the bloodstream. The soft spots and the joins between the bones in the skull widen and the skull increases in size. If the condition is not diagnosed early in life, serious brain damage can result, and an early death is likely from infection.

If hydrocephalus occurs in the womb, it can cause problems with delivery, necessitating a Caesarean section. Ultrasound and x-ray can detect the condition during pregnancy, if it is well-established.

Treatment
Until recently, treatment was possible only after birth, but the operation can now be performed in the womb. Its success depends on the severity of the condition.

A small hole is drilled in the skull and a fine tube or shunt with a one-way valve is inserted. The other end of the tube is inserted into a major blood vessel or the left atrium of the heart. The excess fluid is drained off into the bloodstream, so the swollen head can reduce in size. In some cases the shunt has to be left in place for an indefinite period.

HYPERACTIVITY

Hyperactivity is the term used to describe excessive physical and mental activity in children.

The main feature of hyperactivity is that the child is continuously on the go. He or she is full of energy, fidgety, can't settle, has short attention spans and doesn't have normal sleep patterns.

Obviously hyperactivity is a serious problem to parents. The child can be aggressive, irritable, and emotionally immature. Such traits can develop into antisocial behaviour, with learning difficulties at school being part of the problem.

Causes
The causes of hyperactivity are unknown. It has been suggested that 'minimal' brain damage might be one explanation. There is some evidence to back this up, but it is rather poor. Another theory is that the child inherits a tendency to hyperactivity from its father.

Children with mental retardation, cerebral palsy, or temporal lobe epilepsy may also be hyperactive. A popular theory is that it is connected with food

During treatment of hydrocephalus, children have to have their heads measured regularly. An accumulation of fluid will prevent the normal development of the brain.

SEE ALSO — Hysterectomy, Menopause

MEDICAL FACT FILE

allergies, in particular with the consumption of food additives/preservatives, although again, evidence for this is poor.

Treatment

Drug treatment is available for some cases of hyperactivity, but careful monitoring, usually in hospital, is necessary.

Counselling the parents of hyperactive children is useful. The children need to have formal educational and psychological assessment as many need help with school work. In many cases, hyperactivity disappears completely at puberty. In some cases, it is replaced by depression, sluggishness and moodiness. Sometimes hyperactivity can continue into adult life.

HYPERCALCAEMIA

Hypercalcaemia is an excess of calcium in the blood, which may be due to a number of possible causes.

The most common cause is cancer, which can increase the calcium levels in the blood by releasing it from the bone. Another common cause is hyperpara-thyroidism, or overproduction by the parathyroid hormone, which helps control the blood calcium level. Excessive dosages of vitamin D have the same effect as they increase the absorption of calcium from the intestine.

Symptoms and treatment

The symptoms of hyper-calcaemia include nausea, vomiting, diarrhoea, possibly anorexia; mental disturbances such as depression, fatigue and even dementia; and extreme thirst.

If the condition is caused by an excess of Vitamin D, then the patient should go on a diet to exclude it. If the hypercalcaemia is due to

hyperparathyroidism, this should be treated. Another possible cause is an excess of milk and alkali eaten by ulcer patients.

HYPERGLYCAEMIA

Hyperglycaemia is the condition where there is an abnormally high level of glucose or blood sugar in the blood.

This condition occurs in people who are suffering from untreated or poorly controlled diabetes mellitus. It can also occur in diabetics as a result of an infection, stress or surgery, which may upset the blood sugar levels.

Symptoms and treatment

The symptoms of hyperglycaemia are excessive thirst, passing unusually large amounts of urine, glycosuria (glucose in the urine) and ketosis (an accumulation of ketones — a product of fat breakdown — in the body). These last two symptoms can be detected by testing the urine with special indicator papers. In severe cases, hyper-glycaemia can lead to coma — this requires emergency treatment with insulin and intravenous infusion of fluids.

HYPERLIPIDAEMIA

Hyperlipidaemia is an excess of lipids, or fats, in the blood, usually due to a poor diet, but sometimes due to an inherited condition.

Hyperlipidaemia is linked to a number of serious illnesses, most notably atherosclerosis (the narrowing of arteries by deposits of fatty material) and coronary artery disease.

There are six types of hyperlipidaemias, which are categorised according to the

different forms of lipids which are in excess of normal levels in the blood.

Fats (or lipids) are carried in the blood in several forms, chiefly cholesterol, triglycerides and lipoproteins.

Symptoms and treatments vary according to which type of lipoprotein is in excess in the blood.

For instance, an excess of one type of lipoprotein manifests itself in fatty nodules around tendons and over joints; an excess of other types results in fatty nodules on the eyelids as well as a white line around the rim of the cornea.

What can be done?

Treatment aims at reducing blood lipid levels by reducing the amount of fats, particularly saturated fats. The safest drug treatment is to use a resin that binds fat in the digestive tract. If it does not work, or causes side effects, more powerful drugs may be prescribed.

The tendency towards hyperlipidaemia may be inherited or may be a consequence of another disorder such as hypothyroidism, alcohol dependence, kidney failure, diabetes mellitus and Cushing's syndrome. The condition may also result from treatment with corticosteroid drugs or oestrogen drugs.

HYPERMETROPIA

Commonly known as longsightedness, hypermetropia is caused by the eye being too short from front to back, so that images are not clearly focused on the retina.

The condition is present at birth and tends to run in families. Mild or moderate hypermetropia is actually not a problem, as the ciliary muscles act on the lens to bring the point of focus foward to produce a clear image, a process known as 'accommodation'.

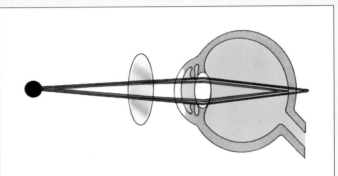

Long-sightedness first becomes noticeable when viewing close objects. The lens focuses the object beyond the retina (blue line). A convex lens corrects the problem.

The power to accom-modate declines with age so symptoms generally do not appear until later life. The more severe the condition, the younger the age at which people experience difficulty in viewing close objects. Eventually distant objects become blurred. Treatment is by wearing convex lenses to reinforce the focusing power.

HYPERTENSION

Hypertension, or high blood pressure, is not a disease in itself. It may, however, be a sign of some diseases and the cause of others.

Huge sums of money are spent every year detecting and treating hypertension but

▶▶ SEE ALSO — Diabetes, Hypocalcaemia, Hypoglycaemia, Thyroid

much of this is wasted, either because the blood pressure was never really high or because the side effects of the treatment outweigh its benefits.

Monitoring the problem

Blood pressure was originally measured by inserting a needle attached to a tube of water into an artery. The higher the column of water the blood could support, the higher the blood pressure. Now, blood pressure is normally measured using a sphygmomanometer. This consists of a bladder that can be pumped up and a device for measuring the air pressure inside the bladder. The bladder is wrapped around the arm and inflated. The bladder exerts a pressure on the arm equal to the pressure inside itself. The pressure that completely closes the artery, which can be detected by feeling the pulse, is equal to the highest pressure the heart can produce. The measurement is further refined by using a stethoscope to detect the minimum pressure the heart can produce. The two figures are expressed as a fraction, such as 140/80. Blood pressure is raised by fear and stress. For many people just seeing a doctor is

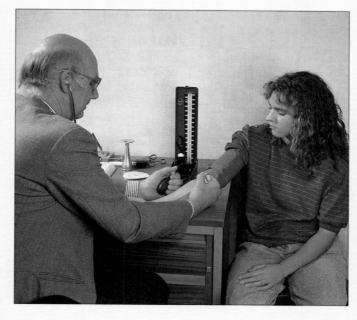

Blood pressure is usually measured with a sphygmomanometer, although electronic gadgets have now been developed.

enough to put their blood pressure up! This so-called 'whitecoat hypertension' can be minimised by repeating the readings several times and taking an average.

What are the effects?

There is little doubt that a high blood pressure (hypertension) puts a strain on the heart and can cause heart attacks and heart failure. It can also cause strokes as the high pressure causes blood vessels inside the brain to leak. Controversy arises over what levels of hypertension are significant.

Most doctors now agree that the higher the blood pressure the higher the chance of disease, yet a blood pressure of below 160/105 should not be treated with drugs. Below this level, the side effects of the tablets usually cause more problems than the hypertension itself.

Who is at risk?

Twenty per cent of the adult population suffer from hypertension and are thus at an increased risk of heart attack and stroke. Men are more often affected than women and old people more often than young. Young people, however, have an increased risk of heart attack and stroke compared to their elderly relatives with the same blood pressure.

Hypertension can only be detected by measuring the blood pressure. There are no symptoms of hypertension. Headaches, nosebleeds and so on are just as likely to occur in the normal population as in the hypertensive.

No cause can be found in 90 per cent of the cases of

hypertension. The other 10 per cent may be due to narrowing of the aorta (the main artery of the body), kidney disease, steroids or rare tumours. Treatment of this 10 per cent is aimed at correcting the underlying cause, treatment of the rest is aimed at simply controlling the blood pressure.

Treatment of hypertension

In some cases drug treatment can be avoided and you should look at your life style before taking drug therapy (see box). There are several groups of drugs for treating hypertension. All work by reducing the demands on the heart. Beta-blockers reduce the strength of the contractions in the heart muscle. They are very effective but can cause tiredness, wheezing and impotence.

Diuretics (water pills) have been used for many years. Losing fluid means that the heart does not need to pump as hard to keep the circulation going. Again they can be very effective but they can have side effects, the most serious being gout and sugar diabetes.

The latest group of drugs to be used in hypertension are the ACE inhibitors. These act on a specific enzyme system in the kidney and actually block the production of the hormone that causes blood pressure to rise. Apart from an irritating cough they seem to have few side effects and are likely to become the standard treatment for hypertension.

HYPERTHERMIA

The medical term for extremely high body temperature. Malignant hyperthermia is an abnormal reaction to a general anaesthetic.

The patient's temperature rises soon after

Self Help For Hypertension

What if your blood pressure is high? If your doctor has ruled out any of the serious causes of hypertension you should first examine your life style. Consider the following points before considering drug therapy.

● Giving up cigarettes will do more good than any amount of drug treatment to cure the problem.
● Losing weight lowers the blood pressure if you are overweight; try to reach your ideal weight and adjust your diet to maintain that weight.
● Exercise more, at least three times a week.
● Salt and alcohol both raise the blood pressure; cut down and if at all possible cut out both.
● The contraceptive Pill can cause hypertension. If another form of contraception is acceptable see what a few months off the Pill will do.

administration of the anaesthetic. At the same time, acidosis occurs as large amounts of lactic acid are released from the muscles into the blood. The muscles then stiffen and the patient turns blue — without emergency treatment the person may have seizures and die.

Treatment is by immediately stopping the anaesthetic and cooling the patient with ice packs. The acidosis is treated with pure oxygen and intravenous injections of sodium bicarbonate.

This condition is very rare — about one in 50,000 cases — and it seems that people who suffer from certain muscle disorders are most at risk.

HYPERVENTILATION

This condition is when the person starts breathing abnormally deeply or rapidly.

It is usually caused by anxiety or stress, but can also be a result of uncontrolled diabetes mellitus, an oxygen deficiency, kidney failure and some lung disorders.

Hyperventilation causes an abnormal loss of carbon dioxide from the blood which can lead to alkalosis (increase in blood alkalinity). It causes carbon dioxide to be lost from the blood, which changes some of the chemicals in the blood. One of these, calcium, controls the transmission of nerve impulses. When the level of calcium changes, a number of unpleasant symptoms can occur, including anxiety, pins and needles, numbness of the extremities, faintness, muscle spasm in the jaw and a sensation of not being able to take a full breath. The effects of alkolosis also increase the feelings of anxiety, possibly leading to 'hyperventilation syndrome' where the sufferer feels impending doom.

Easy solution
If hyperventilation is confirmed the patient is encouraged to carry a paper bag at all times. In the case of an attack, he/she breathes in and out inside the bag, rebreathing their own air. This quickly brings down the acid/alkali balance of the blood and relieves the symptoms.

HYPHAEMA

Hyphaema is blood in the front chamber of the eye, almost always as a result of an injury that ruptures a small blood vessel in the iris or the ciliary body.

In hyphaema, blood is clearly visible in front of the iris in the front chamber of the eye.

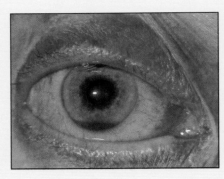

The person's vision is blurred while the blood remains mixed with the aqueous humour, but eventually clears as the red cells sink. In most cases, the blood disappears within a few days and vision is fully restored. Occasionally, there is a risk of delayed bleeding a few days after the injury.

HYPNOSIS

Hypnosis is a state of altered awareness, where the patient goes into a trance and is very open to suggestion.

In hypnotherapy, techniques of hypnosis are used to treat emotional illness and phobias and to 'cure' people of bad habits such as smoking, alcoholism and other drug dependencies. Because the patient becomes very relaxed during the process, it is often used to help relaxation, particularly in patients who suffer from anxiety and panic attacks.

Techniques
In order to undergo hypnosis, a patient must want to be hypnotised, have confidence in the practitioner, and feel very relaxed. The doctor (or psychiatrist) will usually ask the patient to lie on a couch, and repeat relaxing phrases in a soft, low tone, while the patient is looking at a particular object. As the patient becomes more and more relaxed she loses awareness of everything except the psychiatrist's voice. However, this state of total relaxation is not the same as sleep.

In this state, she will act out roles, hold out and describe imaginary objects, and obey certain orders (such as being told to forget everything they have done during the hypnosis). However, patients will not obey orders to do anything that is contrary to their natural inclination.

When they are told to wake up, they snap out of the trance and return to their normal state of awareness.

Autohypnosis
After several therapy sessions, it is possible for patients to learn how to take themselves into a state of hypnosis, which can be particularly useful as an aid to relaxation.

Some people are more receptive to hypnosis than others. Some research seems to indicate that the more imaginative a person is, the more easily hypnotised she is.

Breathing in and out in a paper bag will alleviate hyperventilation by limiting the loss of carbon dioxide

HYPOCALCAEMIA

Hypocalcaemia is the technical term for an abnormally low level of calcium in the blood.

We need calcium for healthy growth and maintenance of bones, nails and muscles. In order to maintain calcium levels, we not only need to eat sufficient calcium-rich foods, we also need enough vitamin D to ensure that the calcium is absorbed into the system.

Hypocalcaemia is usually due to vitamin D deficiency, which may result from a poor diet or a lack of sunshine. It may also be due to chronic kidney failure or hypo-parathyroidism (underactivity of the parathyroid glands).

Symptoms

In adults there are not usually any obvious symptoms; in children, the softening of the bones caused by the deficiency is known as rickets, with characteristic bandy-leggedness, while in old people it is known as osteomalacia, and there is extra risk of bone fractures. Occasionally, sufferers may feel twitches in the muscles of the hands and feet.

Treatment

Rickets cannot be cured, so the problem is one of prevention (and ensuring the condition does not worsen) rather than cure — see box. In other cases, doctors will recommend a calcium- and vitamin D-rich diet, which is an important consideration for all women, particularly towards the menopause.

Evasive Action

In order to avoid hypocalcaemia, you must ensure there is an adequate amount of vitamin D and calcium in your diet.

Vitamin D-rich foods include cod liver oil, herring, mackerel and salmon, egg yolk, liver, fortified milk, butter and cheese.

Calcium-rich foods include cheese, yoghurt, milk, tinned sardines (complete with bones), watercress, yeast, fortified white flour, cabbage, eggs, brown rice and wholemeal flour.

HYPOCHONDRIASIS

Hypochondriasis is a debilitating fear that you are suffering from a serious illness.

People suffering from hypochondriasis (hypochondriacs) will interpret the most trivial symptoms as a sign of a serious disorder (often heart disease, lung disease or cancer). They constantly read medical dictionaries, consult their doctor and demand to be referred to specialists. In some cases, particularly in countries where private medicine is the norm, they may even go so far as to demand exploratory operations.

Treatment

In some cases, the hypochondriasis is a complication of a more serious psychological complaint, such as schizophrenia, depression, dementia or generalised anxiety disorder. In such cases, treatment of the underlying illness should relieve the hypochondriasis.

In other cases, it is not clear what causes the symptoms, although it does seem more prevalent in people who suffered illness, or were exposed to a lot of illness, in their childhood. An understanding doctor and, possibly, a psychotherapist, may help sufferers.

HYPOGLYCAEMIA

Hypoglycaemia is the term for an abnormally low level of sugar (in the form of glucose) in the blood.

The condition is normally due to diabetes mellitus, where the production of insulin in the pancreas is restricted. Insulin is needed to regulate the amount of sugar in the blood, and diabetics usually have too much blood sugar because of the lack of insulin. However, if the sugar-lowering drugs that are prescribed are taken in too large a dose, or if a diabetic does not eat enough carbo-hydrate or takes too much exercise, the blood may become too low in sugar.

Hypoglycaemia may also result from drinking a large amount of sugary alcohol (such as gin and tonic or a sweet liqueur), or it may be due to a tumour in the pancreas causing overpro-duction of insulin.

Symptoms

The main symptoms include sweating, hunger, dizziness and trembling, weakness, headache, palpitations, confusion and double vision. Movements become uncoor-dinated and sometimes aggressive, and if the condition is prolonged and left untreated, the patient may fall into a coma.

Treatment

Hypoglycaemia is a serious condition, which may lead to permanent impairment of the brain. Insulin-dependent diabetics should always carry some sugar with them. A sugar lump or glucose sweet may be all it takes to correct the balance in the short term. If the patient is unconscious, call a doctor who can give a dose of glucose or a hormone (glucagon) by injection.

If you find that you suffer from hypoglycaemia in the early hours of the morning, after a heavy night's drinking, try using low-calorie (sugar-free) mixers with spirits.

HYPOSPADIAS

Hypospadias is a congenital malfor-mation of the penis, where the opening of the urethra is on the shaft or underside of the head of the penis, rather than at the tip of the penis.

In some cases, the shape of the penis may be

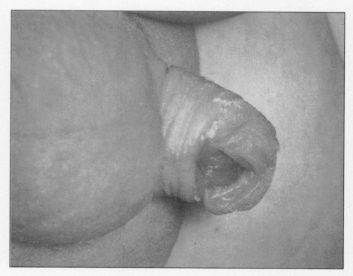

This congenital malformation of the penis (known as hypospadias) can be corrected by surgery.

⏩ SEE ALSO — Thyroid, Diabetes

M E D I C A L   F A C T   F I L E

distorted, and the foreskin may not be complete.

Treatment

The defect is dealt with surgically, within the first couple of years of life. A new opening is formed in the right part of the penis, creating a tube from part of the bladder or the foreskin. In most cases, this enables the child to pass urine normally, and allows satisfactory sexual intercourse in later life.

HYPOTENSION

Hypotension is low blood pressure. It is used to describe a blood pressure that is so low that the person experiences dizziness and fainting because blood flow to the brain is reduced.

The most common type of hypotension is postural hypotension which occurs when people stand or sit up quickly. In normal people, the change of posture is accompanied by an increase in blood pressure but people with postural hypotension don't have this increase.

The condition is sometimes brought on as a side effect of taking antidepressant drugs or antihypertensive drugs. It can also occur in sufferers of diabetes mellitus. Another type of hypotension develops when someone has serious burns or such bad injuries that they go into shock.

Treatment depends on the underlying cause.

HYPOTHERMIA

Hypothermia is defined as a core body temperature of below 35°C (95°F), the normal being 37°C (98.6°F).

Severe hypothermia, which is often fatal, exists if

First Aid for Hypothermia

If a baby's temperature drops, wrap her warmly; hats help prevent further heat loss.

Adults suffering from the first stages of hypothermia should take steps to warm up.

the core temperature drops below 32°C (90°F). There are three main situations in which hypothermia may occur.

In the home

If the home is poorly heated, there is a possibility of hypothermia, particularly if the occupant is badly nourished. Several factors increase the chance of hypothermia. Sleeping tablets, especially barbiturates, and alcohol reduce the amount of heat the body can generate. Any illness may increase the risk, but this is especially true of an underactive thyroid. The elderly are most at risk. Not only are they generally less well off than average, but they have less body fat and tend to feel the cold. If they try to economise on food and heating, the results can be fatal. At the other end of the age range, infants and small children are also at risk. Compared with adults, they have a large surface area of skin relative to their weight, and so they can lose heat very quickly.

Outdoor activities

Those most at risk are climbers, skiers and walkers who venture out ill-equipped against wind and rain. In these circumstances wind chill factor and dampness are as important as actual weather temperature in causing loss of body heat.

Cold water

Immersion in cold water can cause hypothermia. The water will conduct heat away from the body, cooling it down in a way that does not happen to such an extent in cool air. Even in the height of summer, British seas can be lethal if you are in the water for too long.

The stages of hypothermia

At a body temperature of 35 - 32°C, the adult sufferer will complain of intense cold and shiver — this is the body's way of trying to warm itself up. At this stage, the sufferer should be able to take the appropriate action to warm herself up. In the case of babies, they should be kept well wrapped in a warm room if they feel cold.

Below 32°C the sufferer does not feel the cold and

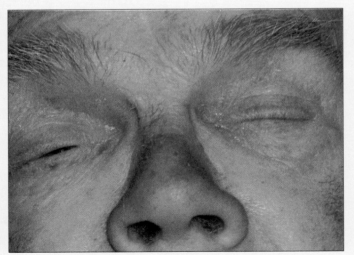

Visual symptoms of hypothermia include pale skin, puffiness about the face and eyes and a withdrawn attitude.

SEE ALSO — Hypertension

Avoiding Hypothermia

If you climb, walk or sail, there are certain precautions that will help you to avoid exposure and hypothermia.

● Never go out alone. If you are injured, it may be hypothermia that kills you rather than your injury, so travel with others who can raise the alarm.

● Survival bags, lined with space blankets are essential lightweight equipment to carry in case you are stranded.

● Wear suitable clothing: complete waterproof overalls are the best in case you get caught in mist or rain. If you don't have waterproof trousers, it is better to wear shorts, so that you can dry your legs when the rain stops. Wet jeans will keep your body temperature down.

● In an emergency, sharing a sleeping bag, so that you can benefit from someone else's body heat, can be a life saver.

often acts irrationally, taking clothes off, for example. At temperatures much below this, coma will set in, followed by death.

Death is due to heart irregularities brought on by a lack of oxygen in the blood.

Diagnosis and treatment

Diagnosis is easy, with a low-temperature thermometer. Rectal temperature is a good guide to the core temperature of the body. Anything under 35°C warrants admission to hospital.

Treatment is aimed at gradual warming. Indoors this can be achieved using blankets and keeping the sufferer in a warm room. In old people, hypothermia is a social disease. It can be avoided if sufficient help is given to old people to enable them to keep at least one room warm.

HYSTERECTOMY

Hysterectomy is the surgical removal of the uterus (womb).

The operation may involve total removal, in which case the cervix is removed, or 'sub-total', when the cervix is left. Because of the possibility of developing cancer in the stump of the cervix, the sub-total hysterectomy has fallen into disfavour. The operation can be performed in one of two ways — either through an abdominal incision, roughly along the bikini line or through the vagina. The 'transvaginal' route is more popular with the patient because it leaves no scar. It is not suitable for everybody, however, as the uterus needs to be fairly small and it needs to be mobile enough to be pulled into the vagina.

As well as the choice between total or sub-total, transvaginal or abdominal, the gynaecologist needs to decide whether to leave the ovaries behind or not. Leaving them behind has the advantage of avoiding an early menopause but if the blood supply to them is damaged by surgery, as it often is, they will fail anyway.

Reasons for hysterectomies

Most gynaecologists now avoid performing hysterectomies in all but the most serious of cases. The commonest reason for performing a hysterectomy is heavy periods, be they caused by hormonal upsets or fibroids. In the case of fibroids the uterus is often so big and distorted that the operation must be done through an abdominal incision. Endometriosis (growth of the lining of the womb in unusual places) in a woman who does not plan to have any more children, can be treated by hysterectomy. In this case the ovaries would be removed to prevent production of ovarian hormones which perpetuate

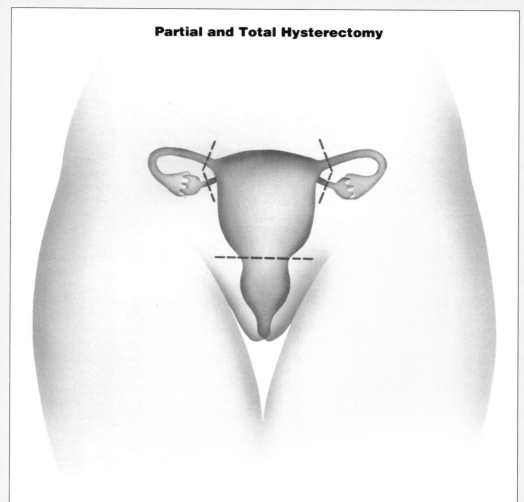

Partial and Total Hysterectomy

In a total hysterectomy, an incision is made in the lower abdomen (red dotted line) so that the uterus, fallopian tubes and ovaries can be removed. In a partial hysterectomy, further cuts are made (blue dotted lines) so the ovaries can be left behind.

▶▶ SEE ALSO — HRT

residual endometriosis elsewhere in the pelvis.

Hysterectomy for cancer is fortunately fairly rare. It is usually performed for cancer of the cervix that has spread up the cervical canal into the womb or for cancer of the womb itself. Cancer of the womb usually starts in the lining, the tissue that in the premenopausal woman is shed monthly. Cancer of the womb may be caused by oestrogen treatment. To avoid this, progestogens are prescribed at the same time — these help to protect the lining of the womb.

After the operation
The average hospital stay after a hysterectomy is about a week but this varies according to the 'pre-op' health of the patient and the policy of the hospital. Most patients wake up with a catheter in the bladder but this is a short term measure and it is usually removed the same day. Most surgeons restrict drinks for the first day after the operation to give the bowel a chance to recover from having been pushed out of the way. With the return of normal bowel sounds the nurses will remove any intravenous drip and give fluids freely. If these are kept down, normal food can be taken. Most patients are up and about the next day and many find their wound suprisingly painless. Nonetheless it may take up to six months before the patient is restored to normal health. Certainly, patients should not lift heavy weights or do any exercise more vigorous than walking for the first month after the operation.

Many women worry about the effects of a hysterectomy on their sex life. They shouldn't. The vagina is left intact and normal sexual relationships can be resumed six weeks after the operation.

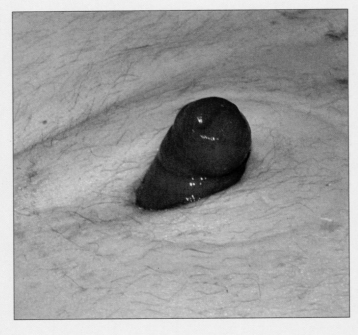

The operation scar and impression of the pad which holds the ileostomy bag in place can be seen around this stoma.

HYSTERIA

Hysteria is a type of neurosis which people under extreme stress can display. The hysteric has apparent physical illness as well as psychological disorders.

Hysterical people tend to be very selfish and are obsessed with attracting attention and admiration from others. Psychiatrists have theorised that a childhood trauma, or insensitive treatment during adolescence may cause the malaise, but this doesn't explain every case.

The hysteria appears in particular circumstances. The person goes blind, deaf or mute, or may suffer from paralysis. They may complain of pain and headaches; backaches and lumps in the throat are common. But once the circumstances which have caused the symptoms go, so do the symptoms.

Treatments include hypnotism or psychotherapy. Tranquilisers only offer temporary relief after a fit.

ILEOSTOMY

An ileostomy is a surgically created opening between the abdominal wall and the ileum, the terminal part of the small bowel.

An ileostomy is only necessary if the entire colon and rectum have to be removed. Unlike a colostomy, a similar opening into the colon, an ileostomy is usually permanent.

Reasons for the operation
The colon and rectum are usually removed as a result of cancer or ulcerative colitis. Ulcerative colitis is an inflammatory condition that tends to affect young adults. The inflammation produces profuse diarrhoea, but this can be treated with steroids and immunosuppressant drugs. Unfortunately, as well as acute complications, such as bleeding or a twisted bowel, sufferers of ulcerative colitis are at a much greater risk of bowel cancer. As this cancer can affect any part of the colon, some surgeons advocate the removal of all of the 'at risk' bowel. To enable the surgeon to plan the best

operation, many hospitals employ a specialist ileostomy nurse. She interviews new patients to find the best position for the ileostomy bag. These nurses are often very much involved in the psychological preparation that surrounds this major operation. It is often a great help if members of the local ileostomy club visit the patient before surgery.

After the operation
The main function of the colon is to remove water from the bowel contents; the main function of the rectum is in the evacuation of waste matter. An ileostomy by-passes both these functions and the patient passes large amounts of semi-liquid faeces into a bag. An ileostomy is permanently open so the bag must be in place 24 hours a day and has to be emptied regularly. Patients soon get used to managing their bag, and the Ileostomy Association can give helpful advice.

Possible problems
The main complication of surgery is infection, but modern techniques and broad spectrum antibiotics have very much reduced the risk. Sexual dysfunction affects about 10 per cent of ileostomy patients. This may be psychological, or due to nerve damage at the time of the operation.

Counselling
Coming to terms with an ileostomy can be a very distressing time for both the patient and his loved ones. However, most people quickly accept their condition and live a perfectly normal life. It is advisable to contact your local ileostomy association before the operation for counselling and advice.

SEE ALSO — Colostomy

THE IMMUNE SYSTEM

The immune system is the body's mechanism for defending itself against foreign material that enters the body.

The immune system provides protection against a wide range of micro-organisms, from viruses, fungi and bacteria to parasites such as those that cause malaria. The first barrier of the body's defences is physical: for example, our bodies are covered with skin, our mouths and eyes are protected by enzymes in the saliva and tears, and our noses have hairs, all of which help to prevent the entry of some microorganisms. Once microorganisms have got through these barriers, our bodies have to learn how to recognise and destroy them.

The science of immunity is based on the fact that immunologists have found that it is rare to suffer a second attack of an infectious disease.

Immunity must be acquired — the body must meet the foreign material once before it can start to destroy it the next time. The level of specific immunity can be raised by repeated exposure. Before this can occur, however, the body must recognise the invading organism as foreign, different from itself. Immunologists call the foreign substance an antigen — something that can trigger an immune response. The body's response is to produce antibodies — proteins that bind to specific antigens and either destroy them or make them more readily attacked by white blood cells.

Each antibody and antigen fit together like a lock and key. An important point about immunity is that any protection is specific. An attack of measles does not protect against a future attack of chicken pox, for example.

Producing antibodies

Antibodies are produced by a type of white blood cell, called a lymphocyte. These lymphocytes are found in the spleen, intestine and blood. There are vast numbers, as many as one billion, in the average adult. When one of these lymphocytes recognises its 'own' antigen, it starts to multiply and to transform itself into a different type of cell — a plasma cell — which produces antibodies.

Disorders of the immune system

Occasionally, the immune system fails to develop properly at birth. The affected baby is healthy for the first few weeks of life, as it still has some of its mother's immunity. After a time, this passive immunity dwindles and the child develops repeated infections. All of these immune deficiencies are serious. Some can be treated with regular injections of antibodies, but others are fatal within two years.

As the name implies, AIDS (Acquired Immune Deficiency Syndrome) is similar to congenital deficiency, but it is acquired or caught. It is due to a specific virus that destroys one type of lymphocyte. Without this lymphocyte the body is unable to mount an immune response and develops repeated

---

How HIV Attacks the Immune System

Normally, when a microorganism (left) invades, the appropriate lymphocytes (green) latch on to the invader, rendering it harmless. Other lymphocytes (blue), help the killer lymphocytes to multiply.

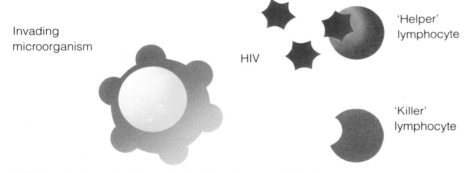

Invading microorganism

HIV

'Helper' lymphocyte

'Killer' lymphocyte

If HIV (purple) invades, it attacks the lymphocytes which help the multiplication process.

Disabled 'helper' lymphocyte

Invading microorganisms are no longer attacked (above) and can proliferate (below).

microorganisms invade

>> SEE ALSO — AIDS, HIV

COLDS AND 'FLU

How is it that we go on catching colds and 'flu year after year?

A single attack from an antigen usually confers life-long protection. Two obvious exceptions are colds and influenza. In the case of colds, there are several hundred viruses that can cause the disease and infection only protects against future attacks of that specific virus. The virus that causes influenza has learned to outwit our immune systems by changing its appearance every few years. This ability to, quite literally, change its coat means that the body's immune system does not recognise it as the same virus that caused an infection last year.

infections. A rare cancer of the immune system, a multiple myeloma, produces a vast excess of one type of plasma cell. These cells produce so much antibody that the blood becomes too thick to circulate properly.

Immunodeficiency disorders may be caused by severe malnutrition, some forms of cancer or may also develop with age.

Antibodies and allergies

Allergies are also related to a disorder of the immune system. Allergy is a common problem, affecting 10 per cent of the population in one form or another. It is due to excessive production of one group of antibodies, the E group. These antibodies occur at the surface of the body — the skin, the lungs and so on. They fight invaders not by destroying them but by causing yet another set of white cells, mast cells, to produce highly toxic chemicals such as histamine. These chemicals poison and destroy the invaders. Allergy sufferers tend to overreact to substances such as pollen, which, whilst they are indeed foreign, are harmless. So much histamine is released that the body feels the effect as irritation and pain — typical hay fever. Treatment of allergy is aimed at avoiding the antigen and blocking the effects of any

excess histamine with antihistamine tablets.

In certain life-threatening hypersensitivities, such as to wasp venom, the patient can be 'desensitised'. This involves regular injections of minute amounts of venom. Over the course of two or three years the body produces other antibodies against the venom and these destroy it before the E group can come into play.

Auto-immune diseases

Almost as common as allergy is the group of disorders known as the auto-immune diseases. Normally, the body is very good at distinguishing between self and non-self. If this ability is lost the body's immune system can be fooled into attacking itself. Antibodies that act against the body itself are known as auto-antibodies. Auto-antibodies cause several common diseases such as sugar diabetes and rheumatoid arthritis. No one knows what triggers these diseases, but some rare conditions, such as rheumatic fever, are well understood. In rheumatic fever, the germ responsible has a coat that closely resembles normal heart muscle. Antibodies produced to fight the germ attack heart tissue as well, weakening it.

IMMUNISATION

This is the process whereby a person is given artificial immunity against a particular virus or bacteria.

Immunisation of babies and children has meant that several infectious diseases have been eradicated or have become very rare — including smallpox, diphtheria, whooping cough and tuberculosis.

How it works

By injecting small quantities of a virus, bacteria or substance closely related to that which causes a particular illness, the body becomes sensitised to that disease. The mechanism that produces antibodies is stimulated so that the body can recognise and fend off the particular micro-organisms if they invade in the future. Immunisation can give life-long protection against many diseases: smallpox, poliomyelitis, measles, mumps and rubella, for example. To immunise against these viral infections, a vaccine is used which contains a similar, but less potent, virus to the one being immunised against. Because this is a live virus, the patient may suffer some of the symptoms of the disease

after immunisation. In other cases, inoculation may have to be repeated from time to time to keep up immunity. The vaccine contains dead viruses or bacteria, and the effect may not be long lasting. Examples include cholera and typhoid, which are often immunised against before foreign travel.

Another type of inoculation contains toxoids — substances similar to the toxins which cause the disease. The immunity is fairly long lasting, but regular boosters may be needed (tetanus is an example of this). Yet another form of immunisation, known as passive immunisation (see overleaf), involves taking plasma from a person who is known to have immunity through having been exposed to a specific disease and injecting it into a person who has been exposed to that disease, but has not yet shown any symptoms. Tetanus-prone wounds are treated in this way, and those going to tropical countries should be immunised against Hepatitis A in this way. Immunity only lasts a few weeks.

When to immunise

Several inoculations are routinely given during the first couple of years of life: your

The Heaf test is used to find out whether a person has an immunity to tuberculosis. A special instrument is used to puncture the skin and carry a little of a highly concentrated solution of tuberculin, from the tuberculosis bacteria, into the body. If the puncture marks swell, the person has immunity.

doctor or heath visitor will recommend when.

● Children should have DPT (diphtheria, pertussis or whooping cough and tetanus) and poliomyelitis immunisation before they are six months.

● MMR (measles, mumps and rubella) is usually given at about 15 months.

● Boosters for poliomyelitis, diphtheria and tetanus are normally given at five years (the pre-school booster).

● If skin tests show it is necessary, tuberculosis inoculation is usually carried out in the early teens. (see opposite)

● Girls who have not previously been inoculated against rubella (and who do not have natural immunity through having contracted the disease) should be inoculated at about 14 years.

● Smallpox vaccinations are no longer necessary, because this disease has been eradicated by a world-wide immunisation programme.

● Tetanus boosters should be given to everyone, with additional boosters at not less than 10-year intervals.

● Influenza vaccinations are available, but only work for known strains of virus.

When not to immunise

Only very few people should not have inoculations, and anyone who thinks they are at risk should discuss this with their doctor. Anyone with an immunodeficiency disorder must not have an inoculation, as the normally harmless antigens in the vaccine may take over. Similarly, anyone with widespread cancer and anyone taking high doses of oral steroid drugs should not be immunised. The whooping cough vaccination is not normally given to any children with a history of fits, or if there is a history of serious reactions in other members of the family. 'Flu and MMR vaccinations should not be given to

---

TERMINOLOGY

Immunisation: the process of giving a person immunity to a disease.

Inoculation: an injection of an antigen which gives immunity.

Vaccination: another term for inoculation, originally used for the smallpox vaccine, which used the cowpox virus (vaccinia is the medical term for cowpox).

Types Of Immunisation

Active Immunisation

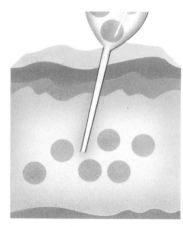

The vaccine contains a dead or modified microorganism.

The immune system creates antibodies to protect the body from the vaccine.

When the harmful microorganism attacks, the antibodies render it harmless.

Passive Immunisation

Blood and plasma, containing antibodies, are taken from an immune person.

The antibodies are injected into the person to be protected.

When the harmful microorganism attacks, the antibodies render it harmless.

MEDICAL FACT FILE

▶▶ SEE ALSO — Diphtheria, DPT, German measles, Measles, MMR, Mumps, Poliomyelitis, Tetanus, Vaccination, Whooping cough

people who are allergic to eggs. Vaccination should be delayed if the person to be vaccinated has a fever. Pregnant women should not have certain inoculations during pregnancy, as they may affect the foetus — discuss this with your doctor.

IMMUNOSTIMULANT DRUGS

Immunostimulant drugs are used to increase the effectiveness of the body's immune system.

Common examples of immunostimulant drugs are those used for vaccination. Another example is interferon — used to treat cancer (particularly leukaemia) and is being used in the treatment of Kaposi's Sarcoma, a skin cancer that is common in AIDS sufferers.

The effect of interferon is currently being tested on viral infections which become life-threatening when they affect people with immuno-deficiency disorders.

IMMUNOSUPPRESSANT DRUGS

These drugs are used to suppress the working of the immune system.

They are used to treat auto-immune disorders, in which the body's immune system turns on itself, and to prevent rejection after transplant surgery.

The disadvantage of using immunosuppressant drugs is that they lay the body open to infection and invasion by relatively harmless microorganisms.

There are other side effects: some are thought to be cancer-causing, and one group — the steroid drugs — causes fatty deposits around the face, neck and trunk.

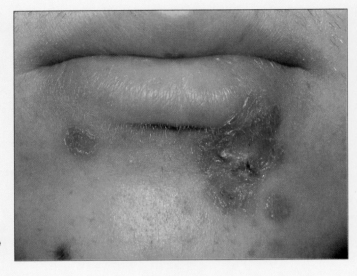

An impetigo sufferer with the characteristic crusty blisters.

IMPETIGO

Impetigo is a highly contagious skin condition, in which inflamed patches and fluid-filled blisters develop.

The infection begins when staphylococcal bacteria invade a cut, cold sore, patch of eczema or other broken skin. Impetigo used to be extremely common, but now there are only occasional outbreaks — usually among children.

Symptoms

The infection starts as puffy, inflamed patches, and then fluid-filled blisters develop. As the blisters burst, the fluid dries and may form a brown crust. The patches may grow around the edges, or spread as the sufferer scratches the blisters, making them burst, and then touches another part of the body.

Treatment

The condition responds well to antibiotics, particularly in cream form. Children should be kept away from school until the inflammation has subsided. Sheets and towels should all be boiled to prevent transmission through the family.

IMPOTENCE

Impotence in men is the inability to achieve or maintain an erection.

Impotence may have psychological or physical causes, and may be a short-lived problem, or a long-term or permanent one.

In the short term

Impotence is often only temporary, caused by anxiety, stress or fatigue. It may affect adolescent boys at their first sexual encounter, and is common in middle-aged men who are suffering stress and fatigue due to emotional or other forms of crisis. In older men, falling testosterone levels may also contribute to impotence.

Physical causes include a lack of sexual drive due to a general illness (such as 'flu or a more serious illness), and certain drugs may cause impotence. Indeed, the most common physical cause is overindulgence in alcohol. Other drugs which may cause temporary impotence are barbiturates, diuretics and other drugs that are used to treat hypertension. Potency returns after the course of drugs is ended.

Removal of the prostate gland may also cause temporary impotence for some weeks after the

operation, although in some cases the problem may be permanent.

Impotence in the long term

Long-term or permanent impotence may have a number of causes. Impotence may be due to psychological disturbance, with long-term depression, or feelings of guilt and anxiety that stem from childhood.

Damage to the lower spine will interrupt the transmission of messages from the brain to the sexual organs. Certain types of tumour and diseases of the spinal cord and nerves will cause impotence in the same way. And removal of the testes is also a cause of impotence.

An imbalance in the endocrine system is another cause, although treatment of the underlying imbalance will restore the libido. Diabetes mellitus is also a common cause of impotence.

Treatment

Sexual psychotherapy may be recommended for those who have deep-seated worries about sexual intercourse. If the problem is physical, and cannot be sorted out by treating the underlying cause, there are certain drugs which can be helpful if there are physical problems, and penile implants may be a solution.

Doctors may also recommend injections into the base of the penis, to cause a spasm which allows blood to flow into the penis but not out again. The solution only works for an hour or two, so patients have to be taught how to inject themselves.

A good self-help treatment for psychological impotence is to ask the partner to press on the perineum (the skin between the testicles and the anus) during sexual intercourse.

INCONTINENCE

Incontinence is the inability to control the passing of urine or faeces.

Urinary incontinence is more common that faecal incontinence, and takes several forms.

Types of incontinence

A complete inability to control the bladder is normal during the first couple of years of life, and may continue at night for some years to come.

In later years, incontinence may return in various forms and for several different reasons. It may be total incontinence, where there is no control at all; urge incontinence, where a strong desire to urinate is coupled with a lack of control of the bladder, so there is an involuntary contraction of the bladder and once urination starts it continues until the bladder is empty; stress incontinence, a female problem, results in an involuntary escape of a small amount of urine, which may happen when a person coughs or laughs, or during strenuous activity; or overflow incontinence, which occurs when the sufferer is unable to empty the bladder normally, so that it is always full, and there is a constant dribble of urine.

Causes of incontinence

Total incontinence, in the young, mentally disabled and elderly, is usually caused by a lack of control by the brain. Similarly, damage to the brain or spinal cord by injury may cause incontinence. Total incontinence may also be due to a malformation of the urinary tract, where the ureter bypasses the bladder, or there is a hole between the bladder and the vagina. Prolapse of the uterus and prostate·disorders can also cause incontinence.

A degree of incontinence is common during pregnancy and/or after giving birth, due to the pressure on the bladder and weakening of the pelvic muscles which control urination.

Incontinence may also be caused by disorders such as bladder stones, urinary tract infections, cancer and irritable bladder.

Sudden shock and anxiety can also cause involuntary emptying of the bladder (in a car accident, for example).

Treatment

Malformation of the urinary tract can be treated surgically. Incontinence caused by lack of brain control (in the mentally handicapped or paraplegics, for example) is difficult to treat. Catheterisation (inserting a tube to empty the bladder) is possible in some cases. Otherwise it is a question of alleviating the problem with adequate social support for the carers.

In other cases (infections, prostate problems or prolapsed uterus, for example) it is the underlying cause of the incontinence which must be tackled. Surgery may be necessary. In some cases after childbirth, surgery is used to repair any damaged pelvic floor muscles.

Faecal Incontinence

Faecal incontinence is the inability to control defaecation.

We normally associate this condition with the elderly, suffering from dementia, or with mentally handicapped people, who have never learned to control their anal sphincter. However, there are some other causes of faecal incontinence.

A common cause, which is more prevalent among the elderly, is faecal impaction, which is usually caused by long-term constipation. Faeces collect in the rectum and irritate the lining, so that small pieces of faeces are passed involuntarily. Severe diarrhoea may also cause incontinence of this type.

Injury to the anal muscles and paralysis of the lower limbs are also causes of incontinence.

Faecal incontinence due to impaction can be avoided with a high-fibre diet, and suppositories or laxatives may be recommended. If the incontinence cannot be treated, the condition can be eased by using enemas or suppositories to empty the rectum regularly.

Pelvic Floor Exercises

This type of exercise is included in ante- and post-natal classes, and is a useful exercise for any woman, to strengthen the pelvic muscles.

The exercise can be done at any time – while you are washing up or standing in a bus queue, for example, or during an exercise session.
1 Clench together all the muscles around your vagina and urethra (as though you were trying to stop yourself going to the toilet).
2 Imagine these clenched muscles are a lift, going up in a department store. Clench them tighter, to take you up to the next floor!
3 Repeat step two, tightening your muscles even further.
4 Relax your pelvic floor muscles slowly.
Another helpful exercise to improve muscle control is to try to stop the flow half way through urination.

INDIGESTION

Indigestion, or dyspepsia, to give it its medical term, is a group of symptoms, usually brought on by overindulgence in food and alcohol.

Symptoms of indigestion include pain or discomfort in the abdomen, wind, nausea and acid reflux (a slight regurgitation of acids from the stomach up the foodpipe) and heartburn (a burning pain in the centre of the chest).

Causes

These symptoms may be caused by gastritis (inflammation of the stomach lining), which is caused by eating and/or drinking too much, and is made worse by smoking. If an unsuitable diet continues, ulcers may develop, causing a long-term problem. Indigestion may also be caused by a hiatus hernia and gallstones.

Relieving the symptoms

Antacids (tablets or liquids, such as Milk of Magnesia) or even a glass of milk may relieve the symptoms. However, if indigestion is recurrent, doctors will

▶▶ SEE ALSO — Enuresis, Gall bladder, Gastritis, Hiatus hernia

recommend their patients to look carefully at their diet.

Chronic dyspepsia

If indigestion is caused by certain conditions, including ulcers, gallstones or a hiatus hernia, drug treatment or surgery may be necessary.

INFECTIOUS DISEASES

An infectious disease is one that is caused by microorganisms such as viruses, bacteria and fungi.

Plague and pestilence have been part of life since earliest times. Such calamities were originally held to be caused by the wrath of God, but people soon realised that one sick person could infect a whole community. Lepers were shunned in Biblical times — and are still isolated in many communities. This treatment may seem sensible, although advances in medical science have shown that the disease is less easily contracted than was originally thought.

Historical background

In the 16th century, the physician Frascatorius realised that not only could some diseases be spread by personal contact, but also through the air and via personal possessions. Because the infectious agent could not be seen, his ideas were largely forgotten, at the cost of much human misery.

Two centuries later the rod-like bacteria that cause anthrax were detected in the blood of a diseased cow. In a famous experiment, blood from a diseased animal was shown to cause the same illness if injected into a healthy beast. Blood that did not contain the bacteria could be injected freely without causing disease.

A century later, an English GP, Edward Jenner,

laid the foundations of vaccination with his discovery that an inoculation of cowpox virus protected against the deadly smallpox. As a result of his work, smallpox has been almost universally eradicated.

Louis Pasteur, a French chemist, is recognised as the father of modern medical microbiology, the study of disease-causing germs. His original work was on the yeasts that cause wines to ferment, but he carried his knowledge and techniques to the study of human and animal diseases. He saved the silk industry from ruin when he discovered the cause of a disease that was decimating stocks. He developed a vaccine against anthrax and on the human side discovered the cause and treatment of rabies. His studies firmly established the relationship between bacteria and disease.

A new cleanliness

A few years later, a Scottish surgeon, Robert Lister, revolutionised surgery by recognising the link between wound infection and poor hygiene. Up until that time, most doctors would operate in clothes caked in blood and pus from previous patients. Small wonder that many of those who survived the operation died later of wound infections. Lister's technique of misting the air with carbolic acid spray was effective — but very uncomfortable for the surgeon. Modern surgeons, using sterile theatres, gloves and masks, try to banish bacteria altogether.

Naturally occurring chemicals that kill germs have been around for centuries. Quinine, extracted from the bark of the cinchona tree, has been used against malaria since at least the early 1600s. Apart from a few, highly toxic drugs based on arsenic, the first really effective antimicrobial drugs

were the sulphonamides developed in the 1930s. Now just about all bacterial and fungal infections can be treated effectively and an ever-increasing range of anti-viral agents is available.

The microorganisms that cause diseases can be divided into five groups — the bacteria, the viruses, the fungi, the protozoa and the chlamydia.

Bacteria

Bacteria are single-celled organisms that reproduce by splitting into two. There are many thousands of different types of bacteria and medical microbiologists divide them according to their shape, size, whether or not they need oxygen and what colour they are stained by certain chemicals.

Most bacteria are harmless or positively helpful. Those that cause disease do so by deliberate intent or accident. Gonorrhoea, for

Infectious or Contagious?

Strictly speaking, infectious diseases are those diseases that can be carried in water or air, whereas contagious diseases can only be spread by direct contact. In both cases, microorganisms are responsible for causing the disease, and 'infectious' is often used as a blanket term to cover both infectious and contagious diseases.

example, is caused by a bacteria that will only infect humans and will die almost at once outside the body. Other bacteria, such as pseudomonas, will only cause disease if its host is weakened in some way — resulting in a chronic leg ulcer, for instance.

Bacterial infections can be spread in many ways. The staphylococci, which cause boils and other skin infections, can be spread by contact with an infected person or by droplets from the nose and throat. Some bacteria, such as the gonococcal bacteria, can only be spread through sexual contact. Still others can only be spread through water contaminated by faeces. In the case of cholera the organism is often concentrated in the bodies of shellfish and causes disease when they are eaten raw. The bacteria that causes plague is spread from person to

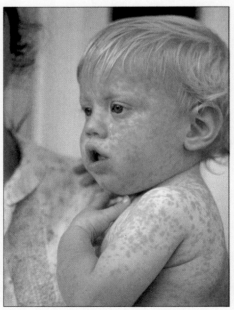

The rash of measles is a symptom of a viral infection, rubeola. Because it is a virus, the body will become immune to the virus after contracting the illness. Inoculation is recommended at 15 months. The blotchy rash starts behind the ears, spreading to the face and the rest of the body. It is infectious from three days before the rash appears, until it subsides.

➤➤ SEE ALSO — Gonorrhoea, Leprosy, Measles

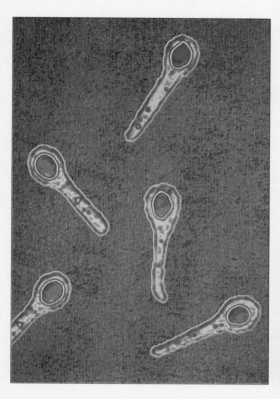

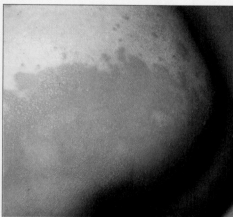

Left: The bacteria which cause tetanus, clostridium tetani, are found in the soil. They enter through wounds and produce a toxin which acts on the nerves that control the muscles. Booster vaccinations against tetanus are recommended every 10 years. Below: Thrush (candida albicans) is a yeast-like fungus which can cause infection in many parts of the body (here the rash is covering a baby's nappy area).

person by the bite of fleas which live on the ears of rats!

The wonder is that anyone survives a day, but as the bacteria have developed so have our protections against them, and the body fights countless bacteria every day without our even knowing.

Viruses

Just as bacteria are too small to be seen with the naked eye so viruses are too small to be seen with an ordinary light microscope. Viruses do not reproduce by splitting but by 'replication' — the virus takes over a cell and uses it to produce millions more viruses. Most of the ones that affect man will only live in humans, although some can infect other animals. Spread is usually through droplets and most infections therefore affect the nose and throat — the common cold, for example. Other infections, such as measles, start off in the nose and throat and then spread through the body. Some infections, such as polio, colonise the gut, and may occur after swallowing water

which has been contaminated by the virus. A few viruses need to pass through the skin to cause an infection. If they were swallowed, they would be destroyed by acid in the stomach. HIV and hepatitis B are the modern examples of this type of virus, but in the past, bites from animals (rabies) and insects (yellow fever) were more common examples.

Viruses, because they live inside host cells and use the cell to their own ends, are very difficult to destroy. Antiviral agents are often so toxic that they cannot be used outside the laboratory. Several 'flu virus vaccines are in use. Progress is being made, and a treatment for infections such as colds is only a matter of time.

Fungi

Fungi are generally larger than bacteria and are usually made up of many cells. Fungi often live in harmony with us, but occasionally they can cause disease. The organism that causes thrush, for example, is present in most women's vaginas. It

only causes the well-known symptoms of intense itching and discharge if something disturbs the vagina's natural defences.

Most fungal infections are spread by contact but some can be transmitted as spores (like seeds), which have the ability to survive outside the body.

Chlamydia

Chlamydial organisms are midway between bacteria and viruses. Like the bacteria, they reproduce by splitting, but, like the viruses, they cannot reproduce without the aid of a host cell. Some forms of chlamydia will only live in man, while others normally affect animals but can also infect people — psittacosis, for example, normally affects birds. The tetracycline group of antibiotics is effective against chlamydial infections.

Protozoa

Protozoa are complex creatures made up of only one cell and, while they are much bigger than bacteria, they are still invisible to the naked eye. Not many

protozoa attack humans, but those that do cause some serious diseases including malaria, dysentery and certain sexually transmitted diseases.

The life cycles of the protozoa are usually complicated. Malaria is transmitted by the bite of a specific mosquito, but only after a specific protozoan has bred in the mosquito's stomach.

Spread of infection

'Coughs and sneezes spread diseases' — but even talking and breathing cause a constant mist of saliva laden with bacteria and viruses. Large droplets fall to the ground and their bacterial content joins the general dust. Small droplets evaporate before they hit the ground and their viral load can stay airborne for many hours. Meningitis, colds, 'flu and pneumonia all spread in this fashion.

Some microorganisms, those that cause the venereal diseases, for example, are spread by direct contact.

Some bacteria live in the soil and can cause serious disease if wounds are contaminated. Tetanus is present almost everywhere and it is only our vaccination policy that stops it becoming a scourge.

INFERTILITY

The inability to have children is very common, affecting 10 per cent of British couples.

Some couples manage to adapt to their childless state, but many visit their doctor looking for help.

The average woman takes six monthly cycles to become pregnant, but 10 per cent of women take more than a year to conceive successfully. This used to mean that doctors were unwilling to investigate couples who had been trying for less than a year, but this has changed with the realisation that the reassurance of seeing a gynaecologist often results in a pregnancy with no treatment at all.

Causes and treatment

In some cases there is no single, readily identifiable cause, but a number of factors work together to prevent fertilisation.

Twenty-five per cent of cases are due to non-ovulation: the woman fails to produce an egg. Treatment usually involves the use of a drug called clomiphene. Most women who are having periods can be induced to ovulate in this way. If this drug fails, others can be used, but they carry the risk of multiple pregnancies.

Defective semen accounts for another 25 per cent of infertility cases. Semen can be defective in one of three ways: the sperm may be abnormal, so that they do not function properly; they may be absent altogether; or they may only be present in small numbers. Little can be done to improve the quality/quantity of abnormal or absent sperm, but drug treatment is available to increase the sperm count. However, wearing looser underpants, taking regular cool baths and drinking less alcohol also help equally well.

Blocked fallopian tubes cause 15 per cent of cases. This is usually as a result of previous infections, but may occur for no apparent reason. If a gynaecologist suspects this as the cause of infertility, she may order an x-ray investigation called a hysterosalpingogram. Dye is squirted through the cervix and its progress up the uterus and along the tubes is followed on a TV screen.

If the tubes are blocked, then surgery is an option.

In Vitro Fertilisation

What is involved in the process of artificial insemination?

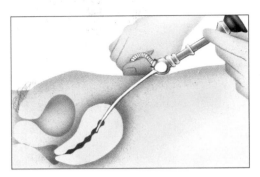

1 The mother-to-be is given drugs to stimulate her ovaries. Ripe eggs are removed, using a laparoscope which is inserted through the wall of the abdomen. Usually more than one egg is taken and fertilised, to save repeating the whole operation.

2 The eggs are placed in a flat dish (not, in fact, a test tube) and sperm from the 'father' are introduced. If conditions are right, fertilisation will take place. Cells from the fertilised egg may be taken and analysed at this stage if there is a chance of genetic disorders.

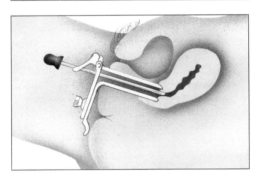

3 Once the egg has started dividing, it can be injected back into the womb. After this, the mother has regular injections of progesterone to combat miscarriage. Often, more than one egg is replaced in the womb, to offset the possibility of rejection.

Unfortunately, tubal surgery has a poor success rate, and it may be simpler to bypass the blockage altogether by injecting sperm and egg directly into the womb end of the tube.

Other gynaecological abnormalities, such as fibroids, cause about 10 per cent of cases. Two or three per cent are due to medical conditions such as an underactive thyroid. This leaves about 20 per cent of infertile couples with no clear cut cause for their problem. In some of these cases, the cervical secretions of the woman create an environment which is hostile to her partner's sperm.

General advice such as achieving an ideal weight, cutting out alcohol and so on is often helpful.

Solutions

Test-tube or in vitro fertilisation occurs outside the body, as opposed to in vivo fertilisation which occurs inside the body (see above). It is used as a treatment for women who have problems with their fallopian tubes.

In vitro fertilisation has some spectacular successes, but it is not a cure-all for infertility. Its 'take home baby rate' is rarely more than 15 per cent. Other forms of treatment should be tried first. Although still at the experimental phase, progress in in vitro analysis raises the hope that carriers of genetic disorders, such as cystic fibrosis, could undergo in vitro fertilisation and only the healthy embryos would be implanted.

Artificial insemination (by husband) is used in some cases where the sperm count is low, where the cervical mucus is hostile, and also where penetration is impossible (in paraplegics, for example).

Artificial insemination by donor may be used if the sperm count is non-existent or the sperm is abnormal.

►► SEE ALSO — Artificial insemination, Fertility, Polycystic ovary

INFLAMMATION

Inflammation describes redness, swelling, heat and pain in a tissue which is caused by injury or infection.

When tissue is damaged, special cells known as mast cells release a chemical called histamine which increases blood supply to the injured area, thus resulting in the redness and heat. Histamine also makes the blood capillaries more leaky, and the leaking fluid causes swelling at the site of injury.

Inflammatory chemicals stimulate nerve endings, creating the sensation of pain. White blood cells gather at the site of infection, to fight off microbes and bacteria, and what is known as pus accumulates — a combination of dead white blood cells, dead tissue cells and dead bacteria

Treatment
Ice packs, applied to the inflammation may help to soothe and reduce swelling. Inflammation may have other causes besides injury or infection — for example rheumatoid arthritis or auto-immune disorders. Treatment is by administering corticosteroid or nonsteroidal anti-inflammatory drugs.

INFLUENZA

Influenza is not simply a bad cold. It is a potentially serious, often debilitating disease which can be fatal to the old and infirm.

Influenza exists throughout the world and may occur as single cases, epidemics or worldwide pandemics. Except during an epidemic, it is difficult to make a diagnosis of influenza and many diseases labelled as 'flu are in fact other respiratory infections.

Types of virus
To the scientist the 'flu virus is fascinating. It can be found in many species of birds and animals as well as man. There are three types of virus, A, B, and C. Type A is responsible for the majority of epidemics and type C for individual episodes. Type A viruses have the unique ability to change their appearance so that the body's immune system fails to recognize and destroy them. This can occur slowly or suddenly. A sudden change, where no one in the world is immune, is often a sign of an impending pandemic. Virologists — doctors and scientists who study viruses — are continually searching for new types of 'flu viruses. When they are discovered they are usually named after the area where they were first found — Hong Kong, for example.

After the discovery of a new strain comes a race against time. The aim is to produce a vaccine before the virus can spread. Every advance in vaccine technology is confounded by the increasing ease of world travel; a business man can pick up the virus in Australia and be spreading it around his local pub 24 hours later.

How is it spread?
Influenza is spread through contact with another person's saliva, mucus or tears, either through coughs and sneezes or by hands contaminated with saliva or phlegm. The incubation period is short, only a day or two, as unlike many diseases the site of infection and the site of entry of the virus are the same. The virus that causes influenza is very hardy and can survive for several weeks in household dust.

The illness is usually shortlived, lasting only two or three days. Symptoms include a high fever, shivering, aches and pains, particularly in the muscles

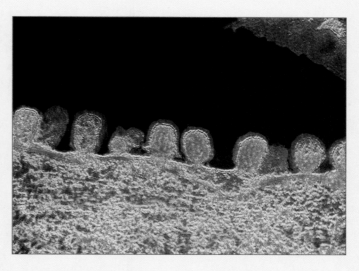

Influenza virus cells growing from an infected cell: the virus cells have a particular affinity for mucus.

and joints, sore throat, headache and a runny nose.

Colds and 'flu
There is often much confusion between colds and 'flu. As a rule, anyone fit enough to go to work is not suffering from influenza. Although recovery from the physical illness is relatively rapid, a feeling of debility and depression can last for many months.

The most serious effects of 'flu are on the chest, especially in people with weak chests such as asthmatics and smokers. The 'flu virus itself can cause a form of pneumonia or it can lower the body's resistance to other germs so that a bacterial infection may ensue. The bacteria that causes the most damage is staphylococcus. This germ is found on most people's skin and sometimes causes boils. In the chest of a 'flu sufferer, it can cause rapid abscess formation and may even lead to death unless antibiotic treatment is given.

Treatment
There is no specific therapy as the cause is a virus. Treatment is aimed at supporting the patient through illness and treating any complications. Rest, aspirin or paracetamol and extra fluids are essential. Hot honey and lemon drinks seem to help but, unfortunately, the old wives' remedy of a bottle of whisky will only make things worse!

Except in the case of the very old or the very young there is no need to consult a doctor unless there are complications. If the patient becomes short of breath, coughs up a lot of green or yellow phlegm or suddenly gets worse, medical advice should be sought.

Immunisation
Immunisation against 'flu is effective so long as the type of 'flu in the environment is the same as the type of 'flu in the vaccine. To ensure that this is the case, the make-up of 'flu vaccine is reviewed annually. If there are any new vaccines they can be included in that year's batch.

Vaccination gives about 70 per cent protection and lasts for a year or so. To derive maximum benefit immunisation should occur every autumn against the strains expected that year. Because of the expense and possible side effects, vaccination is usually reserved for the elderly. Those at special risk from lung, heart or kidney disease, people with diabetes or patients on

SEE ALSO — Immunisation, Infectious diseases

immunosuppressive drugs should also have the injection.

Minor side effects such as swelling, redness and pain at the site of the injection are common. Occasionally a mild 'flu-like illness may occur but this settles rapidly.

Influenza and pregnancy

Some studies have shown an increase in deaths amongst mothers and malformation and leukaemia in new-born children during 'flu epidemics. An equal number of studies have failed to show any tie-up. The position at the moment, therefore, is unclear but it would be wise to try to avoid 'flu in the early stages of pregnancy.

INSECTS

Of the million or so species of insects only a few affect mankind — but they still cause more disease and death than all the lions, tigers, snakes and sharks put together.

Insects cause problems by stinging, biting, or spreading disease — sometimes all three! Insects that bite do so to obtain food (blood). Those that sting do so in self-defence.

Wasps, bees and hornets are the usual culprits as far as stings are concerned. Of these, hornets are rare in the UK, and bees rarely sting except in the immediate vicinity of their hives.

Insect bites cause most deaths by spreading disease. Occasionally the bite itself is painful, though the worst biters of all are not insects proper, but tropical or Australian spiders. Mosquito bites are very common in the summer, but their effect varies from individual to individual. Some people seem to get

Insects In The Tropics

Fortunately, in the UK we are spared the tropical diseases malaria and yellow fever, which are spread by the bites of certain mosquitoes.

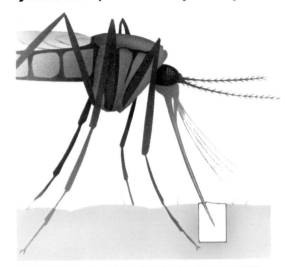

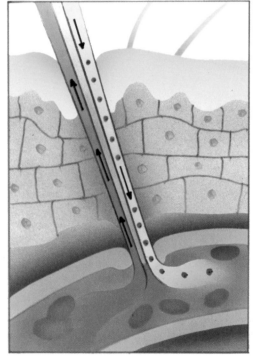

In Roman times malaria was common in England, but these days it's restricted to tropical and sub-tropical areas. Man becomes infected by being bitten by the female Anopheles mosquito. As she bites (top left), sucking blood through the proboscis, she injects a minute amount of gastric juice and with it the microorganism that causes malaria (see detail, below left). The parasite enters the liver and reproduces. After a few days it leaves the liver to enter the red blood cells, where a similar cycle occurs. Some of the parasites in the red blood cells are eaten by the mosquito and they set up home in its stomach, to be injected into a fresh victim the next time the insect feeds.

Travellers to malaria-infested areas should consult their doctor for the latest advice on what antimalarials to take. Treatment is not 100 per cent effective, and it is advisable to use insect repellants, nets at night, and cover up from top to toe, especially in the evening.

Yellow fever is spread in much the same way, causing jaundice in severe cases. In the tropics there are flies who lay their eggs in open sores so that their young will have a plentiful supply of food. In this country, maggots – the larvae of flies – live on dead flesh. It has even been suggested that they be used to clean dead flesh away from wounds!

bitten much more than others, but no one knows why. The reaction is due to a local allergic response; the more you're bitten, the worse the reaction is.

Treatment for bites

A bee sting is usually left behind in the victim's skin. They are easily removed by scraping with a fingernail or handkerchief. A wasp's sting

is not such a problem and little can be done other than to put something soothing on it. The best first aid is ice, or frozen food, but this is rarely available on a picnic! A useful alternative is Wasp-eze, a pocket-sized cold spray with a built-in local anaesthetic. Bee and wasp stings contain about a dozen different chemicals — so forget all those old wives'

tales about dabbing them with bicarbonate of soda or vinegar.

Insect stings are certainly painful, and now and again they may even be fatal. In the UK, an average of four people a year die because of an allergic reaction to wasp or bee stings. If you are stung and your face and tongue swell or if you have difficulty

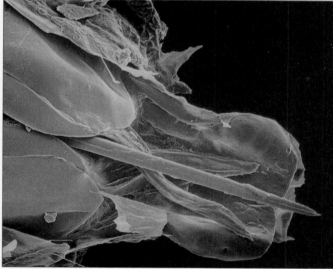

The sting's in the tail: a wasp stinging someone on the arm (top) and a detail of a bee's tail, showing its needle-like sting which paralyses its victim by injection (above).

breathing, you must consult a doctor at once.

Spread

Flies and bluebottles spread disease by their feeding habits. They think nothing of starting a meal on dog's faeces and continuing it with your steak. A fly is unable to swallow solid food and must digest it first. It does this by regurgitating its stomach contents and then trampling it with its six feet. When it's nice and soft, it sucks it up — no wonder they spread disease so efficiently!

INSOMNIA

Insomnia is the inability to sleep as expected. Most adults suffer from this condition at some time in their lives.

It is usually associated with anxiety but can be caused by physical disorders such as sleep apnoea (when breathing is interrupted), restless legs, misuse of sleeping drugs, or life style factors such as excessive coffee consumption.

Our sleep requirements change throughout our lives. Pregnant women need more sleep, as do younger people and the sick. As we age, we need less and less sleep — often the elderly imagine that they suffer from insomnia when in reality they need very little sleep.

Insomnia can also be a symptom of a psychiatric illness. People with mania tend not to sleep very much; schizophrenics often pace around at night; and people suffering dementia may be afraid of the dark and become restless and noisy. Insomnia may also be a symptom of depression.

Treatment

Often the best advice to an insomniac is to stop worrying about the condition, and to reassure them that sleep will come when the body needs it. In order to promote 'sleep hygiene', sufferers should make sure they have a comfortable bed and pillow, with adequate blankets, and curtains that cut out the light. A little exercise before bed (some simple stretching exercises) and a warm, milky drink are also helpful. Sufferers should avoid alcohol and late-night meals.

Relaxation, meditation and psychotherapy are ways of tackling the problem if it persists. Antidepressants might be prescribed if the patient is also a depressive. Only as a last resort will sleeping tablets be prescribed.

INSULIN

Insulin is a hormone that is produced in the pancreas, a sausage-shaped organ in the upper abdomen. Insulin has an effect on the way the body deals with carbohydrates, fats and proteins.

Insulin is said to be 'anabolic' — that is, it increases the storage of these foods. Its main effect is on the metabolism of glucose. The higher the level of insulin in the blood, the lower the blood glucose level and vice versa. The actual secretion of insulin into the bloodstream is triggered by an increased level of glucose — after a meal, for example.

In health, the amount of food we eat and the levels of insulin work together to keep the level of glucose in our blood stable. An excess of insulin will make the blood glucose level drop dangerously, while a deficiency of insulin leads to very high levels of glucose and diabetes mellitus.

Insulin therapy

In some forms of diabetes, insulin treatment is a life-saver, but it must be given by injection, until an implantable artificial pancreas is developed. In the normal individual, insulin is released in a constant trickle which can be instantly increased if and when food is taken. Doctors can try to mimic this in two ways: first, through the use of a pump, worn like a personal stereo, with a needle under the skin. The pump delivers a constant supply of insulin which can be increased at the touch of a button. Secondly, insulin can be modified by binding it to certain chemicals. They can slow the breakdown of insulin so that a single injection in the morning is still effective in the evening. This method of taking insulin can be improved if there is a low background level of a long-acting type of insulin booster, plus fast-acting insulin given with meals.

Until recently insulin was taken from the pancreases of dead pigs and cows. Although very similar to human insulin, it sometimes caused problems with adverse reactions, usually at the site of the injection. This has largely been overcome by the use of genetically engineered 'human' insulin. A small number of diabetics have found this purer form more difficult to manage, and prefer the animal insulin.

The main problem with insulin therapy is accidental overdosage which leads to hypoglycaemia.

INTELLIGENCE

Intelligence is taken to encompass the ability to learn from experience, form judgments and handle abstract concepts.

Intelligence is not fixed for ever — it can be influenced by experience, such as education and upbringing. The extent to which an individual uses her intelligence depends on factors such as motivation and maturity.

There is no doubt that intelligence runs in families, but it's due to more than just heredity. Intelligent parents tend to have intelligent children — but it's not a hard and fast rule. It is more probable that only the basic building blocks of intelligence are inherited, and it can be nurtured or neglected depending upon the atmosphere in which the child is brought up.

Identical twins, separated at birth, would be expected to show the same level of intelligence — but in practice, differences have been observed which seem to be due to their different upbringings. A child raised in an atmosphere of deprivation or abuse will almost always score lower in an IQ test than children from happier homes.

Controversial tests

Measuring intelligence is difficult, for unlike height, it can vary from day to day or even from hour to hour, depending on a range of factors, which include the child's mood. The usual method of assessing intelligence is by means of

The Brain

Left-hand side — Reason, mathematics, logic; Language skills; Analysis

Right-hand side — Recognition of faces, patterns etc; Visual coordination; Processing and synthesis

Intelligence does not lie in one particular area of the brain, but rather in the ability to coordinate the different messages that the brain receives. It has been noticed in children that girls tend to develop better linguistic skills at an early age, while boys develop better spatial awareness and coordination. Indeed, men have faster reaction times from mid-childhood on, whereas women tend to be more sensitive, and more interested in people.

the IQ (Intelligence quotient) test, which consists of a large number of questions, usually written, that test the ability to solve problems and interpret new material. They have been heavily criticised because they do not take cultural and educational backgrounds into account. Completing them successfully may also be seen as something of a knack, and not a true test of inherent intelligence, but nevertheless they are now taken as the accepted way of measuring intelligence.

The average score is 100; scores above this show

above average intelligence and those below it a lower level. The 'normal' range is accepted as being between 70 to 130. It is estimated that 95 per cent of the population score between these figures. Severe handicap is diagnosed if the IQ is less than 50. Children with IQs below this score are unlikely ever to be able to go out to work except in very sheltered environments. The recognition of intelligence levels significantly above or below average is important if people are going to be helped to attain their potential.

Some people with low IQs are simply at the bottom of the scale in the same way that some people are at the bottom of the scale for height. That's just the way they are. But just as some people never grow to their full height because of a deficiency of the growth hormone, perhaps due to physical damage, some people may never achieve their intelligence potential because of various factors — brain damage, or chromosome disorders such as Down's syndrome.

SEE ALSO — Diabetes, Brain

INTERCOURSE, PAINFUL

Painful intercourse (dyspareunia) is a condition that affects both men and women and can have mental and physical causes.

Primary dyspareunia is when the sufferer has always found intercourse painful. Vaginismus is one cause of this, which can only occur in women. An unusually thick hymen, or remnant, can also be a reason for painful intercourse; a simple operation will break it.

Secondary dyspareunia is used to describe painful intercourse which develops after some years. In women, likely physical causes are inflammation of the vulva, vagina or bladder. These inflammations can be due to various infections, including chlamydia, trichomonas vaginalis, or other sexually transmitted diseases. Treatment is by antibiotics or fungicides.

In older women the skin lining of the vagina may shrink, a condition called senile vaginitis. A simple lubricant or, failing that, a hormone cream will help.

Alternatively, the cause of deep pain during intercourse may be pelvic disorders (fibroids, ectopic pregnancy, inflammatory disease); ovarian cysts; or endometriosis. Indeed, in some cases, painful intercourse may be the first symptom of such disorders. Successful treatment of the underlying cause should remove the dyspareunia.

Dyspareunia in men

Physical causes of painful intercourse in men could be due to inflammation of the penis (balanitis); a tight foreskin (phimosis); inflammation of the prostate or even a bowed erection.

INTESTINE

The function of the gastro-intestinal tract, which is made up of the oesophagus, the stomach and the intestines, is the storage, digestion and absorption of foodstuffs.

Storage and, to a lesser extent, digestion occur in the stomach, but most of the nutrients and water are absorbed in the intestine.

The intestine is divided into two functionally different regions, known as the small intestine and the large intestine. Some diseases can affect any part of the intestine, but many are only to be found in one particular section of the tract.

Structure of the intestine

The small intestine extends from the valve of the stomach to the start of the large intestine. It is about five metres long, but its length varies according to the level of activity of its muscles.

The first part of the small intestine is called the duodenum, which is only 25cm long. Two ducts, the common bile duct from the liver and the pancreatic duct from the pancreas, bring digestive juices into the duodenum. The partially digested food continues along the jejunum and the ileum to the caecum at the bottom of the right-hand side of the abdominal cavity. The digestive tract from here on is known as the large intestine.

The main part of the large intestine is the colon, which encircles the small intestine, descending to the bottom left of the abdominal cavity, where it connects to the rectum. The colon acts as a reservoir for waste. Food residues from the ileum take about 18 hours to reach the rectum. During its passage the waste has most of the water removed. The faeces left from the digestive process are eliminated through the anus.

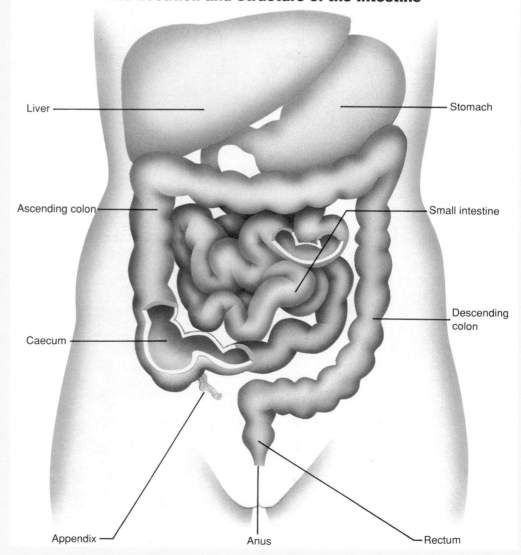

The Location and Structure of the Intestine

Liver — Stomach — Ascending colon — Small intestine — Caecum — Descending colon — Appendix — Anus — Rectum

INTESTINE, DISORDERS OF

There are many problems which can affect the intestine, some of which can be quite serious.

Although some problems can affect the whole of the intestine, it is easier to look at the major disorders according to which part of the tract is affected.

Disorders of the duodenum

The commonest disease to affect the duodenum is peptic ulceration. (Peptic ulcers in the duodenum are known as duodenal ulcers; peptic ulcers in the stomach are known as gastric ulcers.)

Duodenal ulcers are more common in middle age, affecting one in 10 of all men and women betwen the ages of 45 and 55.

The actual cause of peptic ulceration is still unclear. It was originally thought to be due to an excess of stomach acid but infection may well play a role as well. Stress, alcohol and smoking all make ulcers worse. Duodenal ulcers are more common in the spring and autumn and more likely to affect men than women.

The main symptom of a duodenal ulcer is pain, often just below the breast bone but occasionally between the shoulder blades. The pain tends to come on an hour or two after food and often

wakes the sufferer at night. Left untreated the ulcer may burn through the wall of the duodenum so it spills its contents into the abdomen. This causes peritonitis, an acutely painful condition which may be fatal.

If your doctor suspects a duodenal ulcer she may suggest you have a barium meal — a type of x-ray that uses a dye to outline the bowel walls. In some areas, endoscopy is available and this is a more reliable test.

Treatment is simple. Avoid smoking, alcohol and spicy foods as these all make ulcers worse. A six-week course of an acid-suppressing drug is usually sucessful, but this may have to be repeated.

Cancer of the duodenum is extremely rare.

Disorders of the jejunum and ileum

The commonest severe problem affecting this part of the small intestine is obstruction. This may be due to disorders of muscle activity, blockages within the bowel cavity or swelling of the bowel wall. The most common cause of obstruction is a hernia. Hernias occur wherever there is a weakness in the musculature of the abdominal wall. Men commonly suffer from inguinal hernias. These appear along the line that the testicles took in their descent from the abdominal cavity to the scrotum. Simple hernias are painless swellings full of abdominal contents. They may be huge — as large as a coconut — but cause little problem unless they strangulate. Strangulation occurs if the blood supply is cut off. When this happens the hernial swelling becomes tense, red and very painful. Unless emergency surgery is performed, the intestine may become gangrenous.

Foreign bodies in the small intestine are rarely a

cause of obstruction. If an object is small enough to leave the stomach it is too small to cause problems. Rarely, a large gall stone may leave the gall bladder and lodge in the bowel. Like other forms of intestinal blockage, this will cause pain and vomiting.

A rare, but often fatal, condition is blockage of the blood supply to the small intestine. This is usually due to a blood clot. Like all clots it is commoner in smokers. Pain is severe and situated around the umbilicus. Surgery to remove any segments of gangrenous bowel is highly dangerous as patients frequently have heart disease and other signs of arterial thickening.

Crohn's disease is an inflammation of the intestine — usually the ileum and jejunum, although it can occur anywhere in the digestive tract. The cause is unknown, and it affects both men and women, usually between the ages of 10 and 30. The symptoms are vague. Repeated attacks of central abdominal pain and diarrhoea may suggest the condition, but it can ony be confirmed by a barium meal. The diagnosis is sometimes only made when the surgeon has opened the abdomen expecting to find appendicitis. The affected bowel is thickened and rubbery as a result of swelling. It may involve all of the intestine or just small segments, in which case the lengths of bowel between the lesions are normal.

Crohn's disease is a long-term problem and most doctors go to great lengths to avoid surgery, though acute obstruction may make it necessary. Medical treatment with steroids or immuno-suppressant drugs may give long-term remission.

Children with sore throats often complain of tummy ache. This is due to mesenteric adenitis, a

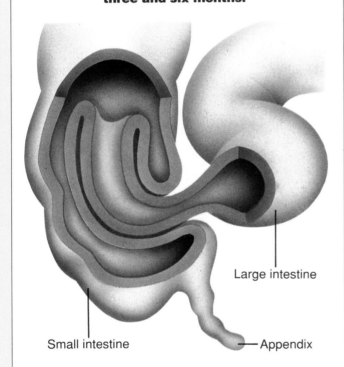

Intussusception

This intestinal disorder only affects small children, usually between the ages of three and six months.

Large intestine

Small intestine

Appendix

One part of the small intestine telescopes back on itself, rather like a coat sleeve being pulled inside out. The symptoms are severe pain and blood-stained stools (said to resemble redcurrant jelly).

A barium enema is usually given to diagnose the problem, and this may clear the intussusception.

 SEE ALSO — Abdominal pain, Crohn's disease, Hernia, Peritonitis, Ulcers

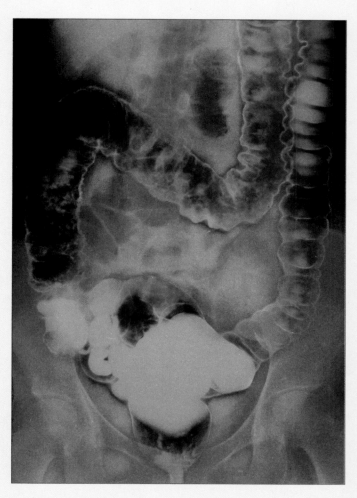

Above: a false colour x-ray of a patient who has had a barium meal. The colon and rectum show clearly, and dark patches on the ascending colon (left) indicate ulcerative colitis.

condition in which the lymph glands in the lining of the bowel wall swell up. Mesenteric adenitis is often confused with appendicitis and many children undergo needless operations.

Appendicitis
The appendix, which branches off the caecum used to be thought to be a 'redundant' part of the digestive tract. It is composed of lymphoid tissue (like tonsils) and it is now thought to be an important part of the body's immune defence system. However, its exact function is still unclear. It may become inflamed, a condition known as appendicitis. The accompanying symptoms are pain, which starts in the centre of the abdomen and

shifts to the right, a mild fever, loss of appetite and vomiting. The patient may have bad breath and a coated tongue.

Treatment is by surgery: laparoscopy can now be used, inserting the laparoscope (a kind of medical telescope) through a small incision in the navel.

Disorders of the colon
Cancer of the colon is a relatively common form of cancer. It usually affects 55 to 70-year-olds. It is slightly more common in women than in men. The onset of the disease is slow and insidious. The patient may be generally under the weather for a year or two before the diagnosis is made. The most important early warning signs are rectal bleeding and a

change in bowel habit. At a later stage, weight loss, diarrhoea and obstruction may occur.

Treatment of bowel cancer is primarily surgical. If possible, the tumour is removed and the remaining sections of the colon are re-joined — the body soon adjusts to the slight shortening of the colon. If this is not possible, the patient may require a colostomy.

Like so many cancers, bowel cancer is most easily treated and most often cured if it is caught early. Any change of bowel habit or rectal bleeding should be reported to your doctor.

Many people have outpouchings of the inner lining of the gut through the muscle layer — diverticula. They are not normally a problem, but because the pouches are not covered by muscle they do not have the ability to empty themselves and tend to become inflamed. This inflammation is known as diverticular disease, and may affect all the large bowel. If a diverticulum becomes perforated, it may cause peritonitis or an abscess.

The symptoms and signs of diverticular disease are very similar to the early signs of bowel cancer and it often takes a barium enema to distinguish the two.

Treatment consists of increasing the amount of fibre in the diet. Acute attacks need painkillers, rest and antibiotics.

Ulcerative colitis is a quite common disease, the cause of which is not known. It usually starts in early adulthood and affects more women than men. The colon becomes inflamed and ulcerated. This causes pain and frequent diarrhoea. The stools often contain blood, mucus and pus. All sufferers have to have regular check up as perforation, abscesses and cancerous changes may occur. Medical treatment with

steroids and immuno-suppresive drugs will reduce the symptoms but most sufferers will end up having surgery to remove the colon.

IRRITABLE BLADDER

An irritable bladder is the intermittent, uncontrolled contractions of the muscles in the bladder wall.

It can be caused by several factors, most commonly by a urinary tract infection. A bladder stone or an enlarged prostate can also be a cause. If the person has a catheter in the bladder the condition may arise. Treatment is by antispasmodic drugs, or by finding the underlying cause.

IRRITABLE BOWEL SYNDROME

Irritable bowel syndrome is the name given to a series of symptoms affecting the large and small intestine. It is commoner in women than in men, and tends to affect the younger age groups.

The root cause seems to be increased bowel activity which leads to a host of unpleasant symptoms.

Symptoms
Diarrhoea is common, often as a matter of urgency first thing in the morning. In some cases, the bowel is so active that it goes into spasm, causing constipation and abdominal bloating. Pain is usually felt as a dull ache in the lower abdomen, but may be colicky and severe enough to raise worries

SEE ALSO — Appendicitis, Colon cancer

about appendicitis.

Irritable bowel syndrome seems to be related to stress, and many sufferers recognise the connection between emotional upsets and a bowel upset.

Diagnosis

The symptoms of IBS are similar to those of several more serious, but fortunately much rarer disorders, such as bowel cancer, ulcerative colitis and Crohn's disease. Most doctors, when faced with a patient complaining of bowel symptoms, exclude these serious conditions before making a firm diagnosis. For this reason, people suffering from IBS may well have rectal examinations and a barium enema or colonoscopy before the condition is confirmed.

Treatment

Reassurance is a very powerful treatment for irritable bowel syndrome. Many people are so relieved by the benign nature of the disease that their stress levels drop and the problem is solved. A high-fibre diet gives the colon something to squeeze on and stops the painful spasms. Simple painkillers such as paracetamol are also useful,

but if these do not work, antispasmodic drugs may be needed. The antispasmodic with the least side effects is probably peppermint oil, which is available in a sealed capsule that will dissolve in the large bowel, where its calming effect is most needed. In severe cases, counselling or even antidepressants may be needed.

ITCHING

Everybody knows what an itch is, but it is hard to describe. It can be defined as a feeling of irritation in the skin.

Doctors know that the nerve impulses that tell us we have an itch run along the same fibres as pain, but how the body differentiates is not known. There is a great variation in people's capacity to feel itchy. Rashes that are intolerable in one person are barely noticed by another.

Itching may be generalised — felt all over — or localised.

Generalised itching

All-over itching is very common and is usually worse at night in bed. Itching is also a symptom of

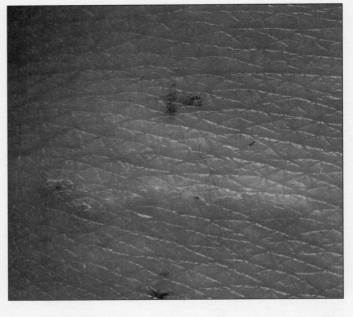

The scabies mite burrows into the skin, leaving characteristic tracks. It is highly contagious and causes intense itching.

urticaria, a condition that commonly affects young women. It is due to an allergic reaction, often to a foodstuff. The skin is intensely itchy and breaks out in swellings similar to nettle rash. The condition can be very troubling but will burn itself out in time. Treatment with non-sedating antihistamine is very effective.

During pregnancy, some women suffer from generalised itching, often with red spots on the abdomen. This is quite harmless, and is best treated with calamine lotion.

More seriously, generalised itching can be the external sign of an internal disease such as anaemia, liver failure, kidney failure or even some forms of cancer. If a general itchiness is accompanied by an increased need to urinate, this may be a symptom of diabetes mellitus, but this has several other symptoms as well.

In older people, generalised itching, or more localised itching on the hands and feet, may be caused by the removal of natural oils.

Localised itching

Itching on the scalp is likely to be due to dandruff, head lice or a fungal infection; itching which is confined to the anus is probably due to threadworms; for itching of the vaginal area see below.

Itchy patches on the skin may be due to scabies, with their characteristic burrowing patterns. Eczema and dermatitis are also accompanied by itching: diagnosis is straightforward, but treatment may take time.

Relieving the symptoms

Treatment should be through identifying the cause of the itching, and treating that, where possible. However, it may be necessary to relieve the itching, in which case calamine lotion is the first option. If this fails, antihistamine tablets can be used. These are available from the chemist, without prescription. The sedating effect of the old-fashioned antihistamines such as Piriton is useful in helping patients to sleep at night. If itching is persistent, consult your doctor, who may be able to help further.

Feminine Itching

Itching in the vulval area can be very irritating, and awkward to soothe.

In many cases, particularly in older women, this type of itching indicates that the natural oils and lubricants are drying out, leaving the delicate skin dry and itchy. Often, soaps, perfumes and bath preparations are responsible for a slightly allergic reaction. If the itching is accompanied by an unusual discharge, you may have a vaginal infection and should consult your doctor.

To help prevent this type of itching:

● Always wear cotton knickers.
● Never use douches or vaginal deodorants.
● Wash the genital area at least once a day with plain water – do not use soap, bath salts, etc.
● Wear stockings rather than tights, and don't wear tight trousers.

»» SEE ALSO — Lice

JAUNDICE

Jaundice is not a disease in itself, but is a symptom of various disorders. It refers to the yellow discoloration of the skin and whites of the eyes caused by the deposition of bilirubin, a yellow-coloured waste product from the liver.

Bilirubin is a waste product made from haemoglobin, the substance that makes red blood cells red. It is released when red blood cells are broken down. Normally the liver excretes the bilirubin, and it is then excreted into the digestive tract with the bile. Bile is used in the digestion of fats and, after use, is excreted in the faeces. This is what gives them their characteristic brown colour. Bilirubin may be deposited in the skin for three possible reasons.

Haemolytic jaundice

In haemolytic jaundice, too much bilirubin finds its way into the blood because of an excessive breakdown of red blood cells. This can be due to red blood cell defects, which cause their premature destruction, or defects affecting the red cells from external sources. The cells might be attacked by the body's own antibodies in a

form of auto-immune disorder, or by micro-organisms, such as malaria, in the blood. Or the destruction might be due to mechanical buffeting, for example if the blood has to flow through replacement heart valves.

Treatment is by removing the spleen, the main site of destruction of the red blood cells, or by administering antimalarial drugs or immunosuppressant drugs. If the jaundice is caused by the wear and tear of the red blood cells, treatment will be to reduce the forces causing this damage.

Hepatocellular jaundice

In hepatocellular jaundice, the liver itself isn't working properly and fails to deal with the production of bilirubin adequately. This damage is

often due to hepatitis and it is the commonest cause of jaundice in adults. Hepatitis is the medical term for inflammation of the liver. This inflammation results in bilirubin not being excreted properly and levels subsequently build up in the blood. Hepatitis is often due to viral infections. These may take many forms including glandular fever.

A rare cause of hepatitis is the contraceptive pill. Women who have been jaundiced are at an increased risk and should remind their doctor of their previous problems before accepting a prescription.

Obstructive jaundice

Obstructive jaundice is caused by an obstruction in the bile duct so the bile does not pass freely into the gut. It is rare in young people.

The usual cause is a gall stone impacted in the common bile duct. This is painful and often follows a long history of dull pains under the right ribs. The skin is bright orange, the stools are the colour of putty and the urine the colour of strong tea. The stone may pass out of the gall bladder spontaneously but, if not, surgery is required.

Another cause of jaundice in the elderly is cancer of the head of the pancreas. This painless tumour presses on the bile duct and blocks it. If the

diagnosis is made soon enough surgery may be curative but it is usually simply a question of bypassing the blockage to relieve the symptoms.

Neonatal Jaundice

Did you know that almost everyone is jaundiced as an infant, soon after birth?

At birth, the foetus has an abundant supply of red cells to act as an oxygen reservoir during the delivery. After the birth they are no longer needed and the body must break them down. This releases large amounts of bilirubin into the blood and gives new-born babies their orange-brown tinge.

Some babies suffer a more serious form of jaundice in which their blood breaks down excessively. This is due to antibodies from their mother's blood. Fortunately modern antenatal blood tests make this condition very rare.

JAW

At birth the jaw bone, or mandible, consists of two separate segments. These fuse to form a solid bone at the age of one.

The main part of the jaw bone holds the teeth while the neck of it hinges with the temple region of the skull; hence it is called the temporomandibular joint. The temporomandibular joint is an example of what is known as a synovial joint (see overleaf) but it is more than a simple hinge. To enable us to chew, it must also allow movement from side to side.

Unlike any other joint in the body each jaw joint must work in perfect harmony with its partner. Any dental problem such as a missing tooth or an abnormal bite will throw the balance out and lead to the very common complaint of 'popping' and pain in the joint. If the problem is ignored it can lead to degeneration of the joint, which may require major surgery to correct.

X-rays with the mouth open and closed should confirm the diagnosis. Treatment in the early stages consists of dental work to realign the bite.

Dislocation

Dislocation of the jaw is a common problem that often affects both sides of the face at once. If only one side is affected the jaw is displaced towards the affected side. Dislocation may be the result of a blow to the side of the face but usually occurs during laughing or yawning. There is a sudden pain over the temporomandibular joint

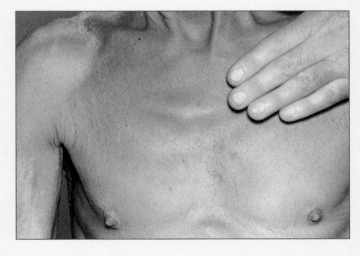

Above: The marked yellowing of the skin on the upper body of a man suffering from jaundice.

» SEE ALSO — Gall bladder, Hepatitis

and the victim is unable to close her mouth. Treatment, which should only be done by properly trained people, consists of forcing the jaw downwards and then back into position.

Repeated dislocation is usually a sign of the teeth being out of alignment.

Fractures

Fracture of the jaw is usually the result of a direct blow. Because of the shape of the joint, fractures often occur not only at the site of the blow, but also on the other side of the jaw. The neck of the jaw that hinges with the skull may snap if the blow is particularly severe.

In either case treatment is the same. If the face is seriously misshapen the jaw is manipulated and wired, otherwise it is left to heal of its own accord.

Arthritis

The jaw is often affected by systemic diseases such as rheumatoid arthritis. Seventy per cent of sufferers complain of pain on chewing. If anti-inflammatory drugs and analgesics do not work, the specialist may prescribe injections of a steroid/local anaesthetic mixture directly into the joint. This may be painful for the first day or so but offers dramatic relief in most cases.

JOGGER'S NIPPLE

This is a common ailment affecting sportspeople. Nipples are irritated by continuous friction with clothing during jogging or long-distance running.

Jogger's nipple can be prevented by applying petroleum jelly to the nipple before going for a long run. Sweat can also aggravate the condition, so wearing clean clothing helps. In severe cases, the nipple should be covered with a bandage to prevent chafing.

JOINTS

Joints are unions between two or more bones. There are four types — bony, fibrous, cartilaginous and synovial joints.

The stability or strength of a joint depends on several factors, mainly the type of joint.

Bony joints

Bony joints are the strongest type of joint. They are fixed and are completely immobile. To all intents and purposes they form a solid unit. Bony joints occur in the hips.

Cartilaginous joints

Cartilaginous joints are joined by cartilage, and allow limited movement. Examples of these are the joints in the spine between the vertebrae.

Fibrous joints

Fibrous joints are rigid and unyielding. The bones are joined together by thick fibrous tissue. The skull is made up of relatively flat bones which are formed into a sphere by fibrous joints.

Synovial joints

The majority of the joints in the body are synovial. Unlike the other types, synovial joints are freely mobile. The two ends of the bones, the articular surfaces, are covered by smooth cartilage. A fibrous capsule grows from the edge of the joint and completely encloses it. The cartilage and the capsule are lined with a synovial membrane which secretes a watery lubricant, which is called synovial fluid.

The capsule may be strengthened by ligaments and the joint itself may be strengthened by ligaments between the articular surfaces. These ligaments are particularly important in the knee where the cruciate ligaments stop the thigh bone from sliding across the top of the shin bone.

Types Of Synovial Joints

There are several different types of synovial joints, each giving different degrees of mobility to the connecting bones.

Pivot Joint

A pivot joint has a bony projection pivoting within a ring, or a ring pivoting on an axis, for example between the first and second vertebrae. Movement is limited to rotation.

Ball-and-Socket Joint

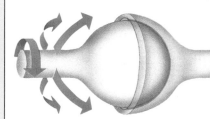

Ball-and-socket joints permit the widest range of movements, in the shoulder and hip, for example.

Ellipsoidal Joint

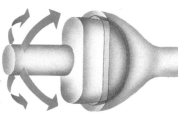

In an ellipsoidal joint an oval-shaped section of bone fits into an elliptical cavity, allowing all types of movement except pivoting.

Hinge Joint

The hinge joint allows bending and straightening movements, as in the fingers.

Synovial joints can be divided into a number of types (see diagram above), which are grouped according to the range of movements possible. Hinge joints are at the elbow, knee and ankle; ball-and-socket joints are at the hip and shoulder.

The shape of the joint, the thickness of the capsule and the presence of ligaments or muscles outside the joint are all important indicators of its strength.

As a general rule the more mobility the joint has, the weaker it is. As long as our joints are in good working order, we are hardly aware of them. But there are many disorders, including cartilage problems and arthritis, and they can be excruciatingly painful.

Joint injuries

If the forces on a joint exceed its strength, the surfaces which are supposed to meet become displaced, causing dislocation. Because of its great mobility, the shoulder is particularly liable to dislocate. Dislocations are often associated with fractures. However tempting it may be, you must never attempt to replace a dislocation. Leave it to the nearest accident and emergency department at your local hospital where the doctors will be able to x-ray it to see the exact problem.

A less severe dislocation is called a subluxation. If bone ends are fractured, this can lead to bleeding at the joint (haemarthrosis) or accumulation of fluid in a joint (effusion).

Sprains

Rupturing or stretching the ligaments which hold the joint together causes a sprain. Contrary to popular belief, this can often be more serious than a fracture and it may need surgical repair.

Arthritis

Almost everybody over the age of 30 has some degree of osteoarthritis. This is an inflammatory condition that roughens the articular surfaces of the joints. This

condition, which may be extremely painful, seems to be due, in part at least, to wear and tear. It is common in retired sportspeople, especially those who have suffered injuries of one sort or another.

Rheumatoid arthritis is another inflammatory condition but this affects the synovial membrane that lines the joint. It causes severe pain and deformity.

Treatment for arthritis

In the early stages both forms of arthritis are treated with weight reduction (where appropriate) and physiotherapy to try and relieve the strain on the joint. In more severe cases, analgesics and anti-inflammatory drugs are helpful. Injections of steroids and local anaesthetic directly into the joint can control the symptoms for many months but often surgery to replace the most damaged joints (particularly the hips) is the only answer.

Bursitis

In some joints, the tendons (which are connected to the muscles and operate the joints) have to be prevented from rubbing against the bones. At the pressure point there is a small fluid-filled pad, called a bursa. Bursitis (inflammation of the bursa) may occur as a result of local

irritation or strain.

The joints most often affected are the knees (which causes conditions commonly known as housemaid's knee and clergyman's knee, the elbow (tennis elbow) and the shoulder.

The main treatment is rest, and the swelling normally subsides as the fluid is reabsorbed into the bloodstream. If the condition persists, it may be necessary to drain the fluid. Very occasionally the bursa has to be removed surgically.

KAPOSI'S SARCOMA

This condition is a prominent feature of AIDS, and consists of malignant skin tumours which look like blue-red nodules.

The tumours usually first appear on the feet and ankles, and then spread further up the legs, before eventually appearing on the sufferer's hands and arms.

In people with AIDS, the tumours can attack the gastrointestinal and respiratory tracts, possibly causing internal bleeding.

Kaposi's sarcoma used to be extremely rare, but now it is much more common and also much more aggressive

in its infection of the body. Treatment is by low doses of radiotherapy in mild cases, or anticancer drugs when the condition is more severe. cases.

KIDNEYS

The two kidneys lie at the back of the abdomen, one on either side of the backbone. Their main function is to filter the blood and excrete waste products in the form of urine.

Most of the kidney is protected by the ribs but because of the size and position of the liver, the right one is slightly lower than the left. Each is about 10cm long, 5cm wide, 3cm thick and weighs about 100g. As the diaphragm contracts when you breathe in, the kidneys move up and down by 2-3cm. Each kidney is enclosed in a tough, fibrous capsule and this in turn is surrounded by a thick layer of fat.

What they do

The main function of the kidney is the selective secretion of waste products. Many of these substances are toxic and would result in death if allowed to accumulate in the body. They may only be present in

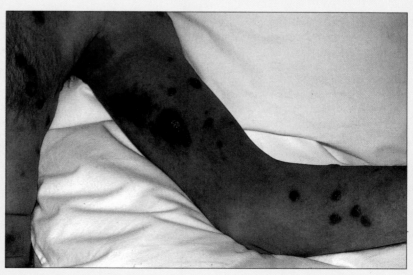

Dark patches (tumours) on the right arm and chest of a man who has AIDS and is suffering from Kaposi's sarcoma, a type of cancer. Until the spread of AIDS, this cancer was only seen in elderly people of Jewish or Mediterranean background.

» SEE ALSO — Hip, Knee, Sprain, Tennis elbow

MEDICAL FACT FILE

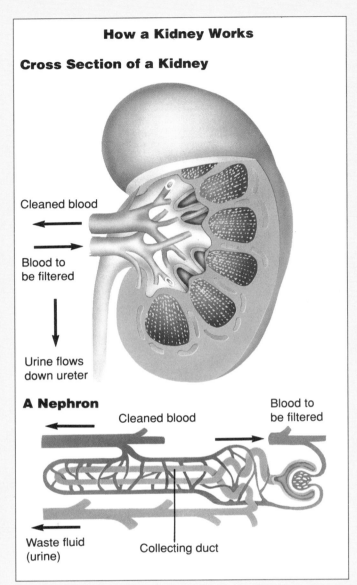

How a Kidney Works

Cross Section of a Kidney

Cleaned blood

Blood to
be filtered

Urine flows
down ureter

A Nephron

Cleaned blood

Blood to
be filtered

Waste fluid
(urine)

Collecting duct

minute quantities and the task of the kidney is to eliminate them without losing essential amino acids, sugars, minerals and so on.

It is obviously impossible for the kidney to recognise and eliminate each and every toxic substance that could come its way in a lifetime. It gets round this by filtering and excreting most of what passes through it. It then reabsorbs substances, such as potassium, that it knows the body needs.

The kidney is unable to excrete waste matter in anything other than a dissolved form. To do this it must excrete water at the rate of at least 600ml per day. In the average day the kidney receives 1300 litres of blood as it circulates round the body and filters 180 litres of water, 179 of which are reabsorbed, leaving about a litre of waste water (urine). In certain conditions, such as sugar diabetes (diabetes mellitus) or in heavy beer drinkers, the kidney can quite happily process 10 or 20 times as much as this.

The nephron

The nephrons in the kidneys actually do the work. Each nephron is tiny — there are about a million in each kidney — and each has a minute artery that feeds it and another, even smaller, that takes the clean blood back towards the heart. Water and

dissolved substances pass through microscopic holes between the arterioles into a collecting duct. From the collecting duct the dilute urine flows out of the nephron, but before it has a chance to leave it is filtered again and most of the water and useful substances are retained.

From the nephron the urine passes through thicker and thicker ducts, which are arranged like the branches of a tree. Urine leaves the kidney through the renal pelvis and passes straight into the ureter, a 25cm tube that connects each kidney to the bladder.

Other functions

In addition to their major role in cleansing the blood, the kidneys are also part of the endocrine system. They produce two hormones, one of which controls blood pressure. The other has a role in the production of normal red blood cells — without it the sufferer becomes anaemic.

KIDNEYS, CANCER OF

The commonest tumour of the kidneys, the renal cell carcinoma, is highly malignant. It tends to affect the over-fifties and more men get it than women.

The first sign is usually blood in the urine. Unlike cystitis this bleeding is painless. Because of the kidney's role in blood formation, anaemia is often an early sign. In the first place the diagnosis is based on examining the abdomen — occasionally the tumour is so big it can be felt.

An IVU — an x-ray investigation that examines the whole of the urinary tract — is usually needed to confirm the diagnosis. A dye

is injected into the patient's arm vein and is then taken up by the kidneys and excreted in the urine. This process highlights the structure of the kidneys, and, if an x-ray is taken every few minutes, it can also show how quickly the kidneys are working to clear the blood.

Treatment is surgical but the specialist will often want an arteriogram, which shows the blood supply of the kidney, to help him plan his operation.

Other tumours

Nephroblastoma is one of the few malignant tumours to affect children. It usually affects them before the age of two — rarely is it seen in children over the age of seven. Bleeding is usually the first sign that anything is wrong — this shows up in the urine. If the cancer grows quickly, the parent may feel it as a swelling in the child's abdomen when bathing the child — again, the diagnosis is confirmed by an IVU.

The faster the tumour can be treated the greater the chance of survival. Surgery to remove the growth is essential but this may prove very difficult as it grows around and through the surrounding structures. If the tumour has reached this stage, then radiotherapy may be used prior to surgery in an attempt to shrink it to a point where it is possible to remove it.

The outlook for this particular cancer used to be extremely gloomy but nowadays the prospects of successful treatment have improved immensely because of the use of radiotherapy and cytotoxic drugs.

Benign tumours of the kidney are rare. Despite their benign nature, these tumours may bleed so much that surgery is needed to remove the kidney.

▶▶ SEE ALSO — Adrenal glands, Endocrine system

KIDNEY DISORDERS

There are many disorders of the kidney, ranging from a mild infection of the urinary tract to complete kidney failure, which could be due to anything from a heart attack to overuse of painkillers.

Infection

The commonest form of kidney disease, especially in women, is an infection. When this affects the bladder alone (cystitis), sufferers have to go to the toilet frequently, and experience pain when they pass water.

If the infection spreads up the ureters into the kidney it causes infection of the kidneys (pyelonephritis). Again this causes pain when passing water; other symptoms include fever, pain in the hips and inner surfaces of the legs, and vomiting.

There may be an obvious cause such as pregnancy, but failing this a significant number of pyelonephritis sufferers have some structural abnormality of the urinary tract.

A first kidney infection is usually fully investigated by urine tests and might well involve x-rays of the kidneys. Treatment with antibiotics is usually curative but some infections recur very quickly and patients may need to be on drug therapy permanently.

Polcystic kidneys

In some people, probably as a result of a dominant gene abnormality, the kidneys develop multiple cysts. This can happen to people any time between the ages of 20 and 50; the patient is usually developing kidney failure before the cysts are identified.

Symptoms include pain, bleeding or repeated infection. An IVU or an ultrasound scan can clinch the diagnosis. This condition tends to be hereditary, so doctors and patients are often on the look-out for it. The condition, if allowed to develop, causes high blood pressure, kidney infections and kidney failure. Dialysis and transplant are the only effective treatment.

Nephrotic syndrome

The nephrotic syndrome is a condition resulting in the loss of large amounts of protein in the urine. This loss lowers the protein content of the blood, which causes swelling and water retention.

There are many causes, from poisoning to cancer but

Kidney Dialysis And Transplants

Although the work the kidneys do is essential, it is possible to live a normal life even if your kidneys have failed completely.

Dialysis and kidney transplant techniques have been greatly refined over the last 20 years.

Dialysis

If the kidney is so badly damaged that it is unable to cope even on a special diet then dialysis is needed, either as a long-term treatment or until a suitable donor organ can be found.

Dialysis relies on the concept of osmosis, by which dissolved salts will always diffuse from an area of high concentration to an area of low concentration. If salts are present in the blood in large quantities then they can be made to cross a membrane into pure water. This is what dialysis is basically all about.

Unfortunately pure water cannot be used as this would leach out all the salts, not just the waste ones. To overcome this a special dialysis fluid, with set concentrations of salts, is used. This fluid may be inside a machine (haemodialysis), or loose inside the abdomen (peritoneal dialysis). Either way, the treatment is costly and time consuming and not all patients can have this treatment.

Kidney transplant

In theory, kidney transplant is simple – remove the old kidney, replace it with a new one, reconnect the artery, vein and ureter and the patient will lead a normal life. In practice, rejection makes the procedure much more complicated. The body sees the new kidney as a foreign object and mounts an immune response. This is overcome by trying to match donor and recipient, but unless they are identical twins some form of drug treatment will be needed to reduce the effect of the immune response. This will increase the likelihood of infection and all such patients need careful follow up. Despite the drawbacks, patients who have undergone a transplant describe the changes in their health as 'miraculous'.

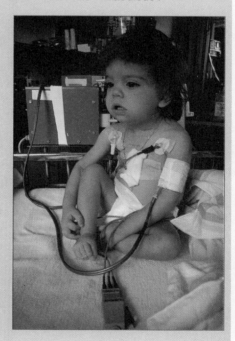

Left: A kidney from a donor arrives at a hospital operating theatre.
Right: A young girl suffering from diabetes undergoes renal dialysis on a kidney machine, while awaiting a suitable kidney donor. The machine removes waste from inefficient kidneys.

the commonest is glomerulo-nephritis. This is one of the auto-immune disorders and in this case antibodies attack the glomeruli in the kidney. Ninety per cent of children and 70 per cent of adults make a full recovery from this type of affliction but they may require large doses of immunosuppressant drugs and even dialysis in the acute phase.

Acute kidney failure
This is defined as a urine output of less than 400ml in 24 hours although sometimes the kidneys may still produce normal amounts of urine even though they have completely failed as a filter.

Acute kidney failure most often happens when people suffer severe physiological shock caused by injury or a serious underlying illness. Blood pressure is reduced and the supply of blood to the kidneys falls below a critical level. The kidneys may stop working altogether as glomeruli die.

Kidney failure may also be caused by back pressure on the kidneys from what is known as 'outflow obstruction'. As the name implies, urine is unable to leave either the ureters or the bladder and the pressure in the ureters builds up to the point where the kidneys cannot overcome it. An enlarged prostate in men or kidney stones in women are the commonest causes.

Acute symptoms
Many diseases of the kidney itself, such as glomerulo-nephritis and heavy metal poisoning, can cause acute kidney failure. Apart from the decreased urine output the signs of acute kidney failure are confusion, hiccoughs, fits and fluid retention. Unless treated swiftly, coma and death will occur within days.

Treatment of acute kidney failure is based on removing the cause, an enlarged prostate for example, and nurturing the kidney in the hope that it will recover spontaneously. This will mean a non-protein diet, careful fluid balance and in some cases dialysis may be needed (see previous page). If the kidneys fail to recover, long-term dialysis or a transplant will be needed.

Chronic kidney failure
The onset of chronic kidney failure is insidious, with many months of vague ill-health and anaemia. The kidney continues to produce urine but fails to excrete waste substances or to reabsorb useful ones.

Chronic failure can be due to a number of diseases such as chronic infection, sugar diabetes, urinary obstruction or drug abuse.

Chronic symptoms
The patient usually complains of lethargy, ill-health, passing large amounts of urine and having to get up at night to pass water. If left untreated, the patient develops weight loss, bruising, itching and hiccups. The skin takes on a 'dirty yellow' colour and brown lines appear on the finger nails.

Treatment
Again, causes must be identified and treated. Stones can be removed surgically; infections treated with drugs. If such measures fail, regulating fluid intake and putting the patient on a high-carbohydrate, low-protein diet is started. Dialysis or a transplant may be needed if the patient deteriorates.

Kidney stones
Urine contains many dissolved salts. In conditions where there is a low urine volume, these salts can crystallise out, like salt water left to evaporate. Layer upon layer will build up to form a rock-hard stone. If the stone is small enough it can slip into the ureter causing severe colicky pain, felt in the side and the groin.

With luck, and given the benefit of painkillers, the stone may be passed naturally. If the stone is too large to enter the ureter, it may grow until it fills the entire kidney, causing pain, infections and chronic kidney failure. Surgery, using a flexible telescope, is needed to remove such stones.

KNEE
The knee joint is between the femur (thighbone) and tibia (shinbone) and is the largest hinge joint in the body. It relies on the surrounding ligaments, tendons and muscles for its strength.

Some degree of rotation is possible in the knee. This rotation locks the knee and means that, when the joint is straight, the thigh muscles can be relaxed.

The knee cap acts as a pulley and functions to stop the thick tendon of the quadriceps, or thigh muscle, from rubbing on the joint.

Ligaments and cartilage
There are two sets of ligaments, those inside the joint and those outside. The ligaments outside the joint are thick fibrous bands which stop the lower leg moving from side to side. The ligaments inside the joint form a cross, hence their name, the cruciate ligaments. They connect the thighbone and the shinbone and serve two purposes: they stop the shinbone from sliding backwards and forwards, and also help to twist it to lock the knee joint when rigidity is needed.

The other important structures inside the knee are the cartilages. These are pads of fibrous gristle which deepen the cup made by the upper end of the shinbone. They increase the stability of the joint by stopping the thighbone slipping on its surface.

Knee cap
Despite its great size and great strength, the knee has more than its share of problems. Fractures of the knee cap occur as the result of a direct blow. The bone may be smashed into several pieces or split in half. Surgery is usually needed to wire the

---

Kidney Function Tests

The kidney excretes some substances and retains others. Measurement of any of these substances in the blood or urine will give an idea of how well it is doing its job.

● Urine tests to measure protein are a valuable screening test. Not only will they pick up infections but also the many conditons, such as the nephrotic syndrome, where protein is lost.
● Blood tests to measure urea, a breakdown product of protein, can be used to give an accurate level of kidney function. Combine this with the measurement of two common salts and you achieve a test of kidney function so reliable that it is the commonest test the hospital chemical laboratory is called upon to perform.
● Kidney biopsy, using a fine needle, aids diagnosis and helps to tailor treatment but may cause complications. Plain x-rays show up kidney stones and an ultrasound can be used to show back pressure and distension.

➤➤ SEE ALSO — Dialysis, Joints

Knee Replacement

Almost as important as the surgery is the aftercare, with physiotherapy and rehabilitation being vital.

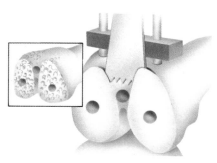

1. The ends of the shinbone and thighbone are removed.

2. A metal hinge is then fitted to the trimmed end of the shinbone.

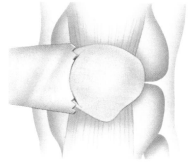

3. Part of the kneecap has to be removed.

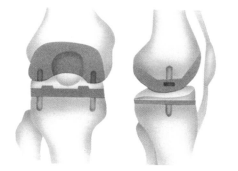

4. The knee with the hinge in position.

KNOCK-KNEE

Knock-knee, or genu valgum, is the descriptive term used for the inward curving of the legs so that the knees touch. The feet are kept further apart than usual.

Many children go through a phase of being knock-kneed between the ages of three and five years and then grow out of it. The condition can develop, however, through rickets; rheumatoid arthritis or osteoarthritis of the knee; or a fracture of the lower thigh bone (femur) or upper tibia (shinbone) that hasn't healed in a straight line.

If knock-knee persists in children after the age of 10, then wearing heel wedges in the shoes can help. Often an operation called an

The characteristic inward-curving legs of knock-knee. The knees touch and the feet are wide apart.

fragments together. Dislocation of the knee cap usually occurs in a weak joint and is the result of a blow to the inner edge. The dislocated bone is easily replaced but the leg must be immobilised for a period of several weeks.

Ligament problems
Tearing of the ligaments is usually an injury that afflicts fit young adults with strong muscles and tough bones. If the thigh is kept still and the shin bent sideways, the ligaments both outside and inside the joint may tear. Again surgery is often needed to repair the damage but even this may leave the knee weak and prone to further injury.

Cartilage problems
Damage to the cartilage is usually the result of the foot being anchored, by a football boot for example, and the body twisting away from the

foot. The resulting force tears the edge of the cartilage causing pain and swelling. Unless the torn cartilage is removed surgically the damage may be permanent.

Other problems
The knee is a common site for osteoarthritis, rheumatoid arthritis and gout. Osteoarthritis is the commonest and is the result of wear and tear. This wear and tear usually occurs in later years but may strike the very active at an early age. Osteoarthritis and rheumatoid arthritis can be treated with drugs to ease the pain and inflammation. In the end, surgery to replace the whole joint may be the only solution.

Total knee replacement is still in its infancy compared with hip replacement, which is now one of the commonest operations performed.

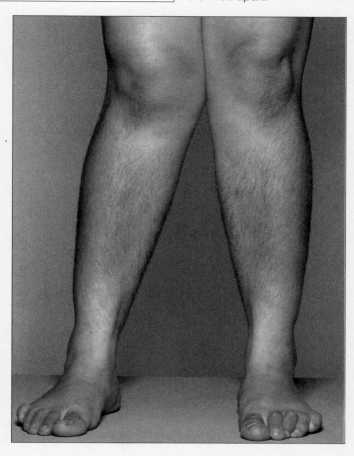

▶▶ SEE ALSO — Arthritis, Cartilage, Ligament

osteotomy is required where the tibia is cut and realigned to straighten the leg. Adults require the same operation or even a knee-joint replacement.

KYPHOSIS

Kyphosis is the medical term for excessive curvature of the upper part of the spine, usually resulting in a 'humpback'.

This abnormal curvature is called Pott's curvature in men, while in women it is known as dowager's hump. Kyphosis tends to develop in the elderly, but the condition can be congenital or present at birth. It can be caused by a number of spinal disorders, including osteoporosis, fracture of a vertebra, or a tumour of a vertebra. In the past, another common cause was spinal tuberculosis. Kyphosis can also be attributed to poor posture having contributed to weak musculature over a number of years.

Treatment
Treatment is rarely successful. Good remedies are exercise, physiotherapy, an orthopaedic brace or surgery.

LABOUR

Labour is the process of giving birth.

Labour is said to have started when muscular contractions of the uterus are occurring regularly at intervals of 10 minutes or less, and finishes with the delivery of the afterbirth or placenta. Two things might also occur to mark the beginning of labour. The mucous plug that has been blocking the cervical canal may be expelled, an event called a 'show'. Or the

The Three Stages of Labour

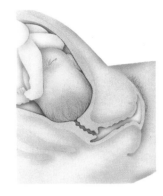 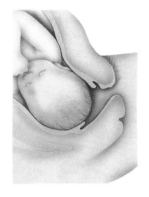 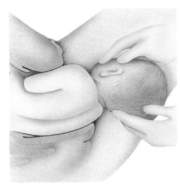

Contractions of the uterus result in the cervix dilating and the foetus moving further down the pelvis.

The mother starts to push, contractions become more frequent, and the baby's head stretches the vagina.

Even after the baby has emerged, the uterus continues contracting, to expel the afterbirth.

Inducing Labour Naturally

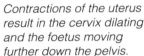

If your baby is 'late for dates', how can you get things moving?

There are many Old Wives' Tales, involving hot curries and long country walks, but the simplest way of inducing labour naturally is through having sexual intercourse. Semen contains prostaglandins that stimulate the uterus to contract and this, coupled with orgasm, may start

labour in the last week or two of pregnancy.

If you are enjoying a normal, healthy pregnancy, it is certainly a good idea to keep up some gentle exercise right up until labour starts (and even during the first stage of labour) to help keep your pelvic muscles in shape.

membranes that surround the baby may break, causing a leakage of the amniotic fluid, commonly known as 'breaking of the waters.' Labour is divided into three stages.

First stage
Over the first three hours or so of a normal labour, the contractions of the uterus increase in strength and frequency. They reach a steady rate with contractions coming every three minutes and lasting about a minute. During this stage the cervix thins out and then opens up, or dilates, to reach a maximum width of 10cm. As the cervix dilates the foetal

head descends further into the pelvis, aided by hormones that relax the fibrous joint at the front.

Second stage
When the cervix is fully dilated the descent of the head becomes more rapid and the mother feels an overwhelming desire to push. At this stage contractions come every two minutes and last a minute or so. The skin and muscles of the mother's vagina are progressively stretched by the emerging baby's head.

Third stage
Even after the baby is born the uterus continues to

contract. This shears the afterbirth from the wall of the uterus and forces it into the vagina from where it is delivered. As the uterus contracts it closes any bleeding blood vessels left by the delivery of the afterbirth.

Artificial induction
The exact trigger for the onset of labour is unknown but as the pregnancy approaches 40 weeks the uterus becomes more sensitive to hormones produced by the foetus and the placenta. If labour doesn't begin at term, then it may have to be induced.

If the pregnancy is prolonged or abnormal the doctor may wish to start labour artificially. A hormone pessary is inserted into the vagina to thin the cervix. This may be sufficient, or it may also be necessary to tear the bag of fluid around the baby. This usually starts contractions but a hormone drip may be needed to keep them coming regularly. Artificially induced labour can be more painful than normal and is often associated with an increased risk of complications.

SEE ALSO — Childbirth

LABYRINTHITIS

This is the medical term for inflammation of the labyrinths, which are the fluid-filled chambers within the inner ear.

The inflammation, caused by infection, causes the sensation of vertigo — the feeling that one's surroundings are spinning.

Causes

Labyrinthitis is caused by bacterial or viral infections. If the culprit is a virus, then labyrinthitis can develop through a 'flu-like illness or during an attack of mumps or measles.

If the cause is bacterial, the infection often begins in the middle ear and if this infection is inadequately treated, vertigo results.

In some cases, an infected collection of dirt and dust, technically known as a cholesteatoma, may have developed and eroded a pathway into the inner ear.

Other ways for the infection to begin are via the bloodstream or from a head injury.

Symptoms

Besides the dizziness, the sufferer may also experience nausea, vomiting, hearing loss, tinnitus (ringing in the ears), and nystagmus (abnormal jerky movements of the eye).

Treatment

Viral labyrinthitis usually clears up without treatment, but antihistamines are sometimes prescribed to help relieve symptoms.

Bacterial labyrinthitis requires antibiotics; lack of treatment can lead to permanent deafness or even meningitis. Occasionally, surgery is necessary in order to drain pus from the ear and remove any debris that may still be in there.

LACTOSE INTOLERANCE

This is the inability to digest lactose, or milk sugar.

Lactose intolerance is caused by a deficiency in the enzyme, lactase, which is normally present in the cells of the small intestine, and which breaks down lactose.

Types

Young children often suffer an inability to digest cow's milk, although this may be only a temporary condition. It occurs because the enzyme has not yet matured, and the condition is most common in premature babies.

The permanent inability to digest cow's milk is very common in many cultures, for example, in those of African and Asian origin. And about five to 15 per cent of those of European descent suffer from the affliction. Lactase deficiency may also be a result of other disorders, such as coeliac disease and gastroenteritis.

Symptoms and treatment

Symptoms include severe abdominal cramps, bloating, flatulence and diarrhoea. This is due to the undigested lactose fermenting within the intestinal tract.

Diagnosis is on examination of the blood and faeces. Treatment is normally by excluding all lactose products. Patients can, however, eat fermented milk in the form of yoghurt. In some cases, enzyme replacements may be given, which break down the lactose partially or fully.

LANUGO HAIR

Lanugo hair is the soft, fine, downy hair that covers a foetus.

It begins to appear while the foetus is in the womb at

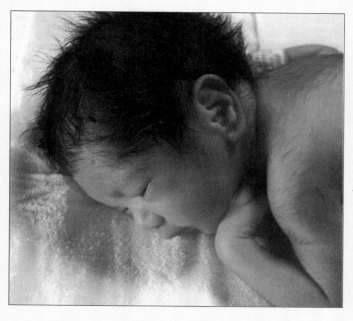

Fine, downy lanugo hair is clearly visible on the shoulders of this baby, who is two months premature.

approximately the fourth or fifth month of gestation. By the end of the ninth month, it has normally vanished — it is usually only seen on babies who are premature.

Occasionally adults develop this hair. It can occur in people who have cancer, particularly cancer of the breast, bladder or lung. Anorectics sometimes grow lanugo. It is also one of the side effects of taking certain drugs such as cyclosporin.

LAPAROSCOPY

Laparoscopy is a technique used to examine directly the interior of the abdomen.

It is usually performed if the patient has pelvic pain or

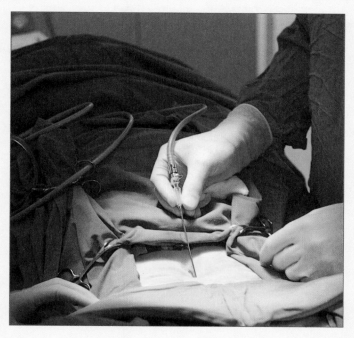

Carbon dioxide is pumped into the abdomen through a needle inserted below the navel during laparoscopy.

▶▶ SEE ALSO — Coeliac disease, Ear disorders, Gastroenteritis, Hairiness

gynaecological problems and is also used to check on the condition of the fallopian tubes if a patient is infertile. It is now used increasingly for gall bladder, appendix and kidney operations in what is known as keyhole surgery.

What happens

The surgeon inserts a hollow needle into the abdomen just below the navel. Carbon dioxide is introduced into the abdominal cavity, via the needle, to expand it. The laparoscope, a type of viewing instrument, is then inserted through another incision. In addition to some abdominal discomfort, the patient may also feel some discomfort in the shoulders for a few days, until the gas in the abdomen has passed out of the body.

LAPAROTOMY

The term laparotomy describes any surgery done to investigate the state of the abdomen.

It is usually performed when other diagnostic tests, such as CT scanning, ultrasound scanning and laparoscopy, have failed to detect any abnormality. Because of the increasing sophistication of scanning methods, laparotomies are growing less common.

The operation involves making an incision in the abdomen and opening up the abdominal cavity. The area is examined for signs of disease, and any defective organs are repaired or removed. The incision is then sewn up. The operation is often done when someone is suffering from recurrent abdominal pain and peritonitis. It is also performed in cases where the abdomen has been seriously damaged in an accident.

LARYNX

The larynx serves two functions. It acts as a valve to stop food entering the lungs and it is responsible for voice production.

The larynx forms part of the tube in the throat that carries air to and from the lungs. It is made up of pieces of cartilage, the largest of which is the thyroid cartilage. This projects outwards to form the Adam's apple.

The voice box is situated in the mid-part of the larynx, where it dilates. The vocal cords, thin ligaments covered in skin, cross the larynx from the back to the front. They vibrate to produce sound, the pitch depending on their length and how taut they are. The length and tension can be altered by the movement of muscles.

Two valves between the mouth and the lungs prevent food and drink entering the trachea. The first is at the top of the larynx and closes every time we swallow. The second valve is the vocal cords, which shut if food enters the larynx.

The vocal cords also play a part in coughing and sneezing. After we breathe in they are shut tight. When they are opened suddenly they allow a jet of compressed air to shoot out and this should dislodge any foreign body in the respiratory tract.

LARYNX, CANCER OF

Malignant tumours of the larynx often cause hoarseness. They account for about two per cent of cancers.

There is a premalignant condition of the larynx in just the same way as there is in the cervix. This condition, known as leukoplakia, appears as white patches around the vocal cords. ENT surgeons remove the patches and send them for microscopic analysis. If they prove to be malignant the condition can be cured by localised radiotherapy.

The treatment and outlook for established cancer depends on which part of the larynx is affected. From this point of view the larynx is divided into three areas: the vocal cords, and the area above and below.

Tumours of the vocal cord region vary in size from minute nodules on the cords themselves to large growths extending throughout the surrounding tissues. The first sign of a tumour is almost always persistent hoarseness. Symptoms of a more advanced growth are, among others, coughing up blood. Both should be investigated. Radiotherapy cures 95 per cent of cases. If there is a recurrence, laryngectomy may need to be performed.

Because of the very good lymphatic drainage in this area of the body, tumours above the vocal cords spread very easily. This means that despite treatment, the survival rate is low. Total laryngectomy and radiotherapy together save 10 per cent more lives than radiotherapy alone, but at the cost of the patient's voice.

Cancer below the vocal cords is rare, which is fortunate as the survival rate is much lower than for the other types of tumour. Cancer in this area is almost always a result of smoking.

Location And Structure Of The Larynx

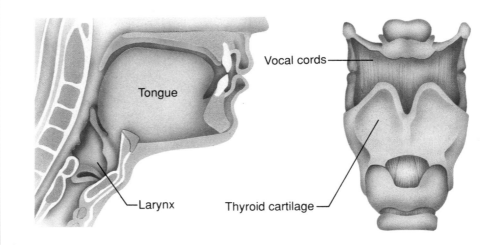

The larynx is in the neck, forming part of the windpipe. It is made up of rings of cartilage.

Tongue

Larynx

Vocal cords

Thyroid cartilage

LARYNX, DISORDERS

The commonest disease of the larynx is laryngitis, the most serious, cancer (see left). Apart from these, there are many other disorders, from paralysis of the vocal cords to tuberculosis.

Inflammation of the larynx, or laryngitis, may be due to infection with a virus, a fungus, bacteria or just because of irritation.

Whatever the cause, the laryngitis sufferer will notice a change in the quality of the voice. It may become hoarse or be lost altogether. If the inflammation is due to infection the sufferer will also feel ill with a temperature and a sore throat.

Causes of laryngitis

The commonest cause of laryngitis is irritation, usually through shouting. Cigarette smoking, even passive, can cause severe laryngitis in some people. This often occurs in those with a generally sensitive nose or skin but can affect anyone if they are feeling a bit under the weather.

The great majority of infections that cause laryngitis are viral in origin. Thrush may be a problem to some, especially to those people taking inhaled steroids for asthma.

Treating laryngitis

Treatment is the same whatever the cause. Rest the voice, write notes if need be but do not whisper — this puts more of a strain on a voice than normal talking. Plenty of moisture in the form of drinks and steam will help. Steam inhalations can be sweetened by the addition of menthol or Friar's Balsam. Painkillers such as aspirin are helpful but antibiotics are often ineffective. Gargles, mouth washes and sprays simply do not reach the affected part.

Vocal cord paralysis

Damage to any part of the nerves which supply the vocal cords will cause paralysis and a change in the quality of the voice. The commonest cause is cancer of the left lung; the tumour spreads to the lymph glands at the top of the lung and these press on the nerve as it loops downwards. Other causes such as meningitis, strokes, thyroid disease and even heart disease have been described.

Trauma

After head injury the commonest cause of roadside death after a traffic accident is respiratory obstruction. This is often the result of trauma to the larynx. Other causes of trauma are knife and bullet wounds and blows during rugby or karate when the neck is bent back and the throat unprotected.

Below the age of 40 the larynx is fairly elastic and will recoil after a blow. After this the larynx tends to shatter. If the patient survives the immediate breathing difficulties he may still encounter trouble.

Several weeks after the damage was initially suffered, the larynx may start to close up as the damaged tissues are replaced by inelastic scar tissue.

Laryngotomy

A laryngotomy is an emergency operation performed to open the larynx and thus relieve an acutely obstructed windpipe. It is an easier operation than the more famous tracheotomy and, in unskilled hands, much safer.

The operation involves inserting a knife into the larynx just below the Adam's apple. Needless to say it should never be performed except in a dire emergency and even then only if the patient has lapsed into unconsciousness and the airway cannot be cleared with the fingers.

Laryngoscopy

Inspection of the larynx and vocal cords is possible using a technique known as laryngoscopy.

Direct examination is most useful in diseases of the vocal cords where the actual movement has to be studied as it happens.

The simplest form of laryngoscopy is 'indirect'. A small mirror, mounted on a long handle, is placed at the back of the mouth. Using a lamp and after a lot of practice, a view of the larynx can be obtained.

The alternative is 'direct' laryngoscopy, used when a close-up view is needed. A laryngoscope, a rigid or flexible telescope, is passed down the larynx and the cords and other parts are inspected.

LARYNGECTOMY

Laryngectomy is a major operation involving the removal of all or part of the larynx. It is sometimes necessary for patients with cancer of the larynx, if the tumour hasn't responded to other forms of treatment.

The type of operation performed depends on the type, size and position of the tumour. Total laryngectomy will destroy the vocal cords, requiring the patient to relearn how to speak. This is very difficult for most people. The patient must learn to regurgitate swallowed air in the form of a belch. As this air comes up the throat, the patient uses an electronic larynx, a gadget which is held to the top of the throat and which emits a buzzing sound. This vibrates the air to create a sound, and the patient uses tongue, teeth and lips to convert the buzz to speech.

Partial laryngectomy may preserve the vocal cords, and if combined with radiotherapy, gives results as good as a total. Either way, the two ends must be joined and this usually means reconstructive surgery using the surrounding muscle tissue. In the case of a total laryngectomy, the upper end of the trachea is brought up to the skin as a permanent tracheotomy.

The survival rate after laryngectomy depends on the type of tumour excised but varies between 40 and 95 per cent.

LASER TREATMENT

Laser stands for 'light amplification by stimulated emission of radiation'. A laser is a device which produces a concentrated beam of light of one, pure colour.

The beam of light can be so intense that it would burn through metal, but different

MEDICAL FACT FILE

intensities are used for different types of operation. Lasers have an increasing number of uses within medicine. A medical laser

treatment of eye disorders. Since the laser can penetrate the fluid in the eyeball, it can be used to repair a detached retina, or to kill any abnormal

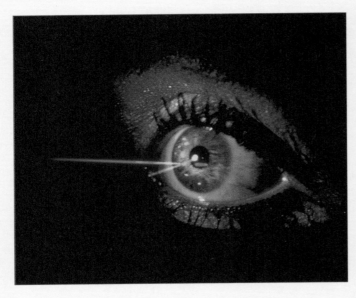

Laser surgery is used to treat many eye disorders.

causes the water inside the cell it is aimed at to boil, destroying it instantaneously. The extent of the destruction depends on the intensity of the beam and the length of time it is focused on any one spot. Low power or rapid movement result in surface destruction; high power or slow movement are for deep destruction.

Low-intensity treatment

Lasers of low intensity are good at stimulating tissue healing, reducing any pain, inflammation and swelling at the site of injury. The laser works by increasing blood and lymph flow, and by inhibiting the production of the prostaglandins which stimulate inflammation.

High-intensity treatment

Lasers of high intensity are employed to kill cancer cells. Because the beam of light is so focused, malignant cells can be destroyed while adjacent healthy cells are left untouched. The laser also stimulates blood clotting, which is useful in surgery. Lasers are also used in the

blood cells growing there if a person has an advanced form of diabetes mellitus. And it is used in some cases of cataract — the laser is used to burn a hole in the lens capsule if it goes opaque after surgery.

Lasers are also useful for gynaecological problems. They can be used in the early treatment of cancer of the cervix, destroying malignant cells, or to unblock fallopian tubes which have become scarred after infection.

Another use for lasers is in cosmetic surgery — they can be used to remove birthmarks and tatoos.

LASSA FEVER

This is an unpleasant and serious viral disease, originating in West Africa.

You catch it by coming into contact with food contaminated by rats, or by being in contact with the vomit, urine, faeces, blood products or saliva of an infected person.

Symptoms

The incubation period is quite short, between three and 21 days. First symptoms are general tiredness and a sore throat. This then develops into a fever which lasts between one and two weeks. The patient suffers severe muscular pains, vomiting, diarrhoea and leukopenia (reduction of white blood cells). The throat becomes inflamed — in severe cases, the pharynx is covered with a thick membrane and begins to ooze blood.

Blood pressure falls and the oxygen supply to the kidneys is cut off, causing excess urea in the blood and reduced excretion of urine. In severe cases, death from kidney and heart damage may result.

Treatment

Treatment has to take place in an intensive care unit. Dehydration is treated as it happens, and the patient might be given immune serum. Actually nursing someone with Lassa fever is very difficult, as the patient remains infectious several weeks after recovery.

LAXATIVES

'Laxatives', 'purgatives', 'cathartics' and 'aperients' are different words for the same thing — drugs taken by mouth that increase the frequency with which the bowels are opened.

All purgatives fall into one of four groups.

Bulk laxatives

These increase the volume of the intestinal contents. They work by encouraging the bowel to contract normally. They are the safest group and may be taken on a long-term basis with little risk of side effects. The most natural bulking agent, though not necessarily the easiest to

take, is a vegetable fibre, such as bran. Large doses can cause intestinal obstruction. One of the most widely used laxatives, lactulose, contains a sugar that the gut cannot break down. When it reaches the large bowel the sugar is fermented, producing gas that bulks up the stool and gives the bowel something to 'bite on'.

Lubricant laxatives

These include products such as liquid paraffin and should be avoided. Not only is their long-term use dangerous but they need to be taken in such large doses that leakage (through the anal sphincter) is a frequent side effect.

They also coat the intestine and interfere with vitamin absorption.

Irritant laxatives

These work in several different ways but the net effect is to increase the frequency and strength of colonic contractions. Cascara and senna both act in this way and both may cause painful cramps.

Osmotic laxatives

These act by causing the bowel to retain fluid, thus increasing the water content and volume of the faeces. An example of this type of laxative is Epsom salts, which contain magnesium sulphate. However, prolonged use of these products can cause a chemical imbalance in the blood.

Very few people actually need laxatives; the frequency and consistency of the stools varies normally from person to person and from day to day. Chronic laxative abuse can cause diarrhoea, weight loss, potassium loss, and weakness. Never take irritant laxatives for undiagnosed 'tummy pain' — they could rupture a grumbling appendix.

≫ SEE ALSO — Constipation

LEAD POISONING

Lead is a cumulative poison — it is not broken down by the body and builds up in the tissues.

Symptoms

Lead poisoning causes nausea, constipation, abdominal colic and weight loss. It interferes with the production of red blood cells and chronic exposure to lead (in the work situation, for example) causes anaemia.

Lead also affects the brain: in severe cases it causes brain damage and coma but in lower doses it adversely affects mental capacity and intelligence levels.

Treatment and prevention

Acute poisoning can be treated with drugs that bind the lead and allow it to be excreted, but the damage done by past exposure is permanent.

It is important to look at the causes of the problem in order to prevent it. Lead used to be widely used in industry and many workers suffered from chronic lead poisoning. The advent of new industrial methods and a greater awareness of safety at work now means that industrial exposure is decreasing. Workers in the scrap and smelting industries are required, by law, to have regular medical checkups.

Large quantities of lead used to be found in the home in paints and pipework. The victims of domestic poisoning were usually children. Not only were they more likely to be chewing lead-painted furniture and toys but their immature brains were damaged by a much smaller dose than the brains of adults were.

The effect of constant exposure to low levels of lead is unknown but it is certainly not beneficial. In an effort to decrease the amount pumped into the atmosphere, many western nations are advocating the use of lead-free petrol.

LEGIONNAIRES' DISEASE

Legionnaires' disease has 'flu-like symptoms. It is caused by bacteria which are found everywhere, but large numbers are needed to cause disease.

Such numbers are sometimes found in cooling plants and hot water systems, especially if they are poorly maintained.

Inhaling droplets laden with the particular bacteria causes pneumonia. However, before the patient starts coughing she suffers a 'flu-like illness with fever, malaise and joint pains. Occasionally sickness and diarrhoea are the first signs of infection.

Making a diagnosis

The changes in the lungs caused by Legionnaires' disease are not specific enough to show up on an x-ray and the doctor has to rely on blood tests to confirm the diagnosis. In severe cases the bacteria can be identified in secretions removed from deep inside the lungs.

Treatment

A few years ago, up to 20 per cent of sufferers died but with an increased awareness this figure has fallen. Treatment is with an antibiotic, either erythromycin or rifampicin.

A recent survey has shown that Legionnaires' disease, despite the headlines, is actually a relatively rare cause of chest infection.

The infection was first diagnosed in a group of American legionnaires (army veterans), hence its name.

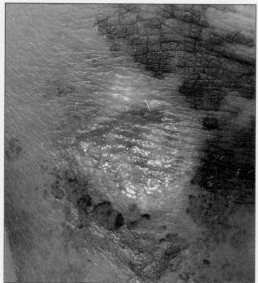

Leg ulcers are unsightly and they are also a source of great discomfort. There are several different causes, but they are all characterised by open sores, often with a red, inflamed area around the site of the ulcer.

LEG ULCER

Leg ulcers are persistent open sores, which are usually due to poor circulation. They affect mainly elderly people.

Most leg ulcers are surrounded by red, inflamed skin, and may take months or years to heal.

The different types of leg ulcer can be categorised according to the cause. Venous ulcers (also known as varicose ulcers) are due to valve failure in the veins: the blood does not flow properly and ulcers tend to form on the ankles and lower legs. Similarly, thickening of the arterial walls may restrict blood supply and cause ulcers to form. They may also be the result of pressure and immobility, combined with poor circulation, in the bedridden. In this case, they are called bedsores.

Diabetes mellitus is a cause of circulatory problems which may lead to leg ulcers. And it is possible for ulcers to develop after an injury has become infected. In hot countries, micro-organisms may cause such infection.

Treatment and prevention

Ulcers should be treated as soon as they are noticed for the best chance of quick healing. They may persist for many years. The best treatment is for the patient to put her feet up as much as possible. While it is essential to keep dressings clean, they should be changed as little as possible to encourage new skin to form beneath the dressing.

Anyone who is likely to be susceptible to leg ulcers should keep as mobile as possible, should try to avoid leg injury, and obese elderly people should be encouraged to lose weight.

LENS DISLOCATION

Lens dislocation is when the lens in the eye is moved out of position. This is almost always due to injury.

The lens is held in place in the eye by small fibres. If these are ruptured, the lens may slip sideways, upwards, or downwards, causing visual problems such as double vision.

Such injuries need urgent medical attention and the lens may have to be removed.

» SEE ALSO — Diabetes

MEDICAL FACT FILE

Implant Surgery

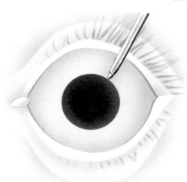

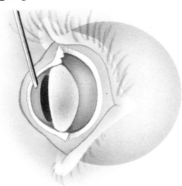

1. The cornea (a transparent dome over the eye) is cut around the top of the lens.

2. A gel is injected to keep the cornea away from the lens.

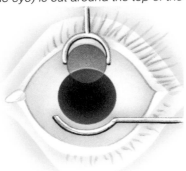

3. The defective lens is removed and a new, plastic lens, held in place by special loops, is inserted in its place. The slit around the top of the cornea is then stitched up with fine nylon thread.

absolutely clear. About 15 million people worldwide suffer from leprosy, most of them in Africa and Asia. There are small pockets of infection in the USA and the USSR but none of the several hundred sufferers in the UK acquired it here.

Infection and disease

Like a lot of diseases, not everybody who is infected goes on to develop the full-blown syndrome. Whether the disease progresses or not seems to depend on several factors such as nutrition, heredity (it tends to run in families) and sex (men are twice as likely to be affected as women).

The incubation period can be anything up to 20 years, and this in itself makes the study of leprosy very difficult. The onset of the disease is usually insidious but an acute reaction can occur with rash, fever and

LENS IMPLANT

A lens implant involves inserting a plastic lens in the eye. It is used to replace opaque lenses in cataract operations.

A lens implant usually provides a great improvement in distance vision, although glasses are needed for close vision.

The operation is performed under local anaesthetic, and requires a stay of only a day or so in hospital.

LENTIGO

A lentigo is a pale brown patch of skin which looks similar to a freckle.

Unlike freckles, lentigines (the plural of lentigo) appear on unexposed areas of skin, and do not respond to sunlight in the way that freckles do. They are more common in older people, and in people who have spent a lot of time in the sun.

They are not normally a problem, but they should be watched: any changes in colour or texture (for example, a dark brown or raised patch in the centre of a lentigo) should be reported to your doctor, as they can develop into malignant melanomas.

LEPROSY

Leprosy is a chronic, infectious disease, caused by an organism similar to a bacterium, called a myco-bacterium.

Because of its association with pestilence and plague many doctors try to avoid use of the word leprosy and refer to it as 'Hansen's disease' instead.

It is probably spread via nasal secretions, though how it gets into the body is not

This man has lost one of his legs below the knee, and the toes on the other foot, due to Hansen's disease (leprosy).

➤➤ SEE ALSO — Cataract, Melanoma

MEDICAL FACT FILE

loss of sensation. The mycobacterium sets off an overwhelming local immune response, similar to tuberculosis.

Symptoms

The reaction centres on the skin and nerves though it can affect other sites. It causes thickening of the skin with a loss of pigmentation and the loss of all sensation.

These two effects not only make the skin more liable to damage but mean that, when the skin is damaged, it takes far longer to heal. The inevitable result of this is that fingers and toes become more and more traumatised and in the end they literally fall off.

The diagnosis is suggested by patches of numb, de-pigmented skin but it can be confirmed by examining a skin smear under the microscope.

Treatment

Treatment with modern antibiotics halts the progress of the disease and limits its spread but nothing can be done to restore sensation to the damaged part. Surgery and physiotherapy, both in short supply in the Third World, are essential components of the treatment.

With effective treatment and the development of a vaccine, the hope must be that leprosy, like smallpox, can be eradicated.

LEUKAEMIA

Leukaemia is a form of cancer, in this case a cancer of the organs that form the white blood cells.

White blood cells are manufactured in the lymphatic system or in the cavity inside certain bones, the bone marrow.

The leukaemias take several forms depending on whether the fault lies in the

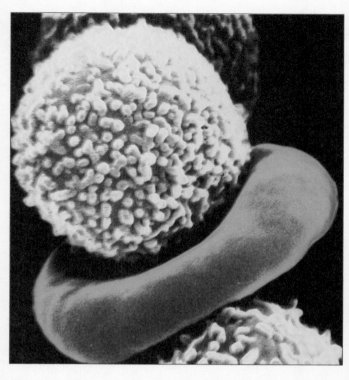

The 'furry' white cells (shown yellow) of chronic lymphocytic leukaemia suppress normal production of red and white cells.

lymph cells or the marrow. The main distinction is between lymphoblastic (of the lymph glands) and myeloblastic (of the marrow). These two types are further divided according to how quickly they progress if left untreated. Thus the disease can be acute, with a rapid onset, or chronic, with a slow onset. These distinctions are very important as treatment and outlook vary considerably according to the type.

Symptoms and causes

Whatever the type of leukaemia the end result is the same: a vast overproduction of white blood cells. These cells may be produced at such a rate that the earliest recorded case of leukaemia describes the patient as having 'blood like gruel'.

About one person in 10,000 contracts leukaemia each year. It occurs more frequently in men than women. Leukaemia can occur at any age, although acute lymphoblastic is

commonest in children below the age of five.

In most cases the cause of the leukaemia is unknown. Several factors, such as exposure to certain chemicals or drugs and radiation, increase the risk. The tendency to develop leukaemia seems to be inherited in that identical twins tend to suffer in pairs, but a non-identical twin with an affected brother runs less risk of contracting it.

The patient usually complains of vague 'flu-like symptoms or of feeling run-down. If the disease is progressing rapidly there may be a deficiency of the other blood cells so that anaemia (lack of red cells) or bleeding (lack of platelets) may give a clue. In lymphoblastic leukaemia the lymph glands in the neck may be huge.

Diagnosis

Occasionally chronic leukaemia is found by chance during a routine blood test but if a doctor suspects leukaemia she can

request a 'full blood count'. This measures the number of white cells, red cells and platelets in a drop of blood. If the white count is high and the others low, this suggests leukaemia. This can be confirmed by examining a few white cells under the microscope.

Leukaemia cells are produced at such a rate that they are still maturing when they enter the circulation. These immature cells are easily recognisable in a blood film. A special test, a bone marrow aspiration, is needed to confirm the diagnosis and to plan treatment. A fine needle is inserted into the bone marrow of the breast bone and a small sample sucked out. The marrow can then be stained and examined under a microscope.

Treatment

Treatment is often unpleasant and some patients, particularly the old and infirm, may not be able to go through with it. The aim is to destroy all the leukaemia cells but without killing off all the normal ones. The first stage of treatment is cytotoxic drugs. As these often destroy most of the normal bone marrow, the patient needs to be under the care of a specialist hospital with experienced doctors and nurses who can cope with the physical and psychological problems. Once remission has been achieved the next task is to 'mop up' any remaining cancer cells. The highly toxic cocktail of drugs which is used initially is stopped and the patient can return home: further courses of treatment with drugs or radiotherapy are then given on an outpatient basis.

If the patient responds well, repeated courses of treatment will mean that fewer and fewer cancer cells remain. When the number of such cells reaches zero, the

➤➤ SEE ALSO — Blood, Cancer, Immune system, Lymphatic system

patient is cured. For many, however, the only hope for a permanent cure is a bone marrow transplant. This is only suitable for young people, under the age of 40, with acute lymphoblastic or acute myeloid leukaemia. It is generally undertaken in the remission phase.

Transplant procedure

The patient is first matched with a compatible donor, usually a brother or sister. The bone marrow is then destroyed by massive doses of drugs and radiation.

In normal circumstances this destruction would be rapidly fatal so great care is taken to avoid infection. A pint or so of donor marrow is drip-fed into a vein. If all goes well, it settles in the empty bone and begins to grow. After three or four weeks the new marrow should be producing some blood, but it will take two or three years to reach full capacity. During this time precautions must be taken to avoid infection.

The outlook for leukaemia sufferers varies according to the type of disease and the age of the patient. Children with acute lymphoblastic leukaemia are usually cured but adults with the same disease only rarely so. Chronic lymphoblastic leukaemia may be so mild that a third of sufferers die with it, rather than from it.

LICE

There are two common sorts of lice — head lice and pubic lice.

Pubic lice are sexually transmitted and are usually called 'crabs' because of their appearance (although the French use the more poetic term, 'butterflies of love'!). Head lice are very common; most children get them once or twice and some never seem to be free of

Facts About Head Lice

● Head lice are tiny, brown insects, about the size of a pinhead. They live for several weeks, and the female can lay hundreds of eggs in her lifetime.
● The eggs, or nits, are paler and smaller than the lice, and are attached to the hair near the scalp.
● The eggs are most commonly found behind the ears or round the back of the neck.
● The eggs take a week or two to hatch, and once hatched the empty shells are white. Empty shells can easily be combed out of the hair, but unhatched ones are harder to shift.
● Lice do not jump; they creep from one head to the next, and need to be near

the skin to survive. It is very unlikely that you could catch head lice from, say, sitting where an infested person has just been sitting: if the lice have left their host, they are on their last legs and unlikely to have the strength to climb on to a new host.
● Pubic lice are smaller than head lice, and can also infest armpits, beards, eyelashes and hairs on the legs or around the anus in hairy men.
● If you find you are infested, you should inform anyone you think you could have passed them on to (or picked them up from). With head lice, the whole family should be treated if one member becomes infested.

them. Like pubic lice, they're spread by close contact, usually as children sit with their heads close together. Short, clean hair is just as likely to be infested as long, dirty hair. In severe cases the infestation can be bad

enough to cause 'flu-like symptoms — the origin of the word 'lousy'.

Lice are easily killed by a range of products obtainable over the chemist's counter. A word of warning, however: alcohol-based lotions used to

treat crabs should be applied with great caution as they are likely to sting.

LIFE EXPECTANCY

Life expectancy statistics predict the amount of life left at any particular age.

Life span and life expectancy are often used to mean the same thing but they have distinct, well-defined uses. Life span is the length of time from birth to death. As such it is an individual figure and can only be measured after death. Life expectancy is more useful. It is based on statistics and can be applied before death as in 'the life expectancy of a smoker is less than that of a non-smoker', for example. As age increases, life expectancy decreases. A 90-year-old would obviously not expect to live as many more years as a 30-year-old.

Life Expectancy

	At birth	Age 50	Age 65
1948			
M	66.3	22.8	12.2
F	71.3	26.6	14.6
1978			
M	70.0	23.6	12.5
F	76.2	28.9	16.6

Source: Health and Personal Services Statistics, 1982, table 5.

Women have always, on average, lived longer than men and more boys than girls are born each year. As a result of better living conditions and medical knowledge, life expectancy is increasing steadily but it is rising at a faster rate in women than men. Every year the ratio of old men to old women falls further.

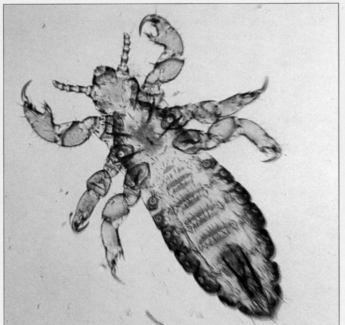

The head louse (pediculus capitis) is little bigger than a pin head, but its translucence makes it difficult to see in the hair.

▶▶ SEE ALSO — Mites, Scabies

LIFE SUPPORT

Life support is the process of keeping a person alive.

It involves the use of a respirator to keep the lungs working, and/or a pacemaker to keep the heart functioning.

The patient has to be supplied with nutrients intravenously, and it may also involve keeping the kidneys functioning through dialysis.

LIGAMENTS

Ligaments are tough bands of tissue which connect the bones within a joint, or hold certain organs, such as the uterus, liver or diaphragm in place. They also support the breasts.

Ligaments are slightly elastic, allowing movement at the same time as giving support. They become a problem only when there is an injury.

Injuries

If excessive strain is put on a joint, particularly the ankle or knee, the ligaments may be sprained or torn. These injuries can be very painful, and it is important not to exercise or use the injured joint excessively.

Minor sprains cause a swelling around the joint and are treated with ice packs to reduce the swelling, then bandaged to support the joint. Physiotherapy may be necessary.

Torn or ruptured ligaments are often difficult to repair. The joint may have to be immobilised for several weeks to give the ligament the chance to repair itself.

In some cases surgical repair is also a possibility — but this is a long and painful process.

LIMB DEFECTS

There are many types of limb defect, with many different causes.

In some cases, amputation is necessary and artificial limbs have to be fitted (see below).

Congenital problems

In some cases, limbs never form properly in the womb. This may be as a result of infections with viruses (such as rubella) or due to toxins such as the drug Thalidomide. Occasionally a limb may be damaged by a band of the mother's tissue, or even the threads of a contraceptive coil, getting wrapped around a limb and cutting off the blood supply.

Amputations

In later life, limbs may need to be amputated because of severe injury, infection, cancer of the bone and soft tissues or because of impairment of the blood supply. (This is usually due to furring up of the arteries.) Poor blood supply accounts for 70 per cent of all amputations in the UK.

The site and type of amputation depend on two main factors: the reason for the amputation and the need to provide a stump that can be fitted with a prosthesis (artificial limb). In a cancer patient, for example, the need to excise the diseased area is a more important consideration than leaving an adequate stump.

In general, the longer the stump the better the results with the artificial limb. If a leg is being amputated, operations that preserve the knee joint give the patient the best chance of walking.

LIMP

A limp, or uneven gait, may have a number of causes. In adults it is relatively easy to tell what is causing the limp, but children may find it difficult to describe the pain which is causing it.

Most limps are due to injury to a muscle or joint in the leg, or they may be caused by foot problems, such as corns, verrucas or ill-fitting shoes. Another possible cause is a hernia in the groin. Limps may be a permanent result of certain illnesses and disorders, such as polio, which affects the spinal nerves and may restrict movement in the legs, and various congenital defects. Sometimes injuries cause permanent limps.

Artificial Limbs

Artificial limbs can mean a new lease of life for those who have lost a limb, whether through injury or as a result of circulatory disorders.

An artificial leg has given this girl the chance to enjoy normal sporting activities.

The production and fitting of new limbs used to be a matter of carving a piece of wood to roughly the right length. Artificial limbs – particularly legs – are now so sophisticated that most large hospitals have a centre staffed by doctors and technicians who do nothing else but fit limbs.

The most important part of artificial leg fitting is to provide a socket through which the stresses and strains of walking can be transmitted without undue pressure. When the weight is off the artificial limb it is generally held in place by a suction cup or suspended by a harness.

Artificial knee joints are usually operated by the wearer throwing the weight of the limb forward and striking her heel on the floor. There are now piston-driven 'bionic' limbs, with electronic circuitry that picks up electronic messages from the nerve endings in the stump. These are more popular with young amputees who can relearn what nerves to use to fire off the electric motors.

In the case of Thalidomide, the victim has some function and power in the defective limb. Although artificial limbs may look better cosmetically, they are often less use than the defective limbs and many victims are happier without artifical limbs.

LINCTUS

A linctus is a thick, usually sweet, liquid which is taken to ease inflammation of the throat.

A linctus does not necessarily contain any drugs, but may be combined with cough suppressants or anti-inflammatories to ease symptoms further.

LINIMENT

A liniment is a liquid which has been formulated to soothe aching muscles and joints.

Most liniments are alcohol-based, and should be rubbed into the affected area two or three times a day, but should never be used on broken skin.

Some contain special ingredients which stimulate the flow of blood in the affected area.

LIP CANCER

Cancerous growths on the lip affect mainly older people, particularly if they smoke or have been exposed to sunlight a lot in the past.

It is usually the bottom lip that is affected. Lip cancer is the most common form of mouth cancer, but only about one per cent of all cancers are lip cancers.

Symptoms and diagnosis

The growth starts as a white patch on the lip, which then becomes scaly and crusted. If untreated, the cancer may spread to the neck and lymph system.

Sores on the lip which persist for a month or more should be seen by a doctor. A biopsy is necessary to confirm the diagnosis.

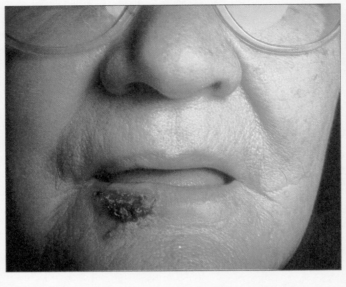

A cancerous growth on the lip is clearly visible, developing into a crusty sore. Seek medical advice immediately.

Treatment

The cancer may be removed by surgery, radiotherapy or a combination of the two. If the cancer has spread to other parts of the body, further treatment will be necessary.

LIPID DISORDERS

These are imbalances of the body's metabolism which result in an excess of fats and oils in the body.

Lipid disorders are most often due to an imbalanced diet, although other factors, such as heredity and digestive disorders, may be involved.

LIPOMA

A lipoma is a benign tumour which occurs in fatty tissue. Lipomas are a relatively common type of tumour.

A lipoma may occur anywhere in the body, but is more frequently found on the thigh, shoulder or trunk. It causes a soft swelling, which grows slowly.

Lipomas are painless, and do not need treatment, although they may be removed surgically for cosmetic reasons.

LIPOSARCOMA

A liposarcoma is a rare cancerous growth which develops in fatty tissue. It is more common in middle age.

Liposarcomas are most often found in the abdomen

LISP

A lisp is a speech defect which occurs because the tongue extends between the teeth so that 's' sounds come out as 'th'.

In most cases, children who lisp when they are very young manage to overcome the problem by the age of five or so. If not, speech therapy may be needed. In some cases, the lisp is due to a congenital defect such as a cleft palate, and although speech therapy can help, the lisp is never eradicated.

LISTERIOSIS

Listeriosis is a bacterial infection (food poisoning) caused by listeria monocytogenes.

This strain of bacteria is widespread and is found or on the thigh. They show up as firm swellings, and they should be removed surgically, although they do tend to recur.

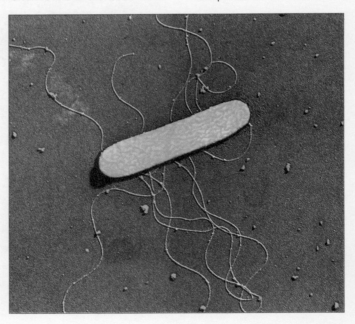

The bacteria which cause listeriosis, a type of food poisoning, thrive on unpasteurised milk products and processed meat.

particularly in the soil. It only becomes harmful when it gets into our food in large quantities.

The number of cases is very low, although it does seem to be growing. Most cases are contracted through eating cheese made from unpasteurised milk, and from processed cold meats — particularly pâté.

Symptoms

In most cases, the only symptoms are fever and aches and pains. There may also be diarrhoea, stomach ache, a sore throat and conjunctivitis. The condition is life-threatening in the elderly. It is particularly dangerous during pregnancy, as affected women may have stillborn children, and it may be a cause of repeated miscarriage. It is also dangerous to people whose immune system is suppressed and to newborn children.

Diagnosis is through analysis of urine and blood samples, and treatment is with antibiotics.

LITHOTOMY

Lithotomy is the removal of a stone from the bladder or any part of the urinary tract.

Lithotomy is one of the earliest known surgical operations: in the past, the patient was made to lie on her back with her knees bent, and an incision was made between the thighs to get at the bladder. This gave rise to the term 'lithotomy position', which is still used for gynaecological examinations (and for childbirth).

Now, stones in the urinary tract or kidneys are more often removed with the aid of endoscopes or broken down with ultrasound.

LITHOTRIPSY

The technique of breaking up stones in the kidney, urinary tract and sometimes the gall bladder with ultrasonic waves.

Small stones can be broken up without having to make an incision in the patient using what is known as extracorporeal shock-wave lithotripsy (ESWL). A special machine is used to emit shock waves which are focused on the stones. The pieces which are left are small enough to be passed with the urine.

In other cases, the operation is carried out using endoscopy. If the stone is in the kidney, an endoscope known as a nephroscope is used, and an ultrasound probe attached which shatters the stone. The pieces are removed through the nephroscope. Only a small incision is required.

After lithotripsy there may be blood in the urine for a day, and the abdomen may be bruised (as a result of ESWL). There may also be some pain as the fragments of stone are eliminated.

LIVER

The liver is the largest and most complicated organ within the body.

In an average man, it weighs about 1500g. It is situated at the top of the abdomen, just under the diaphragm. It is roughly wedge-shaped, with the thick end under the right ribs.

Despite its size it is a delicate organ and its position means that the ribs help to protect it. In thin people it is sometimes possible to feel the bottom edge as it protrudes below the ribs. In some diseases the liver may be swollen so much that it grows below the level of the navel.

Liver Function Tests

Liver function tests are used to detect disease, to measure its severity and to monitor its treatment.

● **Bilirubin levels** Measurement of the amount of bilirubin, the dye that causes jaundice, is the commonest test performed and is perhaps the most useful. Most diseases that damage the liver raise the level of bilirubin in the blood.

● **Enzyme detection** Damage to individual liver cells means that their contents leak out into the blood. Under these circumstances certain enzymes can be detected in increased amounts. The type and the level of these enzymes is very helpful in deciding on the type of liver damage.

● **Albumin tests** The liver produces many sorts of proteins. One, albumin, can be measured in the blood. As the level of liver damage rises so the level of albumin in the blood falls. Of all the so-called 'liver function tests' this is the only one that actually measures function.

● **X-rays** X-rays on their own are of little value but if a dye can be injected into the liver, usually through a vein or directly into a bile duct, the x-ray can then show up tumours or obstructions.

● **Ultrasound examinations** These can be very useful in showing up cysts or dilated bile ducts.

● **Biopsy** A biopsy is the removal, for analysis, of part of a living tissue. The commonest reason for needing a liver biopsy is to determine the cause, and hence the treatment, of jaundice. A fine needle is slipped between the ribs and a fine core of liver removed. The liver may bleed and the patient must rest for 24 hours afterwards.

Functions

One of the liver's many functions is the processing of digested food. To do this it has a unique system of blood circulation. Not only does it receive the conventional supply, bringing oxygen-rich blood from the heart and lungs, but it also receives blood directly from the gut. This blood is rich in all the foodstuffs — and all the toxins — that we eat.

Many of the toxins are destroyed at once and never emerge to poison the rest of the body. Alcohol is an example of one such substance broken down by the liver. Not only is it digested to harmless carbon dioxide and water but the body even gains energy from the process.

As well as dealing with poisons from outside the body the liver also detoxifies many chemicals produced as by-products of the body's own reactions. If the liver fails for any reason these toxins build up and death follows in a matter of days.

The liver plays a central role in handling and storing carbohydrates, and produces many of the proteins in the blood, including the most abundant, albumin. Many hormones and proteins produced elsewhere in the body need to be activated before they can function. As well as all this, the liver produces bile, an essential component of fat digestion.

Regrowth

Being in the front line of the body's defences means that the liver is often damaged, but it has remarkable powers

⟫ SEE ALSO — Bile, Cirrhosis, Endoscopy, Liver, diseases and disorders of

Structure And Location Of The Liver

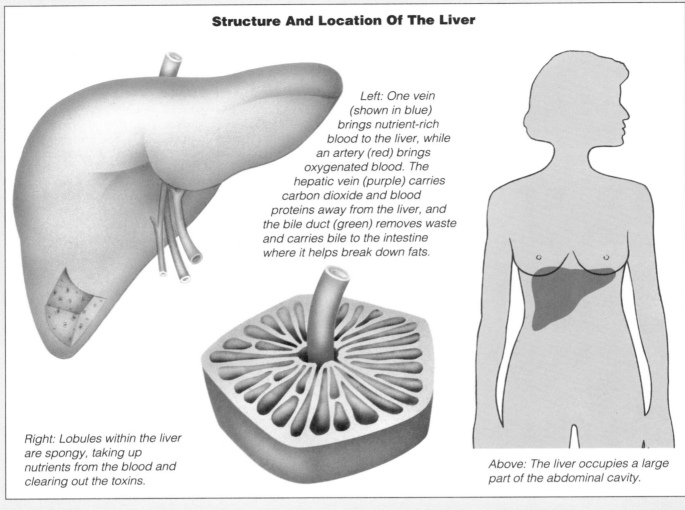

Left: One vein (shown in blue) brings nutrient-rich blood to the liver, while an artery (red) brings oxygenated blood. The hepatic vein (purple) carries carbon dioxide and blood proteins away from the liver, and the bile duct (green) removes waste and carries bile to the intestine where it helps break down fats.

Right: Lobules within the liver are spongy, taking up nutrients from the blood and clearing out the toxins.

Above: The liver occupies a large part of the abdominal cavity.

of healing and regrowth. Cut off a finger and you have a stump for life; cut the liver in half and the remainder will quickly grow back to the original size.

LIVER, CANCER OF

Liver cancer is a relatively common form of cancer, but the majority of tumours are secondary, rather than primary.

Secondary tumours are those which develop after cancer has started elsewhere in the body, spreading to 'secondary' sites. Most often, the cancer has spread from the breast, intestine or lung. The presence of secondary growths in the liver is a very bad sign indeed and sufferers usually die within a few months.

Primary cancer
Primary liver cancer (when the cancerous growth starts in the liver), is rare in the western world, but common elsewhere. It is known as hepatoma. It is a disease of middle age, and is rare over the age of 50. Men are more often affected than women.

Causes of hepatoma
Unlike most cancers, the cause of hepatoma is well known. The commonest cause is the hepatitis B virus — in China, research has shown that 90 per cent of hepatoma sufferers have been infected with the hepatitis B virus. In the West, cirrhosis, particularly the alcoholic type, is the commonest predisposing factor. Rare causes include a fungus found on rotting corn and certain toxic solvents. It used to be thought that there was an association with the contraceptive pill, but this has still to be proved.

Symptoms and diagnosis
The patient, who is usually known to have cirrhosis, loses weight rapidly and complains of a fever. There is usually a vast excess of fluid in the abdomen, sometimes many litres. The doctor may be able to feel a tender, swollen liver.

A specific blood test is available that will confirm the diagnosis in up to 50 per cent of cases. Ultrasound can be used either on its own, to see the size and extent of the tumour, or to guide a biopsy needle so the surgeon can remove a sample for microscopic analysis.

Treatment
With luck, a primary cancer will be single and situated in an area where the surgeon can remove it without too much damage to the normal tissue. Liver surgery is fraught with difficulty as the organ is so soft it will not hold stitches. Chemotherapy and radiotherapy are of little value and the sufferer is usually dead within six months of diagnosis.

Benign growths
Benign tumours of the liver do occur, and are more frequent in young women on the Pill. The first sign is usually pain, either from the tumour itself or from bleeding into the abdominal cavity.

Surgery is sometimes required but the survival rate is excellent.

LIVER, DISEASES AND DISORDERS OF

Although the liver has an extraordinary ability to repair itself, there are many serious problems which can reduce its efficiency.

These may be congenital, or due to infections, or they may be the result of an excess of alcohol or other poisons.

Congenital disorders

The liver may be affected by several congenital disorders. These range from a condition known as Gilbert's syndrome, which is so mild as to be completely harmless, through to malformations of the collecting ducts that can cause death unless there is treatment by surgery or transplant.

Hepatitis

The most frequent liver disorder is viral hepatitis. Hepatitis actually means inflammation of the liver. It is usually due to infections with hepatitis A or B viruses but may be caused by glandular

Alcohol And Your Liver

Alcohol is the commonest cause of liver disease in the western world.

The risk of developing alcoholic liver damage varies from person to person but is directly related to the amount of alcohol drunk.

Women are more prone to develop alcoholic liver disease than men and this is reflected in the recommended maximum weekly intake. At least five years of steady drinking is required to produce cirrhosis; more if the liver is given a chance to recover between drinking bouts.

In the early stages the condition is completely reversible but only if alcohol is stopped altogether. Unfortunately there may be no symptoms to start with so the drinker does not have any early warning.

If the fatty liver is subjected to further abuse it becomes scarred and the cells replaced by fibrous tissue, cirrhosis. Once this stage is reached, the liver can no longer perform its task of detoxifying the blood, and poisons accumulate.

Excessive consumption of alcohol damages the liver, causing it to swell. Sometimes it becomes so large that the whole abdomen is distended.

The most important treatment is total abstinence – all other therapies are of limited value. Good nutrition helps, but the chances for an alcoholic cirrhosis sufferer surviving five years are only 50 per cent.

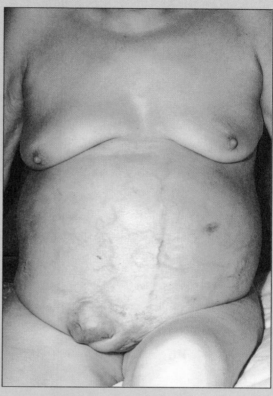

fever or yellow fever. In the Third World, amoeba are frequently to blame.

Treatment is to make the patient comfortable. Most make a full recovery, though a few may go on to develop chronic liver damage or even liver cancer. Toxic chemicals or certain drugs including some anti-TB agents may also cause hepatitis.

Poisoning

Some drugs may induce cirrhosis or rarely, cancer. The damage is usually related to the amount of the drug taken. Paracetamol, for example, is perfectly safe in the standard dose but if this is exceeded it can cause liver failure. Certain drugs are perfectly safe in some people but in others cause an unexpected and severe response.

Cirrhosis, a common consequence of long-term alcohol abuse, results in scarring of the liver. The scar tissue is inactive and tends to block the drainage ducts, so the liver does not work efficiently.

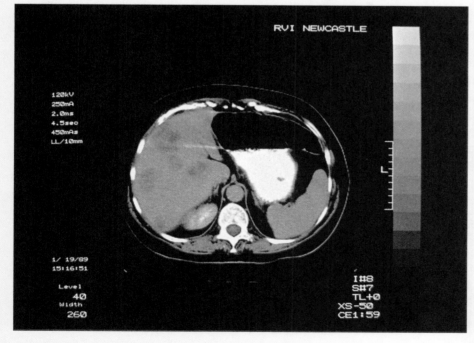

CT scanning plays a major role in diagnosing liver disorders. In this case, the liver is pale blue (left) and several dark patches indicate secondary cancer.

» SEE ALSO — Cirrhosis, Hepatitis, Liver, cancer of

MEDICAL FACT FILE

Iron in the liver

Haemochromatosis is a rare condition in which the total amount of iron in the body is increased. Some of the excess is deposited in the liver, causing a characteristic set of symptoms including cirrhosis, a swollen liver and skin pigmentation. Treatment is by regular blood-letting.

Liver abscess

Liver abscesses are rare but may be caused by bacterial or amoebic infections.

Bacterial abscesses arise as a result of infections carried by the blood, usually from the gut or the appendix. Occasionally bacteria find their way up the bile duct between the gall bladder and the liver.

The symptoms of a liver abscess are vague but it is sometimes suggested by a persistent fever. Treatment consists of surgical drainage and antibiotics.

An amoebic abscess is a tropical disease that is sometimes a complication of dysentery.

Liver failure

The eventual effect of any disorder left untreated may well be liver failure. There are two sorts of liver failure, acute and chronic.

Acute liver failure is rare. It comes on swiftly and is often fatal. The commonest cause of acute liver failure is viral hepatitis but drug poisoning, especially paracetamol overdosage, is another cause. Toxins build up rapidly and the patient becomes disoriented and confused. She develops jaundice and vomiting and rapidly slips into a coma.

Treatment consists of intensive life support with artificial ventilation and nutrition in the hope that spontaneous recovery may happen or a transplant can be found.

Chronic liver failure is often a result of cirrhosis. Jaundice is rare but the sufferer is wasted, retains fluid and looks pale due to anaemia. Men, because the liver can no longer cope with their sex hormones, develop breasts. Sufferers are often confused.

Treatment aims to decrease the work the liver has to do, by a low protein diet for example. Alcohol must be avoided at all costs.

LIVER FLUKE

Liver flukes are part of a family of small worm-like animals that have a fascinating life cycle.

Liver flukes can cause disease in many animals including man.

Life cycle

The adult fluke sets up home in the liver or lungs of its host (a human or other mammal) and releases eggs. These eggs pass out of the body into the environment and burrow into water snails and fish. After a series of changes they end up as cysts on the leaves of water plants. These cysts are taken in by the main host and the cycle starts all over again. Infection only occurs in the tropics where the right sort of snails live.

Problems and treatment

In large numbers, the liver fluke can cause obstruction and jaundice but it is easily treated with anti-worm tablets.

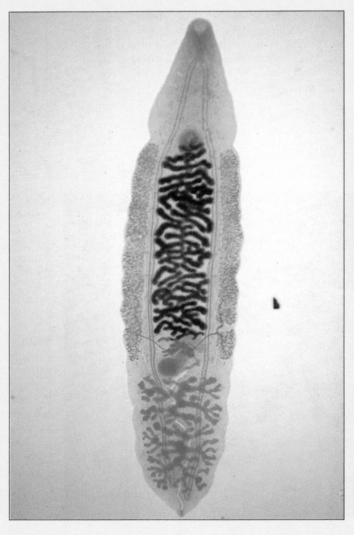

The Chinese liver fluke lives in snails and freshwater fish, and can be caught by humans as a result of eating raw fish.

LIVER TRANSPLANT

Liver transplant surgery is well advanced, with a relatively high success rate but the operation is a very complicated one.

It is possible to see the day when medical science has progressed to the point where many of today's organ transplants are unnecessary. Artificial hearts, kidneys and pancreases will be implanted instead. The liver, however, performs such a vast number of complicated tasks that these could never be duplicated by a machine.

About 3000 people a year between the ages of five and 60 years die in the UK alone from liver disease. Many would be suitable for liver transplantation but the sad fact is that more than half the patients on the transplant waiting list die before an organ can be found.

Reasons for transplants

The commonest reason for transplantation is liver failure, either as a result of toxic damage or hepatitis. Liver cancer might be curable if the diseased organ could be removed and replaced by a transplant. Transplants are also used in the case of children born with livers that have failed to develop properly. Another reason is the condition known as biliary atresia, in which bile, instead of draining into the gut, builds up in the liver and causes damage.

For some reason, a transplanted liver is much less prone to rejection than other transplanted organs. The main problems with surgery are the complications of bleeding and bile leakage.

The operation

Two sorts of operation are performed. The first involves removing the patient's liver and reconnecting the new one in its place. This is essential in the case of cancer and also in the case of babies where their tiny abdomens simply do not have room for two organs. Slightly easier is to leave the diseased organ in place and to connect the new one to it. This allows what remains of the old one to take the load off the new one while it is 'settling in'.

Liver transplantation is still in its early stages and is only used as a treatment as a last resort. However, as techniques improve it may be used to treat non-life-threatening conditions such as congenital enzyme abnormalities, where the transplanted liver will make the missing enzyme.

LOBECTOMY

A lobectomy is an operation to remove a part (or lobe) of a certain organ.

The lobe may be part of the lungs, the brain or a gland. Because lobes are only joined to the rest of the organ by a small amount of connective tissue, they can be removed relatively easily, without affecting the rest of the organ.

Lobectomies are most often performed to remove tumours, or (particularly in the case of the lungs) to remove chronically infected areas.

LOBOTOMY

A prefrontal lobotomy is an operation which involves cutting some of the connections in the frontal lobes of the brain.

The operation was widely used to treat serious psychiatric disorders during the middle part of this century, but the aftereffects of apathy and lack of

judgment mean that the operation is now hardly ever performed.

LOCKJAW

This is the common name for tetanus.

The name came into use because the jaw goes into spasm, stiffening up so that it is difficult to speak or eat.

LONGSIGHTEDNESS

The medical name for this is hypermetropia.

Longsightedness is a defect of the eye, which tends to become more noticeable with age.

LORDOSIS

A type of curvature of the spine, where the small of the back curves inwards.

A certain amount of lordosis is normal. However, bad posture and kyphosis (outward curvature at the shoulders) can cause excess lordosis, which may lead to disc prolapse and osteoarthritis in later life.

LUMBAGO

Lumbago is a general term for pain in the lower back.

It may be a symptom of various disorders — sometimes no precise cause can be found. The pain may come on suddenly — after a twisting or wrenching of the back muscles and ligaments, or it may come on slowly. Common reasons for the pain include slipped disc, a subluxation (a partial dislocation) or catching a bit of the synovial membrane between the vertebrae.

Treatment usually involves rest, although physiotherapy may be needed. Painkillers may be prescribed if the symptom is pronounced.

LUMBAR PUNCTURE

Lumbar puncture involves inserting a needle into part of the spine, to diagnose certain diseases or to treat others.

Some cerebrospinal fluid (which surrounds the spinal cord and brain) is drawn off and tested to diagnose such problems as meningitis or encephalitis.

In other cases, drugs may be injected into the fluid to treat certain diseases of the central nervous system and to inject anticancer drugs in leukaemia patients.

The area is anaesthetised and a hollow needle inserted between two of the vertebrae at the base of the spine. The operation takes less than half an hour, but may leave the patient with a headache.

LUNGS

The function of the lungs is to remove oxygen from the air and pass it to the blood where it is taken up by the red cells.

The two lungs occupy most of the thorax, the space above the diaphragm and below the neck (see overpage). They are protected by the 12 pairs of ribs. The ribs serve a dual function: besides protecting the lungs, they work with the diaphragm, moving up and down to draw air into the lungs.

The lungs resemble sponges but they are, in fact, highly developed for the task they perform. As well as oxygenating the blood, the

How The Lungs Work

● Air laden with oxygen is drawn into the lungs by the action of the diaphragm and muscles between the ribs. It comes down the trachea and branches into the two bronchi. Each bronchus branches into smaller and smaller passages, known as bronchioles.
● The pulmonary artery (the only artery to carry deoxygenated blood) carries blood from the heart to the lungs. It divides into smaller and smaller vessels.
● The oxygen passes through the walls of the finest capillaries, in what is known as an alveolus (see overleaf), and is taken into the bloodstream. At the same time, carbon dioxide passes from the blood into the fine airways.
● The oxygenated blood travels along venous capillaries which join together to form the pulmonary vein, carrying oxygenated blood to the heart to be circulated around the body.

lungs also take carbon dioxide from the blood and remove it in exhaled air.

Oxygenating the blood

The large airways at the entrance of the lungs branch again and again until they form minute sacs only visible under the microscope. Each of these sacs has an artery and a vein which are so small that red cells have to pass down them in single file. The gases in the inhaled air are dissolved in a thin film of fluid that is very close to the blood vessels. Because the concentration of oxygen in this film is high compared to that in the blood, the oxygen

➤➤ SEE ALSO — Back pain, Encephalitis, Hypermetropia, Kyphosis, Leukaemia, Meningitis, Tetanus

Structure And Location Of The Lungs

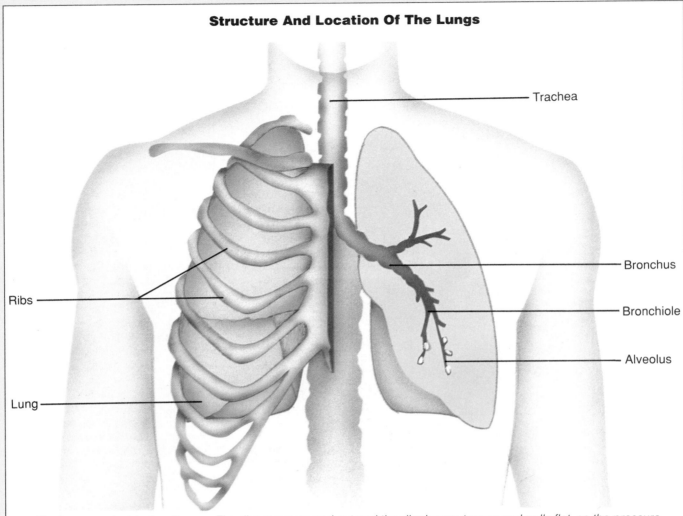

Trachea

Bronchus

Bronchiole

Alveolus

Ribs

Lung

The lungs are inside the ribcage. The ribs move up and out and the diaphragm tenses and pulls flat, so the pressure around the lungs drops and air is drawn down the trachea to the alveoli where the oxygen goes into the bloodstream.

floods into the red cells to be carried to the heart and circulate round the body. In the same way, carbon dioxide passes from the blood to the airways.

LUNG CANCER

Lung cancer is very common. It produces a range of symptoms, according to where the growth forms.

In men, lung cancer accounts for half of all cancer deaths. It is less common in women but this sex difference is decreasing. Most cases of lung cancer occur between the ages of 50 and 75.

The link between lung cancer and smoking is well known. The chances of a smoker developing the disease are proportional to the number of cigarettes smoked and their tar content. Perhaps because of pollution there is a slightly higher rate of this cancer in city dwellers.

Symptoms

The commonest symptom of lung cancer is a cough. However, as lung cancer usually affects smokers it is sometimes difficult to distinguish cough due to cancer from a smoker's cough. If the tumour affects one of the large airways the patient may cough up blood. Breathlessness occurs if the tumour obstructs one of the

major airways and causes part of the lung to collapse. Tumours at the edge of the lung may cause breathlessness by secreting fluid. The fluid collects and the lung is unable to expand.

Because of the lungs' very good blood supply they are often affected by tumours spreading from other parts of the body.

Diagnosis

Doctors may not be able to detect any abnormality by examining the chest so a chest x-ray is essential in any case of suspected lung cancer. However, the dose of radiation involved means that doctors need to balance the benefits and the risks. If the x-ray suggests a tumour the

doctor may wish to remove a sample of tissue for analysis (a biopsy). In the majority of cases this can be done using a bronchoscope (a type of endoscope).

Treatment

Surgery to remove all or part of the affected lung offers the best hope of cure but unfortunately few cases are suitable. Radiotherapy and chemotherapy, either alone or in combination, may cause the tumour to shrink but they rarely do more than relieve the symptoms.

In fact, the number of patients still alive five years after the diagnosis of lung cancer is only 10 per cent.

LUNG, COLLAPSED

In a collapsed lung, part (or all) of the lung stops working because air has leaked between the pleurae (the lubricated membranes which allow movement of the lungs in the ribcage).

The condition may be caused by injury, obstruction or infection. In order for us to breathe, the ribs and diaphragm have to work together to create a change in the shape of the ribcage which alters the air pressure within the lungs, drawing air in or forcing it out.

Each lung is covered by a two-layered membrane, the pleura. The pleurae secrete a lubricating fluid that allows the lungs to expand and contract as the chest and diaphragm move. If some foreign substance comes between the two layers of pleura the increased pressure will cause the lung to collapse.

Causes

The commonest cause is air, either from the outside, through a stab wound, or from the inside, through a hole in the lung. Holes may appear for a number of reasons but the usual cause is bronchitis or emphysema. The pressure may also alter and cause the lung to collapse if there is an obstruction of the airways, which prevents air from being breathed out. The air in the obstructed part of the lung is absorbed into the blood, and that part of the lung collapses. This is a defence mechanism: if part of the lung stops working, it is 'closed down' and other parts of the lung have space to take over. Such blockages may be caused by inhaling foreign bodies (such as a small part of a toy or piece of food), excess secretions from the bronchioles (at birth, in asthma or after a chest operation); a tumour; or inflammation of lymph nodes due to TB or cancer. Blood or pus in the pleural space will also lead to the collapse of a lung but the patient is generally more ill and the onset tends to be slower.

Symptoms and treatment

In most cases the onset is sudden with a sharp pain where the air leak occurs. The patient will be short of breath but the degree of breathlessness depends on the site of the collapse. Treatment consists of inserting a tube through a chest wall and draining the air. If the condition recurs an operation may be necessary to fuse the two layers of pleura together.

LUNG DISEASES AND DISORDERS

There are many diseases and disorders which affect the lungs, causing problems with breathing.

These range from allergies and minor infections to chronic, life-threatening diseases.

Benign lung tumours

Benign lung tumours are rare. They affect a younger age group than do malignant growths, and occur equally in men and women.

Symptoms, which may occur for several years, include coughing up blood and repeated chest infections. A tumour which shows up on a chest x-ray in a young person may be benign but to be sure the chest specialist will need to perform a biopsy (remove some cells from the tumour for testing) using a bronchoscope.

Treatment is surgical. The affected segment is removed if possible. If not, a laser may be used to clear the airways.

Chronic obstructive lung disease

This very common disease, almost always due to smoking, affects the older age group, and men more than women. It is due to narrowing of the small airways in the lungs. Unlike asthma, this narrowing is permanent and is not reversed by drugs such as Ventolin (which is used by asthma sufferers).

The obstruction leads to emphysema and the sufferer is generally barrel-chested and short of breath.

The aim of treatment is to keep the airways as open as possible, and to minimise infections. Oxygen therapy (breathing oxygen-enriched air through a face mask) 18 hours per day helps to relieve the shortness of breath. The patient must stop smoking.

Embolism and emphysema

Pulmonary embolism is potentially one of the most serious disorders of the lungs. It occurs when a blood clot, formed elsewhere in the body, is carried into the lung. If it is large enough to block the pulmonary artery (carrying blood to the heart) it is likely to lead to death.

Emphysema is another condition where the effectiveness of the lungs is severely impaired: the alveoli, where the oxygen moves out of the airways and into the bloodstream, break down, so that the blood cannot absorb all the oxygen it requires.

Respiratory distress syndrome

This is a lung disorder which needs intensive care. It involves severe breathing problems due to a lack of surfactant, the fluid that lubricates the inside of the lungs. There are many causes, including asthma, pneumonia, drug overdose, septicaemia and some auto-immune disorders, but it is most common in premature infants.

Other problems

There are many other problems which affect the lungs and breathing. Infections include bronchitis, tuberculosis, croup (a virus which affects young children), colds, influenza and fungal infections.

LUPUS ERYTHEMATOSUS

This is an auto-immune disorder which causes inflammation of the connective tissue.

The condition is long-term, and may be life-threatening, particularly if it

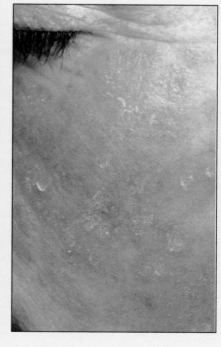

This red scaly rash is a symptom of lupus erythematosus (SLE), which may also cause internal inflammation.

➤➤ SEE ALSO — Asthma, Bronchitis, Coronary heart disease, Embolism, Endoscopy, Lung cancer

affects the kidneys.

There are two forms of the disorder, one affecting the skin, known as discoid lupus erythematosus (DLE) and the more serious form, which is known as systemic lupus erythematosus (SLE), which affects the internal organs and body systems.

The cause of the disease is unknown, but it does seem to be related to heredity and hormonal influences. It affects women more than men, and some ethnic groups (particularly Chinese and those of African origin) more than others.

Symptoms

The symptoms of DLE include red, circular patches on the skin, which turn to white scar tissue as they heal.

With SLE, the symptoms vary, according to the area affected. There is often a reddened patch over the bridge of the nose, and general malaise including fever, loss of appetite, pain in the joints and loss of weight.

In both cases the symptoms come and go, and may be triggered by particular factors.

Treatment

There is no cure for the disease, so treatment involves reducing inflammation and relieving other symptoms. Anti-inflammatory and immunosuppressant drugs may be prescribed.

LUPUS PERNIO

A rare disease of unknown cause in which purple, chilblain-like swellings appear on the face.

The disease is related to sarcoidosis (in which swellings may appear in any of the body's tissues), and is more common in women than men.

LUPUS VULGARIS

This skin complaint is a type of tuberculosis. It usually affects only the head and neck.

Small, painless nodules appear and turn into open sores, which eventually heal, but leave deep scars.

LYME DISEASE

Lyme disease is an infection due to a small organism called a spirochaete which is transmitted by the bite of a deer tick.

Similar diseases may also be carried by ticks which live on other animals. It is called Lyme disease after a place in Connecticut, USA, where it was first described. It is more common in the countryside than in towns.

Symptoms

Symptoms include painful joints and a rash but the main problem is in the nervous system. Problems there range from pins and needles to paralysis and meningitis.

Diagnosis depends on clinical examination and discussing with the patient whether she has been walking in a known infected area.

Treatment with antibiotics is usually successful.

LYMPH AND THE LYMPHATIC SYSTEM

Lymph is a watery liquid which fills the spaces between the cells in the body, and is part of the body's defence mechanism.

Lymph is similar to the watery part of the blood. It contains lymphocytes (see separate entry), proteins and fats. As well as forming part of the immune system, lymph also plays a part in transferring food from the gut to the general circulation.

The lymphatic system

As the blood flows into the fine arterial capillaries, the

Deer ticks may carry a bacterium, Borrelia burgdorferi, which is the cause of Lyme disease in humans.

blood pressure forces the excess fluid out into the spaces between the cells of the body.

Part of this liquid is drawn back into the venous capillaries but the excess, called lymph, is removed via a system of vessels called the lymphatics. These vessels carry the lymph back towards the heart, where they join the veins just before the main vein (the inferior vena cava) enters the heart.

Lymph nodes

At various points around the body, the lymphatics pass into the lymph nodes. These are small (1mm – 2.5cm long) bean-shaped swellings. They are individual organs which produce lymphocytes, and through their own small blood supply allow the lymphocytes to enter the circulation. They also filter dust and bacteria from the lymph.

Intense activity (for example, when draining an infected area) causes the lymph nodes to swell.

How the system works

The lymphatic system plays a major part in the body's defences against invading bacteria and viruses. Any bacteria in the tissue fluid will find their way into the lymphatic system and will eventually reach a lymph node. Their presence there will stimulate the node to grow and to produce large numbers of white cells. These will fight the invaders by means of antibodies and chemicals.

In addition the lymph node contains cells that can engulf the bacteria and thus neutralise them. If the defenders in a lymph node are overwhelmed, by cancer or a severe infection, for example, the lymph vessels may actually speed the spread of disease. This is why it is particularly important to diagnose breast cancer early. It spreads

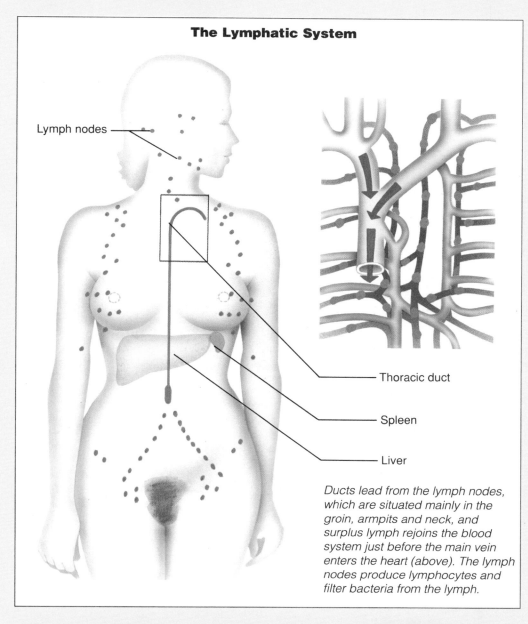

The Lymphatic System

Lymph nodes

Thoracic duct

Spleen

Liver

Ducts lead from the lymph nodes, which are situated mainly in the groin, armpits and neck, and surplus lymph rejoins the blood system just before the main vein enters the heart (above). The lymph nodes produce lymphocytes and filter bacteria from the lymph.

quickly via the lymph system.

The other role of the lymphatic system is to remove excess fluid from the tissues. This may measure several litres per day.

LYMPHATIC SYSTEM DISORDERS

There are several disorders of the lymph system, including auto-immune disorders and problems with swollen glands.

Besides these disorders, there are symptoms which arise from infections and cancerous growths — and may indicate serious problems.

Lymphangitis

Lymphangitis appears as a red line extending up the arm or leg from an infected hand or foot.

The line may stretch for as much as 45cm and is warm and painful to the touch. It is due to infection travelling along a lymphatic vessel. It can be a sign that the body's defences are being overwhelmed by 'invaders' and medical treatment should be sought.

Lymphoedema

Anything that blocks the flow of the lymphatics will cause a build up of fluid known as lymphoedema. This excess fluid will cause the tissues in a limb (usually one or both legs) to swell and harden.

Lymphoedema may be congenital, but it is not always present at birth. Indeed it may take several years to develop. In this case the problem is due to a deficiency in the lymphatic system which results in poor absorption of lymph. Three times as many women are affected as men and the condition is often confined to just one leg.

The commonest cause of acquired lymphoedema on a worldwide basis is parasitic blockage of the lymph vessels. This is called elephantiasis and is due to a worm transmitted by insect bites. Lymphoedema of the scrotum may be so massive that the victim is unable to walk unaided.

In this country most lymphoedema is due to cancer, either the disease itself or as a result of the surgical treatment of it.

Raising the affected limb above the level of the heart helps reduce the oedema. Massage will also increase lymph flow. This can be achieved by wearing a special sleeve fitted with a bladder that is repeatedly inflated and released.

Lymphoma

The lymphomas are a group of malignant diseases of the lymph nodes. There are two main types: Hodgkin's lymphoma and non-Hodgkin's lymphoma.

Hodgkin's lymphoma

The main feature of this disease is a progressive, painless enlargement of the lymph glands, usually those of the neck. At a later stage, the disease may spread to involve the liver and spleen. Men and women are affected in equal numbers and there is a peak in the late teens, with another rise in incidence in middle age.

Apart from the enlarged glands, symptoms include weakness, loss of weight and drenching night sweats. Once the diagnosis is confirmed, treatment will depend on how far the disease has spread. A few years ago this would mean a laparotomy to examine the spleen and liver, but now new CT scanning methods are used instead.

Chemotherapy and radiotherapy are successful, even in advanced disease. Ninety per cent of the

▶▶ SEE ALSO — Glands, swollen, Immune system

patients treated are cured, but untreated, the disease is invariably fatal.

Non-Hodgkin's lymphoma

This includes a whole spectrum of cancers where there is a proliferation of T and B lymphocytes. At their most aggressive they have many features in common with lymphocytic leukaemia. These lymphomas can occur at any age, but the incidence increases with the years. The symptoms are similar to Hodgkin's lymphoma and biopsy may be needed to distinguish the two. Treatment is also similar, but the survival rate is not as good, with only 50 per cent of sufferers being alive two years after diagnosis.

LYMPHOCYTES

There are normally about 7500 million white cells in every litre of blood. Of these about 30 per cent are lymphocytes.

Lymphocytes are white cells which recognise and fight infection. Some are formed in the bone marrow but most are produced by the lymph nodes, the thymus and the spleen. Lymphocytes enter the blood through the lymphatic system at the rate of up to 35,000 million per day. They kill invading bacteria and viruses by chemical warfare. There are two sorts, B lymphocytes and T lymphocytes.

B lymphocytes have areas on their cell walls that recognise specific 'invaders'. When they meet an invader they multiply rapidly to form a cell type that produces antibodies. The antibodies bind to the invaders and cause a reaction that ends in the death of the invader.

T lymphocytes play an equally important role in fighting infection. When a T lymphocyte meets an invader it destroys it by releasing powerful chemicals. The T lymphocytes are responsible for rejecting transplanted tissue. Research is under way to try to discover a way of suppressing the action of T lymphocytes which will leave the other defence mechanisms intact.

Some lymphocytes are involved in 'remembering' the various invaders that have caused problems in the past, so that the appropriate antibodies can be produced.

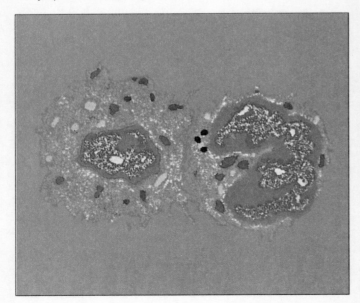

A killer T lymphocyte (left) has latched on to its target cell.

MALARIA

Malaria is a serious disease which is spread by the bites of the anopheles mosquito.

The mosquito is host to a parasite, which spends part of its life cycle in humans. Once it gets into the blood-stream, it infects the red blood cells. When the victim/carrier is bitten by another, uninfected mosquito, that mosquito picks up the parasite, so the disease is passed on.

It can take anything from a week to a year from the time the anopheles mosquito bites until the time the symptoms emerge. If the victim is taking anti-malarial drugs, these may suppress the symptoms, rather than preventing the invasion of the parasites.

The symptoms appear when the red blood cells which are infected rupture and release parasites into the bloodstream. They go on to infect more blood cells.

Symptoms

The main symptoms are shaking, chills and fever. In most cases, the malarial fever has three stages: first the patient starts to shiver; then the temperature rises to around 40.5°C (105°F); finally, the patient gets drenching sweats. The illness may be accompanied by headache and vomiting. As the parasites continue to invade red blood cells, they rupture and spill more parasites into the blood stream, and the patient suffers further bouts of fever, which may recur every two or three days, according to the type of parasite.

One type of malaria, caused by the parasite plasmodium falciparum, is more dangerous, as it attacks the full range of red blood cells and makes them sticky. The infected cells may then block blood vessels and vital organs, including the kidneys. The spleen becomes enlarged, haemolytic anaemia and jaundice are likely to occur, and the brain may also be affected, leading to coma. In some cases, the initial symptoms are milder than in other types of malaria, but left untreated this type of malaria may be fatal within days.

Diagnosis

The disease is readily diagnosed through blood samples: the parasites can be identified by microscopic examination.

It is important to realise that antimalarial drugs may only suppress the symptoms and not prevent the disease, so if you have been to an area where malaria is prevalent (most tropical countries) and contract a fever after your return, you should see your doctor and let her know about your recent travels.

Treatment

In most cases, admission to hospital is necessary. The illness is treated with anti-malarial drugs, but blood transfusions may be necessary in severe cases. Some parasites have become resistant to certain drugs, so a knowledge of the type of parasites involved is important.

Prevention

Anyone travelling to a part of the world where malaria is prevalent should consult their doctor and take antimalarial drugs. In most cases, you have to start taking these before going abroad.

When abroad, it is important to avoid getting bitten by mosquitoes. At night you should use nets over the bed, or you can buy an electrically operated mosquito repellent machine. Wear protective clothing in the evening and apply insect repellent to your skin.

➤➤ SEE ALSO — Insects, Jaundice

MAMMOGRAPHY

Mammography is a method of examining the breast using x-rays. It is used to investigate breast lumps and to check women for breast cancer.

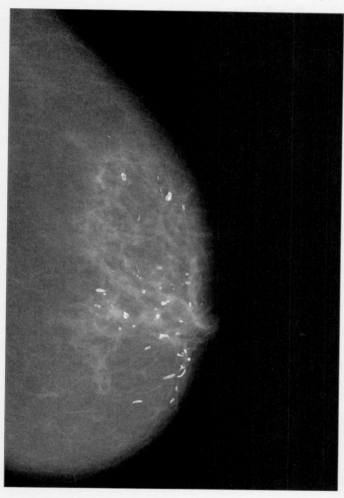

A mammogram of a breast, with the nipple on the right, showing small calcified lumps (which look like white flecks). In this case, the calcification is benign.

It is important to diagnose breast cancer at an early stage in order to treat it successfully. Regular examination is important to detect lumps, and once found, most doctors advise a mammogram or biopsy. Some women's clinics recommend mammography as a regular screening check, because equipment can detect lumps which may be too small to be found by a physical examination.

What happens

The woman being screened has to undress to the waist and put on a lead apron to protect her abdomen from any stray x-rays. The radiographer will help her manoeuvre her breast into position between two x-ray plates. Sometimes, quite uncomfortable angles are involved, and the pressure between the plates may be quite heavy.

In some cases, the x-ray will have to be taken at several different angles. The x-ray will show any tumours, but further investigation (a biopsy) is necessary to check whether the tumour is malignant.

MANIC DEPRESSION

Manic depression is a recurring condition in which the patient's mood swings between being very negative and depressed to being elated, often with long periods of normality between episodes.

Most people experience mood swings from day to day and from month to month. Patients suffering from the psychiatric illness of manic depression experience exaggerated swings from having delusions of grandeur to being plunged into the depths of despair.

Signs and symptoms

It is often difficult to distinguish depression in its psychiatric meaning from the feelings of being 'fed up' that we all experience. In general, the signs of severe depression are a loss of energy and lack of interest in sex and food coupled with constipation, sleep disturbance and a preoccupation with oneself.

On the other hand, full-blown mania is easy to recognise. The patient is extravagant in word and deed, elated and self-assertive. She is so full of ideas that her speech is impossible to follow, with disconnected thoughts and words jumbling to get out. Overspending by vast amounts, without thought for the consequences, is almost universal in sufferers. Before this stage is reached friends and family might note an increased wakefulness and an unusually buoyant mind.

Prevention and treatment

Treatment at this 'hypomanic' stage may prevent serious problems later.

The depressed patient is at risk from suicide and the sufferer of mania is at risk from her extravagance. Compulsory admission to hospital may be the only solution. Treatment consists of drug therapy and electric shock treatment, both of which can be successful. Lithium may be used on a long-term basis to prevent violent mood swings.

MANIPULATION

Manipulation is the use of the hands and knees by doctors or therapists to move muscles, bones and joints.

It is used to treat dislocated joints, moving the bones back into position. It may also be tried as a first stage in treating a fracture: the doctor will try to manipulate the bones into position, so that the patient does not have to undergo surgery. If the treatment is successful and the bones re-align well, a plaster cast can then be used to hold the limb in position while the fracture repairs itself. Similarly, manipulation may be used to stretch muscles or tendons which have become shortened, and physiotherapists will use it to treat certain sports injuries.

Manipulation is the skill learned by osteopaths and chiropactors in order to treat a wide range of disorders, and particularly back pain. However, it has not proved helpful in treating one of the main causes of joint problems, arthritis.

MASTECTOMY

A mastectomy is the surgical removal of a breast. This is almost always as the result of cancer of the breast.

The medical profession's attitude to mastectomy has changed over the years. At one time radical mastectomy or even extended radical

» SEE ALSO — Breast cancer, Mental illness

MEDICAL FACT FILE

mastectomy (see Different Types of Mastectomy, below), were the accepted treatment. It is now accepted that this extensive surgery confers no greater benefit on the patient and causes far more distress.

Surgery today
A patient with breast cancer today may well elect for the removal of the lump and radiotherapy, rather than mastectomy. A proportion, however, feel safer with a mastectomy and many surgeons still prefer this approach. No woman should submit to surgery without a thorough explanation of the options and risks involved. Many hospitals employ specially trained nurses to help patients choose the right type of surgery for them. If a mastectomy is performed it is usually restricted to a simple mastectomy or an extended simple mastectomy.

A mastectomy, devastating though it may be, is a simple operation. The skin is marked, cut open and freed from the breast. The breast is removed and the overlying skin stitched together. A pressure bandage stops fluid accumulating beneath the scar. In some hospitals general surgeons and plastic surgeons work side by side and a new breast is constructed as the old one is removed (see Your Health, Mastectomy).

Afterwards
If you have had a lumpectomy which has changed the shape of your breast, a partial prosthesis or artificial breast can be made to fit, and this is worn inside your bra.

MASTITIS

Mastitis is an inflammation of the breast tissue which may occur during breast feeding or as a result of hormonal changes.

Acute mastitis, which occurs during breast feeding, is usually caused by bacteria entering through the nipple. It is more common in mothers who are suffering from cracked nipples.

Occasionally, acute mastitis results when infection spreads from another part of the body in women who are not breast feeding.

Symptoms and treatment
The problem starts as a slight swelling and tenderness in the breast. If it is not treated at an early stage, there will be more swelling and a permanent feeling of fullness in the breast; an abscess may result, and there is usually fever.

The infection can be treated with antibiotics. If the abscess does not subside, doctors may choose to lance and drain it under local anaesthetic. Painkillers may be prescribed if the condition is very painful.

Prevention
It is important for all breast-feeding mothers to take precautions to prevent mastitis. The breasts and clothes around them must be kept clean. It is also important to ensure the breasts are completely emptied at every feed, as bacteria breed quickly in stagnant milk.

It is advisable to stretch and massage the nipples (particularly if they are retracted or inverted) during the last few weeks of pregnancy to condition them. Once breast feeding begins, the mother should take precautions to prevent cracked nipples by keeping them as dry as possible. If nipples do become cracked,

---

The Different Types Of Mastectomy

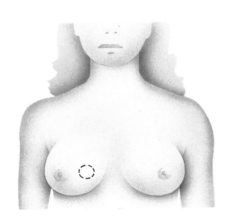

A lumpectomy involves removing only the lump, so it is not a true mastectomy. Radiotherapy may be needed to ensure there is no further growth.

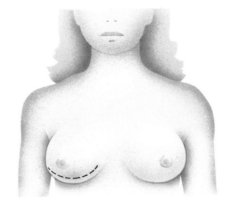

A subcutaneous mastectomy involves cutting a slit in the breast so that the breast tissue can be removed. An implant can be used to reshape the breast.

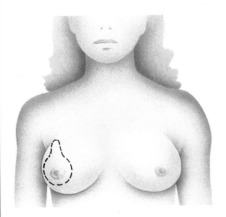

In a quadrantectomy, a large part of the surface of the breast has to be removed along with the underlying tissue. Plastic surgery is more complicated.

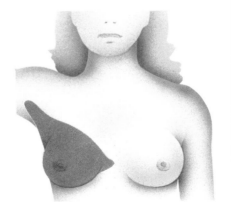

In a total mastectomy, the breast is removed, together with some of the lymph glands in the armpit, which have to be checked for signs of cancer.

Location Of Mastoid Bone

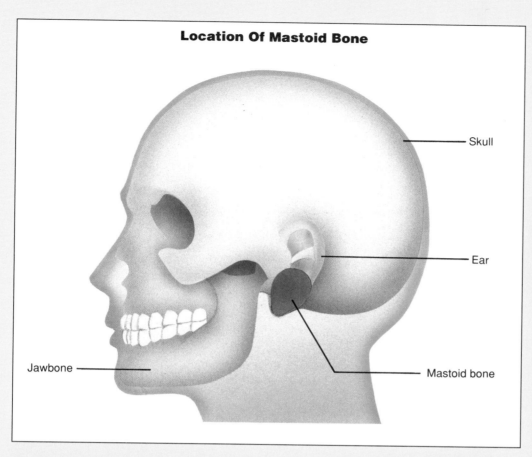

Skull

Ear

Jawbone

Mastoid bone

Officer compiles a report that involves everybody connected with the pregnancy. All the reports are analysed and published every three years. This has highlighted problem areas and these have been systematically tackled.

ME

ME (or myalgic encephalomyelitis) is an illness (probably caused by a virus) which affects the brain and muscles.

The first reported case of ME was in the USA in 1938, and there have been sporadic cases ever since. The cause is almost certainly a virus, though, as yet, no one germ has been shown to be responsible for all the cases. ME usually strikes fit young adults and almost three times as many women as men are affected.

Symptoms

The symptoms include poor concentration, muscle fatigue, loss of short-term memory and irritability, all following a 'flu-like illness. The disease can last for anything from six months to 20 years. Depression is also a symptom, but this may be brought on by the length of the illness and the financial burdens it may impose.

The subject is still controversial and many doctors remain firmly convinced that it is purely a psychiatric condition.

Treatment

Most patients will recover without any treatment. It is important that they do not overdo things while waiting for nature to take its course. Antibiotics are of no value, but painkillers and antidepressants may be prescribed.

antiseptic cream will help to prevent infection. Nipple shields are available, which cover the nipple during feeding so that the baby's mouth does not come into contact with the nipple.

Chronic cystic mastitis

The chronic form of mastitis has many different names, including fibroadenosis and mammary dysplasia.

This condition affects menstruating women, and is worse before the start of a period. Small, painful lumps appear, and doctors may prescribe painkillers and diuretics. Vitamin B6 and evening primrose oil are often recommended to alleviate the problem, which is thought to be due to hormonal imbalance.

Similar symptoms may, very rarely, appear in newborn children or in girls at puberty, but the problem seems to correct itself without treatment.

MASTOIDITIS

This is inflammation of the mastoid bone, which is an air-filled bone behind the ear.

The inflammation is caused by the spread of infection from the middle ear. It causes severe pain, and there may be complications such as meningitis or a brain abscess. Treatment is with antibiotic drugs, although in rare, severe cases surgery may be needed to remove the infected part of the bone.

Mastoiditis is now rare since the widespread use of antibiotics to treat middle ear infections.

MATERNAL MORTALITY

A maternal death is defined as one 'occurring during pregnancy or labour or as a result of

pregnancy, within one year of delivery or abortion'.

It seems almost incredible that at the turn of the century five out of every thousand pregnancies ended with the death of the mother. By 1975 the figure was one in 10,000.

There are many reasons for this fall. Antibiotics and blood transfusions have helped but much of the improvement is due to higher living standards and better nutrition. The fall in infant mortality has meant that women have fewer children so they are better prepared for pregnancy than their grandmothers. Antenatal care was almost non-existent 50 years ago but doctors and midwives today would hope to detect potentially life-threatening conditions at an early, safer stage.

Another important advance has been a series of Reports into Maternal Deaths. In the case of any maternal death, the Area Medical

>> SEE ALSO — Breast feeding, Ear disorders

MEASLES

Measles is a very infectious viral disease spread by droplets of saliva. It is a serious condition that used to carry a high mortality rate, mainly in the under threes.

Measles usually affects children between the age of one and six, but with the introduction of vaccination targeted at this age group, it has become fairly rare.

Symptoms

The incubation period is about 14 days and the first sign of infection is fever and lethargy. A profuse, watery nasal discharge develops over the next few hours and this is followed by a rash one or two days later. As the rash develops the child becomes more and more catarrhal and miserable.

A characteristic that distinguishes measles from the other infections that cause similar rashes is the presence of Koplick's spots. These are found in the inside of the cheek and resemble grains of salt. They are only present in the first few hours of the disease and fade rapidly. The rash itself starts as millions of tiny pinpoint, dark red spots that join together to form irregular blotches. They eventually fade to leave a light brown stain that may be present for several months.

Complications

Measles is a serious disease and complications are frequent. The commonest cause of death is pneumonia and this may carry off as many as one in 20 children in the poorer parts of the world. In this country the most serious complication is encephalitis or infection of the brain. This occurs in about one in a thousand cases and causes coma, convulsions and paralysis. Most patients recover but many are left intellectually impaired.

Treatment

Unfortunately there is no specific treatment for measles. Supportive measures such as fluids and paracetamol will ease the discomfort. The incidence of bacterial pneumonia is so high that some doctors treat all cases with antibiotics, but most would reserve them for children with suspected chest infections. The affected child should be isolated for 10 days: if he or she has been in contact with other children they may be protected by the injection of serum from an infected individual.

Prevention

The MMR injection, normally offered at about 14 months, gives nearly 100 per cent protection against this life-threatening disease.

MELANOMA

A melanoma is a skin growth which arises from overactivity of a type of cell called a melanocyte, which produces the brown pigment melanin.

Melanocyte overactivity may be benign (as in a mole) or malignant (as in a malignant melanoma).

Malignant melanomas

Malignant melanomas are relatively rare and very dangerous, and are one of three different forms which skin cancer can take. They may be found anywhere on the body, usually, but not always, at the site of pre-existing moles. Malignant melanomas are four times as common today as they were 20 years ago, presumably as a result of increased exposure to sunlight, which has been implicated in causing the condition. In Australia, a health education

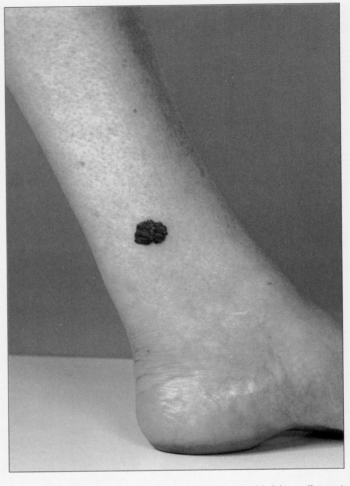

This melanoma on the lower part of a leg is a highly malignant tumour. Malignant melanomas commonly spread to other parts of the body, particularly the lymph nodes and liver, if they are not treated promptly.

programme has been introduced to try to catch melanomas early. Malignant melanomas are very rare before puberty but thereafter affect all ages.

Looking at melanomas

Malignant melanomas differ from benign moles in several respects. They are irregular in outline and of patchy colouring, but above all they grow very rapidly. They can often be felt as raised, irregular nodules. The centre may ulcerate or bleed and it is often itchy or sore. If you have a mole that shows any of these features it is well worth asking your doctor to have a look.

Treatment

The success of treatment depends on the stage of growth: melanomas spread very quicky and it is vital to treat them as soon as possible.

Treatment consists of surgical removal together with a wide margin of normal skin. Chemotherapy and radiotherapy are used in advanced cases but the survival rate is still disappointing.

Juvenile melanoma

This condition only affects children, and is a benign growth which looks similar to a malignant melanoma. It may be removed for cosmetic reasons, or if the specialist suspects a form of skin cancer.

SEE ALSO — Cancer, MMR

MENIERE'S DISEASE

This very unpleasant condition normally affects the middle-aged. There are repeated attacks of nausea, vomiting, deafness and tinnitus (ringing in the ears).

These acute attacks may last from a few hours to a few days. In between attacks the patient suffers progressive deafness and tinnitus. Attacks don't stop until the sufferer is stone deaf but the condition may progress so slowly that this never happens.

The cause of Ménière's disease is unknown but it seems to be due to an excess of fluid in the inner ear. This causes a build-up of pressure and the delicate sensory organs are damaged.

Ménière's disease is difficult to treat. The symptoms may be reduced by the use of antihistamine drugs but the condition continues to progress. Hearing aids and tinnitus maskers (which deliver a constant background noise) may help in some cases. As a last resort, in severe cases the inner ear can be surgically destroyed, causing complete deafness but relieving the tinnitus and nausea.

MENINGITIS

Meningitis is an inflammation of the meninges, the membranes that cover the brain and the spinal cord.

Meningitis is usually due to infection with a virus or bacteria and may be so mild as to pass almost unnoticed or be severe enough to cause death.

Meningitis is usually a disease of childhood, 80 per cent of cases occurring in children under five. The most commonly affected group are six- to 12-month-olds — an age group which cannot describe their symptoms.

Types of meningitis

Viral meningitis is commoner and less severe than bacterial meningitis, and does not require emergency treatment or antibiotics. It may be caused by mumps, but often in such cases the symptoms of the mumps are not obvious. Polio used to be a common cause of viral meningitis, but immunisation has made this very much a thing of the past in the UK.

Meningitis caused by bacterial infection is more likely to lead to death or permanent brain damage. The most common form of bacterial meningitis in the UK is meningococcal meningitis, while in parts of the world where TB is prevalent, tuberculous meningitis is more common. It most often

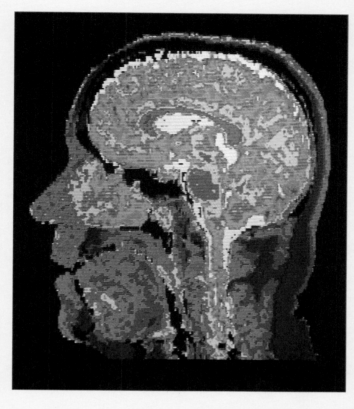

This false colour image shows a white area around the top of the brain, and continuing down the spinal cord. This is the cerebro-spinal fluid which is enclosed by the meninges.

occurs as isolated cases, although there have been small epidemics. Several types of bacteria may be responsible for the infection, different bacteria affecting children of different ages.

Symptoms

The early signs of meningitis are non-specific, especially in small children. Irritability, headache, fever and vomiting are the main symptoms, but these may equally well be the first signs of many other childhood illnesses.

As the condition worsens, older children may complain of neck ache (younger children will not be able to describe the pain, and often rub their ears). In severe cases, the child or adult may have convulsions and slump through drowsiness into a coma.

In older children and adults the neck is so stiff that it is impossible to bend it. A good test for this is to ask the patient to try to kiss her knee.

Diagnosis and treatment

If a doctor suspects meningitis she will perform a lumbar puncture. A thin, sterile needle is inserted into the spine and a small quantity of spinal fluid is drawn off. The hospital laboratory can examine the fluid, confirm the diagnosis and even advise what type of antibiotic to use.

Bacterial meningitis is treated by injecting antibiotics directly into a vein and an improvement is usually apparent within 36 hours. Early treatment is usually accompanied by complete recovery.

Even with prompt treatment meningitis is still a very serious condition — some patients may die and others may suffer deafness or other handicaps.

Vaccines are being developed against the common bacterial causes of meningitis and some of them are in general use, though as yet they are not given to every child.

MENOPAUSE

The menopause is the end of a woman's fertile life, when her periods stop.

The menopause usually occurs at about 51 years, but anything from 44 to 58 years is considered normal. In practice, doctors do not recognise the menopause until six months have elapsed from the last period. The age at which periods stop is not related to when they started or to the number of pregnancies.

What happens?

Periods may stop suddenly, or the cycle may get longer and longer. The menopause is due to failure of the ovaries. This means that they stop producing eggs and the hormones needed to nurture them. The most distressing

SEE ALSO — Encephalitis

MEDICAL FACT FILE

short-term problem and the one which women most often consult their doctors over is the problem of hot flushes. These are short-lived, but often very frequent, bouts of intense dilatation of the skin of the upper body. The sufferer turns bright red, feels intensly hot and sweats profusely. Many women experience hot flushes for a year or two but in some they continue into their sixties.

Side effects

Unfortunately, the hormones produced by the ovaries have many other functions outside the reproductive system. In the long term, oestrogen deficiency leads to a loss of elasticity in the tissue in the genital area, leading to dryness, irritation and sometimes bleeding. The breasts tend to shrink and the normal female fat distribution is lost. Without the stimulus of oestrogen the bones gradually thin and this may lead to problems such as fractured hips and compression of the spine.

Psychological disturbances such as depression and insomnia are very common at the time of the menopause. They may be due to hormonal changes but

equally the late forties and early fifties can be very difficult times for women, with the loss of fertility, children leaving home and feelings of 'loss of attractiveness' all colouring the picture.

Treatment

Treatment will only alleviate the symptoms of flushes and dryness. It may prevent thinning of the bones (osteoporosis), but cannot reverse it. There are several treatments available, but the most popular, and by far the most effective, is hormone replacement therapy, HRT. In the past, HRT was only used to replace the missing oestrogen, as its absence is the main cause of the menopausal symptoms. Unfortunately, oestrogens on their own were found to cause an increase in the likelihood of cancer of the lining of the womb. Adding progesterone for half the month reverses this effect, but does mean that 'periods' return. Women who have had a hysterectomy are, of course, able to use the oestrogen-only treatment.

Hormonal treatment is very effective and results in a considerable reduction in deaths from heart disease

and fractures. Balanced against this there may be a small increase in the risk of developing breast cancer. This risk, if it exists at all, is very small compared to the advantages of HRT.

MENORRHAGIA

Menorrhagia is an excessive blood loss within a normal menstrual cycle.

The amount of blood lost varies, but 'normal blood loss' is less than 80ml per period. It is difficult to measure blood loss, but there are simple guidelines to distinguish normal from excessive loss. In excessive loss, the blood flow is heavy enough to clot and cannot be contained by tampons alone (if you use them). Sanitary towels may have to be used as well.

With or without pain?

Doctors distinguish between painful and painfree menorrhagia. Painful periods may be due to pelvic infections or endometriosis and both can be treated. In practice, a cause is often hard to find.

Painfree heavy periods,

especially in the older age group (over 40), are often due to the presence of fibroids. These are easily detected by a vaginal examination, but may need surgery to rectify.

Subtle changes in the hormone balance may cause excessive bleeding and this is best controlled by use of the combined contraceptive pill. If this is ineffective, progesterone tablets in the last half of the menstrual cycle may work. Various other treatments, usually acting on the blood vessels, are available if hormones are not considered safe.

In some cases, hysterectomy or the latest treatment of endometrial ablation, removing the lining of the womb using a laser, may be needed.

MENSTRUATION

Menstruation is the shedding of the lining of the womb and bleeding which occur at the end of every menstrual cycle, unless a woman has conceived.

A woman's menstrual cycle is controlled by two

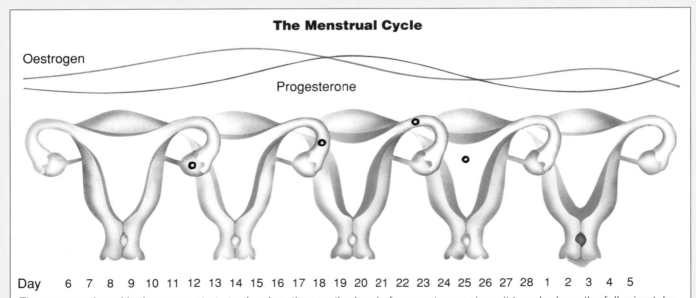

The Menstrual Cycle

Oestrogen

Progesterone

| Day | 6 | 7 | 8 | 9 | 10 | 11 | 12 | 13 | 14 | 15 | 16 | 17 | 18 | 19 | 20 | 21 | 22 | 23 | 24 | 25 | 26 | 27 | 28 | 1 | 2 | 3 | 4 | 5 |

The egg, produced in the ovary, starts to develop, then as the level of progesterone rises, it travels down the fallopian tube. Meanwhile, the lining of the womb thickens. If fertilisation does not occur, the lining breaks down and menstruation occurs.

➤➤ SEE ALSO — Fertility, HRT, Hysterectomy

Menstrual Disorders

This chart deals with the common menstrual disorders, with some suggestions as to the cause of the problem. While in some cases irregularities are harmless, they may also be symptoms of serious underlying disorders, so it is important to consult your doctor or visit a well-woman clinic.

Symptom	Proper name	Possible causes
Excessive loss of blood (in that you have to change your sanitary protection every two to three hours), but periods remain regular.	Menorrhagia.	If there is not an unusual amount of pain, menorrhagia may be due to fibroids. If heavy bleeding is accompanied by pain, the cause may be pelvic infection or endometriosis. Periods may become heavier after having a coil fitted.
Bleeding occurs after intercourse.		This may happen when you first have intercourse. Later, it is a symptom of cervical cancer. See your doctor straight away. After the menopause, it may be due to dryness.
Periods are both heavier and longer than they used to be.		The most likely cause is fibroids, particularly if you are over 35 years old.
Periods are heavy with a longer cycle than normal.	Dysfunctional bleeding.	The cause is usually a hormonal imbalance, so that a deficiency of progesterone and excess of oestrogen cause a prolonged growth in the lining of the womb, which leads to heavy periods and a long cycle.
Normal periods, but a short cycle (less than 21 days).	Polymenorrhoea.	If the cycle is too short, no egg will be released. The cause is hormonal and must be rectified if pregnancy is to be achieved. If you are on the Pill, this may be breakthrough bleeding due to not taking your Pill on time.
Scanty blood loss – no more than a smear and only lasting a couple of days.	Hypomenorrhoea.	May be normal, but is often associated with hormonal imbalance (not enough oestrogen being produced). This may also be associated with the Pill (see above). Occasionally due to damage to the lining of the womb following D and C or childbirth.
Absence of periods. Doctors define this as a failure to menstruate for more than six months, but because the cause could be pregnancy, it is important to have the possible causes checked earlier than this.	Amenorrhoea.	If you have never had a period (primary amenorrhoea), you may simply be a late starter. If your periods stop after being regular, the most common cause is pregnancy, but there could be hormonal causes. If you are in your 40s or 50s (or even younger) amenorrhoea may be due to the menopause. Other causes of both primary and secondary amenorrhoea include thyroid imbalances and other hormonal problems, as well as anorexia.
Delayed periods, where your cycle extends to anything from six weeks to six months.	Oligomenorrhoea.	Causes are similar to amenorrhoea.
Painful periods. Some pain is normal in all but your first couple of cycles. The pain is usually described as cramping or colicky. An analgesic (such as paracetamol) may be all that is needed to ease the symptom, but for some women the problem is more serious and period pains are a common cause of absenteeism from school or work.	Dysmenorrhoea.	If periods have always been painful (primary dysmenorrhoea) there may be no underlying cause, simply an exaggeration of normal pain. Primary dysmenorrhoea is becoming less frequent, possibly as a result of improved sex education. Treatment with oral contraceptives is highly effective. If your period pains have become worse (secondary dysmenorrhoea) there may be a more serious cause. In contrast with primary dysmenorrhoea, pain builds up before your period starts. The cause may be a physical abnormality, such as endometriosis or pelvic infections. The Pill may help to relieve the symptoms, but specific therapy aimed at the cause is frequently more effective.

MEDICAL FACT FILE

»» SEE ALSO — Amenorrhoea, Cervical cancer, D and C, Dysmenorrhoea, Endometriosis, Miscarriage, Thyroid disorders

hormones. Oestrogen promotes the growth of the lining of the womb, and progesterone stops it from falling away. Just before the menstrual period, the lining starts to shrink as blood vessels constrict. This cuts off the blood supply and the lining of the womb falls away. The menses, or blood flow, therefore consists of blood and fragments of the lining of the womb.

Time scale

The menstrual period lasts four days on average, but anything between two and seven is considered normal. The average blood loss is about 70ml, with the heaviest day being the second.

The menstrual cycle, measured from the first day of one period to the first day of the next, is generally 28 days, though periods tend to become more frequent with age (until the start of the menopause). Anything between 21 and 42 days is normal, even in women who consider themselves 'as regular as clockwork'. Irregularity is much more likely in the first few or the last few years of the reproductive life. Cycles of less than 21 days are not usually associated with production of eggs as these take at least 14 days to mature.

MENTAL HANDICAP

Mentally handicapped people are those with very low IQs.

Mental handicap may be inborn (genetic) or acquired, due to damage from infections in the womb, difficulties at the time of birth (such as problems with breathing), or injury.

Measuring mental ability

Mental ability is measured with IQ (intelligence quotient)

tests. The average IQ is 100. An IQ of below 50 is described as severely educationally subnormal (ESN), and an IQ of 50 to 80 is moderately ESN. Severely mentally handicapped children often have physical handicaps as well, and are rarely able to live outside an institution. About 85 per cent of mentally handicapped children are only moderately handicapped, and may be able to cope with mainstream education.

Causes

Severely handicapped children have parents who come from all walks of life, and all sections of society. Moderately handicapped children, on the other hand, tend to come from the lower socio-economic groups. This would suggest that some of the cause of mental handicap is environmental, although the way in which environment has an effect on mental ability is not clear.

Some mental handicap is

inborn, in that it results from chromosome abnormalities, metabolic disease or a group of disorders known as the neurocutaneous syndromes that affect the skin and brain together.

In many cases, the cause of mental handicap is never found. Blood and urine tests, as well as chromosome studies, may offer clues and this can be important for parents planning a future pregnancy.

Mental handicap may also result from cutting off the oxygen supply to the brain for more than a couple of minutes. This can happen at birth, if a baby has problems with breathing, and there are cases of people becoming severely handicapped after being given the wrong mixture of gas during surgery. It can also happen as a result of serious injury.

Symptoms and treatment

Unless it is accompanied by physical handicap, even severe mental handicap may

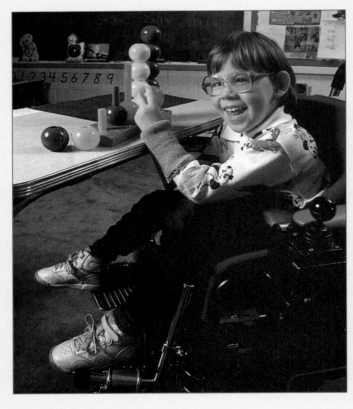

Brain damage during pregnancy, at birth or in the early years of life, may cause physical and mental handicap.

not be obvious at birth. Handicapped children are slow to develop normal skills, though they often sit up and even crawl at the normal age. This is because posture and movement are the skills least affected by intelligence.

Mental handicap can rarely be treated as the brain damage cannot be reversed. However, many ESN children can, with intensive teaching and proper therapy, improve their skills remarkably. Therapy should help the whole family come to terms with the situation, allowing the child to realise his or her full potential, however limited.

MENTAL ILLNESS

Mental illness is a psychiatric disorder which can take many different forms.

Mental illness is divided into two broad categories, neuroses and psychoses.

Psychosis and neurosis

Psychotics (who suffer from a range of psychoses) are not aware that their behaviour is abnormal, losing touch with reality. Psychotic illnesses include manic depression and schizophrenia, and some psychiatrists include paranoia. Symptoms include hallucinations, delusion, depression, loss of emotion and manic behaviour.

Neurotics (who suffer from various neuroses) may be more distressed by their behaviour because they are aware that it is abnormal. Neurotic disorders include some forms of depression, phobia, hypochondria and some forms of obsessive and compulsive behaviour. Symptoms tend to fluctuate in intensity, often according to the stresses imposed on the sufferer. Neuroses can restrict the patient's ability to work and socialise normally.

➤➤ SEE ALSO — Depression, Hypochondriasis, Manic depression, Obsessive-compulsive behaviour, Paranoia, Phobias, Schizophrenia

MERCURY POISONING

Mercury poisoning results from swallowing liquid mercury, inhaling mercury fumes, or coming into physical contact with certain compounds of mercury.

In the average household, mercury is only likely to be present in thermometers. Swallowing the small amount which is in a thermometer is unlikely to have a toxic effect, because absorption of mercury via the intestines is extremely slow. However, mercury gives off a toxic vapour, and in industry it is important to guard against poisoning. In the past, hat-makers suffered particularly because mercuric compounds were used in making felt hats (hence, 'Mad as a hatter').

Symptoms

If mercury fumes are inhaled the mercury will pass into the bloodstream via the lungs; if very large quantities of mercury, or toxic compounds of mercury, are swallowed the mercury will pass into the bloodstream via the intestine. Mercury is eventually deposited in the brain and kidneys. Symptoms include tiredness, lack of coordination, numbness in the limbs and tremors. In severe cases there may be dementia. If mercury is deposited in the kidneys it may lead to kidney failure.

Contact with toxic compounds of mercury may lead to inflammation of the skin, and swallowing mercury may lead to nausea and vomiting.

Treatment

Inducing vomiting if someone has swallowed mercury is only helpful within a few hours of the event. Special chemicals are administered (chelating agents) which combine with the mercury to create a less toxic compound. A form of dialysis may be necessary if the kidneys are affected.

METABOLISM

Metabolism is the process by which chemical reactions go on in the body to produce the different substances which make up the body and make it function.

Just about every substance in the body is the end result of a long series of chemical reactions, each slightly metabolising or changing the molecules of the preceding substance. These reactions produce new tissues for growth and repair of the body, and produce the energy we need. Digestion breaks down the food we eat and sorts it into proteins, carbohydrates and fats, and then these are further broken down (by enzymes) so that they can enter the bloodstream. The rate at which the metabolism works is controlled by the endocrine system. It changes in response to stress, fear, excitement, exertion, illness and other emotional and physical factors.

Defects and disorders

Abnormalities in the body chemistry will result in an increase in the 'building block' chemicals, and a lack of the 'finished product' chemicals. These may be a result of disorders in the endocrine system, which lead to over- or underproduction of various hormones (such as thyroid problems, diabetes and Cushing's syndrome). Metabolic disorders also include those diseases which are due to imbalances of some nutritional elements, such as hyperlipidaemia, hypercalcaemia, gout, osteoporosis and rickets.

In some, very rare, cases, there are metabolic defects from birth. More and more of these errors of metabolism are recognised each year. They are usually genetic, often recessive and always rare. They are often associated with mental handicap (as with Hurler's syndrome, left).

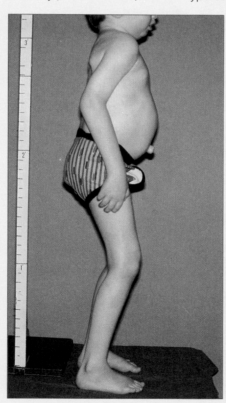

Hurler's syndrome is an inherited enzyme defect, which causes skeletal abnormalities, heart, liver and spleen problems and mental retardation.

Phenylketonuria

Phenylketonuria affects about one in 10,000 births. A single enzyme (a chemical agent which is part of the metabolic chain) is missing, and as a result, the child is unable to produce an amino acid called tyrosine. Instead, a large amount of the building block, phenylalanine, accumulates. This build-up causes physical stunting, mental handicap and convulsions. The disorder can be treated by excluding all phenylalanine from the diet, but this has to be done from a very early age (eight weeks). All babies have a blood test about a week after birth to check they do not have this disorder.

Galactosaemia

Galactosaemia is another very rare metabolic error. It occurs when an enzyme responsible for the breakdown of milk protein is missing. The body accumulates large amounts of a sugar called galactose. Symptoms appear as soon as the child starts drinking milk and include vomiting, weight loss and jaundice. If the condition is not treated it will lead to cataracts, mental handicap and cirrhosis. Treatment involves excluding milk sugars from the diet, but is not always successful in preventing mental handicap.

Funny smells

There is also a whole host of conditions noted for the production of secretions with strange smells. These are usually a result of the build-up of large amounts of metabolites (chemicals in the metabolic chain) in the urine. These very rare conditions are often named after the smell they produce: 'maple-syrup urine disease', 'oast-house disease' and 'sweaty-feet disease'.

MICROBE

Microbe is a common term for microorganism.

The term, microbe, is used particularly to describe microorganisms which cause disease.

⏩ SEE ALSO — Genetic disorders, Gout, Hypercalcaemia, Hyperlipidaemia, Osteoporosis, Rickets

MEDICAL FACT FILE

MICROORGANISM

Microorganisms are tiny, usually single-celled, living organisms which can only be seen through microscopes.

The microorganisms which are of most significance in the medical world are those which cause disease. These include bacteria (which cause problems including boils, some types of food poisoning, typhoid and pneumonia); protozoa (which cause diseases such as malaria and amoebic dysentery); fungi (which cause problems such as thrush and ringworm); rickettsiae (which cause some rare, feverish infections); and chlamydiae (the cause of many genital, eye and respiratory infections).

Most people would include viruses in the definition, though whether a collection of molecules which can reproduce themselves (a virus) can be described as a living organism is still not clear.

MICROSCOPES

A microscope is an instrument which is used to look at small objects — in the case of medicine, the objects are usually collections of cells.

There are various types of microscope available. For many purposes, an ordinary light microscope is sufficient. The cells to be examined are illuminated on a small glass plate, and viewed through an eyepiece. More sophisticated electron microscopes produce an image by bombarding the cells with a beam of electrons. In the case of the transmission microscope, the image is focused on photographic film or a fluorescent screen which can be viewed through an eyepiece. The scanning electron microscope also fires electrons at the specimen, and secondary electrons bounce off it, to be picked up by a detector, which produces a three-dimensional image on a special visual display unit.

There are various other types of light microscope, which enable specialists to look at stained cells using UV light, or with different methods of illumination to enable doctors to examine living tissue.

Degrees of magnification

Degrees of magnification vary from 100 times to 100,000 times, depending on the type of microscope. The different degrees of magnification enable doctors to analyse abnormal cells, look for bacteria and viruses, for example, and allow surgeons to perform microsurgery.

MICROSURGERY

Microsurgery involves the use of sophisticated microscopes during surgery to enable the surgeon to perform very detailed work.

The surgeon aims the microscope at the precise area of the operation, and views the site through a pair of eyepieces. He can adjust the focus and position of the microscope by operating a series of foot pedals.

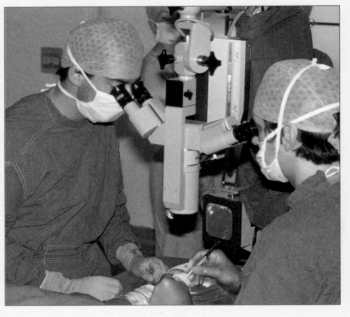

During microsurgery, surgeons look through microscopes so that the tissues they are working on are greatly magnified.

MIGRAINE

Migraine in adults is a severe headache, coupled with other symptoms, which lasts from a couple of hours to a couple of days.

Migraine is a common disease — it affects one person in 50, which gives a total of over a million sufferers in the UK. Despite this number, nobody knows exactly what causes migraine, though it is known that the blood vessels inside the brain are dilated during an attack.

Classical migraine

Attacks of migraine may take several forms, but the term is generally used to describe the features of what is more correctly called classical migraine. In this form, the attack starts with a sense of ill-health, followed by a visual upset known as an 'aura'. This consists of shimmering lights, jagged vision or a complete loss of part of the field of vision. The headache that follows is usually severe, throbbing and only on one side of the head.

During an attack the sufferer often suffers from loss of appetite, and is withdrawn. Light hurts the eyes and there is often nausea and vomiting. In severe cases there may even be weakness on one side of the body. If it is not treated, an attack of migraine may last for several days.

Classical migraine frequently starts in adolescence and is often preceded by a condition known as 'abdominal migraine' or 'the periodic syndrome'.

Belly-ache

Abdominal migraine is commonest in the children of migraine sufferers and usually starts in the five to 10 age group. The symptoms are the same as in classical migraine except that pain is felt in the abdomen rather than the head. These children are often labelled as whingers. Indeed, 'little belly-achers' is a common term among doctors for the condition.

Triggers

Patients can often identify personal trigger factors and by avoiding these things may be able to reduce the number of attacks. In order to identify trigger factors it may be helpful to keep a detailed diary of food, drink, the time of the month, and your emotional state.

Common triggers include chocolate, citrus fruits, alcohol, anxiety, shock and change of routine (it is often worse on the first few days of a holiday, for example). Migraine is more common in

➤➤ SEE ALSO — Bacteria, Chlamydial infections, Fungal infections, Protozoa, Rickettsiae

women taking the Pill. If migraine is caused by the Pill or made worse by it, then another form of contraception should be sought. This is very important if attacks involve symptoms of weakness, as some such episodes precede strokes.

Treatment

Drugs may be used to treat an attack or to prevent one in the first place. Treatment of an established attack is very difficult as the associated nausea and vomiting mean that the drugs cannot be taken by mouth. In the past, erotamine has been used but side effects with its long term use have forced doctors to look for a safer alternative. Most treatment today consists of an analgesic combined with an anti-emetic and tranquilliser. A self-administered injection has just become available and early reports suggest that it will be highly effective.

Preventative treatment is usually reserved for those who suffer frequent or disabling attacks. A once-a-day drug called sanomigran is very effective, though it may cause weight gain.

MISCARRIAGE

Any pregnancy ending before the twenty-eighth week is said to have miscarried.

Miscarriages are very common and at least one in six pregnancies ends this way, usually before the seventh week. The vast majority of miscarried pregnancies are abnormal in some way — the foetus was not formed properly, or the womb did not do its job properly. Most of these abnormalities are 'one-offs' and the chance of miscarrying after one, two or even three previous miscarriages is not greatly increased. Most

gynaecologists would wait until a woman had had three consecutive miscarriages before looking for a cause such as an abnormal womb.

Doctors divide miscarriages into several types.

Threatened miscarriage

A threatened miscarriage is diagnosed when there is any vaginal bleeding before the 28th week, so long as the neck of the womb is closed and no foetal parts have been passed.

Seventy five per cent of threatened miscarriages settle down and the babies do not show any increased risk of abnormality. Unfortunately no treatment, not even total bed rest, has been shown to have any benefit in the remaining 25 per cent of cases, which go on to be completely miscarried.

Inevitable miscarriage

An inevitable miscarriage occurs when the neck of the womb has opened or foetal parts have been passed. There is usually a considerable amount of bleeding and 'cramping' pains in the abdomen. Because of the risk of infection and continued blood loss, almost all doctors would prefer all women who suffer such symptoms to be admitted to hospital for a D and C.

Complete miscarriage

If the entire contents of the womb have been expelled, the miscarriage is complete. There is no appreciable

blood loss and the uterus is small and non-tender. There is no need for treatment but if there is any doubt a D and C may be needed.

Infected miscarriage

An incomplete miscarriage, where parts of the foetus are left behind, may become infected. This is particularly likely following an unsterile, illegal abortion. The infection may spread to the abdomen and, untreated, may be fatal.

Late miscarriage

Miscarriages occuring in the second three months of pregnancy are described as late, and are less common. They are usually the result of abnormalities in the womb or foetus and often recur. Late miscarriages should be investigated to eliminate treatable causes such as an incompetent cervix.

MITES

Mites are tiny animals with eight legs, similar to lice and ticks.

Mites measure less than 1.2mm in length, and some species are human or animal parasites.

Problems caused

Several mites cause intense itching and rashes. The scabies mite burrows in human skin, leaving red, itchy tracks, and various mites which live in grass, fruit or grains can also cause irritation. The house-dust mite lives in bedding and furnishings, and is a major irritant for asthmatics and hay-fever sufferers.

Some mites carry rickettsiae. These are microorganisms which transfer infections from the rodent world to humans.

This false-colour photograph shows a house mite in a sample of dust picked up in a vacuum cleaner.

Terminology

All pregnancies which end before the twenty-eighth week are called abortions in medical terminology. Doctors will use this description on the patient's medical notes.

SEE ALSO — Abortion, D and C, Pregnancy

MEDICAL FACT FILE

MITOSIS

Mitosis is the process of cell division, whereby each new daughter cell carries exactly the same chromosomes as the original cell.

The Process Of Mitosis

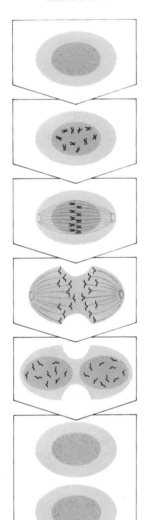

Before the cell divides, the chromosomes copy themselves, but remain joined, in an X shape. As the cell begins to split, a complete set of chromosomes is drawn away to form the nuclei of the new cells, then the rest of the cell divides.

From the fertilised egg, the single cell, the process of mitosis continues until death. Every human being is composed of millions upon millions of cells, and further divisions occur at the rate of thousands per second, to replace dead cells.

A slightly different process goes on in the ovaries and testes, where the new cells receive only half the chromosomes of the original cell.

MITRAL VALVE DISORDERS

The mitral valve is located in the heart between the left atrium and the left ventricle. It resembles a bishop's mitre, which gives it its name.

During a normal heartbeat, blood enters the left atrium, passes through the mitral valve to the left ventricle and then out to the body. Any disease which affects the mitral valve will interfere with the smooth pumping of the heart and may lead to chronic ill-health or even death.

Mitral stenosis

Normally the fully opened valve leaves a hole of about 5 sq cm for blood to pass through. If this hole is narrowed the valve is said to be 'stenosed'.

Almost all cases of mitral stenosis are due to rheumatic heart disease. This now rare, inflammatory condition used to affect children and young adults and is the result of a streptococcal infection. Rheumatic mitral stenosis is much more common in women than men and is due to a gradual thickening of the valve tissue. The extra strain that this places on the heart means that pressure builds up in the lungs so that a number of serious complications occur.

The first symptoms of mitral stenosis are usually shortness of breath and a cough which produces blood-flecked plegm. As the disease progresses, the pulse becomes irregular and the lower limbs swell.

A diagnosis of mitral stenosis is often suggested by an abnormal chest x-ray or ECG, but an echocardiogram, a moving picture of the valve using sound waves, is needed to confirm the diagnosis.

In mild cases the only treatment needed may be antibiotic therapy for chest infections. In severe cases the valve may need to be forced open or replaced with an artificial valve.

Mitral regurgitation

In mitral regurgitation the valve allows blood to pass in both directions. Contractions of the ventricle will thus force blood back into the atrium causing it to swell and become more and more muscular. Again, most cases are due to rheumatic fever, but a considerable number are caused by a floppy, or prolapsing, valve.

Mitral regurgitation may be present for many years without causing any apparent problem. In the later stages of the disease it can cause breathlessness and fatigue. Untreated it can lead to heart failure and death.

Mild mitral regurgitation can usually be controlled with diuretic drugs. More severe symptoms indicate the need for surgery to replace or repair the damaged valve.

MMR VACCINATION

The MMR vaccine protects against mumps, measles and rubella (German measles).

MMR is recommended for children of either sex between the ages of one and two years. It is also recommended for pre-school children who missed out the first time round, regardless of whether they have had mumps, measles or rubella.

The MMR vaccine is very effective and has a low incidence of side effects. Some children develop a mild viral illness about a week after the immunisation, about one in 100 develop mumps-like swellings and one in 1000 suffer convulsions. Alarming though they may sound, these convulsions are harmless and may well be prevented by giving paracetamol between the fourth and tenth days after the injection.

Who should not be immunised?

There are very few children who cannot be immunised but immunisation should be delayed if the child has a temperature. Children who should not receive the vaccine include those with untreated cancers, immune disorders and severe allergies to egg. If the MMR vaccine is given to women of child-bearing years, pregnancy should be avoided for one month.

Unimmunised adolescent girls and women contemplating pregnancy should be checked for immunity to rubella and immunised with the pure rubella vaccine if necessary.

MONONUCLEOSIS

Mononucleosis is a viral infection which causes a fever and swelling of the lymph nodes.

It is more commonly known as glandular fever, and used to be called the kissing disease, because it mainly affects adolescents.

>> SEE ALSO — German measles, Glandular fever, Heart failure, Measles, Rheumatic fever

MEDICAL FACT FILE

MORPHINE

Morphine is a painkilling drug which is derived from the opium poppy.

Morphine is a narcotic drug; it induces numbness and stupor at the same time as relieving the pain. It is used only for very severe pain, in such cases as heart attack, cancer, after major surgery and in cases of serious injury.

Side effects and abuse

Morphine may cause constipation, nausea, drowsiness, dizziness and constipation. Its euphoric effect means that it is illegally abused, and long-term use may lead to craving, tolerance and physical dependence.

MORTALITY

Mortality is the death rate of the population. It is expressed as the number of deaths per year per 100,000 of the population.

In the UK, statistics are published which indicate the cause of death, and mortality statistics also indicate other factors, such as the sex, age and socio-economic group. In the UK, heart and circulatory problems are by far the biggest cause of death, while cancer and respiratory diseases are other major causes.

MOSQUITO BITES

Mosquito bites are irritating in temperate climates, but in some parts of the world the mosquito can carry infection and disease.

There are three main groups of disease-carrying mosquito: the anopheles mosquito (which transmits

malaria and filariasis, a disease which affects the lymphatic system), the culex mosquito (which transmits viral encephalitis and filariasis) and the ades species, (which can transmit yellow fever, viral encephalitis and dengue, a tropical disease with symptoms of fever, headache and rash).

Avoiding mosquito bites

There are many precautions to take against mosquitoes (in all parts of the world) including the use of spray repellents, special burners and electrically heated pads. It is also advisable to keep ankles and arms covered at dusk, when mosquitoes seem to be at their hungriest.

Treating bites

If you are bitten, wash the bitten area thoroughly and apply a soothing ointment or lotion, such as calamine. It is important to avoid scratching mosquito bites, and if children are bitten, keep their fingernails clean to help prevent the bites becoming infected.

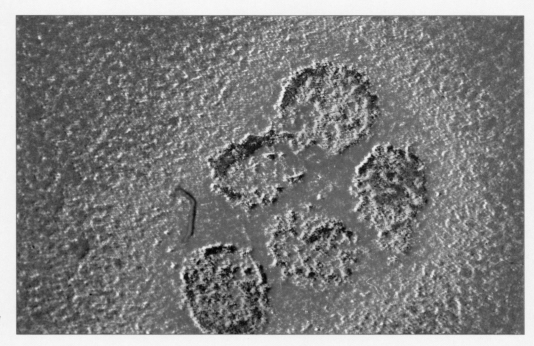

This false colour image shows virus particles of the yellow fever virus, which is carried by mosquitoes. Infection in humans occurs following a bite by a yellow-fever-carrying mosquito.

MOTOR NEURON DISEASE

Motor neuron disease, or MND, is a degenerative disorder in which the spinal nerves that control movement, the motor neurons, are destroyed.

The main symptoms of MND are weakness and wasting of all the muscles in the body, usually starting with the small muscles of the hands and feet and gradually spreading up the arms and legs. At the same time as they are wasting, the muscles are often overcome by a form of movement known as fasciculation — small, unco-ordinated twitches, due to the random contraction of tiny pieces of muscle.

Variations occur in the symptoms, depending on which groups of muscles are affected most. If the muscles of the pharynx are damaged the patient has great difficulty swallowing and speaking.

A rare, fatal disease

Eventually the whole body becomes paralysed and the

disease is always fatal within two to 10 years of diagnosis, usually due to respiratory problems and pneumonia.

Motor neuron disease affects about six people per 100,000 and men and women are affected equally. Unlike multiple sclerosis, it is a disease of middle age and rarely affects the under 50s.

The diagnosis can be confirmed by nerve conduction studies, but the pattern of the illness is so typical that there is rarely any doubt. As yet, no treatment has been shown to be of any value, and the cause of the disease is unknown.

MOUNTAIN SICKNESS

Mountain sickness is a disease caused by reduction of atmospheric pressure, which affects climbers and skiers who ascend mountains too quickly.

In mild cases the symptoms include headache, nausea and

➤➤ SEE ALSO — Insects

dizziness, often with mental confusion. In more severe cases, fluid builds up in the lungs, causing coughing and breathlessness and the phlegm becomes frothy. If fluid builds up around the brain, there may also be vomiting, hallucinations and sometimes a coma.

Causes

The exact mechanism which causes the condition is not known, but it only occurs in people who climb to over 2400m, and do so at the rate of more than about 600m per day, without allowing rest days to acclimatise. The reduced oxygen in the blood at high altitudes, and other changes in the body's chemistry, affect the heart, lungs and nervous system.

Treatment

At the first sign of a problem, the climber should rest. In a couple of days, symptoms should disappear. If there are more serious symptoms the climber should be brought down from the mountain immediately, and be given oxygen. If the brain has been affected, the sufferer may need to rest in hospital. Delay in treatment can cause brain damage and death.

MOUTH CANCER

Cancerous growths in the mouth may occur on the lips or the tongue, or elsewhere in the oral cavity, including the floor of the mouth, the inside of the cheeks, the gums and the roof of the mouth.

There are several factors associated with the development of mouth cancer, particularly heavy drinking of spirits, smoking, badly fitting dentures and dental decay. Oral cancers are more common in men, and rarely develop before the age of 40. They account for about five per cent of all malignant growths.

Symptoms

The most noticeable pre-cancerous condition is leukoplakia, small raised white patches in the mouth, which are usually painless. Although only five per cent of cases of leukoplakia develop into cancer, it should not be ignored. It is more common in smokers. All cases should be treated by surgery or by freezing the lesion with a liquid nitrogen probe.

As tumours grow, they may develop into crusty growths or deep cracks (particularly in the case of the

tongue) and the condition gradually becomes more painful.

If the growth spreads to the tonsils, swallowing and speech become very difficult.

Mouth cancers often become infected and this may cause severe halitosis.

Diagnosis and treatment

Any sore patch, lump or discoloration in the mouth which does not clear up within a month should be reported to your doctor. He will examine the problem, and may do a biopsy.

Before treatment can start, the mouth must be cleaned with antibacterial mouthwashes and any rotten teeth removed. All cancerous tissue should be removed surgically, and radiotherapy may also be necessary. If the growth has spread to the lymph nodes, more extensive surgery is necessary.

The earlier the cancer is diagnosed, the better the chances of successful treatment. However, surgery may be very disfiguring, and cause problems with eating and speaking.

MOUTH DISORDERS

Disorders of the mouth are very common and often cause pain and suffering out of all proportion to the severity of the disease.

Doctors distinguish between diseases of the lips and oral cavity, and disease of the tongue.

Stomatitis

Inflammation of the lips and oral cavity is called stomatitis. It may be due to infection with viruses, bacteria or fungi. Viral stomatitis can be caused by the herpes simplex virus. This may produce cold sores or a more generalised, very

painful inflammation. The condition is recurrent but treatment is possible with the antiviral agent Zovirax.

The commonest cause of fungal stomatitis is candida or thrush. This is usually only a problem in babies, often as a result of poor hygiene. It is rare in adults and generally only affects individuals already weakened by illness. White patches, often joining together to form a film, are seen over the cheeks and tongue. The area between the patches looks very red and sore. Treatment, which may take many weeks, is with specific anti-fungal lozenges or gels.

Bacterial stomatitis is rare in this country, except as an accompaniment to tonsillitis.

The glandular fever virus, as well as affecting the throat, may cause a red, irritating rash on the palate. There is no specific treatment, but sucking ice cubes may relieve some of the discomfort.

Ulceration

The commonest non-infective mouth condition is aphthous ulceration. This consists of very painful ulcers which affect the top layer of skin and are surrounded by an area of redness. They are often multiple and recurrent, and tend to affect teenagers and young adults the most. Nobody knows the cause of aphthous ulcers, but they are common in anaemic patients and in the pre-menstrual phase. In mild cases, analgesic gels such as Bonjela may be effective but in severe cases steroids will have to be applied.

Tongue disorders

Diseases of the tongue are so common that most doctors will ask patients to put their tongues out as a matter of course in examinations. The tongue also gives valuable clues to disease in other organs. A smooth, pale

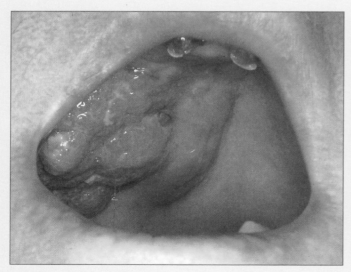

A cancerous growth on the roof of the mouth may be caused by heavy drinking, smoking or by poor oral hygiene.

SEE ALSO — Lip cancer, Teeth, Tongue

tongue, for example, may be a sign of iron-deficiency anaemia. Many patients are alarmed by what is known as a 'geographical tongue'. This describes a raised, pale area with clearly demarcated edges. It looks exactly like a relief map of an island, hence its name. It is completely harmless and can safely be ignored.

MRI

Magnetic resonance imaging (MRI) is a diagnostic tool which is used to build up images of internal organs.

MRI is becoming more widely used as fears over the safety of x-rays increase.

How does it work?
The patient lies in a circular electromagnet. A powerful magnetic field is used to line up the protons in the hydrogen atoms inside every body cell.

A radio wave is applied at right angles to the magnetic field and the protons rotate through a right angle. When the electric field is switched off, the protons flip back to their original position, and, in so doing, generate energy.

The amount of energy produced depends on the amount of water in the cell and this differs according to

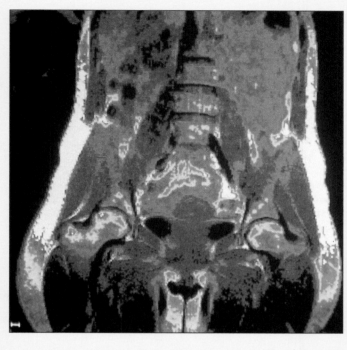

This false-colour NMR scan shows quite clearly the hip joints, thigh bones and spinal vertebrae of a normal female torso.

whether it is blood, bone or other tissues.

Using a computer, a complex picture can be built up, just like a slice through the body. From the point of view of the patient, the magnetic field and the radio waves are painless.

Uses of imaging
The uses of MRI are growing daily, but its original and possibly its most useful application is in the field of neurology. It can show up minute scars and tumours on the brain or even detect the nerve damage of multiple

sclerosis. MRI scans of the spine can pinpoint pressure and help the surgeon plan operations.

Imaging the heart is made more difficult by its constant movement, which blurs the image. This can be overcome by arranging to take each picture at exactly the same moment in each heart beat. Scans of the heart are now reaching the stage where cholesterol deposits can be seen before they block the arteries, thus giving the patient a chance to reverse the damage.

The uses of MRI in the future are only limited by its enormous cost.

nobody knows why.

The commonest age of onset is 20-35 and there are an estimated 50,000 sufferers in the UK. Although MS occurs worldwide, it is more common the further you live from the equator. Statistically, sufferers are likely to have certain genetic features in their blood, but inheritance seems to play only a minor role in the cause of the disease. Many theories have been proposed as to the actual cause, including infection and diet. So far, all attempts to transmit MS artificially have failed and it seems certain that MS is not an infectious disease.

Symptoms
There are two forms of MS — relapsing and remitting (where the symptoms appear and then disappear, only to reappear in a different site) and chronic progressive (where symptoms stay and get steadily worse).

Whichever the form, MS may present itself in several ways, depending on which nerve is damaged. If the optic nerve is affected, the patient will complain of blurred vision and possibly pain in one eye. Typically, vision deteriorates over the course of a few weeks and then recovers spontaneously. Recovery may seem complete but an optician can often spot telltale signs on the retina.

If demyelination affects the base of the brain, it can cause double vision, dizziness, and numbness of the face. If it affects one of the spinal nerves it can cause weakness, pins-and-needles, numbness and paralysis. The nerves to the bladder are commonly involved and this often causes incontinence.

In the later stages, both types of MS can cause severe disability with complete paralysis and dementia. Death is usually the result of kidney failure or

How Safe?

A major concern when any new technique is developed is safety.

So far, MRI seems to be free of any side effects, but its long-term safety cannot be guaranteed. It is known, however, that workers in physics laboratories have been exposed to much higher magnetic fields without coming to any harm.

Obviously, a magnet will attract some metals, so the technique should be used with discretion on certain patients. Most metal joints are not a problem, but some of the metal clips used in brain surgery may be twisted or pulled off and this seems to be the major safety fear.

MS

Multiple sclerosis (MS) is a relatively common, but incurable, disease affecting the nerves in the brain or spinal cord.

The nerves become stripped of myelin, the insulating coat that surrounds them. This 'demyelination' may occur anywhere within the brain or spinal cord but

▶▶ SEE ALSO — X-ray

bronchopneumonia. There is no clear way of predicting how the disease will progress in any one individual. Many MS sufferers live full and useful lives, whilst others become disabled rapidly.

Diagnosis and treatment

Diagnosis is usually made by looking at the symptoms, because until recently no test was sufficiently reliable. MRI can show areas of demyelination within the brain and is useful in cases where the diagnosis is in doubt.

Not surprisingly in a disease that tends to come and go, there have been many claims of 'wonder cures', all of which have proved to be useless. Amongst the suggestions have been heat, cold, high pressure, vaccines, diet, sunflower seed oil and even arsenic. Short courses of steroids seem to have some

benefit in that they can shorten the course of an attack, but the overall outlook remains the same.

MUCUS AND MUCOUS MEMBRANES

Mucus is a sticky, lubricating fluid which is secreted by the mucous membranes.

The mucous membranes are a red/pink, skin-like layer which form the lining of many parts of the body. These include the respiratory passages, the digestive tract, the lining of the eyelids and the genital passages.

Mucus helps to keep the moisture of the body in, and lubricates the passages involved. In addition to acting as a lubricant, mucus is also

part of the body's defence against invading bacteria.

In the digestive tract, the mucus facilitates swallowing and prevents stomach acid and enzymes from breaking down the walls of the intestine. In the respiratory system, the mucus helps to prevent foreign bodies from reaching the lungs. Mucus also lubricates the eyeball to protect it from foreign bodies, and in the vagina it lubricates the lining during sexual intercourse.

MUMPS

Mumps is a highly infectious viral disease.

The main feature is swelling of the parotid glands, the salivary glands at the angle of the jaw.

Spreading infection

Mumps is spread by droplets of saliva, direct contact, or through shared use of personal objects such as knives and forks.

No age is exempt from infection but, because of maternal antibodies, it is rare before the age of two. School-age children and young adults are most frequently affected. The incubation period is about 18 days. The patient is most infectious two or three days before and two or three days after the swelling appears.

Symptoms

The first sign of an attack is generally a 'flu-like illness with fever, malaise and loss of appetite. This is followed, a day or two later, by severe pain at the angle of the jaw. The swelling usually affects both sides, though in some cases only one side is affected. The swollen gland hides the angle of the jaw and may displace the earlobe. At this stage the pain may be so intense that the sufferer is unable to open her mouth.

Vaccination

Vaccination against mumps has proved very successful.

Live, specially weakened virus can be used to vaccinate children over the age of one year. This vaccine may be given on its own or as part of the three-in-one MMR vaccine. Vaccination should not given to immunosuppressed individuals, to children with fever or during pregnancy.

Complications are common, with five per cent of patients developing meningitis. Fortunately this settles without treatment. Thirty per cent of men who develop mumps after puberty suffer acute epididymo-orchitis — swelling of the testicles. In a small number of cases this can cause permanent sterility. A small percentage of women develop oophritis, an inflammation of the ovaries. Mastitis, hepatitis and pancreatitis may also occur.

Diagnosis and treatment

The diagnosis of mumps is usually made through examination, and the doctor's experience of the disease. However, the new MMR vaccine is so successful that a whole generation of GPs is growing up without ever having seen a case. Blood tests can confirm the diagnosis if there is any doubt.

Treatment involves strong analgesics for the pain, and plenty of fluid must be drunk. Fresh pineapple helps to keep the mouth clean and refreshed. Some doctors advocate the use of steroids to suppress testicular or ovarian swelling.

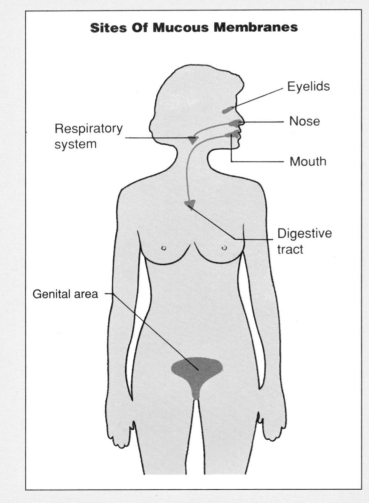

Sites Of Mucous Membranes

- Eyelids
- Nose
- Mouth
- Respiratory system
- Digestive tract
- Genital area

➤➤ SEE ALSO — Meningitis, Orchitis

MEDICAL FACT FILE

MUNCHAUSEN'S SYNDROME

A rare disorder in which the sufferer claims to have various symptoms in order to get attention.

People suffering from Munchausen's syndrome will invent or induce symptoms in order to get treatment from doctors. Commonly invented symptoms include abdominal pain, dizziness, fever, rashes and so on. Many patients aim to get themselves admitted to hospital for investigatory operations and treatment.

In Munchausen's by proxy, parents claim that their children are showing particular symptoms, and there have been cases where children have had to undergo unnecessary operations.

The causes of Munchausen's are not understood, but sufferers are clearly seeking attention. Treatment is aimed at discovering underlying psychological causes and preventing unnecessary treatment.

MUSCLE TYPES

There are three types of muscle in the body, classified according to their structure and the way they operate.

The only function of a muscle, whatever its type, is to contract.

Skeletal muscle
The bulk of the muscle in the body is skeletal. This is the name given to the muscle that produces movement of the skeleton. Skeletal muscle is under voluntary control — we can make a conscious decision when to contract it. When skeletal muscle is activated the two ends, or insertions, are brought closer together, tensing the muscles or altering the relative positions of the bones to which they are connected. Skeletal muscles are usually arranged in such a way that when they contract they pull two bones closer together. They often work in pairs, so that another muscle pulls the bones back again.

Smooth muscle
Smooth muscle is found in many places, including the gut and in the valves that keep the bladder and rectum closed. It also forms the wall of the uterus, which contracts during childbirth. Smooth muscle is under involuntary control. Its state of contraction depends upon hormones and the autonomic nervous system.

In contrast to skeletal muscle, the fibres of smooth muscle are usually joined to each other to form a ring. When the fibres are activated, the ring constricts. If the activity is sufficiently well controlled, a wave of contraction can be made to pass along a hollow tube such as the gut.

Cardiac muscle
Cardiac muscle is only found in the heart. It has the property of spontaneous and rhythmical contraction without outside control.

MUSCLE DISORDERS

Muscle disorders may be due to injury or part of a generalised muscle disease.

Muscle diseases are usually characterised by weakness and spasms or twitching. In addition, there may well be pain.

Diseases of the voluntary muscles, grouped under the medical term myopathies, have a number of causes, but their main characteristic is weakness in the muscles, often leading to wasting.

Inflammatory myopathies
The group of disorders known as inflammatory myopathies is characterised by weak, painful muscles, often with a skin rash. The disease is commonest in the thirties and forties. In its early stages it affects the shoulders and thighs and makes rising from a chair difficult. As the disease progresses, weakness may affect the respiratory muscles and the heart. Steroid drugs reduce the symptoms and in time the disease burns itself out.

Similar inflammatory myopathies may result from infections with parasites, viruses and bacteria.

Metabolic myopathies
Many muscular disorders are caused by hormonal and endocrinal imbalances. Among the commonest are diseases of the thyroid, which cause muscular weakness.

Cushing's syndrome, a

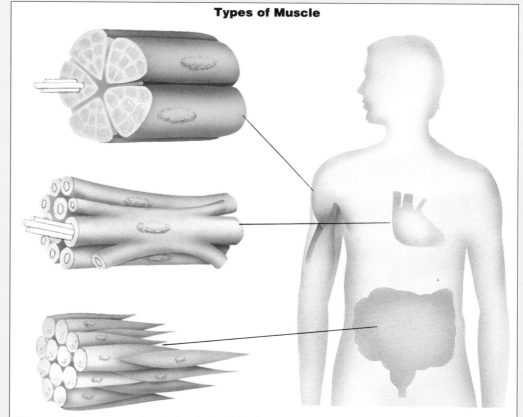

Types of Muscle

There are three types of muscle: skeletal (top), cardiac (centre) and smooth muscle (bottom).

⟫ SEE ALSO — Hypochondriasis

condition in which the body produces an excess of cortisol, causes weakness and swelling of the large muscle groups.

Acute alcohol poisoning produces a severe myopathy with weakness, muscle pain and even muscle death. A similar but less severe condition occurs amongst chronic alcohol abusers.

Myasthenia gravis

Another rare disorder of the muscles is myasthenia gravis, which causes extreme fatiguability: the muscles become extremely weak after exercise. The exact cause is unknown, but it is commoner in patients suffering from auto-immune disorders. It is probably due to destruction of the chemical transmitter that translates nerve impulses into muscle contractions. About one in 25,000 are affected, and twice as many women as men. The peak incidence is in the late twenties.

Sufferers may experience difficulty in speaking; they can start a sentence normally, but their mouth muscles are overcome by such weakness that they are unable to finish it. Eating a meal is nearly impossible. Drugs to replace the missing chemicals are highly effective in most cases. Surgical removal of the thymus aids recovery in the under 40s.

Myotonia

Conditions known as myotonia are characterised by continuing muscle contraction after the patient has stopped trying to move a muscle. Such conditions are inherited, often as part of a whole syndrome of abnormalities, including mental impairment and cataracts. Progression of the disease is slow, and patients often only come to light after surgery, as sufferers tend to react very badly to general anaesthetics.

Periodic paralysis

The condition known as periodic paralysis is inherited. Sufferers become unable to move. Paralysis is linked to a low potassium level in the blood. The weakness often comes on after a heavy meal and may last several hours. It is commonest in teenagers, and tends to remit in the thirties.

Cancers and growths

Tumours may develop in either the smooth or skeletal muscles, and may be cancerous or non-cancerous. The commonest non-cancerous tumours are those of the uterus, known as fibroids. Cancerous growths in muscles are almost invariably primary growths (rather than secondary growths which have spread from elsewhere in the body).

Other disorders

Muscles may be infected by bacteria, viruses and other organisms, causing such disorders as gangrene, tetanus and toxoplasmosis.

Genetic skeletal muscular disorders are described under muscular dystrophy.

Muscles need a good blood supply, and if this is reduced (due to respiratory or heart problems) there will be weakness and pain in the muscles.

MUSCLE SPASM

This is a sudden, involuntary contraction of a muscle.

Muscle spasm is often a result of injury, poor posture, or pressure on a nerve from a slipped disc. It is a common reaction to painful and inflamed joints. Treatment is aimed at alleviating the cause of the spasm, but muscle relaxant drugs may be needed.

MUSCULAR DYSTROPHY

The muscular dystrophies are a group of inherited disorders in which the muscles become progressively weaker.

The different types of muscular dystrophy are classified according to the groups of muscles affected; in all cases, the muscle fibres swell and are then replaced by scar tissue and fat.

Duchenne muscular dystrophy

This serious form of the disease is almost completely confined to boys and is usually apparent before the age of five. The disease starts in the hips and then spreads to the shoulders. The first sign is usually difficulty in walking, often with a waddling gait. Within a year or two the boy has difficulty climbing stairs, though coming down is no problem. Weakness of the pelvic muscles means that the child has difficulty rising from the ground. He overcomes this by rolling on to his side and then on to all fours. He then looks for further support. In the past the disease has progressed rapidly, with the child being unable to walk by the age of 10. Deformities developed and death, usually due to infection, was common in the late teens. The outlook is a little better now, however. The cardiac muscle is often affected and some of the victims die as a result of heart failure.

Duchenne muscular dystrophy is a sex-linked recessive disorder. Chorionic villus sampling allows affected male foetuses to be detected at an early stage and gives the parents the option of choosing termination.

Landouzy-derjerine muscular dystrophy

This type may start any time from childhood to middle age and the sexes are affected equally. This disorder is also inherited but is so mild that patients generally live to a normal age. The muscles of the face are most affected, giving the sufferer a mask-

---

Muscle Injuries

Muscle injuries are part and parcel of many sports. To a lesser or greater extent, all muscle injuries are aggravated by bleeding from the torn muscle fibres. This bleeding causes the characteristic signs of swelling and pain.

 DO

✔ Raise the affected part: put your feet up if ankles or knees are affected, put an injured wrist, hand or finger in a sling, lie flat if your back is damaged.
✔ Apply ice packs to help the muscle to contract.
✔ Fit an elastic bandage to support the injured muscle.
✔ Try to get the affected muscle moving again as quickly as possible.

 DON'T

✗ Take hot baths – this may make things worse as the muscle may become too relaxed and bleed further.
✗ Rest for too long as the muscle and joint may become stiff and difficult to get going again – keep moving the affected joint gently, without straining it.
✗ Take strenuous exercise until pain has gone from the affected muscle.

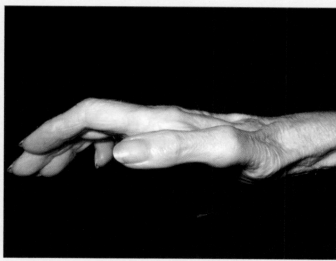

Muscular dystrophy leads to a wasting of the muscles. The rate at which it progresses depends on the type of dystrophy.

like expression. The mouth drops, giving affected children a pout.

Limb-girdle muscular dystrophy

This type usually starts in late childhood, and the shoulders and arms are affected equally. The condition is inherited through a recessive gene. The disease is slow to progress and the patient is usually able to walk for 20 or 30 years before being confined to a wheelchair.

Treatment

As yet there is no specific treatment for the muscular dystrophies. Active and passive physiotherapy is important in slowing the progression of deformities, if not of the disease itself. Like so many of these conditions there is a tightrope to be

walked between too much rest, which seems to lead to weakness, and overexertion, which seems to hasten the loss of muscle tissue.

Children with Duchenne muscular dystrophy are prone to chest infections and steps need to be taken to minimise these and to treat them as soon as they occur.

Research and support

There is a great deal of research going on to try to discover and replace the missing muscle enzyme that will allow muscles to work normally.

The serious forms of muscular dystrophy are a severe psychological stress on sufferers and families alike, and there are support groups to give advice and counselling, and raise funds for further research into the different forms of the disease.

MUSHROOM POISONING

In the UK, most cases of poisoning due to mushrooms can be traced to a couple of varieties.

Although there are many species of poisonous mushroom, most taste too unpleasant to be eaten in

large enough amounts to cause a problem.

Risk of fatality

The death cap and destroying angel earned their names from causing fatal poisoning in some cases. They contain poisonous chemicals which attack the lining of the small intestine, the liver and sometimes the kidneys. There is no known antidote, and sufferers should go straight to hospital for supportive therapies. Those who survive make a rapid recovery after the illness.

Fly agaric is not eaten as a result of being confused with a field mushroom: it is more often children who are affected because they are attracted by its colouring. Sufferers should get medical help immediately. A stomach pump (or gastric lavage) is usually recommended to flush out the poison.

The magic mushroom is a brown mushroom with a

Mushrooms And Mushroom Poisoning

Mushroom poisoning is most often caused by the amanita species.

Name	Proper name	Description	Symptoms
Death cap	*Amanita phalloides*	Similar shape and size to the edible field mushroom. Has an olive/yellow cap with white gills on the underside of the cap. Grows in deciduous woods.	Symptoms for death cap and destroying angel develop within eight to 14 hours. Severe abdominal pain, vomiting and diarrhoea. Later there may be liver inflammation and jaundice. Ten to 15 per cent of victims die of liver failure.
Destroying angel	*Amanita virosa*	Brown with characteristic white ruff on stalk.	
Fly agaric	*Amanita muscaria*	Similar shape to death cap, but the cap is red with white spots.	Symptoms develop more quickly than with the death cap or destroying angel – in 20 minutes to two hours. Nausea, vomiting, drowsiness, visual disturbance and muscle tremors.

➤➤ SEE ALSO — Poisoning

MEDICAL FACT FILE

Fly agaric (amanita muscaria) has very distinctive colouring. Closely related to the death cap, it is not normally lethal, but on no account should it be eaten.

smaller, more pointed shape than the poisonous mushrooms described in the chart. It causes hallucination in adults, but in children may also cause high fever which should be treated professionally.

MUTISM

Mutism is the inability (or refusal) to speak.

It may have a number of causes, including severe psychological disorders such as manic depression and schizophrenia.

In children, an inability to speak may be caused by profound deafness. In some, rare, cases, children may choose not to speak. This disorder, known as elective mutism, affects children around the age of five, and may be caused by shyness, anxiety or personality disorders. It usually only lasts a few months.

Mutism may also be caused by disorders of the brain, including tumours and hydrocephalus.

MYELITIS

Myelitis is an inflammation of the spinal cord.

The nerve fibres of the spinal cord are sheathed in a fatty substance called myelin. Some viruses (in particular, poliomyelitis, measles or herpes simplex) may cause this to become inflamed. The swelling puts pressure on the nerves, causing a range of symptoms, depending on the nerves affected.

Symptoms include headache, fever, a stiff neck and pain in the back and limbs. In some cases the muscles become weak, and

the patient is left paralysed.

Poliomyelitis is now a rare disorder in western countries (due to vaccination) and measles is becoming more rare as most children are now vaccinated. The vaccination programme keeps the diseases at bay, but it is important that all children should continue to be vaccinated.

Any child with unexplained high fever and stiffness in the neck and back should be taken to the doctor.

MYOPIA

Commonly known as shortsightedness, myopia occurs when the eye is too deep from front to back, so that images are focused in front of the retina.

Shortsighted people are able to focus on objects which are close to them, but distant objects look blurred. The disorder, which tends to be inherited, usually first appears in the early teens, and stabilises after about 10 years. However, myopia which begins in early childhood may continue to progress throughout adult life, becoming very severe.

Treatment
Concave lenses are used to alter the focal length of the eye, so that images from distant objects are focused on the retina.

MYRINGITIS

Myringitis is an inflammation of the eardrum.

Inflammation may occur, to a greater or lesser degree, in any infection of the middle ear (otitis media).

MYRINGOTOMY

A myringotomy is a surgical operation to make an opening in the eardrum.

Children who suffer from glue ear have a build-up of sticky secretions behind the eardrum, which reduces the efficiency of the ear and causes a hearing loss. If the condition is untreated, permanent deafness may occur.

The operation
Under general anaesthetic, the surgeon makes a small hole in the eardrum and sucks out the 'glue'. She also inserts a small valve (a grommet) in the eardrum to equalise the pressure in the ear. After the operation, hearing is greatly imporved, and children may find that loud noises are painful.

The grommet is ejected after six months or so, and hearing should remain normal. In some cases the operation (which only requires a day in hospital) may have to be repeated, if there is a further build-up of fluid in the ear.

In the past, before antibiotics were used to clear up infections, myringotomy (without the insertion of grommets) was used to drain the pus due to infections of the middle ear.

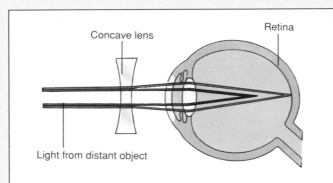

Concave lens | Retina

Light from distant object

Myopic people are unable to see distant objects clearly. The problem can be corrected by using concave lenses – images from distant objects can be focused on the retina.

➤➤ SEE ALSO — Ear disorders, Poliomyelitis

NAPPY RASH

Nappy rash is a skin irritation in the nappy area, causing redness and soreness.

Nappy rash is a condition which affects most babies at some stage in their early life. The irritants are substances in the faeces or urine, and the condition may result from not changing the baby's nappy frequently enough.

Babies vary in their susceptibility, and many mothers find that it is more likely to occur when the child has other problems, such as an upset stomach, or when the baby is teething. Children in families with a history of asthma, eczema and hay fever are more susceptible. The condition may simply involve small patches of redness, but in more severe cases the whole nappy area becomes inflamed and there may be blistering and raw patches. The area may become infected by bacteria in the faeces, or thrush may develop.

Prevention and treatment

Prevention is better than cure: it is important to keep the nappy area as clean and dry as possible. It is recommended that newborn babies are changed before and after every feed: they are likely to be wet before a feed, and most babies have a bowel movement during or soon after every feed.

At all nappy changes, the nappy area should be washed with clean water and dried thoroughly. Then a water-repellent cream should be applied (but these are not suitable for many types of disposable nappies).

If nappy rash does occur, the best treatment is to leave the nappy off as much as possible. Nappy-changing routines should be observed meticulously. There are various antiseptic creams which may help prevent infection. Doctors may prescribe mild cortico-steroids to reduce any inflammation.

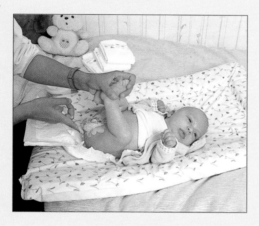

Regular changing and applying plenty of cream will help to prevent nappy rash.

NARCOSIS AND NARCOTIC DRUGS

Narcosis is a state of stupor induced by narcotic drugs or other chemicals.

Narcotics are painkillers, prescribed for moderate to severe pain. In high doses, these drugs induce a state similar to sleep, with low awareness and response to stimuli, from which the person cannot be aroused. Repeated doses (particularly by drug abusers) lead to tolerance and physical and psychological dependence.

NAUSEA

Nausea is the feeling that you are going to be sick, although vomiting doesn't always occur.

The sensation is often accompanied by sweating, pallor, excessive salivation, a rise in the heart beat and sometimes dizziness. The causes of nausea are similar to the causes of vomiting.

Causes

Probably the most common cause is overindulgence in food and/or drink. Nausea may also indicate a disorder of the digestive tract (including food poisoning, ulcers and appendicitis), or of the organs associated with it (the liver, pancreas or gall bladder). Some people are prone to nausea due to particular movements (travel sickness), and the same mechanism may cause nausea if there are disorders of the inner ear (Ménière's disease or labyrinthitis). Migraine can also cause nausea. Disorders in the endocrine system may cause nausea (Addison's disease), and some metabolic disorders (diabetes mellitus) may cause vomiting.

Finally, nausea is very often a side effect of certain drugs and anaesthetics.

Nausea During Pregnancy

Many women experience nausea in the early months of pregnancy.

Nausea and vomiting are a common reaction to the hormonal changes taking place in early pregnancy. Although known as morning sickness, this sensation may happen at any time of day. In later months, some women feel nauseous after eating, due to pressure on the stomach. Light, frequent meals are recommended.

NEBULIZER

A nebulizer is a gadget which is used to administer drugs for asthma and similar conditions.

A nebulizer consists of a face-mask, chamber and pump (electric or foot-operated). Air is pumped into the chamber, and over a solution of the drug, which is dispersed as a fine mist, which is easily inhaled through the face-mask.

NECK

The neck is particularly vulnerable to a large number of disorders.

The neck has to be flexible, to allow our heads to move easily, giving us a very wide field of vision and good hearing. But it also has to carry all the nerve messages from our bodies to our brains and back again, important arteries and veins run through it, taking blood to and from the brain, and the windpipe and food pipe have to run down the neck.

The neck gets its flexibility from the shape of the bones in the neck part of the spine.

Glandular swellings

Swelling of the neck is usually due to disorders of the lymph glands, salivary glands or of the thyroid.

The lymph glands are part of the body's defence system and swell in respose to infection in the area that they drain. Lymph glands can also swell as the result of generalised infections such as glandular fever or certain cancers.

The thyroid gland produces hormones that control the rate at which the body works. Enlargement of the thyroid is a common cause of swellings at the front of the neck. It may be due to cysts or cancer, but

>> SEE ALSO — Addison's disease, Brain, Diabetes, Encephalitis, Labyrinthitis, Ménière's disease, Migraine, Morphine, Travel sickness

MEDICAL FACT FILE

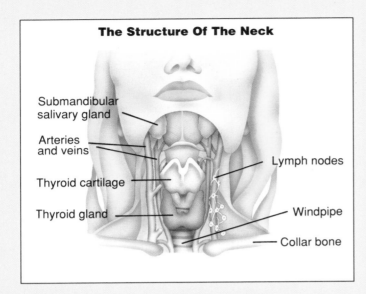

The Structure Of The Neck

- Submandibular salivary gland
- Arteries and veins
- Thyroid cartilage
- Thyroid gland
- Lymph nodes
- Windpipe
- Collar bone

more often it is a sign that the thyroid is having to work harder than usual.

Mumps used to be a common cause of swelling of the salivary glands (before widespread vaccination for mumps).

Swelling of the sub-mandibular gland in the floor of the mouth is likely to be due to stones. The stone blocks the passage of saliva and the floor of the mouth swells, usually at meal times. Surgical removal of the stone is a simple procedure.

A pain in the neck

'Stiff neck' is a common complaint that is usually due to muscle spasm. It is often caused by sleeping at an unusual angle or in a draught. One side of the neck is painful and tender to the touch. Looking over one's shoulder is often impossible. Analgesics, such as aspirin, and massage may be helpful but in severe cases, anti-inflammatory drugs and physiotherapy may be needed.

Occasionally, stiff neck is a sign of a prolapsed cervical disc (a slipped disc in the neck). This causes severe pain and pins and needles in the arm and hand. Surgical treatment is difficult, but the condition often responds to physiotherapy and traction.

Injuries

The neck is more mobile than the rest of the back and is thus more prone to injury. Nature has compensated by leaving more room running through the vertebrae in the neck for the spinal cord than in the main part of the spine. So while the neck is more liable to be broken than the back, a broken neck often causes less damage since the spinal cord is less likely to be injured.

Injury may result from throwing the head back, usually in a car accident (known as whiplash). Another cause of injury is excessive bending of the neck (in a rugby scrum, for example). Treatment may be simple, consisting of little more than physiotherapy and a neck support, or highly complex, involving surgery.

NERVOUS BREAKDOWN

Nervous breakdown is generally used to describe a state in which the patient is unable to function normally due to an acute mental illness.

The term, much loved by the media, is almost never used by the medical profession. All medical diagnoses are based on the idea that to name a disease offers some clues as to its cause, treatment and likely outcome. 'Nervous breakdown' is too vague and too subjective a description.

The term is commonly used to describe a mental abnormality of sudden onset, and the hope is that the sufferer will recover fully. This precludes many of the progressive illnesses, such as Alzheimer's disease, and all of the psychoses, such as schizophrenia. Most nervous breakdowns are due to acute anxiety or depression. Acute anxiety attacks may only last a few minutes but can be completely incapacitating. Depression tends to last longer but the two are closely interwoven.

Treatment

Treatment should be supportive as well as medical. The doctor may prescribe antidepressants or anxiolitics such as valium. (Despite its bad press, short courses of valium can be very useful in acute anxiety.) Beta-blockers are effective in relieving the symptoms of panic attacks and are safe in long-term use.

NERVOUS SYSTEM

The nervous system, in conjunction with the endocrine system, controls all the functions of the body.

The nervous system is highly complex, carrying tens of thousands of tiny electrical impulses every second. These impulses allow the central nervous system (the brain and spinal cord) to monitor every organ continually and to react if change is needed.

The nervous system is divided into three parts: the sensory division, the motor division and the central nervous system.

The sensory division

The sensory division of the central nervous system receives information from specialised sensory receptors. These receptors are on or near the surface of the body, and detect heat, cold, vibration (sound), light (vision) and pain, as well as many other sensations. There are other types of receptors, the action of which we are not normally aware, which monitor things like blood pressure and the passage of food through the digestive tract. A third set of receptors constantly inform the brain about the positions of our joints, although we do not consciously think about them all the time.

Sensory nerve impulses travel along nerve fibres to the spinal cord. Once in the spinal cord, the impulse travels up to one or more sensory areas in the brain, and the signal is processed and passed on to all the other areas in the brain.

The motor division

The motor division controls the body's activities. This involves sending messages to skeletal muscles, to smooth muscles in the internal organs or, in some cases, to glands, telling them to secrete certain hormones.

Some actions are

Nerve Block

The link between nerves can be blocked by certain drugs.

One such drug, Curare, extracted from plants, was used by South American Indians to paralyse the animals they hunted. Modern medicine uses the drug to block the nerve transmission to muscles so surgeons can operate on a relaxed, numb body.

How Nerves Work

Our nerves carry messages all through the body about the sensations and stimuli we feel and about controlling movement.

The sensory nerve fibres pick up sensations and transmit them to the central nervous system. Once the message reaches the spine, the motor nerves come into play, to move the hand away from the source of pain. At the same time, a message goes to the brain so we become aware of the pain.

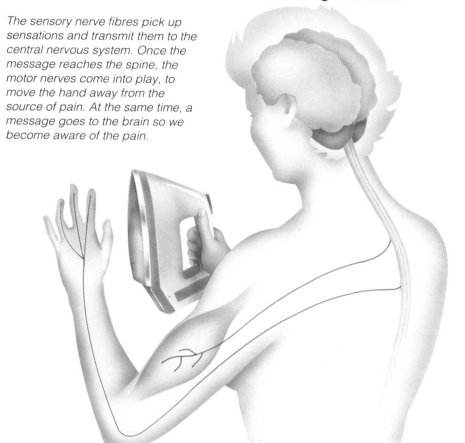

All cells in the body, by their chemical nature, act as tiny batteries with a voltage difference inside and outside the cell wall. Some cells, such as nerve and muscle cells, can transmit this electrical excitement from one cell to the next, and are said to be excitory.

The resting nerve cell or neuron maintains a voltage difference across its cell membrane of about one tenth of a volt. This difference is held steady by the cell actively pumping electrically charged chemicals (neurotransmitters) across its cell membrane. Any factor that changes the way these chemicals pass in and out will cause a change in the voltage. This change is transmitted to the next part of the nerve, often at speeds of many metres per second.

Excitable nerves

Any chemical altering the rate that sodium and potassium pass in and out of the nerve cells has the potential to interfere with its correct workings. A common cause of excitable nerves is a low level of calcium in the blood and in the fluid surrounding the cells. This low level of calcium may be due to hormonal upsets or it may be due to hyperventilation (breathing abnormally quickly or deeply, sometimes due to anxiety).

Hyperventilation alters the acidity of the blood, and this changes calcium into a new, electrically different form. This change mimics the effect of a low calcium level and causes light-headedness, giddiness and tingling around the mouth. In extreme cases, the motor nerves cause the muscles to go into spasm.

Nerve cells (neurons) in the brain showing branching nerve fibres.

premeditated: you decide to lift a finger and the voluntary system controls the muscles involved. In other cases (for instance, the movement of food through the bowel) the movement is involuntary and the autonomic nervous system takes over.

Skeletal muscles can be controlled at several levels within the nervous system. If you touch a painful stimulus, it is important to move your hand quickly before any damage is done. In order to save time, nerve impulses are acted upon by the spinal cord (see left).

The great majority of sensory inputs are ignored. Even whilst just sitting and reading a magazine the nervous system is continually bombarded with information about contact with clothes or the chair; the eye sees the whole room and the nose constantly smells the air. Only relevant changes, such as a smell of gas, are allowed to penetrate the consciousness.

The central nervous system

As the human brain has become more complex, so it has retained some characteristics from earlier stages of development.

From an evolutionary point of view the spinal cord is the most primitive part of the central nervous system, retaining many of the features found in creatures such as the earthworm. Certain actions (reflexes) are controlled automatically and

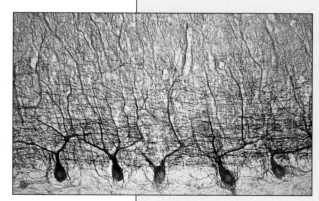

Disorders of the Nervous System

There is a wide range of disorders of the nervous system. Symptoms include tingling sensations, pain, numbness, paralysis, dizziness, vomiting, nausea, memory loss, confusion, fits, loss of consciousness and loss of bowel or bladder control. Disorders may also be the result of a loss of blood supply to the nervous system or due to injury to the brain or spinal cord.

Disorder	Description
Abscesses and tumours	Brain abscesses and tumours of nerve fibres or brain cells cause a range of symptoms.
Carpel tunnel syndrome	Numbness and tingling in the fingers, due to pressure on the nerves in the wrist.
Epilepsy	A sudden surge of electrical signals upsets the balance in the brain and causes fits or convulsions. The cause is not known. May follow brain injury.
Headache and migraine	May be side effects of another disorder, or occur on their own.
Huntington's chorea	Degenerative nerve disease, causing swift, jerky movements.
Meningitis and encephalitis	Inflammation of nerve cell coverings or nerve cells themselves in the brain.
Motor neuron disease	Degenerative disease of motor nerve cells.
Multiple sclerosis	Inflammation of the myelin sheath that covers the nerves in the brain and spinal cord, leading to a range of disabilities.
Myasthenia gravis	Muscle weakness caused by breakdown of neurotransmitters.
Neuralgia	Pain from a damaged nerve.
Trapped nerve	Nerves may get pressed on, producing numbness, tingling and weakness or pain.
Parkinson's disease	Deterioration of nerve centres in the brain that control movements, leading to tremors and loss of control of automatic physical movements.
Peripheral neuropathies	Damage to nerves other than those in the brain and spinal cord due to long-term disorders such as diabetes mellitus, alcoholism or vitamin deficiences; overdoses of exposure to certain minerals and other chemicals; infections such as poliomyelitis and tetanus. May cause tingling, numbness and wasting of muscles.
Pre-senile dementia	Deterioration of brain cells leads to intellectual and emotional dysfunction. May be due to brain tumour or hypothyroidism.
Poliomyelitis	Viral form of infection which attacks motor nerves.
Vertigo	Disturbance in brain and/or inner ear, causing sensations of spinning and dizziness.

Tuberculosis bacteria may infect the brain, causing tuberculous meningitis.

almost instantaneously by transmissions within the spinal cord.

The next most developed part of the system is the 'lower brain'. Most of the subconscious activities of the body, such as heart rate are regulated by this region.

Cerebral thinking
Most of the functions needed to sustain life occur in the spinal cord and lower brain, but 75 per cent of the nerve cells of the entire body are in the higher brain (or cerebral cortex). These areas, which are much bigger in humans than other animals, act as vast storage areas. They contain memories of previous sensory inputs and literally thousands of complicated, learned, muscle responses — such as the ability to keep our balance once we have learned to ride a bike.

Large areas of the cortex, the prefrontal, the parietal and the temporal lobes have no role in either sensory or motor activity. They are given over to abstract thought.

>> SEE ALSO — Brain, Numbness, Spinal cord

NETTLE RASH

Nettle rash is the common name for urticaria, a rash which is usually the result of an allergy.

Nettle rash, also known as hives, may have a number of different causes (besides nettles). Allergens and irritants include milk, eggs, wheat, nuts, chocolate, strawberries, insect bites, vaccinations, plants, shock, water and sunlight. Often the rash appears and fades with no apparent cause.

Symptoms and treatment
The rash is intensely itchy, red and often patchy with white weals. It may cover the whole body, or just the arms or trunk. It usually goes within a day or so but may recur. Apply soothing lotions, such as calamine. In serious cases, doctors may prescribe antihistamines, or corticosteroids.

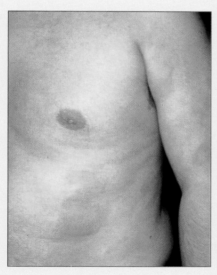

The red patches of nettle rash.

NEURALGIA

Neuralgia is brief bouts of often very severe pain, which sometimes shoots along the affected nerve.

Neuralgia is caused by irritating or damaging a nerve. It may be a symptom of a disorder such as migraine or shingles, or a result of damage to a particular nerve.

Analgesics such as paracetamol may relieve the pain, and stronger painkillers are prescribed for particular forms of neuralgia.

NEURAL TUBE DEFECTS

A defect in the neural tube — the part of the embryo which becomes the spinal column.

At an early stage of pregnancy, the neural tube is transformed into the spinal column, brain and nerves of the body, and the bones of the spine form a protective sheath. If this development is interfered with, the nervous system does not form properly and the spine does not close, leaving the spinal cord exposed (a condition known as spina bifida).

Various degrees of severity may occur, from the insignificant 'hidden' spina bifida to the most severe, 'open' spina bifida.

Open spina bifida
In open spina bifida, the delicate spinal cord is exposed to the air and soon dries out. This, and the disruption of nerves, means that the baby's legs are partly or completely paralysed. A build-up of fluid around the brain is common and this will require surgical correction. If the nerves of the bowel or bladder are affected the child will be incontinent.

Open spina bifida affects about 2000 babies a year. The incidence is decreasing as a result of screening and possibly as a result of better nutrition. Open spina bifida requires urgent surgical closure to prevent further damage.

The cause of neural tube defects is still unclear, but there is growing evidence to suggest that vitamin and folic acid deficiencies before conception may play a role.

Neural tube defects may be detected in early pregnancy by blood tests or an ultrasound scan.

NEUROBLASTOMA

Neuroblastoma is a highly malignant tumour. It grows in the immature nerve cells of the sympathetic nervous system.

Neuroblastoma usually occurs within the first four years of life. It is most often found in the adrenal gland.

Diagnosis
The tumour usually grows very quickly, and most are not noticed until the abdomen is visibly distended. By this stage the tumour has usually spread and the child is extremely ill. Because the adrenal gland is so close to the kidney there is sometimes a problem deciding where the tumour is sited. CT scans and x-ray-guided biopsies may be used, but there is a simple urine test that can make the diagnosis in most cases.

Treatment
A neuroblastoma disappears spontaneously in some cases, or it may transform into a benign growth. Most tumours, however, are too far advanced for surgery and the prospects of survival are slim. Radiotherapy and cytotoxic drugs help to relieve pain. Younger children — those under a year — tend to do better than the older age group.

NEUROSIS

A neurosis is a mental disorder in which the sufferer does not lose touch with reality.

Such disorders include some forms of depression, anxiety, obsession and phobia. Neurotics tend to worry excessively, but because they are aware of their problems, the problems may take on an even greater significance in the mind of the sufferer. In some cases, worries become self-fulfilling. If a person is neurotic about the possibility of losing their job, for example, it may be that they become so overwhelmed by their worry that they do not perform well, and do end up being made redundant.

Many neurotics are able to accept that they have a problem and find ways of avoiding or coping with it. For example, people with a phobia about flying can take classes in learning how to overcome their fear.

Treatment may involve drug therapies (tranquillisers and antidepressants) and counselling sessions.

Psychotics, on the other hand, have more serious mental illnesses, and at times lose touch with reality.

NEUROSURGERY

Neurosurgery is the term used to describe operations involving the nervous system, particularly the brain and spinal column.

The operations may involve structural changes to relieve pressure on a nerve (for example, in the wrist, in carpel tunnel syndrome, or in the spine, in some cases); removal of tumours of the brain and spinal cord; surgical treatment of certain types of epilepsy; and operations to correct problems with the blood

⟫⟫ SEE ALSO — Depression, Nervous system, Obsessive-compulsive disorder, Phobia, Spina bifida

MEDICAL FACT FILE

supply to the brain, including aneurysms and brain haemorrhages.

NIGHT BLINDNESS

Some people find that they are unable to see well at night (when driving, for example).

Night blindness may be caused by a number of factors: in some cases it is hereditary; it may be the result of vitamin A deficiency; or it may be an early sign of retinitis pigmentosa.

NIGHT TERROR

This is a distressing condition in which the sufferer wakes suddenly, screaming and frightened.

It is most often children between the ages of four and seven who are affected by night terror. They become semi-awake, and are difficult, or impossible, to calm because they do not appear to recognise familiar faces. There may be other physical symptoms, such as sweating. They gradually slip back into a state of sleep, and have no memory of the event in the morning.

Night terror seems to have no significance, but it is distressing to parents. Children grow out of it; in adults, night terror may be a sign of an anxiety disorder.

NIPPLE DISORDERS

The main symptom of a disorder of the nipples is a discharge. Some people have misshapen nipples or even extra nipples.

Discharges can take many forms, and may be a sign of various disorders. It is difficult to pinpoint the cause

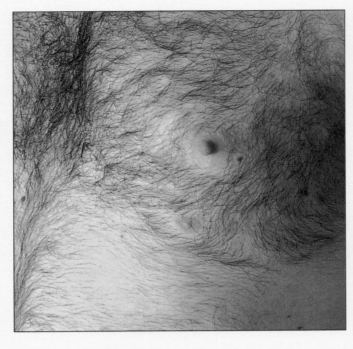

Extra nipples are usually smaller than normal nipples, and in general, do not present any problems.

of many discharges, and most doctors would suggest a mammogram to rule out serious disease.

Discharges

A clear and watery discharge may be due to long-term use of the contraceptive pill. It may also be due to a benign polyp or, rarely, cancer of the breast or nipple.

A blood-stained discharge is surprisingly common. Again, the majority of cases are due to benign polyps, but it is important to have the breast checked out in case cancer is present.

A milky discharge is, of course, quite normal after childbirth, and it may occur right through pregnancy. Milk may also be produced in women who are on the contraceptive pill.

Physical injury — a severe blow to the ribs — may also cause a milky discharge, since the damage to the chest wall stimulates the nerve that supplies the breast and can start them working. Pituitary gland disorders may also stimulate milk production. Milk production coupled with

infertility may be a sign that the pituitary gland is producing an excess of the hormone prolactin.

Extra nipples

Some women, and some men too, have what are called supernumerary nipples. These extra nipples — as many as six or eight — occur along an imaginary line from the armpit to the groin. They are rarely as well developed as normal nipples and are completely harmless.

Inverted nipples

In some women, one or both nipples are retracted, and when slightly aroused the nipple may invert into the breast rather than protruding. In most cases, the nipple becomes erect when further stimulated. Doctors usually check pregnant women, to see that breastfeeding will not be a problem.

If an inverted nipple appears in a woman who has not previously had the condition, it may be a sign of breast cancer.

NITS

Nits are the eggs of headlice.

Nits are the most obvious indication of headlice, and steps should be taken to eradicate them as soon as they are spotted.

NOISE DAMAGE

Hearing may be damaged by exposure to unusually loud noise, or by continual exposure to lower levels of noise.

The loudness of noise is measured in decibels. It is generally agreed that noise levels of over 130 decibels can cause permanent damage: 130 decibels is the level of noise from a jet engine 30 metres away. Continuous exposure to levels over 90 decibels (very loud music, or a pneumatic drill 1 metre away) carries a risk of injury.

How it happens

Normally, as noises get louder, the muscles within the ear restrict the movement of the bones in the ear, dampening down the sound. If the noise is sudden and loud, the muscles do not have time to operate in the middle ear, and the full vibration is passed on to the inner ear, damaging the cells which pick up the sounds, and sometimes damaging the eardrum.

More often, the damage is due to long-term exposure to noise.

Symptoms and prevention

Very loud noise usually causes pain and may lead to deafness for a few minutes — or hours. If there is damage, there is likely to be ringing in the ears after the noise has stopped.

After prolonged exposure to noise, patients may become deaf to high

»» SEE ALSO — Jogger's nipple, Lice, Retinitis pigmentosa

Legislation ensures that people in certain occupations are provided with ear protectors to prevent noise damage.

tones, but later they are likely to find that their whole range of hearing is impaired.

There are regulations about noise levels in the workplace, and those who cannot avoid exposure are obliged to wear ear protectors.

NON-SPECIFIC URETHRITIS

Inflammation of the urethra due to problems other than gonorrhoea.

Urethritis, inflammation of the urethra (the tube from the bladder to outside) may be due to physical stimulation or chemical irritation, for instance from a bubble bath. Rarely, a urinary tract infection may cause urethritis.

The commonest cause, however, is infection with gonorrhoea or some other (non-specific) organism.

The majority of cases of non-specific urethritis (NSU) are due to chlamydia, but they may also be due to trichomonas, candida, herpes or warts. All are sexually transmitted. In about a quarter of cases, no infecting agent can be found, and strictly speaking, the term NSU should be reserved for these cases.

Men are more often affected than women.

Symptoms and diagnosis

The commonest symptoms are a urethral discharge and a burning pain when passing water. A specimen of the discharge can be examined under a microscope and in most cases an immediate diagnosis made.

Treatment and prevention

Treatment is usually simple. A thorough examination is needed, including blood and urine tests, before the final 'all clear' can be given.

As well as their protective role against AIDS, condoms are highly effective against NSU.

NOSE

The nose warms, moistens and filters the air as we breathe, and is a sense organ, enabling us to smell.

The nostrils and nasal cavity behind are shaped and constructed to perform a variety of functions. The large number of blood vessels in the nose readily give up their heat. This ensures that inhaled air is near to body temperature before it reaches the lungs. At the same time, the nose filters the air. By a clever combination of turbulence and hairs, almost all particles bigger than a hundredth of a millimetre are trapped. The nose is particularly effective at filtering bacteria.

Inside the nasal cavity, sensory receptors pick up scents as the air passes through.

Cold symptoms

The symptoms of a runny or blocked nose and sneezing are extremely common. In one study, school-age children were shown to have, on average, one cold a

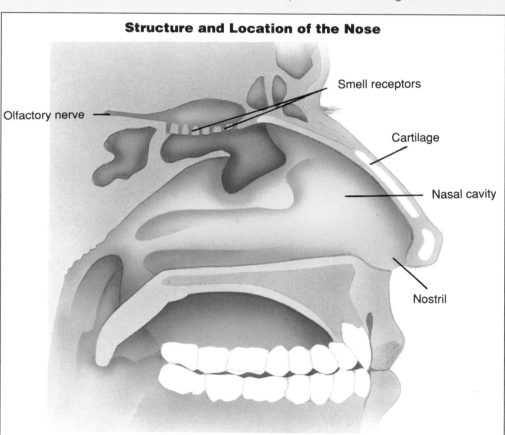

Structure and Location of the Nose

Olfactory nerve

Smell receptors

Cartilage

Nasal cavity

Nostril

The nose consists of two parts, the external nose and the nasal cavity. The front third is divided into two halves by the nasal septum. The nose has a very good blood supply and there is a large number of veins and arteries just below the surface. The upper part of the nasal cavity is lined by specialist cells that give us our sense of smell.

⏩ SEE ALSO — Chlamydial infections, Cystitis, Deafness, Ear disorders

Nose Bleed

Nose bleeds can occur at any age. In the majority of cases no cause can be found.

Nose bleeds are often due to injury. Other causes include infection, foreign objects and blood disorders. Nose bleed is often thought to be due to high blood pressure. This is not the case.

● If you have a nose bleed, squeeze the soft part of the external nose as shown below.

● Keep up the pressure for at least 10 minutes.

● A cold compress on the back of the neck may speed things by causing a reflex constriction of the blood vessels in the nose.

● If the bleeding persists for more than half an hour and is severe, medical help should be sought. The doctor may be able to cauterise the bleeding vessel. In severe cases, a blood transfusion may needed.

● Avoid spicy food for 24 hours.

month. Other than the common cold, a frequent cause of these symptoms is allergic rhinitis (hay fever and other allergies). It is sometimes very difficult to tell the two apart but, in general, the symptoms of allergic rhinitis may be seasonal (following exposure to certain pollens) or generalised. The most common cause of generalised allergic rhinitis is the house-dust mite.

Colds are episodic and more frequent during the winter. The cold sufferer often feels ill. There is no cure for colds although nasal drops may be used to dry up the secretions, and decongestants (a safer long term alternative) can be used to loosen phlegm. Drinking alcohol makes nasal secretions worse.

Allergic rhinitis can be treated with a combination of antihistamine tablets and steroid nasal sprays.

Blocked nose may also be caused by nasal polyps. Polyps are often a sign of nasal allergy and their initial symptoms may mimic those of rhinitis. They may shrink with steroid treatment, but the only cure (which is not always permanent) is surgery.

A broken nose

A blow on the nose may fracture the nasal bones. The nose may be flattened and unsightly or the septum may be buckled to one side. This displacement may cause obstruction and repeated infection.

Many doctors argue that there is no point in x-raying a broken nose unless evidence of the damage is needed. If it is displaced it needs straightening. If it does not look too unsightly it should be left. Either way, a decision should be put off for a week or so after the injury so that an objective assessment can be made once the swelling has settled.

If surgery is needed, the patient is anaesthetised and the nasal bones are straightened with a pair of long-bladed forceps. A splint of plaster or strapping is applied externally to hold the bones in position.

More severe nasal fractures may occur if the whole of the face is pushed in. In this case the whole of the face is pulled forward and held in position by special wire splints.

NOTIFIABLE DISEASES

Notifiable diseases are those which have to be reported to local health authorities so that steps can be taken to ensure the disease does not spread.

In the UK, doctors have to report notifiable diseases (see list), and in some cases, where the disease is very rare or very contagious and dangerous, steps will immediately be taken to trace all contacts.

Certain occupational diseases (such as poisoning due to working with certain chemicals or radiation) are also notifiable, so that steps can be taken to ensure that working conditions are up to standard.

Some congenital disorders are also classed as notifiable diseases.

Cancer statistics are registered nationally, and international agencies have pooled all their information on the subject.

The list is subject to change and may vary from one country to another. In addition, certain diseases (including cholera, plague, relapsing fever, smallpox, typhus and yellow fever) have to be reported to an international agency.

Notifiable Diseases

In the UK, the following diseases are notifiable:

Cholera
Diphtheria
Dysentery
Encephalitis (acute)
Food poisoning
Infective jaundice
Lassa fever
Leptopirosis
Malaria
Green monkey disease
   (Marburg disease)
Measles
Mumps
Meningitis (acute)
Ophthalmia neonatorum
Pasteurella pestis
   (plague)
Poliomyelitis (acute)
Rabies
Relapsing fever (due to
   lice or ticks)
Rubella
Scarlet fever
Smallpox
Tetanus
Tuberculosis
Typhoid and paratyphoid
Typhus fever
Viral haemorrhagic
   disease
Whooping cough
Yellow fever

▶▶ SEE ALSO — Hay fever

NUMBNESS

Numbness, which is often coupled with tingling sensations, is rarely a sign of serious disease.

By far the commonest cause, especially when it occurs in the arms or hands, is a trapped nerve. Pressure on the nerve causes numbness and tingling in the areas supplied by it.

Carpel tunnel syndrome

In carpel tunnel syndrome, for example, the median nerve is compressed at the wrist due to fluid retention. This causes altered sensation, including pain, numbness and weakness, in the first three fingers of the hand. The sufferer is often a pregnant woman.

A similar sensation is produced by knocking the 'funny bone', except that in this case the numbness affects the fourth and fifth fingers.

Generalised numbness

Numbness in several parts of the body at the same time is less common and may be a sign of underlying disease.

Diabetes, kidney failure, alcoholism and vitamin B12 deficiency can all cause what is known as 'glove and stocking' numbness in the extremities. In all these cases, simple blood tests can supply the diagnosis. Treatment is aimed at the cause of the numbness.

Rarer causes

Patches of numbness in a recent immigrant from a third-world country, especially if they are around areas of depigmentation, may be a sign of Hansen's disease (leprosy).

Another rare cause of numbness is syphilis of the spinal cord. In this case, the numbness has a strange effect on the feet. The patient is unable to feel his footfall, and adopts a stamping style of walking.

Damage to the sensory region of the brain may occur as a result of an accident or a stroke. In many cases the patient can still feel major sensations, but is unable to perform complex tasks such as identifying an object by its feel.

OBSESSIVE-COMPULSIVE BEHAVIOUR

Obsessive-compulsive behaviour is a neurotic disorder.

Sufferers make repeated, compulsive actions due to a persistent idea which takes them over. One example of the disorder is an obsession with cleanliness — the sufferer spends all her time cleaning — herself, her home, even other people's homes.

Sometimes the obsession takes the form of constant questioning in the mind: should the door be open or closed? How should the cushions be arranged on the sofa? How many slices of bread are in the packet? The sufferer keeps checking and double checking the effects or facts, to no particular end.

Causing problems

In severe cases, the ritualised and repetitive acts mean that the sufferer cannot lead an ordinary life, becoming housebound because of her indecision. Obsessive-compulsive behaviour is something that affects many people from time to time, but in rare cases it takes over. It usually starts in adolescence, and it is often associated with anxiety and depression.

The condition appears to be sparked by hereditary and environmental factors, or may be due to certain forms of brain damage.

Treatment

Therapy, in the form of psychoanalysis (to establish the root of the problem), behaviour therapy and drug therapy (antidepressants) all help to relieve the symptoms.

OCCLUSION

Occlusion is a term which is used by doctors to describe a blockage of any of the tubes in the body.

Occlusion produces different effects, depending on the part of the body affected. An occlusion of a blood vessel, for example, is very serious.

In dentistry, the term refers to the way in which the

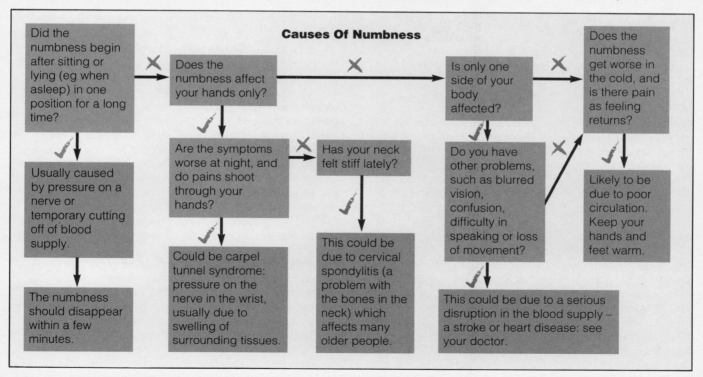

Causes Of Numbness

Did the numbness begin after sitting or lying (eg when asleep) in one position for a long time?

✗ → Does the numbness affect your hands only?

✗ → Is only one side of your body affected?

✗ → Does the numbness get worse in the cold, and is there pain as feeling returns?

✓ Usually caused by pressure on a nerve or temporary cutting off of blood supply.

Are the symptoms worse at night, and do pains shoot through your hands?

✗ → Has your neck felt stiff lately?

Do you have other problems, such as blurred vision, confusion, difficulty in speaking or loss of movement?

✓ Likely to be due to poor circulation. Keep your hands and feet warm.

The numbness should disappear within a few minutes.

✓ Could be carpel tunnel syndrome: pressure on the nerve in the wrist, usually due to swelling of surrounding tissues.

✓ This could be due to cervical spondylitis (a problem with the bones in the neck) which affects many older people.

This could be due to a serious disruption in the blood supply – a stroke or heart disease: see your doctor.

⊳⊳ SEE ALSO — Phobia

MEDICAL FACT FILE

teeth fit together when the jaw is shut. A bad fit, malocclusion, can cause serious problems.

OCCUPATIONAL HEALTH

Occupational health is the branch of medicine involved with making the workplace as safe as possible.

There has been a number of Acts of Parliament which lay down standards that are to be met in offices and workshops. Legislation covers such things as heating, lighting, ventilation,

New legislation covers the use of computers and word processors in the workplace.

overcrowding and sanitary arrangements. It also covers particular health hazards connected with specific industries: workers exposed to lead, mercury and other chemicals, and new regulations cover those working at computer keyboards and VDUs.

The law also recognises that certain diseases are due almost entirely to one particular environmental hazard. Mesothelioma, a form of lung cancer, is unheard of outside the asbestos industry. Diseases which are related to

occupation are included in the list of notifiable diseases, and sufferers, or their widows, may be entitled to special help.

Occupational physician

Many of these diseases are so specific to the workplace that there are now medical specialists, known as occupational physicians, whose job is to monitor the health and safety of workers.

The occupational physician does this in several ways. On their first day at work, many new employees have to give a detailed work history describing where they have worked and what hazards they have been exposed to. This helps the

occupational physician to diagnose work-related illness and also allows management to minimise a worker's exposure to a hazard. This is particularly important in fields such as radiation, where the risk is proportional to the length of exposure.

The occupational physician advises on control of the work environment, extraction of dust and so on. She is also responsible for advice on personal healthy measures, such as ear protectors and goggles.

After an accident or an illness it is the responsibility

of the occupational physician to assess recovery and suggest alternative work where necessary.

OCCUPATIONAL THERAPY

Occupational therapy is treatment to enable people to lead as normal a life as possible after illness, injury or when incapacitated by mental illness or handicap.

Some severe injuries and diseases leave sufferers weak and uncoordinated. Therapists are trained to help them re-learn the use of muscles so that they can cope with everyday tasks and find some form of employment. In some cases, handicap may be due to birth defects, and therapy can help in some of these cases as well.

Occupational therapy also involves helping disabled people to occupy their time constructively — often in hospitals or day centres — with crafts and other tasks.

OEDEMA

Oedema or fluid retention describes a type of swelling that is due to an excess of fluid in the tissues.

Oedema is most commonly seen around the ankles and can be distinguished from other forms of swelling by the fact that gentle pressure leaves a dent which takes a few seconds to smooth itself out.

The fluid excess is of a type known as extracellular. This forms a halfway house between fluid inside the cells and the fluid in the general circulation (blood and lymph

system). Extracellular fluid exists in equilibrium with these other fluids and is readily exchangeable with either. In the normal individual this equilibrium is maintained by a combination of factors including the blood pressure in the arteries and veins and the concentration of various salts and proteins in the blood. Anything that upsets this balance can cause oedema.

Common causes

The vast majority of oedema sufferers are perfectly fit and healthy. In hot weather the capillaries on the skin surface dilate. This dilation causes fluid to leak out and oedema is the result. A similar condition occurs on long haul air flights. Lack of exercise, low cabin pressure and alcohol all contribute to the swelling of feet. This form of oedema can largely be avoided by regular walks up and down the aisle and by exercises involving the legs and feet.

Oedema in women

The fluid retention most women suffer before a period is due to a hormone imbalance. If severe, it can be treated with diuretics (water tablets) or the contraceptive pill. Although there is a hormonal element in water retention during pregnancy, the main cause of the oedema is pressure on the pelvic veins by the pregnant womb. In late pregnancy, a sudden increase in the amount of oedema, especially if it is accompanied by visual disturbance or high blood pressure, may be a sign of pre-eclampsia or toxaemia. Medical advice should be sought at once.

Heart or kidney failure

There are several serious causes of oedema in the middle-aged and elderly.

Heart failure, when the heart loses its pumping

▶▶ SEE ALSO — Notifiable diseases, Pre-eclampsia, Toxaemia

efficiency, causes a build-up of fluid. This can be particularly serious if the build-up is in the lungs. Symptoms of heart failure include swollen legs and a shortness of breath which is made worse by lying down. Treatment with powerful diuretics is very effective.

Less easy to treat is the fluid retention of kidney failure. Again, this is due to a number of factors, but in such cases water tablets are less effective and kidney dialysis may be needed.

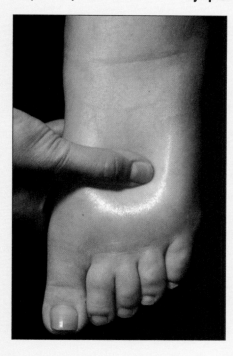

Swelling due to oedema becomes indented when pressed: the dent stays for a while before the fluid returns.

Other causes

Any factor that slows the return of blood to the heart will cause oedema. Common causes include varicose veins or thrombosis. Tumours in the pelvis sometimes cause oedema by blocking the veins that return blood to the heart.

Oedema, like anaemia, is not a disease in itself, just a sign of one. It is essential to find and treat the cause of the oedema, and not just the oedema itself.

OESOPHAGUS

The oesophagus is a muscular tube that extends from the pharynx to the stomach.

During swallowing, the valve at the top of the oesophagus, which is normally closed, is opened. A wave of contraction sweeps down the oesophagus, taking the food with it.

Symptoms of disorders

The main symptoms of oesophageal disorders are difficulty in swallowing, heartburn and painful swallowing.

Difficulty in swallowing may be due to problems in the mouth or due to obstructions (see below). The feeling of a 'lump in the throat' but with no difficulty in swallowing is called globus hystericus. As the name implies, the problem is a psychological rather than a physical one.

Pain during swallowing may be a sign of local injuries, such as a scratch from a fish bone, or it may be the result of oral infections such as thrush (a fungal infection).

Congenital disorders

In some, very rare, cases, part of the oesophagus is missing from birth. Urgent surgery is required to correct the defect.

Some babies are born with web-like constrictions, which do not usually require surgery, since they become less constricting by the time the child is on to solids.

Acid reflux

Oesophagitis (inflammation of the oesophagus) is usually due to acid reflux. There is a valve at the top of the stomach, and if the acid from the stomach comes back through this valve, it causes the sensation known as heartburn. It is normally described as a hot or tight sensation behind the breast bone. The pain is often worse at night or if the patient bends down. The pain is made worse by hot drinks and alcohol and soothed by milk.

Most cases are mild and can be treated with antacids. They are all effective — in particular look for tablets or suspensions containing magnesium trisilicate. If the pain is not relieved by antacids, a doctor should be consulted. In some cases it is difficult to differentiate heartburn from angina and doctors may request an x-ray to confirm the diagnosis.

In some cases, acid reflux is due to a hiatus hernia — part of the stomach protrudes above the

diaphragm. In itself, a hiatus hernia is painless, but it does allow stomach acid to burn the delicate lining of the oesophagus. In the past, surgery was used to correct hernias, but this is so major, and modern treatment is so effective, that surgery is now rarely used.

Oesophagitis may also be caused by swallowing corrosive chemicals.

Benign oesophageal stricture

If food sticks in the throat, it may be due to an oesophageal stricture. Acid from the stomach causes tiny ulcers that scar when they heal. The scar tissue forms a ring and as the scar contracts the oesophagus is narrowed. A similar stricture is caused by swallowing corrosive liquids. A simple operation using an endoscope to overstretch the oesophagus is successful in most cases, but surgery may be necessary.

Mallory-Weis tear

Sometimes, there is a physical injury to the lining of

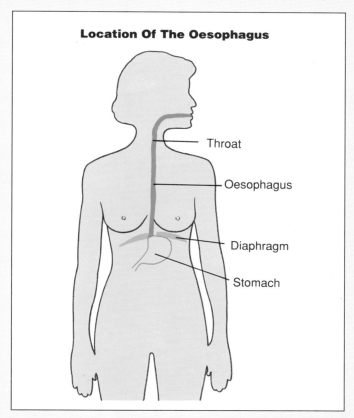

Location Of The Oesophagus

Throat

Oesophagus

Diaphragm

Stomach

▶▶ SEE ALSO — Heartburn, Hiatus hernia

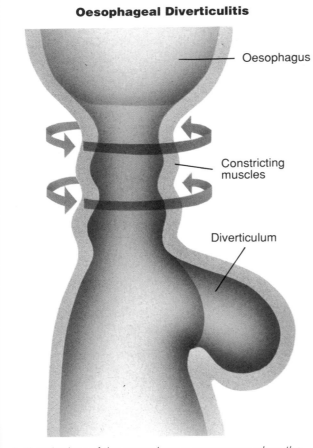

Oesophageal Diverticulitis

Oesophagus

Constricting muscles

Diverticulum

A diverticulum of the oesophagus may occur when the muscular wall of the foodpipe fails to relax.

the oesophagus, usually just above the stomach, as a result of a sudden rise in abdominal pressure. This may be a result of coughing or retching. It is commonest of all following retching on a full stomach. For this reason, it is most frequently seen in young men following a night in the pub and a curry. The tear in the lining causes blood in the vomit. The amount of blood lost can be alarming, but most cases do not require treatment. If blood loss continues, surgery may be needed.

Achlasia
One rare condition can occur at any age. In achlasia, for some unknown reason, the muscles of the oesophageal wall fail to act in a coordinated fashion. This means that food may stick and that the oesophagus

may go into a very painful spasm. Many patients learn to overcome their difficulty by drinking large quantities of fluid. This increases the pressure in the oesophagus and dilates the constricted segment. An operation to stretch the oesophagus using endoscopy is usually successful.

Oesophageal diverticulitis
As in the colon, pockets, or diverticula, may form if the lining of the oesophagus is forced through the wall. If these are near the top of the oesophagus and fill up with food, the patient may get bad breath and have difficulty in swallowing.
Diverticula may be removed surgically. Lower down the oesophagus they do not present a problem.

OESOPHAGUS, CANCER OF
Cancer of the oesophagus accounts for 2.5 per cent of all malignant tumours in the UK.

The incidence of cancer of the oesophagus varies considerably from country to country. It is higher in most other countries than it is in the UK, particularly in China and parts of Africa. In areas of Iran, the incidence is the highest for any cancer anywhere in the world. There may be as much as a hundredfold difference between two regions very close to each other.

Dietary and other factors are suspected as the cause of such growths, but as yet no links have been proved. Cancer of the oesophagus in the UK is commoner in men and in heavy drinkers and heavy smokers, and it usually affects the 60 to 70 age group.

Symptoms and treatment
Difficulty swallowing is the commonest first symptom. Difficulty is initially confined to solid food, but in time even liquids stick.

Cancer of the oesophagus causes rapid weight loss, which is partly due to difficulty in swallowing and partly due to the action of the cancer itself.

Treatment is very disappointing: only 25 per cent of sufferers are alive five years after diagnosis. The simplest treatment is to place a tube in the oesophagus to keep it open.

Surgery to remove the tumour is difficult and rarely offers further advantages over the tube.

Recent attempts to burn a hole through the tumour using a laser have been successful and this may become more widely used in the future.

OESTROGEN
Oestrogen hormones are chemical messengers released mainly by the ovaries.

Oestrogen is essential for the sexual development of girls and for the normal functioning of the menstrual cycle, as it is involved in the build-up of the lining of the womb. During pregnancy, the placenta releases oestrogen.

Oestrogen drugs
Synthetic oestrogen has been developed for use in the Pill, or to supplement or replace oestrogen hormones in certain conditions. Oestrogen drugs work by suppressing the production of other hormones which cause the egg to be released from the ovaries.

Oestrogen drugs are also used (together with progesterone drugs) for hormone replacement therapy at the menopause.

Side effects
Oestrogen may cause weight gain, breast tenderness, nausea, migraine, reduced sex drive, depression and bleeding between periods. More significantly, it may also increase the risk of blood clotting, and for this reason it should not be taken by heavy smokers.

Oestrogen may also lead to a tendency to high blood pressure, so it is important to have regular medical check ups when taking the Pill.

OINTMENT
A skin preparation, normally based on petroleum, wax, or other greasy substances.

Ointments are used to soothe, moisturise and protect the skin — for example, against nappy rash.

▶▶ SEE ALSO — Endoscopy

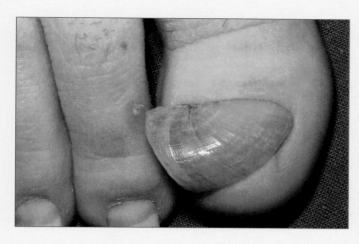

In this case of onychogryphosis, the thickening big toenail has curved round and is growing into the adjoining toe.

ONYCHOGRYPHOSIS

Onychogryphosis is an abnormal thickening of the nails, particularly the toenails.

The condition most often affects elderly people. The exact cause is not known, but it is thought to be connected with fungal infections. If nails affected by this condition are not kept trimmed, the nail will curve round as it grows. It is usually the big toe which is affected.

OOPHORECTOMY

Oophorectomy is the surgical removal of one or both ovaries.

The operation is carried out to treat certain conditions, such as ovarian cysts, cancer of the ovaries and extreme cases of endometriosis.

Oophorectomy may also be carried out at the same time as a hysterectomy, in women past the menopause or in cases where disease has spread from the uterus.

Operation and recovery

The operation is performed under general anaesthetic, taking less than an hour. A small scar is left in the abdomen. The length of time for full recovery is usually about six weeks, although this may be longer if a hysterectomy has been performed at the same time.

Most specialists try to avoid removing both ovaries in younger women, to give them the maximum chance of remaining fertile.

Women who have had both ovaries removed at an early age may be prescribed hormone replacement treatment to reduce the risk of heart disease and osteoporosis.

Oophorectomy used to be a common treatment for some types of breast cancer, since the oestrogen produced in the ovaries may promote growths in the breast. However, anti-oestrogen drugs are now used instead.

OPHTHALMITIS

This is a general term for any disorder of the eye which involves inflammation.

The term is also used to describe two particular disorders.

In sympathetic ophthalmitis, inflammation occurs in one eye some 10 days after the other eye has been severely injured. It may be necessary to remove the injured eye in order to save the sight of the other eye, which has become inflamed 'in sympathy'.

In neonatal ophthalmitis, very young babies develop a discharge from their eyes (within 21 days of birth). This is due to infection with sexually transmitted diseases, carried in the mother's vagina, while the baby is being born.

OPHTHALMOPLEGIA

Ophthalmoplegia is the paralysis of the muscles which move the eye.

The muscles may be totally or partially paralysed. The disorder has various causes, including muscular disorders such as Graves' disease and neurological disorders such as a brain tumour, a stroke, encephalitis or multiple sclerosis.

OPTIC ATROPHY

Optic atrophy is the degeneration of optic nerve fibres, leading eventually to complete loss of vision.

Optic atrophy is caused by injury or disease in the optic nerve.

OPTIC NEURITIS

Optic neuritis is an inflammation of the optic nerve.

Optic neuritis is most often found in multiple sclerosis patients, although it may also result from infection of the area around the optic nerve.

Other symptoms which accompany the complaint are pain, particularly when moving the eye. It may cause loss of vision, especially in the centre of the visual field.

Attacks usually come and go, lasting about six weeks, and may be eased with corticosteroid drugs, although the condition may eventually lead to optic atrophy.

ORAL CONTRACEPTIVES

Oral contraceptives (the birth control pill) are the most effective reversible method of contraception.

Oral contraceptives contain hormones similar to those produced by the ovaries. The most widely used form of oral contraception is the combined oestrogen-progestogen pill. It owes its popularity to its reliability and its good cycle control. The mini-pill is slightly less reliable, but may be recommended in some circumstances.

The combined pill

Most makes of the combined (oestrogen-progestogen) pill have 21 active pills to be taken each month. Some makes also have seven sugar pills, which some women find helpful to keep up a regular habit of pill-taking throughout the month, making up a 28-day cycle. Some makes have 22 active pills, for a 29-day cycle.

The main effect of the combined pill is to suppress egg production. It does this by interfering with the formation of hormones in the pituitary gland and the ovaries. At the same time, it alters the lining of the womb, changes the cervical mucus and interferes with the transport of the egg along the fallopian tubes.

Since the link between oestrogen levels and thrombosis was discovered, the manufacturers have been steadily decreasing the amount of this hormone in their pills. Some pills now contain as little as 20mg of

SEE ALSO — Contraception, Eye disorders, Ovary

MEDICAL FACT FILE

oestrogen — a fifth of the levels of 20 years ago.

During the break from the combined pill (one week per month), the withdrawal of hormones causes period-like bleeding (although some women go without a period at all).

If a pill is missed, contraceptive cover will continue provided the missed pill and the next one are taken within 24 hours. If more than one pill is missed, the situation is more complicated and it is usually advisable to back up the contraception with other methods. If you suffer an attack of vomiting or diarrhoea soon after taking a pill, you may not be protected, and it is advisable to use other methods of contraception for the rest of the month.

Side effects

Side effects from the combined pill are uncommon. Most are trivial, but a few may be serious. In order to eliminate the possibility of side effects, doctors do not normally

Starting To Take The Pill

It is important to follow the manufacturer's instructions when you start taking the Pill.

With most brands, you are advised to start taking the Pill on the fifth day after your period starts (day five of your natural cycle). Protection may not be complete, so manufacturers usually advise you to combine the Pill with other methods of contraception. In some cases, starting to take the Pill on the first day of your period (day one) will give complete protection.

prescribe it for women who smoke, who have a history of blood clotting disorders or heart problems, or for women over 35.

There is an increased incidence of thrombosis in the veins in the legs: on average one in 100,000 women die each year as a result of taking the Pill. However, the risk of death through taking the Pill is one tenth of the risk of dying in childbirth, and is minimal compared to the risks of death through smoking. Nevertheless, it is vital that you consult your doctor if you get any unexplained pains in your chest or legs.

Other side effects include a mild tendency to diabetes and a slight rise in cholesterol levels. Both are easily reversed. A few women taking the Pill become depressed, but this depression can be treated quite effectively by a daily vitamin B6 tablet.

Mini-pill

The progestogen-only pills work in a similar way to the combined pill except that they do not suppress ovulation. They alter the mucus discharged from the cervix, making it too thick for the sperm to penetrate. The pills are taken daily, with no pill-free interval. It is vital that the pills are taken at the same time every day, preferably in the morning. Again, other methods should be used if you have an attack of vomiting or diarrhoea.

Periods may become irregular or unpredictable, but they normally settle down after a few months.

The main disadvantage is unwanted pregnancy. On average, two to six women per year become pregnant while taking the mini-pill, and a higher-than-average proportion of these pregnancies will be ectopic.

ORCHIDECTOMY

Orchidectomy is the surgical removal of one or both of the testicles.

Removal of a testicle is a treatment for cancer of the testicle and for gangrene caused when the blood supply to the testicle has been cut off. Orchidectomy is sometimes part of the treatment for cancer of the prostate gland, because the testosterone hormone, which is secreted by the testicles, may promote the growth of such a cancer.

Operation and recovery

The operation is performed under general anaesthetic. Painkillers and an ice pack to relieve swelling are usually needed after the operation.

If only one testicle is removed, sex drive and fertility are not diminished. 'False' testicles can be inserted for cosmetic effect.

Hormone Levels And The Combined Pill

How does the Pill affect the levels of hormones in your body?

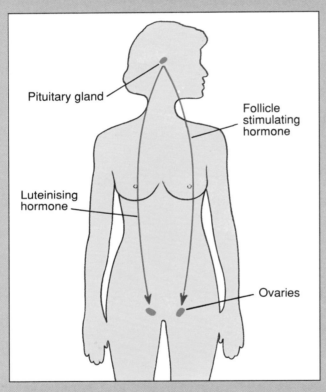

Pituitary gland

Follicle stimulating hormone

Luteinising hormone

Ovaries

● Higher-than-normal levels of oestrogen and progestogen interfere with production of the follicle-stimulating hormone (from the pituitary gland), so the egg does not ripen in the ovary.

● Levels of luteinising hormone (also from the pituitary gland) are reduced, so the egg is not released from the ovary.

● Withdrawal of the extra progestogen and oestrogen after 21 days induces menstruation.

▶▶ SEE ALSO — Penis, Testicles

ORCHITIS

Orchitis is the inflammation of a testicle.

Orchitis is most often seen in men who contract mumps. It is painful and accompanied by high fever. Epididymo-orchitis is caused by infections travelling to the testicles down the vas deferens.

Orchitis is treated with painkillers, ice packs and, in the case of bacterial infections, antibiotics. Occasionally, the affected testis is permanently damaged.

ORTHODONTIC APPLIANCES

Orthodontic appliances are devices (commonly known as braces or plates) which move the teeth and correct crookedness.

Crooked teeth are not only unsightly, they may lead to serious dental problems because they are difficult to clean. Orthodontic devices may also be used to correct a 'bite' — the position of the jaws in relation to each other when closed. For example, if the top front teeth overhang the bottom teeth a long way, this may lead to straining and stiffness, and even arthritis.

Crooked teeth may be inherited, may be caused by thumb-sucking beyond a certain age, or they may be due to overcrowding, in which case extraction could be necessary before straightening can take place. Often there is a combination of factors.

Types of appliance

All braces work by putting steady pressure on the crooked teeth, slowly moving them to a better position.

Orthodontic appliances may be fixed, attached to the teeth with special cement, or they may be removable, usually in the form of wires fitted to a plastic plate which goes in the roof of the mouth. The plate may cause some problems with speech, but removable braces are usually easier to keep clean than fixed appliances.

Most types of appliance have to be checked regularly by an orthodontist and tightened to maintain the pressure.

Braces may have to remain in place for anything from six months to several years, until teeth are straight.

OSTEOARTHRITIS

Osteoarthritis is the most common form of the disease arthritis, involving pain and swelling in the joints.

Osteoarthritis is due to excessive wear on joints, which may be caused by being overweight or by slight deformity putting unusual strain on a joint, or it may be due to age. Although normally associated with the older age group, it can affect young people who have overexercised in their youth — some gymnasts who started training very young have been crippled by the disease.

Wear on the joint breaks down the cartilage protecting the ends of the bone, or may cause extra bony growths at the joints. Most people over the age of 60 have some degree of osteoarthritis, although painful symptoms are not always present. It is three times more common in women than in men.

Symptoms

Pain, stiffness, swelling and creaking of joints are all symptoms of osteoarthritis. The joints most often affected are the hips, knees and spine, which bear a lot of weight. Shoulders, elbows, wrists and hands are often

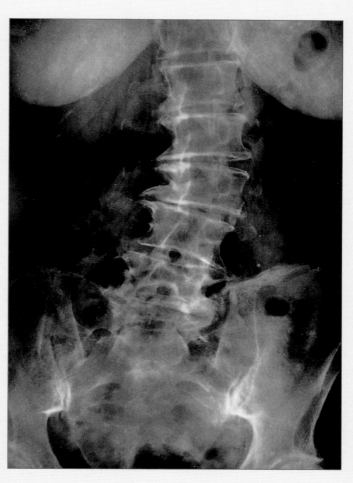

This x-ray of the lower part of the spine of an 80-year-old woman shows bone degeneration due to osteoarthritis.

affected too. Because movement is so painful in some cases, the disease may lead to muscle wasting, due to the fact that the muscles are used less.

Diagnosis and treatment

The disease is usually diagnosed by physical examination and description of symptoms. X-rays may be used to determine the extent of the degeneration of the cartilages.

Symptoms can be relieved by painkillers and non-steroid anti-inflammatory drugs, and corticosteroid injections may be given. It is important to keep weight down and to exercise gently as much as possible. Swimming is particularly helpful as the limbs are supported.

Sticks to take the weight off the limbs, and physiotherapy are also helpful. Joint replacement operations may be advised.

OSTEOCHONDRITIS DISSECANS

A condition affecting joints in which part of the bone breaks away.

Osteochondritis dissecans usually affects adolescents, and it is thought that it is normally due to disruption of the blood supply to the bone following injury. The fragments of bone may grow back into place, but often further fragments break off.

The condition causes aching pain, with swelling of the affected joint from time to time. The joints which are most often affected are the knee and elbow.

MEDICAL FACT FILE

MEDICAL FACT FILE

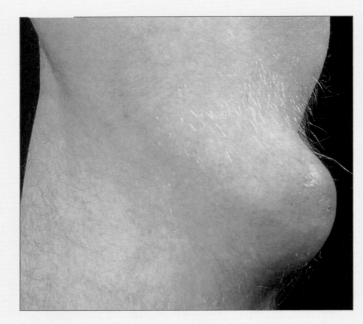

The deformity below the knee of this young person is due to osteochondritis of the shinbone.

Treatment

X-rays will show the extent of the damage and the position of fragments of bone. Endoscopic surgery can be used to remove fragments of bone, or the joint may be immobilised in a plaster cast so that the fragments can grow back into place. The condition is likely to lead to osteoarthritis in later life.

OSTEOCHONDRITIS JUVENILIS

Osteochondritis juvenilis is an inflammation of the growing part of the bone.

Osteochondritis juvenilis is thought to be due to a disruption of the blood supply to the bone. There are various types, named according to the joints affected. The condition usually occurs in children and adolescents. The bones most often affected include the thighbone, vertebrae, certain wrist bones and bones in the feet.

The inflammation causes pain and tenderness in the affected area, and leads to softening of the bone, which may cause deformity.

Treatment

The affected bones are usually immobilised with a plaster cast or orthopaedic brace in severe cases, but for some patients, surgery is necessary.

The bone usually recovers and grows normally again within three years, but there is an increased risk of osteoarthritis in later life.

OSTEOCHONDROMA

Osteochondroma is a benign growth on a bone — usually at the end of the thighbone or upper arm, near the knee or shoulder.

The growth has a neck of bone capped with cartilage, growing out of the side of the affected bone. It starts growing around adolescence and stops once the skeleton is fully developed. If the growth interferes with movement, it can be removed surgically.

OSTEODYSTROPHY

Osteodystrophy is used to describe any bone defects caused by an upset in the body chemistry.

Osteodystrophies may be caused by dietary deficiencies (eg rickets and osteomalacia, caused by a deficiency in vitamin D) or by a hormonal imbalance (eg osteoporosis and Cushing's syndrome). It may also be the result of long-term illnesses. The condition can be treated in adults if the underlying cause can be treated effectively. Once bone deformity has occurred, treatment may not be possible.

OSTEOGENESIS IMPERFECTA

This rare condition is usually known as 'brittle bone disease'.

Children suffering from osteogenesis imperfecta have very fragile bones that can fracture at the slightest knock. Cartilage growth is unaffected, so the bones look normal, but the mineral deposits that give bones their strength are missing.

The condition is hereditary, inherited as a dominant gene. Two forms exist. In the more severe form, multiple fractures occur while the baby is in the womb. The trauma of birth is so great that these babies seldom survive more than a few hours. A milder form exists and, at first, these babies appear normal. Fractures are often wrongly put down to child abuse, and insensitive questioning of parents can cause a great deal of grief. Babies with osteogenesis imperfecta often have a blueness in the whites of their eyes and a slight flattening of the skull. They may become deaf in later life.

Diagnosis and treatment

When brittle bones are suspected a bone biopsy may be needed to confirm the diagnosis. The broken bones heal rapidly but often become distorted. In severe cases, broken bones can have metal rods threaded through them. As the child grows older, the bones become thicker and fewer fractures occur.

OSTEOMA

A benign tumour of bone which may cause pain by pressing on surrounding structures.

An osteoma is hard and usually small — about 1cm in diameter. If it causes pain it may be surgically removed

A baby's eye showing the characteristic blueness of the rare condition, osteogenesis imperfecta.

➤➤ SEE ALSO — Brittle bones, Cushing's syndrome, Rickets

OSTEOMALACIA

Osteomalacia is the weakening of bones in adults due to a deficiency in vitamin D.

Healthy bones need calcium and phosphorus, which come from various foods. In order to absorb these minerals properly, a certain amount of vitamin D is required. This may come from diet (fish, eggs, butter and margarine) or sunshine. If the bones do not get the supply of minerals they need, they become softer, weaker, and are susceptible to fractures. In children this condition is known as rickets.

Osteomalacia is rare in developed countries, except as a side effect of some other conditions, such as coeliac disease, kidney failure and some inherited metabolic disorders.

Pains in the bones, muscle weakness and muscle spasms in the hands, feet and throat are all symptoms of osteomalacia. It is treated by careful attention to diet with vitamin and mineral supplements in some cases. Patients who have problems in absorbing the minerals and vitamins through their intestines, may be given injections.

OSTEOMYELITIS

Osteomyelitis is the term used to describe an infection of the bone and bone marrow.

As with all living tissues, bone is liable to infection. This infection may arise as a result of germs entering the bloodstream via a skin wound — in a compound fracture, for example — or as a result of an infection somewhere else in the body.

Acute osteomyelitis usually occurs in children and adolescents. The patient complains of a sudden, very severe pain in a limb. In the early stages there is a high fever and the limb is very tender to the touch. As the disease progresses the affected area becomes reddened and swollen. Even at this stage any x-rays look normal. Besides listening to the patient's description and examining the area, diagnosis may be made by a blood test to see if there is an excess of white blood cells.

Treatment
Strict bed rest, with the affected area raised, together with intravenous antibiotics may cure the disorder. In difficult cases, surgery may be needed to remove the infected bone.

Long-term problem
If the infection is not completely eradicated it may lie dormant for many years, walled off in a cavity in the bone. Now and again the condition flares up, often following a knock. This chronic osteomyelitis is very difficult to treat even with surgical removal of the affected bone tissue and long courses of antibiotics.

OSTEOPATHY

Osteopathy is a therapy involving the manipulation and massage of joints, muscles and tendons throughout the body.

Osteopathy is based on the idea that many disorders are the result of the misalignment of bones and the disruption of nervous and muscular activity.

Osteopaths use various diagnostic techniques, including taking a detailed history and sometimes x-rays. Treatment involves massage and manipulation, sometimes followed by stronger pressure. Sometimes tension is released with heavy pressure, causing a loud but relatively painless crack, followed by great relief.

Osteopathy is generally agreed to be a useful therapy for some types of back and neck pain. Many practitioners claim that they can use the technique to treat conditions such as asthma, migraine and digestive disorders, since they claim that all body systems operate in unison, and that disturbances in one area can affect the way other parts of the body work.

Osteopaths have to do a four-year course of study. Practitioners should belong to a recognised association.

OSTEOPOROSIS

Osteoporosis is the term used to describe thinning of the bones.

Osteoporosis itself is painless, but the loss of bone makes the sufferer more likely to develop fractures, particularly of the hip and wrist. Compression fractures of the spine cause a loss of height and the bending of the shoulders, known as dowager's hump, which affects many older women.

Osteoporosis is generally thought of as a disease of old age, but there are many causes, some of which affect the young and previously healthy.

The causes
To grow and mature normally, bone must be continually stressed and strained. Any condition that results in immobility will cause osteoporosis of the affected limb. This is common after severe fractures, and accident victims who have been in

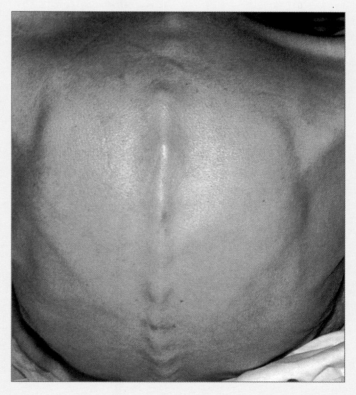

This elderly woman is suffering from osteoporosis, a loss of bony tissue, which has resulted in a 'dowager's hump'.

⏩ SEE ALSO — Bone, Rickets

Calcium-Rich Foods For Strong Bones

Milk
Cheese
Butter
Green leafy vegetables
Citrus fruits
Sardines with the bones in
Shellfish

plaster for several months require careful physiotherapy if they are to avoid further fractures. This is even more true of astronauts, who have spent prolonged periods in the weightlessness of space.

Several drugs, including steroids and heparin, have been known to induce osteoporosis. For this reason it is important that patients on these treatments maintain a high calcium intake.

All post-menopausal women suffer from osteoporosis because their ovaries are no longer secreting oestrogen, which helps to maintain the density of bone. The degree to which they are affected depends on two things: their age at the menopause and the density of the original bone. For this reason, it is important to ensure that calcium intake is adequate, particularly in the last 10–15 years before the menopause. Bone density can be measured and this gives a very good indication of the likelihood of fractures occurring in later life. Unfortunately the test is not yet generally available.

The disorder is generally painless and often the first indication is when a minor injury or 'fall' causes a broken bone.

Treatment and prevention

Once the bone has thinned, it cannot be replaced, but it is possible to minimise the progress of osteoporosis. The first stage in the treatment is to remove the cause of osteoporosis where at all possible. However, in women who have reached

the menopause, treatment is aimed at trying to preserve the remaining bone, usually through hormone replacement therapy (HRT). Most doctors would agree that any woman who has had a premature menopause (due to a hysterectomy, for example) or who has a family history of osteoporosis, should be on HRT. A high protein, calcium-rich diet and regular exercise will all help to minimise the risk.

OSTEOSARCOMA

Osteosarcoma is a malignant tumour of the bone which spreads to the lungs if not treated.

Osteosarcoma occurs in young people and, as yet, the causes are unknown. Normally the main symptom is swelling and pain in the affected bone — often one of the long bones in an arm or leg, or around the shoulder, knee or hip.

Diagnosis and treatment

Diagnosis is usually based on x-rays or other techniques such as MRI (magnetic resonance imaging).

Treatment with radiotherapy may be possible, but in most cases removal of bone is the best treatment. This may mean amputation, but sometimes a bone graft or artificial bone can be used to replace the diseased bone.

Anticancer drugs will be necessary to ensure that the growth does not spread through the body.

Paget's disease

Osteosarcoma may also develop as a rare complication of Paget's disease — a bone disorder in which there is an imbalance between the cells which break down bone tissue and those which form bone tissue.

Paget's disease is a condition that only affects older people.

OSTEOTOMY

Osteotomy is an operation on a bone to change its position, shorten it or lengthen it.

The most common reason for osteotomy is to treat bunions, by operating on a deformed big toe bone, and it is also used to treat congenital hip deformation. It may also be used in plastic surgery or cosmetic surgery.

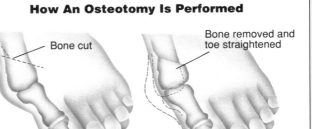

How An Osteotomy Is Performed

Bone cut

Bone removed and toe straightened

1

2

To correct a bunion, first the bone is cut (1), part of it is then removed and the toe is straightened (2).

OTITIS EXTERNA

Otitis externa is an inflammation of the outer ear canal.

Inflammation may initially be due to irritation or infection: the warm, moist environment of the outer ear means that the two usually go together. Infection is usually due to fungi or bacteria and may be localised or widespread. The commonest localised infection is a boil. This may be extremely painful, due to the build up of pressure. Home treatment with painkillers and hot compresses may have to be supplemented with antibiotics.

Susceptibility to infection

Normally, the outer ear is protected by wax and skin. If these defences are breached, otitis externa is the result. The outer ear is a self-cleaning organ: cotton

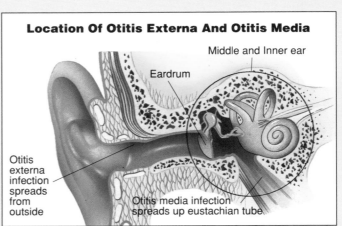

Location Of Otitis Externa And Otitis Media

Middle and Inner ear

Eardrum

Otitis externa infection spreads from outside

Otitis media infection spreads up eustachian tube

➤➤ SEE ALSO — Deafness, Ear disorders, Paget's disease

buds, hairgrips and finger nails will all push old wax back towards the eardrum and cause scratches that let in infection. Prolonged immersion in water will soften the skin of the external ear and otitis externa is more common in swimmers than non-swimmers.

Any ear infection can lead to deafness if it is not treated. In mild cases, the doctor may clean the ear canal and prescribe ear drops. In severe cases, however, oral antibiotics and an ear pack soaked in antiseptic may be needed.

OTITIS MEDIA

Otitis media is inflammation of the middle ear.

Inflammation is usually infective and the cause is almost always a bacteria or a virus. Infection is more likely if the normal secretions of the middle ear are unable to drain away. The usual cause of this condition is if there is a cold blocking the eustachian tube (which links the middle ear to the back of the nose, and allows for changes in pressure).

Children, who have very narrow eustachian tubes, are more commonly affected than adults.

Symptoms and diagnosis

In older children, pain, deafness and discharge make the diagnosis fairly easy. In babies and infants, however, the only signs to be recognised may be a fever and irritability.

Examination of the ear with an auriscope or otoscope will reveal a red bulging eardrum. If this bursts, a trickle of blood and pus is released and the relief from pain is instantaneous.

Treatment and outlook

Treatment is usually very straightforward, with a combination of painkillers and antibiotics.

Mastoiditis, meningitis and brain abscesses are very rare complications.

However, chronic otitis media, or glue ear, is relatively common in children under the age of about seven. Thick, sticky mucus accumulates in the ear, causing deafness. Efforts to clear the glue with antibiotics and decongestants frequently fail, and grommet surgery is required. This involves inserting grommets, tiny plastic valves, in the eardrum, allowing the middle ear to drain freely.

OTOPLASTY

Otoplasty is cosmetic surgery to correct bat or protruding ears.

To operate on ears which stick out, the surgeon will cut away some of the skin behind the ear, and re-shape the cartilage. The scar is hidden in the crease behind the ear.

In the case of non-existent ears (some children are born without ears) or ears which have been torn off in an accident, the surgeon sculpts a new ear from a piece of cartilage taken from elsewhere in the body (usually from the ribs) and fits it into a pocket of skin which is at the side of the ear. As long as the other ear works normally, the surgeon does not concern himself with making the new ear function fully. It is primarily a cosmetic operation.

OTOSCLEROSIS

Otosclerosis is a disorder of the middle ear, in which one of the bones (the stapes) becomes immobile.

The cause of the disorder is not known. The bone which forms the stapes overgrows, so that it can no longer transmit sound vibrations, causing progressive deafness.

The condition tends to run in families, and affects as many as one in 200 people. it is more common in women than in men.

Symptoms and diagnosis

Sounds become muffled, although they may be easier to hear if there is some background noise. The condition progresses slowly over a couple of decades, and is often accompanied by tinnitus (ringing in the ears). To start with, the sufferer tends to speak very quietly. If the condition gets worse, high tones may become difficult to hear, and the sufferer starts to talk much more loudly.

Anyone who suspects that their hearing may be failing them should go for a hearing test to try and diagnose the problem.

Treatment

A hearing aid will usually improve the quality of hearing and, in some cases, an operation may be performed to replace the stapes with an artificial bone.

OVARY

The ovaries are a pair of almond-shaped organs which are vital in the female reproductive system.

The ovaries are about 2cm by 4cm, and are attached to the side of the pelvis by ligaments. Each ovary has a dual role: the production of an egg each month and the secretion of the female sex hormones, oestrogen and progesterone, which affect the condition of the wall of the uterus. The ovaries are very sensitive to compression and it is possible for an over-enthusiastic gynaecologist —

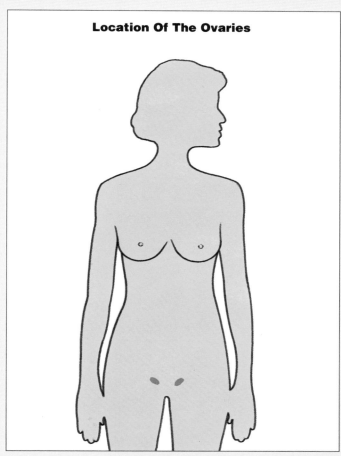

Location Of The Ovaries

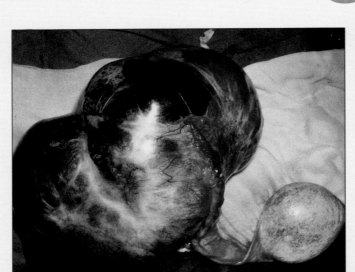

Ovarian cysts are usually non-malignant, but they may become very large and painful and have to be removed.

or lover — to cause you severe pain.

There are several disorders of the ovary, some of which are quite serious.

Ovarian cysts

Ovarian cysts are common. Most come from the site of the maturing egg and do not cause problems. These 'follicular cysts' may reach up to 5cm in diameter. Larger cysts may also occur: they are often the result of hormonal imbalance, and may cause irregularities in the menstrual cycle.

Endometrial cysts of the ovary are uncommon. They are due to the endometrium, the lining of the uterus, spreading outside the confines of the womb. Since they are made up of the same tissue as the lining of the womb, these cysts bleed in monthly cycles. This bleeding can be intensely painful and in severe cases, removal of the ovary is the only treatment.

The most spectacular of the ovarian cysts are those known as serous cysts. They are filled with a clear, watery fluid, and may be as large as a pregnancy (the foetus and liquid surrounding it) at full term. Twenty per cent of these cysts prove to be

malignant and it is common practice to remove both ovaries and the womb in all affected women past childbearing age.

Ovarian cysts often cause surprisingly few symptoms. Often, the first sign is tight clothing. At this stage, the cyst is often some 10–12cm across, and can be detected in a pelvic examination. Accidental twisting of the cyst, so that the blood supply is cut off, causes severe pain in the lower abdomen. Simple cysts may go away of their own accord: dermoid cysts and malignant growths do not.

Dermoid cysts

The majority of ovarian tumours in young girls are benign 'dermoid cysts'. These tumours are made up of primitive cells, and often contain hair, teeth and bones. They should be removed, as they may become malignant.

Polycystic ovaries

Polycystic ovaries are a poorly understood condition caused by an excess of male sex hormone. This has many effects, including absence of periods, male hair distribution and clitoral enlargement. The excess of male hormones is often due to a minute tumour of the ovary that would otherwise pass unnoticed. In polycystic ovaries, the ovaries are covered in tiny cysts, each about 5mm in diameter, and each representing a failed egg. There may be so many cysts that the ovary is enlarged and takes on a 'cobblestone appearance'

If a tumour is the cause of the condition, it should be removed. If not, hormonal treatment to counteract the effects of testosterone is prescribed. Obesity seems to play a part in maintaining the syndrome and dieting may also help.

OVARY, CANCER OF

Some growths on the ovaries may originate from the ovaries themselves, or they may be secondary growths which have spread from another part of the body.

Ovarian cancer usually occurs after the menopause. It is more common in women who have never had children, and not so common in women who have been on the Pill. It affects about one woman in a hundred, and, although it only accounts for a quarter of all female genital cancers, it is the fifth leading cause of cancer death in women after breast, lung, colon and stomach cancer. This is because the tumour is usually completely symptomless until it has spread beyond the pelvis.

There is no completely reliable test for the early detection of ovarian cancer (as there is with cervical cancer), but it can be detected with ultrasound, and mass screening for ovarian cancer may soon be more common than screening for breast cancer.

Symptoms and treatment

The commonest symptom of ovarian cancer is abdominal swelling, either as a result of the tumour itself, or as a result of the excessive production of fluid.

Laparoscopy (examination with a surgical telescope) or laparotomy (an exploratory operation) may be needed to confirm diagnosis. As much of the malignant growth as possible has to be removed, so a hysterectomy may be necessary in some cases. In any case, once the ovaries have been removed, the patient is no longer fertile. It is possible that radiotherapy and chemotherapy will also be necessary.

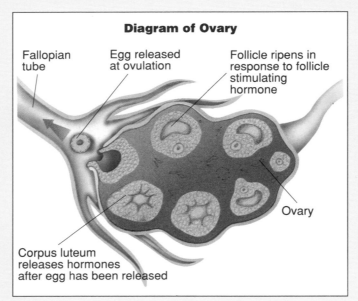

Diagram of Ovary

Fallopian tube

Egg released at ovulation

Follicle ripens in response to follicle stimulating hormone

Ovary

Corpus luteum releases hormones after egg has been released

SEE ALSO — Chemotherapy, Laparoscopy, Radiotherapy

PACEMAKER

An artificial pacemaker is a device which provides a stimulus to the heart, to supplement its natural pacemaker.

The normal cardiac pacemaker is a collection of cells in the wall of the heart. It has the unique property of being able to generate a wave of electrical activity which spreads through the heart muscle and controls the heart rate. In certain conditions the natural pacemaker may fail and the heartbeat becomes erratic. In these circumstances an artificial pacemaker may need to be fitted.

Artificial pacemakers are battery operated devices designed to provide a regular stimulus to the heart. In the past, some pacemakers have been nuclear powered, but the latest lithium batteries can guarantee 15 years trouble-free running. The type most commonly fitted is the 'on demand' pacemaker. This only comes into operation if the natural heart beat drops below 70 beats per minute. Newer and more sophisticated models are being developed which can detect and treat an increasing range of cardiac irregularities.

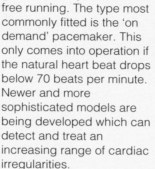

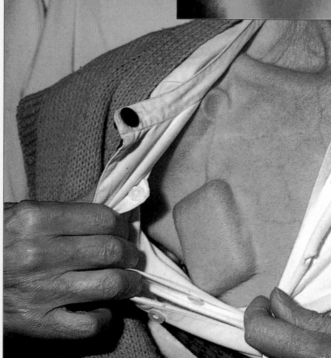

Above: An elderly man with an artificial heart pacemaker inserted beneath his skin. This device provides a stimulus which supplements the heart's natural pacemaker. Inset: An x-ray of a heart pacemaker in position in a patient's chest.

PAGET'S DISEASE

The term Paget's disease has been applied to a number of disorders which were first described by Sir James Paget.

Sir James Paget was Queen Victoria's surgeon in the nineteenth century. There are two disorders which are of particular importance.

Paget's disease of the bone

Paget's disease of the bone is a common disease amongst the elderly.

In normal individuals, all the bones in the body are in a constant state of flux, with new bone being laid down as old bone is reabsorbed into the blood-stream. But in Paget's disease of the bone this delicate balance is lost and the consequence is deformity, pain and fractures. This form of Paget's disease may be diagnosed by x-ray or by characteristic changes in the bio-chemistry of the blood. The condition can be largely controlled, if not cured, by the patient receiving regular injections of the thyroid hormone calcitonin.

Paget's disease of the nipple

Paget's disease of the nipple is a form of breast cancer which manifests itself as irritation of the nipple. This irritation mainly affects elderly women and resembles eczema. A particular characteristic of Paget's disease of the nipple is that it only affects one breast. Treatment depends on how far the disease has spread, but mastectomy and radiotherapy are frequently needed.

PAIN

Pain is a sensation which is picked up by various nerves in the body and transmitted to the brain.

Pain and its relief have always fascinated mankind. As long ago as 2250 BC the Babylonians were using plants such as opium and cannabis to relieve pain.

Modern theories about pain are complex, with newer, ever more complicated systems of pain transmission being described almost yearly.

What is pain?

The sense organs for pain are naked nerve endings found in almost every organ of the body except the brain. Pain messages are transmitted to the brain by the two distinct types of fibre: one type transmits signals very quickly and the other relatively slowly. Both types of fibre end in the spinal column and other nerve fibres relay the message to the brain and muscles.

The presence of two types of pain fibre explains the observation that there are basically two types of pain. One type is described as 'bright' and 'sharp' and the other as 'dull' or 'boring'. A painful blow causes an immediate sharp pain, which is followed a few moments later by a dull ache.

Under certain circumstances the pain messages leaving the sense organs are modified before they reach the level of consciousness. It seems that pain carried along the fast fibres can stop the perception of pain travelling along the slow fibres. It is known that prostaglandins, fatty acids which act rather like hormones, have a role in causing pain and inflammation in damaged tissues. These facts are being exploited in the search for more effective painkillers.

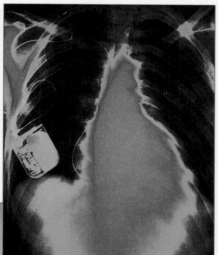

Levels of pain

Besides this difference in types of pain, it seems that different people perceive levels of pain in different ways. For example, sudden, unexplained pain (from sitting on a sharp pin or needle, for example) may seem more alarming than the pain from an injection, which you are prepared for. The same is thought to be true in childbirth: if you approach the event feeling relaxed, and prepared for a certain amount of pain, it may be more bearable than if you have not practised any relaxation techniques. Once a person has come to terms with the cause of pain, for example if they have cancer, they often find that the pain is less crippling.

Pain is perceived more strongly in a person who is irritable, tired, run down or anxious. And many women find they become more sensitive to pain around the time of menstruation. On the other hand, it has been noticed that people who have their mind on something that is important to them, whether it is winning a battle or saving a child from some terrible threat, become immune to certain types of pain, so that even if they have a broken arm or a badly cut foot they will continue in their task.

Treating pain

The most effective therapy in treating pain is to remove the painful stimulus: some sources of pain can be treated surgically or medically. Unfortunately, depending on the cause of the pain, this is not always possible and doctors must try to suppress the effects of the painful stimulus. Most hospitals run a specialist Pain Clinic where the medical team offer a wide range of treatments, and some hospitals even offer complementary therapies such as hypnotherapy.

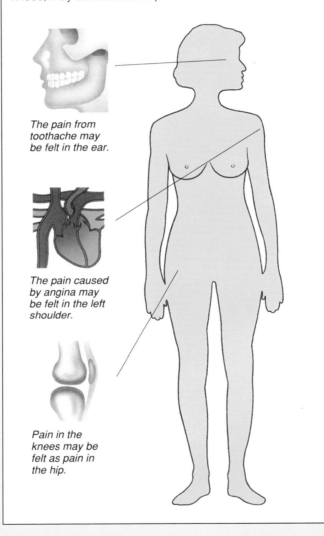

Referred Pain

A referred pain is felt somewhere other than where the injury or disease is. Sometimes it is not clear where the source of the pain is.

Referred pain occurs because some nerves converge before they transmit their messages to the brain, so that the brain cannot identify the exact nerve which is affected.

For example, a bad tooth may cause earache; angina (a heart disorder) is felt in the left shoulder; and some disorders, such as arthritis, which cause pain in the knees, may be felt in the hip.

The pain from toothache may be felt in the ear.

The pain caused by angina may be felt in the left shoulder.

Pain in the knees may be felt as pain in the hip.

Drug treatment is the most common form of pain control: the medicine comes in many forms: liquid medicine, pills, injections, liniments and suppositories. Such painkillers, or analgesics, are divided into two types: narcotic and non-narcotic. The narcotic drugs are all based on the chemical structure of morphine. Some are more powerful, some have fewer side effects, and some are safer in overdose, but they all work in the same way. They bind to sites in the brain that are normally reserved for naturally occurring chemicals. In so doing they do not abolish pain, but remove its unpleasant consequences. Tolerance

occurs and as time goes on, bigger doses are needed to exert the same effect. This is not the same as addiction, which is rarely a problem if narcotics are used properly.

Most other drug treatments, including aspirin, paracetamol and the non-steroidal anti-inflammatories, act by inhibiting prostaglandins.

Pain pathways

TENS (transcutaneous electrical nerve stimulation) is a therapy which involves irritating the nerve fibres by passing minute electric shocks through electrodes which are placed on the skin. This closes the pain pathways before they reach the brain. It may provide relief only while the electrodes are in place, or the relief may continue for some time. It is not suitable for people with pacemakers.

Local anaesthetics work by interfering with the electrical transmission of nerves. When anaesthetics are injected around a nerve fibre, they abolish pain in the area that the nerve supplies. A similar, but more permanent, effect can be produced by injecting alcohol into the nerve.

Alternative therapies, such as acupuncture, and psychological techniques such as hypnosis and biofeedback, can be used to treat painful muscle conditions, such as spasm, or tension headaches.

PALLOR

Pallor is a term which is used to describe abnormally pale skin. Pallor may be a symptom of an illness or disorder.

Pallor shows in the mucous membranes as well as the skin, and doctors may check under the eyelids for this sign.

➤➤ SEE ALSO — Albinism, Anaemia, Blood

Possible causes

Pallor is commonly caused by the narrowing of blood vessels which may occur as a result of various upsets to the body, including shock, pain, heavy blood loss and extreme cold. Pallor usually accompanies fainting.

It may also be the result of various metabolic disorders, including kidney and thyroid disorders. It could be due to anaemia, which takes many forms, but involves a lack of haemoglobin, which gives blood its red colour.

Pallor is also a feature of albinism and melanin deficiency.

PALPITATION

Palpitations are the sensation of a very rapid or forceful heartbeat.

Such sensations are normal after heavy work or exercise, after a sudden shock or in tense situations when the adrenal gland is preparing the body for 'fight or flight'. However, if they occur when you are resting, they could be an indication of certain problems.

Ectopic heartbeats

An ectopic heartbeat is an irregularity in the rhythm: the heart gives an early beat, followed by a pause, and it feels like a fluttering in the chest. Ectopic heartbeats are completely harmless.

Common causes include drinking too much coffee or overindulgence in alcohol.

PALSY

Palsy is an old-fashioned term for paralysis.

It is still used to refer to certain types of palsy, including cerebral palsy and facial palsy (also known as

Bell's palsy). Facial palsy, a weakness and paralysis caused by damage to the facial nerves, is usually only a temporary condition.

PANCREAS

The pancreas is a soft, tapering, sausage-shaped organ which produces enzymes and secretes the hormone insulin.

The pancreas is situated against the back of the abdomen, just below the stomach.

What the pancreas does

The digestive enzymes secreted by the pancreas are used to break down carbohydrates, fats and proteins. The juices collect in the pancreatic duct which joins the common bile duct leading into the duodenum. These digestive juices are produced in response to hormones which are released by the stomach.

Insulin is produced in distinct clumps of cells known as the islets of Langerhans. A high blood glucose level causes the release of insulin directly into the circulation. From a functional point of view, the insulin-producing islets are completely distinct from the rest of the pancreas.

In certain conditions (cystic fibrosis, for example), the pancreatic duct is blocked and the digestive juices are absent. This leads to malabsorption, malnutrition and vitamin deficiencies, since the foodstuffs are not broken down and nutrients cannot be absorbed.

Disorders of the pancreas

The most common disorder of the pancreas is diabetes mellitus. Insulin-deficiency diabetes, the most serious form, involves a relentless rise in the concentration of glucose in the blood. The body tries to get rid of the excess glucose via the urine. To do this, large volumes of fluid are needed and the commonest symptoms of diabetes are therefore thirst and the passage of large

MEDICAL FACT FILE

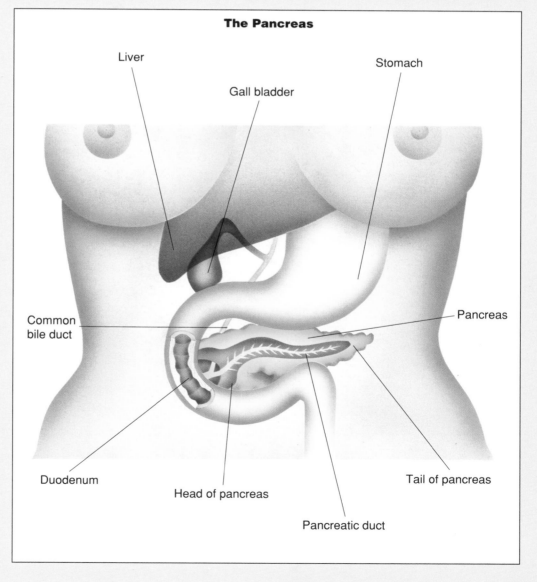

The Pancreas

Liver

Gall bladder

Stomach

Common bile duct

Pancreas

Duodenum

Head of pancreas

Tail of pancreas

Pancreatic duct

▶▶ SEE ALSO — Diabetes, Gall Bladder, Phobias, Hyperventilation

amounts of urine. If untreated, diabetes mellitus is fatal. Treatment consists of regular injections to replace the missing insulin.

Cysts may develop in the pancreas: the commonest cyst is the pseudocyst. This is usually the result of an injury which crushes the pancreas. Eventually, the cyst may grow to fill the whole of the abdomen. Treatment consists of internal drainage, in which the contents of the cyst are emptied into the bowel via a permanent opening.

Pancreatitis

Acute pancreatitis is a very painful condition, in which the pancreatic juices digest the organ itself. The condition is commonest in alcoholics but may occur as a side effect of mumps or gall stones.

The first sign of acute pancreatitis is severe upper abdominal pain, often spreading through to the back. The abdomen is acutely tender to the touch. The diagnosis can be confirmed by a simple test that will show a very high level of digestive enzymes in the blood. Treatment is medical rather than surgical. Large doses of opiates are given to combat the pain and a tube is passed into the stomach to remove the gastric juices and thus relieve the strain on the pancreas. Intravenous fluids are given in an attempt to combat shock.

Ninety five per cent of sufferers make a complete recovery and subsequent attacks are rare.

PANCREAS, CANCER OF

Pancreatic cancer is a rare condition, which affects mainly the older age groups.

Pancreatic cancer is rare below the age of 50, and about twice as many men are affected as women. Pancreatic cancers are highly malignant and spread readily. As the pancreas swells it obstructs the bile duct, causing jaundice. Indigestion, loss of appetite and rapid weight loss are common symptoms.

Diagnosis and treatment

Pancreatic cancer may be confirmed by an ultrasound scan or by injecting dye into the bile duct and taking x-rays. Small growths may be removed surgically but in the majority of cases, the best that can be hoped for is an operation to bypass the tumour. This relieves symptoms but it does not increase life expectancy.

PANIC ATTACK

Panic attacks are short periods of extreme anxiety. They are often a symptom of phobia or an anxiety disorder.

Panic attacks usually last only a few minutes. The sufferer feels intense fear, and feels physical symptoms such as tightness in the chest, palpitations, dizziness and faintness, trembling and sweating. There is often fast, shallow breathing (hyperventilation), which can be relieved by breathing into a paper bag.

Treatment for panic attacks is aimed at finding the trigger for the attack, and learning to avoid the trigger or overcome the problem with relaxation techniques or beta-blockers.

PAPILLOEDEMA

Papilloedema is a swelling of part of the optic nerve, and is usually a symptom of a serious disorder.

Papilloedema can be seen by looking at the retina

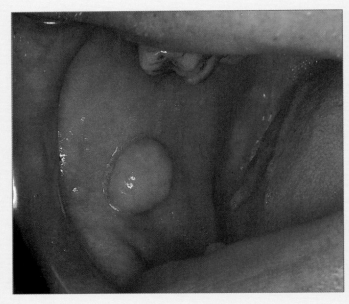

A papilloma which has grown on the inside of the cheek. This benign growth occurs on the skin or mucous membranes.

with an opthalmoscope. This may indicate that there is a rise in the pressure of cerebrospinal fluid in the skull, which could be due to a brain tumour, or it may be due to damage to the optic nerve itself.

PAPILLOMA

A papilloma is a small growth of skin, which resembles a wart, but which is often attached to the body by a very small 'neck'.

The outer layer of skin or mucous membrane, the epithelium, grows extra cells, and a small knot of skin develops. These growths are common in older people, and are almost always benign.

They may be removed by your doctor for cosmetic reasons. This is usually done by tying a silk thread around the base of the papilloma, thus cutting off the blood supply. Bigger ones may be snipped off and the base cauterised.

Papillomas may grow anywhere in the body, but they are most commonly found internally — in the throat, urinary and digestive tract — as well as on the surface of the skin.

PARACETAMOL

Paracetamol is an analgesic drug, or painkiller.

Paracetamol is a mild painkiller, which is used by many to treat headaches, toothache, period pains, rheumatic pains, and so on. It also relieves the symptoms of colds and influenza.

The main advantage of paracetamol over aspirin is that it does not irritate the stomach, and is therefore useful for treating stomach ulcers. However, unlike aspirin, paracetamol is not an anti-inflamatory drug and so it is less effective than aspirin in treating injury to muscles and ligaments.

Paracetamol is considered by doctors to be the safest painkiller for children and it is available in syrup form.

PARALYSIS

Paralysis is the loss of function of one or more muscles.

The cause of the paralysis can vary from the short-lived effects of a heavy blow, to the life-threatening consequences of a stroke.

Causes of paralysis

Stroke is the third commonest cause of death in the western world. Strokes that do not cause death often cause varying degrees of paralysis. Strokes may be the result of a blood clot blocking an artery in the brain or of bleeding into the brain itself. Smoking, high blood pressure and sugar diabetes are all known to increase the risk of a stroke. In the same way that angina can warn of an impending heart attack, so some strokes may be heralded by transient ischaemic attacks or 'mini-strokes'. These have all the characteristics of strokes, including paralysis, but the effect is short-lived. Such an attack requires urgent investigation and possibly long-term treatment to prevent further clotting.

Brain tumours often have similar effects to strokes, but the onset is gradual and is usually accompanied by headache and vomiting. The outlook is usually poor as 85 per cent of all brain tumours are malignant.

Multiple sclerosis is a relatively common cause of paralysis in the UK. In the early stages it usually causes a mild weakness of short duration. It may take many years for the disease to progress to the stage where paralysis affects the sufferer's life style.

Parkinson's disease may affect as many as one person in every 100 in the over-50s age group. Weakness develops slowly and is often not as obvious as the classical tremor.

Another common condition which mainly affects the elderly is cervical spondylosis. This is a form of osteoarthritis which affects the neck so that nerves are pinched as they leave the spinal cord. Neck pain is often a prominent feature and weakness of the hands only develops slowly.

Other causes

Other, less common, conditions can cause paralysis, including vitamin B12 deficiency, myasthenia gravis and muscular dystrophy.

Treatment

Treatment depends on the cause of the paralysis. In many cases, the outlook is poor. Hospital examination is often necessary to check the cause of the paralysis.

Strokes cannot be reversed, though the effects may be minimised with physiotherapy aimed at utilising the unaffected parts of the brain. Underlying diabetes or high blood pressure should be controlled to try and minimise the chance of further paralysis.

Surgery may be possible on brain tumours, but often it is only possible to use chemo- or radiotherapy to try to control them. Cervical spondylosis can be treated surgically but there is a danger of worsening the paralysis. Modern treatment of Parkinson's disease may be highly effective during the early stages.

Other than these specific conditions, the most that can be done for the majority of cases of paralysis is rehabilitation. The aim is to improve the patient's functional capacity through the use of splints, sticks and other aids.

PARANOIA

Paranoia is commonly used to describe a feeling of persecution — that everyone is out to get you.

The feeling of persecution is only one manifestation of the condition of paranoia: in medical terms, the condition involves a feeling that everything that is going on hinges around oneself. Besides persecution, there may be delusions of grandeur and jealousy. Other symptoms include hallucinations, but more often it is abnormal behaviour such as sudden anger, suspicion and self-

isolation which indicate that there's a problem.

Types and causes

Paranoia may be a long-term problem, caused by brain damage, alcohol and drug abuse, or it may be a symptom of a serious psychosis. For some, it is a short-term condition, due to a change in circumstances (such as leaving home, or in some cases bereavement). In shared paranoia, the sufferer develops delusions as a result of a close relationship with someone who is already paranoid.

Treatment

It is important to treat the illness in its early stages, with antipsychotic drugs and psychological therapy, to prevent the delusions becoming entrenched.

PARASITES

A parasite is any organism which lives in or on another plant, animal or person, and derives its nutrition from that host without benefiting the host.

Technically, bacteria, viruses and fungi are parasites, which may cause disease but often actually assist correct bodily function (in the case of some bacteria in the digestive system).

However, the term is more often used to describe small creatures which may live inside the body (tape worms, liver flukes, etc) or on the surface of the body (head lice, ticks and bedbugs, for example). Many types of parasites multiply rapidly, and may become a drain on the host, causing fever and illness. Most are relatively easy to treat, the type of treatment depending on the parasite involved.

Paralysis in young children is usually due to injury. Modern development in wheelchair technology and campaigns for wheelchair access have made life easier for paraplegics.

MEDICAL FACT FILE

➤➤ SEE ALSO — Brain, Chemotherapy, Lice, Liver fluke, MS, Muscular dystrophy, Radiotherapy, Roundworm, Scabies, Stroke, Tapeworm

PARATHYROID GLANDS

The parathyroid glands, situated on or in the thyroid glands, produce a vital hormone which controls the amount of calcium in the blood.

The parathyroid glands are yellowish-brown bodies about the size and shape of grape pips. Most people have four, but some people have six or even eight. The parathyroid glands are intimately associated with the thyroids, to the extent that they are sometimes embedded within them.

Functions

The parathyroid glands produce a hormone, parathormone, which is essential for life. The hormone acts on the gut, the kidneys and the bones, and has the overall effect of increasing the amount of calcium in the blood. The levels of parathormone and calcium are tightly linked: if the level of calcium in the blood falls, more parathormone is produced, which has the effect of increasing the calcium levels by absorbing more from the bones and gut, and conserving it by not excreting it through the kidneys. If there is too much calcium in the blood, the level of parathormone will fall so that less calcium goes into the bloodstream.

Disorders of the parathyroid fall into two groups: hyperparathyroidism and hypoparathyroidism.

Hyperparathyroidism

Hyperparathyroidism is an excess of parathormone. It is usually the result of a benign, hormone-producing tumour of one of the parathyroid glands. Symptoms are due to the high serum calcium level and include loss of appetite, nausea, vomiting, thirst, constipation and muscle fatigue. In about five per cent of cases the first sign of a high serum calcium level is an acute psychiatric illness.

There are many other causes, and to confirm the diagnosis, blood levels of parathormone must be measured. Surgical removal may be necessary to control the level of the hormone, but this is made harder by the fact that the position of the glands varies from individual to individual. Sampling blood from specific sites may give the surgeon clues as to which gland is affected.

Hypoparathyroidism

The commonest cause of hypoparathyroidism is accidental removal of the glands during thyroid surgery. Occasionally, an auto-immune disease destroys the glands. Symptoms of a low calcium level depend on the actual level, but tingling around the mouth, cramps and even convulsions may occur.

Blood tests will reveal a low serum calcium level and a very low serum parathormone level. Parathormone is rapidly destroyed by the kidneys and so it is not given as a treatment. In emergencies, calcium may be given intravenously to control convulsions. Long-term therapy consists of calcium and vitamin D supplements.

PARKINSON'S DISEASE

Parkinson's disease is a condition which affects older people and causes a disturbance in the function of the voluntary muscles.

The disease was first recognised by James Parkinson at the end of the eighteenth century. It affects about one person in a thousand.

Symptoms

The main features of Parkinson's disease are rigidity, tremor and slow movements. Walking is slow, with arms hanging by the side of the body, and short, jerky steps. The face is expressionless and the eyes unblinking. In long-standing cases, the sufferer is unable to rise from his chair, falls frequently and develops minute handwriting.

The tremor is most obvious in the hands, and the head nods backwards and forwards rhythmically. Not surprisingly, depression is also a common side effect of the disease.

Causes

The commonest form of Parkinson's disease is 'idiopathic', a term which means 'of unknown cause'. It usually starts in the 50 to 60 age group and affects more men than women. It seems to be caused by an imbalance in the chemical make-up of the brain.

Hardening of the arteries can cause many diseases such as heart attacks, strokes and dementia. It can also cause Parkinson's disease, but in this case there tends to be less tremor than in the idiopathic kind. Drugs, especially those used in psychiatry, can cause Parkinsonian symptoms. In these cases, abnormal writhing movements of the face and mouth are common.

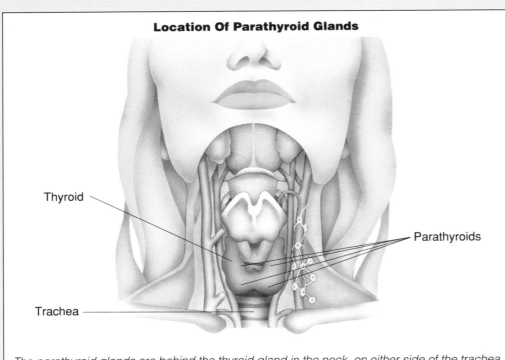

Location Of Parathyroid Glands

Thyroid

Parathyroids

Trachea

The parathyroid glands are behind the thyroid gland in the neck, on either side of the trachea.

▶▶ SEE ALSO — Hypercalcaemia, Hypocalcaemia, Thyroid

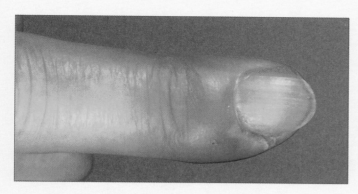

An infection down the side of a fingernail, known as paronychia, causes the skin around the nail to become very tender and inflamed. Women in particular are susceptible to such infections.

Rarely, Parkinson's disease may follow certain types of poisoning or viral infections.

Treatment

Physiotherapy can play a useful role, especially in the more extreme cases of Parkinson's disease. Drug therapy has advanced considerably in the past few years and whilst it is not curative, it can very largely control the symptoms allowing the sufferer to live a near normal life. Surgery to destroy part of the brain was used in the past but this may have serious side effects and was often found to be only of short-term benefit.

The so-called 'brain transplant' heralded as a cure a few years ago involves the insertion into the brain of material taken from aborted foetuses. This had a benefit in some cases but advances in medical treatment have meant that surgery is becoming rare.

Many doctors overlook the symptoms of depression but most patients respond very well to treatment with antidepressants.

PARONYCHIA

Paronychia is an infection of the skin down the side of the nail.

Paronychia may be due to infection with bacteria, or it may be more long term, due to infection with candida albicans. It is more common in women, particularly if their hands are constantly immersed in water, and if they have poor circulation. Treatment for bacterial infections is with antibiotics, and for candidal infections is with antifungal drugs.

PATERNITY TESTING

Paternity testing is the use of blood tests to help reveal whether or not a specific man is the father of a specific child.

Blood samples are taken from the child involved, from the man who is thought to be the father, and sometimes from the child's mother. They are examined for the presence of genetic material such as proteins in the blood plasma and small pieces of DNA itself. Comparison of samples from the people involved will show that if, for example, a certain genetic 'marker' is present in the child's blood but not in its mother's, then it will definitely be present in its father's blood. Any man without this 'marker' will not be the father of the child.

Using the latest techniques in 'genetic fingerprinting', an investigator would be able to prove that such marked similarities between a child's and a man's DNA would only occur accidentally — that is, without any family connection — with a chance of one in 30 thousand million.

PELLAGRA

Pellagra is a nutritional disorder, due to a deficiency of niacin (part of the vitamin B complex).

The deficiency occurs in poor countries, particularly in places where maize is the staple cereal.

Causes

Niacin is present in maize, but it can only be absorbed under certain conditions: as in Mexico, where the maize is soaked in an alkaline solution before cooking, and eating maize and beans together also helps with absorption of niacin. Some other disorders, such as inflammatory bowel disease (which restricts the absorption of certain amino acids and minerals) may also cause pellagra.

Symptoms

As a result of the deficiency, the body becomes run down. There is lethargy, weakness, loss of weight and depression, together with physical symptoms such as inflammation and itching if the skin is exposed to the sun. Blisters may develop, and in severe cases the skin becomes rough, dry and darker in colour. Diarrhoea is a common symptom.

Treatment

Replacing the missing vitamin (either in food or tablet form), together with a healthier, more balanced diet, leads to complete recovery.

PELVIC INFLAMMATORY DISEASE

Pelvic inflammatory disease (PID) is a broad term that covers infections of any part of the uterus, fallopian tubes or ovaries. Organs such as the gut which are part in the pelvis and part in the abdomen may also be affected.

The commonest cause of PID is an infection ascending from the vagina, usually as a result of sexual intercourse. Gonorrhoea and chlamydia are the most frequent culprits. Infection may also be introduced directly into the uterus at childbirth or following an abortion.

PID may be acute or chronic. Acute infections cause severe pain, usually low down in the abdomen and often on both sides. The patient usually complains of vaginal discharge and pain on intercourse.

Diagnosis and treatment

External examination reveals a tender abdomen, and internal examination can be very painful. Movement of the cervix causes pain. Laparoscopy will reveal pus in the abdominal cavity. However, this is rarely needed as most doctors base their diagnosis on the patient's description of her symptoms, plus an examination. Swabs from the cervix can be very helpful in pinpointing the infecting organism and suggesting the correct treatment.

Acute PID is treated with high doses of antibiotics, painkillers and bed rest. Early, effective treatment is vital if chronic PID is to be avoided. If treatment in the acute phase is delayed or inadequate, then bacterial waste products produce adhesions between the pelvic organs.

MEDICAL FACT FILE

Chronic PID causes persistent lower abdominal pain and a chronic discharge. If adhesions affect the fallopian tubes the normal passage of an egg is interrupted. This can cause infertility or even ectopic pregnancy. Acute flare-ups are common and need to be treated with antibiotics. Surgery to free adhesions is rarely successful and in many cases a surgical 'total pelvic clearance' is needed.

PELVIS, STRUCTURE AND DISORDERS

The pelvis is the region of the trunk that lies below the abdomen.

Pelvic Examination

In the few seconds it takes a skilled doctor to perform an 'internal', she will have gained a great deal of information about the condition of the pelvic organs.

A look at the vulva may show eczema, scratches or pubic lice. A vaginal examination will reveal a discharge or the characteristic white plaques of thrush. Looking at the cervix may reveal a discharge or even cancer. The softness of the cervix is an indication of pregnancy, and pain on moving it gently from side to side will suggest infection. The size, shape and position of the uterus are all important. The feel of the pelvis above and to the side of the vagina gives clues as to the health of the fallopian tubes and ovaries.

The pelvic and abdominal cavities are continuous, but for convenience, doctors regard them as distinct regions.

Structure

The bony pelvis is made up of four bones: the two hipbones, the sacrum and the coccyx. The bones of the pelvis contain and protect the lower parts of the gastrointestinal and urinary tracts and the internal organs of reproduction.

The shape of the pelvis differs between men and women and, to some degree, from woman to woman.

Problems and disorders

Deformities of the pelvis in women lead to difficulties in labour and in severe cases

Pelvimetry

Pelvimetry involves taking x-rays of a pregnant woman's pelvis to ascertain whether a normal delivery is possible.

If an obstetrician suspects deformity of the pelvis there are several ways in which she can assess the mother to see if a vaginal delivery is practical.

In less severe cases it may well be that the best policy is to allow labour to proceed normally but to have a surgical team ready for an emergency Caesarean delivery. In some cases, x-rays of the pelvis and the baby's head may indicate the need for avoiding a vaginal delivery altogether.

may cause obstruction so that the baby gets stuck in the pelvis and can't be delivered normally. The use of pelvimetry (see box above) helps to prevent any complications that may arise

as a result of deformity.

Congenital deformities are very rare. Most problems are acquired through injury or disease such as rickets.

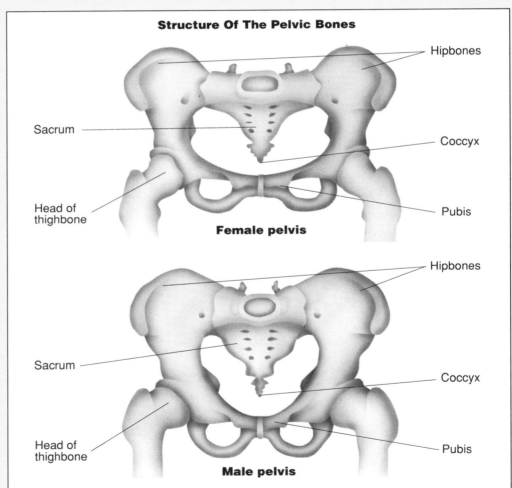

Structure Of The Pelvic Bones

Hipbones

Sacrum

Coccyx

Head of thighbone

Pubis

Female pelvis

Hipbones

Sacrum

Coccyx

Head of thighbone

Pubis

Male pelvis

The bones of the pelvis have fixed joints, forming a basin. At the back, the sacrum connects to the spine, while the hipbones have sockets for the thighbones on either side. The male pelvis is much narrower than the female pelvis.

SEE ALSO — Caesarean section, Childbirth, Labour

PENICILLIN DRUGS

Penicillin, discovered in 1941, was the first of the antibiotics.

The original form of penicillin, Penicillin G, was obtained from a mould, penicillin notatum. Penicillin G was easily broken down by stomach acid into a different chemical, before it got to the bloodstream and had to be given by injection.

Nowadays 'penicillin' is used to describe a whole group of antibiotics obtained either naturally or semi-synthetically from the penicillin mould. Some, such as Amoxycillin, are active against a wide range of infections, while others are most effective against specific bacteria.

All penicillins work by interfering with the growth of bacteria. Animals build their cell walls in a different way from bacteria, and penicillin cannot damage human cells.

Except in the case of specific allergy, which is rare, penicillins are remarkably safe, even in overdose. Their main side effects are diarrhoea (due to interference with 'helpful' bacteria in the gut) and thrush. Both may be minimised by eating live yogurt during the course of treatment.

As with all antibiotics, it is vital that patients finish the course, otherwise bacterial resistance may emerge.

PENILE IMPLANT

Most cases of impotence are due to psychological factors. Those that are not may be helped by penile implants designed to stiffen the penis.

The simplest form of implant is a silicone splint embedded in the body of the penis, which becomes semi-erect permanently, but at least penetration is possible.

A more sophisticated device incorporates a wire rod that can be bent and unbent at will. The most natural — but most expensive — device consists of a fluid-filled balloon inflated through a pump inserted into the scrotum.

PENIS, CANCER OF

Cancer of the penis is usually found in the skin under the foreskin. It is very rare in the young and almost never affects those who have been circumcised.

In its early stages, cancer of the penis is confined to the skin, but it can spread deep into the shaft of the penis.

The first sign is often a bloody discharge from the foreskin. Occasionally penile cancer can cause extensive swelling.

Treatment

In any suspected penile cancer, circumcision is performed and the affected area biopsied. Small lesions can be treated with radio-therapy. More extensive cancers are amputated through the shaft of the penis. In advanced cases amputation of the penis and scrotum may be needed. The outlook after this kind of surgery is very poor.

PERICARDITIS

Pericarditis is an inflammation of the membrane surrounding the heart (pericardium).

The inflammation may be caused by a number of things, including infections, heart attack, cancer or injury. It sometimes occurs with other disorders including rheumatoid arthritis, systemic lupus erythematosus and kidney failure. Sometimes, no cause can be identified.

Symptoms

Fever and chest pains are the main symptoms of pericarditis. The pain is behind the breastbone, and may also be felt in the neck and shoulders.

As a result of infection, there may be an accumulation of pus in the space between the two layers of the pericardium, which may press on the heart and interfere with its action. Where the pericarditis is caused by cancer, there may be an accumulation of blood in the pericardial space. If the fluids restrict the action of the heart, blood pressure will fall, leading to difficulty in breathing and swollen veins in the neck.

In some cases, if the inflammation is long term, the pericardium becomes scarred and thickened, so that there is oedema (which shows as swelling of the abdomen and legs).

Diagnosis and treatment

A thorough examination and description of symptoms may be adequate for diagnosis, but x-rays and an ECG can confirm the diagnosis.

Treatment should be aimed at the underlying cause, but painkillers and/or anti-inflammatory drugs may be prescribed to ease the problem. Fluid may be drawn off by inserting a needle into the pericardial space.

Penile Implant

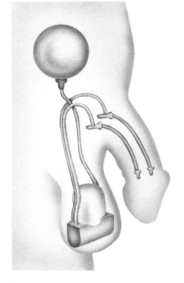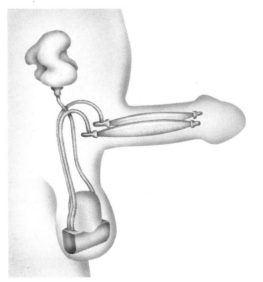

A penile implant can be inserted into the penis, with a reservoir in the abdomen. A control in the scrotum enables the penis to become erect when necessary.

▶▶ SEE ALSO — Antibiotics

MEDICAL FACT FILE

PERIODONTAL DISEASE

Periodontal disease is a general term to describe disorders of the tissues which hold the teeth in place.

The most common periodontal disorder is gingivitis, an inflammation of the gums. If untreated, this develops into periodontitis.

PERIODONTITIS

Periodontitis is an inflammation of the membranes which hold the teeth in place.

Infections can get to the periodontal membranes in two ways: through bacteria entering the tooth via holes in the enamel due to dental caries, or through untreated inflammation of the gums (gingivitis). In either case, the root cause of the problem is poor dental hygiene.

If the inflammation is not treated, the bacteria will eventually erode the bones surrounding the teeth, the inflamed periodontal membrane will come away from the teeth, and the teeth will drop out.

Symptoms

If periodontitis has resulted from gingivitis, the gums will have been red, tender and prone to bleeding for some time. There is also likely to be bad breath and an unpleasant taste. There may be gum boils and, eventually, loosening of teeth.

If periodontitis has developed due to dental caries, there will be toothache, and abscesses or cysts may develop. Dental x-rays are used to confirm the problem.

Treatment and prevention

Dentists scale and polish the teeth to prevent gingivitis. This should be done regularly, and teeth-cleaning techniques must be improved. If the gingivitis is advanced, gingivectomy may be necessary. This is an operation to trim away part of the gums.

If there are cysts or abscesses, they will have to be drained. If affected teeth cannot be filled they will have to be extracted.

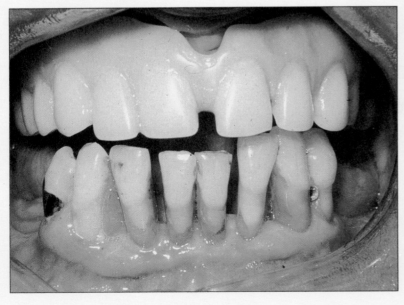

Periodontitis leads to an erosion of the gums and bones holding the teeth in place, giving the effect of being 'long in the tooth'. The disorder can be avoided with meticulous attention to dental hygiene.

PERIOD PAIN

Period pains are cramping abdominal pains at the time of menstruation.

The medical term is dysmenorrhoea, and while some dysmenorrhoea is normal, there may be an underlying reason for excessive pain.

PERIOSTITIS

Periostitis is an inflammation of the periosteum, the tissue which covers all the bones in the body.

The periosteum provides the bones with nutrients and also contains nerves. If it is damaged (either by disease or injury), there is pain and swelling in the affected area.

PERIPHERAL VASCULAR DISEASE

Peripheral vascular diseases affect any artery other than those of the heart or brain.

There are three main types of peripheral vascular disease:

Acute obstruction

This is usually caused by a clot, which blocks the supply of blood to a particular limb. The affected limb is painful, pale and cold. Surgeons can often remove the clot using a fine bore catheter.

Intermittent claudication

This is a symptom of thickening of the arteries. There is cramping pain in the calf during exercise. It is very rare except in elderly men who smoke. Therapy is based on exercise and giving up smoking. In some cases the blockage can be bypassed surgically.

Raynaud's disease

This usually affects young women. The arteries of the fingers go into spasm in colder weather. Affected fingers turn white and then blue. Treatment is not very successful but the condition usually abates with time. Several drugs are available to treat the disease, but none of these is as effective as a good pair of warm gloves.

PERITONITIS

Peritonitis is the inflammation of the peritoneum — the lining of the abdominal cavity. This may be due to infection, perforation of an organ or gangrene.

Blood, bile, urine and other fluids leaking into the abdominal cavity are intensely irritant. Perforation of the peritoneum allows rapid bacterial proliferation which often spreads to the bloodstream.

A common cause of peritonitis in the younger age group is appendicitis. If the diseased organ is not removed it can burst, releasing gut organisms into the lower abdomen.

Symptoms

Up to the point of rupture the pain of appendicitis is felt just below the navel. With the onset of localised peritonitis the pain shifts to the left, only to become more diffuse as the condition spreads.

In the early stages of peritonitis, the sufferer lies very still, and the pain is intense and unremitting. Both temperature and pulse are raised slightly. As a result of muscle spasm the abdomen

>> SEE ALSO — Dysmenorrhoea, Gingivitis

is as hard as a board. In a matter of hours the patient becomes dehydrated, shocked and confused. Unless treatment is started at once, death follows rapidly.

Treatment

Once the diagnosis has been made, surgery is performed urgently. Sometimes the patient's condition is so bad that intravenous fluids must be given before she is fit for the operation.

The abdomen is opened at the midline and the inflamed organ removed. The abdominal cavity is cleaned out with warm saline solution and the wound then closed. A broad spectrum antibiotic is usually given during the course of the operation and for several days thereafter. After the operation, recovery is usually trouble-free.

PERNICIOUS ANAEMIA

Anaemia is a reduction in the level of the oxygen-carrying pigment, haemoglobin, in the blood. In pernicious anaemia, this is caused by a failure to absorb vitamin B12.

In pernicious anaemia, there is a disorder of the stomach lining so that vitamin B12 is not absorbed from the intestine. This leads to the production of abnormal red blood cells, and anaemia.

Causes and symptoms

The condition is usually caused by an autoimmune disorder. It has a tendency to run in families, and usually starts in middle age. It may also be associated with disorders such as diabetes mellitus.

The symptoms are not obvious, but include tiredness, headaches, weight loss and, in severe cases, breathlessness and tingling in the feet.

Diagnosis and treatment

Diagnosis is with blood tests, and it can be confirmed with a bone-marrow biopsy, or a special test which looks at how vitamin B12 is absorbed into the bloodstream.

If the disorder is diagnosed, injections of the vitamin directly into the muscle are necessary for the rest of the patient's life.

PERTHES' DISEASE

Perthes' disease is an inflammation of the growing head of the thighbone.

It is a form of osteochondritis juvenilis, caused by a disruption of the blood supply to the growing bone. It usually affects only one hip, and is more common in boys than girls, affecting children in the five to 10 age range.

The disease causes pain in the hip and movement may be restricted. Diagnosis is made through x-rays of the hip, and treatment includes bed rest, splinting of the hip to hold the hipbone in place or surgery to alter the position of the thighbone in its socket.

The disease usually rights itself after a few years, although there may be osteoarthritis in later life.

PESSARY

Pessary is a term which describes medications administered in tablet form in the vagina, or a device placed in the vagina to correct the position of the uterus.

Medications include treatments for thrush or trichonomiasis, as well as hormone treatments. They are usually administered with a special applicator, which positions them at the back of the vagina.

Spermicides are also available in pessary form.

Pessaries to support a prolapsed uterus have to be inserted under medical supervision.

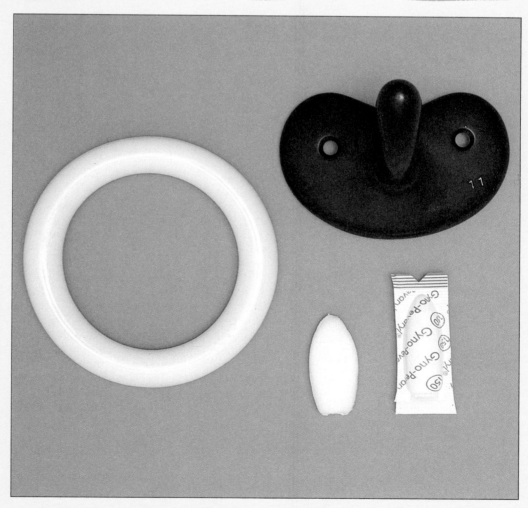

Two devices for supporting a prolapsed uterus – a ring pessary (above left) and a shelf pessary (top right). The medications shown here are for treating pre-menstrual tension and for the treatment of thrush. Spermicides are also available as pessaries.

➤➤ SEE ALSO — Osteochondritis juvenilis, Osteoarthritis

PEYRONIE'S DISEASE

Peyronie's disease is a disorder of the penis, which causes it to bend at an unusual angle when it is erect.

The disorder usually only affects men over 40, and may cause pain and difficulty during intercourse. The sideways bend in the penis is caused by a thickening of the sheath of connective tissue, which may be felt as a nodule in an unerect penis. It may improve without treatment, but it may be necessary to give local injections of corticosteroids. In severe cases, surgery may be an option but this may cause scarring, which can make the problem worse.

PHARYNX, CANCER AND DISORDERS OF

The pharynx is a funnel-shaped tube that connects the back of the nose and the mouth to the oesophagus.

Through most of its course the pharynx lies behind the larynx and cannot be felt from the outside. The part that is seen — the throat — is more properly called the 'oropharynx'. The pharynx is lined with mucus-producing cells and has a thick muscular wall that constricts during swallowing.

Sore throat

The commonest disease of the pharynx is pharyngitis — a sore throat. This may be caused by physical irritants such as dust or smoke, but is usually due to an infection. Most infections are caused by viruses, often part of a generalised upper respiratory infection such as a cold or 'flu.

About a quarter of all sore throats are caused by bacteria, usually the streptococci. Very rarely an acute bacterial sore throat will cause further problems, such as rheumatic fever in other parts of the body.

Thrush in the mouth and pharynx is generally only found in infants, who may contract it throughout the gastrointestinal tract, but can be seen in adults who use steroid inhalers or who practise oral sex.

Treatments

Sore throats, whether caused by viruses or bacteria, usually resolve in a few days. Several studies have shown that even bacterial infections get better nearly as quickly without antibiotics as with them. A warm gargle of soluble aspirin, followed 30 seconds afterwards by swallowing the mixture, and honey and lemon drinks are all that are needed in the majority of cases. If symptoms persist for more than three days, or if the patient has difficulty swallowing, consult a doctor.

Cancer

Cancer of the pharynx is rare. When it does occur, it is commoner in men than in women, and in smokers rather than non-smokers. The cancer quickly spreads to the lymph glands in the neck, which may degenerate and become infected. Surgery is very difficult and most cases are treated by radiotherapy in the form of x-rays or radioactive implants.

Other disorders

Diphtheria, now very rare in the UK, causes acute pharyngitis with severe upset to the system. Urgent hospital treatment is needed as the condition still has a high mortality rate.

An unusual problem is the formation of a pharyngeal pouch (an oesophageal diverticulum in the pharynx). This starts as a protrusion of the mucous membrane through the muscular wall of the pharynx. The pouch grows and becomes filled with rotting foodstuff. Pharyngeal pouches may cause halitosis, difficulty in swallowing, or even aspiration pneumonia. Treatment is surgical.

Location And Structure Of The Pharynx

Pharynx

Tongue

Epiglottis

Vocal cords

Windpipe

Foodpipe

The pharynx lies at the back of the nose and mouth, connecting them to the foodpipe (or oesophagus). It is the part of the throat which is often the first to be affected when you have a sore throat.

PHENOBARBITONE

Phenobarbitone is a barbiturate drug, which acts as an anticonvulsant.

In the past, phenobarbitone has been used as an anti-anxiety drug and as a sleeping drug. However, its main use now is in treating epilepsy — although even in this role it is being replaced by newer anticonvulsants.

Side effects may include drowsiness, dizziness, clumsiness and confusion.

▶▶ SEE ALSO — Oesophagus

PHENYLKETONURIA

Phenylketonuria is an inherited condition, caused by a recessive gene, in which there is a missing enzyme.

The lack of the enzyme which is needed to digest phenylalanine leads to an accumulation of this amino acid, interfering with the functioning of the nervous system and causing mental retardation.

Affected children tend to have paler colouring than other members of the family. If the condition is not treated, they develop epilepsy in early childhood, and have a 'mousy' smell.

Screening

All babies have their blood tested to check that they do not have phenylketonuria. (The test is known as the Guthrie test, and is carried out between eight and 14 days after birth.) If they are found suffer from the condition, they will have to follow a diet which excludes certain forms of protein.

PHIMOSIS

Phimosis is a tightness of the foreskin, which may cause difficulty in urination and difficulty in getting an erection.

In infancy, all boys have a degree of phimosis, and the foreskin cannot be pulled back over the glans. However, if the problem is severe, there will be difficulty in passing urine. Later in life, the foreskin may remain too tight to pass over the glans.

The condition may also lead to balanitis — infection of the glans — due to hygiene problems, and sufferers are more prone to cancer of the penis.

Treatment

Phimosis is treated with a simple circumcision operation, which is performed under general anaesthetic.

PHLEBITIS

Phlebitis is the commonly used term for a condition correctly known as thrombophlebitis.

The condition involves an inflammation of a vein, due to tiny blood clots.

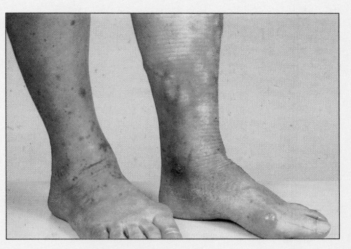

As a result of thrombophlebitis there is swelling, redness and tenderness along the affected veins.

PHOBIA

A phobia is a form of mental neurosis whereby the sufferer develops an irrational fear of something.

Common phobias include: agoraphobia (fear of open spaces); claustrophobia (fear of enclosed spaces); zoophobias (fears of different animals, such as snakes, mice, spiders, birds and dogs), as well as fear of flying and fear of heights.

If the fear becomes debilitating, as with agoraphobia when the sufferer may become too nervous to go outside the home, treatment may be necessary. Counselling and behavioural therapy are appropriate in the long term, although tranquillisers may be a short-term solution.

PHOTOPHOBIA

Photophobia is an aversion to light, due to a physical disorder.

Photophobia is a sign of a number of disorders, such as injury of the cornea, inflammation of the iris, glaucoma and meningitis.

PHOTOSENSITIVITY

Photosensitivity is a reaction to sunlight whereby the skin develops a rash.

The condition may be the result of exposure to a sensitiser (in the form of a chemical, such as a dye, a drug or an ingredient in cosmetics or soap), or a particular plant.

In some cases, exposure to light aggravates an existing condition, such as lupus erythematosus.

PIGEON TOES

Pigeon toes is a minor deformity, in which the toes point inwards.

The disorder normally corrects itself before puberty. If it persists, and the sufferer feels it is a problem, special insoles may be used to help keep the feet straight.

PILES

Piles is the common name for haemorrhoids.

The condition involves varicose veins in the anus. Surgery may be required in serious cases.

PINK EYE

Pink eye is the common name for conjunctivitis.

The inflammation of the conjuctiva (the membrane behind the eyelid and over the white of the eye) may be due to a bacterial or viral infection, or it may be an allergic reaction. As well as pinkness, there may be a feeling that there is grit under the eyelid. In some cases there is a yellow discharge which forms a crust on the eyelashes, sometimes preventing the eye from being opened on waking up.

Treatment

The condition may be contagious, so it is important to pay attention to hygiene, and not use the towel of someone with an infection.

Viral infections usually clear up on their own, but bacterial infections may need antibiotics. Allergic reactions may be treated with antihistamines.

PINS-AND-NEEDLES

Pins-and-needles is a tingling sensation, usually in an extremity (hands or feet).

Pins-and-needles is often accompanied, or preceded, by numbness. It

▶▶ SEE ALSO — Balanitis, Conjunctivitis, Glaucoma, Haemorrhoids, Lupus erythematosus, Meningitis

MEDICAL FACT FILE

may be caused by interference in the sensory nerves, (for example, due to sitting in an awkward position for some time).

If it goes on for weeks it may be a symptom of an underlying disorder of the nervous system such as multiple sclerosis.

PITUITARY GLAND

The pituitary gland secretes hormones which affect every aspect of our daily lives.

The pituitary gland is situated at the base of the brain, behind and just below the eyes. It is no bigger than a pea and is made up of three more or less separate lobes that secrete at least 10 different hormones.

Structure and function

The anterior lobe secretes thyroid-stimulating hormone, adrenocorticotrophic-stimulating hormone, luteinising hormone, follicle-stimulating hormone, prolactin and growth hormone. With the exception of growth hormone and prolactin, all the other hormones regulate the function of the main hormone-producing glands of the body.

The posterior lobe secretes the hormones oxytocin and antidiuretic hormone.

The middle lobe secretes melanocyte-stimulating hormone, which acts on pigment-producing cells in the skin to control its colour.

The secretions of the anterior pituitary are under the control of the hypothalamus, another tiny gland at the base of the brain. Locally active hormones from the hypothalamus are released into the bloodstream to make the 1cm journey between the two glands. Hypothalamic hormones cause the release or inhibition of pituitary hormones.

Disorders of the pituitary

Diseases and disorders of the pituitary depend on the lobe affected. Failure of secretion or underproduction of hormones is more common than overproduction.

Underactivity

If the pituitary is underactive, a condition known as Simmond's disease, the slowing down in secretions, tends to occur in a fixed pattern. The hormone most susceptible to underactivity is the growth hormone, and the least likely to be affected is the antidiuretic hormone.

The commonest cause of underactivity is a tumour: so much of the gland is taken up by a tumour that there is not enough tissue left to produce hormones. There is usually loss of sexual function. Men may find that they no longer need to shave. Lack of melanocyte-stimulating hormone means that sufferers are often deathly pale. Low cortisol levels mean that coma may occur. Tumours of the pituitary gland often press on the optic nerves and cause loss of part of the field of vision.

Pituitary glands may be underactive from birth, due to congenital defects, leading to perfectly proportioned dwarfs, known as Peter Pan dwarfs.

Another, now rare, cause of damage to the pituitary gland is childbirth. In the days when women bled heavily at childbirth, the very delicate pituitary gland could be starved of oxygen long enough to kill it.

Overactivity

An excess of growth hormone before puberty causes giantism. Children who are affected grow very tall — eight or nine feet in some cases — but the overactivity soon turns to underactivity, so in spite of their vast size, affected individuals are not usually strong or virile.

If the excess occurs after puberty it causes a condition known as acromegaly. After puberty the bones can no longer grow and any overgrowth will only affect soft tissues. In consequence, the tongue enlarges, the face changes shape and the hands become long and shovel like.

Life expectancy in giants and acromegalics is reduced.

Treatment

Problems due to tumours are treated by the removal of the

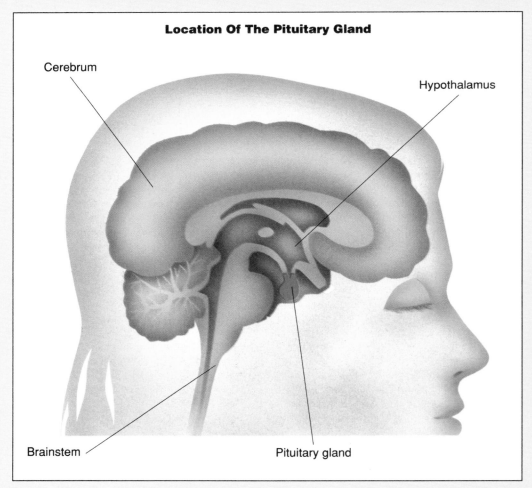

Location Of The Pituitary Gland

Cerebrum

Hypothalamus

Brainstem

Pituitary gland

>> SEE ALSO — Nervous system, MS

Hormones Secreted By The Pituitary Gland

Hormone	Action
Thyroid-stimulating hormone	Stimulates thyroid secretion and growth.
Adrenocorticotrophic hormone	Stimulates adrenal glands to produce cortisol.
Growth hormone	Accelerates body growth.
Follicle-stimulating hormone	Stimulates egg production in women and sperm production in men.
Luteinising hormone	Stimulates release of egg in women and production of testosterone in men.
Prolactin	Stimulates production of milk and maternal behaviour.
Antidiuretic hormone	Causes retention of water.
Oxytocin	Causes ejection of milk.
Melanocyte-stimulation hormone	Promotes production of skin pigment.

gland. Missing hormones such as oestrogen, cortisol and thyroid hormones are replaced with drug therapy to control any disorders.

In the case of giants and acromegalics, radioactive implants are sometimes used to destroy the gland without resorting to surgery.

PITYRIASIS

Pityriasis is a common skin condition which takes three forms.

Pityriasis mainly affects children and young adults and clears up easily.

Pityriasis alba
In this condition, caused by mild eczema, pale, irregular, scaly patches appear on the face. The condition clears up if emollients are applied.

Pityriasis rosea
In this condition, which may result from a viral infection, a rash of flat, round or oval dark spots with scaly edges appears over the trunk. The rash is usually preceded about a week beforehand by a single larger spot. The rash may be itchy, and usually lasts for about eight weeks. It can be soothed by calamine lotion or antihistamine drugs.

Pityriasis versicolor
This condition, due to a fungus (which is normally present on most skins) involves white or brown patches of flaking skin over the body and neck. It may become more pronounced after exposure to sunlight.

It is treated with antifungal creams or lotions, applied at night. All clothing in contact with the skin must be thoroughly washed to prevent reinfection.

PLACEBO

A placebo is a 'false' medication, which has no physical effect, given in place of a drug.

Placebos are given for two main reasons. Firstly, they are given in trials of new drugs: one group of volunteers takes the drug being tested, while another group takes a placebo. This is because of the 'placebo effect': people taking medicines expect to get better. By comparing the progress of the two groups of volunteers, the effect of the drug can be measured.

Secondly, the placebo effect is used to treat some disorders which do not actually need medication. For example, sufferers from fatigue and nervous disorders, which are not caused by a physical illness, may actually benefit from a placebo if they think the medication (which they do not know is inert) will make them better.

PLACENTA

The placenta is an organ which develops in pregnancy, allowing the exchange of nutrients and waste between the mother and the foetus.

The placenta develops in the uterus from the outer layer of cells of the fertilised egg. It is connected to the foetus by the umbilical cord.

How it works
The mother's blood circulates to the wall of the uterus, and oxygen and nutrients pass into the placenta. Tiny blood vessels carry waste products from the foetus, and nutrients and waste are exchanged in the chorionic villi — finger-shaped extensions in the placenta.

The placenta produces hormones, to prepare the mother for pregnancy and childbirth, including human chorionic gonadotrophin, which is excreted in the mother's urine, and is used to detect pregnancy.

After giving birth, the last stage of labour involves delivery of the placenta (or afterbirth).

Cancer of the placenta
Very rarely, benign or malignant tumours may develop in pregnancies when the embryo does not develop normally. Symptoms include vaginal bleeding and excessive morning sickness.

Malignant tumours may develop after an abortion, or, very rarely, after a normal pregnancy.

Benign tumours are treated with a D and C. Malignant tumours must be detected early if they are to be cured: anticancer drugs or a hysterectomy may be needed.

Placenta praevia
Placenta praevia is a cause of vaginal bleeding during pregnancy, and is still a cause of death during childbirth. If a woman has a placenta praevia, the placenta is at the lower end of the uterus, often over the cervix. The condition occurs in about one in 200 pregnancies, and the severity depends on the proximity of the placenta to the cervix. The condition is detected during routine ultrasound scans.

The main symptom of placenta praevia is vaginal

bleeding — usually in late pregnancy. This may be alleviated by bed rest, but if the pregnancy is near term and the bleeding is heavy an immediate delivery may be necessary.

If a woman is diagnosed as having a placenta praevia, she is normally admitted to hospital during the last month of her pregnancy due to the danger of haemorrhage. The baby is usually delivered by Caesarean section.

PLASTIC SURGERY

Plastic or reconstructive surgery is the field of medicine concerned with the surgical restoration of the body's form or function.

Plastic surgery has been practised for 2500 years, but modern techniques have their basis in the treatment of the horrendous injuries of the two World Wars.

Although some surgery is for strictly cosmetic purposes, the idea of a plastic surgeon as someone who makes vast profits from the vanities of the super-rich is unfair. The best plastic surgeons work in the NHS and all have trained for many years to master other surgical specialities such as orthopaedics and ENT (ear, nose and throat surgery).

Reconstructive operations

After injury and burns, a number of techniques may be used to reconstruct the skin and structure of the face or body. For example, skin grafts (using a thin layer of skin) and skin flaps (using a deep layer of skin and tissue, complete with blood supply) may be used to replace damaged skin; noses can be re-built with portions taken from a rib; and congenital defects such as hare lip and hypospadias can be corrected with appropriate surgery at an early age. Silicone implants may be used to reconstruct breasts after mastectomy.

Cosmetic surgery

Plastic surgery on an otherwise healthy person is known as cosmetic surgery, and involves operations such as face lifts and breast improvement.

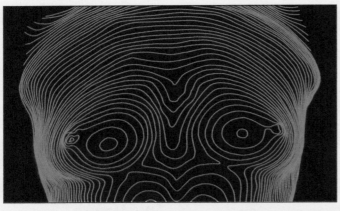

Before and after cosmetic surgery: these graphic 'relief maps' of a woman's breasts show how a surgeon can re-shape sagging breasts (top) to create a fuller bustline (below).

PLEURISY

Pleurisy is the inflammation of the pleura — the membrane lining the lungs and chest cavity.

Pleurisy is usually caused by a viral or bacterial infection, and is often a result of pneumonia. It may have a more serious underlying cause, such as a pulmonary embolism (blood clot), lung cancer or tuberculosis.

Symptoms and treatment

The main symptom is a sudden pain in the chest on breathing in. The pain arises because the inflamed membranes rub together.

The disease is treated by bed rest, together with antibiotics if the infection is bacterial.

Pleural effusion

Sometimes, pleurisy leads to an excess of pleural fluid, a condition known as pleural effusion. There is no pain, but the fluid may put pressure on the lung, causing breathing difficulty. Doctors may tap the chest to listen for a dull sound, indicating pleural effusion. Pleural fluid can be drawn off with a needle to help breathing, but the underlying cause must also be treated.

PMS

PMS is the abbreviation for premenstrual syndrome.

The condition involves a range of unpleasant symptoms, including sore breasts, tension, irritability and headaches.

PNEUMOCONIOSIS

Pneumoconiosis, or dust disease, is a group of occupational illnesses only found in workers from specific industries.

Many types of dust can settle in the lungs and cause problems in later life. Of these, the commonest are coal, causing 'coal-miner's lung', silica from rock drilling, causing 'silicosis', and asbestos. Asbestos can cause asbestosis — a type of scarring — lung cancer or cancer of the pleural space.

Symptoms

In the early stages of pneumoconiosis there are no symptoms, but there are characteristic x-ray changes. As the disease progresses, which it will do even if further exposure is avoided, the patient becomes increasingly short of breath on exertion. As the scarring worsens, chronic bronchitis and pneumonia will develop. In the terminal stages the strain of pumping blood through diseased lungs causes an enlarged heart and ultimately heart failure.

Treatment

There is little that can be done to help sufferers of the dust diseases other than to treat the complications.

Workers, or their widows, who can prove that their lung disease is related to their employment are entitled to compensation.

▶▶ SEE ALSO — Caesarean section, Childbirth, Hypospadias, Premenstrual syndrome, Skin flaps, Skin grafts

PNEUMOCYSTIS PNEUMONIA

Pneumocystis pneumonia is an infection of the lungs caused by the microorganism pneumocystis carni.

The infection is life-threatening to anyone who has a deficient immune system, and as many as 50 per cent of AIDS sufferers may be affected by it at one time or another. It also affects people who have leukaemia.

It is likely that infection also occurs in healthy individuals but in such cases the symptoms are so mild as to pass unnoticed.

PNEUMONIA

Pneumonia is an infection of the alveoli, the part of the lungs where gas exchange occurs.

In the past, the term single pneumonia was used to describe an infection of one lung and double pneumonia an infection of both, but this terminology is rarely used now.

Two forms of pneumonia exist: bronchopneumonia, which affects all of the lung tissue, and lobar pneumonia, which affects only one lobe or segment.

Bronchopneumonia

Bronchopneumonia rarely affects normal, healthy adults. In the majority of cases it attacks lungs already damaged by conditions such as bronchitis or cancer. In children it often follows measles or whooping cough, and in adults it often follows 'flu.

The patient usually suffers from fever, tiredness and general ill-health for a day or two before the onset of a productive cough. Sputum is green or yellow and may smell foul. Examination of the chest reveals loud crackles and wheezes, but in case of doubt the diagnosis is easily confirmed by x-ray.

Bronchopneumonia may be due to viral or bacterial infections. As a rule, viral infections are milder, which is fortunate because antibiotics are of no use in their treatment.

Lobar pneumonia

Lobar pneumonia used to be a frequent cause of death, but it has become less common since the advent of penicillin. The onset of lobar pneumonia is sudden, with cough, blood-streaked sputum and a very high temperature. Most patients with lobar pneumonia require urgent hospital admission for treatment with intravenous antibiotics.

Underlying disorders

Infection by the staphylococcus bacteria causes a serious form of pneumonia in patients with an underlying disorder such as cystic fibrosis. The infection spreads throughout the lung, causing abscesses to form. The organism is often resistant to penicillin and special antibiotics are needed.

In the absence of chronic bronchitis, repeated attacks of pneumonia arouse suspicion of an underlying disease. In an adult, especially a smoker, the commonest cause is probably a cancer blocking one of the airways. For this reason, patients with recurrent pneumonia should always have a chest x-ray.

POISONING

Poisoning is the result of consuming a substance (poison) which disrupts the normal functioning of the body.

Poisoning can take many forms, from the accidental swallowing of poisonous substances (when children

DO

✔ Find out what the victim has swallowed.
✔ If it is tablets or berries and they are conscious, try to induce vomiting by putting your fingers down their throat.
✔ Call an ambulance.
✔ Move them into the recovery position if they are unconscious.
✔ Keep medicines and cleaning materials out of the reach of children.

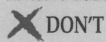

DON'T

✗ Induce vomiting if they have swallowed anything corrosive (bleach, petrol, cleaning materials). Instead, make them drink a lot of milk or water.
✗ Keep cleaning materials in any container other than the child-proof containers they come in.

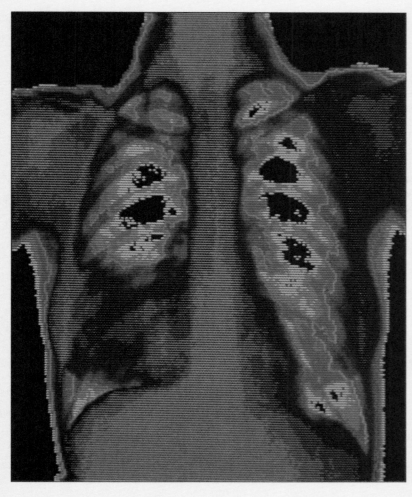

This colour-enhanced x-ray of the chest of a patient with lobar pneumonia indicates how the right-hand lung (on the left of the picture) is reduced in effective size. Only the coloured parts of the lung work normally.

▶▶ SEE ALSO — Food poisoning, Lung cancer, Lung diseases and disorders, Mercury poisoning, Mushroom poisoning

MEDICAL FACT FILE

drink cleaning materials, for example) to snake bites. In some cases, poisoning comes from within the body, for instance when liver failure or kidney failure means that poisonous substances build up in the body.

Many cases of poisoning are deliberate suicide attempts: the patient takes a drug overdose, often in combination with alcohol.

POLIOMYELITIS

Poliomyelitis, or polio, is a highly infectious disease caused by one of three types of virus.

Since the advent of routine immunisation in the UK in 1957, it has become a rarity, but in Third World countries up to 95 per cent of children are infected before their third birthday.

The virus is spread by droplets of saliva or by faecal contamination of drinking water. In the first instance, the virus multiplies in the gut. From there, it spreads to the blood and then to the central nervous system. At any stage in its journey the virus can be defeated by the body's defences, but in rare cases it may cause paralysis.

Silent polio
This is the commonest type of infection. The virus is confined to the gut and causes few or no symptoms.

Abortive polio
If the virus spreads from the gut to the bloodstream, it causes a 'flu-like illness with headache, fever and diarrhoea. In most cases, the illness sorts itself out at this stage without treatment and without the sufferer knowing the true cause of their illness.

Non-paralytic polio
In some cases, the second stage does not recede and after a day or two there is a second rise in temperature. This is caused by the virus entering the central nervous system. Headache, vomiting and a stiff neck occur — the classic symptoms of meningitis. Activity increases the risk of paralysis. Strict bed rest for at least a week is essential.

Paralytic polio
Only a very small proportion of cases progress to paralysis. The first sign is usually pain and tenderness in the muscles. Paralysis may increase over the course of 48 hours and can affect the muscles which enable us to breathe — with disastrous consequences. Other than strict bed rest, little can be done to halt the progression of the paralysis. After two or three weeks, physiotherapy can be started. The condition usually improves with exercise, but patients are often left severely handicapped.

An extra toe is a relatively rare birth defect: in this case, the angle of the toe will make it easy to amputate.

POLYDACTYLY

Polydactyly is a birth defect in which the baby has extra fingers or toes.

The extra digits are sometimes no more than fleshy stumps, but in other cases they are perfectly formed. The deformity may be accompanied by other congenital problems, including mental handicap, but there may be no other abnormalities. The condition affects about one in 2000 babies.

POLYHYDRAMNIOS

Polyhydramnios is an excess of amniotic fluid, the liquid that surrounds the unborn baby.

In the later stages of pregnancy, the uterus contains up to 1.5 litres of amniotic fluid. Any more than this, and polyhydramnios is present. The disorder takes two forms.

Acute polyhydramnios
The relatively rare, acute form occurs between the 20th and 30th weeks and is often due to an identical twin pregnancy. The abdomen swells rapidly and becomes extremely painful. Premature labour is common.

Under these circumstances, the mother-to-be is usually admitted to hospital for scans of the foetus. If the pregnancy looks normal, then strict bed rest is prescribed, and drugs are usually prescribed to try to delay birth.

Chronic polyhydramnios
Chronic polyhydramnios may be associated with foetal abnormality or sugar diabetes in the mother, but in the majority of cases no cause can be found.

Women with chronic polyhydramnios do not need to stay in hospital but must admit themselves at the first sign of labour as the excess fluid often makes for a difficult delivery.

Immunisation

Immunisation has made polio a rarity in the UK.

An immunisation course consisting of three oral doses has eliminated the epidemics of polio which used to sweep the western world. However, it is still endemic in many countries and any traveller outside Europe or North America must have a booster.

➤➤ SEE ALSO — Paralysis

POLYP

A polyp is a small growth that may appear on any mucous membrane.

Polyps are often on stalks: they are found on the lining of the nose, the larynx, the cervix, the intestine and other mucous membranes. They should be examined so they can be removed if they cause symptoms or are likely to become malignant. Nasal polyps (usually due to allergies) may block the sinuses, laryngeal polyps may cause hoarseness and cervical polyps cause a watery, blood-stained discharge.

PORPHYRIA

There are six forms of porphyria — uncommon inherited disorders due to an excess of porphyrins.

Porphyrins are chemicals that are formed in the body as part of the process of manufacturing haemoglobin, which carries oxygen in the blood. The build-up in porphyrins is due to deficient enzymes which may be genetic or acquired due to excess alcohol. Common symptoms include rashes and blistering when there is exposure to sunlight. Other symptoms include psychiatric disturbances, red coloured urine, reaction to certain drugs, excessive hair growth and anaemia. One type of prophyria gives all the characteristics of a werewolf.

Diagnosis involves testing urine and faeces. Treatment may involve extra glucose or haematin (to replace haem, used in the process of manufacturing haemoglobin). One type is eased by bloodletting — taking blood from a vein.

PORTAL HYPERTENSION

Portal hypertension is a rise in the pressure of the blood between the gut and in the liver.

Under normal circumstances, the blood pressure in and around the gut and liver is less than in general circulation.

The commonest cause of portal hypertension is cirrhosis and, in the UK, the commonest cause of cirrhosis is alcoholism.

The rise in blood pressure causes oesophageal varices — enlargement of the blood vessels at the bottom of the gullet. If these burst — and they often do — the sufferer can bleed to death in a matter of seconds.

Treatment

Treatment of bleeding varices consists of blood transfusions and inflating a special balloon in the gullet which puts pressure on the points which are bleeding. If the acute bleeding is controlled, the dilated blood vessels can be cauterised.

In some cases of portal hypertension the main blood vessel from the liver is reimplanted to lessen the pressure. This is a major operation, especially in alcoholics, who often have circulatory disorders.

POSTNATAL CARE

Postnatal care involves checking on the health of a new mother from birth until the baby is about six weeks old.

Immediately after delivery, the mother will have her temperature, pulse and blood pressure checked, particularly if there have been any complications such as pre-eclampsia or heavy bleeding. If the mother has had an episiotomy, or if the birth has caused a tear around the vagina, wounds will be checked daily while the mother is in hospital. Advice on pelvic floor exercises and stomach-flattening exercises may be given, together with advice

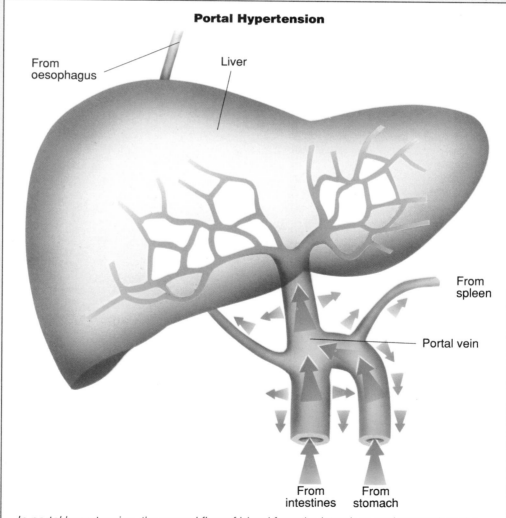

Portal Hypertension

From oesophagus

Liver

From spleen

Portal vein

From intestines

From stomach

In portal hypertension, the normal flow of blood from the intestines and stomach to the liver (large arrows) is under so much pressure that it may be reversed (small arrows).

SEE ALSO — Alcoholism, Antenatal care, Cirrhosis, Endoscopy, Liver, Papilloma

MEDICAL FACT FILE

When the midwife makes postnatal visits she will check breastfeeding mothers for sore nipples and can advise on different positions for feeding which may alleviate any problems.

on contraception. After return from hospital, checks will continue when the midwife visits the home to check on the early development of the baby. She will also ask about the mother's vaginal discharge, which should change from red to brown.

Six weeks after the birth, new mothers will be asked to visit their doctor or clinic for a final examination, to be weighed and to ensure that there are no complications which may have been overlooked. At the same time, the baby usually has a checkup to ensure all is well.

POSTNATAL DEPRESSION

Postnatal depression is the term used to denote a particular change in a patient's mood in the first year after childbirth.

Most new mothers experience the 'baby blues' on the second or third day after delivery. Although they are weepy, most mothers actually describe themselves as happy or even elated. This is often a reaction to the excitement of the previous few days and an expression of fears over the future. The baby blues are harmless, and, with support, settle after a day or two.

Not just in the mind

Postnatal depression is a much more serious matter which affects about one in a hundred women. It is commoner in women who have had previous pre-menstrual tension or depression.

The cause is still unknown, but most doctors accept that it is due to an imbalance between the hormones oestrogen and progesterone.

The onset may be delayed for several weeks after delivery and is usually slow and insidious. The mother feels low, has no interest in either herself or the baby, and may even be suicidal.

Treatment

Untreated, the depression usually lifts in time, but this may take anything up to a year. Treatment consists of antidepressant drugs and hormone pessaries or patches.

In some severe cases, postnatal psychosis occurs with delusional thoughts. This is an emergency and requires immediate admission to hospital to protect mother and child.

POTT'S FRACTURE

A Pott's fracture is a serious injury to the ankle, involving both fracture and dislocation.

Pott's fracture is caused by violent twisting of the ankle. The fibula — the outer, thinner bone in the calf — breaks, and the tibia — the shinbone — also breaks or dislocates.

Treatment

Treatment involves manipulating the bones back into position, and sometimes a pin is used to hold the broken bones together. The lower part of the leg and the foot are immobilised in a plaster cast for at least two months. After the fracture has healed, physiotherapy is needed to restore the use of the muscles and give maximum flexibility to the ankle, which may always remain stiff. Osteoarthritis is likely in later life.

PRE-ECLAMPSIA

Pre-eclampsia is a disease of the second half of pregnancy, which may become life-threatening if left untreated.

Pre-eclampsia is said to exist if a mother shows three clear symptoms: raised blood pressure, oedema (swelling of the feet and ankles) and protein in the urine. Every mother-to-be has these things checked at each antenatal appointment. Untreated, pre-eclampsia may lead to eclampsia, a potentially fatal disease in which the mother-to-be loses consciousness and suffers epileptic-type fits.

Nobody knows the cause of pre-eclampsia, but it is probably due to an auto-immune disorder. It is commoner in first pregnancies, multiple pregnancies and in mothers already suffering from high blood pressure or sugar diabetes.

In the past, pre-eclampsia and eclampsia were the major causes of maternal deaths. Antenatal care has changed this, and most cases that 'slip through the net' are women who have missed antenatal appointments.

The main treatment is bed rest, which may be in hospital in severe cases. If the problem becomes serious, and the mother is close to term, labour may be induced or a Caesarean section performed.

» SEE ALSO — Caesarean section, Fracture

PREGNANCY

Pregnancy, from conception to giving birth, lasts an average of 40 weeks.

Pregnancy produces a number of changes in the whole of a woman's body — not just in the reproductive organs. Most of these changes are beneficial to the mother and the foetus, but some seem to increase the strain on the mother's health.

Hormones at work

Most of the changes of pregnancy are brought about by the influence of hormones from the placenta and the mother's ovaries. Usually, the most obvious change is that the mother's periods stop (although there have been women who have had regular vaginal bleeding for most or all of their pregnancy).

The principal hormone in early pregnancy is Human Chorionic Gonadotrophin (HCG). This is produced almost as soon as fertilisation has taken place and has a vital role in the maintenance of the early pregnancy. It also acts on the embryonic testicles to stimulate them to produce male sex hormones.

Progesterone also helps to maintain the early

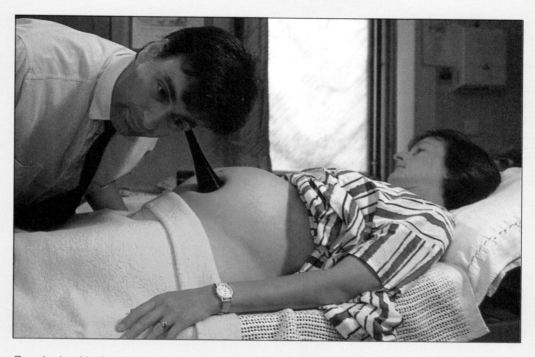

Regular health checks are essential throughout pregnancy – for the sake of the child as well as the mother. One thing doctors will check is the foetal heartbeat.

pregnancy. A deficiency can lead to recurrent miscarriages. In the first few weeks of pregnancy, the mother's ovary is the main site for the production of progesterone, but as the pregnancy progresses the placenta takes over.

Vast quantities of oestrogen are produced throughout pregnancy, both by the placenta and the maternal ovaries. Quite why so much is needed is unclear. In some rare cases a lack of enzymes in the placenta means that very little oestrogen is produced, but despite this, these pregnancies seem to progress normally.

Human Placental Lactogen (HPL) is produced by the placenta and can be detected from about the tenth week onwards. Levels continue to rise until the time of delivery. HPL has many actions, including stimulating

Drugs In Pregnancy

The thalidomide disaster of the sixties (when thalidomide was prescribed as a sedative and was found to cause terrible deformities in foetuses) has made the public and the medical profession much more aware of the risks of taking drugs during pregnancy.

In general, all drugs should be avoided during the first three months of pregnancy. The oral contraceptive pill, taken when you don't realise you are pregnant, seems to be perfectly safe. If you are prescribed drugs, or even if you buy them over the counter, it is vital to tell the pharmacist if there is any chance you might be pregnant.

Antisickness drugs The only drug in this group in common use is Avomine, and this seems safe. Most women can avoid the need for any drugs by taking small, regular meals and avoiding fatty foods.

Antibiotics These are often needed for the treatment of urinary infections. Unfortunately, many can cause problems, although penicillin has been used for many years without adverse effects.

Painkillers The safest painkiller in pregnancy seems to be paracetamol. Aspirin should be avoided, as it may cause bleeding in the mother and the baby.

Visiting The Doctor

It is important to get proper health care throughout your pregnancy, so when should you visit your doctor?

This depends on a number of factors, such as your general health and any problems with previous pregnancies. Most doctors like to see pregnant women as soon as is practicable. Some variables such as blood pressure and haemoglobin alter in the early stages, and it is important to establish a base-line against which future changes can be measured. Some doctors prefer to wait until 10 to 12 weeks before the visit, to allow for accurate sizing of the uterus in confirming the date of delivery, but ultrasound techniques have largely negated this delay.

Sensible Advice

There is plenty of advice for pregnant women, but here are the six main areas where a sensible attitude is important.

Alcohol A modest alcohol intake (a unit a day) is not harmful. Heavy drinking can cause the foetal-alcohol syndrome of physical and mental retardation.

Smoking Smoking in pregnancy is definitely harmful. Not only does it cause an increase in deaths amongst babies, but it also stunts growth and causes mental retardation in the survivors.

Diet An increased intake of protein (meat, dairy products and fish) and calcium (dairy products) is needed, but avoid cheeses made with unpasteurised milk. An increased intake of fruit and vegetables helps to prevent constipation and provides extra vitamins.

Sexual intercourse It is perfectly safe to have sex throughout pregnancy unless the doctor has specifically warned against it, which she may do in some cases of threatened miscarriage. Intercourse at term may induce labour.

Rest Pregnancy is very tiring, especially if there are other children. If at all possible, rest for an hour or two in the afternoon. Moderate exercise, such as walking and swimming can be continued throughout pregnancy, but violent sports and those which may involve serious accidents, such as ski-ing and horse riding, should be avoided. Water ski-ing, because of the risk of water being forced up the vagina, may even be lethal.

Dental care This is free during, and for a year after, pregnancy. Gingivitis occurs in 50 per cent of pregnant women and many develop caries.

the growth and development of the breasts.

Relaxin is the name given to a hormone which has not been isolated. It is thought to soften connective tissue, particularly in the pelvis. This allows the pelvic bones to separate during childbirth and facilitates delivery. The existence of relaxin has never been proved and its effects may be due to a combination of other hormones.

Bigger and better

As well as these hormonal changes, many of the body's organs and glands enlarge. The thyroid tends to swell, especially if the intake of iodine is low. As a result the metabolic rate increases and the body burns more

Pregnancy And Problems

Pregnancy is divided into three trimesters or terms. Problems can occur at any stage,

The first term lasts until the 13th week of pregnancy. During this time the embryo develops from a fertilised egg to a foetus, recognisable as a baby, with fingernails, toenails and sex organs which can be identified.

The second term lasts from week 13 to week 27. During this time the mother can actually feel the baby move, and the foetus steadily gains weight. By about the 16th – 20th

week, the mother's abdomen will definitely 'show' and normal clothes may no longer fit.

The third term covers the last three months of pregnancy. The foetus continues to develop. By about the 32nd week the baby should settle head down, and at about the 36th week the head normally engages – moves into the bony part of the birth canal.

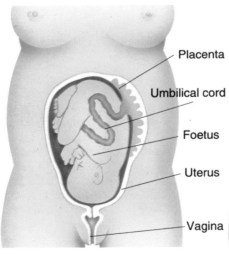

Placenta
Umbilical cord
Foetus
Uterus
Vagina

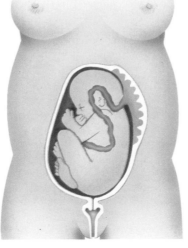

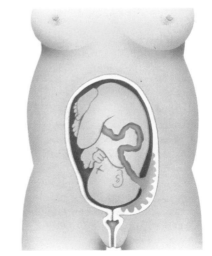

About a month before the baby is due, the uterus has become very large, and much of the digestive tract is pushed out of the way by the growing foetus.

In a breech birth, the baby 'presents' bottom first. Vaginal delivery is possible, but there is a risk of complications.

In placenta praevia, the placenta is at the lower end of the uterus, sometimes blocking the cervix. In this case a Caesarean section may be necessary.

Pregnancy Tests

Pregnancy tests are used by doctors and prospective parents to confirm or deny suspected pregnancy.

Many types of pregnancy test have been used in the past, but nowadays all rely on the detection of HCG, a hormone produced by the placenta. HCG can be detected in the urine on the first day of the missed period, but positive results at this stage should be re-tested a few days later. (Most tests give a negative result at around 20 weeks.) Home pregnancy tests are widely available and with a little care they are just as reliable as the hospital ones. Most tests specify that you should test the first urine of the day. This is the most concentrated and the HCG is easier to detect.

calories. Outside the genital organs, the greatest change is probably in the heart and circulation. The cardiac output increases by about a third during the course of the pregnancy, most of the extra blood being diverted to the kidneys, skin and uterus. The rise in blood flow to the skin explains why pregnant women tend not to feel the cold as much as others.

Despite this increased cardiac output, blood pressure actually drops during pregnancy. A rise in blood pressure may be a sign of a serious disease such as pre-eclampsia.

Veins become engorged, especially in the legs. This may lead to swollen ankles, piles and varicose veins.

The amount of blood in the circulation also increases by about a third, though some of the extra is just water. Despite this increase in blood volume, anaemia is a very common complication of pregnancy. This is because the growing foetus needs to build its iron stores to allow it to cope with the first few months of life, when the amount of iron in the baby's diet is low.

The work of the kidneys rises by about 50 per cent during pregnancy and the amount of water conserved increases. This extra fluid load also contributes to swelling of the ankles. Ankle swelling, or oedema, is only a problem if the blood pressure is raised. In women whose blood pressure is normal, ankle oedema is associated with healthier, heavier babies.

Signs and side effects

The first sign of pregnancy is often morning sickness. Pregnancy-induced changes in the gastrointestinal tract can persist throughout the whole nine months. These changes include the reflux of stomach acid, causing heartburn; vomiting during labour; constipation, often leading to piles; and an increased predisposition to gallstones.

Major changes

Important though these changes are, they are minor compared with the effects of pregnancy on the genital tract. In a non-pregnant woman, the uterus weighs about 50g. At the time of delivery it weighs 20 times as much. The blood supply to the vagina also increases several fold and the walls become softer and smoother with an increase in the activity of the mucus-producing glands.

During pregnancy the breasts increase in volume by an average of half a pint each! To develop properly, breast tissue must receive an adequate supply of oestrogen, progesterone, prolactin, HPL, insulin, cortisol and thyroxine.

Multiple Pregnancies

Multiple pregnancies are those where more than one baby develops – twins, triplets or even more.

In the UK the natural incidence of twins is one in 80. The incidence of triplets is one in 6400 and the incidence of quads is one in 500,000. Use of the fertility drugs clomiphene and HCG to induce pregnancy means the actual rate is higher, with a disproportionately higher incidence of quads and quins. Multiple pregnancies are more common in some nationalities – Nigerians, for example – and less common in others such as the Chinese.

Twins may develop from one fertilised egg (uniovular or identical) or from two (binovular or non-identical). Identical twins often have a common placenta. This can cause growth problems if blood is diverted to one twin at the expense of the other.

Multiple pregnancy is more common if there is a close family history of twins, in women taking fertility drugs or if there is excessive morning sickness. In most cases there are no known risk factors and the diagnosis comes as a complete surprise.

Complications are more common with multiple pregnancies and the risk of complications rises with the number of babies. An especial risk, because of the increased size of the uterus, is prematurity (giving birth before full term). Prematurity is so common, that although only 1.55 per cent of pregnancies are twins, they account for 15 per cent of all premature births.

Good ante-natal care is vital for the well-being of mother and babies. Vitamin and iron supplements are usually given as a matter of course. Rest is vital and some doctors routinely go so far as to admit all multiple pregnancies to hospital for the last two months of pregnancy.

Delivery of twins is often complicated, and this is one case where all mothers should be in hospital.

PREMATURITY

A premature baby is one born before full term – that is at 37 weeks gestation or less.

Modern paediatric care means that more and more premature babies are surviving. Ninety-six per cent of all babies born at 32 weeks, and 50 per cent of babies born at 28 weeks survive to lead a normal life.

Complications at birth

Any woman who goes into labour prematurely should be admitted to hospital at once. In many cases an intravenous drip of a drug called ritodrine will slow or even stop the contractions. If childbirth looks inevitable the hospital team will try and ensure that all the preparations for a premature

» SEE ALSO — Breech birth, Caesarean section, Childbirth, Fertilisation, Labour

MEDICAL FACT FILE

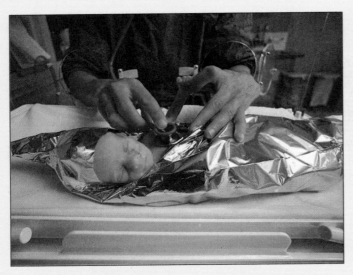

Many premature babies are placed in incubators in intensive care to maintain their body heat and keep their respiration, heartbeat and other functions normal.

birth are made before delivery. If the pregnancy is very early this may involve transfer of the mother to a hospital with intensive care incubators.

Premature babies, because of their soft heads, are more prone to birth trauma. Most doctors would perform an episiotomy and a forceps delivery, and some would even go as far as a Caesarian section to try to protect the baby.

The small baby

At the time of birth, premature babies are at special risk from complications. In all such cases a paediatrician, with special knowledge of very small babies, should be at the delivery. Very small babies cool rapidly and great care is needed to keep them warm. Breathing difficulties are common and many premature babies need artificial ventilation for a time.

Even after the birth, premature babies, because many of their systems are not fully formed, require special care. One problem peculiar to premature babies is respiratory distress syndrome. In a normal infant the lining of the lungs is coated with a detergent-like substance that allows the lungs to expand fully. In very premature babies this substance is missing and the effort of expanding the lungs is often more than the baby can manage. In the past, artificial ventilation at high pressure has been needed, and recent trials with an artificial detergent blown into the lungs have also been very promising.

PREMEDICATION

A premed (as premedication is commonly known) is a drug given to a patient an hour or two before going in to surgery.

The drug is intended to prepare the patient for anaesthesia and surgery. It usually contains a painkiller and something to induce drowsiness and relieve anxiety before going into the operating theatre.

For some types of operation, the premed also contains a drug to reduce the secretions in the airways. Premedication tends to make the patient irritable and dry in the throat.

PREMENSTRUAL SYNDROME

Premenstrual syndrome or PMS describes a whole range of symptoms occurring in the few days every month before the onset of menstruation.

PMS is a serious problem. Forty-nine per cent of female prisoners in Britain committed their offence during the premenstrual period. The number of suicides and emergency admissions to mental hospitals of women double in the week before their period. In studies, 20 to 30 per cent of women report feeling irritable, anxious or depressed in the premenstrual period. Many more complain of bloating, headache, swelling of the hands and feet, dizziness and palpitations.

Causes and treatments

The timing of the complaint suggests that the problem is hormonal in origin but there is a debate about treatment amongst doctors, nutritionists and alternative therapists.

The oral contraceptive pill or high doses of progesterone are helpful in some, but not all, cases. Water tablets (diuretics) and fluid restriction help to prevent fluid retention and bloatedness, but they do not seem to help with the psychological symptoms.

In trials, vitamin B6 and oil of evening primrose were found to be more effective than placebos. However, they may need to be taken for several monthly cycles before the benefit becomes plain to see.

Some doctors advocate frequent, small, high-carbohydrate meals to help alleviate the problem — it's a form of treatment which is certainly worth trying.

PRESBYOPIA

Presbyopia comes with age and is a gradual loss of focusing power in the eye.

In a young, healthy eye, the ciliary muscles which hold the lens in place in the eye contract when the eye needs to focus on a near object. This fattens the lens, so that the near object is focused on the retina. With age, this ability is gradually lost — from the age of about 45 — until by the age of about 65, the lens has lost all its elasticity and can no longer adjust to focus on near objects.

Treatment

'Reading glasses' with convex lenses are used to correct the defect, focusing near objects on the retina. The prescription for the reading lenses will depend on the degree of elasticity still remaining in the lens, so that several changes of glasses may be necessary as the condition develops.

PRESCRIBED DISEASES

Prescribed diseases are those diseases which may be contracted as a result of working in a particular occupation, and for which financial compensation is available.

Claimants have to prove that they have a particular prescribed disease and have worked in an occupation which leads to a higher incidence of that particular disease. Obvious examples are pneumoconiosis and occupational deafness.

Some of these diseases are notifiable (mercury and lead poisoning, and radiation sickness, for example).

➤➤ SEE ALSO — Hormones, Myopia, Notifiable diseases, Oestrogen, Progesterone

PRESSURE POINTS

Pressure points are those points on the body where pressure can be applied to stop or limit arterial bleeding.

Arterial blood is bright red, and pumps from wounds in regular spurts, in time with the beating of the heart. Where arteries lie near the surface of the skin and against a bone, it is fairly easy to apply pressure at certain points to limit the bleeding from an injury further away from the heart.

The technique cannot be used to stop bleeding from a vein (which is darker and flows more evenly than arterial blood).

PRIAPISM

Priapism is a dangerous condition in which the penis remains erect.

The condition is painful, and the erection persists without any sexual arousal. It occurs because blood fails to drain from the tissue in the penis due to a nervous disorder, a blood disorder that causes clotting in the penis, or occasionally because the blood is blocked by an infection such as prostatitis or urethritis.

Treatment
Emergency treatment is necessary to prevent permanent damage to the penis. This may involve simply draining the blood from the penis with a needle, or spinal anaesthesia, which dilates the veins so that the priapism goes.

PRICKLY HEAT

Prickly heat is a disorder of the sweat glands. It is common in the tropics but almost unheard of in temperate areas such as Britain.

In normal circumstances, water from the sweat glands evaporates from the surface of the skin to cool the body. In prickly heat, the body surface is so hot that the skin cells swell and the sweat pores become blocked. The sweat glands continue to produce sweat and the result is an intensely itchy rash resembling tiny, red blisters. The trunk is usually the worst affected area.

Treatment
The condition settles rapidly with cooling and most of the traditional remedies, such as application of eau de Cologne, help by imitating natural perspiration. Calamine lotion is an effective soothing lotion.

A similar condition sometimes affects children with an acute fever. In this case, the sweat glands become blocked with the salt left behind by the evaporation of sweat. This produces tiny, red blisters on the surface of the skin. The skin condition returns to normal spontaneously after a day or two.

Pressure Points

Knowing where the pressure points are can be very useful in cases of serious injury.

● The first step in trying to stop arterial bleeding is to apply pressure to the wound itself.
● If this does not stem the flow, apply pressure at a pressure point. Use your fingers, pressing the artery against the underlying bone.
● If possible, raise the injury so that it is the highest point in the body, and gravity will help to stem the flow as well as the pressure.

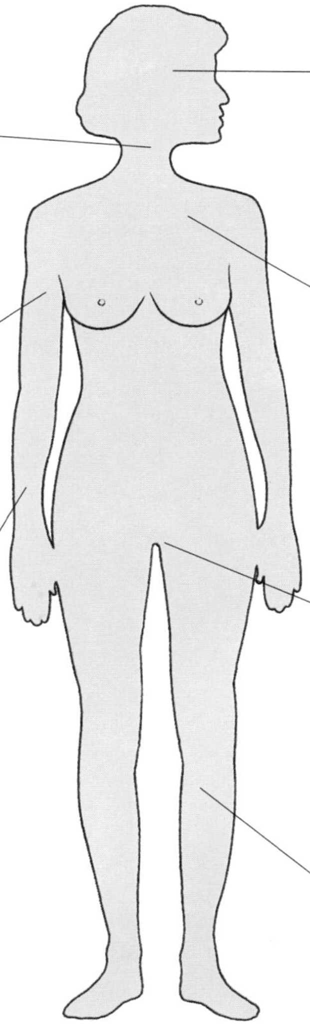

Under the jaw
Prevent bleeding from the head and neck by applying pressure at the side of the neck, below the jaw.

Upper arm
Prevent bleeding from the lower arm and hand by applying pressure half way down the inside of the upper arm.

Lower arm
Prevent bleeding from the hand by applying pressure half way down the inside of the forearm.

Temples
Prevent bleeding from the scalp by applying pressure in front of the ear.

Under the collarbone
Prevent bleeding from the shoulder and upper arm by applying pressure between the collarbone and first rib.

Groin
Prevent bleeding in the upper leg by applying pressure in the fold in the groin.

Back of the knee
Apply pressure behind the knee joint to control lower leg bleeding.

➤➤ SEE ALSO — Rash

MEDICAL FACT FILE

PRIMARY TEETH

The primary teeth are the teeth we grow in early childhood, which are eventually replaced by permanent teeth.

Primary teeth, also known as milk teeth or deciduous teeth, start to appear at about six months. It is usually the two bottom front teeth which appear first. Altogether, children grow eight incisors at the front of the mouth, four eye teeth or canines, and eight molars, the chewing teeth at the back of the mouth.

Children start to lose their primary teeth at about the age of six.

PROGESTERONE

Progesterone is a female sex hormone that prepares the lining of the womb for pregnancy.

The main action of progesterone is to produce and maintain a thickening of the lining of the uterus. The hormone is produced during the second half of the menstrual cycle by the corpus luteum — the scar left on the ovary after ovulation (the release of the egg). After two weeks, unless the egg is fertilised, production of progesterone ceases and the lining of the womb falls away. If pregnancy ensues, the role of progesterone production is taken over by the developing placenta.

Progestogen drugs

Progesterone, usually in the form of synthetic drugs called progestogens, is one of the most widely used drugs. In combination with oestrogen it is the basis of the oral contraceptive pill. Given in the second half of the menstrual cycle it decreases the amount of menstrual blood loss and often makes the cycle more regular. On its own, as the mini-pill, it can still prevent pregnancy.

Progesterone injections in early pregnancy can prevent some types of miscarriage. In older women, progesterone is known to slow the growth of cancers of the womb.

PROLAPSE

A prolapse is a displacement of an organ or certain other parts of the body from its normal position.

Disc prolapse is the correct term for a slipped disc. Another common form of prolapse, which affects mainly older women, is a prolapse of the uterus.

Degrees of prolapse

Normally, the uterus is held in position at the head of the vagina by ligaments. If these ligaments become stretched (which may happen as a result of the strain of childbirth), the uterus is no longer held in position and pushes down into the vagina. In some cases, the cervix reaches the opening of the vagina. In severe cases, the uterus can actually be seen protruding from the vagina, which turns inside out.

Treatment

In women who are past the menopause, and in very severe cases, hysterectomy and repair surgery is needed. Prolapse repair is a major operation, requiring an abdominal incision, and recovery takes many weeks.

In women who do not want, or cannot have, surgery, a pessary device (in the form of a ring or a hook) can be inserted into the vagina so that it holds the uterus in position. Such pessaries should not be worn for very long periods (particularly in older women) as friction may damage the tissues around the cervix.

Prevention

In order to reduce the risk of prolapse, pelvic floor exercises should be practised, particularly during pregnancy and after childbirth. Pelvic floor exercises help to tone the muscles of the vagina, and may also help to prevent incontinence. Another way to strengthen the muscles around the vagina is to use vaginal cones. A quite heavy plastic-coated cone is inserted in the vagina, stretching the muscles which contract as a reflex action, strengthening them.

PROSTATE GLAND

The prostate gland is situated at the base of the male bladder. It secretes fluid and nutrients that help to feed sperm.

The prostate gland is shaped like an inverted pyramid. The urethra, the tube that carries urine from the bladder to the penis, runs through the centre of it. The ejaculatory ducts which carry mature sperm also run through the prostate, and the gland adds a milky fluid to the sperm. (Further secretions are added before the final semen mixture is ejaculated.)

At birth, the prostate is tiny, but when boys reach puberty, male hormones, secreted by the testes and adrenal glands, stimulate the prostate to grow to about the size of a walnut.

Prostatic problems are extremely common.

Enlarged prostate

With increasing age, most men's prostates enlarge and this is a frequent cause of urinary symptoms. The main problem is distortion of the urethra as it runs through the gland. This blocks the outflow and may eventually lead to pressure damage in the kidneys.

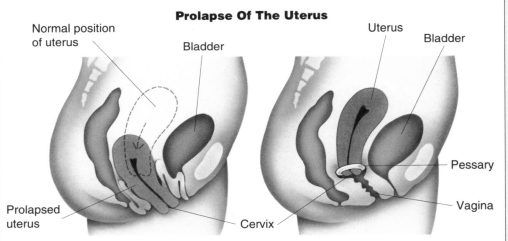

Prolapse Of The Uterus

Normal position of uterus

Bladder

Prolapsed uterus

Cervix

Uterus

Bladder

Pessary

Vagina

A prolapsed uterus (above left) can be corrected by inserting a specially designed pessary into the vagina. This supports the cervix, holding the uterus in place above the vagina.

SEE ALSO — Contraception, Disc prolapse, Incontinence, Menstruation, Oestrogen, Oral contraceptives, Pessary, Uterus

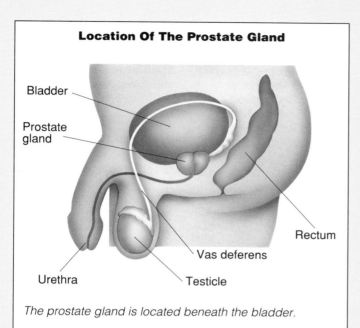

Location Of The Prostate Gland

Bladder

Prostate gland

Rectum

Vas deferens

Urethra

Testicle

The prostate gland is located beneath the bladder.

Benign prostatic enlargement is uncommon under the age of 60 and is rare in Asians. The cause of the enlargement is unknown but is clearly connected to male sex hormones.

The first symptom of an enlarged prostate is frequency in passing urine, which is often worse at night. Trouble with starting and stopping the flow of urine and a reduced force of the stream are also common. In some cases it becomes impossible to pass water, and fluid must be drawn off using a catheter passed up the penis.

Treating enlarged prostate
Until recently the only real treatment for prostatic enlargement was surgery. Most prostatic surgery is performed using a cystoscope, a rigid tube that allows the lining of the urethra and the bladder to be visualised. A hot wire loop is used to pare away the prostate until a sufficiently large hole has been bored for the urine to pass through freely.

Now, however, drug treatment has been shown to be of some value in shrinking the prostate. An even newer development is the use of

microwaves. A microwave aerial is threaded up the urethra and is activated in the area of the prostate, causing it to shrink. This method should be effective, safe and almost painfree.

Prostatitis
A condition that affects younger men is prostatitis — inflammation of the prostate. Prostatitis may be caused by a urinary tract infection but is more usually a consequence of urethritis — bacterial infection (which may or may not be sexually transmitted) spreads from the urethra to the prostate. It causes pain in the lower abdomen and penis, often worse on ejaculation. In acute cases, which are usually due to gonorrhoea, there is fever, frequent need to urinate and pain on passing water.

Diagnosis and treatment
In order to make an accurate diagnosis a sample of prostatic fluid is needed. This is obtained by massaging the prostate through the wall of the rectum. The fluid can be stained to identify the organism causing the inflammation. Treatment is with appropriate antibiotics.

PROSTATE GLAND, CANCER OF

Prostatic cancer is a malignant growth in the outer part of the prostate gland.

Prostate cancer is one of the commonest cancers in men. Indeed, seven per cent of all cancers in men occur in this tiny gland, and up to 80 per cent of 80-year-old-men are affected. In most cases it causes few problems, but in some cases, probably as a result of hormonal influences, the cancer grows rapidly.

Symptoms and treatment
Prostatic cancer causes the same symptoms as benign enlargement — frequency and other problems with urination. However, if the cancer spreads rapidly it often affects the bones, and the first sign is often severe bone pain.

Surgery to remove the gland relieves any obstruction to the urethra, but if the cancer has spread, hormonal treatment to shrink the secondary growths is needed. The simplest form of hormonal treatment is castration. Without the drive of the sex hormones, secondary growths may melt away.

PROSTHESIS

A prosthesis is an artificial replacement for part of the body.

Prostheses may be fitted to help the body function normally (as with artificial limbs or artificial heart valves). Whole branches of research are dedicated to improving the performance of such devices. The term is also used to describe devices fitted for cosmetic (and psychological) reasons after a mastectomy.

PRURITIS

Pruritis is the medical term for itching.

Three areas where pruritis is often noticed are around the anus (pruritis ani), around the female genitals (pruritis vulvae) and between the scrotum and the leg (which is commonly known as jock itch).

Pruritis ani is used to describe anal itching with no obvious cause — it is often due to a dryness of the skin which comes with age, but other possible causes, such as threadworms, should be checked out.

Vulval itching may be a symptom of infection, or may be caused by irritants such as soap or bath preparations. As with pruritis ani, there may be no obvious cause, and it becomes more common in older women. Avoid using soaps, and make sure you wear cotton underclothes if you are affected by this condition.

Jock itch is usually due to a fungal infection, and a fungicidal cream may be prescribed.

PSORIASIS

Psoriasis is a very common condition in which skin cells multiply at a faster rate than normal.

Psoriasis affects more than a million people in the UK alone. It first appears in the five to 25 age group. In the early years, twice as many girls are affected as boys but by adult life the ratio is nearer 50:50. It often affects scar tissue.

Symptoms
The skin becomes thickened and covered in masses of silvery scales. The rash of psoriasis consists of islands of pink or red scaly skin against a background of normal tissue. In acute

» SEE ALSO — Itching, Limb, artificial, Mastectomy

MEDICAL FACT FILE

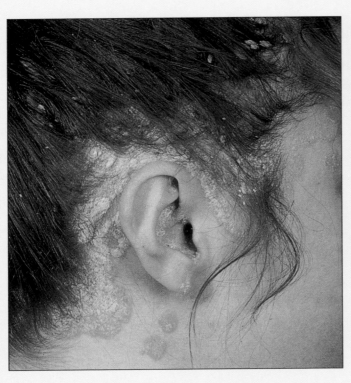

The chronic skin disease, psoriasis. In addition to being unsightly, the red, scaly patches are also extremely itchy.

psoriasis the rash appears as tiny discs that often extend over the whole body. These acute lesions often remit, to be followed, usually on the knees and elbows, by the larger, thicker plaques of chronic psoriasis.

Psoriasis may also affect the scalp. In this case the hairs anchor the scales in place until the skin is a centimetre or two thick. In 25 per cent of patients, psoriasis affects the nails, which become pitted — sometimes so badly that the nail resembles a thimble. In a few cases, psoriasis affects the joints, causing arthritis.

Finding the cause
Several factors are implicated in the cause of psoriasis but in many cases no connection can be found. Inheritance plays a role — most sufferers have a family member with the disease. Infection may be a cause in some cases — especially with children — as attacks often occur 10 to 12 days after an infection. Stress does not usually cause

psoriasis but there is no doubt that emotional upset can make an attack worse.

Sunlight seems to help the condition. It is commoner in northern climes, but rare amongst white people living in the tropics. Most sufferers find the condition improves in the summer.

Therapies
Moisturising creams can help acute psoriasis until the condition remits. Chronic psoriasis is usually treated with creams containing tar or steroids, but these are likely to make acute psoriasis worse. In some cases, ultra-violet light, with or without local applications, can be very effective. In severe cases, ultraviolet light is shone on to skin already primed by oral drugs. This increases the absorption of light and promotes healing.

In severe cases anti-cancer drugs are used to slow the growth of the skin. These work very well but side effects limit their usefulness.

PSYCHOSIS

A psychosis is a type of psychological disorder in which the sufferer is debilitated, losing touch with reality.

Psychotic disorders include schizophrenia and manic depression. Symptoms include delusions, depression, hallucinations, loss of emotion and mania.

The causes of psychoses are thought to lie in malfunctions of the neurotransmitters in the brain, but no specific causes have yet been isolated.

Drug therapies and, in some cases, extensive rehabilitation, are used to treat psychotics.

PSYCHOSOMATIC DISORDERS

Psychosomatic disorders are those in which symptoms are actually caused by psychological factors.

Some physical symptoms have obvious physical causes, but in some cases it may be that emotional upsets trigger physical problems.

Disorders which are commonly agreed to have psychosomatic bases in some cases include eczema, asthma, headaches, irritable bowel syndrome and some forms of ulcer.

PTERYGIUM

Pterygium is a thickening of the conjunctiva.

The conjunctiva is the membrane covering the white of the eye and the inside of the eyelids. Some people, if they are exposed to strong sunlight through living in the tropics, for example, develop a thickening of the conjunctiva extending from the inner and outer corners of the eye to the cornea.

The condition does not usually cause any problems, but if it starts to extend on to the cornea, or if it feels uncomfortable, it may be removed surgically.

PTOSIS

Ptosis is a condition where the upper eyelid droops.

Ptosis may be congenital, it may develop spontaneously or as a result of injury, or it may be a side effect of a serious neurological disorder such as myasthenia gravis.

If the condition is severe in young children, it can be corrected with surgery.

In later life, any unexplained development of ptosis should be checked by a doctor, as it may be a sign of a brain tumour, aneurysm or other neurological disorder.

The upper eyelid of this baby is drooping, a condition known as ptosis. This case is congenital, but ptosis can have other causes.

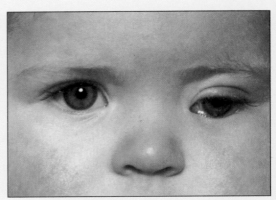

➤➤ SEE ALSO — Depression, Manic depression, Schizophrenia

The Structure Of The Heart

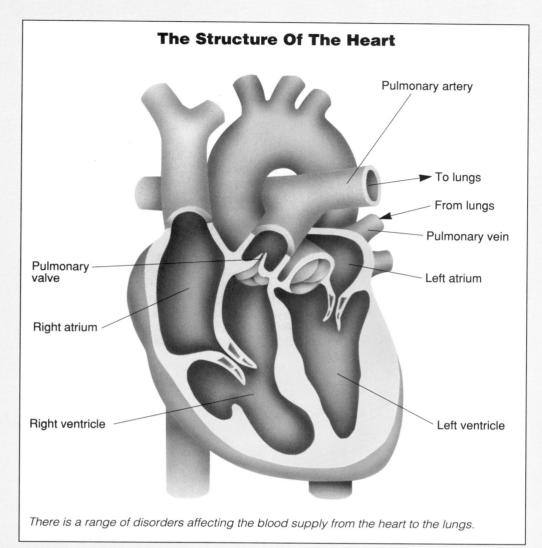

Pulmonary artery

To lungs

From lungs

Pulmonary vein

Left atrium

Pulmonary valve

Right atrium

Left ventricle

Right ventricle

There is a range of disorders affecting the blood supply from the heart to the lungs.

symptoms and sudden death may occur with no warning.

Physical examination may reveal a number of features which might suggest the disease, but the diagnosis should be confirmed using x-rays and an ECG.

Treatment depends on the underlying condition. Water tablets relieve some of the pressure. Other treatments such as drugs that dilate the blood vessels in the legs have been tried but have little effect. In the younger age group, heart and lung transplants offer hope of a cure.

PULMONARY INCOMPETENCE

Pulmonary incompetence involves a fault in the valve between the right ventricle and the pulmonary artery, which carries blood to the lungs.

If the pulmonary valve is incompetent, then the heart is unable to pump deoxygenated blood to the lungs. Surprisingly, this seldom causes too many problems. The main symptom is a loud heart murmur. If the condition is caused by pulmonary hypertension, this must be treated, rather than the defective valve.

PULMONARY OEDEMA

Pulmonary oedema is the proper name for a disorder commonly referred to as fluid on the lungs.

There are many causes of the condition, including anaemia, liver failure and kidney disease, but the commonest is heart failure. In heart failure, which usually

PULMONARY EMBOLISM

A pulmonary embolism is an obstruction of the pulmonary artery (the artery leading to the lungs) by a blood clot.

The condition may be life-threatening if the clot is large or if there are many smaller clots, as it deprives some of the lung tissue of blood. The condition is more commonly referred to as an embolism.

PULMONARY FIBROSIS

Pulmonary fibrosis is a thickening of the lung tissue as a result of serious lung disease.

Pulmonary fibrosis may occur throughout both lungs, or just in small patches. It is usually the result of a disorder such as pneumonia or tuberculosis. Shortness of breath is the main symptom. The disorder may be diagnosed by x-raying the lungs, but in many cases no treatment is possible.

PULMONARY HYPERTENSION

Pulmonary hyper-tension is raised blood pressure in the artery between the heart and the lungs — the pulmonary artery.

There are many causes, including chronic lung disease, holes in the heart

and blood clots. A rare condition, seen predominantly in young women, is primary pulmonary hypertension. This name is given to the disorder when the cause is unknown: however, slimming tablets and the contraceptive pill have been suggested as possible causes.

If pulmonary hypertension is left untreated the right ventricle increases in size in order to compensate for the increased work load. In the end, however, it is unable to cope and the patient deteriorates rapidly.

Symptoms and treatment
Chest pain, shortness of breath and fatigue are common symptoms. In some cases there are no

⟫ SEE ALSO — Anaemia, Embolism, Fibrosis, Heart, Lung diseases and disorders

affects the elderly, the heart pumps less efficiently. As a result, back pressure in the lungs leads to fluid leaking into the tissues.

Symptoms and treatment

The main symptom is shortness of breath, especially when lying down.

Water tablets help to restore the fluid balance and improve symptoms, at least in the short term.

PULMONARY STENOSIS

Pulmonary stenosis is a thickening of the pulmonary valve so that blood cannot pass through it freely.

Pulmonary stenosis is usually a congenital defect, but may be acquired as a result of rheumatic fever.

Obstructing the blood flow from the heart leads to an increase in pressure in, and an increase in the size of, the right ventricle. This leads to an increase in the size of the right atrium. Severe obstruction usually means death within a few minutes of birth. Lesser degrees of obstruction can give rise to fatigue, breathlessness and loss of consciousness. Mild cases may be symptom free.

Diagnosis and treatment

Blood rushing through the tight valve causes a loud heart murmur — so loud it may even be felt by placing a hand on the chest. Chest x-rays and ECGs show any enlargement of the heart.

Treatment of severe cases involves opening up the valve to allow the blood to flow freely. This can be done by open heart surgery, or with endoscopy, threading a balloon through the heart and inflating it momentarily to open the valve.

PULSE

The pulse is the rhythmic pumping of blood through an artery, which can be felt by compressing an artery against a bone.

The pulse can be felt at many points, but the one most often used is at the wrist, on the radial artery. When a doctor takes a pulse she is feeling for several different things. The rate of the pulse reflects the heart beat. The normal resting pulse in an adult may lie anywhere between 60 and 100 beats per minute. The pulse rate is higher in children and lower in the super fit. Increases in the pulse rate may be due to emotion, infection or an overactive thyroid. Slowing of the pulse occurs in some forms of heart disease and with an underactive thyroid.

The normal pulse is regular, except for the occasional missed beat. A completely irregular pulse, especially if it is very fast, may be a sign of heart disease or an overactive thyroid. Feeling two pulses together may give valuable clues to narrowing of an artery. A delay between the wrist and the groin, for example, may indicate a narrowing in the aorta.

A weak pulse, one that is difficult to feel, is usually due to a deep-seated artery. If the patient is obviously very ill, a weak pulse may indicate that the heart is failing to pump efficiently.

PUNCH-DRUNK

This term is used to describe the effects of brain damage caused by several incidents of loss of consciousness due to head injury.

Symptoms include a general slowing of thought processes and actions, slurred speech and lack of concentration. It gets its name because boxers are most often affected by the disorder.

PUPIL, DISORDERS

The pupil is the circular opening in the centre of the eye, which looks black.

The pupil is surrounded by the iris and covered by the cornea, and many disorders affecting the pupil may actually be disorders of the iris or cornea. The pupil may have an irregular or distorted shape due to a congenital problem with the iris, or due to injury.

One disorder, which is caused by syphilis, is known as Argyll Robertson pupil: the pupil does not adjust its size according to the amount of light (becoming smaller in bright light and dilating in the dark), although it does adjust to help focus on objects.

Some drugs have an affect on the pupil: atropine makes it larger and pilocarpine makes it smaller.

PURPURA

The term purpura describes a number of disorders characterised by bleeding under the skin, which shows up as purple or reddish-brown patches.

The patches (also known as purpura) may be anything from the size of a pinhead to

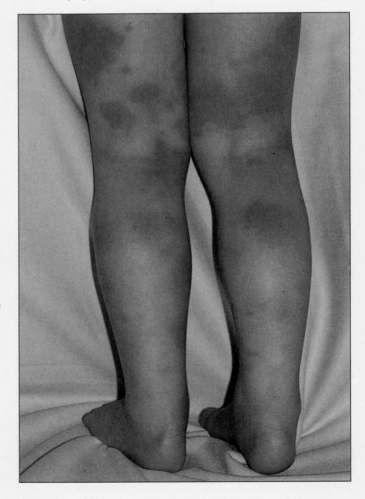

This form of purpura, known as Henoch-Schönlein purpura, which affects children, shows as raised patches of dark skin. Its cause is not known, but it may be an allergic reaction.

➤➤ SEE ALSO — Brain damage, Syphilis

MEDICAL FACT FILE

the size of a 2p piece. There are many different types of purpura, with various causes.

Common purpura
Common purpura, also known as senile purpura, is the most common bleeding disorder. It mainly affects elderly women. As the hormone balance changes after the menopause, the tissue thins so that blood vessels rupture easily.

Other forms
The disorder may also occur as a result of inflammation of the blood vessels, which is sometimes the result of an allergic reaction. It may be more serious — resulting from a lack of platelets which are needed for the blood to clot. This in turn may be caused by another under-lying disease such as leukaemia or aplastic anaemia, or it may be a side effect of radiation or certain drugs.

Purpura is also a symptom of scurvy, auto-immune disorders and kidney failure.

Diagnosis and treatment
The doctor will make a thorough investigation of the signs and symptoms, and take samples of blood for testing. If common purpura is diagnosed, it may be helped by hormone replacement therapy. Other types of purpura may be treated with corticosteriod drugs and immunosuppressant drugs. In some cases, transfusions are needed to replace the platelets. The removal of the spleen (which processes platelets) may be necessary with some forms of purpura.

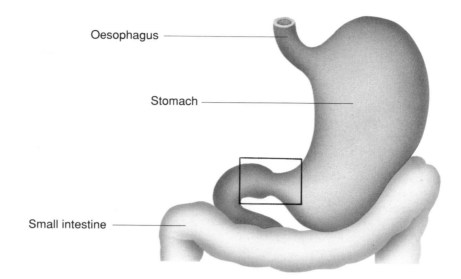

Location Of The Pyloric Valve

Oesophagus

Stomach

Small intestine

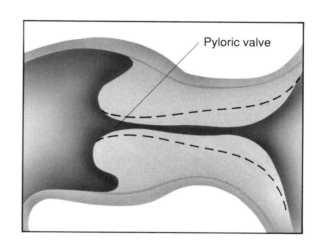

Pyloric valve

Pyloric stenosis affects the pyloric valve, which controls the flow of food out of the stomach (above). The valve becomes constricted, stopping the flow of nutrients and waste from the stomach to the intestine. The dotted lines (see detail, right) indicate the normal width of the valve.

PYELONEPHRITIS

Pyelonephritis is an inflammation of the kidney, usually due to a bacterial infection.

The disorder may occur as a sudden attack (acute) or it may be a chronic condition, in which case there may be permanent kidney damage.

The acute form is most common in women, particularly in pregnant women. It usually occurs following an attack of cystitis, when the infection spreads to the kidney. Symptoms include a high fever, chills and back pain.

The chronic form is usually due to a backflow of urine into one of the ureters from the bladder, which in turn is usually due to a congenitally faulty valve. If the backflow is persistent, there may be permanent

damage to the kidney. Anyone who has persistent kidney infections should have special tests to check whether the cause is a faulty valve, which can be corrected surgically.

PYLORIC STENOSIS

Pyloric stenosis is a disorder of the valve between the stomach and the small intestine.

If the valve, known as the pyloric valve, is too tight, it can no longer regulate the emptying of the stomach. Food becomes trapped in

the stomach. The condition is usually congenital, although it may occur in an adult as a result of peptic ulceration.

A congenital problem
Congenital pyloric stenosis is quite common. It affects seven times as many boys as girls, and seems to run in families. The cause seems to be an overgrowth of valve muscle, and it usually takes several weeks to develop after birth.

The main feature of the disorder is vomiting. Initially this is light, but by the time the child is six weeks old, no milk stays down. The vomit can come up with such force

>> SEE ALSO — Kidneys, Radiation, Ulcers

that it is projected several feet across the room.

Treatment

Treatment is surgical. In an operation known as pyroplasty, the valve is divided along its length and restitched. If the child is too weak for surgery, a tube can be passed into the small intestine and liquid feeds given. Although the condition should resolve itself as the child grows, it may take many months.

PYURIA

Pyuria is the presence of white blood cells in the urine.

Pyuria causes the urine to become cloudy, which is an indication of infection and inflammation of the kidneys or the urinary tract.

In order to diagnose the cause, your doctor will send a specimen of urine for testing, and if the cause is found to be a microorganism, antibiotics will be prescribed.

QUICKENING

This term is used to describe the first movements of the foetus during pregnancy.

Quickening usually occurs in mid-pregnancy, at 16 – 20 weeks. Movements, which feel rather like a fluttering in the abdomen, may be felt earlier in subsequent pregnancies.

QUINSY

Quinsy is an abscess on the tonsil.

The condition usually occurs as a complication of tonsillitis, causing a painful throat, fever, and swollen glands (or lymph nodes) in the neck. Patients may dribble and have difficulty opening their mouth. Antibiotics should clear up the infection if it is caught at an early stage, otherwise the abscess may have to be drained surgically.

RABIES

Rabies is a viral disease, transmitted to humans by animals, which is usually fatal once symptoms have developed.

Rabies has been eradicated in Britain, most of Scandinavia and Australia, but in other parts of the world it is carried by skunks, bats, jackals, wolves and, the animal which most often passes it on to humans, dogs. Anyone bitten by a dog (or any other mammal), in an area where rabies is rife, should seek medical attention, as immunisation is available (see box above).

The microorganism causing rabies is present in animals' saliva. If it gets into the human blood stream (from a bite, or from an infected animal licking an open wound) it travels through the nervous system to the brain where it causes inflammation which leads to several symptoms.

Symptoms

The incubation period can be anything from just over a week to several months, although somewhere between one month and two-and-a-half months is most usual. The first symptoms are a slight fever, coupled with a number of problems, including delusions, disorientation and, in some cases, seizures. The main feature is an extraordinary reaction to water: even if the patient is thirsty, he or she will suffer spasms of the throat on trying to drink. Such spasms are even triggered by the sight or mention of water. This is what gave the disease its former name, hydrophobia. The face muscles may become paralysed, and after anything from a few days to three weeks, the patient falls into a coma and dies.

Treatment

There are a few cases of patients surviving rabies, due to intensive care to maintain breathing and heartbeat. Other treatment involves sedatives and painkillers.

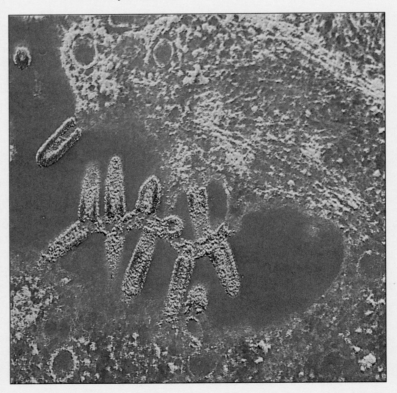

The virus which causes rabies can be seen as a red, elongated particle budding away from the host cells (in green on the right).

>> SEE ALSO — Blood, Pregnancy

RADIATION

Radiation is the emission of energy in the form of particles or waves.

Light, x-rays and radiowaves are all examples of radiation. Many forms of radiation are harmless — or even beneficial — but some may be hazardous to health.

All radiation can cause disruption to cells, but the severity and the extent of the damage depends on the type of radiation and the dose. Radiation is either penetrating (x-rays, gamma rays) or non-penetrating (alpha or beta particles). Absorption of large doses, following a nuclear explosion for example, can cause immediate sickness of varying severity. Long-term effects may take years — or even a whole generation — to appear.

Acute radiation sickness

Acute radiation sickness may be mild or severe. It may follow a nuclear explosion or accidents in atomic power stations or other nuclear establishments. Radiation sickness may also occur as a result of radiotherapy treatment for cancer.

In mild cases, the symptoms include nausea, vomiting and general malaise. A week or two after exposure, the white blood cell count may fall.

Victims of mild doses of radiation recover, but run an increased risk of developing leukaemia in later life.

In severe cases of radiation sickness, most of the organs in the body are affected, but as a rule, the faster the turnover of cells in an organ the more it suffers. Bone, for example, is scarcely damaged at all, whilst the much faster-growing bone marrow may be devastated. Damage to the bone marrow and other blood-forming organs causes anaemia, bleeding and an increased sensitivity to infection.

Absorption of high doses of radiation causes almost immediate nausea and vomiting. This settles after a few hours but as the damaged cells are shed, the initial symptoms are followed by severe diarrhoea. The skin is particularly badly affected, showing redness and blistering, followed by infection. Complete hair loss is common, and usually a sign of a fatal dose. Dehydration and infection are common causes of death following exposure to massive doses of radiation. Huge doses of radiation can also make the brain swell, leading to confusion, coma and rapid death.

After exposure

Survivors of severe, acute radiation sickness are at an increased risk of subsequent illness and have a lowered life expectancy. Leukaemia and cancer — particularly of the thyroid, salivary glands and skin — are all more common. Infertility and cataracts may also occur.

There is also an increased risk of birth defects in the children of those who have been exposed — sometimes many years later. There is even the suggestion that the children of survivors suffer more cancers than expected.

No one knows if such genetic changes affect grandchildren and great grandchildren of those who have been exposed to radioactive materials, but evidence is beginning to show that it might.

Following exposure to radiation, the victim should be undressed and washed in an effort to minimise the dose absorbed. Other than this, the treatment of acute radiation sickness is largely supportive, with the emphasis on preventing dehydration, infection and haemorrhage.

Specific antidotes are available for some radioactive materials: large doses of iodine will prevent the thyroid absorbing radioactive iodine, for example.

RADIOTHERAPY

Radiotherapy is the branch of medicine concerned with the use of ionising radiation in the treatment of disease — mainly cancer.

The principle behind radiotherapy is that normal cells have a greater ability to recover after a given dose of radiation than tumour cells. Tumour cells grow faster than normal cells, but they are more easily destroyed.

Administering radiotherapy

Radiotherapists may use electromagnetic radiation such as x-rays and gamma rays, or particles such as electrons or neutrons. The type of radiotherapy used depends on the size of the tumour, its sensitivity to radiotherapy, its site and its spread.

Radiotherapy may be administered by directing a beam of radiation on to, and into, a specific part of the body or by inserting radioactive needles directly into the tumour. In some cases, particularly thyroid tumours, a radioactive dose

Protective clothing and strict safety measures are essential for those who work in situations where they may be exposed to harmful radiation.

▶▶ SEE ALSO — Leukaemia, Salivary glands, Skin, Thyroid, X-rays

During sessions of radiotherapy, the site of the growth and 'target' of the radiation is usually marked on the skin. The patient has to be positioned accurately, and doses are very carefully controlled, in order to reduce the chance of healthy cells being affected by the radiation to an absolute minimum. Comfort and reassurance from the medical staff are essential, as the process (and the equipment which is used) seems quite alarming and impersonal.

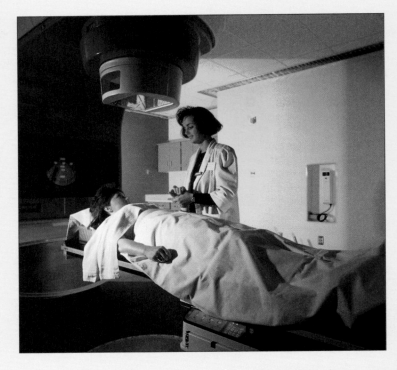

is taken by mouth but finds its way to the target organ.

Tumours vary greatly in their sensitivity to radiotherapy. Many childhood tumours and the lymphomas such as Hodgkin's disease are highly sensitive. Slow-growing, solid tumours, such as those of the gut, are much less sensitive to radiotherapy.

The size of the tumour is another factor that influences the effectiveness of radiotherapy. The larger the tumour, the harder it is to treat. Conventional surgery to remove most of the tumour followed by radiotherapy is often more effective than either treatment on its own.

What are the side effects?
Unfortunately, radiotherapy is not the 'cure-all' for cancer. The factor that limits its usefulness is its effects on normal cells. Again, some normal cells are more sensitive than others, amongst the most sensitive are the eye and the kidney.

Although these organs can be protected by lead shields or by splitting the dose up over several days, side effects are almost always a problem.

Depending on the area irradiated, these may include reddening of the skin, nausea, diarrhoea and anaemia. Long-term effects include scarring or even further cancers.

Success rates
Despite its problems, radiotherapy, especially in localised tumours, can be highly effective. In cancer of the larynx, 80 per cent of patients who receive radiotherapy are cured. Even in patients with cancer which is so advanced that there is no hope of a cure there may be considerable benefit in radiotherapy. The excruciating pain of secondary bone cancer, for instance, can be abolished with a single treatment.

RAPE

Rape is a criminal offence in which the victim is forced, through violence or threats, to have sexual intercourse against their will.

There has been much research into the nature of

rapists and their crimes. Rape is not usually sexually motivated — it is usually committed by men with a deep distrust or hatred of women. In a surprisingly large number of cases, the victim knows the rapist; physical abuse is often involved but its absence does not mean the victim led the rapist on.

Number of cases
The number of rape cases reported has increased dramatically over the last 10 years or so. This may be due to an increase in the number of incidents, but is more likely to be due to an increase in the proportion of cases reported. Women are often reluctant to report rape to the police, due to feelings of shame, worry that they may not be believed or fears of the trauma of an investigation and trial.

Tests and treatment
It is advisable to report rape to the police as soon as possible, but victims should try to get the support of a close friend or relative. The Rape Crisis Centre (a counselling and research organisation) can provide

emotional support and advice if you need it.

It is necessary to perform a physical examination, and any deposits of saliva, semen, and so on will be taken for analysis. The doctor will also check the victim's fingernails for samples of hair, skin or clothing of the rapist. The clothes worn by the victim will be taken for examination.

Cuts and bruises are treated as soon as possible, and the 'morning after' pill can be prescribed if necessary. However, the incident may leave emotional scars, and psychiatric help is available, together with self-help support groups organised by local hospitals.

RASH

A rash is an eruption of the skin in spots or patches.

Rashes are extremely common. In one community surveyed, 22 per cent of the population were found to be suffering from a rash of one sort or another.

Doctors examining rashes and trying to find a cause divide them into two groups. The first group, mainly affecting children who were previously well, develops over the course of a day or two. The rash may be localised to start with but rapidly spreads to become widespread and symmetrical. Such rashes are often due to childhood diseases, and are accompanied by 'flu-like symptoms (see chart opposite). Since the

» SEE ALSO — Hodgkin's disease

Common Rashes: Symptoms And Treatment

Name	Symptoms	Treatment
Chickenpox	The illness usually starts with a widespread rash. In adults, there may have been vague 'flu-like symptoms for the preceding day or two. The rash starts as flat spots which rapidly turn to blisters. After a day or two, the blisters scab over and new crops appear.	There is no specific treatment for any of these viral infections. Rest, fluids and paracetamol are all that is usually required. It is advisable to consult a doctor, to confirm the diagnosis. You should also consult a doctor if the condition persists for longer than expected, or if a 'productive' cough develops.
Measles	The patient is usually miserable with conjunctivitis and a runny nose for a day or two before the onset of the rash. The rash itself consists of flat, dusky red spots which join together to form irregular blotches. After two or three days the rash fades to leave a brown stain that may persist for many months.	
Rubella (German measles)	The onset is usually mild, with vague feelings of ill-health for 24 hours or so. The rash starts behind the ears and rapidly spreads over the whole body.	
Non-specific viral infections	Many viral infections produce rashes, especially in children. Many resemble rubella and most fade within a day or two.	
Urticaria and similar rashes	Generalised, itchy rashes are usually harmless. The commonest is urticaria, an intensely itchy rash that resembles the weals of nettle rash. The rash usually subsides after a few hours, but may recur over many months. Drugs such as aspirin may be responsible, but often the cause remains unclear.	Antihistamines are a highly effective treatment.
Eczema	Eczema or dermatitis is very common. The rash starts as redness and swelling, followed by blistering, scaling and ultimately thickening of the skin. In acute cases there are septic spots and the whole area may ooze. In most cases, the itchiness is very troublesome. Powerful irritants or prolonged exposure will produce eczema in almost any skin, but some skins are more sensitive than others. Exposure to a powerful irritant such as caustic soda for a short time has the same effect as exposure to a mild irritant such as detergent for a longer period. The site of the rash may give a clue to the cause.	Sensitising substances must be identified and avoided. Creams and ointments soothe the condition. Steroid creams are highly effective in eczema, but long-term use may cause thinning of the skin.
Psoriasis	The characteristic rash consists of numerous raised, red, scaly plaques. The rash most commonly affects the knees and elbows.	Coal tar soap and steroid creams.
Scabies	The rash, which is due to a parasitic mite, consists of burrows under the skin about half a centimetre long, usually ending in a small blister. It commonly appears between the fingers, on the wrists and at the elbows and armpits, and is extremely itchy.	Mild insecticide lotions, available from the chemist, will kill the mite.

MEDICAL FACT FILE

introduction of the MMR vaccination, measles and rubella have become something of a rarity.

Generalised rashes which are itchy, but not accompanied by other symptoms are usually harmless. Urticaria is the most common, and it usually disappears fairly quickly. If it does re-appear, it can be treated (see above).

The second group of rashes consists of either a localised rash or a more widespread rash that has taken several weeks to develop. There are hundreds of causes of localised rashes — eczema, for example, may be caused by any number of sensitising substances, whereas psoriasis is due to an irregularity in the skin cells. The chart above describes the commonest rashes and treatments.

DRUG RASHES

Almost any drug can cause a rash in a sensitive individual.

Drug rashes may appear on the first occasion the drug is taken, or they may only appear after the drug has been used several times.

Drug rashes are usually flat, red and widespread. In some cases they are extremely itchy, and there may also be facial swelling and breathing difficulty if the patient reacts particularly badly to the drug. Drug rashes usually disappear within a day or two of stopping the drug.

▶▶ SEE ALSO — Chicken pox, Eczema, German measles, Measles, Mumps, Nettle rash, Psorias

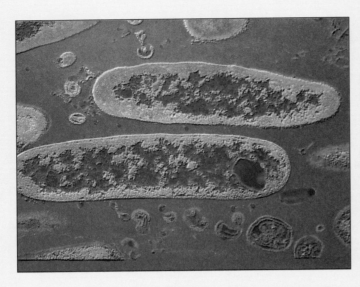

Yersinia pestis is the causative agent of bubonic plague (the Black Death). It is carried by fleas which transfer to suck human blood when their rat host dies.

RATS, DISEASES FROM

Rats (and their fleas) can infect humans in a number of ways.

Rats were responsible for the 'Black Death', the plague which killed 25 million people in Europe during the 14th century, and rats also carry diseases such as typhus, rabies and Lassa fever. Rat bites can cause serious fever, and water contaminated with rat urine can also transmit infection.

Plague
The plague which affected Europe in the Middle Ages was caused by a type of bacterium, yersinia pestis, which is spread from one rodent to another by fleas. The plague killed off the rats, and the fleas then moved to human hosts, killing them off too. A bite from an infected flea causes the lymph glands (or buboes) to swell up (hence the name, bubonic plague). Pneumonic plague can occur as a complication, when the lungs are affected. Once humans are infected they can infect each other if infected droplets (from coughing, for example) are inhaled or swallowed.

Symptoms include fever, shivering and severe headache, with swellings of the lymph glands in the armpits, neck and (most often) the groin. Dark patches may appear around the affected glands if they bleed under the skin. If pneumonic plague develops, there will be heavy coughing with frothy, blood-stained phlegm.

Plague can now be treated with specific antibiotics if it is diagnosed in time. The disease is now confined to areas of Africa, Southeast Asia and South America, but there are still quite a number of cases in the US every year, where the fleas are carried by cats and squirrels.

Immunisation is available if you are travelling in a high-risk area, or work in a job which may bring you into contact with infected rats.

Weil's disease
Weil's disease, or leptospirosis, is a disease which is carried by rats, the bacteria responsible being excreted in the rat's urine. Canals and stagnant water in rat-infested areas may well harbour Weil's disease.

Symptoms include fever, chills, a throbbing headache, chills and muscle aches, as well as eye inflammation and skin rash. More severe problems occur if the kidneys and liver are affected, as there may be liver damage and jaundice.

The disease can be treated with antibiotics, but in a large proportion of cases, recovery is slow, and the nervous system may also be affected, with signs of meningitis (inflammation of the membrane covering the brain and spinal cord).

Rat-bite fever
Another disease, which is transmitted by rat bites, is rat-bite fever. The symptoms of this disease include swelling at the site of the bite, swelling of nearby lymph nodes, fever, rash, and sometimes inflammation of the joints. Rat-bite fever can be treated with antibiotics.

Other diseases
Other diseases spread by rats include typhus, which is spread by rat fleas; rabies, which is transmitted in bites and which can infect any mammal; Lassa fever, a viral disease carried in the urine of rats, which is limited to West Africa; and other rare viral and bacterial diseases.

The number of diseases carried by rats indicates the importance of controlling rat populations.

RAYNAUD'S DISEASE

Raynaud's disease is a disorder in which the blood vessels supplying the fingers and toes close up, cutting off the flow.

This closing up of the blood vessels only occurs when the sufferer is cold. It most often affects young women. The main symptom of the disorder is a paleness of the fingers (more often than the toes). This may be accompanied by tingling and numbness. As the blood flow returns the affected fingers turn blue and then they turn bright red.

The symptoms may occur for no known reason. If there is an underlying cause, the disorder is referred to as Raynaud's phenomenon (see below).

Treatment
The best treatment for the disorder is prevention — keeping the hands and toes warm in cold weather.

Sufferers who smoke should try to give up the habit, as smoking is likely to make the problem worse. It is possible to treat the disorder with drugs to dilate the blood vessels, or even surgery (to cut the nerves controlling the dilation of the blood vessels) in severe cases.

RAYNAUD'S PHENOMENON

The symptoms of Raynaud's disease may occur as a side effect of another disorder, in which case it is referred to as Raynaud's phenomenon.

Common causes of Raynaud's phenomenon include atherosclerosis, thrombosis, rheumatoid arthritis, lupus erythematosus and drug therapies such as certain heart drugs and beta-blocker drugs. It is a condition which is an occupational hazard for people who operate vibrating machinery or even typists and pianists, whose fingers are subject to constant impact.

▶▶ SEE ALSO — Lassa fever, Lupus erythematosus, Rabies, Rheumatoid arthritis, Typhus, Weil's disease

RECTUM

The rectum is a short segment of bowel between the large bowel and the anal canal.

The rectum is about 12cm long. It acts as a reservoir for solid waste until a convenient time and place for defecation can be found. In the rectum, the absorption of fluids begun in the large bowel continues.

One of the main symptoms of a disorder of the rectum is rectal bleeding (mainly on defecation). This may be a symptom of a number of common (but uncomfortable) disorders, but may be a symptom of something more serious.

Common disorders

The junction between the rectum and the anal canal is the site of internal piles (or haemorrhoids). These resemble varicose veins and, like varicose veins, the cause is unclear. There is a hereditary tendency but anxiety, constipation and straining to pass a motion may also play a part.

The main symptom of piles is bleeding on defecation. There may be a feeling of fullness or irritation as well. Pain is not necessarily a feature of piles, but it may be a symptom if the piles become strangulated at a later time.

In early piles, simple regulation of bowel habit, with plenty of fibre, may be enough. They can be treated by injecting them (in the early stages) or banding them (in the second stage). If the condition is well advanced, surgical removal may be necessary.

Cancer of the rectum

Rectal cancer is the commonest cancer of the digestive tract. It is more common among the elderly, but it can affect younger people too. Bleeding on defecation is the main symptom, and many people, mistakenly, diagnose themselves as having piles. It is important that you consult a doctor if you have any signs of rectal bleeding; a simple internal examination can detect a cancer.

Besides bleeding, other symptoms may include a change of bowel habit, with increasing constipation and bouts of diarrhoea. There may be a 'dragging' discomfort and a feeling that the bowel is never quite empty. There may also be bloodstained and offensive mucus. Later on, if the cancer is untreated, there may be anaemia and weight loss, and the bowel may become completely blocked.

Treatment involves major surgery: if the growth is high in the rectum, a single abdominal incision is made, but if it is lower down, it has to be removed through the abdomen and the perineal area (between the legs) at the same time, and a colostomy is necessary. However, the outlook is generally good if diagnosis is made early.

Benign growths

There are several types of benign growths which may develop in the rectum. Villous papilloma, which only occurs in adults, is a growth which resembles seaweed with numerous fronds. It may fill the whole rectum, causing obstruction and a copious bloody discharge. However, the tumour can be removed through a sigmoidoscope (see above).

Familial polyposis of the rectum is a rare, inherited disorder in which the whole rectum becomes filled with tiny polyps. Although these growths are benign, they almost always become malignant in time. If the polyps are present throughout the colon there is no alternative to widespread surgery. If the polyps are confined to the rectum, local

Sigmoidoscopy

Sigmoidoscopy is a quick and simple form of endoscopy. It is a vital investigation in anybody suffering from rectal bleeding.

A sigmoidoscope is a surgical telescope with a light source and a lens. It is passed into the rectum, and then air is pumped up the tube. When the rectum is distended the internal surface can be seen easily. Surgical instruments can be passed along the sigmoidoscope and growths can be removed totally, or partially for biopsy. The whole procedure takes no more than a few minutes and is almost pain free.

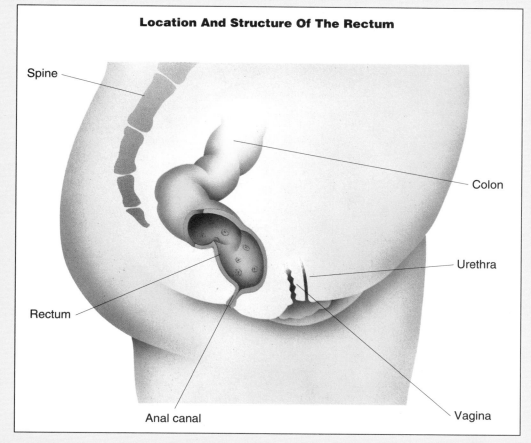

Location And Structure Of The Rectum

Spine

Colon

Urethra

Rectum

Vagina

Anal canal

» SEE ALSO — Colostomy, Crohn's disease, Haemorrhoids, Suppository

MEDICAL FACT FILE

treatment and regular review through a sigmoidoscope may avoid the need for a colostomy.

Proctitis

Inflammation of the rectum is referred to as proctitis, and it is usually accompanied by bleeding, and sometimes a discharge of mucus and pus. It is often associated with an inflammation of the colon, a symptom of ulcerative colitis or Crohn's disease. In male homosexuals, proctitis may be due to a sexually transmitted disease. Treatment of proctitis involves treating the underlying disorder.

Other disorders

A fistula is a crack which leads from the skin around the anus to the rectum. It is usually the result of an abscess and once established requires surgery to close it. There is always a discharge of mucus or pus, and if the track of the fistula lies outside the sphincter muscles, there is also a leak of faecal matter.

Rectal prolapse — collapse of the rectum, so that part of it (or all of it in severe cases) protrudes from the anus — is relatively common. In children, partial prolapse is the usual type, and is only seen when straining to pass a motion. In the elderly, as a result of poor muscle tone, complete prolapse may happen.

Prolapse in children does not have to be treated, since the problem rights itself as they grow, and the rectum 'fits' better. Plenty of liquids and fibre in the diet will help to prevent constipation, and straining to pass a motion must be discouraged. In some, rare cases, rectal prolapse is a sign of cystic fibrosis. Adults with rectal prolapse get worse rather than better, and all require surgery at some stage.

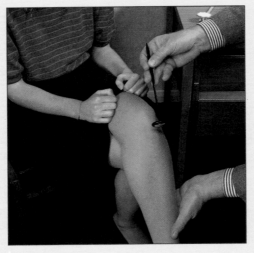

Knee-tapping tests a person's reflexes, to check that the nerves are responding as they should. Other tests include the response of the eye to light and the toe-curling reflex when the sole of the foot is irritated.

REFLEX

A reflex is an involuntary or automatic action in response to a stimulus.

There are several types of reflex, the simplest being the reflex arc.

This consists of a short chain of nerve cells connecting a receptor to a gland or a muscle. An appropriate stimulus will always lead to the same response. The simple reflex arc avoids the brain and is useful in situations where speed is essential.

Knee tapping

Tendon reflexes, such as the knee jerk, are due to a reflex arc consisting of a stretch receptor in the body of the muscle, a series of nerve cells and the muscle fibres

themselves. The instant the muscle is stretched it automatically contracts so as to preserve the status quo. Stretch reflexes allow us to stand up without constantly thinking about our balance.

Reflex arcs may be protective as well as postural. A light touch on the cornea makes us blink both eyes almost immediately. Doctors use this reflex to detect patients who are feigning unconsciousness.

Conditioned response

Another type of reflex, the conditioned reflex, is a psychological term. In this case a response normally associated with stimulus A can be produced in response to stimulus B, through the constant association of A with B.

In Pavlov's famous experiment, it was shown that by always ringing a bell when food was served a dog could be conditioned to respond to the bell rather than to the actual food.

REFLEXOLOGY

Reflexology is a form of alternative therapy involving massage.

Practitioners massage different parts of the feet in order to treat disorders in different parts of the body.

REITER'S SYNDROME

Reiter's syndrome is a condition in which a number of disorders arise after a particular infection.

Urethritis, arthritis and conjunctivitis are symptoms of the syndrome. The condition usually only develops in people with a particular genetic predisposition. It occurs after an attack of dysentery or non-specific urethritis.

Symptoms

The first symptom is usually a urethral discharge, followed by conjunctivitis and then arthritis in one or two joints. The syndrome is the commonest cause of arthritis in young men.

The pain, due to inflammation in the affected joint(s), will come and go for varying periods. There may also be a skin rash.

Treatment

The symptoms can be treated with analgesics and nonsteroidal anti-inflammatory drugs, but there are usually periods of remission and relapse.

Reflexes In Babies

Newborn babies possess primitive reflexes. These are often quite complex behaviour patterns in response to specific stimuli.

The function of many of these reflexes is unknown, but because they disappear by a certain age they can be very useful in assessing a baby's development.

Probably the best-known primitive reflex is the walking reflex. Hold a baby up and press its heel on to a firm surface and it will make walking movements with its legs. This reflex disappears at about six weeks of age in the normal infant. Another primitive reflex, but one which is lost a little later, is the grasp reflex: stroke the palm of a small baby's hand and it will grip your finger firmly enough to be lifted up in the air.

➤➤ SEE ALSO — Arthritis, Conjunctivitis, Nervous system, Urethritis

RENAL COLIC

Renal colic is the term used to describe a particular type of pain around the kidneys.

The pain is usually due to kidney stones. Patients suffer spasms of severe pain on one side of the back as the kidney stones start to pass down the ureter.

There is often a continuous, dull pain behind the spasms, and there may be other symptoms such as nausea, vomiting, sweating and blood in the urine.

Treatment

The disorder is treated with painkillers (by injection), bed rest and plenty of fluid.

REPETITIVE STRAIN INJURY

Repetitive strain injury describes any disorder which is caused by repetitive movements of a particular part of the body.

With the increasingly widespread use of computer keyboards, there is increasing concern about the disorder, but this is not the only cause. Golfer's elbow, tennis elbow, housemaid's knee and clergyman's knee are all examples of the disorder. Inflammation develops on bony prominences in the affected joints, due to the pull of the muscles attached to them.

Symptoms include pain and stiffness in the affected joints, which should disappear with rest. Often, a slight change in technique (such as altering the position of a chair or keyboard) will prevent the condition from recurring. Regular rest periods and relaxation of muscles should prevent the condition from arising.

RESPIRATORY ARREST

Respiratory arrest is the term which describes the sudden stopping of breathing.

Respiratory arrest may have a number of causes including electric shock, a drug overdose, a heart attack, head injury, stroke or respiratory failure.

It is an emergency condition, which requires immediate artificial respiration. If the condition is not reversed there will be cardiac arrest (the heart will stop working), brain damage, coma and death within a few minutes.

RESPIRATORY DISTRESS SYNDROME

Respiratory distress syndrome is due to a lung disorder that causes difficulty in breathing.

The condition may affect premature babies, or it may occur in adult life. In premature babies, the condition occurs because the lungs have not developed enough to breathe independently after birth. In adults, the condition may be present after injury or damage to the lungs — for example, as a result of pneumonia, inhalation of an irritant gas, partial drowning or a drug overdose.

Symptoms

If the condition is present, the patient starts to breathe faster, and then breathing becomes laboured. Babies make grunting noises, and the patient turns blue as the blood oxygen level falls.

Treatment

The condition is life-threatening and requires intensive care. Oxygen can be given by mask, and a tube may be inserted through the nose or mouth to help breathing. A ventilator is then used to maintain breathing. In premature babies, an artificial detergent may be blown into the lungs to replace a substance which is missing at birth.

Ninety per cent of premature babies who suffer from the condition now survive, but in adults the survival rate is less than half. Some survivors are left with permanent lung damage.

RESPIRATORY FAILURE

Respiratory failure is a condition in which the lungs stop working properly, so there is a fall in the level of oxygen in the blood.

The condition is caused by any disorder which affects the normal exchange of gases in the lungs, such as severe asthma, bronchitis or emphysema.

The patient becomes breathless, turns blue, and the breathing rate may speed up or slow down. The condition is life-threatening, and oxygen has to be given. Intensive care on a ventilator may be needed.

Treatment involves treating the underlying cause of the failure.

RESPIRATORY TRACT INFECTION

This term covers a number of illnesses which are caused by viruses or bacteria.

The infection may affect any part of the breathing passages, from the nose to the smallest airways in the lungs. Upper respiratory tract infections, which include the common cold, pharyngitis,

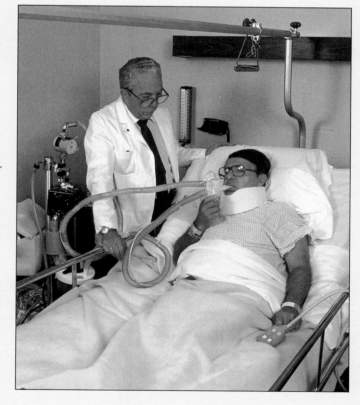

In cases of respiratory arrest or respiratory failure, a ventilator is used to pump oxygen into the patient's lungs.

» SEE ALSO — Asthma, Bronchitis, Drowning, Emphysema, Occupational health, Prematurity

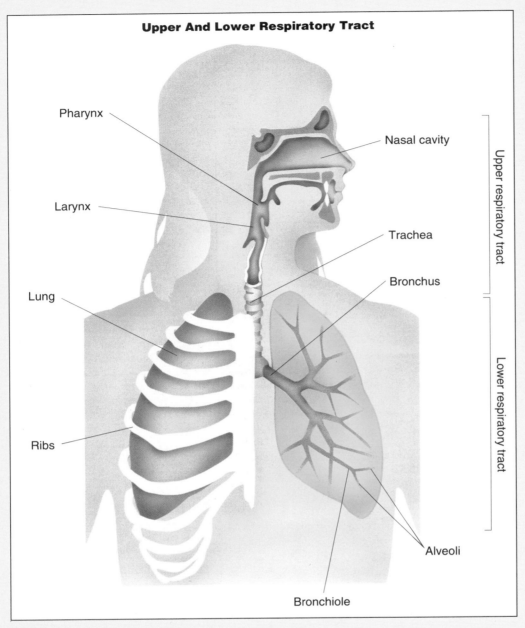

Upper And Lower Respiratory Tract

Pharynx

Larynx

Lung

Ribs

Nasal cavity

Trachea

Bronchus

Alveoli

Bronchiole

Upper respiratory tract

Lower respiratory tract

---

used to convert a photosensitive pigment in the retina, known as visual purple, into two separate molecules. This reaction releases a minute amount of electrical activity which is transmitted to the optic nerve, and then to the brain.

Rods are extremely sensitive to light and are the receptors for night vision. Cones need more light to operate but are capable of much finer discrimination of detail. The electrical activity produced by the cones varies with the colour of the light, thus creating colour vision.

Medical significance

The retina is particularly important to a doctor. Not only is it subject to a whole range of disease, but it also gives the doctor an opportunity to see living arteries, veins and nerves without any incision.

For example, patients with high blood pressure show a series of changes in the retina. Indeed, so characteristic are these changes that the first person to detect high blood pressure is often the optician.

Another disorder which affects the retina is diabetes. Diabetic retina disease is common and used to be commoner still. Diabetes is still the most frequent cause of blindness in the under 60s. Diabetes mainly affects the retinal blood vessels, making them swell and leak. Blood oozing from the vessels causes minute haemorrhages whilst fat-rich serum causes yellow staining. These changes do not, in themselves, constitute a threat to vision, but if they are not treated, vision may deteriorate.

Laser treatment of the long-term retinal changes now saves many diabetics from blindness.

---

laryngitis, tonsillitis and sinusitis, are very common, particularly in childhood. Lower respiratory tract infections include acute bronchitis, acute bronchiolitis and pneumonia, and may be more serious.

RESTLESS LEGS

Restless legs is a condition in which the leg muscles ache, tingle, or burn.

The condition comes on at night, or after a long period of sitting still. The

unpleasant sensations can only be relieved by getting up and walking around.

The condition most often affects middle-aged women, and is more common in people who drink a lot of coffee or smoke. The exact cause is unknown, but some drug treatments are helpful.

RETINA

The retina is the layer which coats the inside of the back of the eye.

The retina is light-sensitive, receiving images

via the lens which are picked up by special cells. The images are translated into electrical activity which the brain can interpret.

Rods and cones

The cells that pick up the light images (light receptors) are of two sorts: rods and cones. The central, most sensitive part of the retina consists of nothing but cones, each with its own tiny nerve. The outer portion of the retina is made up of rods, and several rods may serve a single nerve. When light strikes a rod or cone it is absorbed and its energy is

⮞ SEE ALSO — Blood pressure, Bronchitis, Colds, Diabetes, Eye disorders, Laryngitis, Pharynx, Pneumonia, Sinusitis, Tonsillitis

RETINA, DETACHED

A detached retina occurs when the retina separates from the other layers at the back of the eye.

The disorder may occur as a result of injury, but more often it is something which happens spontaneously, without any obvious cause. The disorder is more common in people who are very shortsighted, in the elderly and in those who have had cataract surgery.

Symptoms

The main symptoms are to do with the disturbance of vision. There may be flashing lights at the edge of the field of vision and 'floaters', shadowy blobs, moving around the field of vision. For some, the first symptom is a blackness and loss of vision, the amount and position of the blackness depending on the site of the detachment. It is often described as being rather like a dark curtain being lowered.

Treatment

Treatment usually involves surgery: if the point of detachment is at the top of the retina, the sufferer must lie down to prevent it from worsening. As long as the

Torn Retina

A tear in the retina may precede retinal detachment.

A torn retina may be the result of injury, but is more often due to degeneration of the retina. Symptoms include flashing lights and floaters. The hole in the retina can be repaired with laser or very low-temperature treatments.

central part of the retina, where the central vision occurs, is not damaged, the outlook is good.

RETINAL TUMOURS

Tumours of the retina may occur at any age, and there are various different forms.

Retinoblastoma is a tumour of early infancy. At this age, the child is unaware of visual changes and the first sign is often a white mass visible through the pupil. Retinoblastomas can be treated with radiotherapy, but surgery to remove the eye is sometimes needed.

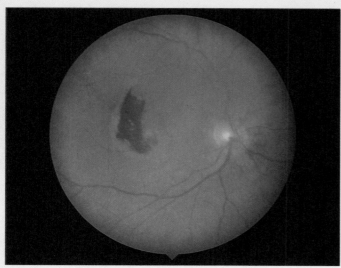

The part of the retina which has become detached from the choroid shows here as a brown discoloration.

Malignant melanomas, more common on the skin, may also affect the eye. They usually occur in the middle-aged, and rapidly spread to other parts of the body, especially the liver. Treatment consists of surgery and radiotherapy, but the mortality rate is disappointingly high.

RETINITIS PIGMENTOSA

Retinitis pigmentosa is the commonest of a number of diseases, all of which cause gradual degeneration of the retina and a steady loss of vision.

The retina is slowly obliterated by an overgrowth of black pigment. This overgrowth starts at the edge of the retina and tends to affect night vision first.

The condition starts in late childhood and progresses remorselessly. There is no treatment but occasionally the degeneration shows an irregular course, giving rise to spurious hopes of a cure.

RETROLENTAL FIBROPLASIA

This is a condition which affects newborn babies who are given too much oxygen therapy.

Retrolental fibroplasia used to be a major cause of blindness in premature babies. The more immature the baby, the greater the risk.

A very high concentration of oxygen in the blood, usually as a result of overenthusiastic oxygen therapy in children who have breathing difficulties at birth, causes intense constriction of the retinal veins. This can very rapidly lead to swelling and detachment of the retina.

Now that the relationship between retrolental fibroplasia and oxygen therapy has been established, the disease has largely been prevented.

RETT'S SYNDROME

Rett's syndrome is thought to be caused by a genetic disorder.

Rett's syndrome was first described (by an Austrian, Andreas Rett) in the 1960s, but was only recognised by the medical establishment in the 1980s. The condition only affects girls.

Symptoms

Symptoms start to appear when the child is about one year old. The affected girls gradually lose the skills of walking and talking which they have learned, and show signs of autism. There are often repetitive movements and sudden outbursts of laughing or crying for no apparent reason.

There is no known cure, and parents should receive genetic counselling.

REYE'S SYNDROME

Reye's syndrome is a set of serious (and sometimes fatal) symptoms which may occur when a child is recovering from certain childhood illnesses.

The worst effects include liver and brain damage. The syndrome rarely occurs in children over the age of 15.

Causes and symptoms

The disorder develops as a child is recovering from an infection, such as chickenpox, 'flu or respiratory tract infection. It is often (though not invariably) associated with taking aspirin (to ease the symptoms of the original

➤➤ SEE ALSO — Chickenpox, Eye disorders

disease). For this reason, doctors now always recommend paracetamol, rather than aspirin.

Affected children become lethargic and disoriented, and there is uncontrollable vomiting. If there is swelling of the brain, the child may have seizures, fall into a coma and heart and breathing rates may be erratic. There will be jaundice if the liver is damaged.

Treatment

Drugs are given to control swelling of the brain, and kidney dialysis or blood transfusions may be necessary if the blood chemistry is upset.

The death rate from Reye's syndrome has fallen since the syndrome has been understood, so that only about 10 per cent of those affected now die. However, serious attacks will cause brain damage.

RHESUS INCOMPATIBILITY

Rhesus incompatibility is one of a group of diseases in which the newborn baby's red blood cells are attacked by its own mother's antibodies.

Red blood cells from the baby's circulation leak into the mother's bloodstream, usually at the time of birth. The mother's immune system recognises these cells as foreign and produces defensive antibodies against them. The first child is not affected by the disorder.

Problems arise in subsequent pregnancies when these antibodies cross the placenta and destroy the baby's red cells. The disorder most often occurs where the mother is rhesus negative and the baby is rhesus positive.

The antibodies which the mother has developed will

Rhesus Factor

The system of dividing blood groups into rhesus positive and negative depends on the presence of certain substances in the blood.

The system is named after rhesus monkeys, in whose blood the different factors were first identified.
● Rhesus positive blood contains a factor known as D antigen, rhesus negative blood does not.
● The genes dictate whether a person's blood is rhesus positive or negative.
● If a mother is rhesus negative (about one in six people are), her baby can only be rhesus positive if the child's father is rhesus positive.

attack the red blood cells of the foetus. In mild cases, the only symptoms in the newborn baby are mild jaundice and anaemia. In severe cases, there is serious anaemia in the foetus before it is born, which may lead to swelling and stillbirth.

Treatment

In order to prevent rhesus incompatibility developing, rhesus negative women who

have been sensitised to rhesus positive blood (through their first child, or through being given a transfusion of rhesus positive blood by mistake), can be given Anti-D immunisation. If the injection is given within a couple of days of delivery of her first child (or after an abortion, miscarriage or amniocentesis), the injection will 'mop up' the baby's cells before the mother can

Rhesus Incompatibility

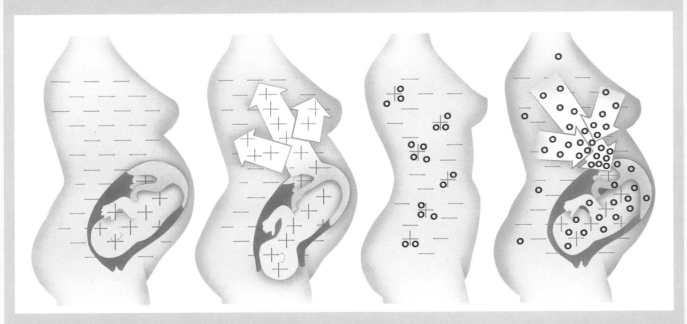

1. A mother with rhesus negative blood carries her first child who, in this case, has rhesus positive blood, inherited from its father.

2. At the actual birth, some of the baby's blood may 'leak' into the mother's bloodstream.

3. The mother's immune system treats the baby's blood as an invader and develops antibodies to defend her against it.

4. In later pregnancies, if the baby is rhesus positive, the antibodies which were developed previously attack the new foetus's red cells.

▶▶ SEE ALSO — Blood, Jaundice

produce any antibodies against them.

If the disease (with symptoms of anaemia and jaundice) does develop in subsequent babies, it can be treated by exchanging the baby's blood with fresh blood from a donor.

RHEUMATIC FEVER

Rheumatic fever is a disorder which may follow certain bacterial infections. It often damages body tissues, including the heart valves.

Rheumatic fever is caused by certain kinds of streptococcus bacterium. It is thought to be a form of auto-immune disorder. It is most common in children and adults up to the age of 30. It has been less widespread since the introduction of penicillin.

Symptoms
The disease usually starts with a sore throat, which may clear up very quickly. A week to six weeks later there is fever, and other symptoms which depend on the parts of the body affected.

If the heart is affected, there are few other symptoms. If the joints are affected, they will become inflamed, tender, hot and very painful.

There may well be a blotchy rash which comes and goes on different parts of the body, particularly the affected joints. Lumps may develop on knees, elbows, wrists and knuckles.

Diagnosis and treatment
The doctor will listen to the patient's heart with a stethoscope and may take blood specimens for analysis. She may also suggest chest x-rays and an ECG to check for heart problems. Fluid may also be taken from joints for analysis.

Bed rest, with aspirin to relieve pain and reduce inflammation, are normally prescribed. If the inflammation does not subside, steroid anti-inflammatory drugs may also be prescribed.

A long-term course of antibiotics is usually prescribed to prevent recurrence. This helps to prevent heart damage.

In the past, most patients did have a recurrence, and more people suffered heart damage as a result. Now, an increased risk of joint disease is a more common long-term result of rheumatic fever, rather than heart disorders in later life.

RHEUMATISM

Rheumatism is the common term for any disorder of the muscles and joints which causes aches and pains.

The term is often used to describe quite minor aches and pains, as well as more serious disorders, properly known as rheumatoid arthritis or osteoarthritis.

RHEUMATOID ARTHRITIS

Rheumatoid arthritis is due to inflammation of the surface of joints.

In the early stages of the disease, the inflammation causes pain and swelling, but in the later stages the articular surfaces may be completely destroyed. As well as affecting the joints, rheumatoid arthritis may also involve the tendons, the heart, the lungs and many other organs.

Rheumatoid arthritis is commoner in women, and generally starts in early middle age. There is often a family history of the disorder.

Juvenile Rheumatoid Arthritis
This form of rheumatoid arthritis is a childhood disease.

The disease starts suddenly, with skin rash and fever. Despite its name, joint pain is not always a feature. The eyes, heart and lymphatic system may also be affected.

At least 50 per cent of children who contract the disease make a complete recovery, but in the others the disease may drag on into adulthood. Just as in the adult condition, the mainstays of treatment are aspirin and physiotherapy.

Symptoms
The small joints of the hands and feet are most frequently affected, usually in a symmetrical fashion. The onset may be sudden, with an acute, 'flu-like illness or gradual with progressive pain and early morning stiffness. The joints are tender to the touch and movement is painful. In long-standing cases the muscles of the hand are so under used that they waste away. Instability of the joints produces multiple dislocations with deformities of the fingers and wrists. The lungs are affected in about

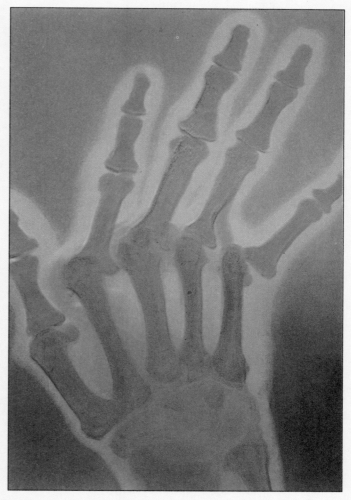

An x-ray of a hand with deformed finger joints which have been caused by rheumatoid arthritis.

» SEE ALSO — Arthritis, Osteoarthritis

MEDICAL FACT FILE

50 per cent of cases, but only a few patients show symptoms of breathlessness. Raynaud's phenomenon, a condition in which the small arteries of the hands and feet go into spasm in the cold, is very common.

The clinical picture of advanced rheumatoid arthritis is unmistakable, but in its early stages it may be confused with other conditions. Blood tests may be necessary to confirm the diagnosis.

Treatment

The object of treatment is to reduce pain and to allow the patient to live as near normal a life as possible. To achieve this requires a team approach involving health-care workers, social services and the family.

Anti-inflammatory drugs such as aspirin and indomethacin are the first line of attack and may be very effective. However, their usefulness is limited by the high incidence of side effects with long-term use.

Resting the joints, even to the extent of wearing splints at night, can be helpful. Physiotherapy to maintain movement and strength is an important part of treatment.

If these simple measures fail, specific treatment may halt the progress of the disease. Gold injections are often very beneficial, but in view of their serious side effects they are usually reserved for non-responsive cases. Steroids are sometimes used when all else fails, but the high doses required often cause serious complications. The total dose of steroids administered can be reduced by injecting them directly into the joint. This gives immediate relief, but if repeated too often it can cause further destruction of the joint.

In the long term, 60 per cent of patients suffer little or no disability; 30 per cent suffer some restriction of activities and 10 per cent suffer so badly that they are almost completely disabled.

RHINITIS

Rhinitis is an inflammation of and discharge from the mucous membranes in the nose.

Rhinitis is a symptom of the common cold. More than 200 viruses are responsible for this disorder, and we gradually build up resistance to them. Some children seem to have constantly runny noses, as they succumb to viruses they have not met before. But viruses are constantly developing, so there will always be viruses around to which we have not built up an immunity.

The symptoms may also be caused by a blockage of the nasal passages or sinuses.

The other common cause of the symptoms is hay fever, or allergic rhinitis. Common allergens are pollen, house dust (and the mites) and pet dander (dried saliva left after grooming).

Less common causes of rhinitis are a thickening of the mucous membrane due to repeated nasal infections, and the wasting of the mucous membrane due to ageing, as a result of nasal surgery or due to long-term bacterial infections.

Treatment

Colds can only be eased with rest in a warm, humid room, aspirin or paracetamol to ease pain, and plenty of fluids to drink in the form of fruit juice and comforting hot drinks (but not alcohol).

Allergic rhinitis may be treated with antihistamines, and decongestants may help if the problem is severe. The sufferer should take measures to avoid allergens where possible. Thickening of the mucous membrane

can be treated with surgery, while thinning of the membrane can be treated with antibiotics, or sometimes with oestrogen drugs. (It has been found that oestrogen from the combined Pill or during pregnancy may increase the secretions from all the mucous membranes.)

RHINOPHYMA

Rhinophyma is a deformity of the nose, in which it becomes bulbous and red.

The condition normally only affects elderly men. It is a complication of rosacea. If rosacea persists, it may cause the blood vessels in the nose to enlarge and the sebaceous glands to become overactive.

The condition can be remedied by an operation to pare away the excess tissue.

RHINOPLASTY

Rhinoplasty is plastic surgery to alter the shape of the nose.

The operation may be performed after injury has disfigured the nose, or for psychological reasons to re-shape a particularly large or unsightly nose.

The operation

The surgeon makes incisions inside the nose so that he can get at the septum (the cartilage which divides the nostrils and gives the nose its shape). The position of the septum can be altered, some of it can be pared away, or extra cartilage can be grafted on, depending on the original problem.

After the operation there may be extensive bruising, which can persist for weeks or months. Complications are rare, but there may be repeated nosebleeds at the site of the incisions.

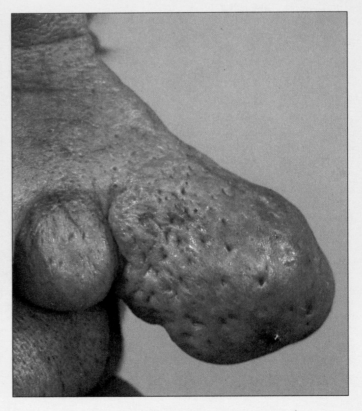

A bulbous nose and pitted skin are characteristic of rhinophyma, a condition which affects some elderly men.

⟩⟩ SEE ALSO — Colds, Hay fever, Raynaud's phenomenon, Rosacea

RIB

The ribs are curved bones, arranged in pairs, which form a cage around the chest.

Men and women possess twelve pairs of ribs. All are hinged to the backbone but only the top seven join the breastbone. The lower five ribs are joined to each other by a strip of thick cartilage.

The ribcage serves several functions, including protecting the lungs and heart and helping in movement, but its main function is in respiration.

Breathing technique

During respiration, the ribs, which normally point downwards, move upwards and outwards, altering the volume of the chest and sucking air in.

Disorders

In some, rare cases, people are born with an extra pair of ribs (an extension of the lowest neck vertebra) at the top of the ribcage. This may cause problems if the ribs press on nerves.

Fractures of one or more ribs are common, usually as the result of a direct blow. The main feature of a fractured rib is pain, especially with pressure, movement or breathing.

Complications

Occasionally, a broken rib will puncture a lung, which causes the pleural cavity to fill with blood. The pleural cavity then has to be drained.

Fracture of a single rib requires no treatment and even if several are fractured, strapping is of little benefit. The primary concern should be to give strong painkillers. Without pain relief, the victim will not take deep breaths and the result can be pneumonia.

RICKETS

Rickets is a disease of childhood in which the bones are deprived of calcium and other salts.

If the bones are not properly nourished, they become soft and easily deformed. The classic example of rickets is the stunted, bow-legged child whose own weight has caused his legs to bend. A similar condition, osteomalacia, occurs in adults.

The commonest cause of rickets is vitamin D deficiency, but this is now much rarer than it used to be. In some circumstances, vitamin D is synthesised from sunlight, particularly through dark skins in hot countries. Vitamin D deficiency may still be a problem in Asian immigrants, particularly females. Not only is their diet low in vitamin D, but their way of life prevents them from getting sunlight which helps to synthesise it.

Rickets may also occur after stomach surgery or in cases where there is a particular problem with absorption. There is also a form of rickets known as vitamin D-resistant rickets, which is inherited.

Diagnosis and treatment

Although rickets may be suggested by the clinical picture and by measuring certain blood salts, the only certain diagnosis is with a bone biopsy.

Treatment consists of regular doses of vitamin D, either on its own or in a modified form. Because an excess of calcium in the blood can lead to problems, any child on high-dose vitamin D therapy needs regular blood tests.

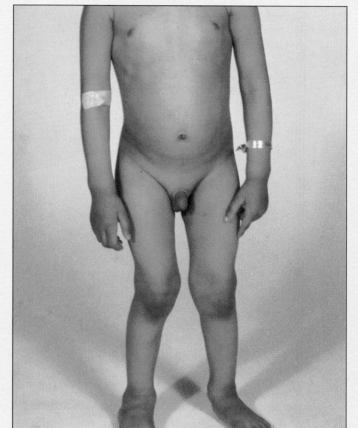

Deformities of the legs and spine are the most obvious symptoms of rickets.

RICKETTSIA

A rickettsia is a parasitic organism which is responsible for a number of relatively rare diseases.

Rickettsiae multiply when they invade other living cells, rather like viruses. They live mainly on insects such as lice, fleas and mites, which in turn live on larger animals and mammals, including humans.

The insects can pass the rickettsiae on to humans when they suck blood or when they pass faeces at a point where the person's skin is broken.

Diseases which are caused by rickettsiae include typhus, Q fever (a 'flu-like illness which may lead to hepatitis and endocarditis) and Rocky Mountain spotted fever (a rare disease which occurs in America).

RIGOR MORTIS

Rigor mortis is the stiffening of muscles which occurs after death.

The muscles start to stiffen some three or four hours after death, and the body is completely stiff after about 12 hours (at normal temperatures).

The process is due to the gradual degeneration of the chemical which is normally responsible for the relaxation and contraction of muscles.

After two to three days, the stiffness in the muscles disappears again as the chemical involved degenerates further.

Rigor mortis is used as a rough guide in determining the time of death. It is interesting to note that if the dead person was active just before death, rigor mortis will set in faster.

» SEE ALSO — Osteomalacia, Typhus

MEDICAL FACT FILE

RINGWORM

Ringworm is a fungal infection of the skin.

The fungus which causes ringworm is called tinea. It usually affects the scalp or trunk of children, but may affect the limbs. A similar fungus is responsible for athlete's foot.

The fungus is contagious, and can be picked up from dogs or cats as well as people. It is found more commonly in children than adults.

Symptoms

Ringworm starts as a small, round red patch, which is scaly and itchy.

It gradually grows bigger, and the skin in the centre begins to heal, so that rings up to about 25mm in diameter develop. If the scalp is affected, bald patches will appear.

Treatment

As soon as symptoms appear, medical advice should be sought. An antifungal ointment or cream will be prescribed. If the scalp is affected, the medication will be in the form of a lotion or shampoo.

After a full course of treatment, ringworm is unlikely to recur. If you suspect a pet is infected, consult a vet.

ROOT-CANAL TREATMENT

Root-canal treatment, or deep-root treatment, involves clearing out the pulp in the tooth and then re-filling the canals.

Root-canal treatment is performed on teeth when the pulp — the live tissue in the centre of a tooth — has decayed to such an extent that the only other alternative is extraction. The pulp decays as a result of bacteria penetrating the outer enamel of the teeth so that the dentine beneath decays and the bacteria can invade the pulp.

Diagnosis and treatment

If tooth decay has set in, the dentist will x-ray the affected tooth to ascertain the extent of the damage.

If the roots are affected, the dentist will drill out all the diseased pulp, fill the cavity with antibiotic paste and put in a temporary filling.

A week or so later, the patient goes back to the dentist, who removes the filling and checks that there is no further infection. Then the final filling can be done, extending right down into the roots with a cement seal on top.

Possible problems

It is essential that the cavity is completely sterile before the final filling is done, and that nothing can penetrate the new filling, or further infection may set in. Such infection may have to be treated by making an incision in the gum and bone to drain out the pus.

In some cases, the treated tooth turns grey and discoloured, in which case it may be necessary to use a technique known as bonding to restore the whiteness. Bonding involves using an acrylic or porcelain 'veneer' to cover discoloured teeth.

ROSACEA

Rosacea is a form of acne in which the cheeks and nose become flushed and red.

To start with, the patient suffers flushes after a particular trigger — eating spicy food, or drinking alcohol, for example. Eventually, the patient becomes permanently flushed and pus-filled spots appear. The condition mainly affects middle-aged people and may persist for many years.

Treatment and outlook

It can be treated with courses of antibiotics. In severe cases, rhinophyma develops.

Root-Canal Treatment

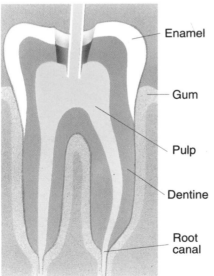 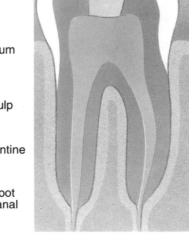 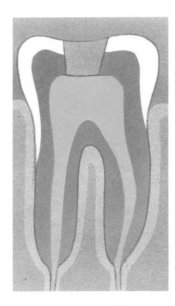

Enamel

Gum

Pulp

Dentine

Root canal

1. All the infected pulp is drained from the centre of the tooth, and the root canals may be drilled out further.

2. The resultant cavity is filled with an antibiotic paste to clear the infection and is sealed with a temporary filling.

3. When the infection has gone, the tooth is re-filled with a permanent filling and cement seal.

SEE ALSO — Acne, Athlete's foot, Caries, Dental problems, Rhinophyma

ROSEOLA INFANTUM

Roseola is a relatively common, infectious disease, which mainly affects children under the age of two.

Symptoms include fever, which may rise to 40.5°C (105°F) over the course of four days. The temperature then drops suddenly, and a rash appears on the body, sometimes spreading to the face and limbs. The rash only lasts a day or so.

The main complication is that, as with any fever, the child may have febrile convulsions. Treatment involves keeping the child cool (by sponging with tepid water if necessary) and giving paracetamol in syrup.

ROUNDWORM

Roundworms are long, cylindrical parasites which live in animals and can be passed on to humans.

There are many different types of roundworm, including threadworms, hookworms, porkworms and the common roundworm.

Prevalence and infestation

Most types of roundworm enter the body when the eggs are swallowed accidentally after they have contaminated food or fingers. (In many cases, the eggs come from human or animal faeces, so hygiene is important in preventing the spread of infestation.)

In the UK, threadworm is the only common type of roundworm. One type, porkworm, used to be prevalent in Central and Eastern Europe: it is picked up by swallowing the larvae in undercooked pork.

In some countries it is possible to pick up larvae from the soil if you walk barefoot. Hookworm is a particularly unpleasant form which can be picked up in tropical countries.

The worms do not cause any symptoms, apart from an itchy bottom, unless they are present in large numbers. However, if you do notice any thread-like pieces in your faeces you should consult a doctor. The worms are easily eradicated with special tablets.

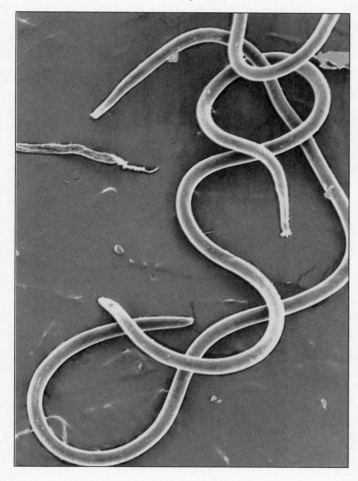

Roundworms (enlarged and coloured) can be seen in faeces, and cause itching of the anus, particularly at night.

RUBELLA

Rubella is a childhood disease which is caused by a virus.

It is more commonly known as German measles.

RUNNING INJURIES

There are several disorders which may result from jogging or running.

Compared with contact sports such as football or rugby, the chance of injury during jogging or running is slight. But injuries can happen. The knee, followed by the ankle, hip and groin, are the commonest sites of more serious injury.

Types of injury

Injuries usually involve the soft tissues (muscle strain), but damage to the ligaments (ligament strain, for example) or even to the bones themselves can occur if the runner falls. Treatment of soft-tissue injuries consists of aspirin, rest and applying ice packs for 24 hours followed by gentle exercise.

Long-distance running frequently upsets the gastrointestinal tract. Diarrhoea and even rectal bleeding are common consequences of marathon running.

The condition is probably due to oxygen starvation of the gut as a result of too much blood going to the muscles. It is rarely necessary to consult a doctor unless unpleasant symptoms persist.

The commonest problems, however, are blisters and stiffness. It is advisable to stop running if blisters begin to form. Never run while you are still feeling stiff from the previous run.

Prevention

The key to avoiding running injuries is graded preparation. The would-be marathon runner should train on level ground, preferably parkland with smooth grass, using well-fitting equipment.

RUPTURE

A rupture is the common name for a hernia.

The term is used to refer to an abdominal hernia, where part of the abdominal contents protrudes through the wall of the abdomen.

SACRALISATION

Sacralisation is the fusion of the lowest vertebra with the sacrum, which forms the centre back of the pelvis.

In some people, the joint is fused from birth. This causes no ill effects. In people who have had a serious disc prolapse or displacement of vertebrae, the joint may be fused surgically in order to prevent further symptoms.

MEDICAL FACT FILE

➤➤ SEE ALSO — Disc prolapse, German measles, Jogger's nipple, Hernia

SACROILIITIS

Sacroiliitis is the inflammation of one or both of the sacroiliac joints in the pelvis.

The sacroiliac joints are fixed joints at the back of the pelvis between the sacrum (the triangular section at the centre back of the pelvis) and the ilium (the side sections of the pelvis). The joints may become inflamed as a result of ankylosing spondylitis, rheumatoid arthritis and various other forms of arthritis. It may (rarely) be due to infection which has spread from other parts of the body.

The main symptom is pain in the lower back, sometimes accompanied by fever. The disorder is diagnosed with x-rays, and fluid may be taken from the joint if infection is suspected. It is treated with nonsteroidal anti-inflammatory drugs, or antibiotics if infection is present.

SAD

Seasonal affective disorder (SAD) is a form of depression which is influenced by the season.

Sufferers become depressed during the autumn months, and worse in the winter, recovering in the spring. The disorder seems to be related to the amount of daylight the sufferer is exposed to. Susceptible people benefit from exposure to artificial daylight for a couple of hours every morning.

SALIVARY GLANDS

The salivary glands are in the mouth, and they produce saliva.

There are three pairs of salivary glands, and numerous smaller ones in the mouth cavity. Together they produce about three pints of saliva a day.

The largest pair of salivary glands are the parotids. These are situated at the angle of the jaw and pass unnoticed until an attack of the mumps. The submandibular glands are situated on the floor of the mouth and open at the side of the frenelum, the fibrous band at the base of the tongue. The sublingual glands are also situated beneath the tongue but their secretions are mainly mucus.

Disorders

The commonest salivary gland problem is infection and the commonest type of infection is mumps. Bacterial infections of the parotid gland also affect patients who suffer from dehydration or who have poor dental hygiene. In this case the bacteria travel up the salivary duct to cause an infection. Acute parotid infection causes pain, redness and swelling at the angle of the jaw. Unless antibiotic treatment is given an abscess may form. An abscess usually needs to be drained through an incision in the inner cheek.

Children often suffer from mild infections of the parotid gland though usually these settle without treatment.

Tumours of the parotid gland are quite common in relation to other forms of tumour. Benign tumours are slow growing but need surgical removal, a difficult task because of the nerves and blood vessels that pass through the gland. Malignant tumours are fast growing and spread rapidly. Removal is very difficult and recurrence is common.

The submandibular duct is the usual site for salivary stones. These can often be felt through the floor of the mouth and removal under local anaesthetic is usually straight forward, although small ones can find their way out of the salivary duct of their own accord.

A rare condition, but one that is very distressing is Sjorgen's disease. This is an auto-immune process in which the salivary glands (and tear glands) dry up, causing a dry mouth (and dry eyes). Keeping the mouth moist with artificial saliva helps, but there is no effective cure.

Saliva

Saliva has many functions:

- It aids swallowing.
- It acts as a lubricant during chewing.
- It facilitates speech by lubricating the tongue and lips.
- It is a solvent which carries the molecules that convey the taste of food to the taste buds.
- It assists in the digestion of starch.
- It has an antibacterial effect.
- It helps to prevent mouth infections and tooth decay.

Location Of The Salivary Glands

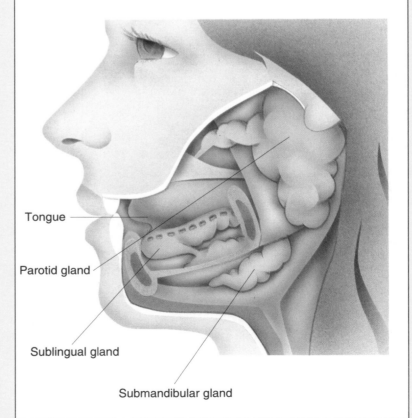

Tongue

Parotid gland

Sublingual gland

Submandibular gland

» SEE ALSO — Arthritis, Pelvis, Rheumatoid arthritis

SALMONELLA

The name salmonella covers a group of bacteria which can cause a range of diseases.

The most common forms of infection are grouped together under the label 'food poisoning', but salmonella bacteria are also responsible for typhoid fever.

The chicken and the egg

During the 1980s, a large increase in cases of salmonella food poisoning was reported. In many of these cases, chicken meat and eggs were found to be responsible, and battery-raised fowl were found to be particularly likely to have the infection. If these products are properly cooked and correctly handled after cooking, even infected chicken meat and eggs should cause no problems, but if they are not fully cooked, the salmonella bacteria multiply quickly.

Symptoms

The main symptoms of salmonella food poisoning are nausea and diarrhoea, usually accompanied by feverishness and often a headache. The symptoms come on suddenly, usually 15 to 24 hours after eating the infected food. In most cases symptoms pass in a day or two, but occasionally (particularly when the sufferers are small children, elderly or infirm) special treatment is necessary.

Diagnosis and treatment

If salmonella food poisoning is suspected, samples of faeces will have to be sent for laboratory analysis to isolate the strain responsible. If the patient has lost a lot of liquid through persistent diarrhoea, it may be necessary to admit the patient to hospital in order to rehydrate with an intravenous drip. If the poisoning gets into the blood stream (septicaemia), antibiotics have to be prescribed.

SALPINGITIS

Salpingitis is the infection of the fallopian tubes.

The infection is almost always part of a more generalised pelvic infection such as gonorrhoea. The fallopian tubes are delicate structures, easily damaged, and a common consequence of salpingitis is blockage of the tubes, which is a cause of infertility.

Causes and course

Infections may ascend from the vagina and uterus, usually as a result of sexual intercourse with an infected person. Gonorrhoea used to be the commonest cause of ascending salpingitis but this has largely been replaced by chlamydia. Occasionally, infection is due to direct damage during childbirth, or from a ruptured appendix.

A rare cause of infection in the western world, but a common cause of infertility worldwide, is TB. This infection spreads through the bloodstream, usually at the time of puberty. Tuberculous salpingitis is usually symptomless but the chronic infection causes severe scarring and distortion of the fallopian tubes.

The acutely infected fallopian tube is swollen, reddened and filled with pus. In the first instance this pus escapes into the gut cavity, causing a low grade peritonitis. Left untreated, the tube becomes blocked and the pus causes it to swell like a balloon.

Symptoms

The patient with acute salpingitis feels unwell, has a temperature and is tender in the lower abdomen. Vaginal examination is painful, especially when the doctor presses high up and to the sides of the vagina or 'wiggles' the cervix. Acute salpingitis always affects both sides (assuming the patient has both fallopian tubes, of course). If only one side is painful, the cause may be appendicitis, an ovarian cyst or an ectopic pregnancy.

Diagnosis and treatment

Swabs from the vagina or cervix are very often misleading. The diagnosis can only be confirmed by laparoscopy. In practice, most doctors tend to use high dose antibiotics whenever they suspect salpingitis.

Chronic salpingitis is very difficult to treat and in the end the only solution may be surgery to remove the infected tubes.

SARCOMA

A sarcoma is a malignant tumour of the connective tissue.

The term is used to describe cancerous growths originating in the bones, cartilage, tendons, ligaments and muscles.

SCABIES

Scabies is a skin infestation which is highly contagious.

The scabies mites burrow under the skin to lay eggs, causing a trail of tiny itchy lumps and swellings.

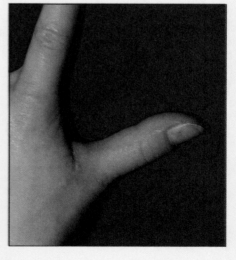

The raised trails left by a scabies mite show between the finger and thumb.

Preventing Salmonella Infections

It is important to take sensible precautions to prevent infection by salmonella bacteria.

● Always cook chicken thoroughly.
● Do not leave chicken (or other meat) lying around in a warm kitchen. If you have cooked it, put it in a refrigerator as soon as it has cooled.
● Do not store cooked and uncooked meat together.
● If re-heating meat, ensure that it is thoroughly heated to kill any bacteria which may have multiplied.
● Beware of home-made mayonnaise which has been sitting at room temperature.
● Do not give under-cooked or raw eggs to the very young, the very old or the infirm.
● If you contract a salmonella infection, be even more meticulous than usual about personal hygiene: the organisms can remain in the intestine, being excreted with the faeces.

SEE ALSO — Appendicitis, Cancer, Ectopic pregnancy, Food poisoning, Chlamydial infections, Gonorrhoea, Ovary, Typhoid fever

MEDICAL FACT FILE

The most common sites are between the fingers, on the wrists, in the armpits and in the genital area. Itching gets worse at night, and sores may develop.

Treatment

The infestation is easily eradicated with insecticide lotions, available from chemists or on prescription. All members of a family (or all people in institutions) should be treated at the same time. The itching may persist for some time after treatment.

SCAR

A scar is the mark left after injured tissue has healed.

The healing process involves the production of a protein, collagen, to knit the injury together. This leaves a scar on the skin, which is usually white, although it may be red or purple if the skin was torn and not held together (with stitches, for example) as it healed.

Scarring can also be internal, after penetrating wounds, surgery or ulceration, for example. In some cases, adhesions may become a problem, when scar tissue blocks ducts or causes parts of different internal organs to stick together.

SCARLET FEVER

Scarlet fever and the milder form, scarlatina, are rare diseases, caused by one of the streptococcus bacteria.

It is more common in children than in adults, and also causes more severe symptoms in children.

Symptoms and course

The incubation period is two to five days, and the main symptoms, a sore throat followed by a rash, develop suddenly, accompanied by a fever and loss of appetite. The tongue is furred and swollen. At a later stage, this fur peels off, leaving the tongue clean and red, the 'strawberry tongue'.

The rash generally appears on the second day, as a background reddening, with minute, intensely red spots. The rash fades on pressure. After a few days the skin peels off in flakes.

The most common complication is earache, if the infection spreads to the ears. In some cases, the germ spreads to the bloodstream and may infect the bone, heart or brain.

Treatment

All patients should be treated with penicillin. Because the disease is so infectious, it is advisable to isolate the sufferer, keeping them at home for seven days.

These adult larvae are responsible for schistosomiasis. When they are in the intestine, they release spiked eggs which cause anaemia, inflammation and scarring.

SCHISTOSOMIASIS

Schistosomiasis, also known as bilharzia, is a tropical disease, caused by a parasite.

The parasites are flukes, whose life cycle is dependent on humans and snails.

The life cycle

The snails pick up the eggs and act as hosts until the larvae hatch. The larvae can penetrate human skin, settling in the bloodstream of the intestine where they grow to adult flukes. They lay eggs which cause inflammation of the skin and other organs, and there may also be bleeding, ulceration and the formation of scar tissue in the intestine, the bladder and the liver. Eggs are excreted and picked up by snails, who pass the larvae on to new human hosts.

Symptoms

Apart from an itchiness where the parasite entered the body, symptoms may be slow to develop. When the adult flukes lay eggs, there may be a 'flu-like illness. Later there may be blood in the urine, abdominal pain and enlargement of any organs which are affected.

Diagnosis and treatment

The presence of the flukes is easily diagnosed from blood samples, and laboratory examination of urine or faeces reveals the eggs. The flukes are easily dealt with by a single dose of medicine.

Avoiding infestation

The flukes are prevalent in freshwater lakes, rivers and irrigation systems in many tropical countries. There is no vaccination, so travellers should avoid wading or bathing in fresh water which may be infested. Under-developed tropical countries are encouraging the use of proper sanitary facilities to eliminate the problem.

Keloids

A keloid is a form of scar which is more common among black-skinned people.

A keloid scar continues to grow in size as the body produces protein, even after the wound has healed. The scars can occur anywhere on the body. There is little that can be done to treat them but they may gradually flatten of their own accord.

Surgical removal only leads to the development of further keloids in most cases, although injections of steroids when the wound is stitched up may help.

SCHIZOID PERSONALITY

A schizoid personality shows a range of paranoid and fanatical characteristics, and an inability to carry on normal social relationships.

Assessing personality is a difficult and often subjective task. Although it is generally agreed that a schizoid personality does exist as a disorder, and it often occurs before the onset of acute schizophrenia, there is controversy over how frequently it occurs and whether it is an accurate signpost to later problems.

Schizoid personalities are most common in the near relatives of schizophrenics, perhaps an indication that full-blown schizophrenia and the personality trait are inherited.

Symptoms and treatment

Schizoid individuals display characteristic traits of secretiveness, abnormal shyness, emotional indifference, fanaticism and hypochondriasis.

It is treated with therapy to try to prevent further deterioration. Sufferers are not usually able to carry on a normal life, and occupational therapy or work which does not involve social interaction are usually the best options.

SCHIZOPHRENIA

Schizophrenia is a psychotic disorder in which the sufferer shows abnormal social and emotional behaviour.

The schizophrenic has a bizarre way of thinking and behaving and sees her environment in an abnormal fashion. She lives an inner life, crowded with fantastic ideas and images and as a result she is cut off from her fellows and appears withdrawn. Schizophrenia is not a split personality, though abrupt mood swings and lack of communication sometimes give the impression that the sufferer is two separate people.

The incidence of schizophrenia is about 0.85 per cent and this is remarkably constant, from country to country and across different social groups. Many factors such as body build, personality, heredity and childhood experiences have been put forward as the cause of schizophrenia. In all probability, several factors combine to trigger schizophrenia in a genetically predisposed individual.

Symptoms

The main symptoms of schizophrenia are disordered thoughts and delusions. The schizophrenic's powers of thinking are so disturbed that she confuses cause with effect and draws hopelessly false conclusions. Schizophrenics can speak for hours on end without any of it making any sense at all. The sufferer may appreciate that her thoughts are muddled and say that 'thinking is difficult'. In true schizophrenic style, however, she will often ascribe this to other people either taking her thoughts away or inserting their own thoughts into her brain. Schizophrenics are particularly prone to delusions, maintaining incorrect beliefs in the face of logical argument.

A particularly common delusion is the so-called 'ideas of reference'. This is an experience in which the sufferer feels that even the most mundane happenings have particular relevance to themselves. Strangers in the street, advertising hoardings, newspapers and so on are all discussing and directing the victim.

Another common disturbance is auditory hallucinations — voices commenting on their actions, speaking their thoughts or telling them what to do.

Treatment

Because schizophrenia is so poorly understood, treatment is difficult. In general, therapy is aimed at strengthening the patient's ties with reality. The major tranquillisers such as Largactil not only calm the patient, but also normalise thinking. Injections once a month are now regarded as the most effective medication.

Supportive psychotherapy is helpful but analytical therapy may even be harmful.

SCIATIC NERVE

The sciatic nerve is the largest nerve in the body, running down each leg from the pelvis to the knees.

The sciatic nerves connect the spinal nerves to

Location Of The Sciatic Nerve

Buttock muscles

Sciatic nerve

Nerves branching to upper leg

Thigh muscles

Peroneal nerve

Tibial nerve

➤➤ SEE ALSO — Psychosis

the hips and legs, carrying messages to and from all parts of the leg. The sciatic nerve splits to become the tibial and peroneal nerves below the knee.

Sciatica

Inflammation or injury to the sciatic nerve produces sciatica, a severe pain in the buttock and down the back of the leg. There is usually lower back pain as well, which is made worse by movement. In severe cases there may be numbness in the area supplied by the nerve. The most common cause of sciatica is muscle strain, caused by bending, sitting or lifting awkwardly. It may also be caused by a slipped disc or, rarely, by a tumour, abscess or embolism.

Painkillers and bed rest (on a firm surface) will help to relieve the symptoms, but underlying causes should be investigated. Gentle exercise to keep the back and hips supple may be started after a few days. If the pain persists, medical advice should be sought.

SCLERITIS

Scleritis is an inflammation of the sclera, the white part of the eye and cornea.

Scleritis is a symptom of various disorders, including rheumatoid arthritis and some forms of herpes. Scleritis usually responds to eye-drops containing corticosteroid drugs, but this treatment may lead to thinning and the eventual perforation of the sclera.

SCOLIOSIS

Scoliosis is a deformity of the spine in which it bends to one side.

The condition can start in childhood (juvenile

scoliosis), gradually becoming worse until the child stops growing. It may also result from a congenital deformity of the vertebrae, from poliomyelitis, or in children who have legs of different lengths.

Juvenile scoliosis, and minor but worsening conditions, are treated by fitting a jacket or brace to immobilise the spine. Misshapen vertebrae can be straightened surgically in a spinal fusion operation.

SCREENING

Screening is the process of testing apparently healthy and normal people for various diseases which can be treated more easily if they are detected at an early stage.

Examples of screening include cervical smear tests, hearing tests for young children and chest x-rays to detect lung disorders.

SCURVY

Scurvy is a disease caused by a lack of vitamin C.

In developed countries, an increased awareness of the need for, and availability of, fresh fruit and vegetables means that scurvy is rare.

A lack of vitamin C leads to an irregularity in the body's production of collagen, a protein which helps to form the body's connective tissues. The collagen no longer serves its normal role, so that wounds do not heal as quickly and haemorrhages may occur, showing as bruising under the skin. The gums also bleed, and teeth may fall out in chronic cases. If there is bleeding in the joints, there will be pain. In children, this

may lead to stunted growth.

If there is haemorrhage in the brain, the disorder may be fatal.

Treatment and prevention

The condition is easily treated with large doses of vitamin C. A small daily intake of fresh fruit and vegetables will prevent the condition from developing.

SEBACEOUS GLANDS

The sebaceous glands are found in the walls of hair follicles.

They produce sebum, an oily substance which lubricates the skin and gives it its characteristic sheen.

Sebum is produced inside special cells, which, when they are full, disintegrate, releasing the sebum. The sebum then migrates up the hair shaft to the skin surface. In some areas, such as the tip of the

penis and the lips of the vagina, sebaceous glands empty directly on to the surface of the skin.

Secretion of sebum is under hormonal control. More is produced in pregnancy and adolescence — contributing to acne — and less is produced in old age — leading to dry skin.

If the opening of the gland is blocked, secretions build up and bacteria can multiply, causing pimples and spots. Retained secretions may react with the air, making the oil rancid and dark — the blackhead.

In adolescents, particularly boys, there is sometimes excessive secretion of sebum, a condition known as seborrhoea. The exact cause is not known, but male sex hormones are known to play a part. The condition often gives rise to skin problems, such as acne, but usually disappears of its own accord as the teenager grows up.

Sebaceous Cysts

A sebaceous cyst is a harmless but unsightly, and sometimes painful, lump which may develop under the skin.

The cysts tend to form in blocked sebaceous ducts, and may swell to quite a large size, in which case they become painful. The cysts contain yellow, cheesy matter.

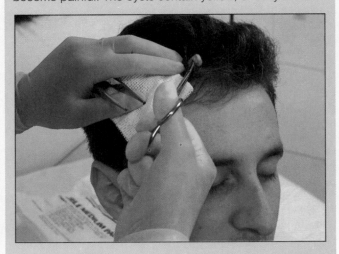

A cyst being removed under local anaesthetic.

➤➤ SEE ALSO — Abscess, Acne, Disc prolapse, Embolism, Kyphosis, Poliomyelitis, Tumour

SEIZURE

A seizure is the effect of an irregularity in the electrical activity in the brain.

The fits of epilepsy are typical examples of seizures, but seizures are only classed as epileptic if they are recurrent. The commonest type is a febrile convulsion — which affects children with a high fever.

Generalised seizures

In a generalised seizure, the abnormal electrical activity spreads throughout the brain, causing loss of consciousness. Such generalised seizures are known as grand mal or petit mal, depending on the length of unconsciousness and other symptoms.

Partial seizures

In other cases, only part of the brain is affected, and the symptoms depend on the part of the brain affected.

In temporal lobe epilepsy, for example, there is a sense of disassociation, déjà vu, hallucinations and anxiety, while in Jacksonian epilepsy, groups of motor muscles are affected, so that there may be twitching of the face or a hand.

Causes and treatment

A tendency to seizures may be due to hereditary factors or metabolic disorders, but seizures are more often due to birth trauma, brain infection (such as meningitis), brain injury, a brain tumour, a stroke, or alcohol withdrawal.

Anticonvulsant drugs may be prescribed for those who have repeated seizures, but in milder cases patients have to learn to recognise warning signals and keep out of dangerous situations, (a grand mal seizure while crossing a busy road, for example, could be fatal).

SEMEN

Semen is the fluid produced by a man on ejaculation.

Semen is made up of seminal fluid from the seminal vesicles, which are behind the bladder, together with secretions from the prostate and Cowper's gland and, most important, sperm from the testicles. The production of semen is controlled by the male hormone, testosterone.

Testing times

Male fertility depends upon the quantity of sperm in the semen, and the ability of the sperm to move (in order to 'swim' up the fallopian tubes to fertilise the egg). In an average ejaculation, about a teaspoonful of semen is produced, containing about 350 million sperm. The semen (produced by masturbation) can be tested for a deficiency or absence of sperm, and their shape and agility can be examined under the microscope. Similar tests are performed after a vasectomy, to check that sperm are not still present in the semen. (After a vasectomy, sperm are still produced, but the tube from the testicles to the seminal vesicles is cut. The sperm are reabsorbed.)

Sign of disorder?

Blood in the semen is usually a harmless condition. The blood comes from small vessels in the prostate or seminal vesicles, but the cause is unknown. However, it may be a symptom of a testicular tumour.

SENSES

The senses pick up sensations — the awareness of a physical experience.

Sensation depends upon the stimulation of sense

A blind musician reading Braille music. If one sense is impaired, other senses usually become more highly developed, and blind people are often good musicians.

receptors, and the transmission of electrical impulses to the brain.

The vivid 'sensations' of dreams are not true sensations as they have their origins in the brain and not the sense organs.

Of the five senses, four (vision, hearing, smell and taste) take place in specific organs and are referred to as the special senses. The fifth, touch, is made up of several components, including soft touch, pain, hot and cold.

Sight

For an object to be seen, light must be reflected from it and focused on the retina. The image is then translated into electrical activity and transmitted via the optic nerve to the visual cortex. The focusing properties of

the eye are often imperfect, leading to uneven focusing (astigmatism, short-sightedness or long-sightedness).

Hearing

Sound is produced by minute changes of air pressure, caused by a vibrating object such as a tuning fork (or a vocal cord). Sound waves strike the eardrum causing it to vibrate. The movements are transmitted, via three tiny bones, to the inner ear where they are translated into electrical impulses.

Any part of the ear can be affected by injury or disease, leading to deafness. Interference with the transmission of sound waves across the outer or middle ear causes

▶▶ SEE ALSO — Brain, Epilepsy, Fertilisation, Hypermetropia, Myopia, Vasectomy

The Tongue

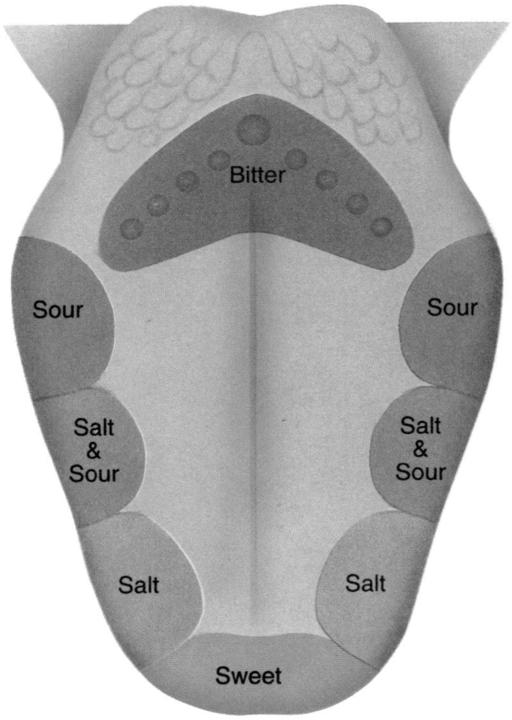

Different parts of the tongue sense different tastes.

conductive deafness. The commonest cause of this form of deafness is wax blocking the canal. In children, glue ear, which dampens the movement of the eardrum, is a frequent cause of deafness. Both are easily treated.

Sensory deafness is due to damage to the inner ear or to the nerve leading to the brain. The commonest cause of sensory deafness is prolonged exposure to high noise levels.

Smell

Compared with the other senses, the sense of smell is poorly understood. The organ of smell is an area the size of a postage stamp high up in the roof of the nasal cavity. The cells in this area are covered in minute, hair-like projections that sample the air as it wafts past them. Each cell is connected, via a short nerve, to the brain.

In order for a substance to be smelled, some of it must be carried by air currents to the nose. It dissolves in the mucus on the surface of the cells and causes minute changes in the electrical charges across the cell wall. Humans are said to be able to distinguish 4000 different odours.

Taste

The human tongue contains about 10,000 taste buds, each of which is able to distinguish one of the four basic tastes — sweet, sour, bitter and salty. In the same way as colour is made up of the three primary colours (and black and white), so the four basic tastes make up the range of flavours which we experience. Our sense of taste is greatly helped by the sense of smell.

Taste and smell are most frequently lost as the result of an upper respiratory tract infection. Occasionally, this loss may be permanent. Frontal brain tumours may cause bizarre symptoms where one smell is mistaken for another.

General disorders

Apart from damage to the individual sense organs, disorders affecting the senses are rare. Multiple sclerosis may affect vision and touch, and brain tumours may affect various senses, depending on the part of the brain affected.

SENSITISATION

Sensitisation is the initial exposure of someone to a foreign body or allergen which produces an immune response.

The next time the person is exposed to it, the reaction is likely to be stronger. The process of sensitisation is the basis of all allergic reactions.

SEPTAL DEFECT

A septal defect is more commonly known as a hole in the heart.

The defect is between the two sides of the heart — either between the left and right ventricles or between the left and right atria.

Septal defects arise before or at the time of birth. Defects before birth usually involve the septum, or wall, between the two ventricles.

At the moment of the first breath, the circulation changes dramatically. No longer does the baby derive oxygen-rich blood from the placenta but instead it must rely on its own lungs and their circulation.

If this changeover does not take place correctly the result may well be a septal defect, which allows blood to cross from the left atrium to the right.

Ventricular septal defect

A hole in the ventricular septum is the commonest congenital defect. The abnormal blood flow causes a loud heart murmur but few other symptoms. In most cases it is discovered soon after birth as part of the doctor's routine examination of the newborn. In some cases the baby becomes breathless during feeding and in a few, rare cases the heart is unable to cope with the strain and fluid builds up in the body and lungs. Drug treatment in the first few days of life may tide the baby over long enough for the hole to close on its own. If it does not close naturally there is a risk of lung damage and surgery is undertaken to patch the hole.

Atrial septal defect

A hole occurring in the wall between the two atria rarely closes spontaneously and the baby usually ends up having open heart surgery. The outlook varies according to where exactly in the septum the defect is. The higher the hole is situated the nearer it is to the mitral valve and the more likely it is to damage it. If the mitral valve needs replacing the operation is technically much more difficult.

Septal defects cause blood from the left side of the heart to be pumped to the right side. This ensures that plenty of blood reaches the lungs and this type of problem does not result in an oxygen-starved 'blue baby'.

SEPTICAEMIA

Septicaemia occurs when bacteria or fungi multiply in the bloodstream.

Septicaemia is often fatal and patients suffering from

SEE ALSO — Allergy, Heart disease, Immunisation, Nose

the condition require immediate admission to hospital.

The germs that cause septicaemia usually enter the bloodstream from an established infection elsewhere in the body, often the lungs or urinary tract.

In some patients, usually the frail, the elderly or those with certain pre-existing conditions such as sugar diabetes, the original infection cannot be traced.

Symptoms and treatment

Fever, uncontrollable shaking and collapse (see Septic shock) are the main features of septicaemia. The onset is usually rapid but the illness is often preceded by vague 'flu-like symptoms.

The diagnosis of septicaemia relies on laboratory analysis of the patient's blood. This may take several hours and, as speed is absolutely essential, doctors usually begin the patient on intravenous antibiotics before the results are available.

The cocktail of drugs used may be varied according to the bacteria which have been isolated from laboratory samples.

SEPTIC SHOCK

Septic shock occurs when the body's defences are overwhelmed by invading bacteria.

The main feature that distinguishes it from septicaemia is circulatory collapse. Untreated, septic shock is rapidly fatal and even with the best therapy available it still carries a high mortality rate.

Infected wounds and body tissues can cause septic shock in one of two ways. The infection may be relatively minor, but localised in an area where even minor damage is fatal — the heart,

for example. On the other hand, the infection may be widespread, causing damage as a result of the body's own defences.

In the normal course of a minor infection, the body produces chemicals that destroy the invader. These chemicals are often highly toxic, but because they are present in such small quantities they do not cause problems. In septic shock the reaction is so widespread that the body's own defences damage healthy tissue.

The early signs of septic shock are similar to those of septicaemia, but the patient's condition rapidly deteriorates.

Treatment, consisting of high-dose antibiotics, often needs to be augmented by artificial life support until the infection is overcome.

SEX CHANGE

A sex change operation involves hormonal and physical changes.

Some people, although their chromosomes clearly show that they are of a definite sex (see Sex determination), feel psychologically that they are of a different sex. In such

cases, it is possible to 'change' sex with courses of hormones and operations to remove existing genitals and build new genitals to simulate the appropriate organs.

SEX DETERMINATION

The biological sex of an individual depends on the sex chromosomes present in their cells.

The mother's egg always contains an X chromosome, so the sexual identity of an embryo depends on whether it receives an X or a Y chromosome from its father's sperm. The sex chromosome make-up of a female is XX and that of a male is XY.

In the very early stages of embryonic life there is no difference between the male and the female foetus. At about seven weeks, probably as a result of chemical changes brought about by genes on the sex chromosomes, the primitive gonad changes.

Within a few days the newly formed testis or ovary is producing the hormones that determine the development of the external sex organs.

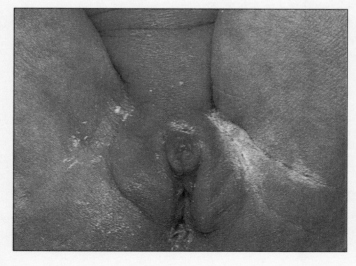

The sex of this child is not apparent: the vagina can be seen clearly, but the clitoral protrusion is like a small penis.

Occasionally the sex of a child is not apparent at birth. This is often not due to chromosome abnormalities, but arises as a result of insufficient sex hormones.

Once chromosome analysis has established the true sex, reconstructive surgery can be used to create the external sex organs, producing remarkably good results.

Very rarely, an extra chromosome or a missing chromosome causes gender abnormality.

SEX-LINKED INHERITANCE

A sex-linked inheritance is one that is carried on the X chromosome.

The most well-known example is haemophilia. A female carrying the abnormal, haemophilia gene is protected by her normal, second X chromosome.

A male, who has an X and a Y chromosome, has no such protection and exhibits the disease. Some congenital abnormalities, whilst not involving sex-linked genes, are more common in one sex than another. Spina bifida is seen more frequently in girls and cleft palate more in boys.

Genetic counselling and testing should be available to any parents of a child with a sex-linked disorder.

SEXUAL INTERCOURSE

Sexual intercourse describes the process of a man inserting his penis into a woman's vagina.

The natural aim of sexual intercourse is to fertilise the woman's egg in order to

➤➤ SEE ALSO — Chromosomes, Cleft palate, Genes, Genetic counselling, Spina bifida

produce a child, but the sensation is very pleasurable, and procreation is not the only aim.

Step by step

The first stage in intercourse is arousal: as a man becomes sexually excited, his penis becomes hard and erect as blood flows into it. The woman's vagina becomes moist as the membrane lining secretes a lubricant. Her clitoris becomes hard.

Next the man penetrates the vagina, making rhythmic, thrusting movements, while the muscles in the vagina contract to grip the penis.

When the man reaches a climax, the vas deferens and epididymis force semen down the penis and into the woman's vagina. Ideally, the woman reaches orgasm at the same time, her vaginal walls contracting strongly, giving an intense, pleasurable feeling throughout the body. There is usually a noticeable increase in secretions at the same time.

Disorders

There are various disorders which may inhibit or prevent sexual intercourse — either physical or emotional. If one or both partners lose interest in sex or fail to reach orgasm, it is worth discussing the problem with a sympathetic doctor, who can put them in touch with a sex counsellor if necessary.

SEXUALLY TRANSMITTED DISEASES

There is a wide range of sexually transmitted diseases (STDs) — disorders which are passed on during sexual intercourse.

Some STDs are more serious than others. The HIV virus and AIDs are very serious, and the number of cases increased throughout the second half of the 1980s in most parts of the world. However, diseases such as syphilis and gonorrhoea are on the decrease, since the introduction of penicillin.

Other STDs include chlamydial infections, trichomoniasis, genital herpes, genital warts, scabies and pubic lice. Some are grouped together as non-specific urethritis.

Clinics

Diagnosis and treatment of STDs is usually carried out at special clinics, attached to hospitals, where there is specialist help and advice. Anyone who is diagnosed as having a serious STD should inform the clinic of all recent sexual partners, so that they can be traced and treated if necessary, preventing further spread.

The symptoms and treatment of various STDs are described elsewhere, according to the individual diseases. Prevention is very important. Safer sex techniques restrict the spread of STDs.

SHIGELLOSIS

Shigellosis is a form of dysentery caused by shigella bacteria.

There are only about a thousand cases of shigellosis in the UK each year, mainly in institutions and in children who attend nurseries, but it is endemic in some countries. The bacteria are passed on in the faeces of infected people.

Symptoms and treatment

The main symptoms are diarrhoea and abdominal pain. The diarrhoea starts suddenly, and after a few days pus and blood may show in the faeces. There is also nausea, vomiting and

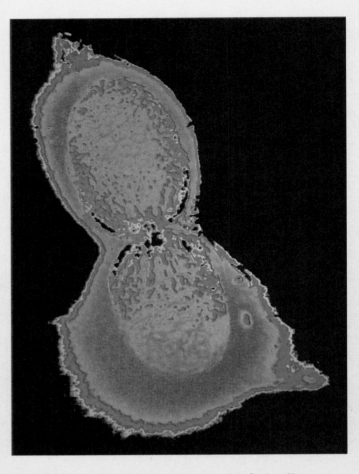

Shigella flexneri is the bacteria responsible for bacillary dysentery. Here, a cell can be seen dividing.

general aches and pains.

If the diarrhoea is persistent, it is important to guard against dehydration. Other possible problems include toxaemia (poisons in the blood).

The disorder usually clears up on its own, although this may take several weeks. It is important to pay extra attention to hygiene whenever there is a bout of diarrhoea.

SHINGLES

Shingles is an infection of the nerves supplying certain areas of the skin, which causes a crusty, blistered rash.

Shingles is caused by the herpes zoster virus which also causes chickenpox.

SHIVERING

Shivering is the involuntary trembling of the body as a normal response to cold.

Shivering may accompany fever, and also may be a response to fear. The trembling occurs because the muscles contract and relax rapidly, in an effort to generate heat. In patients with a fever, the shivering occurs because the body's thermostat is 'reset' at a higher level, and the body feels as though it is cooler than it should be.

Goose pimples often accompany shivering, making the hairs stand on end to trap heat in an effort to warm up the body. In frightening situations, animals' hair stands on end to make them look larger.

⟩⟩ SEE ALSO — AIDS, Dehydration, Dysentery, Ejaculation, Fertility, Herpes, HIV, Impotence, Vaginismus

SHOCK

In medical terms, shock is a lack of oxygen reaching the tissues, usually as a result of heart or circulatory failure.

This description of shock is referred to as surgical or physiological shock, and there are four main types. Another form of shock which has a similar effect is an allergic reaction. The sensations and symptoms following a disturbing physical or emotional event, although commonly referred to as shock, are not included in this medical definition (but see Post-Traumatic Stress Syndrome, above right).

Hypovolaemic shock

This is due to massive circulatory fluid loss, either internally or externally. The fluid loss may be a fall in the level of water in the blood, as a result of diarrhoea, for example, or there may be an actual loss of blood through cuts and other injuries.

Septic shock

Septic shock is the term used to describe the condition of a patient who has been overwhelmed by bacterial toxins.

Cardiogenic shock

Cardiogenic shock occurs when the heart is no longer able to function efficiently as a pump. The usual causes are a heart attack or a pulmonary embolus.

Neurogenic shock

If the brain is starved of oxygen the nervous system collapses and all control over the circulation is lost.

Anaphylactic shock

Anaphylactic shock is a very rare, acute and sometimes fatal allergic reaction. Common allergens which may cause such an extreme sensitivity include insect stings and certain drugs, as well as some foods (certain types of nut for example).

The allergic reaction involves the release of large quantities of chemicals, which widen the blood vessels so blood pressure drops. The airways in the lungs may swell, as may the tongue and throat. There may be a rash, itching and stomachache. Such symptoms need immediate medical attention: an injection of adrenaline may be life-saving.

Post-Traumatic Stress Syndrome

Disturbing events (such as war and torture, rape, serious accidents, natural disasters or bereavement) may induce a range of symptoms known as post-traumatic stress syndrome.

The symptoms of post-traumatic stress are related to a deep-felt anxiety and include:
● Recurrent dreams about the event.
● Disturbance of sleep.
● Loss of concentration.
● A feeling of isolation.
● Nervous twitches.

The symptoms are worse when the sufferer is reminded of the event, and may lead to depressive illness. Treatment involves counselling and emotional support, and letting time heal if possible.

SHORT STATURE

Short stature (also described as dwarfism or restricted growth) is a height which is significantly below the average for a person's age.

Most infants who are taken to a doctor with the complaint 'She isn't growing' are perfectly normal, short children. Their shortness is due either to being small at birth and not having caught up, or to being naturally short — with short relatives and, particularly, short parents. Despite the fact that they are below average size, their rate of growth, if plotted on a graph, is normal.

Most of these children have a delayed growth spurt and eventually reach a normal height. However, if a series of growth measurements shows a child isn't growing, or is growing more slowly than expected, another explanation should be sought.

Causes

In the developing world the commonest cause of short stature is poor nutrition. This may even happen in this country if the child is on a restricted diet or has some form of digestive disorder. Children who are emotionally

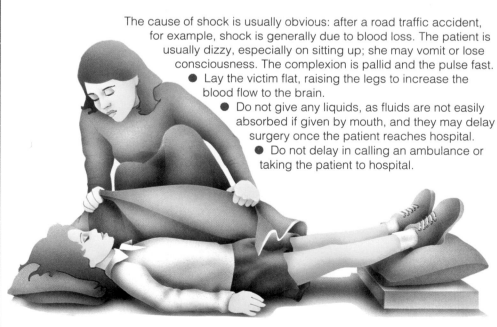

First Aid For Shock

In the first-aid situation, the diagnosis and treatment of shock come second to the diagnosis and treatment of its cause.

The cause of shock is usually obvious: after a road traffic accident, for example, shock is generally due to blood loss. The patient is usually dizzy, especially on sitting up; she may vomit or lose consciousness. The complexion is pallid and the pulse fast.
● Lay the victim flat, raising the legs to increase the blood flow to the brain.
● Do not give any liquids, as fluids are not easily absorbed if given by mouth, and they may delay surgery once the patient reaches hospital.
● Do not delay in calling an ambulance or taking the patient to hospital.

deprived, even if they receive a perfectly adequate diet, may also fail to grow properly and end up stunted in body as well as in mind.

Chronic disease of any sort, including such common conditions as asthma, can cause delayed or restricted growth. Specific conditions, such as an underactive thyroid, are usually detected in very early infancy, but untreated they can still result in short stature.

Deficiency of growth hormone is much less common than a deficiency of thyroid hormone, but without it almost no growth can occur. The level of growth hormone in the blood can be measured and, if it is low, replacement therapy is possible.

Achondroplasia, a condition in which the long bones fail to develop, results in normal heads (often with a high, protruding forehead) and bodies on tiny legs. The condition is hereditary, but expected lifespan, intelligence and sexual development are normal.

Treatment

Lack of growth due to inadequate diet can be corrected by improving the intake of nutrition. If there is a hormonal problem, this can also be corrected by supplementing the natural production of hormones. However, growth hormone treatment is expensive, even with the new synthesised hormones. (In the past, growth hormone was taken from the brains of human corpses, and in the UK there have been incidents of those who were treated later dying from Creutzfeldt-Jacob syndrome, a disorder related to BSE.)

Stretching the legs using steel rods screwed to the bones can add several inches to children with short bones.

SHOULDER

The shoulder is a ball and socket joint, connecting the arm to the body.

Although the shoulder is classed as a ball and socket joint, which allows a wide range of movement, the socket is actually very shallow. So shallow, in fact, that it needs a capsule of muscle to keep it from dislocating under the weight of the arm. These 'rotator cuff muscles', as they are called, are easily injured.

Falling on to an outstretched arm is probably the most common accident of all. The patient may have put out an arm to prevent injury to the face, but the arm is often injured in the process. The damage may be confined to the muscles of the rotator cuff, or it may disrupt the joint completely, causing dislocation. The most important aspect of the treatment of shoulder injuries, especially in the elderly, is preservation of movement. As soon as the swelling has subsided, mobilising exercises and physiotherapy are started. Occasionally an extensive tear needs surgical repair.

Dislocation

Dislocation of the shoulder usually occurs in a forward direction, so that the ball of the joint lies in front of the socket. A dislocated shoulder is usually obvious. It is very painful and the casualty is reluctant to let anyone examine it. The normal, rounded contour of the shoulder is lost and the arm is held at about 30° from the body. Most dislocated shoulders can be manipulated back into position, but this needs a general anaesthetic and plenty of practice.

Dislocation weakens the muscles of the shoulder and recurrent dislocations are common. Surgical repair of the damaged muscles is usually successful.

Fractures

The shoulder region is a common area for fractures. These generally occur at the ball of the upper arm or the shaft of the same bone. As with other shoulder injuries, prevention of stiffness is paramount. The arm is rested in a sling for about two weeks and then mobilised by physiotherapy.

Collarbones

The collarbone runs from the base of the neck out to the shoulder. Fractured collarbones occur most frequently in children and young adults. Fractured collarbones usually unite very quickly, but the patient is almost always left with an unsightly bulge at the site of the injury.

Complications

An unusual complication of shoulder injury is 'shoulder-hand' syndrome. Damage to the upper arm is mirrored by swelling, pain and osteoporosis in the wrist. This is thought to be due to disruption of the autonomic nervous system. Treatment with painkillers and hydrocortisone help but the condition may take up to two years to resolve.

SIAMESE TWINS

Siamese twins are identical twins who failed to separate completely during the development of the embryo from the fertilised egg.

The term 'Siamese' was given to such conjoined twins after the first recorded pair, Chang and Eng, who were born in Siam (now Thailand) in the early 19th century, and lived for 63 years. They were joined at the hip.

Birth may be particularly difficult, and Siamese twins may not survive.

The outlook for Siamese twins depends on the extent to which they are joined. Some only share some connective tissue, or perhaps a section of bone in the leg, while others have major organs (including the heart) in common.

Surgeons can operate to separate twins, but in some cases only one of them can be saved.

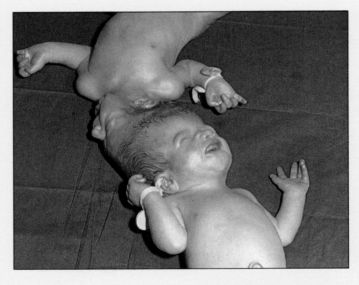

These Siamese twins are joined at the top of the head. There have been cases where twins connected in a similar way have survived, still joined, well into adulthood.

>> SEE ALSO — BSE, Frozen shoulder, Growth, Joints, Thyroid, Twins

SICK BUILDING SYNDROME

Sick building syndrome is a collection of symptoms which are usually ascribed to working in modern office buildings.

Symptoms include dry, itching eyes, loss of energy, headaches and repeated attacks of colds and 'flu. The exact mechanism is not understood, but the controlled environment and air conditioning are often blamed, as well as the lack of natural ventilation and daylight.

Rest and relaxation, together with a good diet, may help to alleviate the symptoms.

SICKLE CELL DISEASE

Sickle cell disease, and the less serious sickle cell trait, are due to abnormalities of haemoglobin.

Haemoglobin is the oxygen-carrying pigment in red blood cells. In unaffected individuals, haemoglobin is in the form of haemoglobin A. In sickle cell disease, most of the haemoglobin is of the abnormal haemoglobin S type.

In many respects, haemoglobin S and haemoglobin A are very similar. Unfortunately red cells containing haemoglobin S become misshapen when they have given up their oxygen. The commonest shape is a crescent moon or sickle, hence the name. These misshapen cells cannot pass through the fine blood capillaries to carry oxygen to the parts of the body which need it. They may actually block the passage of other oxygen-carrying cells.

In sickle cell disease the curved shapes of haemoglobin S contrast with the normal, round haemoglobin A cells.

Inheritance

Sickle cell disease is inherited from the parents and only affects black-skinned people of African origin. For full-blown sickle cell disease the child must inherit an abnormal gene from both parents. If one abnormal and one normal gene are inherited then the child has sickle cell trait.

Problems and symptoms

Sickle cell disease starts as a mild illness in about the third month of life. Untreated, the disease progresses rapidly and most children would die before the age of two. Although the affected baby is often pale, most are only discovered because of a crisis. Two forms of crisis occur, either profound anaemia or severe pain.

Anaemia is often brought on by a minor infection such as a cold.

Painful crises are brought about by thrombosis in the circulation. Pain is usually felt in the bones but it may also affect the abdomen or the joints. Strokes and kidney damage are common.

Treatment

Treatment involves reducing the chance of a crisis and dealing with any symptoms if they do arise. There is no cure for the disorder. Prompt treatment of infections and an adequate fluid intake may stop abnormal cells reaching crisis numbers. General anaesthetics and blood transfusions are avoided, as both may precipitate a crisis.

The outlook is still gloomy, many sufferers dying in childhood or early adult life.

Sickle cell trait

Sickle cell trait rarely causes problems, except if the individual is exposed to an environment low in oxygen. It is best not to fly, as there may be a drop in oxygen even in a pressurised cabin.

SINGER'S NODES

Singer's nodes is a condition which may affect anyone who misuses their vocal cords.

Singers, teachers and politicians are particularly at risk. Small, greyish-white lumps develop on the vocal cords, causing hoarseness and loss of voice. If the condition persists, a sample of tissue may be removed for analysis to ensure there is not a malignant growth. The treatment is rest, but in some cases surgical removal of the nodes may be the only cure.

SINOATRIAL NODE

The sinoatrial node is the heart's natural pacemaker, keeping it beating regularly.

Even when cut off from the brain, the heart continues to beat rhythmically, a fact first recognised by the Ancient Greeks.

The electrical activity which initiates the heartbeat is generated by specialised nerve tissues in the right atrium. The sinoatrial node, or pacemaker, is a knot of tissue buried in the atrial wall just below the point of entry for the vein that drains the head and neck. A minute change in the electrical potential across the cell membranes causes all the cells in the sinoatrial node to fire an electrical discharge. The wave of electrical activity spreads out from the node to all parts of the heart, like the ripples from a pebble tossed in a pool.

Normal and abnormal

The average heart rate is about 70 beats per minute but anything between 60 and 100 can be considered normal. A sinus bradychardia (slow pulse) is said to exist if the rate is less than 60. A sinus bradychardia may be a sign of thyroid or heart disease but it is usually a sign of super-fitness. The heart of an athlete in training works so efficiently that it can pump all the blood the resting body needs with a pulse rate as low as 40.

A regular pulse rate above 100 is called a sinus tachycardia. This may be a sign of gross unfitness, especially if it occurs after mild exertion such as climbing a flight of stairs. More often it is a sign of high emotion or high fever. An overactive thyroid frequently causes a fast pulse, but the pulse is usually irregular and is therefore not a sinus tachycardia.

» SEE ALSO — Anaemia, Blood, Heart, Larynx, Pacemaker, Thyroid

Damage and disease

The sinoatrial node can be damaged by a lack of oxygen, either as an acute episode during a heart attack or as a chronic condition brought on by furred-up arteries. In this case it may cease functioning, either temporarily or permanently.

Fortunately the heart is provided with various fail-safe devices, which are designed to produce rhythmical electrical activity, albeit at a slower rate than the sinoatrial node.

SINUSITIS

Sinusitis is an inflammation of the membranes lining the sinuses.

The sinuses are cavities in the bones behind the nose and eyes. Their exact function is unclear, but they make the head lighter than it would be if the bones were solid and they seem to help the voice to resonate.

Normally, any mucus produced by the membranes in the sinuses drains down narrow passages to the nose. However, these channels enable infection to travel up from the nose to the sinuses. Such infection is normally the result of a cold, but occasionally it travels into the sinuses when an upper tooth develops an abscess.

Some people have a particular tendency to develop sinusitis, and once such a tendency is established the disorder may occur after every cold.

Symptoms and treatment

Sinusitis causes a painful, throbbing, heavy feeling behind the nose and eyes and in the cheeks, depending on which sinus cavities are affected. There is usually a partial or total loss of sense of smell, a change in the tone of voice, and there may be fever.

Steam inhalations help to ease the symptoms, and antibiotics and decongestants may be prescribed. It may be necessary to flush out the sinuses to take samples of bacteria for identification to select the best antibiotic treatment.

In severe cases, the only solution is surgical drainage of the sinuses.

SITUS INVERSUS

Situs inversus is the term used to describe a person in whom the major organs are on the opposite side of the body to normal.

Normally, for example, the heart is on the left-hand side, but very rarely it is on the right, and other organs, such as the appendix and pancreas are also reversed.

The condition needs no treatment, unless the organs are misformed.

SKELETON

The human skeleton consists of 206 bones, which are surrounded by muscle and connective tissue which allow movement to take place.

Despite their solid appearance the bones that make up the skeleton are living tissues, growing and reshaping themselves according to the strains that are placed upon them.

Male and female

Not surprisingly, the area of major difference between the male and female skeleton is in the bones making up the pelvis. The male pelvis is rougher, thicker and heavier. The inlet at the top is heart-shaped rather than round and the pelvic canal is longer and narrower than that of the female. The male sacrum has three bones in contact with the pelvis, the female sacrum has only two.

Functions

The skeleton has five main functions. It acts as a rigid support giving the body form and shape. By means of the muscles and cartilages attached to it, it enables us to move. It provides protection for vital organs such as the brain, heart and lungs. It produces blood cells in the bone marrow; and it acts as a store for many of the minerals the body needs. particularly calcium and phosphorus.

Structure

Anatomists divide the skeleton into two parts: the axial skeleton and the appendicular skeleton. The axial skeleton consists of the skull (28 bones), the vertebrae (26), the ribs (24) and the hyoid and sternum.

The appendicular skeleton consists of the shoulders, arms and hands (64 bones) and the pelvis, legs and feet (26).

The bones that make up the skeleton consist of a rigid, brittle honeycomb of calcium-rich salts inter-spersed with an organic matrix containing the cells that build the bone. A typical skeletal bone such as the femur, the long bone of the thigh, is covered by a thick fibrous membrane, the periostium. The periostium supplies the bone with its blood and nerve supplies.

The actual bone itself consists of a hard outer layer and a much softer, sponge-like inner core. This inner core of porous bone is found in the long bones of the thigh and upper arm, the breastbone, the ribs and the hips and it is where the bone marrow is formed.

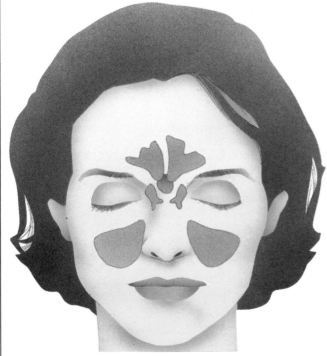

Location Of The Sinuses

The sinus cavities are in the skull, between and above the eyes, and in the cheeks.

» SEE ALSO — Bone, Pelvis

In close up, it is possible to see how the surface of the skin is scaly. The hairs show clearly as fine shafts emerging from between the epidermal (outer layer) skin cells.

SKIN

The skin is the largest organ in the body, serving several functions.

The skin protects the body from the environment, particularly from dehydration, germs and poisons. It acts as an insulator against heat loss. It can signify emotion and, through its touch receptors it is the largest sense organ in the body.

Structure

The skin is divided into two distinct parts, the superficial part, the epidermis, and the deep part, the dermis. The dermis is a layer of connective tissue that is well supplied with blood vessels. In its deeper parts it merges with the subcutaneous tissue. The dermis contains the long, coiled tubes of the sweat glands. These glands are found all over the body except the lips, the clitoris and the tip of the penis.

The dermis also contains the sebaceous glands which pour their secretions over the shafts of the hairs. The hairs themselves have their roots beneath the dermis, deep in the subcutaneous tissue.

The epidermis consists of multiple layers of cells growing up from the supporting dermis. As the cells mature and rise to the surface, so they flatten. On the soles of the feet and the palms of the hands the epidermis may be many thousands of cells deep to withstand wear and tear. In other areas, the armpit, for example, it is very thin.

The cells of the dermis are arranged in parallel lines and a knowledge of the direction of these lines is vital to the aspiring surgeon. An incision along these lines heals quickly and neatly. One across the line puckers and scars.

The skin around joints always folds in the same places. These skin folds (and the lines on the palms of the hands) represent areas where the overlying epidermis is firmly anchored to the deep structures by fibrous bands.

Diseases and disorders

Considering the benign nature of most skin conditions, skin disease is an emotive area. The way we present ourselves to the world and the way we see ourselves depends more than anything else on our skin. A skin disease is immediately apparent to everyone and is hard to ignore. Most skin complaints fit a recognisable pattern and as, unlike other medical conditions, they can be seen and felt there is often little difficulty over the diagnosis. Where doubt does exist it is a relatively simple task to remove a sample of the lesion for analysis.

Common problems include birthmarks; rashes and blemishes due to viral infections (such as the childhood diseases or herpes simplex); inflammation due to dermatitis or eczema; psoriasis; acne vulgaris (which is due to hormonal disorders); problems due to injury, including cuts, grazes and burns; and benign skin tumours, papillomas (raised growths, sometimes on a stalk), sebaceous cysts and cutaneous horns. Other problems include skin cancers, ulceration due to poor blood supply and auto-immune disorders such as lupus erythematosus and vitiligo. These are all described under the appropriate entries.

SKIN CANCER

Skin cancer is a malignant tumour of the skin.

Although malignant tumours of the skin are more common than other types of malignant tumour, the majority of them are easily treated and rarely cause problems.

Basal cell cancers

Basal cell cancers, usually referred to as 'rodent ulcers', possibly because the edge of the lesion looks as if it has been gnawed by rats, are the commonest type of skin tumour. They usually occur on the face, often around the nose and eyes. They seem to be induced by ultraviolet light and are usually seen in the fair-skinned. Rodent ulcers are rare in the young.

Skin Biopsy

A skin biopsy is more often used to eliminate the possibility of cancer than to diagnose particular problems.

Skin biopsy is a simple, almost painless procedure. The suspicious area, usually at the edge of a lesion, is numbed using local anaesthetic. The dermatologist then uses a razor-sharp punch – a fine hollow tube – to remove a sample of skin right down as far as the subcutaneous tissue. Analysis under the microscope, possibly using modern antibody detection techniques, leads to a diagnosis in the vast majority of cases.

▶▶ SEE ALSO — Acne, Birthmark, Cuts, Burns, Dermatitis, Eczema, Leg ulcer, Lupus erythematosus, Rash, Senses, Vitiligo

Mole Watch

Pigmented moles are common, malignant melanomas are rare. The danger signs to look out for are:

● A mole that gets bigger.
● A mole that develops little moles around it.
● A mole that gets darker or lighter in colour.
● A mole that bleeds, itches or ulcerates.

If they do occur it is mainly in people of northern European descent living in areas of bright sunshine such as Australia or South Africa.

The tumour starts as a small nodule which gradually grows outwards, leaving behind an ulcerated centre. In most cases this central ulcer bleeds and scabs over. Rodent ulcers are slow-growing and do not spread to distant parts of the body. They can, however, become very unsightly and plastic surgery may be needed.

Squamous cell cancers

Squamous cell cancers also occur on exposed areas but usually on the hands and ears rather than on the face. Like rodent ulcers, they start as a small nodule that ulcerates as it grows. Squamous cell cancers can spread and early diagnosis and treatment is vital.

Malignant melanoma

Malignant melanoma is a relatively rare tumour that can occur on any part of the body. It may appear from nowhere or it may develop in a pre-existing mole. It is rare in childhood but can affect any age from puberty on.

A malignant melanoma is irregular, pigmented and grows rapidly. Treatment is surgical with wide excision and skin grafting. Chemotherapy and radiotherapy are used if the tumour has spread but by this stage the outlook is generally gloomy.

SKIN GRAFT

Skin grafts are a means of rapidly replacing lost skin by means of an operation.

Skin may be lost by injury or following surgery. There are two basic methods of replacing it. The skin can be replaced by a free graft or a flap graft. Both involve cutting away a piece of skin from another part of the body (the donor site) to replace the damaged skin.

The donor site regenerates itself (or may have to be stitched up, creating some scarring).

Grafting

Skin is a living tissue and requires oxygen and nutrients to survive. With a free graft, a patch of skin is cut away from the donor site, and positioned over the damaged skin. The patch of skin carries enough nutrients to keep itself alive until new blood vessels develop. It is held firmly in place by even pressure to try to ensure that blood does not lift it off.

In mesh grafts, the patch of skin is perforated with small slits, and stretched over the damaged skin.

Flaps

A flap graft is cut away from the donor site with blood vessels still connected to the patch. In some cases the donor site is adjacent to the damaged area, and the blood vessels remain intact. In other cases, microsurgery has to be used to re-connect the blood vessels as the flap graft is positioned.

SKIN TAG

A skin tag is a small flap of skin.

The tag may be brown or flesh coloured, and may appear for no reason, or as a result of unsatisfactory healing of a wound. It can be removed easily by a doctor.

SKULL

The skull is the set of bones which form the skeleton of the head.

The skull is made up of a number of bones united by immobile joints called sutures. The only mobile bone is the jawbone. The bones of the skull are divided into those of the cranium (the round part of the head) and those of the face. The cranium consists of eight bones and the face is made up of 14. The bones are made up of two sheets of compact bone with an inner, much spongier filling.

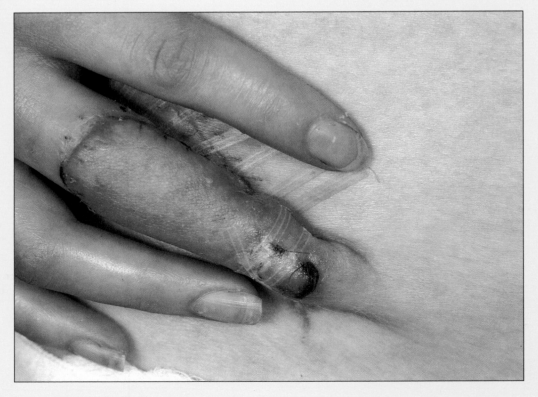

In a flap skin graft, the blood supply from the donor site must be maintained while the skin re-grows. In this case, some skin from the abdomen has been grafted on to a finger. By positioning the finger on the abdomen, the blood supply to the skin graft is maintained.

▶▶ SEE ALSO — Melanoma

The cranium

The bones of the skull form the vault, the cavity that protects the brain. Relatively speaking, the vault of the human skull is larger than that of any other animal.

The base of the vault is pierced by numerous small holes, inlets for blood vessels and outlets for nerves. One hole, the foramen magnum, is very much larger than the others — about the size of a 10p piece. It is through this that the spinal cord passes. Immediately in front of the foramen magnum is the protruberance that anchors the neck muscles. The powerful neck muscles and the position of the bones of the spine make the joint between the head and the neck very secure, but it can be dislocated — usually deliberately — by hanging.

The face

The bones which make up the face start at the forehead with the downward curve of the frontal bone. The base of the frontal bone forms the roof of the orbits — the cavities that protect the eyes. The bone here is paper thin and easily damaged, especially by penetrating injuries. Within the frontal bone, just above the orbits, are the frontal sinuses. These hollow spaces are linked to the back of the nasal cavity, but their function, together with that of the similar hollows in the cheekbones, is unclear. They may have a role in creating resonance of the voice, or they may simply make the skull lighter.

Disorders of the skull

The commonest disorder to affect the skull is sinusitis, which may follow a day or two after a cold. The nasal passages swell up so that mucus cannot drain from the sinuses, leading to infection. Pressure and inflammation cause a severe pain above or below the eye. The pain is made worse by bending or lying down. Treatment consists of analgesics, decongestants and antibiotics if necessary.

Fractures of the skull are more common in adults than in small children. In infants, the bones are more resilient and the sutures between them are fibrous and able to give to absorb some of the force of impact. If the skull of a young child is fractured it tends to form a depression rather than splintering, a bit like a ping-pong ball. This type of fracture is called a pond fracture, and as long as there is no damage of the underlying structures there is no cause for urgent treatment. The depression will usually resolve naturally.

In adults, the need for surgery will depend on the size, shape and site of the fracture. Unlike the ping-pong-ball-like skull of the infant, the skull of the adult can be likened to an eggshell. It has some resilience, but beyond this it will splinter. A heavy, localised blow will cause a depression fracture with splintering radiating out like the rays of the sun. The base

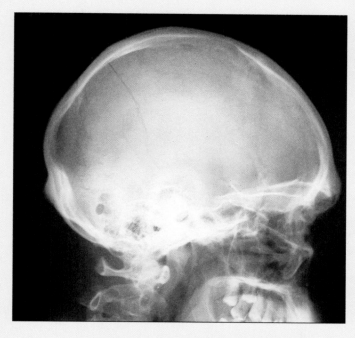

The bones of the cranium butt together at the sutures or joints. In this skull, there is a fracture (top left).

of the skull, with its nerves and blood vessels, is at particular risk from these splinters, but ridges of bone turn them away before they cause damage. Some parts of the skull, particularly the temples, are very thin and are more prone to fractures than the thicker frontal areas.

Skull fractures are no different from any other type of fracture. Given time they will heal, as long as the splinters are not completely displaced. However, they need careful attention because the brain lies so close to the skull. Open fractures rapidly lead to infection and tearing of blood vessels, causing bleeding.

SLEEP

Sleep is a natural behavioural state in which the body renews and restores itself.

During sleep, interaction with the environment decreases, but does not cease altogether. Deprived of sleep for several days, healthy volunteers function less and less ably. They are unable to concentrate, judgment becomes impaired and they become more and more irritable.

Even the immune system functions less effectively and minor infections become more common. A couple of nights of undisturbed sleep are needed to restore normality.

Sleep patterns

Normal sleep consists of at least two distinct types. The two patterns follow a cycle, with each cycle lasting about an hour and a half. Slow wave sleep, named after the characteristic brain waves on an electrical recording, alternates with REM (rapid eye movement) sleep. During REM sleep the eyes jerk, the heart races and dreams and spontaneous erections (in men) are normal. If the body is deprived of either type of sleep it will compensate at a later date.

Sleep disorders

The commonest complaint relating to sleep is insomnia. At any one time about five per cent of the adult population think they do not

Hints For A Good Night's Sleep

● Keep regular hours for going to bed and getting up.
● Take regular exercise.
● Choose a light, easily digested evening meal.
● Be content with your life, accept yourself for what you are and do not worry about sleeping.
● If you can't get off to sleep, don't lie awake – do something else, whether it is reading a (boring) novel, sorting out the washing, or having a warm, milky drink.

▶▶ SEE ALSO — Head injury, Sinusitis

MEDICAL FACT FILE

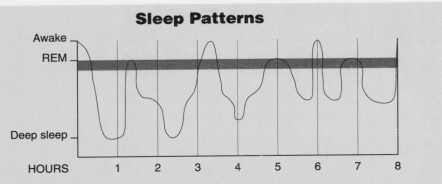

Sleep Patterns

A typical sleeping pattern shows that we plunge into a deep sleep at the beginning of the night, and that our sleep runs in a series of waves, which become shallower towards the morning. Dreaming occurs during REM sleep, when we are nearly awake.

get enough sleep. The requirement for sleep varies from individual to individual, but as a general rule it declines with age. Anything between five and 10 hours is considered normal. Long-term studies show that those who have particularly short or particularly long nights show a slightly reduced life expectancy.

Sleeping pills and alcohol induce sleep, but the type of sleep is abnormal and the sleeper rarely wakes refreshed. Occasional use of sleeping tablets is harmless but regular use, even if only for a week or two, causes compensatory changes in the brain and the patient is soon back to square one, except they may be addicted to sleeping tablets as well.

Sleepwalking, shouting out and night terrors are all common in childhood and adolescence, and may also occur in adults. The sleeper is rarely aware of the problem, and other than guarding against injury, little needs to be done. It is not necessary (and sometimes not possible) to wake a sleepwalker: simply guide them back to bed. In some adults, sleepwalking is a symptom of anxiety, and counselling may help. In some cases, sleepwalking is caused by sleeping tablets or an excess of alcohol.

SLEEP APNOEA

Obstructive sleep apnoea is a condition in which the sufferer experiences collapse of the pharynx and subsequent obstruction of the airway during sleep.

The sleeper awakes with a loud snore and never achieves a deep or satisfying sleep. The patient is profoundly tired during the day, but rarely recognises the cause.

Pressure measurements in the sleeper's pharynx are needed to clinch the diagnosis. The typical sufferer is an obese, middle-aged man who nods off during the day. It is more common in those who drink alcohol, especially in the evening.

Sleep apnoea in children
In children, sleep apnoea may be due to oversized adenoids, and the condition has been linked to sudden infant death syndrome (SIDS). It has also been shown that children who suffer sleep apnoea may grow more slowly than normal, because they do not go into deep, slow-wave sleep, which is when the growth hormone is released.

Treatment
In children, the disorder is easily treated by removing the adenoids, and possibly the tonsils at the same time.

A variety of treatments have been tried for adults, but the most successful is continuous positive airway pressure (CPAP). A tight-fitting nasal mask is worn at night and air is forced down it at a pressure that is sufficient to keep the pharynx permanently open.

In severe cases, if other forms of treatment have not worked, reconstructive surgery to strengthen the pharynx may help.

SLEEPING SICKNESS

Sleeping sickness is an infectious disease, caused by a parasite, typanosoma brucei.

The parasite is carried by the tsetse fly. Sleeping sickness takes two forms: one, found in Central and West Africa, is spread by the tsetse fly from person to person, and the other form, found in East Africa, mainly affects wild animals, but may be transmitted by the tsetse fly to humans.

Symptoms
The first symptom is a painful lump at the site of the tsetse fly bite. As the parasites multiply in the patient's bloodstream and lymph vessels, there are bouts of fever and the lymph nodes become enlarged. In the Central and West African form, the symptoms occur over a period of months or years, and eventually the fever spreads to the brain, causing headaches, confusion and inertia. Without treatment, the patient falls into a coma and dies.

In the East African form, the fever is more severe, and the disease may be fatal within months.

Treatment
The disease is diagnosed by examination of the blood, lymph or cerebrospinal fluid. Drug treatment will cure the disease, but there may be side effects, and if the disease has already spread to the brain the patient may be left with permanent brain damage.

Prevention involves eradicating the tsetse fly in areas where it is prevalent, and travellers to such parts should take precautions against being bitten.

SLEEP PARALYSIS

Sleep paralysis is a sensation of being unable to move at the time of waking up or when going to sleep.

The sensation may be accompanied by hallucinations. Sufferers are usually healthy, and since the sensation only lasts a few seconds, no treatment is necessary.

SLIPPED DISC

A slipped disc occurs when one of the discs of cartilage between the vertebrae in the spine rupture.

The condition is more correctly known as a prolapse of the disc.

➤➤ SEE ALSO — Disc prolapse, Head injury, Hygiene, Sudden infant death syndrome

SLOW VIRUS DISEASES

Slow virus diseases are a group of diseases which affect the central nervous system.

Slow virus diseases may be complications of certain diseases, or slow developments of disease following viral infection. Examples include Creutzfeld-Jacob disease (similar to BSE, the so-called mad cow disease) and brain infections which occur in some cases of HIV.

SMALL CELL CARCINOMAS

Small cell carcinomas, also known as oat cell carcinomas, are the most dangerous form of lung cancer.

About a quarter of all lung cancers are small cell carcinomas. The tumours are so virulent that by the time the disease has been diagnosed it is usually too late to prevent further spread by surgery. The cancer rapidly spreads to other parts of the body.

Treatment is usually with anticancer drugs and/or radiotherapy.

SMALLPOX

Smallpox is a severe, systemic illness with a characteristic rash similar to that of chickenpox.

As a result of a World Health Organisation vaccination programme, smallpox has now been eradicated worldwide.

Apart from two laboratory-acquired infections, the last case was reported in Somalia in 1977.

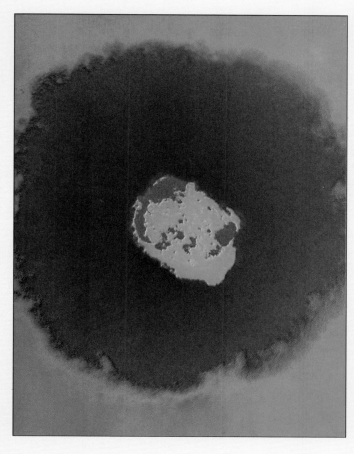

The smallpox virus was transmitted in drops of sputum or through contact with pox: it now only lives in the laboratory.

Course and symptoms

Smallpox was due to one of the pox viruses. The rash, unlike that of chickenpox, was thicker on the face, arms and legs than the trunk. Like chickenpox, the rash went through several stages, including blistering and scabbing, but, in contrast, all the spots changed together. As many as 40 per cent of patients died and many of the rest were left severely scarred. Little could be done to treat smallpox once the disease was established.

The vaccine was developed from the cowpox virus, when it was discovered that people who had been exposed to cowpox did not develop smallpox. Vaccination against smallpox, except in the case of a few laboratory staff working with viruses, is not justified.

SMEAR

A smear is a film of cells spread on a glass plate for analysis in the laboratory.

The most common example is the cervical smear test.

SMEGMA

Smegma is a build-up of sebum, secreted from the sebaceous glands, under the foreskin.

The smegma collects under uncircumcised foreskins, as a result of poor hygiene, or due to a tight foreskin which cannot be pulled back. The smegma may cause a fungal or bacterial infection to develop, and in cases of tight foreskin, a small stone may develop. To prevent the build-up of smegma, men and boys should pull back the foreskin to wash the head of their penis every day.

SMELL

The sense of smell is located in a small area about the size of a postage stamp, located high up at the back of the nose.

In dogs and other animals with a highly developed sense of smell the area is much larger. In humans, there are about 15 million receptor cells in the smell area, interspersed with mucus-producing cells. In order for us to smell a substance it needs to be dissolved in this mucous film.

Smelling smells

When smelly substances react with receptor cells they produce a minute electrical charge: how it is produced is unknown.

The human nose is remarkably sensitive. Methyl mercaptan — one of the smelliest substances known, and the one which gives garlic its odour — can be detected at levels of less than one millionth of a milligram per litre of air.

Most people can distinguish between 2,000 and 4,000 separate smells. The sense of smell is more acute in women than in men and seems to be at its height around the time of ovulation.

The smell receptors are located so far up the nose that during normal breathing most of the air passes them by. Sniffing diverts air to the receptors and greatly increases smell perception. Sniffing occurs whenever a new smell appears and is usually a reflex action we are unaware of.

Smell disorders

Disorders of smell are common. Any condition that blocks the nose will destroy

▶▶ SEE ALSO — Balanitis, BSE, Cancer, Cervical smear test, Chickenpox, HIV, Phimosis

the sense of smell. Usually it returns when the nose is cleared but in some cases it is lost for ever. An altered sense of smell may be a bizarre symptom of a frontal lobe tumour.

SNAKE BITES

Snake bites are potentially dangerous, but most people recover fully within a very short time.

The adder (a member of the Viperidae family) is the only venomous snake native to the UK, but around the world there are many other venomous Viperidae (rattlesnakes, lance-headed vipers and carpet vipers), as well as Elapidae (cobras, mambas), Atractaspididae (burrowing asps) and Hydrophiida (sea snakes).

Bites and symptoms
Members of the viper family make a double puncture wound. This causes massive local swelling followed by a generalised illness including

vomiting, sweating and shock. Viper venom affects blood clotting, and many victims bleed to death internally.

The bite of a snake from the Elapidae group, except for the cobra, does not usually cause swelling at the site of the bite. Vomiting and shock are followed by muscle weakness and paralysis.

Sea snakes kill their victims by inserting a powerful toxin that destroys muscles. This can affect the heart, lungs and kidneys.

Treatment
Most snake bites do not puncture the skin, in which case all that needs to be done is to wipe the skin to remove any venom. In more serious cases a firm bandage should be applied and the limb immobilised. Do not use a tourniquet and do not cut the bite. If the bite is severe, causing generalised illness, antivenom should be used but this carries the risk of a fatal allergic reaction.

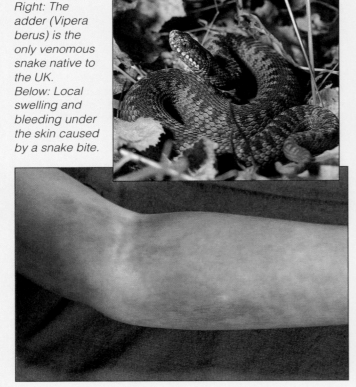

Right: The adder (Vipera berus) is the only venomous snake native to the UK. Below: Local swelling and bleeding under the skin caused by a snake bite.

SNEEZING

Sneezing is a sudden, often violent, exhalation of air through the nose and mouth as a result of irritation.

Irritation in the upper respiratory tract may be due to: an allergic reaction (as in hay fever), a simple irritant such as dust or pepper, or inflammation and secretion of mucus, caused by colds and 'flu.

Sneezes due to colds and 'flu may carry particles of mucus and moisture which are responsible for spreading viral infections.

Sneezing can be quite painful, and violent sneezes can actually cause back problems.

SNORING

Snoring occurs during sleep when inhalation causes the soft palate at the back of the mouth to vibrate noisily.

Snoring is usually due to a blockage of the nasal passages, due to a cold, 'flu or hay fever, for example, or due to enlarged adenoids. It may also occur, particularly in obese people, due to sleeping on the back.

Medications which help to clear congestion in the airways may help to relieve the problem in short-term illnesses; removal of adenoids relieves the problem in children; and re-learning sleep habits to avoid sleeping on the back is a long-term solution.

SOILING

Soiling describes the uncontrolled passing of faeces (after the age when most children are toilet trained).

Soiling may be a side

effect of a disorder such as epilepsy or be caused by emotional shock or trauma (in a serious accident, for example). There may be various medical causes, involving a lack of control of the sphincter muscles (see Incontinence). Leakage may also occur if there is severe constipation (when faecal fluid leaks around solid faeces stuck in the intestine) or diarrhoea.

Soiling may occur in children who have been toilet trained due to anxiety (about a domestic crisis or starting school, for example).

Some children may soil intentionally, defecating in secret places (behind the sofa, for example) due to a psychological problem (perhaps due to too much pressure to use a potty, or an emotional upset such as the birth of a younger sibling).

Soiling by children needs sympathetic treatment, as they usually find it very disturbing.

SOLVENT ABUSE

Solvent abuse ('sniffing glue') means getting high by breathing the volatile fumes of glue, butane, petrol or any of a whole host of chemicals readily found in the home.

Most young people never sniff; most of the remainder only experiment, but a few become habitual users. The effects of sniffing are similar to alcohol but the results are more rapid and wear off more quickly.

Sniffing kills an average of 100 young people in the UK per year. The commonest cause of death is a direct toxic effect on the heart. Exertion or fright after solvent abuse can be particularly hazardous, so if you discover a sniffer, try and stay calm and don't cause alarm. Sniffers face many other

▶▶ SEE ALSO — Colds, Incontinence, Influenza, Senses, Shock, Sleep, Sleep apnoea, Toilet training

MEDICAL FACT FILE

dangers — from fire (most solvents are highly flammable) to suffocation.

Treatment and prevention

Recognising a sniffer can be difficult. They are often moody, but so are normal teenagers. Telltale signs to watch out for include chemical smells, empty containers, mood swings, headaches and spots around the mouth.

Helping a sniffer is never very easy. The majority give up without any outside help. Local agencies can offer expert advice.

SOMATISATION

Somatisation is an example of what psychologists call an immature defence mechanism.

When psychologically fit individuals suffer a crisis, they face it and deal with it. With the psychologically immature, mental pressure can be converted into a bodily affliction which is known as somatisation. The condition used to be described as hysteria.

A somatisation disorder is a psychiatric illness that affects women more frequently than men. It usually starts in the early twenties and tends to run in families. It consists of recurrent and multiple complaints for which medical help is sought.

Symptoms are vague, such as nausea, malaise, heavy periods and so on. Despite intensive investigation, a medical cause cannot be found.

The condition is difficult to treat as the victim often denies that she has an emotional problem, even to herself. Support and finding a sympathetic practitioner are all that can be done.

SOMATOTYPE

A person's somatotype is their physical build, which according to some classifications, can suggest certain personal characteristics.

There have been various attempts to relate psychological make-up to physical build, known as constitutional theory.

Early development

The Greek physician, Galen (120 – 200 AD), identified four basic character types (sanguine, melancholic, choleric and phlegmatic). Earlier this century, a German psychiatrist, Ernst Kretchmer, identified three different body types, each prone to particular disorders. Stocky people were prone to manic depression, slender types were more likely to have schizoid personalities (including schizophrenia), while athletic types were more likely to be mentally healthy (although they may be deliquent).

Somatotype theory

The American psychologist, W.H. Sheldon, (1898 – 1970), described three somatotypes: ectomorphic (tall and willowy), endomorphic (large build, but not athletic) and mesomorphic (a medium, athletic build). He linked these with different types of personality (see below).

SORE THROAT

A sore throat is a raw feeling in the throat which is particularly noticeable when swallowing.

Sore throats are a very common symptom, often accompanied by other symptoms such as a runny nose, cough and general malaise.

Causes

Sore throat is often the first symptom of a cold or 'flu, glandular fever, chickenpox, measles or mumps. It is also caused by pharyngitis, tonsillitis or laryngitis.

Sore throat may also be caused by bacterial infection — usually due to a member of the streptococcus family

Shapes And Psyche

Sheldon's somatotypes related the physical build to certain character traits. The theory describes tendencies, rather than having any scientific basis.

ENDOMORPH
Heavy, with large frame and poorly-developed muscles; sociable, loving 'earth mother' type.

ECTOMORPH
Tall, willowy figure, with light bones and poorly-developed muscles; sensitive, self-conscious, restrained and shy.

MESOMORPH
Well-proportioned with well-developed muscles; physically active, adventurous and aggressive.

▶▶ SEE ALSO — Hypochondria

— in which case it is often known as strep throat.

Treatment

Sore throats due to viral infections do not usually need medical attention. They can be eased with aspirin (for adults), and soothing throat lozenges. Anti-inflammatory sprays are available on prescription. Sore throat due to bacteria should be treated with antibiotics. If a rash develops, consult a doctor.

SPASM

A spasm is an involuntary movement due to a sudden contraction of a muscle.

The commonest manifestation of muscle spasm is hiccups, when the diaphragm contracts to force air out of the chest. Muscle cramps (usually in the calf muscles) are also a form of spasm, as are nervous tics and twitches.

Such symptoms are not normally a sign of a serious underlying disorder, though they may be related to chemical balance in the body and/or anxiety.

Spasms of the small airways of the lungs are the cause of asthma.

Symptom of disorder

Some spasms are a symptom of a disorder of the central nervous system or a muscular disorder. Spasms also feature in tetanus, rabies and strychnine poisoning.

SPEECH

Speech is the use of vocalised sound symbols to convey ideas from one person to another.

Speech is an extremely complicated process that relies on a large number of complex activities.

Speech processes

From an anatomical viewpoint, the production of speech is simple. Air is forced out of the lungs and through the larynx. The vocal cords vibrate and the noise produced is chopped into words by the tongue and mouth. At a higher level the production of speech is under the control of the brainstem which receives its commands from the motor centres of the brain. In turn, these motor areas are under the influence of the language cortex and the speech centre. The language centre acts as a dictionary and the speech centre acts as a control centre to coordinate the muscles and nerves of speech production.

Disorders

The diagnosis and treatment of speech disorders is mainly the province of speech therapists, but many other specialists may be involved, according to the cause of the problem.

A psychiatric patient may have a speech disorder in that the ideas expressed are so fanciful that no-one can understand them, but this is clearly a case for a psychiatrist. Cancer of the larynx can cause speech problems, but this is clearly a case for a surgeon (in the first instance). Similarly, children who have problems with speech may need treatment from an ear specialist, if reduced levels of hearing are causing the problem.

Speech abnormalities are generally divided into those affecting adults and those confined to children. On the whole, children's problems are primarily a failure in development while adults' disorders have more complicated causes such as strokes.

Speech therapy for children consists of individual and group activities designed to identify and practise difficult sounds. Parents are encouraged to join in.

Disruption of the language area, by injury or stroke, causes problems with the content of speech. The patient speaks at a normal rate with a normal rhythm, but the content is nonsense. Damage to the speech area produces a disorder in which speech is slow and halting, but the words are comprehensible. Injuries to the muscles and nerves of the face and tongue cause slurring of the words. Injury to the larynx or soft palate causes an inability to form certain sounds.

Childhood disorders

The commonest speech disorder in children is language delay, in which the three-year old speaks like a two-year-old, and so on. It is often a feature of mental handicap and all development may be slow. In the second group of disorders, control of speech is normal but there is a problem with intelligibility. It may be due to deafness, either total or partial, which may be treatable.

Developing Speech

In normal children, there is a definite pattern in the development of speech.

NEWBORN BABY Produces different cries for different reasons: hunger, fear, discomfort, anger.

UP TO 1 YEAR Learns to distinguish various sounds, and practises them in an apparently meaningless babble. Usually recognises own name, and by first birthday is able to say a few words (which are often recognised only by the child's parents).

1 – 2 YEARS Increases the number of sounds produced rapidly, imitating the sounds heard.

2 – 3 YEARS Begins to learn better control of the speech mechanisms and begins to develop complete sentences, rather than just mimicking sounds.

3 – 5 YEARS Develops a sense of grammar, which may actually cause errors in speech (for example, having learned that when talking about things in the past the verb ends with '-ed', there is a tendency to put an '-ed' or irregular verbs, such as 'goed' or 'eated').

SEE ALSO — Colds, Cramp, Deafness, Development, Influenza, Laryngitis, Larynx, Pharyngitis, Streptococcal infections, Tonsillitis

SPHEROCYTOSIS

Spherocytosis is a rare cause of anaemia.

In normal individuals, the red blood cells are flattened, rather like ring doughnuts. In spherocytosis the wall of the red cell is weakened and the cell swells to form a sphere.

Inherited symptoms

The condition is inherited as a dominant gene. If one parent is affected, half the children will be. The abnormal red cells are broken down by the spleen, often when they are only a few days old. This leads to anaemia and consequent lassitude, but the main symptom is usually jaundice. In some cases the condition maybe mistaken for recurrent hepatitis. Gallstones are more common in spherocytosis sufferers than in the general population. The condition may escape detection until the patient suffers an acute infection of one sort or another. Under these conditions a 'haemolytic crisis' may occur with severe anaemia.

Treatment

The symptoms can be relieved surgically by removing the spleen, but the underlying defect cannot be cured.

SPHINCTER

A sphincter is a ring of muscle which controls the flow of fluids and/or solids through a natural opening or passage.

The anal sphincter, for example, holds the faeces in the rectum, and is under voluntary control to a major extent. The pyloric sphincter, at the exit of the stomach, keeps the partly digested food in the stomach until it is ready to leave. This process is involuntary.

Sphincter problems

In some patients, sphincters may have to be cut open in order to reduce constriction. This operation, known as a sphincterectomy, may have to be performed on sphincters in the digestive tract — to allow passage of stones, for example — or on the anal sphincter as treatment for an anal fissure.

Artificial sphincters have been created in some patients, using part of the ileum, to give control in cases of faecal incontinence.

SPINA BIFIDA

Spina bifida is a relatively common and serious congenital abnormality in which the developing spine

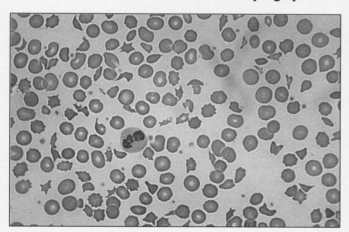

In spherocytosis, the red blood cells are round, rather than flat, due to a weakening of the cell walls.

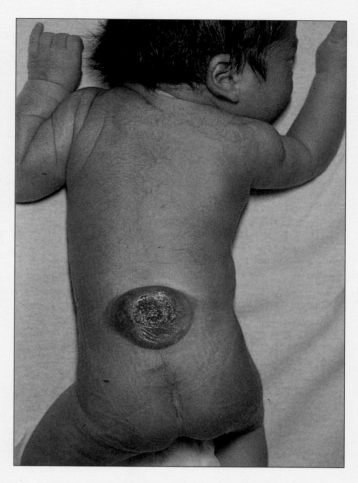

In this newborn baby with spina bifida, the spinal cord is exposed in the lumbar region.

fails to fuse around, and protect, the delicate spinal cord.

In the normal embryo, the primitive spine and spinal cord are flat but they roll in on themselves to form a solid nerve inside a hollow tube. This normally occurs on the 27th day of embryonic life. Failure leads to spina bifida. The severity varies from the very mild, symptomless spina bifida occulta to the devastating meningo-myelocele in which the spinal cord is laid bare. It is more common in Caucasians than Negroes; it occurs more frequently in the lower socio-economic groups; and particularly young or particularly old mothers seem to be more at risk. Couples who have had an affected child are at a tenfold risk in subsequent pregnancies.

Meningomyelocele

The very severe form, meningomyelocele, is also the most common — there are about 2,000 cases a year in the UK. The spinal cord can be exposed at any level but it usually occurs in the lumbar region. The baby is born with a raw wound over the base of the spine. The spinal cord is open to the air, or at best, only covered by a thin membrane. The exposed cord is at risk from infection, injury or drying out.

In addition to the spinal problem there is usually an associated problem in the brain. A tongue of tissue grows down the spinal cord and blocks the free drainage of spinal fluid. Untreated, the build-up of fluid causes the brain and the head to swell. Unless the pressure is released, permanent damage will follow.

» SEE ALSO — Anaemia, Incontinence

MEDICAL FACT FILE

Several physical problems arise as a result of meningomyelocele. The legs are partially or completely paralysed and as a result the feet turn inwards and the hips dislocate. The nerves to the bladder and bowel are damaged and the bladder swells, leading to incontinence and kidney damage. The emotional pressure both on the child and the family are enormous and this can lead to almost as many problems as the physical damage.

Treatment

If the spinal cord is left open, infection and desiccation lead to death within days. A few years ago, doctors operated on all children with open spina bifida, but most now accept that this was misguided. An affected child born these days is usually transferred to a specialist centre where an assessment can be made by the staff and parents. Babies with severe paralysis or multiple associated abnormalities are not usually operated upon.

Some children may be helped by neurosurgery to relieve pressure on the brain, orthopaedic surgery to relocate the hips and urological surgery to control the bladder. Even with this formidable surgical burden, the majority are still handicapped for life.

Meningocele

Meningocele is a less serious form of spina bifida. Whilst there is still a bulge of spinal material, the actual cord is protected by the spinal canal. It is much less serious than open spina bifida, but also much less common. It usually occurs in the upper spine and there is no associated paralysis.

Causes and prevention

The cause of spina bifida is still unknown, though it appears likely that a relative lack of vitamins before conception may be responsible. A good diet before pregnancy is known to reduce the risk.

Spina bifida may be diagnosed by amniocentesis or an ultrasound scan during pregnancy. Most women have a blood test (alpha-fetoprotein) at about the 14th week of pregnancy to screen for the disorder.

SPINE AND SPINAL CORD

The spine, or vertebral column, is the central pillar that supports the body.

The spine takes the weight of the head, neck and trunk, and transmits it, via the legs and feet to the ground. It also houses and protects the delicate spinal cord.

Structure

The spine is made up of 33 vertebrae, though some of the lower ones are fused together. The vertebrae are separated by tough, fibrous wedges called intervertebral discs. This arrangement allows for greater flexibility than a single solid column would, and the slight 'give' in the intervertebral discs means that they act as a shock absorber between the ground and the skull.

The vertebrae are organised into five groups. Each group is different but there are basic similarities between them all. The typical vertebra has a solid body with a rounded, backward-facing arch. The body supports the vertebra above and the arches form a tube around the spinal cord. Each vertebra has several bony projections. These act as anchor points for the muscles and tendons that hold us upright.

Groups of vertebrae

The cervical vertebrae, of which there are seven, make up the neck. Compared with the rest of the spine the

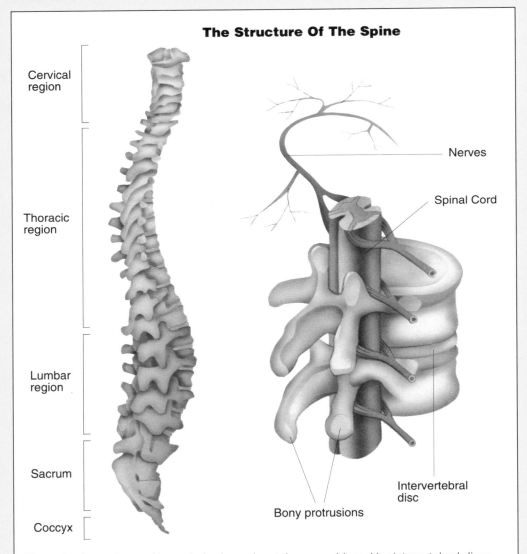

The Structure Of The Spine

Cervical region

Thoracic region

Lumbar region

Sacrum

Coccyx

Nerves

Spinal Cord

Intervertebral disc

Bony protrusions

The spine is made up of irregularly shaped vertebrae, cushioned by intervetebral discs. The spinal cord runs up through the vertebrae, and nerves branch to all parts of the body.

cervical vertebrae are less robust, mainly because they only have to bear the weight of the head and neck. This can lead to problems if the spine is subjected to trauma.

The twelve thoracic vertebrae are joined to the ribs as well as to the vertebrae above and below. They form a near rigid column with very little side-to-side movement.

Most of the flexibility of the spine is concentrated in the five lumbar vertebrae. Because of this mobility, the lumbar spine is the commonest site for wear and tear and muscle strains.

Although there are five bones in the sacrum, they are fused together to form a solid mass that has sufficient strength to articulate with the pelvis. Below the sacrum are the four bones of the coccyx, most of which are fused together. This stump, little bigger than a thimble, is all that remains of what, in our ancestors, was a tail.

Formation

In the foetus the spine has one continuous curve from head to hip. As the baby develops, the shape of the spine alters until, in the adult, it resembles an S with a tail. In a pregnant woman, the flexibility of the lumbar spine increases as the pregnancy progresses, in order to maintain the centre of balance. In old age, the intervertebral discs wear away and the spine reverts to one continuous curve.

Man is unique amongst the vertebrates in adopting an upright posture. Unfortunately, the spine has not evolved as much as the brain, and in its present form, it is better suited to a four-legged animal. Man's unnatural posture gives rise to a number of back problems.

Back disorders

Backache is very common. In the majority of cases, no specific cause can be found and the patient is described as having a back strain. Two main factors make back strain more likely: weak muscles or a structurally abnormal back. Weak muscles may be

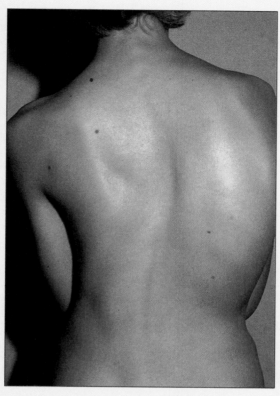

Deformities of the spine may be congenital or develop with growth: in this child, the spine bends to one side, a condition known as scoliosis.

caused by a lack of exercise or by an illness such as 'flu. If a weak back is called upon to exert itself, muscle damage and pain are the likely outcome.

Minor degrees of structural abnormality are very common. Any irregularity of the spine throws excess stresses on to other segments and makes back strain more likely.

Back strain may be acute or chronic. Acute lower backache (lumbago) may be due to a specific condition such as a slipped (prolapsed) disc, but more often it is due to muscle spasm. In normal circumstances, muscle spasm helps protect an injured joint but in the case of the spine the spasm often causes more pain than the underlying injury. Pain is worsened by sitting or standing and eased by lying. The victim's back is usually rigid and lifting the legs causes severe pain. Acute

back pain usually responds to a few days' rest, but this must be strictly enforced. Physiotherapy to relax the muscles and relieve the pain should begin when the patient is mobile. Back strengthening exercises may prevent the problem from recurring. Analgesics and muscle relaxants such as valium may cure the pain, but in the long term physio-therapy is more important. Manipulation of the spine is an effective pain reliever, but because of the slight risk of nerve damage it should not be attempted immediately after an injury.

In the longer term

Chronic backache often follows an episode of lumbago but instead of clearing up, the pain remains as a dull ache. In most cases of chronic backache an x-ray is advisable.

Occasionally the pain can be due to an infection, a tumour or some other serious condition. If there is evidence of nerve entrapment, such as pain or pins and needles in the leg, the doctor may want to inject dye around the spinal cord to check that the spinal canal is of a normal size.

Treatment of chronic backache is difficult, both for the patient and the doctor. In the first instance, treatment is aimed at strengthening the back muscles, thereby protecting the site of weakness. If this fails, external support in the form of a corset may be prescribed. If the pain is

Spinal Cord

The spinal cord is a continuation of the white matter of the brain.

In the adult, the spinal cord terminates a couple of inches below the bottom rib. In the young child it is relatively longer. Along the whole length of the spinal cord, 31 pairs of spinal nerves are attached. These spinal nerves leave the spine between the vertebrae. They provide nervous impulses from the neck downwards. Most of the nervous impulses reaching the spinal cord are transmitted upwards to the brain but some enter simple reflex pathways that provide near-instantaneous responses.

The spinal cord is well-protected by the spine but, especially in the case of a fracture dislocation, it can be disrupted, leading to various degrees of paralysis. Paralysis may also be caused by compression from within the spine itself, usually due to a tumour of the tissue covering the spinal cord.

severe and x-rays have revealed a structural weakness, surgery may be needed. Depression is common and anti-depressants and psycho-therapy can be as rewarding as standard medical treatment.

A broken back

Fractures of the spine may occur as the result of direct trauma (a blow in a fight or a car accident, for example) or as the result of downward compression forces. The latter is common in old ladies with osteoporosis. The body of one or more vertebrae collapses to form a wedge shape. The spinal cord is usually safe but the spine takes on a forward curve known as a dowager's hump.

The most severe form of injury is a fracture dislocation. Not only is the body of the vertebra damaged but the bone is displaced forwards, compressing the spinal cord. The severity of nerve damage depends on the site of the fracture: the higher up the spine the more serious the damage.

Treatment of a fracture dislocation is dependent on the degree of neurological damage. In all spinal injuries the most important first aid principle is not the make things worse. If circumstance permit the casualty should remain motionless until skilled help arrives. If movement is essential, great care should be taken not to bend the spine.

SPLEEN

The spleen is part of the lymphatic system. It is located under the ribs on the left side.

The normal adult spleen is about the size of an apple. Its main functions are to filter, store and sometimes create new red blood cells.

Functions of the spleen

Normal red cells, which are pliable, pass through the spleen easily but old or damaged ones are filtered out. In times of crisis the spleen can also produce new red blood cells. About one third of the body's platelets are stored in the spleen, ready for rapid mobilisation should they be needed.

Disorders

An enlarged spleen may be felt under the left ribs, but in some conditions particularly disease of the bone marrow, the spleen may be so swollen that it reaches below the tummy button.

A moderately enlarged spleen may be a sign of infection with bacteria, viruses or parasites. It is a common sign of malaria. Inflammatory conditions such as rheumatoid arthritis, cancers such as leukemia, and liver disease can also cause an enlarged spleen. Whatever the cause, a large spleen can result in a condition called hyper-splenism. In hypersplenism the spleen performs its various tasks too well. The result is anaemia and jaundice. Treatment depends on the underlying cause but in severe cases surgical removal of the spleen may be needed.

Withering away of the spleen as a result of multiple areas of oxygen starvation is commonly seen in sickle cell disease. The spleen also shrinks in coeliac disease and ulcerative colitis.

Splenectomy

The spleen is a relatively soft organ and easily damaged by trauma. In most cases a damaged spleen cannot be repaired and it has to be removed. Splenectomy, as the operation is called, is a simple matter but there can be side effects. In the short term the platelet count rises dramatically so much so that clots may form. The long-term risk is developing infection, particularly those due to bacteria and malaria. All children who have undergone splenectomy receive regular penicillin, as they are far more susceptible to infection than adults.

SPLINT

A splint is a device to hold part of the body immobile during the healing process.

Splints may be applied as a first-aid measure, to hold a limb or digit, or even the back, in a fixed position until the patient can be taken to hospital. In some conditions, such as carpal tunnel syndrome (where fingers tingle due to pressure on a nerve in the wrist) splints may be worn at night to stretch the ligaments which cause the pressure. Splints may also take the form of body jackets, which are used to correct spinal deformities.

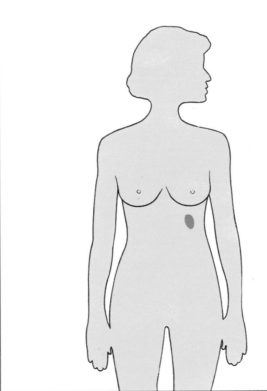

Location Of The Spleen

A Quick Splint

If someone injures their leg badly, what can you do to prevent further damage?

Not all of us have proper, medically-approved splints to hand, but you can help the victim by laying them on their back and binding their legs together. The good leg thus acts as a splint for the injured leg. Pad the patient between the legs (a jacket or rolled-up blanket will do) and then bind the legs and feet together using bandages or strips of sheeting.

Do not delay in calling an ambulance or getting medical help.

➤➤ SEE ALSO — Coeliac disease, Kyphosis, Lordosis, Osteoporosis, Rheumatoid arthritis, Sickle cell disease, Ulcerative colitis

SPONDYLITIS

Spondylitis is an inflammation of the joints in the spine, between the vertebrae.

The condition is most common in older women, since it is often caused by osteoarthritis. It may also be caused by rheumatoid arthritis or ankylosing spondylitis. Rarely, it is due to bacterial infection.

SPONDYLOLITHESIS

Spondylolithesis covers a group of conditions in which one of the vertebrae has slipped forward on another.

Spondylolithesis may follow an injury or it may be due to an abnormality of the spine itself.

Spondylolithesis causes low back pain, often precipitated by some trivial injury. Spinal movements are painful and restricted. The patient has a characteristic 'duck-like' waddle.

Surgical treatment may be needed, especially if pain is severe or there are signs of nerve irritation. The dislocated vertebrae are fused together using a bone graft taken from the hip.

SPRAIN

A sprain is an injury to a joint involving damage to the ligaments around it.

This type of injury is a result of a sudden, forceful movement, such as turning the sole of the foot inwards, so that the weight of the body is misplaced on to the side of the foot or the ankle.

The force causes a sudden, sharp pain, followed by swelling. The joint cannot be moved without causing further pain.

Treatment involves rest,

Bandaging A Sprained Ankle

A cold compress and careful bandaging may help to ease the pain of a sprained ankle.

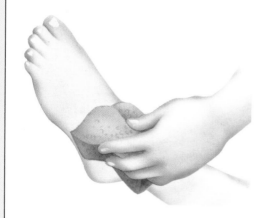

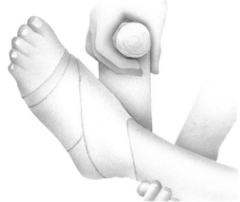

1. Cool down the inflammation by applying an ice pack or a cloth or sponge soaked in cold water.

2. Using a crepe bandage, wrap it twice around the foot and then around the ankle, allowing a generous overlap.

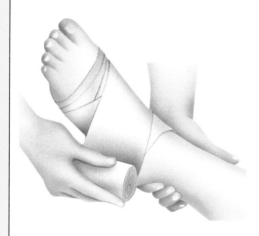

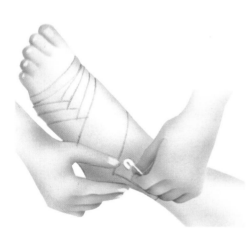

3. Continue wrapping in a figure of eight, around the foot and the ankle, until you have completely bound the ankle.

4. Secure the bandage with a safety pin. Rest with the foot up and seek medical attention if a fracture is suspected.

to give the ligaments a chance to repair themselves, and a cold compress to reduce the swelling. Bandaging (see above) will help to support the ankle while it heals. It is advisable to consult a doctor, who may suggest an x-ray to eliminate the possibility of a fracture.

Once the joint is free of acute pain, it must be exercised gently in order to restore mobility.

SQUINT

A child has a squint if both eyes do not look in the same direction at the same time.

The condition, sometimes known as strabismus, is very common. In one study, as many as 15 per cent of pre-school children were affected. The squint may be convergent (one or both eyes directed too far inwards) or divergent (an eye directed outwards).

Very small babies have no control over the way they direct their gaze and in the newborn a squint is considered normal. Older children may appear to have a squint due to prominent skin folds around the nose.

Diagnosis

To detect a squint, the child is encouraged to look at an object held in various positions. In the commonest form of squint, the eye has the same degree of

▶▶ SEE ALSO — Fracture, Osteoarthritis, Rheumatoid arthritis, Strain

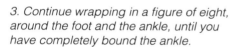

MEDICAL FACT FILE

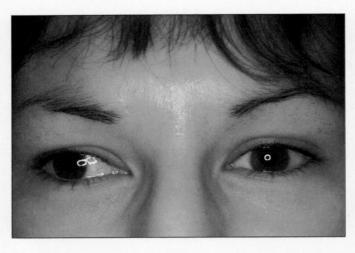

This young woman has a divergent squint: one eye 'wanders' outwards. The brain tends to suppress information from the diverging eye, so that it becomes weaker.

abnormality in all directions. Also known as a lazy eye, if it is not treated it will not improve — and may go blind — since the child will use the correctly directed eye and suppress the information from the squinting eye.

Treatment

The condition may be corrected in some cases by covering the normal eye, so that the child learns to use, and focus correctly, with the lazy eye. In some cases, surgery may be necessary.

Squints in later life

In later life, squint may occur as a result of certain brain disorders, and may be a symptom of diabetes, multiple sclerosis, stroke or an overactive thyroid.

STAPHYLOCOCCAL INFECTIONS

The staphylococcal group of bacteria are probably the most important micro-organisms associated with humans.

Some of these bacteria cause disease, some live in harmony with us and others cause illness in certain conditions.

Routes of infection

Everybody has some staphylococcal bacteria on their skin or in their nose. If the body's defences are working properly they can usually be kept in check. However if the skin is broached they can cause boils, carbuncles and impetigo.

Food handlers with staphylococcal skin infections may easily contaminate cooked foods, giving rise to a severe form of gastroenteritis.

If staphylococci enter the bloodstream they may settle in the heart or brain. Infections of either of these organs can be fatal without antibiotic treatment.

In the lungs, especially after a bout of 'flu, they can cause abscesses or a rapidly fatal pneumonia.

Staphylococcal infections often complicate compound fractures. Once established, staphylococcal bone infection is very difficult to treat.

Treatment

Most staphylococcal infections respond rapidly to standard antibiotics but there is a strain emerging that is resistant to all but the strongest antibiotic.

STERILISATION

Sterilisation is the surgical achievement of infertility.

Sterilisation is available to both men and women, for couples who have completed their family or individuals who have personal or medical reasons for not having children.

Male sterilisation

Male sterilisation, known as vasectomy, is performed by cutting the vas deferens, the tubes that carry sperm from the testicles to the penis. Male sterilisation is simple to perform and only requires a local anaesthetic.

Bruising can be a problem, causing pain for some days after the operation, but serious side effects are rare.

The operation has no effect on the man's ability to ejaculate, it simply removes the sperm from the semen. However, sperm may still be present for up to three months after the operation, so a final sperm count is essential before the 'all clear' can be given.

Female sterilisation

Female sterilisation involves the blockage of the fallopian tubes, to prevent eggs travelling down from the ovaries. The operation may be performed through the vagina, but it is usually performed using a laparoscope. The fallopian tubes may be cut, tied, clipped or burnt. The operation may be performed on an out-patient basis, but in some cases a short hospital stay is necessary.

The menstrual cycle continues as normal after sterilisation, but sperm is unable to travel up the tubes to fertilise the egg.

Hysterectomy operations also involve sterilisation, but they are only performed if there is a disorder of the female reproductive organs.

Outlook

No method of sterilisation is 100 per cent effective. Vasectomy carries a failure rate of one in 1000 and female sterilisation a rate between one in 300 and one in 1000, depending on the type of operation used. There is a greater chance of ectopic pregnancy among those for whom sterilisation has not been effective.

Sterilisation is easy to perform but difficult to reverse. Assessment should involve both partners and once performed sterilisation should be regarded as permanent.

STEROID DRUGS

Steroid drugs are a group of chemicals which are formulated to resemble certain steroids produced naturally in the body.

One of the most commonly prescribed steroids is hydrocortisone, an anti-inflammatory agent, which is similar to the corticosteroids produced naturally in the adrenal glands. Another example is synthetic aldosterone, which is prescribed for those suffering from Addison's disease, in which the production of aldosterone is reduced.

The sex hormones are also steroids which can be manufactured synthetically. For example, oestrogen, used in the combined contraceptive pill and hormone replacement therapy, is a steroid drug.

The most notorious steroids are anabolic steroids, which contain synthetic testosterone, the male hormone. Originally developed to treat male problems such as impotence, they are also now taken by many sportspeople, in order to take advantage of the properties they have in

➤➤ SEE ALSO — Bacteria, Fertilisation, Streptococcal infections, Vasectomy

helping to develop muscles. The testosterone also promotes aggressive competition. Such use has been banned by most official sporting bodies, not only because it gives those who have taken them an unfair advantage but also because they may have permanent side effects.

Controlled administration

Different steroids may have different side effects, but some could be serious so they are carefully monitored by doctors. Some anti-inflammatory hydrocortisone creams, for example, prescribed for skin allergies and eczema, should only be administered in very small amounts, for short lengths of time, as they may lead to a thinning of the skin. Oestrogens may increase the risk of thrombosis, and anabolic steroids may cause acne, oedema, liver damage and adrenal gland problems.

STIFF NECK

A stiff neck is the term used to describe a painful neck with limited movements.

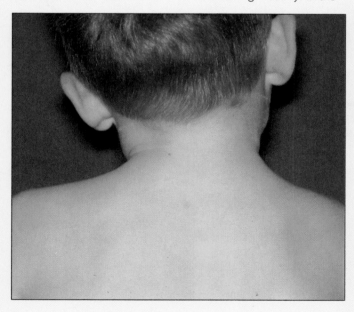

The muscles on one side of the neck have gone into spasm so that the head can only be held at an awkward angle.

Most stiff necks are due to muscle spasm, either as a result of adopting an unusual posture during sleeping or some form of trauma. Muscle spasm causes the neck to be held tilted and slightly twisted. This spasm is a protective mechanism designed to guard the neck from further injury. Occasionally, an acute stiff neck may be due to a prolapsed disc.

Stiff necks usually respond very well to physiotherapy and local heat to reduce the spasm. Analgesics may be required for the first day or two.

STILLBIRTH

A stillborn infant is one that does not draw breath after delivery.

With modern intensive care, this is a slightly outdated definition, as any baby in this position would now be ventilated artificially. Doctors prefer the term 'perinatal mortality', which includes all stillbirths as well as all deaths in the first weeks of life.

The perinatal mortality rate is falling steadily. In the UK for example, in 1940, 40 babies in every 1000 were stillborn or died soon after birth. By 1986, this figure had dropped to about 10 per 1000. Stillbirths account for about half the perinatal mortality rate.

Causes

Amongst the stillborn, many have severe congenital abnormalities that would be incompatible with life. Most of the other stillbirths are due to oxygen starvation during delivery or birth trauma. (The two are often connected).

The stillbirth rate is certain to drop further as better screening tests and more accurate scans detect gross abnormalities at an early stage in pregnancy. Reducing the risk of birth trauma and oxygen starvation requires extra monitoring and a readiness to act swiftly (to perform a Caesarean, for example). Unfortunately this tends to 'medicalise' normal deliveries and may not be in the mother's best interests.

STIMULANT DRUGS

Stimulant drugs work on the central nervous system to increase alertness and reduce drowsiness.

Stimulants (including caffeine and amphetamines) work by increasing the production of certain chemicals released by the nerve endings.

They are used to treat excessive drowsiness, and have also been found to be helpful in treating hyperactivity. In the past, amphetamines were used as slimming pills, to suppress the appetite, but this is no longer advised because of their severe side effects. Similarly, the use of amphetamines in sports is banned by official sports bodies.

Side effects

The side effects of stimulants include shaking, palpitations, sleeping problems, hallucinations and paranoid delusions.

In the long term, larger quantities of a particular stimulant may be needed to produce the same effect, and prolonged use of amphetamines may lead to drug dependency.

Respiratory Stimulants

There is a group of stimulants which work by stimulating the part of the brain which is responsible for controlling respiration.

This group of stimulants is very different from stimulants which work on the central nervous system. It is used for emergency treatment of respiratory failure, both in newborn children and in adults with heart disorders.

STINGS

There is a wide range of animals and plants which sting.

As well as the familiar wasps and bees, there are other stinging insects, scorpions, and sea creatures such as some types of fish, jellyfish, sea anemones and corals. Nettles are a common stinging plant, but there are others which may produce an allergic reaction, such as poison ivy (in the USA).

Treatment

Scorpion stings should be treated professionally: some are no more of a problem than a bee sting, but others may need strong painkillers

⯈⯈ SEE ALSO — Caesarean section, Drug dependence

MEDICAL FACT FILE

and antivenom.

Jellyfish stings may produce no more than an itchy rash, but in severe cases (Portuguese men-of-war, for example) there may be a strong reaction, with vomiting and breathing difficulties. Analgesics (such as aspirin or paracetamol) may be adequate, but hospital admittance is required in severe cases.

The rashes produced by stinging plants are best treated with calamine lotion, once the affected skin has been washed to ensure no traces of the plant remain.

STOMACH

The stomach is a muscular bag, situated in the upper abdomen.

The stomach has several functions but primarily it acts as a food reservoir, allowing us to eat large, infrequent meals. Whilst in the stomach, food is churned and mixed to a uniform consistency. Enzymes start the digestive processes but the majority of foodstuffs are actually absorbed in the small intestine. A major function of the stomach is the secretion of acid, partly to help in the digestive process and partly to kill the millions of germs we eat with every meal. In the small hours of the morning, when the acids secreted are not buffered by food, the acidity (pH) of the stomach juice is close to that of battery acid. The walls of the stomach are protected from this acid by the secretion of a thick coat of sticky mucus.

Recent research has shown that the stomach is also an endocrine gland. It produces several hormones that have effects upon the whole body and the digestive system in particular.

The stomach has two valves: one at the top where it joins the gullet; and one below where it joins the small intestine. The valve at the top of the stomach protects the delicate gullet from the corrosive stomach acid. The lower, pyloric valve regulates the passage of partially digested food into the small intestine. Stomach emptying depends on several factors. In particular, fatty foods delay the passage of food into the small intestine.

STOMACH CANCER

Stomach cancer may develop from ulcers or from previously healthy tissue.

In the older age group in particular, stomach ulcers may turn cancerous, but most cancers arise in previously healthy tissue. Stomach cancer is very common. In the UK, one in 5000 males are affected every year. In some parts of the world, the incidence is even higher. It is higher in lower socio-economic groups and affects more men than women. Many dietary links have been suggested, including spices, alcohol and nitrate ingestion.

Symptoms

The commonest symptom is pain below the breastbone. Clinically, this pain is indistinguishable from that of peptic ulceration and most doctors would wish to investigate all over 35s with severe indigestion.

Stomach cancer causes rapid weight loss.

Outlook

At least 50 per cent of patients have a tumour that can be felt on abdominal examination by the time the diagnosis is made. Most tumours are inoperable because they have developed so rapidly by the time they are diagnosed, and the chances of being alive five years after diagnosis are as little as five per cent.

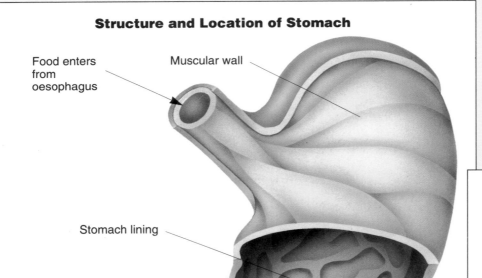

Structure and Location of Stomach

Food enters from oesophagus

Muscular wall

Stomach lining

Food passes to small intestine

Pyloric valve

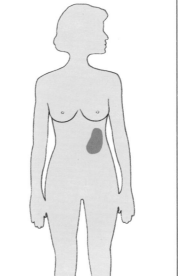

»» SEE ALSO — Insects, Intestine, Nettle rash, Swallowing

STOMACH DISORDERS

The acid balance in the stomach makes it a particularly common site for pain and disorders.

The commonest disorder is gastritis. More serious (and painful) are ulcers.

Gastritis

Gastritis is an inflammation of the lining of the stomach. Acute gastritis is usually a result of consuming spicy food or alcohol, which irritates the stomach lining and causes excessive acid production. Stress also leads to excess acid. In some cases the inflammation is so severe that the stomach lining is destroyed and ulcers form. These ulcers are common after severe physical stress such as a heart attack and usually heal without scarring.

Symptoms include pain below the breastbone, indigestion and vomiting. In most cases a simple antacid such as magnesium trisilicate mixture, available over the counter from chemists, does the trick.

If the condition is long term (chronic gastritis), there

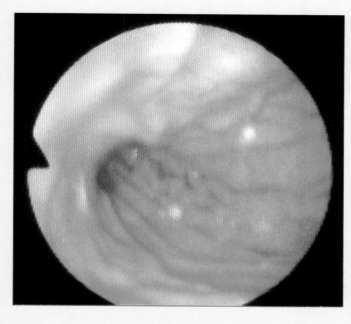

Using fibre optics, it is possible to see right into the stomach, in order to diagnose gastric disorders.

may be few symptoms. Chronic gastritis is less common than the acute form, and is usually only diagnosed incidentally during an endoscopic examination of the gut when diagnosing other disorders. It may be due to an auto-immune disorder, chemical irritants such as aspirin, or a bacterial irritation.

Stomach ulcers

Stomach ulcers are the second commonest type of peptic (or acid-produced) ulcers. (Most peptic ulcers occur in the small intestine.) Some patients with stomach ulcers simply produce too much acid, but the majority have normal or even low acid secretion.

The fault seems to lie in the protective layer of mucus. Once this is broken down the gastric juices quickly burn into the stomach wall. Although still not proven, most doctors believe that infection is the root cause of most ulcers. Stomach ulcers run in families and are much commoner in some parts of the world than others.

The main feature of stomach ulceration is pain, often worse with food. The pain is often severe and is situated just below the breastbone. Nausea is a common complaint, but patients rarely vomit. If they do, the pain is usually eased. Antacids always help the pain, if only for a few minutes.

Stomach ulcers are easily diagnosed using a gastroscope, a flexible telescope that can quickly examine every corner of the stomach. In some areas of

the country, access to gastroscopy is limited and doctors still have to rely on a barium meal and x-rays to make the diagnosis.

Most stomach ulcers respond to acid-suppressing drugs such as Tagamet, but those that don't, usually heal on a combination of acid suppression and antibiotics. Many will recur unless the patient modifies her life style.

STRAIN

Strain is the damage of muscles due to sudden or heavy exertion.

The damage takes the form of tearing or stretching of the muscle fibres, and causes pain, swelling and muscle spasm. There is usually internal bleeding, and a bruise appears a day or so after the injury.

Treatment

Treatment involves applying ice packs to reduce swelling, and the injured muscles may be bound or strapped up to support the muscles as they heal. It is essential to rest the damaged muscles to avoid further damage. Pain relievers will help to ease the pain. Once the pain has subsided, gentle exercise and physiotherapy are important to get the muscles working again.

In order to avoid muscle strain in sporting activities, it is important to do warming-up exercises.

STRANGULATION

Strangulation occurs if the circulation to an organ is cut off, usually as a result of external pressure.

Pressure on the carotid artery as it passes through the neck will cause the brain to become starved of oxygen within a few seconds. Loss of

Stomach Pump

In some cases it is necessary to drain the stomach and wash it out with water – a gastric lavage.

Patients may have to have their stomach pumped as a result of taking poisons – either accidentally or intentionally (in the form of a drug overdose, for example). The patient is placed face downwards, with her head below the level of her stomach. A tube is passed into the throat and down the gullet to the stomach. The open end of the tube has a funnel attached to it, which is held up so that water can be poured down the tube until the stomach is full. The top of the tube is lowered, so that the contents of the stomach flow back down the tube. A sample is usually kept for analysis, and then the process is repeated until the stomach contents have been cleared. In some cases, a neutralising agent or antidote to the poison are poured down the tube, rather than water.

» SEE ALSO — Endoscopy, Gastritis, Sprain, Ulcers

consciousness, brain damage and death follow rapidly. Judicial hanging (in which the neck is dislocated), choking (in which the windpipe is obstructed) and restriction of the windpipe by external pressure are equally fatal but are not classed as strangulation.

Emergency action
If the arteries in the neck get blocked (accidentally or during a fight, for example, the brain will lose its blood supply. The victim will lose consciousness and turn blue. Remove any cords or strings from around the neck and, if breathing has stopped, give artificial respiration while waiting for the ambulance to arrive.

Internal problems
A strangulated hernia is one in which the blood supply to the section protruding through the abdominal wall is disrupted. If the contents of the hernial protrusion are part of the bowel, then gangrene and peritonitis will develop. A strangulated hernia is hot, red and tender. Pain is localised to start with, but as peritonitis develops the pain becomes more widespread. Untreated, the condition is usually fatal.

The testes and ovaries, both of which receive their blood supply via a long stalk, may become strangulated if the stalk is twisted.

STREPTOCOCCAL INFECTIONS

The streptococcal bacteria are a common cause of infection.

There are several different groups of streptococcal bacteria. One group alone, known as the A strain, causes 95 per cent of all human bacterial infections. Unlike the staphylococcal bacteria, which tend to cause localised infections, the streptococcal bacteria have a widespread effect. In the skin, which is readily infected, it can cause impetigo or cellulitis (an infection of the skin and tissues beneath it).

A sore throat
Most sore throats are due to viruses, but streptococcal infections are common. A 'strep throat' is usually very painful and the throat is fiery red, often with beads of pus oozing out of the tonsils.

In children a streptococcal infection of the throat can cause scarlet fever. Scarlet fever used to be a serious infection but antibiotics have rendered the disease less virulent. A generalised, 'flu-like illness is followed, a day or two later, by a bright red rash that peels off, leaving bright new skin. A similar streptococcal infection, but this time affecting the muscles, the joints and the heart, results in rheumatic fever. The streptococcal bacteria are the commonest cause of pneumonia and osteomyelitis, an infection of the bone.

Treatment
Penicillin is the drug most commonly used in treating the streptococcal bacteria. Fortunately, the bacteria have built up little resistance to the drug.

STRETCHMARKS

Stretchmarks are a striped effect which appear on skin when it is distended, or stretched, the marks remaining when the skin returns to its former shape.

The most common reason for developing stretchmarks is pregnancy. They may appear on the abdomen and breasts, starting as pink stripes, which turn purple and then fade as the skin returns to its normal size. The marks are still clearly visible however, sometimes paler than skin colour but sometimes remaining a purplish pink. The stretchmarks are shinier than the unstretched skin. The skin along the line of the strechmark loses elasticity, and may become thinner than the surrounding skin.

Stretchmarks may also appear as a result of a sudden growth spurt in teenage years, or as a result of putting on excess weight. They may also appear as a result of taking steroid drugs. Hips and thighs are common sites for them.

Causes
Stretchmarks do not appear in every pregnant woman. The reasons are unclear. Some women swear by oils and ointments which are rubbed into the skin, but it is more likely that it is the level

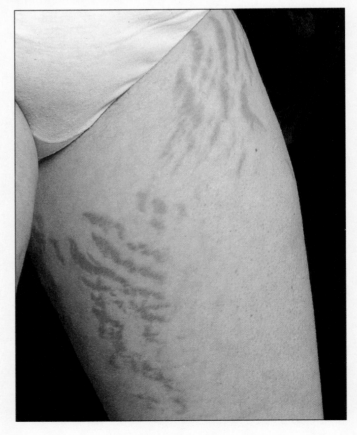

Stretchmarks (or striae) are slightly irregular purple lines which may appear as a result of excess weight gain.

▶▶ SEE ALSO — Impetigo, Osteomyelitis, Ovary, Pneumonia, Rheumatic fever, Scarlet fever, Staphylococcal infections, Suffocation, Testis

of corticosteroids in the body which determines whether or not they form. This could explain why they often appear after long-term treatment with steroid drugs.

STROKE

A stroke is a localised brain defect caused by a sudden decrease in blood flow.

A stroke is usually of sudden onset and the effects last more than 24 hours. The same effect (usually involving paralysis) may be caused by tumours, abscesses or injury — but these are not true strokes.

Causes

The blood supply to the brain may be interrupted in one of three ways. A blood vessel may become furred up over time and suddenly become completely blocked by clot formation, or a blood clot (usually from the heart) may enter the general circulation and eventually reach the brain where it gets trapped in an artery. Thirdly, a blood vessel may burst, allowing blood to ooze into the brain.

The causes of stroke are similar to the causes of heart attacks and both share the same predisposing factors.

The major risk factors include high blood pressure, smoking, diabetes, obesity, a high cholesterol level, excess alcohol consumption and the Pill.

Effects

The effects of a stroke depend on the area of the brain deprived of blood. Damage to the motor areas will cause paralysis, damage to the language area will cause speech problems, and so on. The duration of symptoms depends on several factors.

Generally speaking, strokes due to a burst blood vessel carry the worst prognosis and those due to clots from other parts of the body the best. Within these limits, there is a huge variation depending the area affected and whether other areas can take over the work of the damaged part.

Treatment

The initial treatment of stroke is generally supportive: intravenous fluids and even artificial respiration may be vital. Following a stroke the brain swells and this may cloud the picture in the first few days, making things seem worse than they actually are. High-dose steroids may reduce this swelling. Treatment of anything other than the most minor of strokes requires a team effort from doctors, nurses and various therapists. Most health authorities have specialist 'Stroke units' that employ physiotherapists, speech therapists and occupational therapists. Little can be done to restore the damaged area, but skilled therapy teaches the victim how to overcome difficulties and encourages other parts of the brain to take over some of the role of the damaged areas.

STUTTERING

Stuttering (or stammering) is a speech disorder in which there is hesitation and repetition of certain words or parts of words.

The disorder usually starts in childhood, although it may begin later in life as a result of trauma or stroke, for example. For some people, it is particular consonant sounds which are a problem; for others, the difficulties are more generalised.

The condition affects about one per cent of adults, but is more common in children. Many children stutter temporarily at around the age of two, when their speech is developing. If their stutter remains with them to the age of six, it is quite likely to stay into adulthood.

Causes

There are various theories about the cause of stuttering. Some maintain it is due to a particular form of brain damage, while others put it down to anxiety. It is interesting that the problem usually recedes if the sufferer is singing or speaking in unison, when communication is less crucial. Some people who hardly stutter have problems when speaking in public.

Treatment

Speech therapy is necessary in serious cases. This may involve isolating and practising problem sounds, and giving equal emphasis to all syllables.

STYE

A stye is a small boil on the edge of the eyelid, caused by infection.

The stye usually develops as a result of a bacterial infection of the hair

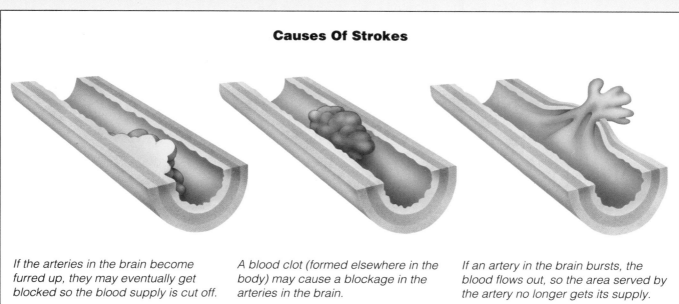

Causes Of Strokes

If the arteries in the brain become furred up, they may eventually get blocked so the blood supply is cut off.

A blood clot (formed elsewhere in the body) may cause a blockage in the arteries in the brain.

If an artery in the brain bursts, the blood flows out, so the area served by the artery no longer gets its supply.

⏩ SEE ALSO — Brain, Coronary heart disease, Embolism, Speech therapy

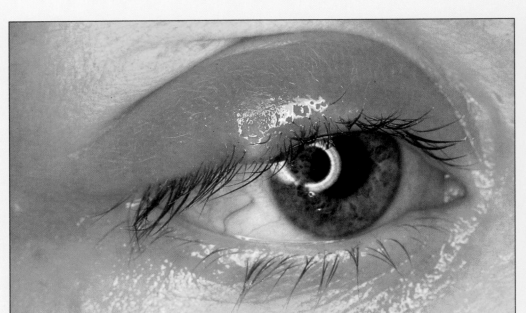

Styes are both unsightly and uncomfortable, developing in the hair follicle of an eyelash as a result of infection. People on poor diets may be more susceptible to such infections.

follicle of an eyelash. There may be a build-up of pus, which can be quite painful.

Treatment
A warm compress may draw out the pus. If this does not work, check carefully which eyelash is infected and use tweezers to pull out the lash. The pus will normally come with it. In severe cases, antibiotics may be needed.

Prevention
Because the infection is contagious, it often passes from one eyelash to another. A doctor can prescribe a cream to prevent this. Anyone with a stye should be careful to use only their own flannel and towel. Tweezers used to treat a stye should be sterilised afterwards.

SUBARACHNOID HAEMORRHAGE

A subarachnoid haemorrhage (SAH) is spontaneous bleeding into the subarachnoid space between the brain and its covering layers.

The condition affects 15 people in 100,000 per year, usually young adults. Most are due to unsuspected weaknesses in the arteries at the base of the brain.

Bleeding in the subarachnoid space due to injury is not classed as a subarachnoid haemorrhage.

Symptoms
The onset is sudden, with devastating headache, usually at the back of the head. Survivors are often convinced that they have been coshed from behind. This is usually followed by vomiting and a rapid loss of consciousness.

Nearly half are dead before they reach hospital and another 10 – 20 per cent die in the next few days.

Neck stiffness is present and this sometimes causes confusion with severe meningitis. A lumbar puncture or CT scan will confirm the diagnosis.

Treatment
The immediate treatment of patients with SAH is strict bed rest and supportive measures. Intravenous steroids combat swelling of the brain and may save lives. Survivors are usually referred to neurosurgical centres for assessment. In some cases, surgery may be needed to avoid recurrence.

SUBCONJUNCTIVAL HAEMORRHAGE

A subconjunctival haemorrhage is bleeding under the membrane covering the white of the eye.

A bright red patch appears on the white of the eye, which looks alarming but is rarely serious. The haemorrhage may occur due to exertion — coughing or vomiting — which causes a rise in pressure in the delicate blood vessels. The condition normally clears up without treatment in a couple of weeks.

SUBCLAVIAN STEAL SYNDROME

Subclavian steal syndrome is a set of symptoms caused when the arteries are so furred up that movement of an arm 'steals' blood from the brainstem.

Symptoms include visual disturbance, dizziness and lack of coordination. It is usually the left arm which is affected. The left subclavian artery, carrying blood to the arm, works adequately while the arm is at rest, but when moved, the muscles demand extra oxygen, so the brain becomes deprived. The symptoms are accompanied by a weak pulse and low blood pressure in the affected arm.

Treatment involves surgery to reconstruct the affected arteries.

SUBDURAL HAEMATOMA

A subdural haematoma is a collection of blood between the brain and its fibrous covering.

An acute subdural haematoma is usually due to major injury, tearing the arteries and veins leading to the brain so that there is rapid blood loss.

A chronic subdural haematoma usually affects the elderly and often follows quite minor injury. A damaged vein oozes blood for several weeks or even months until eventually a blood-filled cyst forms.

As the blood collects, the brain is compressed, leading to a progressive loss of consciousness, facial paralysis and death.

Altered consciousness, vomiting or uneven pupils after a head injury are possible clues to the development of a subdural haematoma and the patient should be admitted to hospital at once. In hospital, burr holes are drilled in the skull to relieve the pressure.

▶▶ SEE ALSO — Boil, Meningitis

SUDDEN INFANT DEATH SYNDROME

Sudden Infant Death Syndrome (SIDS) or cot death is the sudden and unexpected death of a baby in whom a thorough postmortem examination fails to reveal a cause.

In the UK, SIDS kills one in 500 babies and accounts for a fifth of all infant deaths. Most deaths occur in the one- to five-month age group, more often in towns than the country and usually at night.

More boys are affected than girls, and the frequency increases with social deprivation and younger mothers. Most occur in the late winter and early spring, times when colds and 'flu are at their peak. Indeed, most SIDS are preceded by upper respiratory tract infection but this is usually so mild that treatment is rarely sought.

Causes

Many theories have been put forward to explain cot deaths, but in the end it is likely that several factors, some inside the baby and other external factors, all come together at a critical time in the baby's development. The oldest theory of all dates back more than 100 years, when cot deaths were usually registered as being due to 'maternal smothering', but in most cases this can be discounted.

Reducing The Risks

Recent research has revealed four areas in which simple precautions can lower the risk of SIDS.

Smoking Don't. Certainly not near the baby and preferably not at all.
Temperature Babies should be kept warm but not overheated. The baby's room should be kept at the temperature in which the average adult would be comfortable. Lightweight blankets, that can be added or taken away, are better than duvets.
Sleeping position Recent research shows that SIDS is more common in babies who sleep on their stomachs. Lay them on their sides (below) or their backs. Do not worry about them vomiting and choking while lying on their back – this is no longer considered to be a risk. Books published before the late 1980s may give different advice, but current medical thinking is that it is best for children to lie on their sides or back.
Minor illness Any minor illness in a baby under six months may be a warning. If a baby seems unwell, seek medical advice quickly.

SUFFOCATION

Suffocation is caused by a blockage of the air passages, resulting in a lack of oxygen.

The condition may be caused by a blockage of the pharynx or larynx (due to inhaling a small object) or it may be caused by covering the nose and mouth (with a pillow or plastic bag) so that air cannot enter the respiratory tract.

Effects

The effects of suffocation are similar to strangulation: the victim turns blue, and as oxygen fails to get to the brain, there is brain damage and death.

Treatment

The first thing to do for someone who is suffocating is to remove any blockage from the mouth. With children this may involve holding them upside down and giving them a thump between the shoulder blades. If possible, move the person out of doors to give them fresh air.

Check to see whether the victim is breathing normally; if not, give artificial respiration until help arrives. If the victim is unconscious but breathing, lay them in the recovery position.

SUICIDE

Suicide is the deliberate taking of ones own life.

On average, 4500 deaths in the UK each year are recorded as suicides. This is certainly an underestimate as many coroner's courts are very reluctant to bring in a verdict of suicide.

'Success' and failure

For every person who commits suicide, at least 20 'attempt' suicide. The group who succeed are very different from the group who attempt it but fail. Most people who genuinely want to die succeed and the remainder, although they may have convinced themselves that death is the only way out, use attempted suicide as a means to draw attention to their plight or to punish those they perceive as causing the problem.

Attempted suicide is so common that doctors try to reserve this term for those who seriously intended to take their own lives but failed. The term 'para-suicide' is used to describe non-serious attempts.

As a rule, para-suicides are more often female and suicides more often male. Suicides are commoner in the older age group and para-suicides in the younger.

Suicidal intent is often signalled by the method used and the place chosen. Para-suicides rarely use shotguns or throw themselves off cliffs. Suicides usually choose a deserted spot, often with strong personal connections. Para-suicides usually make sure they will be found before too much harm can befall them.

Treatment

Treatment of para-suicides can be very difficult for doctors, family and friends. Many para-suicides have

SEE ALSO — Artificial respiration, Strangulation

good reason to be unhappy and to seek help, but the method they choose to solve their problems tends to create a feeling of 'if we go along with this she is only going to do it again when the going gets tough'. As well as dealing with the underlying problem it is important that the para-suicide is taught less destructive ways of expressing herself.

A tragic consequence of para-suicidal gestures can occur if paracetamol is taken in overdose. In the short term, high doses of paracetamol seem virtually free of adverse effects and this may lull the attention seeker into a false sense of security. Unfortunately even as few as 20 tablets can cause irreversible liver damage. The would-be para-suicide dies a few days later, often with their original problem happily resolved.

Because of such possibilities, and any uncertainty over what may have been taken, all suicide attempts warrant urgent hospital admission for physical and psychological assessment.

SUNLIGHT

Sunlight has both positive and negative effects on our bodies.

Some exposure to ultraviolet light from the sun

is necessary for the body to produce adequate vitamin D — particularly in dark-skinned people.

However, too much sunlight is bad for us. In the short term, overexposure causes sunburn and may result in heat cramps, heat exhaustion or heatstroke (although these conditions may occur through overheating without exposure to sunlight). Heatstroke caused by exposure to sunlight is referred to as sunstroke.

Repeated exposure to strong sunlight causes the skin to age more rapidly, and leads to an increased likelihood of developing keratoses (wart-like growths) and skin cancer.

Photosensitivity

Some people are abnormally sensitive to sunlight, coming up in a rash. Such photosensitivity may have developed naturally, or may be a side effect of a disorder such as porphyria. It may also result from taking certain drugs.

The eyes, too, may be particularly sensitive to light. Wearing good quality sunglasses will not only protect the cornea, they will also stop you from wrinkling your face as a defence against sunlight — another cause of the wrinkles which make you look older.

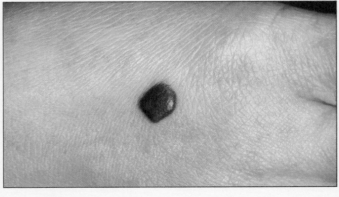

Malignant melanomas, which may result from overexposure to sunlight, are dark in colour, and usually slightly raised.

Treating Sunburn

Sunburn is more common in fair-skinned people, because they have lower levels of melanin, a protective pigment.

Apply calamine lotion or a sunburn cream to affected areas. Painkillers may be taken to relieve tenderness. If there is severe burning, it is advisable to consult a doctor, who may prescribe a corticosteroid preparation.

Prevention

Prevention is better than cure: avoid long exposure to the sun, particularly if you are fair skinned. If you want to get a tan, build up a resistance to sunburn by limiting your exposure to the sun to less than half an hour on the first day, gradually increasing exposure as your skin becomes used to the sun. Remember that even in hazy conditions the ultraviolet rays can penetrate. Reflected light from water and snow may increase the amount of sunlight you are exposed to.

Use suncreams to enable you to stay longer in the sun if necessary, but apply them regularly, and always after swimming.

SUPPOSITORY

A suppository is a form of drug which is administered by inserting it in the rectum.

The suppository melts as it reaches body temperature, so that the active ingredients are released and can be absorbed. This form of medication is used to treat anal/rectal problems such as haemorrhoids and proctitis and it is also used where the drugs might irritate the digestive tract, or if they might cause vomiting if they were taken orally.

SUPRAVENTRICULAR TACHYCARDIA

Supraventricular tachycardia is an abnormally fast heart-beat, lasting for several hours or even days.

The rhythm remains regular during the periods of rapid heart rate but the speed may reach 150 – 200 beats per minute. The condition arises because

electrical impulses in the heart disrupt the working of the heart's natural pacemaker. This causes various symptoms, which include palpitations, faintness, breathlessness and/or chest pain.

Diagnosis and treatment

The disorder is diagnosed through an ECG. In some cases, an attack can be treated by trying to breathe out while holding the mouth and nose closed, or by drinking cold water. In more serious cases it may require treatment with anti-arrhythmic drugs or by defibrillation — applying an electric shock to the heart.

SURROGACY

Surrogacy describes the role of a woman who agrees to bear a child on behalf of a couple who are unable to have children.

The details of the conception depend on the problems of the childless couple: if the woman

➤➤ SEE ALSO — Fertilisation, Haemorrhoids, Heatstroke, Infertility, Melanoma, Pacemaker, Photosensitivity, Porphyria

produces no eggs, the surrogate mother will be artificially inseminated with the man's sperm. In other cases, where the woman's uterus does not accept the fertilised egg, the true mother provides an egg which is fertilised in vitro and then implanted in the surrogate mother.

Surrogacy became very controversial when it was revealed that some women had exchanged large sums of money. Surrogacy for financial advantage is now against the law in the UK and many other countries.

SUTURE AND SUTURING

A suture is the medical term for a stitch, used in the repair of injuries or surgical incisions.

There are various methods of suturing or stitching, depending on the type of wound, and various different materials can be used, including catgut, fine stainless steel, linen, silk and synthetic thread.

Some sutures are absorbable, so that once the wound has begun to heal, the stitches are absorbed into the body; others have to be removed once the repair process has begun.

The method of suturing depends on the depth of the wound or incision. The surgeon uses a curved needle, gripping it with a needle holder (like a fine pair of pliers) while forceps are used to hold the edges of the wound in place.

If the wound is fairly shallow, the surgeon usually chooses simple stitches to hold the edges together, knotting each stitch individually. For deeper wounds, the surgeon may go through the skin twice, first shallowly and then more deeply, again knotting each stitch individually.

Some small wounds do not need stitching: the edges can be held together with medical staples or strong adhesive tape. Surgeons and casualty departments will choose the most appropriate method.

SWALLOWING

Swallowing is a reflex action which conveys food from the mouth to the stomach.

Once the tongue has propelled the contents of the mouth backwards, a wave of involuntary contraction pushes the food into the gullet. As part of the reflex, breathing is inhibited and the

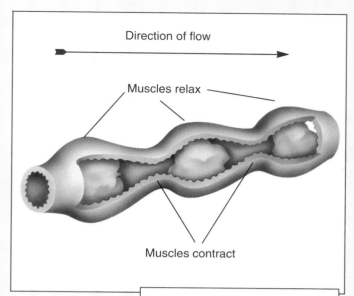

The process of swallowing (known as peristalsis) involves the rhythmic contraction and relaxation of muscles in the oesophagus or gullet (indicated in the diagram on the right).

glottis closes to protect the lungs. Swallowing with the mouth open is nearly impossible.

Down the hatch

When the food enters the gullet a wave of contraction forces it towards the stomach at a rate of about 4cm per second. In an upright position, food generally falls down the gullet at a faster rate and reaches the stomach ahead of the wave of contraction. In humans, who eat and drink in an upright position, swallowing is not as important a process as in grazing animals who are perpetually swallowing 'uphill'. When food reaches the bottom of the gullet a valve opens to allow it to enter the stomach.

Swallowing disorders

Nervous people often swallow large amounts of air whilst eating and drinking.

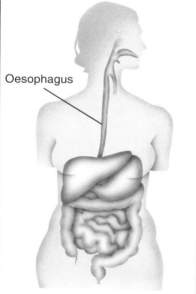

Some of this air is absorbed, some is regurgitated by belching, but most eventually finds its way to the colon.

Dysphagia, the medical term for a difficulty in swallowing, is common. The usual cause is lack of saliva, usually due to excessively dry food, but occasionally due to a medical condition. Extra moisture in the food and plenty of water to drink with it should alleviate the problem.

A feeling that 'food is sticking' is very common, but it is rare that it actually does so. Fish bones and other sharp objects can scratch the wall of the gullet and

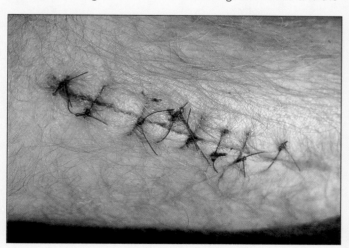

The aim of stitching a wound is to hold the skin in place neatly until the healing process is complete.

➤➤ SEE ALSO — Oesophagus, Mouth, Salivary glands

cause localised swelling, leading to the false impression that food is stuck.

True dysphagia, characterised by difficulty swallowing solids, but not liquids, may be due to a stricture or a tumour. Strictures of the gullet are usually caused by corrosive stomach acid washing up the gullet.

Tumours of the gullet are common, but can usually be removed surgically. Strictures or inoperable tumours may be helped by dilating the gullet with mercury-filled balloons, passed into the stomach.

SWEAT GLANDS

Sweat glands are long, tubular glands distributed over the whole skin surface except the glans of the penis and the clitoris.

Sweat glands help to control body temperature by secreting sweat which evaporates, thus lowering the skin temperature. A certain amount of water is vaporised at all times, usually 50 ml or so per hour, but the amount varies from person to person.

Evaporation of 1ml of sweat removes just over half a kcal of heat. In the tropics, as much as 1.5 litres of fluid can be lost per hour.

Sweating disorders

Hyperhydrosis, as excessive sweating is known, may be generalised, usually as the result of a fever, or localised. Local hyperhydrosis usually plagues young adults and generally affects the soles of the feet, the palms of the hands and the armpits.

Socially crippling though it may be, hyperhydrosis is rarely due to serious illness. Often it has an emotional basis and it improves during sleep. Topical applications of aluminium hydroxide,

available on prescription, are very effective and may only need to be used one or twice a week.

SYDENHAM'S CHOREA

Sydenham's chorea is a disorder of the central nervous system which affects children.

Sydenham's chorea was formerly known as Saint Vitus' dance, because the main symptoms are uncontrollable twitching and fidgeting, together with restlessness and irritability. Controlled movements become clumsy, speech becomes slurred and handwriting deteriorates.

The disorder usually develops after an attack of rheumatic fever (now rare in the UK).

Treatment

Treatment involves bed rest and antibiotic drugs. If there is extreme fidgeting, the child may also be sedated.

The condition usually clears up after a few months, with no long-term adverse side effects.

SYMPATHECTOMY

A sympathectomy is an operation to divide some of the sympathetic nerves as they emerge from the spinal cord.

The sympathetic nervous system works without our conscious knowledge and controls many of the body's functions.

In particular, activity in the sympathetic nervous system causes blood vessels to tighten, so that if the patient already has a disease in which blood vessels are constricted, the further tightening may completely block some

arteries. Sympathectomy prevents this extra constriction, so increasing the blood supply to a limb. The operation is usually performed to relieve the symptoms of arterial disease in the lower limb.

Another function of the sympathetic nervous system is to relay information about pain. Sympathectomy may be used to treat pain due to nerve injury.

Sympathectomy may be performed in severe cases of Raynaud's disease — in which arterial spasm is precipitated by cold. The sympathetic nerves that supply the hands and toes are cut to prevent spasm.

Sweating is also under the control of the sympathetic nervous system and sympathectomy may be performed to control excessive sweating of the hands or feet.

Sympathectomy used to be performed through an incision, but nowadays it is a less traumatic, 'closed' operation. A needle is

guided to the spine using x-rays and an injection of carbolic acid is used to destroy the nerve.

SYNDACTYLY

Syndactyly is a congenital defect in which two or more fingers or toes are joined with webs of skin.

The condition may be inherited, and may be associated with other congenital defects (including dwarfism). It is more common in males than females. In some cases there is not simply a web of skin, the fingerbones are actually fused together, and there may only be a single nail for two adjacent digits.

Treatment

Syndactyly can be corrected by operating on the affected digits at an early age.

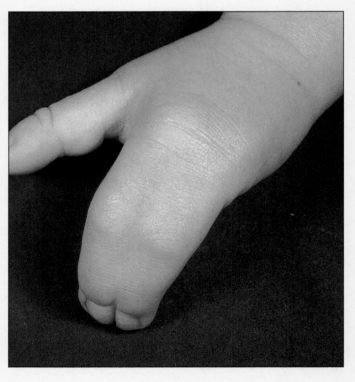

These fingers are not simply webbed, but fused together along their length – a condition known as syndactyly. The condition is present from birth.

➤➤ SEE ALSO — Nervous system, Raynaud's disease, Skin

Synovium In A Finger Joint

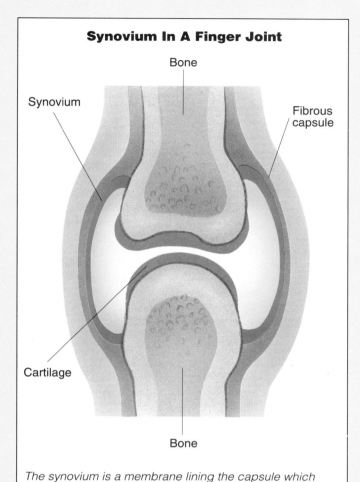

Bone

Synovium

Fibrous capsule

Cartilage

Bone

The synovium is a membrane lining the capsule which encloses a joint. The synovium secretes a lubricating fluid.

SYNOVITIS

Synovitis is the inflammation of the synovium in a joint.

The synovium is a membrane that covers all the inner surface of a joint, apart from where the bone rubs against the adjacent bone. It secretes a clear, slightly viscous fluid that lubricates the joint cavity.

A similar condition may affect the synovial membrane which lines tendon sheaths.

Causes and treatment

The commonest cause of synovitis is rheumatoid arthritis, a generalised disease that most frequently affects young women.

Anti-inflammatory drugs, such as aspirin, may ease the pain of synovitis but there is some evidence to suggest that they speed the eventual destruction of the joint. Specific treatments such as gold injections are helpful but long-term side effects limit their usefulness.

In severe cases of synovitis an operation known as synovectomy may be considered. This is the surgical removal of the proliferating synovial membrane from the joints and tendons. It may be performed on the hands, feet and knees.

SYPHILIS

Syphilis is a sexually transmitted disease, which may be congenital.

Syphilis is due to a minute parasite that enters the body through breaches in the skin or mucous membranes. It is almost exclusively sexually transmitted, though occasionally it may affect non-genital areas in medical staff. Infection can also be passed to the foetus, giving rise to characteristic deformities in the baby. Since the advent of penicillin the incidence of syphilis has declined dramatically. Both sexually transmitted and congenital syphilis have early and late stages.

Primary syphilis

Two to four weeks after infection the primary lesion develops. This starts as a raised lump but quickly ulcerates to form a hard, painless chancre. The commonest sites for chancres are the penis, the labia, the mouth or, in homosexual men, the anus. The primary chancre heals in a few days.

Secondary syphilis

A few months after the primary infection a generalised 'flu-like illness develops. The fever is usually accompanied by a sore throat, a rash and joint pains. The symptoms of secondary syphilis may last several months but subside eventually.

Tertiary syphilis

Before the discovery of penicillin, 10 per cent of patients with secondary syphilis went on to develop the tertiary infection, often as long as 25 years later. Tertiary syphilis may affect the heart, nervous system or the skin and bones. The latter, benign, form produces ulcerated lesions known as gummas. More serious infections affect the heart and circulation which leads to a failure of the valves and consequent death.

Syphilis of the central nervous system may produce symptoms similar to meningitis or it may produce a bizarre condition in which the sufferer holds grandiose delusions about themselves.

Diagnosis and treatment

Syphilis is easily diagnosed with a simple blood test and in the early stages can be cured with a single injection of penicillin. But it does increase the risks of contracting other serious conditions and avoidance is better than cure.

TACHYCARDIA

Tachycardia is the technical name for a rapid heart rate.

In a normal adult, the heart beats at between 60 and 100 beats per minute, with 75 being the average.

During exercise, tachycardia occurs in order to supply extra blood to the muscles. A rapid heartbeat while at rest may be caused by anxiety, heart disease, hyperthyroidism, fever or simply as a result of a high caffeine intake. The condition may also occur as a side effect of certain drug treatments.

Symptoms include palpitations, breathlessness and lightheadedness. Treatment of the condition depends on the cause.

TALIPES

Talipes is a birth defect, commonly known as club foot.

The exact cause is not known, but it appears to be due to pressure on the feet in the uterus during the final stages of pregnancy. There is also a hereditary element.

The disorder can take various forms, but most commonly the feet are turned inwards, and the shinbone may be deformed.

MEDICAL FACT FILE

The tapeworm can hook on to the wall of the intestine, where it lays eggs. The eggs are carried in the faeces to the anus.

TAPEWORMS

Tapeworms are parasites which live in human or animal intestines.

Tapeworms get taken into the body through eating undercooked meat or fish which contain the larvae. The larvae then grow in the human intestines, and lay eggs which are excreted with the faeces. If hygiene is inadequate, the eggs may be passed on to other people, and if sewage control is inadequate the eggs may be picked up by animals.

Infestation is no longer common in developed countries.

Symptoms
If tapeworms do infest the body, there are few symptoms. In some cases, sufferers report abdominal discomfort, sometimes there is diarrhoea — and sometimes both are present.

The main symptom and means of diagnosis is the presence of sections of tapeworm in the faeces. There may be itchiness around the anus.

Treatment
Anti-worm drugs get rid of the worms very easily, although there may be a problem with pork tapeworms. If the eggs of this type of worm develop to the larval stage in the abdomen (which normally only happens in an animal host), the larvae may burrow into the tissues and form cysts, causing muscle pains.

TASTE, LOSS OF

Taste is one of the five senses, the receptors of which are on the tongue.

Loss of taste is usually associated with loss of smell, due to respiratory tract infections. Loss of taste without loss of smell may be due to a dry mouth, which in turn may be due to an infection of the salivary glands, or a side effect of certain drugs or radiotherapy. Taste also fades with age, due to the degeneration of the taste buds. Other causes of loss of taste include mouth cancer and nerve damage, as a result of brain injury or a brain tumour. There may be disturbance of taste in certain psychiatric disorders.

TEETH

Adults normally grow 32 permanent teeth, in a range of shapes and sizes, for breaking up the food in different ways.

In adults, each jaw has four incisors (flat teeth for biting into food); two canines (pointed teeth for tearing tougher food such as meat); four premolars (for grinding food) and six molars (larger than premolars, also for grinding). Wisdom teeth are the last molars to come through, at the back of the mouth.

Teething
Traditionally, teething has been implicated in most of the ills of childhood, with everything from diarrhoea to epilepsy being blamed on a child's teeth. Many doctors

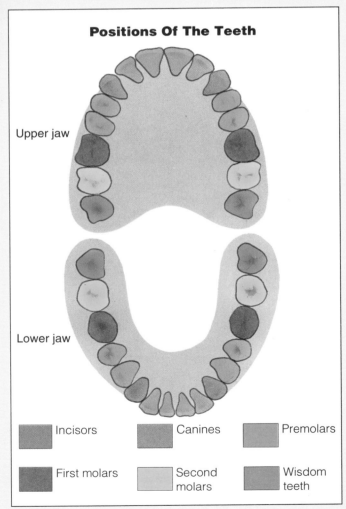

Positions Of The Teeth

Upper jaw

Lower jaw

Incisors | Canines | Premolars

First molars | Second molars | Wisdom teeth

▶▶ SEE ALSO — Roundworms, Parasites, Senses, Threadworms, Tongue

Teething And Milk Teeth

There are 20 milk (or deciduous) teeth, which are eventually replaced by 32 permanent teeth.

Name	Position	Age at which they appear
Central incisors	Lower jaw	6 – 10 months
	Upper jaw	8 – 10 months
Lateral incisors	Lower jaw	2 – 18 months
	Upper jaw	8 – 10 months
First molars		2 – 18 months
Canines		16 – 20 months
Second molars		20 – 30 months

There is considerable variation in the time of eruption of the milk teeth. Some babies are born with teeth and some have none at all until well into their second year. This variation is completely natural and, despite anxiety on the part of parents it is very rarely a sign of any form of disease. The arrival of teeth does not normally preclude breastfeeding (if this is already established).

try to avoid using teething as an explanation for ill health, believing that this may obscure the true cause of a condition.

Teething may well cause reddening of the cheek on the affected side, and often causes excess salivation and dribbling. Many mothers firmly believe that teething is always accompanied by bronchitis, but this is usually due to excess saliva trickling down the windpipe. Similarly, some mothers find that diarrhoea accompanies teething, perhaps because the child is constantly finding things to bite on — which may not be as clean as they should be.

Many babies cut teeth with no apparent effort. Any pain can be relieved with paracetamol syrup, which seems to give results that are at least as good as teething gels. Teething rings may help to prevent small children from chewing things they shouldn't.

Second time around

Permanent teeth start to appear at around the age of six. Usually the lower incisors come first, although the order is more variable than with the milk (or first) teeth. All but the wisdom teeth are usually through by the age of 14 — girls are usually a few months more advanced than boys.

Healthy teeth

Preventive dental health is vital for all children. The earlier good habits are developed, the easier it will be to carry on good dental health practice in adult life. Fluoride drops or tablets (if the water does not already contain fluoride) reduce the rate of dental decay by 50 per cent. They should be sucked or chewed. However, if fluoride toothpaste is used three times a day, tablets should not be necessary.

Sweets encourage dental decay: adults who ate sweets are likely to have both rotten teeth and a weight problem. Keep sweets for special treats only and offer fruit instead.

Regular trips to a dentist should start at about 18 months of age, with visits every six months for both children and adults.

TEMPERATURE

In a healthy adult the temperature deep inside the body is maintained at a remarkably constant 37°C.

The overall control of body temperature is governed by the heat regulation centre in the hypothalamus, a tiny gland in the brain.

Heat is produced by burning fuel in the form of glucose — a chemical reaction that continues in our bodies 24 hours a day. Heat is lost through the skin and through air expelled from the lungs. If more heat is being produced than is being lost, blood vessels in the skin dilate and sweating occurs. At ambient temperatures above 32°C, and during exercise, most people begin to sweat.

If a person from a temperate climate moves to the tropics, the body takes a week or two to acclimatise. There is a gradual increase in sweating, but a decrease in the amount of salt contained in the sweat.

Daily fluctuations

The normal body temperature shows a regular daily fluctuation. It is at its lowest at 6 am, and as much as 0.7°C higher in the evening. In women there is a rise in temperature of about half a degree at the time of ovulation.

A sign of disease

Fever — an increased temperature — is a well-known hallmark of disease. It is almost universal, occurring in fish, amphibians and birds as well as mammals. The benefit of running a high temperature is unknown, but there must be considerable advantages for it to be such a widespread phenomenon. It is thought that the high temperature allows the body's enzyme systems to work faster, and thus combat infection. Very high temperatures are harmful: prolonged temperatures above 41°C can cause permanent brain damage,

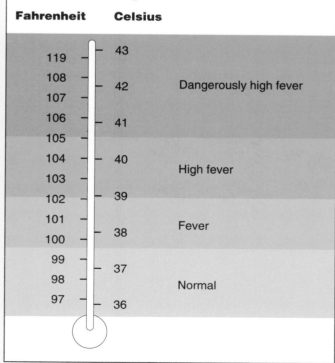

Temperature Chart

Fahrenheit	Celsius	
119	43	
108	42	Dangerously high fever
107		
106	41	
105		
104	40	High fever
103		
102	39	
101		Fever
100	38	
99		
98	37	Normal
97	36	

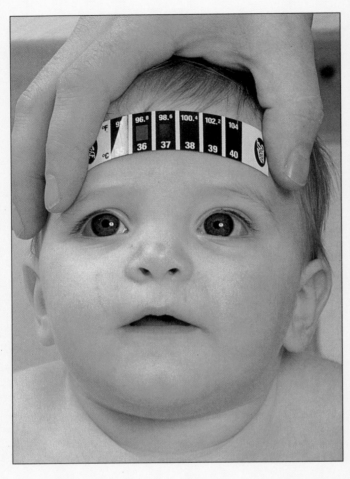

A fever scan is an easy way to take a child's temperature. Panels on the strip change colour according to the temperature of the forehead, and the fever scan indicates the internal temperature.

while a temperature above 43°C causes heatstroke and death.

Measuring temperature

The actual measurement of body temperature is not usually of vital importance, except in a few cases or where the progress of a disease needs to be monitored. It is usually sufficient to feel the skin and to ask the patient how they feel. A patient who is hot to the touch and yet says they feel cold certainly has a temperature.

Fever scans are a safe method of measuring temperature, and usually adequate for most needs. These are strips containing temperature-sensitive liquid crystals and they are held against the forehead. The

reading is usually slightly higher than the actual body temperature. If a more accurate reading is needed, a mercury-filled glass thermometer should be used. This is placed under the tongue, but must be left in place for at least two minutes. Temperature can also be taken in the armpit, but the reading will be a degree or two lower than core temperature.

TEMPERO-MANDIBULAR JOINT

The temperomandibular joint is where the jaw joins the skull just below the ear.

Temperomandibular joint dysfunction is a common condition, giving rise to pain and clicking in the joint. It is due to an abnormality of the bite pattern, and is more common in women, night-time teeth grinders and those of a nervous disposition.

Untreated the condition usually worsens and may eventually lead to arthritis in the joint. Symptoms may be alleviated by an injection directly into the jaw joint, though this can be painful. In most cases, a complete cure can be effected by dental correction of the bite, either through the removal of teeth or orthodontic treatment.

TENDON

Tendons are the cords of fibrous tissue that join muscles to bones.

Tendons are stronger than muscles and allow the muscular forces to be concentrated in a small point. This is particularly important in areas like the wrist where several tendons pass through a small area.

Ruptured tendons

The commonest tendon problem arises when the elastic limit of the tendon is exceeded and damage occurs. This happens in twisted ankles and sprained wrists where the weight of the body is suddenly concentrated in one small area. The tendon itself may rupture or it may tear off the bone. Both these injuries are difficult to treat and in the case of a ruptured Achilles tendon, extensive surgery is required to wire the ends of the tendon together.

Partial rupture

A partial rupture of the tendon is more common — some of the fibres remain intact. Because the remaining fibres hold the torn ends in contact there is a

good chance that, given time and rest, the ends will reunite. A partial rupture is liable to become a full-scale rupture, and most doctors would protect them with a plaster cast for a few weeks, and then start physiotherapy.

Tenosynovitis

Tendons run in synovium-lined sheaths. These sheaths, and the tendons they contain, may become inflamed giving rise to tenosynovitis. This may be caused by repeated blows or by repeated minor strains. Repeated minor strains are most likely to occur in individuals whose job requires them to reproduce the same movement time and time again. Typists, for example, often develop tenosynovitis at the wrist as a result of lifting their fingers hundreds of times a minute. The only sure cure for this condition is rest. Anti-inflammatory drugs and steroid injections may help but there may be nothing for it but to change jobs.

TENNIS ELBOW

Tennis elbow is an inflammation of the elbow, causing pain.

The inflammation occurs in the tendon that attaches the muscle of the forearm to the bone of the upper arm. Although it may be due to overuse of the muscles through playing tennis with the wrong type of grip on the racquet, it may also be due to wrenching the muscles when lifting heavy weights.

Treatment involves rest, application of ice packs to reduce inflammation, and painkillers and anti-inflammatory drugs may help. In severe cases, injections of corticosteroids may be prescribed. Surgery may be an option.

▶▶ SEE ALSO — Fever, Jaw, Joints, Repetitive strain injury, Sprain, Strain

TESTICULAR FEMINISATION SYNDROME

Testicular feminisation syndrome is a rare condition in which a person's external genitals appear to be female, but undescended testes are also present.

The individual is in fact a male, but usually ends up leading life as a woman. The condition is inherited, being carried in female genes.

Symptoms and causes

Throughout childhood, the individual appears to be a girl, and most sufferers develop normal female characteristics at puberty. However, no menstruation occurs, and there is no uterus (although the vagina is present).

It is caused by an enzyme deficiency, which prevents the body from reacting normally to the male hormone, testosterone, even though the body does produce the normal amount of the hormone.

Diagnosis and treatment

In most cases, diagnosis is not made until puberty, when a doctor is consulted about the lack of periods. However, it may be diagnosed earlier if there is an inguinal hernia, or if one of the labia swells and turns out to contain a testis.

Treatment involves the removal of the testes and hormonal therapy with oestrogen drugs.

TESTIS

A testis or testicle is one of the pair of male sex glands, producing hormones and sperm.

The two testes hang in the scrotum, suspended by the spermatic cord. Each is oval in shape, about 4cm by

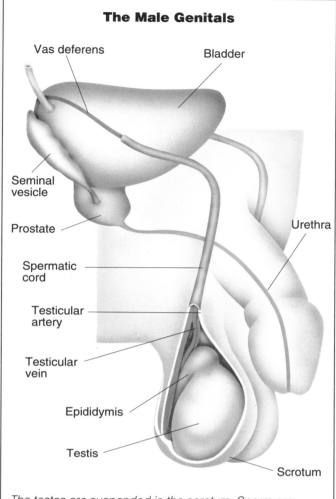

The Male Genitals

Vas deferens

Bladder

Seminal vesicle

Prostate

Urethra

Spermatic cord

Testicular artery

Testicular vein

Epididymis

Testis

Scrotum

The testes are suspended in the scrotum. Sperm are produced in the testes and stored in the epididymis.

2.5cm in size. The back of the testis is covered by the tightly coiled tubes of the epididymis, the main storage area for mature sperm.

Structure and function

The testes are made up of tightly coiled tubes, the seminiferous tubules. The sperm are produced along the walls of these tubes and when they are mature they fall into the centre of the tube to be carried to the epididymis. Between the tubules are clumps of endocrine cells, which produce the male sex hormone testosterone and release it directly into the bloodstream.

Production of sperm is a complicated process that requires optimum conditions.

The testis requires adequate amounts of testosterone and other hormones, and needs to be at the right temperature, considerably below normal body temperature. The temperature of the testis is lowered by heat loss from the scrotum. Hot baths and tight underwear will lower the quantity of sperm in a given sample of semen, but not prevent semen production.

In the unborn baby the testes are formed in the abdomen, high up on the back wall, not far from the kidneys. During development, the testes migrate downwards and pass through the abdominal wall. At or around the time of birth, they finish their journey and lodge safely in the scrotum. The area of the abdominal wall they pass through at this stage is the site of inguinal hernias.

TESTIS, CANCER OF

Tumours of the testes are usually malignant, and most fall into one of two groups.

Seminomas affect the older age group, while teratomas are commonest in 20-40-year-old men. Occasionally, testicular tumours manufacture sex hormones, and if urinary

Testicular Self-Examination

Men should examine their testes regularly to check there are no unusual lumps.

The most common symptom of testicular disease is a painless lump. Most lumps are not cancerous, but it is important you consult your doctor quickly because in the early stages testicular cancer is easily treated. The testes should be examined after a hot bath when the scrotum is relaxed and the contents can be easily felt.

● Start by feeling the epididymis, which should feel soft and slightly tender. The spermatic tube can be felt at the top of the epididymis. It should feel smooth and firm. The testis itself should feel smooth and lump-free. Most lumps are found at the front and the bottom of the testis.

● If an abnormality is found and your doctor is unable to reassure you of its benign nature, he will arrange for a biopsy (laboratory analysis of a section of tissue).

SEE ALSO — Ejaculation, Endocrine system, Penis, cancer of

MEDICAL FACT FILE

pregnancy tests are given, they may be positive.

Symptoms

Testes affected by either type of tumour become hard, insensitive and heavy. As the disease progresses, the testis and the epididymis, which can usually be felt separately, form a solid scrotal mass.

Secondary growths may be found as far away as the lymph glands of the neck. Distant spread via the bloodstream is common, and occasionally an x-ray will show growths in the lungs or liver before the tumour in the testis can even be felt.

Treatment

Treatment of testicular cancer represents one of the success stories of modern medicine. Castration and radiotherapy provide a permanent cure in the great majority of cases. Despite the surgery, men treated in this way can still enjoy a normal sex life by having monthly injections with testosterone.

TESTIS, DISORDERS

There is a wide range of disorders of the testis.

Some disorders are diagnosed at an early age, others only affect older men as a rule.

Undescended testes

Undescended testes are one of the commonest problems at birth and certainly by the age of six months they should both be in the scrotum. The testes of children are highly sensitive and will withdraw into the abdomen at the slightest touch. The best time to check is during a hot bath. If the testes have been in place once, even if they never seem to come back, that is fine. If not, consult a doctor who will probably refer the child for a simple operation to fix them in place. Untreated, an undescended testis will be sterile, because of the high temperature in the abdomen compared with the scrotum. There is also a higher than normal incidence of cancer.

Ectopic testes

Occasionally, the testes descend as normal but still fail to end up in the scrotum. These 'ectopic testes', as they are called, may be found anywhere in the genital area. Like an undescended testis the ectopic testis is more prone to damage and disease and should be returned to the scrotum and fixed in place.

Torsion

The blood supply to the testis travels down the spermatic cord from the main artery of the body. Occasionally, this long cord becomes twisted, cutting off the testicular circulation. The result is severe pain in the lower abdomen, often accompanied by vomiting. The scrotum is swollen and acutely tender. Torsion of the testis, as it is called, usually affects children and young adults. It is an acute surgical emergency because if the blood supply is not restored within a few hours, the testis will become gangrenous and must be removed.

Infection

Infection of the testis, which is much commoner than torsion, causes similar symptoms. Although the age groups affected are different, confusion sometimes occurs. When making a diagnosis, most doctors work on the principle that acute pain in the testes of a young man is due to torsion until proved otherwise. Most infections involve not only the testis but the epididymis as well. The exception is mumps which causes an extremely painful swollen testis. The affected testis often withers and, if both sides are affected, sterility is common.

Infection of the testis and epididymis may be acute or chronic. Acute infections are usually the result of sexually transmitted diseases or urinary infections. In some cases, no infecting organism can be found. It seems that in some circumstances, usually during vigorous exercise, sterile urine is forced down the vas deferens, setting up a chemical reaction very similar to an infection. In an acute infection the testis becomes red, tender and swollen. The epididymis feels thickened and is painful to the touch. There is often a penile discharge and occasionally the testis itself suppurates. Treatment consists of rest, scrotal support and high-dose antibiotics.

Torsion Of The Testis

The tube supporting a testis may get twisted – torsion of the testis.

Other pains

The majority of cases of pain in the testes do not have a sinister cause. The most common problem is bruising, which happens easily, but in some cases of bruising the damaged blood vessel will continue to bleed, leading to haematoma formation. This blood-filled cyst can grow to an enormous size, sometimes as big as a coconut. If bruising seems to be getting worse rather than better, a cold bath and tight underwear may help. If not, surgery to evacuate the blood clot and seal the leaking vessel may be needed.

'Lover's ball' (the popular name for a condition which is common in teenagers) is a result of sexual excitement without ejaculation. Arousal causes the epididymis to become engorged and painful, but the condition is relieved by ejaculation.

TESTS

Conventional western medicine divides the process of treating a disease into five stages, and medical tests may form a part of this.

The first stage is to find out the history of the problem, asking the patient how they feel, where the pain is, what symptoms they have, and so on. Then the patient is examined. On the basis of these two stages, the doctor can decide what further information (obtained from medical tests) is needed. The last two stages are diagnosis and treatment.

The future

In some countries (particularly the USA) tests are taking over from the history and examination as the most important part of a consultation.

Routine Tests

The commonest types of test measure the concentration of various chemicals in the blood, urine, spinal fluid and other bodily fluids.

These usually involve chemical reactions and are now so highly automated that one machine can test for scores of chemicals in hundreds of samples every hour.

More specific tests either visualise the substance of an organ, or measure how well it is working.

Simple x-rays can only differentiate between various concentrations of minerals in the body. Areas of high mineralisation, such as bones, show as dense patches on a photographic plate. Areas of low mineralisation, such as soft tissues, produce light area. X-rays can be made more sophisticated by using a computer to generate 'slices' through a body, but they still only reveal the structure, not the function of an organ.

Ultrasound scans work in a similar way to x-rays, but use sound waves (rather than x-rays) to look at the structure of various parts of the body. It is particularly used in pregnancy (to examine the foetus) and to look at the liver and colon. It can be used in detecting cancer.

Measurement of the electrical activity of an organ such as the brain (EEG) or heart (ECG) allows defects in the working of those organs to be recognised and treated.

An area of hope for the future is in gene profiling. At some stage, and it may only be a matter of a few years, it should be possible to map an individual's genes. This will allow doctors to predict future disease, such as heart attacks, accurately. This may do wonders for health promotion (for example, if a person's genes indicated a very high chance of getting lung cancer, they might be less likely to smoke) but it is also an area in which ethical problems abound (in matters such as life insurance, and when testing the genes of an unborn child, for example).

TETANUS

Tetanus is an extremely serious bacterial infection that leads to muscle spasm and death in 20 per cent of patients.

Tetanus occurs if the spores of the tetanus germ (mainly found in soil and manure) contaminate an open wound. The germs multiply in the wound and produce a powerful toxin that destroys nerve fibres and causes a rigid paralysis. The incubation period varies but may be up to several weeks.

Symptoms and treatment

Vague, 'flu-like symptoms are rapidly followed by muscle spasm, often starting in the jaw, giving the disease its old name, lockjaw.

Patients are sedated, and given artificial ventilation if necessary, which has improved the survival rate, but prevention is more effective than treatment.

Prevention

Immunisation against tetanus is effective and virtually free from serious side effects. Children should receive immunisation in the first few years of life, and boosters should be given every 10 years. (Anyone who does not have immunity should have a course of three injections, one month apart, to give them immunity for the next ten years.)

In the unimmunised who have a tetanus-prone wound, some degree of protection can be obtained by the administration of an antitoxin produced from the blood of immune volunteers.

THALAMUS

The two thalami are walnut-sized structures at the top of the brainstem.

Each thalamus is connected to all parts of the brain. They relay sensory information to the brain. This

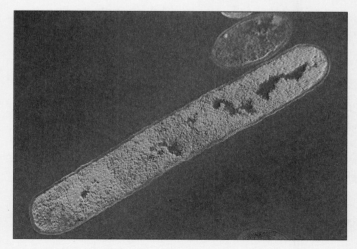

The bacterium responsible for tetanus is called clostridium tetani and lives in the soil and the intestines of animals.

information is received directly from the sense organs (such as eyes and ears) or from sensory receptors via the spinal cord. The thalamus actually interprets some sensations, such as pain, and ensures the body reacts as fast as possible. The thalamus sorts out which bits of information are important, so that we are not constantly conscious of certain sensations and movements.

It makes it easier for us to think about the content of something we are reading, for example, without having to consider how fast to move our eyes over the page to read individual words and letters which register automatically. The thalamus may also play a part in long-term memory.

THALASSAEMIA

The thalassaemias are a group of inherited disorders, all of which cause anaemia.

Thalassaemias were originally thought to be confined to the shores of the Mediterranean, but the problem is now acknowledged as being worldwide.

Thalassaemias are due to structural abnormalities in the protein structure of haemoglobin — the iron-rich compound that transports oxygen round the body. The abnormal haemoglobin means that the red cells break down rapidly, leading to anaemia. The severity of the disease depends on the specific abnormality and the relative numbers of abnormal haemoglobin chains.

In the genes

The gene of the commonest type of thalassaemia, beta-thalassaemia, is carried by 150 million people world wide. Beta-thalassaemia is divided into major, minor and

➤➤ SEE ALSO — Anaemia, Brain, Immunisation, Ultra-sound scanning, X-rays

MEDICAL FACT FILE

intermediate forms, according to the severity of the symptoms. Children affected by thalassaemia major become ill within the first few months of life, with failure to thrive, infections and anaemia. Thalassaemia minor may be so mild as to pass unnoticed.

Treatment and outlook

The aim of treatment is to suppress the production of the ineffective forms of haemoglobin and to combat the anaemia with regular blood transfusions. Further drugs may be needed to counteract the side effects.

As with most genetic disorders, the outlook is rosy. Research has identified the gene abnormality and there is hope that gene transplants may actually cure the disease.

THALIDOMIDE

Thalidomide is a sleeping drug which was withdrawn from the UK market in 1961.

Most of those affected by thalidomide have learned to cope with their disabilities on a practical level.

The drug achieved notoriety because during the 1950s it was prescribed to pregnant women (particularly those who had problems with morning sickness). However, it was found that it caused limb deformities in many of the babies born to women who had taken it, and was withdrawn.

It has now been found to be useful in treating certain forms of Hansen's disease (leprosy).

THIRST, EXCESSIVE

Excessive thirst is most commonly due to dehydration.

If the liquid intake is low, or excessive amounts of liquid are lost through sweating and/or diarrhoea, the sufferer becomes thirsty, and an increased intake of liquid will re-hydrate the body. The same effect may be noticed the morning after a night of excessive alcohol consumption.

Thirst may also be a symptom of diabetes

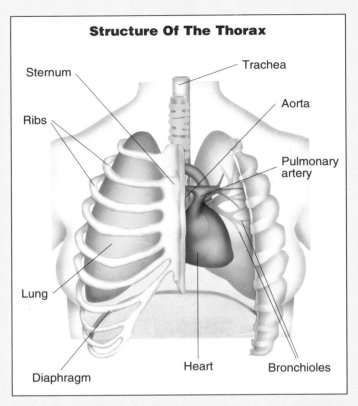

Structure Of The Thorax

Sternum

Ribs

Lung

Diaphragm

Trachea

Aorta

Pulmonary artery

Heart

Bronchioles

(mellitus or insipidus), kidney failure, or a side effect of treatment with certain drugs (prescribed for psychotic disorders or to relieve nausea). Thirst is the main symptom of a psychological condition known as psychogenic polydipsia.

THORAX

The thorax is the area between the diaphragm and the neck.

The contents of the thorax are divided into the lungs, together with their associated coverings, and the mediastinum. The mediastinum is a thick sac containing the heart, great vessels, the thymus, windpipe and gullet. The lungs are surrounded by two very thin but very strong membranes, the pleurae. The pleurae secrete a lubricating fluid that helps the lungs to glide over the ribs during breathing.

Any surgery to the chest, be it open heart surgery or removal of a lung, requires

the thorax to be opened — an operation known as thoracotomy. The usual route for thoracotomy is to split the breastbone with an electric saw and to spread the edges of the wound using a mechanical device rather like a car jack. If a tumour is located at the side of the chest, the surgeon may perform a thoracotomy between the ribs. After thoracotomy the bones are wired back together.

Thoracic outlet syndrome

Normally the ribs join the 12 thoracic vertebrae but occasionally the first rib is connected to the bottom cervical vertebra instead. This extra rib presses on the spinal nerves as they unite to supply the arm. Nerve damage causes pain and wasting of the muscles of the thumb. Occasionally the artery to the arm is also compressed, causing the pulse to fade in certain arm positions. Treatment is simply the surgical removal of the extra rib.

▶▶ SEE ALSO — Diabetes, Heart, Lung, collapsed,

THREADWORM

Threadworms are the commonest parasitic worms in the UK.

Threadworms cause few symptoms, and do little harm. They affect children more than adults.

The worms are about 10mm long. They live in the gut and lay eggs around the anus. Once the worms hatch they cause itching, which is usually worse at night. Unfortunately the sufferer easily transfers the eggs, often directly to the mouth, or passing them on to other children via toys or clothing.

Occasionally the infestation may cause malnutrition (if the child is slightly underfed) or vaginitis (if the infestation spreads to the genital area).

Treatment

The infestation can easily be treated with antiworm tablets. These should be prescribed for the whole family if one member finds they are infested. Ointments may be prescribed to relieve any anal itching.

THROAT

The throat is the common name for the windpipe and gullet, from the back of the mouth down to the base of the neck.

The symptom which most often affects the area is a sore throat.

THROMBOPHLEBITIS

Thrombophlebitis is an inflammation of the veins near the surface of the skin.

The condition is caused by tiny blood clots which irritate the lining of the veins. It is most often the legs which are affected.

The condition may occur after surgery to the legs, in association with varicose veins, in drug users who inject themselves, or in certain disorders of the surface veins.

Treatment

Anti-inflammatory drugs, together with gentle exercise, are usually recommended. Exercise is also a preventive measure. When sitting or lying, the sufferer should ensure the legs are up (on a stool if sitting, or raised on a pillow if lying) to prevent the blood in the legs from stagnating in the veins. Ulceration of the leg may also occur, in which case antibiotics may be prescribed.

THROMBOSIS

A thrombus is a solid mass (or clot) formed in the circulation. The process by which it is formed is called thrombosis.

Thrombosis of one sort or another is very common, accounting for more than half of all adult deaths in the UK. Even if the thrombus itself does not cause problems, fragments of thrombus (called emboli) may break off and move through the circulatory system until they reach fine blood vessels, where they form a blockage. This may lead to serious damage in the part of the body which is supplied by that blood vessel.

Thrombosis may occur in the venous circulation or in the arteries.

Venous thromboses

Unlike arterial thromboses, venous thromboses often occur in healthy blood vessels in healthy people. The most important factors in forming a venous thrombosis are immobility and an increase in the clotting ability of the blood. Immobility is usually the result of enforced rest following an operation or an illness, but may occur after long, cramped aeroplane flights. Many factors make the blood more sticky and more prone to clotting — pregnancy, the Pill, diabetes, old age and obesity being the commonest.

The majority of venous thromboses occur in the deep veins of the legs, giving rise to a deep vein thrombosis, or DVT.

A DVT may be completely symptomless — as many as 50 per cent of patients who undergo some forms of surgery develop one without realising it. More commonly, a DVT causes pain, swelling and redness in the affected calf. Because the superficial veins dilate to carry more blood, the leg often feels warmer too.

The main danger from a DVT is not blockage of the circulation in the leg, though this can occur if the clot is big enough, but pulmonary embolus. A pulmonary embolus is a sudden blockage of one of the major arteries to the lungs, due to a thrombus usually from the legs. Pulmonary embolus is a common cause of death, particularly after surgery.

Treatment

The aim of treatment is to prevent the formation of a pulmonary embolus. The patient is rested in bed and not mobilised until the clotting tendency in the

Deep Vein Thrombosis

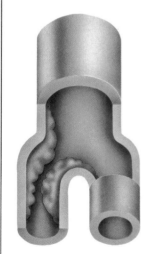

A thrombosis occurs when a blot clot builds up in a blood vessel – either a vein or an artery.

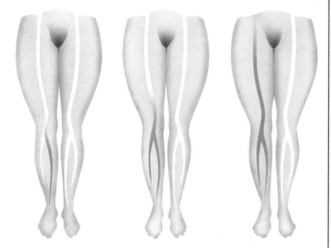

Deep vein thrombosis is most common in the veins of the leg. The symptoms vary according to the position of the thrombus: the higher up the leg the thrombus the greater the extent of pain and swelling up the leg.

⟫ SEE ALSO — Embolism, Larynx, Leg ulcer, Oesophagus, Pharynx, Sore throat

Blood Clot In The Heart

Clots may form inside the pumping chambers of the heart.

Clots are more likely to form inside the pumping chambers if the heartbeat is irregular or if the inside of the heart has been damaged by disease. A clot inside the heart may remain silent for years before flying off to block a vessel some distance away.

blood has been reduced by drugs. Treatment with blood thinning agents, (anticoagulants) is normally continued for three months, but in the case of recurrent disease, treatment may have to be for life.

Superficial thrombosis affecting the veins on the surface of the legs is a far less serious problem. Inflammation and pain is due to the irritant effects of the clot and the vein itself can often be felt as a knotted cord running up the side or back of the calf. Treatment consists of elevation, analgesics and rest.

Arterial thromboses

Arterial thrombosis is usually due to tiny clots formed in the turbulent blood flow around defects on the arterial walls. These defects are usually due to deposits of cholesterol and arterial thrombosis is therefore more common in smokers, diabetics, people with high blood pressure and those with a family history of heart disease or stroke. The oral contraceptive pill does play a very small role, but from a health point of view the Pill is far safer than smoking.

Once formed, an arterial thrombus grows rapidly and quickly cuts off the circulation downstream of the blockage.

A thrombus in one of the arteries supplying a limb will cause the limb to become cold, white and painful. If the blocked artery supplies the heart or brain, the result is a heart attack or stroke.

Treatment

An arterial blockage is a surgical emergency. Deprived of oxygen the limb will die within a few hours.

Call a doctor at once, and while waiting for her to arrive, elevate the limb and keep it warm.

Various intravenous drugs have been developed to dissolve clots, but they are more suited to the very small clots found in the coronary circulation than the large ones found in the limbs.

If drug treatment is unsuccessful, surgical removal of the clot, or thrombectomy, is undertaken. In its simplest form, this involves opening the artery above the blockage and sliding a thin plastic tube down the blood vessel. When the tube is well past the blockage, a balloon is inflated at the end of the tube, and the whole thing is slowly withdrawn, dragging the clot with it. If this is unsuccessful, a major operation to bypass the clot may be needed.

Prevention

Arterial thromboses may be prevented by avoiding risk factors such as smoking, high-fat diets and obesity, and possibly by a regular intake of aspirin. In people who have already suffered an arterial thrombus, doses as low as a quarter of a tablet per day have been shown to lower the risk or recurrence. The role of aspirin in the prevention of clotting in the healthy

population is still unclear, but at present it is not thought that 'an aspirin a day keeps the doctor away'.

THRUSH

Thrush is the common name for a fungal infection caused by the organism candida albicans.

It is most often found in the intestine, the mouth or the vagina.

THUMB-SUCKING

Thumb-sucking is a habit taken up by many small children, as a form of reassurance.

Thumb-sucking is common at bedtime and at times of stress, but most children grow out of the habit by the age of six or seven. The only serious side effect of continuing the habit beyond this age is that it may force the teeth out of position. In some cases, orthodontic treatment may

be necessary once the habit is stopped.

Discouragement

Parents who do not like to see children sucking their thumbs are advised to find an alternative: one theory is that a dummy is better, because it can be 'lost' once the child is old enough to manage without it. The thumb-sucking habit should not be attacked, as this may make the child more insecure and more inclined to suck. However, in older children it is worth discussing the problems of crooked teeth and dental treatment to try to encourage them to give up the habit.

THYMUS

The thymus is a gland which plays an important role in the immune system.

The thymus is situated at the top of the chest, behind the breastbone and in front of the windpipe. It starts functioning at about the 12th week after conception, and

Many babies find thumb-sucking a reassuring habit, but it is not a good idea to continue it after the age of about six.

⟫ SEE ALSO — Fungal infections

continues to enlarge until puberty.

It has two lobes, made up of lymphoid tissue — tightly packed lymphocytes, epithelium and fat. It conditions the lymphocytes to become the killer T-lymphocytes which form the body's defence against viruses and other infections.

Disorders

The most common disorder is abnormal enlargement of the thymus, which may be due to myasthenia gravis, thyrotoxicosis or Addison's disease. In children, abnormal development of the thymus may lead to immunodeficiency disorders.

A tumour of the thymus is known as a thymoma. Such a tumour is rare, but may give rise to serious disorders such as non-Hodgkin's lymphoma, or symptoms which resemble Hodgkin's disease. Tumours of the thymus may cause increased susceptibility to infection. They are commonly associated with myasthenia gravis, an auto-immune disease.

THYROGLOSSAL DISORDERS

The thyroglossal duct is present in the embryo, running from the back of the tongue to the thyroid gland in the neck.

The thyroglossal duct normally closes up before birth, but the duct or part of the duct in which a cyst forms, may be present as a congenital defect.

If a cyst forms in the duct, it becomes infected and swollen, and may be mistaken for an abscess. It (and any remnants of the thyroglossal duct) should be removed surgically.

THYROID GLAND

The thyroid gland controls many of the metabolic reactions in the body.

The thyroid is a butterfly-shaped organ that straddles the windpipe in the lower half of the neck. During the development of the foetus, the thyroid starts at the back of the tongue and grows downwards. As a result, little islands of functioning tissue are sometimes found in the tongue itself and these can cause problems if they swell.

Function

The thyroid gland produces three different hormones, though two — thyroxine (T4) and triiodothyronine (T3) — are structurally very similar.

The exception is calcitonin, a hormone that

has a profound effect on the growth of bone.

T3 and T4 play an important role in controlling the body's metabolism. In children, they are necessary for normal physical growth.

Regulation

The amount of calcitonin secreted by the thyroid gland is controlled directly by the amount of calcium in the blood. If there is a high level of calcium in the blood, calcitonin will be secreted in order to deposit calcium in the bones, lowering the level in the blood.

T3 and T4 are produced in response to a hormone called Thyroid Stimulating Hormone (TSH) which is produced by the pituitary gland. The secretion of TSH is in turn under the control of another hormone, Thyroid

Releasing Factor (TRF), which is produced in the hypothalamus.

THYROID GLAND, CANCER OF

Thyroid cancer is relatively uncommon in the UK.

Thyroid cancer accounts for 400 deaths a year in the UK. The first symptom is nodules on the gland, and then there is enlargement of the gland, together with pain, and irregularity of growth or rapid growth. It is treated by surgery or radiotherapy. The outlook is generally good if the cancer is diagnosed at an early stage.

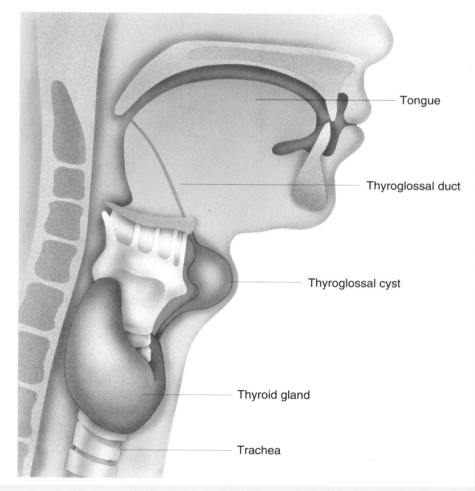

Thyroglossal Disorders And Thyroid Gland

Tongue

Thyroglossal duct

Thyroglossal cyst

Thyroid gland

Trachea

» SEE ALSO — Addison's disease, Hodgkin's disease, Lymph & the lymphatic system, Lymphocytes

THYROID DISORDERS

Thyroid disorders fall into two groups: over- and underactivity of the gland.

Underactivity of the thyroid gland is known as hypothyroidism which causes a disorder known as myxoedema.

Overactivity is known as hyperthyroidism, causing thyrotoxicosis. Graves' disease is another description of the disorder.

Causes of underactivity

Too little circulating thyroid hormone may be due to underactivity of the gland itself or underactivity in the pituitary or hypothalamus.

The commonest cause of an underactive thyroid is an auto-immune disorder, with the substance of the gland being replaced by inflammatory cells. The condition is much commoner in females and the incidence increases with age.

For the gland to function normally, the body must ingest a certain amount of iodine. If it does not, then despite the gland being normal, it cannot produce enough hormone, and underactivity is the result. This used to be common in Derbyshire and other parts of the world which are a considerable way from the sea, but recognition of the problem means that a dietary deficiency of iodine now only occurs in some areas of the Third World.

Symptoms

The classic symptoms of an underactive thyroid include slowness, tendency to put on excess weight, dry and brittle hair, thick skin, and a deep voice. The sufferer feels the cold more than normal and is often constipated. Most patients, however, consult their doctors before such obvious

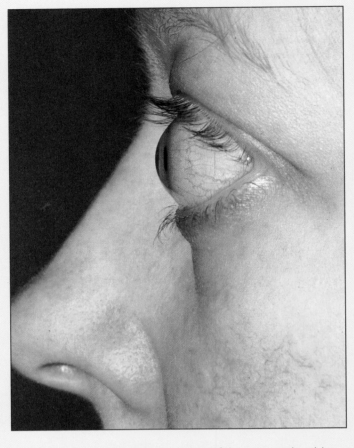

Bulging eyes (exophthalmus) is one of the most noticeable symptoms of an overactive thyroid gland.

symptoms develop, so diagnosis may take some time. In babies, an underactive thyroid will cause severe mental retardation (cretinism). In young women it may cause menstrual abnormalities or general malaise.

Treatment

Treatment of an underactive thyroid is simplicity itself. A daily dose of thyroxine, taken as a single tablet, will restore all functions to normal. Different doses suit different people, and until the dose is stabilised the patient may need several blood tests. Once the dose has been established, a yearly check is adequate.

Causes of overactivity

Almost all cases of overactivity of the thyroid are due to the gland itself rather than a dysfunction of the pituitary gland. Like

underactivity, overactivity is usually a dysfunction of the auto-immune process. The thyroid is tricked into thinking it must produce more and more hormone. Occasionally an overactive thyroid may be caused by a type of cyst.

The condition is common, and affects women more often than men. In one survey, as many as five per cent of women had been affected at one time or other.

Symptoms

The symptoms of overactivity are the opposite of underactivity, though both can cause menstrual irregularities.

The patient loses weight despite an increased appetite and becomes restless and irritable. Heat intolerance and a fast pulse are very common, together with physical and mental hyperactivity (which are often frustrating, because the

activity tends to be unproductive). The thyroid itself becomes enlarged (goitre), a symptom which may also occur with underactivity.

A diagnostic sign, but one which is due to the auto-immune antibodies rather than the overactivity of the gland itself, are bulging eyes. These do not respond to lowering the level of thyroid hormone, and cosmetic surgery may be needed.

Treatment

Controlling the production of thyroid hormone is a more difficult process than treating an underactive thyroid. It may be done in one of three ways — with thyroid drugs, surgery, radiotherapy or a combination of these.

Thyroid drugs stop the synthesis of hormone, but they can cause side effects (including putting a strain on the heart) and many people find they cannot tolerate the thought of taking them for years on end.

Surgery is usually reserved for patients with a large thyroid gland, where reduction is needed for cosmetic reasons, although it may be used to restrict the size of the gland and control overproduction.

One of the most straightforward treatments is to use radiotherapy. A dose of radioactive iodine is given in the form of a drink, and as this is concentrated in the thyroid it destroys it. There is a chance of a problem with underactivity in later years after this treatment.

Other disorders

Thyroiditis (inflammation of the thyroid), may be due to infection (which is very rare), or an abscess. Infections may be treated with antibiotics; if there is an abscess, surgical drainage may be necessary.

»» SEE ALSO — Goitre

MEDICAL FACT FILE

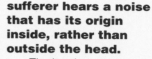

TIC

A tic is a repeated, sudden, involuntary muscular contraction.

Tics commonly affect the muscles of the face and upper trunk. They are usually made worse by stress and anxiety, often disappearing when the sufferer is absorbed or sleeping.

They occur most frequently in children, as a sign of a minor psychological disturbance. They usually go away without treatment after a couple of years, although they may continue into adult life. Tics may also develop later in life, in response to stress (particularly in post-traumatic stress disorder). If they become a problem, psychiatric treatment may be necessary.

Gilles de la Tourette

One manifestation of a tic, which starts in childhood and usually continues into adulthood (although it may disappear at puberty), is a disorder called Gilles de la Tourette's syndrome. This is a psychiatric disorder in which the sufferer has facial twitches and distortions, and is occasionally overcome by an uncontrollable desire to shout out strings of obscenities. The sufferer is mentally and physically normal otherwise. The disorder may be treated with drugs, but since these have to be taken for life, and may have various side effects, patients often choose to suffer the symptoms.

TICKS AND DISEASES

Ticks are tiny, parasitic, eight-legged creatures that feed on blood.

Ticks attach themselves to animal or human hosts with their mouths, and suck blood, increasing in size from about 3mm to around twice that when they are full. They may be picked up in rural grasslands and woodlands.

Apart from the drain on the system, the ticks may transmit bacteria through their bites. Some types of female tick have a particular toxin in their saliva which can cause a form of paralysis. The toxin affects the motor nerves, and if it spreads to the respiratory system it can be fatal.

Treatment

Ticks can be picked off, but may leave their heads behind. If you paint them with silver nitrate first, to kill them, they come off easily.

TINEA

Tinea is a fungal infection which occurs on the skin or nails.

The severity of the infection depends on the type of fungus and its site. Different forms have different names — common names include ringworm and athlete's foot.

Tinea podis (athlete's foot) is the commonest fungal infection in humans. Most cases result from communal use of wash places such as changing rooms. Usually it is the skin between the toes which is affected, and the skin becomes soggy and scaly. There is another form that causes widespread scaling of the soles of the feet.

Tinea of the nails causes them to become yellowed and thickened.

Groin rash

A problem that seems to affect men more frequently than women is tinea of the groin. This affects the upper thigh and produces a red rash with sharply demarcated edges. Often a few blisters appear in the centre of the rash.

True ringworm, or tinea corpora, which looks very similar, affects the scalp, trunk and/or limbs. The rash forms a ring as the lesion slowly expands, leaving the inside almost clear.

Treatment

Most tinea infections respond very well to local creams such as Canesten. More extensive lesions or tinea of the nail need an oral antifungal agent, available on prescription.

TINNITUS

Tinnitus is the subjective sensation of sound in the ear. The

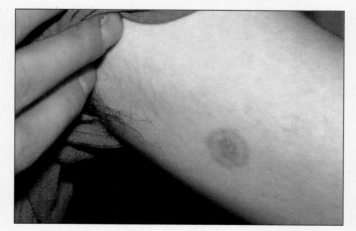

This patch on the arm shows the ring formation of ringworm. In this case, the fungus was picked up from a sheep.

sufferer hears a noise that has its origin inside, rather than outside the head.

Tinnitus is a very frequent complaint and affects almost everybody at some time.

Tinnitus is a sign of irritation of the inner ear, or the auditory nerve, in just the same way as pain is a sign of irritation of the pain receptors.

The sound heard may be continuous, intermittent, or it may pulsate with the heart. Tinnitus may take the form of whistling, rushing, ringing, and so on. It may continue 24 hours a day, and may be so loud as to interfere with sleep. Not surprisingly, tinnitus sufferers are often profoundly depressed. Pulsating sounds are often a sign of infection but frequently no abnormality can be demonstrated.

Diagnosis

Tinnitus that persists for more than a few days may be a sign of a serious underlying disorder, such as kidney failure or even a tumour. Although a doctor will be able to exclude a serious cause, there is little that can be done in the way or treatment. Some forms are helped by drugs, but in the main all that can be done is to mask the sound with either background noise or music.

TIREDNESS

Tiredness or excessive fatigue may have a number of different causes.

Tiredness is one of the most frequent symptoms which cause patients to consult a doctor. One survey suggested that nearly one in five of the population had experienced undue tiredness in the previous two weeks, women reporting the symptom twice as frequently

» SEE ALSO — Lyme disease, Shock

Tiredness Checklist

Tiredness is a common complaint, sometimes a symptom of serious illness, sometimes a symptom of an unhealthy life style. Here is a flow chart to help you analyse the causes of tiredness.

Is it associated with physical activity or interrupted sleep? → Such tiredness is natural. Try to find time to catch up on exertion.

Could you be pregnant? → Consult your doctor – and get more rest.

Are there other physical symptoms: brittle hair, tendency to put on weight, coarsening of the skin or susceptibility to cold? → These are all symptoms of an underactive thyroid. Consult your doctor.

Do you suffer from excessive thirst and need to urinate frequently? → These are symptoms of diabetes. Consult your doctor.

Are you unusually pale, faint, breathless or do you suffer from palpitations? → This could indicate anaemia. If you are getting adequate iron-rich foods, consult your doctor, as laboratory tests to establish the cause may be necessary.

Do you drink too much alcohol? → The depressant effect of alcohol may make you overtired, even if you do feel that you get enough sleep.

Is the tiredness a feeling of mental fatigue, coupled with an inability to concentrate, generally low spirits and insomnia? → Likely to be due to depression. Seek help through your doctor or counselling. If these symptoms are coupled with pressure at work, the tiredness may be due to stress and overwork. Think about changing your life style.

Are you on medication? → Many people, particularly the elderly, find that tiredness is the price they must pay for their medication.

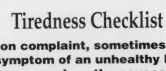

as men. The chart (left) may help you find the cause of any tiredness you feel.

Physiological causes

The feeling of tiredness that follows a day's work or any emotional or physical strain is perfectly normal and most people recognise it as such. Complaints of tiredness under these circumstances may be a sign of unrealistic expectations rather than disease.

Tiredness may also be caused by over- or understimulation and this may be an area where sensitive questioning can reveal a reason for 'burning the candle at both ends'. Sometimes overactivity may be a defence mechanism to escape painful memories and in such cases counselling can be of considerable benefit.

Many people who worry about tiredness have good reason to be tired — holding down two jobs for financial reasons, for example. Most people in this position recognise this and their complaint of tiredness is often a veiled request for a stimulant.

Morning fatigue, usually caused by going to work without breakfast, is a surprisingly common complaint to doctors.

Diseases

All diseases, by definition, lower one's feeling of well-being and this is often felt as a feeling of tiredness. This is especially true of illness such as diabetes, thyroid failure or anaemia, which have an insidious onset when the feeling of tiredness may precede specific symptoms such as thirst.

A common cause of tiredness, and one that is not often recognised by the sufferer, is alcohol abuse. Regular intake of alcohol, especially just before bed, causes a disturbance in the normal sleep pattern and

MEDICAL FACT FILE

leads to unrefreshing sleep. Tiredness on a Monday often follows Sunday drinking.

Psychological causes

Tiredness is a prominent feature of both anxiety and depression. Sometimes it is the only symptom of inner turmoil concerning family relationships, fear of dying, and so on. Tiredness in the elderly is normal and most accept it as part of growing old, but others try to recapture the prowess of their youth. This striving for a perfection they are not physically equipped for causes profound physical and emotional tiredness which requires skilled and sympathetic counselling.

Treatment

Treatment of tiredness is aimed at correcting the underlying problem, if any. In many cases, all that can be done is to persuade the patient that their feelings are normal and try to encourage them to adopt a life style in which rest and sleep play a more prominent role. A better, balanced diet may also play a role in treating tiredness.

Tonics, especially if brightly coloured or foul tasting, can provide a valuable psychological boost if not a physical one. The growing recognition of their potential for addiction and abuse has made the prescription of stimulants, such as amphetamines, a thing of the past.

TISSUE-TYPING

Tissue-typing is the analysis and classification of the tissues (which make up particular organs), to check that donor and recipient are compatible.

The better tissue types are matched, the less likely the recipient of transplanted organs is to reject them. (If tissue types are not matched, the recipient's immune system attacks the new organs.)

The main features which have to be matched are the human leukocyte antigens (HLAs) which are present on the surface of all human cells. The only people with identical HLAs are identical twins. Close relatives are likely to have similar HLAs.

TOILET TRAINING

Toilet training is the process of teaching a child to urinate and defecate in a lavatory, so that they no longer have to wear nappies.

By about 24 months, most children are aware when they are urinating or their bowels are opening. However, they need to be trained to recognise the sensations that warn them this is about to happen.

TONGUE

The tongue is a flexible, muscular organ in the mouth.

The main functions of the tongue are tasting, rolling the food round when chewing, closing the back of the mouth when swallowing and in forming certain sounds in speech.

The taste buds on the tongue are the receptors for taste, different tastes being picked up by different groups of taste buds.

Disorders

Mouth ulcers may develop on the tongue, and leukoplakia (raised white patches) may also affect it.

If there is any soreness which does not disappear within three weeks, consult your doctor because of the risk of cancer. Tongue cancer is a mouth cancer, and it may spread very quickly. It mainly affects people over 40.

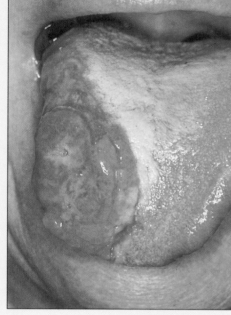

Cancer of the tongue is a relatively rare cancer, but the tongue is the most common site for mouth cancers.

Steps In Toilet Training

For every child, in every household, toilet training will take a different course. However, there are some general points to observe.

1 Introduce the potty gently, at around 18 months. It could be casually discussed in the bathroom, or children who are impressed with something new might be presented with a 'special present'. At this stage, they will not be ready to use the potty, but should be encouraged to practise sitting on it.

2 Once the child tells you she is about to pass urine or a bowel movement, she is ready to use the potty.

3 Do not force the child to sit: if she doesn't want to use the pot, simply put her nappy on again, and let her try later. This may involve several trips to the lavatory before the potty is actually used.

4 Physically, bowel movements are easier to foresee than urination. For many children, it is quite clear when a bowel movement is on its way, and it is easy to take them to the potty in time to 'catch' it. On the other hand, some children become confident about urinating in the potty, but retentive about bowel movements.

5 If you do have any problems with training, do not appear cross or disgusted at their behaviour. Although a certain amount of praise will encourage them to use the pot again next time, telling them off when they 'miss' will only build up a barrier.

6 Night-time control comes later: some parents wait until nappies are normally dry in the morning before leaving them off; sometimes the child refuses to wear a nappy at night; but sometimes occasional (or frequent) bedwetting continues for many years, often coinciding with anxiety.

» SEE ALSO — Enuresis, Mouth cancer, Senses, Soiling, Taste, Ulcers

MEDICAL FACT FILE

An enlarged tongue is a symptom of congenital disorders such as Down's syndrome. An inflamed tongue is a condition known as glossitis. Smoothness of the tongue is a symptom of anaemia, syphilis or glossitis. Roughness of the tongue may be a problem: a rough surface may be discoloured, and deep fissures sometimes develop, which do not cause trouble unless food gets trapped in them. Brushing the roughness with a soft toothbrush and using an antiseptic mouthwash seems to remove the discoloration, although it must be repeated twice daily.

TONSILS

The tonsils are lumps of lymphocyte tissue in the back of the throat.

The tonsils, together with the adenoids at the back of the nose, form part of the lymphatic system, playing an important part in the body's defence mechanism. They enlarge during early childhood, until the age of about seven, and then they shrink.

Disorders

Tonsillitis, inflammation of the tonsils due to infection, is a common disorder, particularly in young children. The tonsils are meant to pick up micro-organisms, so that the defence mechanism can develop the appropriate antibodies. However, the microorganism may infect the tonsils. If the infection is bacterial, antibiotics may be prescribed. The infection may also spread to the middle ear, and repeated infections may lead to glue ear, a condition in which hearing is impaired.

Treatment of tonsillitis involves bed rest and pain killers. Other disorders include abscesses around the tonsils, which need medical attention.

Tonsillectomy

In the past, tonsils were removed as an almost routine operation in children under the age of seven. However, the role of the tonsils is now recognised, and most specialists only recommend their removal if they are abnormally large (possibly causing breathing difficulties and sleep apnoea), or if there are multiple infections at a young age. The adenoids at the back of the nose, which serve a similar function to the tonsils, are often removed at the same time. Rarely, tonsillectomy is performed on teenagers who have repeated infections. It is an uncomfortable operation, leaving the child with a sore throat. Soft food has to be served, and plenty of ice cream soothes the throat and cheers up the child.

TOOTHACHE

Toothache is a pain which is caused by a disorder in the tooth pulp or gums.

The most common cause of toothache is dental decay (caries), in which case the pain is particularly noticeable when eating hot, cold or sweet foods. The pain may also be caused by a broken tooth, an unsound deep filling, or an abscess. The latter is the most painful, causing continuous, severe pain. Infection of the gums and supporting tissues also causes toothache.

Occasionally, sinusitis (an infection of the sinuses) causes pain in the upper molars or premolars.

Painkillers will relieve the pain, but dental attention is necessary to eradicate the problem. If sinusitis is the cause, however, treatment of the disorder solves the problem.

Careful attention to oral hygiene helps to prevent the incidence of toothache.

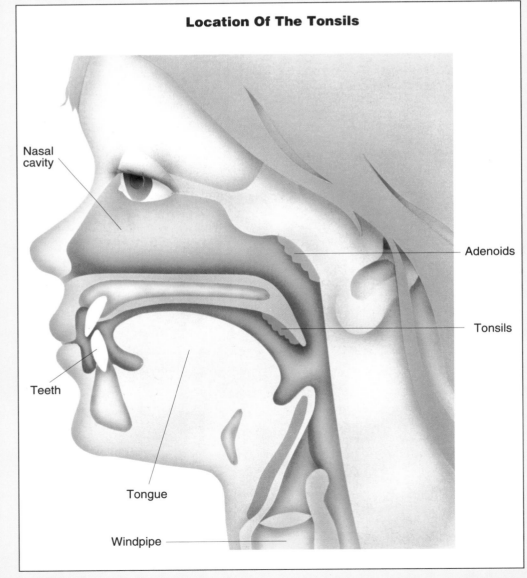

Location Of The Tonsils

Nasal cavity

Adenoids

Tonsils

Teeth

Tongue

Windpipe

TOUCH

The sense of touch allows us to judge the shape, size, texture, position and temperature of an object by feeling it.

Similar receptors to the touch receptors pick up sensations of pain. The touch receptors are distributed over the skin surface, and their distribution seems to change from day to day. The signals from the receptors travel through the nervous system via the spinal cord, to the thalamus in the brain, and then on to the sensory cortex which interprets the signals it receives.

A change of feeling

Touch spots are thickly clustered around hair follicles, and when hairs are removed the sensation of touch is greatly reduced. Some areas of the body are more sensitive than others.

If two points on the skin are touched simultaneously, a blindfolded subject will be able to distinguish two separate points only as long as they are more than a certain distance apart. This critical distance varies from 1mm on the lips and fingertips to 70mm on the middle of the back.

TOXAEMIA

Toxaemia is the presence of poisons (toxins) in the bloodstream.

The toxins are produced by bacteria, and a common route of infection is septicaemia, in which bacteria spread into the bloodstream from a particular site of infection, such as an infected wound.

Symptoms

Symptoms include generalised malaise, with fever and headache. Some toxins cause specific symptoms (such as the stiffness and muscle spasm associated with tetanus). In severe cases, septic shock may develop, with damage to tissue, although this happens most often in hospital patients who are already weak before the toxaemia develops.

Treatment

Antibiotics kill off the bacteria in the bloodstream, and any localised infection must also be treated. In severe cases, treatment for shock is needed, including intravenous infusions of plasma to raise the blood pressure and keep the circulation working.

TOXIC SHOCK SYNDROME

Toxic shock syndrome is a group of symptoms which is thought to be caused by a particular kind of bacterium, staphylococcus aureus.

Symptoms include sore throat, high fever and rash, followed by conjunctivitis, muscle pain and diarrhoea. If not controlled, there may be a fall in blood pressure, kidney failure and death. The syndrome was only identified in the late 1970s.

Routes of infection

It is not clear exactly how the particular bacteria invade the body, but research has shown that the syndrome is more common among menstruating women (although males and post-menopausal women have been infected).

In one study in the US, which looked at women who suffered toxic shock syndrome and used tampons, over 75 per cent of those infected used the same brand of tampon (which has now been withdrawn). It is now thought that the infection may enter the body through an open wound or through the vagina, and that it is very important to pay attention to hygiene when inserting tampons. You should always make sure that your hands are clean, and change tampons regularly before any bacteria have the chance to multiply.

Treatment

The body has little natural resistance to the bacteria involved. Antibiotics are needed at an early stage to combat the spread of infection, together with supportive treatment including a saline drip to maintain blood pressure. Early diagnosis usually leads to successful treatment.

TOXOCARIASIS

Toxocariasis is an infestation which is passed on from worms living in the intestines of dogs (and sometimes cats) via their faeces.

Small children are the most susceptible as they

Toxaemia Of Pregnancy

Toxaemia of pregnancy is an outdated, but still commonly used, term which describes a set of serious symptoms which may develop during pregnancy.

Originally, the disorder was thought to be due to toxins in the blood, but no toxins have ever been identified, and the condition is more commonly referred to as eclampsia. The exact mechanism leading to toxaemia is not fully understood.

The symptoms which warn of eclampsia are raised blood pressure, protein in the urine, visual disturbances, such as flashing lights and lack of focus, and oedema. If two or more symptoms are present the condition is described as pre-eclampsia. If it is not treated (with complete bed rest and possibly early induction of the baby's birth), the patient may have seizures and/or fall into a coma (eclampsia).

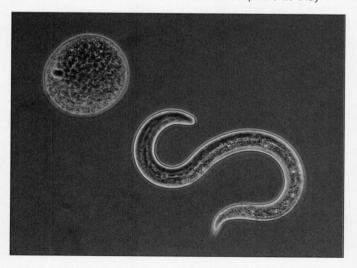

An egg and first larval stage of the dog roundworm, toxocara canis, which causes toxocariasis in humans.

➤➤ SEE ALSO — Blood poisoning, Senses, Septicaemia, Septic shock

MEDICAL FACT FILE

pick up the disease from the faeces of pets, or deposits in public parks.

Symptoms

The infestation causes mild fever and general malaise, although pneumonia and seizures may occur in severe cases. If the larvae travel through the bloodstream into an eye there may well be loss of sight.

Treatment and prevention

In most cases the body rids itself of the infestation, but all possible sources of infestation should be removed. In severe cases, admission to hospital and antiparasitic drugs are necessary.

Pets should be de-wormed monthly to the age of six months, and annually thereafter, to eliminate the chance of human infestation. Meticulous attention to hygiene is important when dealing with animal faeces. Never leave dog or cat bowls lying around where children can touch them, and always wash them separately from human eating utensils.

TOXOPLASMOSIS

Toxoplasmosis is an infestation by a single-celled microorganism, **toxoplasma, which normally lives in the intestines of cats (and sometimes dogs).**

Toxoplasmosis is particularly dangerous if it is caught by a pregnant woman, as the infection may be passed on to the foetus, causing hydrocephalus or brain damage. The only symptoms, which are not always present, are abdominal pains and swelling of the lymph glands. Treatment involves a course of drugs. As for toxocariasis, attention to hygiene when dealing with animals prevents the spread of the infestation to humans.

TRACHEA

The trachea is the section of the respiratory tract which carries the air from the larynx to the lungs.

The trachea is about 12.5cm long and slightly to the right of the centre of the neck. At the lower end it divides into the left and right main bronchi. The walls of the trachea are formed from fibrous tissue which is held open by 20 or so incomplete rings of cartilage.

Disorders of the trachea

In the newborn, these rings

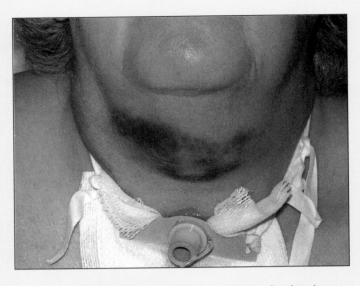

This patient has had a tracheostomy – an opening has been made in the base of her neck and a plastic tube inserted.

are only partially formed, and a 'floppy larynx' is a frequent cause of loud breathing in the first few months of life. Some newborn babies have a connection between the trachea and the gullet. As the baby feeds, milk enters the trachea and causes a fit of spluttering and coughing.

Surgery is needed to close the opening, but if any milk enters the lungs there may be a severe, even fatal, infection.

Acute tracheitis (sudden inflammation of the trachea) is a frequent complication of viral or bacterial infections of the upper respiratory tract. The trachea may also be affected by the upward spread of infection from acute bronchitis. Symptoms include fever, and the patient complains of a burning sensation in the lower throat when breathing in.

Treatment involves relieving the symptoms, with

Tracheotomy And Tracheostomy

Tracheotomy is an operation to make an opening in the trachea, usually to by-pass an obstruction higher up the airway. If the opening is made permanent, the operation is given the name tracheostomy.

The commonest reason for a tracheotomy is a blockage caused by an inhaled foreign body becoming impacted in the larynx or a tumour of the larynx. The larynx may also be inflamed and block the trachea in cases of diphtheria (now fortunately almost eradicated). And damage to the nerves which control breathing (due to barbiturate poisoning, tetanus or serious head injuries, for example) may mean that a temporary tracheotomy has to be performed. A tracheostomy may be performed if the larynx has to be removed because of a tumour.

The operation is relatively simple, but after a tracheostomy the patient is left with a plastic tube opening at the base of their neck. Without the use of the larynx, they then have to learn new methods of communicating (which usually involves burping and using the mouth as a voice box).

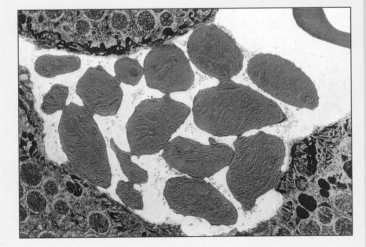

A false colour image of the sporozoan, toxoplasma gondii, which causes toxoplasmosis in humans.

▶▶ SEE ALSO — Larynx, Lungs

painkillers and soothing inhalations of menthol and eucalyptus oil in a bowl of hot water. In severe cases, the doctor may prescribe antibiotics.

Blockage of the trachea (tracheal obstruction) may be caused by tumours in the trachea or enlarged lymph glands around the trachea. These glands usually only become swollen due to the spread of lung tumours or tuberculosis. In severe cases, there may be a crowing sound as the sufferer breathes in. The condition requires hospital admission to establish the cause and proceed with appropriate treatment.

TRANQUILLISER DRUGS

Tranquillisers are those drugs which have a sedative effect (but do not necessarily induce sleep).

There are two groups of tranquilliser drugs: major and minor tranquillisers.

Major tranquillisers
The major tranquillisers are known as antipsychotic drugs, and are used in large doses to treat serious mental disorders such as schizophrenia and manic depression. They are also used to treat people with mental disorders which have made them very aggressive.

Antipsychotic drugs suppress the actions of chemicals which stimulate electrical activity in the brain. They have to be administered under controlled conditions as there may be side effects such as twitching, dry mouth, drowsiness, blurred vision and problems with the digestive and urinary tract.

Minor tranquillisers
The other group of tranquilliser drugs, minor tranquillisers, are known as anti-anxiety drugs. These may be prescribed for short periods to provide relief from anxiety if it interferes with a person's day-to-day life. However, counselling and psychotherapy are the only long-term solutions. There is a danger of compounding problems, since anti-anxiety drugs are addictive. Anti-anxiety drugs are sometimes administered as pre-medication before surgery.

TRAVEL SICKNESS

Travel sickness, or motion sickness, is nausea and vomiting which is caused by the movement of a car, ship, plane — or other form of motion such as a fairground ride.

Travel sickness is thought to be caused by the effect of movement on the mechanisms which control our balance.

The disorder is more common in children.

Control and prevention
Antihistamines, which are available on prescription or over the counter, induce drowsiness and reduce travel sickness. And transdermal patches worn behind the ear may help in cases of sea-sickness (see below). In a car, concentrating on something (such as the road ahead) may ease the feeling of nausea, as may plenty of fresh air. The condition does not usually affect people who are asleep.

Reading often makes matters worse and on a train, try to avoid looking out of the window, as this encourages side-to-side eye movement which may worsen the condition. On a plane, sleep is probably the best option, or listening to something through headphones.

TREMOR

A tremor is an involuntary contraction and relaxation of a muscle or group of muscles, causing uncontrolled shaking.

Tremor is a symptom of a number of conditions. A tendency to tremor seems to run in families.

If tremors occur over an extended period of time, it is advisable to consult your doctor, in case they are due to a serious disorder.

Causes
Tremor has a range of different causes. Delirium tremens (the DTs), is a form of tremor which is caused by withdrawal from alcohol, and similar symptoms may be caused by withdrawal from certain drugs.

Tremor is a feature of Parkinson's disease and it may also be due to hyperthyroidism

A harmless condition known as intention tremor, which occurs when the sufferer reaches for an object, is due to a disorder of the cerebellum (the part of the brain controlling movement of the muscles).

A transdermal patch worn behind the ear is one way of preventing sea-sickness. The patch contains 1.5 mg of the drug scopolamine, which is is absorbed through the skin.

➤➤ SEE ALSO — Brain, Thyroid disorders

MEDICAL FACT FILE

TRICHINOSIS

Trichinosis is a disease caused by a parasite of pigs, the worm trichinella spiralis.

Trichinosis is usually acquired as a result of eating undercooked pork. It is therefore essential to ensure that pork is thoroughly cooked before eating it as this destroys the worm. The disease is serious, and may be fatal if not treated.

Symptoms and treatment

Symptoms include those symptoms which are associated with food poisoning. These are abdominal discomfort, nausea, diarrhoea, an increased pulse rate and a raised temperature. If not treated, the face and eyes become puffed up, and there is chest pain, a cough and breathlessness.

Treatment is with antiworm medication.

TRICHOMONIASIS

Trichomoniasis is an infection of the genital tract.

It is caused by the protozoan, trichomonas vaginalis. As the name suggests, it is mainly women who are affected, as the organism multiplies in the vagina, but it can be passed on to men, where it causes urethritis.

Symptoms and treatment

The main symptom in women is a heavy, offensive, greenish-yellow vaginal discharge. It is easily treated with a short course of drugs. Infected men show no symptoms, but they may re-infect the partner who passed it to them (and any other sexual partners), so they should be contacted and treated at the same time.

TUBERCULOSIS

Tuberculosis (commonly referred to as TB) is an infectious illness due to a type of bacterium, myco-bacterium tuberculosis.

Tuberculosis is one of the oldest infections known to man, and, until 50 years ago, it was so common that virtually everyone in the world had been infected at some time. Even today, in certain parts of the world, the infection is widespread. (In the Indian sub-continent, 80 per cent of adults show evidence of past infection.) In the West, better nutrition and better housing, coupled with higher standards of hygiene, mean that infection is rarely encountered.

Signs and symptoms

Most cases of tuberculosis are sub-clinical. This means that there are no symptoms. The germ is walled off in a small part of the lung, and a cyst filled with a cheesy substance develops. With time, the walled-off area becomes calcified (hard and stone-like) but may still contain live bacteria and if the host's immunity drops sufficiently, they will escape and multiply.

A lowering of the host's immunity may be the result of infection, old age, alcoholism, diabetes or taking immuno-suppressant drugs. If allowed to, the bacteria spread locally and, via the bloodstream, to other parts of the body. Tuberculosis may also affect other organs, including the gut, the genito-urinary tract, bone marrow and heart. Up until the 19th century, tuberculosis of the lymph nodes (scrofula) was known as the King's evil, as people believed that the only cure for it was the touch of the reigning monarch.

Diagnosis

The commonest form of 'post-primary tuberculosis', as the re-infection is called, affects the lungs.

The onset is gradual, with increasing tiredness, weight loss and general malaise, almost always accompanied by fever, cough and night sweats. The sputum is often tinged with blood. An x-ray will usually suggest the diagnosis but sputum samples or even a bronchial biopsy (a sample of tissue taken from the bronchi) may be necessary for absolute confirmation.

Treatment and prevention

Antibiotics have revolutionised the treatment of tuberculosis. A disease that used to be a common cause of death does not even require hospital admission in the majority of cases these days. Antibiotics are usually given for six months or longer.

Vaccination with BCG, a form of tuberculosis found in cows, has been given to British school children since 1954. The gradual improvement in living conditions, which are enjoyed in most areas of the UK, have led to calls to stop vaccination on economic grounds. However, these calls are probably premature, as in some areas, especially where immigration rates are high, the incidence of tuberculosis is actually rising.

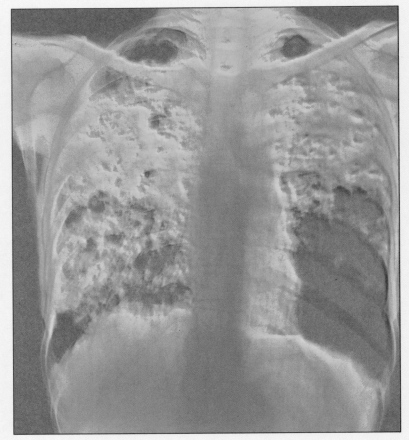

An x-ray of the lungs of a tuberculosis sufferer. Normal lung tissue is shown in blue and the infected areas are in yellow. In this patient, it can be seen that the right lung (left) is more infected than the left.

➤➤ SEE ALSO — Sexually transmitted diseases, Lungs

TWINS

Twins are children conceived by their mother at the same time.

Twins may occur for one of two reasons: a single ovum (egg), fertilised by a single sperm, may develop into twins (which will be identical) or two ova may be fertilised by different sperm at the same time, developing as non-identical twins. Twins face more difficulties than usual, and the neonatal death rate is higher than in single children.

Identical twins

Identical twins, also known as monozygotic or monovular twins, develop from the same egg. Once fertilised, the egg divides completely so that two embryos develop. If the division is incomplete, the identical twins remain joined — Siamese twins. Identical twins look remarkably similar, and may be very similar in character. Some studies show that, even if separated in childhood, they may have very similar life patterns. Their genes match exactly.

Non-identical twins

Non-identical twins, also known as dizygotic twins, are more common than identical twins, occurring in about one in 80 pregnancies. Older women, particularly those who have had many previous pregnancies, and women who have a history of twins in the family are more likely to conceive non-identical twins than other women.

TYPHOID FEVER

Typhoid is an infectious disease, which is caused by the bacteria salmonella typhi.

The bacteria can be picked up by eating contaminated food or drinking water containing the bacteria. In most cases, the contamination arises from carriers. These are people who either have the disease and do not clear it from their system, or those who are unaware that they have the disease as they do not develop the symptoms. Carriers excrete the bacteria in their faeces. The bacteria may get into drinking water if there is poor sanitation, or carriers handling food may pass it on if there is inadequate hygiene. Flies also carry the bacteria from faeces to food.

Once the bacteria get into the body, they enter the bloodstream from the intestine, and then travel to the spleen and liver, increasing rapidly. The organisms are then released back into the intestine via the gallbladder.

Symptoms

Symptoms start to develop one to two weeks after infection. There may be no more than a mild stomach upset, but in some cases the disease is fatal. There is usually a headache to start with, followed by a rise in temperature, then general illness and loss of temperature, and constipation, followed by diarrhoea. A rash appears on the chest and abdomen, and the abdomen becomes very tender as the liver and spleen are invaded.

Diagnosis and treatment

Blood, faeces and/or urine tests are necessary to isolate the bacteria or antibodies. Antibiotics are prescribed to control the disease and prevent complications. And in severe cases, corticosteroids may be needed. If not controlled, peritonitis may develop, which may require surgery.

The disease may take up to a month to clear up.

TYPHUS

The term typhus covers a group of infectious diseases caused by microorganisms known as rickettsiae.

Typhus is spread by insects — particularly body lice — carrying the rickettsiae. The itching caused by the body lice leads to scratching, and if the skin is broken, the rickettsiae are able to enter the bloodstream. This type of infection occurs in epidemics in parts of tropical Africa and South America.

Other forms of the disease are endemic (present all the time in localised areas). These include a form that affects rats, which is carried to humans by fleas and occurs in Central and North America, and a form that is spread by mites, which occurs in India and Southeast Asia.

Symptoms and treatment

The main symptoms are a severe headache, with pains in the back, arms and legs. There is also coughing and constipation, and a high fever develops accompanied by a rash. The patient is weak, and sometimes

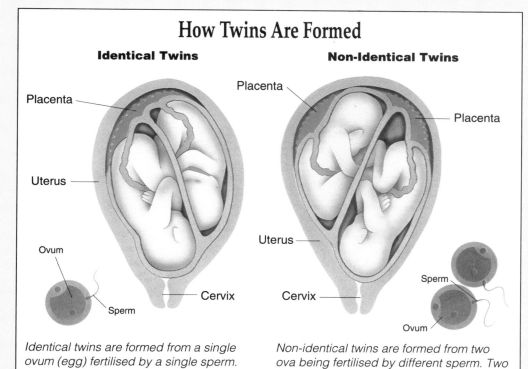

How Twins Are Formed

Identical Twins

Placenta
Uterus
Ovum
Sperm

Non-Identical Twins

Placenta
Placenta
Uterus
Cervix
Sperm
Ovum

Cervix

Identical twins are formed from a single ovum (egg) fertilised by a single sperm. The ovum divides into two embryos which share the same placenta.

Non-identical twins are formed from two ova being fertilised by different sperm. Two separate embryos then develop, each having their own placenta.

▶▶ SEE ALSO — Rickettsia

MEDICAL FACT FILE

becomes delirious. The disorder is treated with antibiotic drugs. It may be necessary to do a blood test first to isolate the type of rickettsia responsible. If not treated, there may be heart failure, kidney failure or pneumonia, causing death.

Prevention
It is important to control infestations with lice, and to keep the rat population under control. Outbreaks of typhus are most common at times of war and natural disaster, when there is overcrowding and lowering in standards of hygiene.

ULCER

An ulcer is an open sore, usually with an area of suppuration at the centre.
Ulcers can occur on any surface, inside or outside the body. They are extremely common — most people suffer from them at one time or another.

In the mouth
Mouth ulcers (aphthous ulcers) only affect the superficial layers of the tongue or gums and are surrounded by an area of redness. They are small, white, usually multiple and extremely painful.

They usually start in adolescence and recur every few weeks until resolving spontaneously in the twenties or thirties. The cause is unknown, though they may, rarely, be a sign of a serious underlying condition such as Crohn's disease. Steroid pellets, available on prescription, may speed recovery, and local anaesthetic gels may relieve the pain, but, as yet, there is no real cure.

On the skin
Most skin ulcers affect the legs. Venous leg ulcers

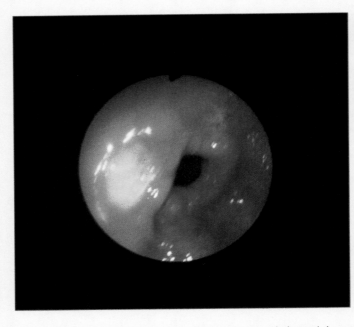

This endoscopic image shows a benign stomach (gastric) ulcer – the oval, yellowish-white area. Gastric ulcers may be caused by diet, alcohol, stress and certain drugs.

usually follow varicose veins or venous thrombosis. Blood plasma leaks from the damaged vein and leaves a deposit around the vessels. In time, this deposit starves the skin of oxygen and it breaks down, forming an ulcer. Skin ulcers away from the ankle are usually due to arterial disease. The surrounding skin is cold, white and hairless. The ulcers themselves have a 'punched out' appearance and are very painful.

Pressure ulcers are a type of ulcer which rarely occurs on the legs. They are found on the buttocks where skin overlies a bony prominence. Under normal circumstances, pressure exerted on the skin causes us to shift position, even in our sleep. In the elderly or bedridden, damage to the skin can cause a ulcer that is extremely difficult to heal.

Treatment for skin ulcers
Whatever their cause, the treatment of skin ulcers is the same. Support bandages, 'putting the feet up' and exercise all help to get the circulation going and encourage healing. If the

surrounding skin is infected, antibiotics sometimes help. The ulcers themselves should be kept clean and there are several types of dressing available, to suit either wet or dry ulcers.

Internal ulcers
Internal ulcers usually affect the gut — most frequently the stomach or duodenum — though they can occur anywhere as the result of a malignancy. Stomach ulcers and duodenal ulcers (both of which are referred to as peptic ulcers) are due to erosion by stomach acid. This may be caused by an excess of acid but usually results from a deficiency in the mechanisms that normally protect the delicate gut lining. The principal feature of peptic ulcer disease is pain, either in the upper abdomen or lower chest. The pain is often related to food and may be accompanied by nausea or vomiting.

Treatment usually consists of suppressing acid production with drugs and giving the ulcers time to heal.

ULCERATIVE COLITIS

Ulcerative colitis and Crohn's disease are the two major forms of inflammatory bowel disease.
Ulcerative colitis (unlike Crohn's disease) is confined to the large bowel. The lining of the bowel becomes reddened, ulcerated and bleeds easily.

Symptoms
The commonest symptom of ulcerative colitis is diarrhoea with blood and mucus. The disease may be chronic with frequent relapses. In an acute attack, the sufferer may pass up to 20 loose, blood-stained motions a day, and quickly develops lethargy and anaemia. The majority of cases, however, are mild and some patients only suffer flare-ups every few years. Severe disease is associated with cancer of the colon, especially if the disease has been present for 10 years or more.

Treatment
In mild cases, symptoms can be controlled with antidiarrhoeals such as codeine, but more severe cases may require anti-inflammatory drugs or steroids. Regular inspections are made of the lining of the gut to exclude cancer.

ULTRASONICS

The technique of ultrasonics uses high frequency sound waves (ultrasound) for diagnostic and therapeutic purposes.
Audible sound falls in the range of 20 to 20,000 cycles per second. Ultrasound employs frequencies as high as one million cycles per second, at which level sound waves can

➤➤ SEE ALSO — Colitis, Crohn's disease, Leg ulcer

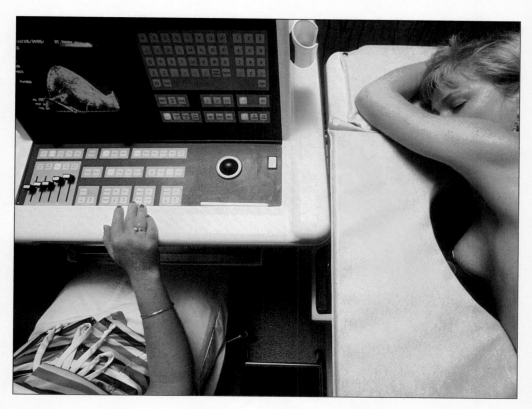

This patient is receiving water-path ultrasonography – a breast-screening technique which can detect the early stages of breast cancer.

be focused and reflected in the same way as light.

Diagnostic ultrasound uses very low power levels to drive a transmitter that can be moved over the body's surface. The sound waves pass through and bounce off the liquid-filled organs and tissues and some return to the probe where they are picked up by a receiver.

The deeper the tissue, the longer the sound waves take to return. By measuring this time interval, a picture can be built up of the body's internal organs. With computer technology, a moving 'real time' image can be produced.

Uses of ultrasound

The most frequent use of ultrasound is in obstetrics, to look at the foetus. The picture obtained is so detailed that the exact age of the foetus can be determined by measuring the size of the skull and spine. Minor abnormalities, such as missing fingers or

toes, can also be detected, as well as more serious conditions such as spina bifida.

Ultrasound is also being used more and more in other medical fields. In cardiology it can be used to study the structure and function of the heart and to measure the speed of blood flow along arteries and veins.

As a diagnostic tool, ultrasound has been extensively investigated and seems remarkably free from side effects.

Its main disadvantage is that the sound waves cannot pass through air and bone — almost all the sound waves are reflected from them, making it impossible to examine some areas, such as the brain and lungs.

Turning up the volume

Ultrasound at power levels of 100 times higher than those used in diagnostic tests has been shown to speed up the healing process of muscle tears and skin ulcers, and

the technique is being used more and more by physiotherapists.

At even higher power levels, beams of ultrasound focused on kidney stones pulverise them, allowing them to be passed out of the body as dust.

UMBILICAL CORD

The umbilical cord connects the foetus to the placenta, carrying oxygen and nutrients.

The umbilical cord is the unborn baby's lifeline. It is usually about 40 – 60cm long, consisting of two arteries and a vein in soft, jelly-like tissue.

The umbilical cord ceases to function after the birth of the baby, when the baby starts to breathe through its lungs. It is clamped with a special plastic clip, and then cut.

After a few days, the remaining stump drops off,

leaving a large scar, called the umbilicus or navel. The end of the cord that is attached to the placenta is delivered shortly after the birth of the baby, when the placenta itself comes away from the mother's uterus.

Complications

In some cases, the cord is incomplete, with only a single artery. This is normally associated with birth defects. And if the cord protrudes through the mother's cervix at an early stage in labour, it may be necessary to perform an emergency Caesarean or a forceps delivery, since there is a danger that the baby's oxygen supply will be cut off. Another problem at birth is that the cord may get tangled around the baby's head. But it's always possible for the doctor or midwife to untangle the cord to facilitate the birth.

Post-natal problems

After the birth, the cord may become infected. It is vital to pay attention to hygiene, and infection can be treated by wiping the stump with sterile cotton wool, although in some cases antibiotics may be necessary.

There are sometimes growths (either granulomas or polyps) on or around the umbilical stump, which need medical attention.

The umbilicus is a weak point in the new-born infant, and hernias may develop if the contents of the abdomen protrude through the weak point. They usually sort themselves out, but if they persist, or if they occur in adults (especially women following childbirth) surgery may be necessary.

Discharges from the umbilicus are rare, but they may be due to a birth defect in which parts of the digestive or urinary tract are wrongly connected. This is a case for surgery.

»» SEE ALSO — Caesarean section, Forceps delivery, X-rays

URINARY TRACT

The urinary tract conveys urine from the kidneys to outside the body.

During the process, urine can be stored in the bladder until a convenient time and place can be found for urination.

The urinary tract is divided into three parts: the pair of ureters, the bladder and the urethra (see right).

The ureters

The ureters are narrow, muscular tubes, about 25cm (10in) long, which leave the kidneys and enter the bladder, via a one-way valve at the top. However, if the valve doesn't function properly and the urine travels backwards up the ureters it can carry infection from the bladder to the kidneys. This backflow may be the result of increased pressure in the bladder due to outflow obstruction or it may be due to narrowing of the ureters.

In some circumstances, salts in the urine crystallise out in the kidney and form stones. If one of these stones enters the ureter the result is the excruciating pain of renal colic. Renal colic is felt in the angle of the back and down into the groin. It is caused by spasm of the ureteric muscles as they struggle to force a stone down into the bladder. In many cases the ureters win the battle and the stone passes painlessly into the bladder.

In this case all that is needed is strong painkillers (such as pethidine) until the stone — and the pain — has passed. If the stone does not pass spontaneously, it may be snared and eased out using an operating telescope.

The bladder

The central portion of the urinary tract, the bladder, is a muscular reservoir that stores urine. At the base of the bladder is the opening of the urethra, which is protected by two valves.

The urethra

In the female, the urethra is about 3cm long, while in men — because it has to pass down the length of the penis — it is about 20cm.

The commonest urethral problem is inflammation — urethritis. Urethritis may be due to infection with a wide range of organisms, such as gonorrhoea and chlamydia, or chemical irritation from bubble baths, douches, and so on. The main symptom of urethritis is pain on urination. In severe cases this is often described as being 'like passing broken glass'. As well as causing pain, irritation of the urethra produces the sensation of urgency — the feeling that if urine is not passed at once incontinence will follow.

Urethritis can be distinguished from cystitis by the 'two glass' test. Pass urine into two clean jars; if the first sample is cloudy with threads of mucus and the second is clear, the problem is likely to be urethritis. If the second glass is the same as the first, it is probably cystitis.

Bacterial urethritis is best treated with antibiotics. Chemical irritation can often be overcome by removing the irritant and taking regular salt baths.

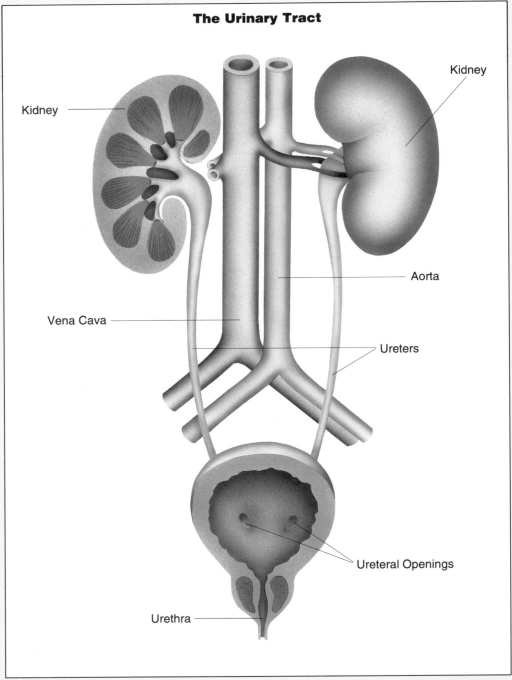

The Urinary Tract

Kidney

Kidney

Aorta

Vena Cava

Ureters

Ureteral Openings

Urethra

>> SEE ALSO — Bladder, Chlamydial infections, Cystitis, Gonorrhoea, Incontinence, Kidneys, Non-specific urethritis

URINARY TRACT DISORDERS

Urinary tract disorders are relatively common, and symptoms are readily apparent.

The term urinary tract infection may be used to refer to an infection anywhere in the urinary tract, including inflamed kidneys (pyelonephritis), bladder (cystitis) or urethra (urethritis). Inflammation is nearly always due to bacterial infection, although urethritis may be due to chlamydia or other types of infection.

Symptoms of a disorder may involve problems with urination, or passing urine which is unusual in appearance.

Urine Tests
Urine is a freely available body fluid and urine tests are an essential part of most medical examinations.

Blood, glucose and protein can all be detected by dipping a dye-impregnated stick into a fresh sample of urine. The method means that widespread screening is very easy and painless, although a blood test may be necessary to confirm the diagnosis.

Blood Except during menstruation, any blood in the urine is abnormal. It is usually the result of cystitis or a kidney infection but it may be due to tumours of the bladder or kidney.

Protein Traces of protein are often found in normal urine but any more than this could signify an infection or kidney failure.

Glucose Glucose in the urine is usually due to sugar diabetes but in some cases, especially after a meal, a completely normal person may have some sugar in their urine.

Other tests
In cystitis or kidney infections a urine sample is extremely helpful. It will reveal blood and pus and the germ causing the infection can be grown, identified and tested against various antibiotics to assess their effectiveness. Even when the diagnosis is obvious most doctors like to see the results of a urine test to ensure the best treatment has been prescribed.

Urine tests can be used to detect many other chemicals. One of the most common is a hormone called Human Chorionic Gonadatrophin or HCG. This hormone is present in large amounts in the first few weeks of pregnancy and the excess can be readily detected by a simple urine test. Some tests are now so accurate that pregnancy can be established before the first missed period.

Problems with urination
The commonest symptoms of urinary problems are frequency, pain and passing blood. There is also a fourth problem, which tends to be restricted to older men. This is difficulty in passing urine, due to prostate problems.

Frequency (passing water more often than normal) is not the same as polyuria (passing more water than normal), though the two symptoms do exist together in sugar diabetes. If frequency involves passing only a few drops of urine, it is the result of cystitis or urethritis. Polyuria may also be caused by a kidney disorder or a hormonal imbalance.

Pain is usually felt at the begining of passing water. If it is coupled with a white vaginal discharge, the cause is probably thrush. Pain sited at the urethral orifice, or over the bladder, when water has been passed is usually a sign of cystitis or local urethral irritation. If the pain is in the small of your back, you may have a kidney infection.

Blood in the urine is usually not serious in the younger age group, being due to readily treatable infection. In the older age group, however, it may be due to a tumour on the wall of the bladder or in the kidney and always warrants investigation.

Unusual appearance of urine
In the normal state, urine is clear, almost odourless and a light straw colour. Most changes in the appearance of urine are perfectly normal and not a sign of disease.

In dehydration the urine becomes very dark and strong smelling. By this stage thirst should have prompted an increased fluid intake, but if ignored, dehydration can cause problems due to the deposition of waste crystals in various parts of the body. Early-morning urine is usually much darker than urine passed later in the day.

In jaundice the urine often takes on a very dark, 'stewed tea' colour as the body loses excess liver salts.

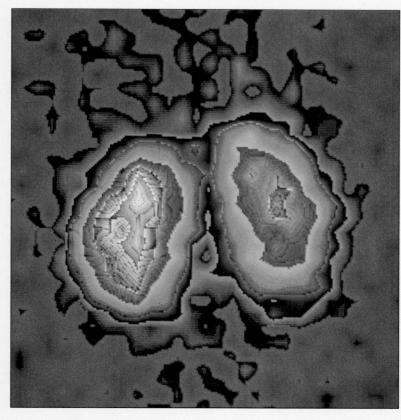

Infection shows up clearly in this kidney scan. A radioactive substance is administered, which has been absorbed by the kidneys. The purple colouring of the right kidney indicates decreased activity.

▶▶ SEE ALSO — Chlamydial infections, Diabetes, Kidneys, Non-specific urethritis, Prostate gland, Sexually transmitted diseases, Thrush

MEDICAL FACT FILE

Causes And Treatment Of Cystitis

Cystitis is one of the commonest disorders affecting the urinary tract. It is due to germs multiplying in the bladder.

Most of the germs that cause cystitis come from the bowel and find their way up the urethra into the bladder. Because of the differences in the length of the male and female urethras, cystitis is far commoner in women than men. Cystitis may be brought on by sexual intercourse. The pumping action of the penis forces germs up the urethra and into the bladder.

Passing water after intercourse helps to flush out the bacteria before they can multiply and cause a problem.

Occasionally cystitis and kidney infections are due to structural abnormalties in the urinary system. For this reason most children, male and female, with a proven urine infection are investigated fully to ensure all is well.

Self help and treatment

Many women with cystitis can treat themselves at home. The aim is to flush the germs out before they have a chance to gain a foothold. At the first sign of stinging or burning, line up four pints of water and drink them within half an hour. If the infection takes hold, flushing the bladder with fluid will ease the pain. The antibiotic which the doctor chooses to treat cystitis depends on the causative germ, but most doctors make a 'best guess' and modify it according to the results of the urine test.

A cloudy urine sample, in the absence of other symptoms, is usually due to the existence of salts that are dissolved at body heat but solid at room temperature.

Bloody urine, urine that smells foul or urine that is cloudy as it is passed is often a sign of infection and a fresh sample should be taken to the doctor for testing. If you do not have a clean glass jar with a screw top, you can get one from your doctor's surgery.

Some drugs, food colourings and natural vegetable dyes (especially beetroot) can stain the urine most alarmingly but most of these can be detected by adding vinegar or bicarbonate of soda. If the colour disappears it is due to a dye and can safely be ignored for a day or two.

Treatment

Since all the above symptoms can be ascribed to various disorders it is essential to consult a doctor if symptoms do not disappear within a day or so. Diagnosis and treatment depend on the symptoms and disorder.

UTERUS

The uterus protects and feeds the developing foetus.

The uterus is situated low down in the pelvis, in front of the rectum but behind the bladder.

Structure and function

The uterus consists of a hollow body and a cervix or neck. The body is shaped like a flattened, upside-down pear with the two fallopian tubes emerging from the upper corners. The cavity inside the uterus is about 6cm long in women who have never had children and about 8cm long in those who have. The cervix accounts

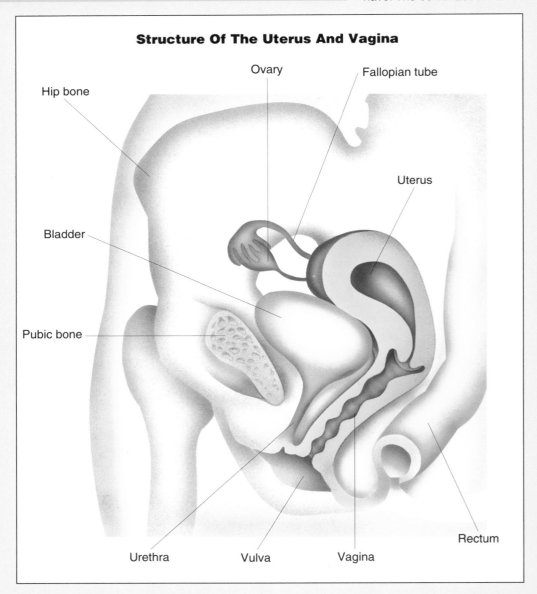

Structure Of The Uterus And Vagina

Hip bone

Ovary

Fallopian tube

Uterus

Bladder

Pubic bone

Rectum

Urethra

Vulva

Vagina

for about two of these centimetres. The walls of the uterus are about 1.5cm thick and consist almost entirely of muscle, arranged in layers.

The lining of the uterus is a specialised tissue, the endometrium, which is well supplied with blood vessels. Over the course of a menstrual cycle it grows from 1mm to 5mm thick before being shed as part of the menstrual flow.

The uterus is held in its normal position, tilted slightly forwards, by two sets of ligaments. In about 25 per cent of the female population the uterus is held, just as securely and just as safely, tilted backwards — a 'retroverted' uterus. Retroversion used to be regarded as an abnormality and it was blamed for a variety of problems from backache to recurrent miscarriage, but in most cases it is no problem, and it may be possible to manipulate the uterus into the more normal position. In some cases, fixed retroversion — in which the womb is tilted backwards and cannot tip forwards — may be due to infection, fibroids or endometriosis. This can cause problems in the fourth month of pregnancy as the fixed uterus is unable to rise out of the pelvis and into the abdomen. The result is urinary retention and eventually miscarriage.

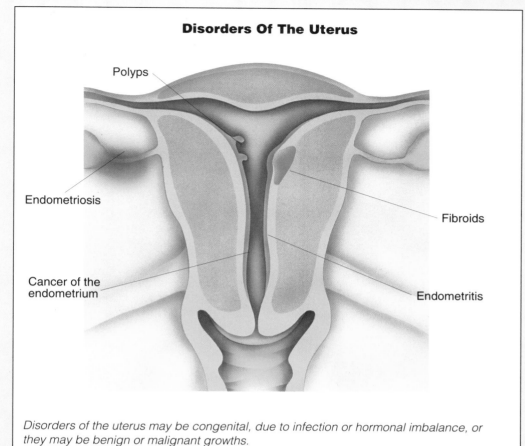

Disorders Of The Uterus

Polyps

Endometriosis

Cancer of the endometrium

Fibroids

Endometritis

Disorders of the uterus may be congenital, due to infection or hormonal imbalance, or they may be benign or malignant growths.

During pregnancy the uterus expands, reaching right up to the rib cage. At the time of delivery, forceful contractions push the baby along the birth canal.

Uterine disorders
Infection of the cervix is very common but the plug of mucus at the cervical opening means that infection very rarely spreads as far as the uterus. It may, however, become infected during abortion or after childbirth. The symptoms are a bloody discharge, fever and pain. The infection usually settles on high doses of antibiotics but occasionally a D&C is needed.

Tumours of the uterus, especially if the cervix is included, are common. Almost 20 per cent of all female cancers are directly related to the genital tract.

Gross enlargement of the body of the uterus is usually due to benign tumours of uterine muscle, known as fibroids.

Fibroids are very common and usually multiple. The origin and the cause is unknown but it is thought they may start in blood vessels rather than in the muscle itself. Several factors are known to increase the risk of fibroids, including delaying the first baby until after 30 years of age and being of Afro-Caribbean origin. They are dependent on oestrogen for their growth and shrink away after the menopause. They grow quickly during pregnancy and may even outgrow their blood supply, in which case the centre of the fibroid breaks down, causing pain.

Outside pregnancy, fibroids cause symptoms for three reasons: their size, their position inside the uterus and accidents to them. Some fibroids may be so large as to cause abdominal swelling but remain symptomless, while others, even small ones, if they distort the uterine cavity will cause heavy periods. Some fibroids may cause infertility by interfering with the normal implantation of the embryo. Very rarely a fibroid may become cancerous, but the risk of this is less than the risk of a general anaesthetic, so most surgeons would only remove a fibroid if it were

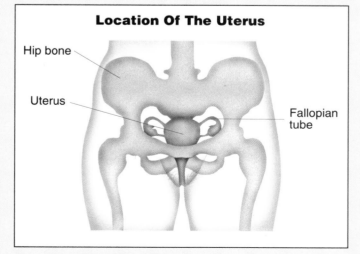

Location Of The Uterus

Hip bone

Uterus

Fallopian tube

⟫ SEE ALSO — Cervix, Dilation & Curettage, Endometriosis, Fibroids, Ovary, Polyps, Prolapse

MEDICAL FACT FILE

causing symptoms. Fibroids can be removed and the uterus left intact but in most cases a hysterectomy is performed.

Other disorders of the uterus include endometriosis, endometritis (inflammation of the endometrium) and polyps.

UTERUS, CANCER OF

Malignant tumours of the uterus may arise from the lining, the muscle layer or from abnormalities associated with pregnancy.

In practice almost all cancers arise in the lining. These tumours are commonest between the ages of 50 and 70 and very rare before the menopause. The first sign is vaginal bleeding usually before the uterus is even enlarged.

Cancer of the uterus lining is associated with higher than normal levels of oestrogen in the absence of progesterone. This may occur naturally or it may be due to the incorrect use of HRT. In general, survival with this sort of tumour is good. Surgery and radiotherapy provide a 90 per cent cure rate if the warning sign of post-menopausal bleeding is heeded.

A very rare tumour that affects women of child-bearing years is choriocarcinoma. This tumour occurs about once in every 20,000 pregnancies. The tumour is very soft, full of blood vessels and grows rapidly. The main symptom is vaginal bleeding, weeks or even months after an apparantly normal delivery.

Treatment with chemotherapy is very effective.

VAGINA

The vagina is an elastic tube between the urethra and the anus. It is made up of muscle and fibre.

The vagina is about 10 cm long and the front and back walls are normally together. The muscles of the perineum (the genital area) distort the vagina into an 's' shape when they are contracted, and these same muscles can be used to hold the vagina shut, either voluntarily or involuntarily. The muscles may go into spasm — a condition known as vaginismus. The cervix, the neck of the womb, protrudes into the upper part of the front wall of the vagina.

Secretions

The vagina is lined with a special type of skin which exudes moisture. The amount of moisture depends on the hormone oestrogen. With increasing age the levels of oestrogen drop and the vaginal walls can become thin and dry.

Normal vaginal secretions, which are a mixture of dead cells, vaginal moisture and cervical mucus, appear creamy. In women of child-bearing age these vaginal secretions are acid which helps to keep the vagina free of infection. This acidity is lost at the time of menstruation, making the vagina more prone to infection.

During sexual activity the vagina becomes more moist to allow painless penetration, and it also increases in size, making it possible to accommodate the penis.

Disorders

Inflammation of the vagina, vaginitis, is very common. Vaginitis can occur if the normal protective environment of the vagina is altered in any way. This may be caused by vaginal deodorants, vaginal douches, antibiotics or anything that destroys the normal protective organisms.

The symptoms of vaginitis are vulvovaginal itching, pain on intercourse and a discharge. The nature of the discharge depends on the type of germ producing the infection and in many cases the doctor can identify the cause from the discharge. The typical discharge of trichomonas, for example, is watery, greenish and foamy with an unpleasant fishy smell.

Atrophic vaginitis affects post-menopausal women. The thin walls of the vagina rub together causing irritation and bleeding. HRT or local oestrogen creams are a very effective treatment in the majority of cases.

Vaginismus (involuntary muscle spasm preventing penetration) is usually caused by a fear that penetration will be painful. This fear may be due to previous experiences (such as rape or child abuse) or to previous discomfort as a result of an infection. Treatment involves psychosexual therapy and special exercises.

Cancer

Vaginal cancer is rare, accounting for less than 2 per cent of genital cancers. It usually affects the post-menopausal age group.

This view of the vagina has been taken through a medical telescope, with the walls of the vagina held open. The cervix protrudes into the vagina, and in this case a patch of inflammation (vaginitis) can be seen clearly.

» SEE ALSO — Discharge, HRT, Menopause, Oestrogen, Progesterone, Pruritis

VARICOSE VEINS

Varicose veins are veins which are irregularly dilated, tortuous and lengthened.

The commonest site for varicose veins is in the legs, but they may also occur around the oesophagus or the rectum, where they are known as haemorrhoids or more commonly, piles.

Causes

Varicose veins tend to run in families and affect up to 20 per cent of adults at one time or another. Varicose veins of the leg may appear out of the blue or they may be the result of thrombosis. They may also affect pregnant women — the pregnant uterus slows the flow of blood along the veins of the pelvis.

Women are five times more likely to suffer from varicose veins than men. The basic weakness seems to lie in the walls of the vein, which are more prone to dilatation than normal. This dilatation destroys the vein's valves, which means that the pressure in the vein, and hence the degree of dilatation, increases.

Diagnosis and symptoms

As varicose veins are usually visible diagnosis tends to be straightforward. However, in some cases, they are more easily felt than seen. Untreated varicose veins cause a decrease in blood flow back to the heart. This leads to fluid retention in the legs, dermatitis and

eventually ulceration. The veins may be painless but patients often complain of a 'dragging sensation', especially after standing for any length of time.

Treatment

Varicose veins can be treated with injections, surgery or pressure stockings. Injections are suitable only for patients with minor varicosities not affecting the main veins. An irritant solution is injected into the vein and the reaction set up obliterates it. More severe varicose veins require surgery. The commonest operation is 'stripping', in which a wire is passed down the main vein from the groin

to the ankle. The wire is then pulled back, turning the vein inside out and pulling it out. Support bandages are applied as the vein is removed and they must be worn for several weeks afterwards. The patient may take up to three months to make a full recovery .

In patients who are too frail for definitive treatment or in those who wish to postpone surgery, pressure stockings can be very effective in abolishing the symptoms of varicose veins. Pressure stockings should be put on before getting up in the morning and not taken off until bed time.

How A Varicose Vein Is Formed

Normal Vein

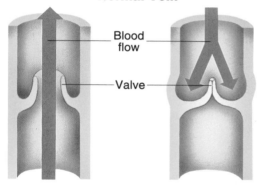

The valves in normal, healthy veins distribute the weight of the blood, preventing it from draining back down the leg.

Varicose Vein

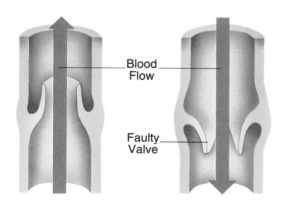

If the valves in the vein fail, the blood drains back downwards, causing the vein to become swollen with blood – a varicose vein.

VASECTOMY

Vasectomy, or male sterilisation, is a simple procedure that can be done under local anaesthetic.

A small incision is made in the scrotum, and each vas deferens — the tubes that carry sperm from the testicles to the penis — is cut, tied and cauterised.

Precautions

Sperm stored above the level of the incision are still produced in the ejaculate for up to four months. Therefore, contraceptive precautions should still be taken. The all-clear cannot be given until a sperm count has shown that no more sperm are present. If precautions are taken, the failure rate of vasectomy is less than one in 1000.

Serious complications are very rare but occasionally a blood vessel will ooze, causing a bruise that can grow to almost the size of a coconut.

Contrary to what many men may fear, vasectomy has no effect on libido or potency. In many cases, sexual pleasure is heightened by the final removal of the risk of accidental pregnancy.

Reversal of vasectomy is possible but difficult and the operation should therefore be regarded as permanent .

VIRUSES

Viruses are the smallest living organisms. They are so small that, on their own, they lack the ablility to grow or reproduce themselves.

Viruses must live as parasites inside a host cell, using that cell for their own synthesis. This can cause major problems for the host cell as it struggles to continue its own function.

⟫ SEE ALSO — Haemorrhoids, Sterilisation

Viruses overtake cells by introducing their own genetic material into them. The cells are tricked into accepting the messages which are contained in the viruses DNA or RNA and they start to produce viral protein.

The fact that viruses hide inside other cells makes them difficult to kill without damaging the host's cells. As yet, very few safe anti-viral agents are available.

Classification of viruses

There are many different families of virus. Doctors classify them according to either the type of disease caused or the shape of the virus. A typical virus would be the rotavirus, so called because of its wheel-like appearance. It is found throughout the world and causes epidemics of

diarrhoea in children, mainly in the winter.

The common cold is due to a viral infection with one of a family of viruses called rhinoviruses. There are at least a hundred strains of rhinovirus, and immunity is only acquired one strain at a time. The average school-age child has about six colds a year; by the age of 20, this has fallen to two or three colds a year; and by the age of 60, the average individual suffers only one cold a year.

Prevention not cure

Although viral infections cannot be cured, they can be prevented or, failing this, their effects lessened. Serious viral infections — poliomyelitis, measles and mumps, for example — can be prevented by vaccination. In most cases, an artificially

weakened virus is introduced into the body. It produces an antibody reaction but not an illness, and the recipient becomes immune to that particular infection. Unfortunately, because there are so many viruses that can cause colds, it is impossible to develop a realistic vaccination against them.

Treatment

In time, the body will rid itself of most viral infections and treatment is aimed at relieving the symptoms until the body's defences can be mobilised. In the case of a cold, this is simply a matter of taking aspirin and getting plenty of rest. However, for severe infections such as poliomyelitis, it may mean artificial life support.

VOMITING

Vomiting is the expulsion of the stomach contents through the mouth.

It is usually preceded by nausea — the feeling of wanting to vomit — which is itself usually accompanied by sweating and pallor.

Vomiting is controlled by a specific area of the brain — the vomiting centre. The vomiting centre can be stimulated by nerve impulses from the brain or gut, or it may by activated by poisons in the bloodstream.

Vomiting has a valuable role in ridding the body of toxic substances eaten by mistake. In the early stages of vomiting, the valves in the gullet remain closed despite the action of the diaphragm and stomach. When the valves eventually open, vomiting occurs and the force may project food several feet.

Causes

Vomiting may occur without nausea, particularly in pyloric stenosis, a condition in which

the valve at the exit of the stomach does not open.

Most conditions which affect the gut will cause vomiting, but vomiting that is sustained over a number of days with no other features of abdominal disease is usually due to causes outside the gut. Any acute infection, such as 'flu, can cause vomiting, especially in children. Vomiting is also a prominent feature of infections of the central nervous system, such as meningitis; it may be caused by motion as in travel sickness or by excess alcohol, migraine, drugs or kidney failure. Vomiting on rising in the morning is sometimes a sign of increased pressure inside the skull; if it persists for more than a day or two or is accompanied by headache, consult a doctor.

Treatment

Although vomiting is very unpleasant, it rarely causes harm, and most doctors would be loath to treat a short-term problem with drugs that dull the vomiting centre. In most cases, all that is required is to abstain from food for a few hours. Sips of water, or better still, diluted lemonade (its sugar content aids rehydration), will replace any fluid lost.

WARTS

Warts are harmless growths, caused by a virus.

Warts are very common and contagious. They affect only the top layer of the skin, but they are unsightly. Over 30 different wart viruses have been identified.

Types of wart

Common warts are firm, usually round lumps, up to 5mm in diameter and flesh-coloured, yellow or brown. Common sites include the

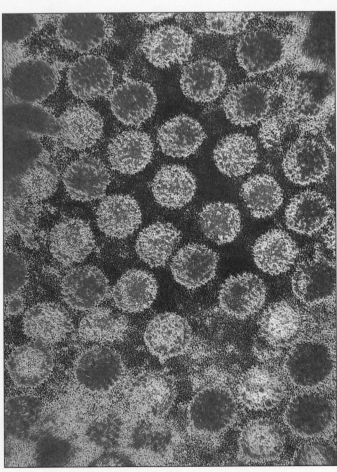

A false-colour image of rotaviruses, which belong to the genus reovirus, and cause gastro-enteritis in children. The virus gets its name from its wheel-like appearance.

➤➤ SEE ALSO — Bacteria, Colds, Immunisation, Measles, Mumps, Nausea, Poliomyelitis, Pyloric stenosis, Rhinitis, Travel sickness

hands, knees, face and scalp. Flat warts have a flat top, and may itch. They usually occur on the wrists or the backs of the hands. Digitate warts are finger-like growths and dark in colour. Filiform warts are long, thin growths, usually occurring on the eyelids, neck or in the armpit. Plantar warts, commonly known as verrucas, are flat warts on the sole of the foot. Genital warts are pink and bumpy in appearance, rather like the florets of a cauliflower. They occur around the genitals and anus, and are sexually transmitted. Since there is some evidence to show that the presence of genital warts pre-disposes a woman to cervical cancer, it is important that they should be removed. Infection is easily passed between partners, so both should be treated and checked regularly.

Treatment

Common warts often disappear of their own accord within a year or so, as do verrucas. However, because of their contagious nature, it is advisable to consult a doctor about treatment. In addition, verrucas may need to be removed because of the pain caused by the pressure of weight on the sole of the foot.

Warts can be treated with liquid treatments, wart plasters, which soften the surrounding skin and lift off the wart, and cryosurgery, in which the wart is frozen, and as the skin thaws it forms a blister, lifting off the wart. Warts can also be cut out and treated with lasers.

WEIGHT LOSS

Doctors tend to classify weight loss as serious only if more than 10 per cent of body weight is lost in less than six months.

What's Causing Your Weight Loss?

Rapid, unplanned weight loss may be a symptom of a serious disorder. Most doctors start by looking for other symptoms.

SYMPTOMS	DIAGNOSIS
Weight loss with ● Excessive urination ● Unusual thirst ● Tiredness ● No periods ● Genital itching	All symptoms of diabetes. Diagnosis involves urine and blood tests. Treatment is with tablets, monitored diet or regular injections of insulin.
Weight loss with ● Sweating ● Bulging eyes ● Lack of energy ● Trembling and weakness ● Feeling of depression and frustration	All symptoms of thyroid disorder. Diagnosis involves blood test and sometimes a scan. Treatment is long term with drugs.
Weight loss with ● Lack of appetite ● Diarrhoea or constipation ● Abdominal pain and/or blood in the faeces	All symptoms of digestive tract disorders. Important to consult a doctor, since cancer is a possible cause, and it must be caught early for best chances of recovery.
Weight loss with ● Lack of appetite ● Low feelings ● Loss of interest in sex ● Insomnia ● Inability to concentrate	Stress and tension can cause loss of weight, but serious depression may be at the root of it. Look carefully at your life style, and consult your doctor.
Are you determined to lose weight, although people are always remarking on how slim you look?	Anorexia nervosa and bulimia are psychological disorders, both causing excessive weight loss. It is essential to consult a doctor, as depression and suicide are common among sufferers.
Could you be pregnant?	Weight loss is common in the first three months of pregnancy.

Weight fluctuates from day to day and also according to the time in the menstrual cycle.

Causes

The commonest reasons for weight loss are either a decrease in calorific intake or an increase in calorific expenditure or exercise. Both are often a result of stress where nervous energy is burned off and appetite is lost without it being apparent to the victim.

Weight may also be lost as a result of disease. Untreated diabetics can lose two or three stones in as many weeks, both from fluid loss and an increased calorie expenditure. An overactive thyroid increases the metabolic rate and sufferers have usually lost several pounds before other symptoms occur. Weight loss is a well-known symptom of many cancers, but by this stage the cancer is often advanced and other symptoms are usually present.

Weight loss in anybody may be a sign of anorexia

>> SEE ALSO — Anorexia nervosa, Bulimia nervosa, Diabetes, Thyroid gland

MEDICAL FACT FILE

nervosa, though this tends to be most common in teenage girls. Bulimia nervosa, in which a normal or even a high calorie intake is accompanied by self-induced vomiting or purges, may be even more common.

Treatment

The treatment of weight loss is entirely dependent on the cause. Physical illness should be diagnosed and addressed before any attempt is made to put weight on.

There are many types of high-calorie supplements available — some come in the form of pure carbohydrate and others as complete meal supplements. In most cases where a serious physical illness is not the cause, simply choosing high-calorie foods is often enough to reverse the trend.

X-RAYS

X-rays are electro-magnetic radiation similar to light and radiowaves but which have the ability to pass through human tissue.

In radiology (the branch of medicine concerned with x-rays), x-rays are used to build up a 'shadow picture' of the internal organs. X-rays, which are produced in an x-ray tube, penetrate a specific region of the body. Some rays are absorbed while the remainder strike, and blacken, a photographic plate.

X-rays pass readily through soft tissue, such as skin and muscle, but not so easily through the bones. Where few x-rays are absorbed, the image produced is dark, as, for example, in an image of the lungs; and where most of the x-rays are absorbed, as happens when bone is x-rayed, the image appears as a white area.

In a CT scan, the simple picture produced by x-rays can be enhanced by the use of moving detectors and computers to produce slices that build up to give a precise picture of the internal organs. In a barium x-ray, the outline of body cavities such as the stomach can be visualised using x-rays and barium, which is opaque to x-rays, so the cavities show up as white areas.

Disadvantages

The main problem with x-rays is their ability to damage the DNA structure of the tissues they pass through. This damage is dose-related and can cause cancer and foetal abnormalities. Modern equipment minimises the risk but doctors still try to avoid using x-rays if at all possible.

YELLOW FEVER

Yellow fever is an infectious disease caused by a virus which is transmitted by mosquitoes.

The fever is usually of short duration, and the main symptom in severe cases is jaundice — yellowing of the skin due to a surplus of bilirubin (the pigment in bile) in the blood, which gives the disease its name. The disease may be picked up only in certain parts of Central and South America, and in large parts of Africa. It is becoming less and less common as the mosquito responsible is gradually eradicated.

Symptoms and treatment

The first symptoms appear three to six days after exposure. There is fever, headache, nausea and often there are nosebleeds. The heart rate is slow.

In most cases, the patient recovers after about three days, but in severe cases the disease continues with pain in the neck, back and legs, damage to liver and kidneys, jaundice and possibly kidney failure.

Treatment is mainly supportive, with intravenous drips to maintain the blood volume. An antiviral agent has not yet been discovered. Death results in around 10 per cent of cases.

Prevention

Once a patient has recovered from the disease they have lifelong immunity.

A vaccination is available, and it is recommended before travel to areas where the disease is prevalent. In some cases vaccination is compulsory before travel. The vaccination lasts for about 10 years, but it should not be given to children under the age of one.

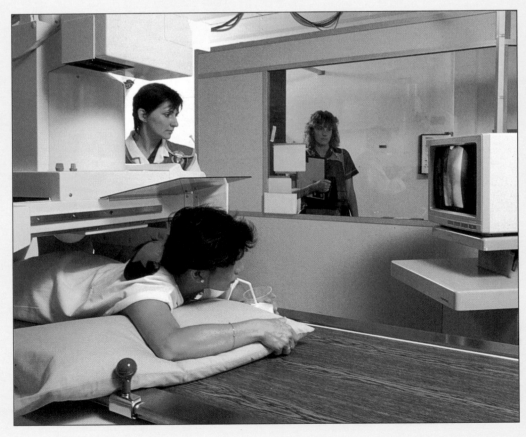

This patient is undergoing a barium meal x-ray examination. In this case, she is drinking a suspension of barium sulphate while lying under the x-ray machine. This process is used to detect problems of the oesophagus, stomach, and intestine.

»» SEE ALSO — Immunisation, Insects, Mosquito bites, MRI, Ultrasonics

INDEX